International Federation of Library Associations and Institutions
Fédération Internationale des Associations de Bibliothécaires et des Bibliothèques
Internationaler Verband der bibliothekarischen Vereine und Institutionen
Международная Федерация Библиотечных Ассоциаций и Учреждений
Federación Internacional de Asociaciones de Bibliotecarios y Bibliotecas
国际图书馆协会与机构联合会

الاتحاد الدولي لجمعيات ومؤسسات المكتبات

About IFLA
www.ifla.org

IFLA (The International Federation of Library Associations and Institutions) is the leading international body representing the interests of library and information services and their users. It is the global voice of the library and information profession.

IFLA provides information specialists throughout the world with a forum for exchanging ideas and promoting international cooperation, research, and development in all fields of library activity and information service. IFLA is one of the means through which libraries, information centres, and information professionals worldwide can formulate their goals, exert their influence as a group, protect their interests, and find solutions to global problems.

IFLA's aims, objectives, and professional programme can only be fulfilled with the cooperation and active involvement of its members and affiliates. Currently, approximately 1,600 associations, institutions and individuals, from widely divergent cultural backgrounds, are working together to further the goals of the Federation and to promote librarianship on a global level. Through its formal membership, IFLA directly or indirectly represents some 500,000 library and information professionals worldwide.

IFLA pursues its aims through a variety of channels, including the publication of a major journal, as well as guidelines, reports and monographs on a wide range of topics. IFLA organizes workshops and seminars around the world to enhance professional practice and increase awareness of the growing importance of libraries in the digital age. All this is done in collaboration with a number of other non-governmental organizations, funding bodies and international agencies such as UNESCO and WIPO. IFLANET, the Federation's website, is a prime source of information about IFLA, its policies and activities: www.ifla.org

Library and information professionals gather annually at the IFLA World Library and Information Congress, held in August each year in cities around the world.

IFLA was founded in Edinburgh, Scotland, in 1927 at an international conference of national library directors. IFLA was registered in the Netherlands in 1971. The Koninklijke Bibliotheek (Royal Library), the national library of the Netherlands, in The Hague, generously provides the facilities for our headquarters. Regional offices are located in Rio de Janeiro, Brazil; Pretoria, South Africa; and Singapore.

IFLA Publications 136-137

Global Library and Information Science
A Textbook for Students and Educators

With Contributions from
Africa, Asia, Australia, New Zealand,
Europe, Latin America and the Carribean,
the Middle East, and North America

Edited by
Ismail Abdullahi

K · G · Saur München 2009

IFLA Publications
edited by Sjoerd Koopman

Bibliographic information published by the Deutsche Nationalibliothek
The Deutsche Nationalbibliothek lists this publication in the Deutsche Nationalbibliografie;
detailed bibliographic data is available in the Internet at http://dnb.d-nb.de.

⊗

Printed on permanent paper
The paper used in this publication meets the minimum requirements of
American National Standard – Permanence of Paper
for Publications and Documents in Libraries and Archives
ANSI/NISO Z39.48-1992 (R1997)

1005851806

© 2009 by International Federation of Library Associations
and Institutions, The Hague, The Netherlands

Alle Rechte vorbehalten / All Rights Strictly Reserved
K.G. Saur Verlag, München
An Imprint of Walter de Gruyter GmbH & Co. KG

Printed in the Federal Republic of Germany by Strauss GmbH, Mörlenbach

ISBN 978-3-598-22042-5
ISSN 0344-6891 (IFLA Publications)

Contents

Part 1
Africa

Part 2
Asia

Part 3
Australia

Part 4
Europe

Part 5
Latin America

Part 6
Middle East

Part 7
North America

FOREWORD

Globalization is with us for better or for worse. Our increasing technological and economic interconnectedness allows the world's population to share in benefits such as more rapid economic growth, improvements in living standards, reduction of poverty, increased foreign direct investment, and the peaceful resolution of international political and economic tension. But these benefits are not evident everywhere. Economic or geographic handicaps and in some cases ideological barriers prevent many countries from taking advantage of globalization. These countries tend to get left behind. The negative consequences of globalization are emphasized by a broad anti-globalist or mundialist movement, which cites a range of problems attributed to globalization, for example, the heavy social and economic costs of economic restructuring required to be competitive in the world market, a growing gap in the standard of living between richest and poorest countries, environmental damage, the use of economic power by the rich to protect their industries from competition by poor countries, and the erosion of national cultures and languages. A more frightening downside of globalization is international terrorism, while the recent international credit crisis, in which the effects of bad decisions by US bankers were rapidly exported to other institutions and individuals worldwide, illustrates the dangers of shifting large amounts of money worldwide with the click of a mouse. Globalization presents us with challenges that can best be faced if we are equipped with increased international understanding.

Librarians have a long tradition of internationalism and cooperation across national borders. This has found expression in, for example, international schemes for interlibrary lending and the sharing bibliographic records, international cooperation in the preservation and conservation of library materials, and international digitization programs. The International Federation of Library Associations and Institutions (IFLA) have played a leading role in many of these international activities. Our interconnectedness, made possible by modern information and communication technologies, facilitates such programs. Globalization opens up new opportunities for cooperation. To seize these opportunities and utilize them for the benefit of libraries and library users everywhere, and to avoid the pitfalls of well-intentioned but badly conceived international programs, librarians need to be well informed about the situations, challenges and values of their colleagues in partner countries. The communication has to be two-way. The time when all new ideas, innovations and standards came from the northern hemisphere, and specifically from the USA, is over. Increasingly we live in a multipolar world, with many sources of insight and influence. This makes global librarianship more complex, challenging and interesting than ever before.

The present book makes a valuable contribution to our understanding of the situations and challenges of our colleagues in other countries. This is not the usual potpourri of chapters on various themes in various countries. Not since Miles Jackson's *International handbook of contemporary developments in librarianship*

(1981)[1] has there been such an ambitious attempt to construct a geographically comprehensive and thematically systematic overview. The editor, Ismail Abdullahi, consulted widely, drew up a logical framework, and recruited regional editors and chapter editors to ensure that a coherent overview could take shape, region by region, and within each region, by type of library. This was a big challenge. Africa, for example, counts over fifty countries and it is no simple task to determine the state of the art in each of them, let alone the state of the art for each type of library, and to combine this information into readable chapters. While gaps inevitably remain to be filled, the result is a significant contribution to the literature of international librarianship, which combines richness and diversity of content within the discipline of a systematic framework. It should be of value not only to teachers and students of international librarianship, but also to area studies librarians, librarians involved in running international programs, and any practitioners of our profession who are open to insights that may be gained from other situations and cultures and are willing to learn from the experiences of colleagues all over our shrinking globe.

Peter Johan Lor

---

[1] Jackson, M.M., (ed.) 1981. *International handbook of contemporary developments in librarianship.* Westport, Connecticut: Greenwood press.

INTRODUCTION

Ismail Abdullahi

Global Library and Information Science: A Handbook for Students and Educators brings together five regions of the world in one volume offering an overview to any one interested in library development internationally. Written by regional experts and scholars from each region, the book offers first-hand knowledge about public libraries, academic libraries, special libraries, school libraries, library and information science education and international library associations in Africa, Asia, Australia and New Zealand, Europe, Latin America and the Caribbean, and North America.

Librarianship always has been international. Its ideas cross many borders and deal with common purposes and missions. The organization of this book is by regions and then by types of libraries. This Global library and information science book will be useful as an introductory textbook for students interested to studying global librarianship. For more than eight decades IFLA has successfully brought together librarians from around the world to discuss, share ideas, understand each other, and work together for the common good. This book is a supplement to IFLA's effort and hard work in making global library and information science a reality.

Dennis Ocholla introduces the section on Africa by explaining that most African countries only gained their political independence from the colonial powers of France, Britain, and Portugal in the second half of the twentieth century. The refusal of Europeans to share library services with indigenous Africans has created a library system in which libraries only serve the privileged. As a result, the majority of the people in Africa have no access to libraries. Failure to exploit the oral traditions also has kept out the majority of the population and marginalized them as far as access to knowledge is concerned,

Stuart Ferguson presents his regional chapters of Australia and New Zealand by describing similar experiences that Ocholla gave for Africa that of British colonial influence on the Islands. But usage of the English language, as well as having most of its people from England, helped them to emulate leading British institutions in culture, reading, and use of libraries. Although Ferguson finds similarities of library development in both countries, he emphasizes that LIS education in Australia and New Zealand allows undergraduate as well as postgraduate pathways to professional membership. Like other regions of the world the library profession in Australia and New Zealand is also going through many changes.

Abdus Sattar Chaudhry and Chihfeng P. Lin describe the Asian library challenges and the complexity of Asia that incorporates many cultures, traditions, religions, languages and differences in development models and geographical distances. At present, they are regarded as challenges to modern development of librarianship on the continent.

The section on North America provides library and library education development in North America from the early colonial period of private libraries to the present and the critical role LIS schools has played in the advancement of library education and ALA's role in establishing and maintaining accreditation standards in North America. Last but not least, Michael Dowling and Keith Michael Fiels provide and an overview of the development of global library association at the local, national, regional, and international levels that include the leadership provided by the International Federation of Library Associations and Institutions (IFLA) as a leading body representing the interests of library and institution services and their users.

Leif Kajberg and Marian Koren talk about Europe as a multicultural continent that is a complex entity. They discuss the endangered languages that rapidly disappearing. The unification of Europe after the downfall of the Soviet also has added challenges when considering the experience of these nations under a totalitarian regime for the last five decades, which left them without much freedom that Western Europe enjoyed. Although the European countries' experience in library development was similar, the continent was unable to unify its library profession under one umbrella, like ALA in the United States. The challenges could be related to coming to grips with tradition and culture that were old as the continent itself.

Filiberto Felipe Martinez-Arellano, in his introduction of libraries and LIS education in Latin America and the Caribbean describes such different challenges as climate, geography, traditions, life style, and social systems that greatly contributed to inequality on educational and library services. On the other hand, university and special libraries are better organized than public libraries in Latin America and the Caribbean.

Sajjad ur-Rehman introduces us to library development in the Middle East, which has a long history of ancient libraries, such as those found in Sumaria, Babylonia, and the valley of Euphrates. But in the last decades, this region, which is also considered a part of Asia, has been a victim of war and regional tensions. The region has many other challenges, such as differences in library development between the oil rich and other nations, between those who hold graduate degrees and the larger number of professionals. In addition there is a lack of professional activities and research.

It is my hope that these well presented and discussed chapters will bring a true insights into librarianship and library development in the six regions of the world covered by this book. Librarians, library students, and all those who are interested in this profession will benefit from the chapters.

ACKNOWLEDGEMENTS

As I bring this project to a close I am grateful to the large number of people who contributed their time, work, and effort in assisting me in the compilation of this book. I express my deepest appreciation to the regional editors Dennis Ocholla, Abdus Sattar Chaudhry and Chifeng P. Lin, Stuart Ferguson, Leif Kajberg, Marian Koren, Filiberto Felipe Marinez-Arellano, and Sajjad ur-Rehamn, Leila Marouf and their chapter authors. It would have been impossible to publish this book without their assistance and contribution. Their insightful essays provide valuable information for many librarians, library science students, and educators who will use this book to better understand global library and information science.

I owe a great debt of gratitude to the following individuals who gave me many encouragements and inspirations that lead to publishing of this book – E. J. Josey, Preben Kirkegaard, Leif Kajberg, Leif Lørring, Ole Harbo, Michael Gorman, Irene Owens, Norman Harrocks, C.R. Karisiddappa, Tony Rodriguez-Buckingham and many others.

No one was more interested in the progress of publishing of this book than Sjoerd Koopman of IFLA, Manfred Link and Barbara Fischer at K. G. Saur, whose support and encouragement made the publication of this book a success. I express my sincere thanks to all of them.

PART 1
AFRICA:
INTRODUCTION

Dennis Ocholla
Regional Editor

Africa is the second largest continent in land size and the first in terms of the number of nations in the world with 53 independent countries and a population of approximately 877,500 million people (see http://worldatlas.com/webimage/ countrys/af.htm as at 2006), but also the poorest in economical terms. Most African countries only received their political independence from colonialists (France, Britain, and Portugal) during the second decade of the 20th Century. It is therefore not surprising that libraries in Africa have always tended to serve the privileged, i.e. the colonialists during the colonial period, and the educated, and economically sated urban 'settlers' of the present. According to my knowledge and observation that is perhaps also shared by others, the view of library services is based on the assumption that library users know how to read and write, or are functionally literate in at least a non-African language (such as English, French, Portuguese), reside in urban areas (where they are closer to the library), and are aware of what the library provides even if the content is not relevant to their needs. A speech by the former Minister of Education of South Africa in 2002 reveals that in South Africa, with its 48 million people, "*3.5. Million adults over the age of 16 have never attended school; another 2.5 million adults have lost their earlier ability to read or write. That makes essentially 6 million South Africans who are essentially barred from the written word, from the whole universe of information and imagination that books hold; and also from the more functional everyday empowerment that written languages gives – for employment, for travel and to be a responsible citizen* (Speech by the Minister of Education, Professor Kader Asmal in Nassimbeni, May 2006:13). A more recent speech by Pallo Jordan (2007), Minister of Arts and Culture South Africa still paints this bleak picture thus "*51% of South Africans have no books in their homes. A mere 14% of the population read books and only 5% of these read to their children*" (Jordan, 2007)

Professor Kader Asmal and Dr. Pallo Jordan's speech provides an example of how an African population can be economically deprived, geographically isolated, and culturally and socially marginalized through illiteracy. Yet even though colonial ideas still dictate literacy in the form of reading and writing, oral traditions have been the dominant mode of knowledge acquisition, storage, dissemination and sharing before, during and post colonial rule amongst most of the African populace. These oral traditions have not been sufficiently exploited in attempts to make libraries more relevant to those who are destitute or marginalized in their own countries due to economic poverty. The marginalized include rural people who are often geographically isolated because of poor communication and trans-

portation systems; those disadvantaged by cultural and social poverty and depriva-
tion, especially the illiterate; the elderly, women, and children; those who are dis-
criminated against because of their race, ethnicity, creed or religion; and the
physically disabled. Oral traditions require librarians to adapt, for example by
scheduling a 'speakers day' in the library to enable community knowledge holders
to share their experiences with active and potential library users, or providing multimedia forums that showcase the visual and performing arts together with textual
media. How can word of mouth (WOM) both traditional and modern (i.e. audio-
visual) be effectively used in libraries?

The chapters in this publication focus on academic, public, school and special
libraries as well as LIS education and training in Africa. Fundamentally, both
availability and accessibility are critical to ensure library development in Africa in
order for libraries to fulfill their role, which is to inform, entertain, enlighten, educate, empower and equip individuals and communities with knowledge and information for life-long learning. Thus, libraries inadvertently enable individuals to fulfill their social roles and obligations in society knowingly and responsibly.

Academic libraries are relatively better equipped and resourced than other libraries in Africa. Their establishment and development has not been stagnant because academic institutions or Higher Education Institutions (HEIs) in most African countries are compelled by most governments to establish libraries as a requirement and maintain them for accreditation. Beyond this, HEIs have been left
alone to equip the libraries as they wish with a fraction of the subsidization they
receive from government or other affiliations, and there is therefore significant
variation in their development and growth, both in quantity and quality. While
there is a general consensus in many studies that academic libraries in Africa do
not have a staffing problem, most studies agree with the problems identified in a
study on the status of academic libraries in Africa by Rosenberg (1997). The study
revealed that libraries are poorly fundedwith budgets that are either non-existent,
declining or rarely honored; collection development is often either minimal or non
existent; there is too much expenditure on staff (some libraries are overstaffed) at
the expense of acquisitions; there is over dependence on [foreign] external funding, which is sometimes estimated to be as high as 90-100% in some libraries;
ICTs aren't sufficiently utilized and networks suffer poor connectivity; and resource sharing is not a common practice. Reggie Raju from the University of
KwaZulu Natal library and Jaya Raju from the Durban University of Technology,
discuss the issues and challenges of academic libraries in the first chapter, and
while agreeing with studies focusing on this library category, recommend minimal
benchmarking for academic libraries. The authors reiterate that cost reduction, income generation, resource sharing, rational staffing, the application of information
and communication technologies (ICTs), and the reduction of donor dependency
engender sustainability and, therefore, need everyone's critical attention.

The next chapter focuses on public libraries. Most public libraries in Africa play
a dual role as Public Libraries and National Libraries, with the exception of coun-

tries such as South Africa where the two types of libraries are separate. Public libraries receive significant attention worldwide, and the UNESCO Public Library Manifesto provides guidelines and moral support for their development. The Manifesto states that, *"The public library, the local gateway to knowledge, provides a basic condition for lifelong learning, independent decision – making and cultural development of the individual and social groups. The Manifesto proclaims UNESCO's belief in the public library as a living force for education, culture and information, as an essential agent for the fostering of peace and spiritual welfare through the minds of men and women"* (IFLA/UNESCO public library manifesto, 1994). Unfortunately, public library development in Africa has received strong criticism. For example, in a report by Issak (2000) on public librarianship in a segment of Africa (10 Anglophone countries), the findings echoed poor services, declining budgets, lack of resources, outdated materials, lack of planning, inadequate knowledge of the information needs of the users, and poverty. This report partly blamed the western model of the public library system on the poor state of the libraries. Other studies concur with Issak report, stating that most of Africa's population has yet to experience the library and its services because of a long history of elitism, urban-centrism and Euro-centrism (e.g. Sturges & Neil, 1990). The argument presented by these authors is that libraries in Africa still remain largely stocked with Western literature, most of which is written in non-African languages.

Several authors in this collected work suggested the need for alternative services such as community information services, and impact assessments of public library services. Government commitment, improvements in the professional commitment of librarians, and the provision of resources were also considered essential areas of focus. The community library concept discussed by Mostert and Vermuelen (1998) is also, by all appearances, a viable way to deliver information to the poor and marginalized from a public library platform. But I would strongly concur with Rosenberg that *"Originating from the initiative of a group from the community or an aid agency, their birth is followed by a year or two of rapid growth and a good deal of local publicity and attention. This is followed by a period of slow decline, accompanied by theft, the departure of the initiators, loss of interest among staff and users – the library still exists but signs of life are barely discernible. Sometimes this period continues indefinitely, but often a final stage is reached when all remaining books are removed, stolen, or damaged beyond repair and the premises and staff are allocated to another activity"* (Rosenberg in Mostert 2001: Lack of sustained effort to find an alternative library framework). However, this does not mean that community libraries or information resource centers are irrelevant. Mchombu (2004) demonstrates how they should work in his chapter on the content of information and knowledge in community resource centers, information sharing and processing, and how to keep the community information resource center alive; and also provides four interesting case studies and lessons learnt at grassroots level on setting up community information resource centers.

Issac Kigongo- Bukenya, a Professor from the East African School of Library and Information Science, Uganda, has a crucial chapter on public libraries in Africa that addresses the issues and challenges of an institution that is highly regarded and trusted by the international information community for changing lives of many people in the world by providing a facility for life long learning. In his final remarks, he observes that although public libraries have existed in Africa for a reasonably long time: their development in different parts of the continent is not uniform; support for public libraries by African governments and civil society is minimal; and in many countries, public library provision and services have declined to an alarming extent. Isaac, like many critics of public library development in Africa, associates the decline with what he calls the "*alien and elitist nature of the public library; the failure of the public library to identify with community needs and therefore offering irrelevant services; lack of appropriate information materials; lack of proper staffing; and finally lack of committed institutional budgets and consequently donor funding dependency*". He recognizes new, sometimes politicized initiatives, such as Reading Tents – Uganda; The Village Reading Rooms Programmed (VRRP) – Botswana; Rural Libraries and Resource Development Programme (RLRDP) – Zimbabwe; and in Kenya, the Camel Library Service (CLS), to name a few. However, whether these initiatives are practical, sustainable, apolitical, and address the gaps created by Western oriented public libraries depends on the outcome of their evaluation or impact assessment, if they last that long.

School libraries, as outlined in the School Library Manifesto, are to provide "information and ideas that are fundamental to functioning successfully in today's information and knowledge-based society. The school library equips students with life-long learning skills and develops the imagination, enabling them to live as responsible citizens" (IFLA/UNESCO School Library Manifesto, 2006). While most countries in Africa have embraced the creation of libraries in tertiary or higher education institutions both as a government requirement and to enable accreditation, schools in Africa are not compelled to establish schools libraries as a statutory requirement. Ultimately, most schools in Africa do not have schools libraries. Therefore the golden objectives of school libraries expressed in the IFLA school libraries Manifesto are irrelevant to most schools on the continent. Even relatively well-developed African countries, such as South Africa, have less than 30% (some sources quote approximately 20%) of school libraries. The most commonly cited reason is the absence of school library policies, the argument being that if library policies work for academic institutions, why not for schools. In this chapter, Robert Ikoja-Odongo, a Professor at the School of Library and Information Science at Makarere University, Uganda, provides an insightful account into the development of school libraries in parts of Africa, and concludes by stating that governments should consider developing and implementing genuine school library policies in every country, recognizing and employing trained professionals for the management of the libraries and the provision of services, providing space and accommodation for the libraries and restoring them appropriately, promoting a local languages publishing programme, and developing a curriculum that demands resource based and learner-centered education.

Special libraries are individual, private or government information centers that serve the information needs of a specific user group, e.g. parliamentarians, the physically disabled, lawyers, researchers or prisoners. From this definition, one can see that it would be difficult to quantify special libraries because of their obscure existence and services. In Africa, special libraries have a multiplicity of other names, such as documentation centers, information centers, etc. Their collections are normally subject specific, i.e. music, art, rare documents/books, etc. Although some may serve both their parent organization and the general public (for example, the library of the blind), they are not considered public, national, academic, or school libraries. In this chapter, Janneke Mostert, a Senior Lecturer at the Department of Library and Information Science, University of Zululand, South Africa, discusses the status, noteworthy developments and challenges of special libraries. She notes that special libraries have existed for a while in Africa, with ancient repositories in Mali (Timbuktu), Egypt, and Ethiopia; and their development has been re-active rather than pro-active, which has hampered their growth. At present, stronger growth and development has been observed in Egypt, Kenya, Nigeria and South Africa, particularly in the government ministries/departments, Non Governmental Organizations (NGOs) and corporate sectors. It was noted that the challenges facing special library development include marginalization, collection development (e.g., local content, digitization), capacity building, the application of ICTs, networking, and resource sharing. These challenges can be turned into opportunities if attention is redirected to the development of consortia, benchmarking and the measurement of value/standards, ICTs, collection development, staff development and the increased visibility of the libraries.

The last chapter in this section focuses on Library and information Education and Training. Essentially, common trends are noted in the following areas: the growth of LIS schools that are now over 55; review and revision of curricula; increased use of information and communication technologies (ICTs); the rise and fall of student numbers depending on market forces; amalgamation and reorientation of LIS programs for viability; relocation of the academic administration of LIS schools; and the expansion and closure of LIS schools (See Ocholla & Bothma, 2007; Minishi-Majanja, 2004.). The chapter by Bosire Onyancha and Mabel Minishi-Majanja, both from the University of South Africa, recognised and discussed the enumerated trends and concluded that LIS education and training in Africa has recorded significant growth in research productivity.

I think that impact studies and benchmarking of libraries in Africa is essential while improving on literacy rates overall and adult basic education by libraries are worth further exploration. A recent (2007) IFLA Publications [series 127] written by Roswitha Poll on "Performance Measurement in Libraries" that describes the indicators and focuses on resources and infrastructure, use, efficiency and potentials and development could be used for benchmarking African libraries.

SELECTED READINGS

Issak, Aissa [compiler]. 2000. *Public libraries in Africa: a report and annotated bibliography.* Oxford: International Network for the Availability of Scientific Publications (INASP). [Online] Available: http://www.inasp.ac.uk. Accessed 1 May 2006.

Jordan, Pallo. 2007. *Budget vote speech delivered by Minister of Arts and Culture, Dr PZ Jordan, MP, National Assembly.* [Online] Available: http://www.info.gov.za/speeches/2007/070612345.htm. Accessed 15 February 2008.

Mchombu, K.J. (2004) Sharing Knowledge for Community and Transformation: A Handbook 2. Quebec, Oxfam Canada [Online] Available: http://www. oxfam.ca/publications/sharing knowledge.htm Accessed 27 April 2006.

Mostert, B.J. (2001) African public library systems: a literature survey. LIBRES: Library and Information Science Research Electronic Journal Volume 11 Issue 1; March 31 [Online] Available: http://libres.curtin.edu.au/libres11n1/mostert.htm. Retrieved on 25th Apr 2006.

Nassimbeni, Mary and May, Bev. (2006) Adult education in South Africa public libraries: a profile of activities. South African Journal of Libraries and Information Science, Vol.72 (1), 12-26.

Ocholla, Dennis and Bothma Theo (2007) Trends, challenges and opportunities for LIS education and training in Eastern and Southern Africa, *New Library World,* Vol.108,N. 1/2, 55-78.

Ocholla, Dennis N.(2006) Information accessibility by the marginalized communities in South Africa and the role of libraries. In Susanne Seidelin and Thomas Skov Jensen, (eds.), IFLA/FAIFE Theme Report, World Report Series, Vol. IV, 15-27.

Rosenberg, D. (ed.) (1997). *University libraries in Africa: a review of their current state and future potential.* Three volumes. London: International African Institute.

Sturges, P., Neill, R. (1990). *The Quiet Struggle: Libraries and Information for Africa.* London. Mansell Publishing Limited.

PUBLIC LIBRARIES

Isaac Kigongo Bukenya

INTRODUCTION

Since time immemorial, Africa has had a strong communication mechanism through families, villages, communities, countries, etc. have disseminated information – formal and informal meetings in which issues of concern were raised, deliberated and resolved. Thus, oral means were mostly used to transfer information. The concept of the public library as a forum created to provide information, through the written word, to communities, was imported to Africa from the West, and appears to have been mooted in a philanthropic philosophy that encourages the equitable distribution of information resources to all people. The idea is that everyone should have equal opportunities for development. The aims and objectives of public library provision in the UK, the USA and Scandinavian countries reflect this philanthropic view.

The Colonization of Africa was a turning point in the colonial powers' establishment of their dominating influence in Africa. The renowned negative aspects of this phase of history will not be delved into in this chapter. But there were also positive developments that took place, such as the phenomenon of humanism, which regarded Africa as a huge arena for missionary work geared towards the betterment of African people. For the most part, the missionaries gave spiritual counselling through Christianity although some used other religions, such as Islam. In doing so, they utilized key religious sources of literature, such as the Bible and the Koran, on top of other development literature. They therefore had to spread literacy among the converts and create new literature for consumption. In turn, this literature had to be processed, stored and retrieved for use whenever necessary. They couldn't have known it then, but this was the first step towards the creation of a reading facility for all. One of the pioneers in this respect was Bishop Anglionby in the former Gold Coast (Ghana), who donated money for library causes and was particularly instrumental in the development of Ghanaian library services. Another example was Bishop Hannington, who started the big Mengo Hospital Library in Uganda. Even then, the idea of the library, let alone the public library, had not taken strong roots.

The upsurge of colonialism in the late 19th and early 20th centuries ushered in a political phase that culminated in the colonial rule of African territories. Colonial powers were represented by governors, under whom a hierarchy of administrators was commandeered. This chapter does not intend to examine the pros and cons of colonialism, but rather seeks to link the advent of libraries, and public libraries in particular, to colonialism. Coming from a background in which libraries were a course of habit, the colonialists soon proceeded to establish libraries for political and administrative purposes, and later for the privileged elite for information and educational purposes. Colonial cultural agencies such as the British Council, Alliance Francaise, and the United States Information Services, etc.; soon followed. Their emphasis was on promoting their culture in colonized countries. This was achieved through libraries – not, strictly speaking, public libraries, but cultural centercenters open to the public under certain arrangements.

The major breakthrough in the growth of the formal public library was initiated by UNESCO, which is the educational, scientific and cultural arm of UN (Gardner, F.M. (1966). The Second World War had just ended, and UN and its functionaries was one of the key strategies created to promote international understanding and peace. In 1949, the UNESCO Public Library Manifesto was published, with core guidelines stipulating the aims, services and beneficiaries of the public library. The UNESCO Public Library Manifesto has since been revised in 1972 and 1994.

UNESCO, in collaboration with the Nigerian Government, organized the first regional seminar on the development of public libraries in Africa at Ibadan. The Ibadanian Seminar focused on and highlighted three main areas:

1. Organizing public library services on a regional basis or national scale
2. Provision, selection and use of publications and audio-visual materials in African public libraries (and)
3. Professional training for public library services

The Seminar further advocated library legislation to ensure functional libraries through adequate financial backing and efficient administration according to national standards (http://www.emeraldinsight.co/Unsught/ViewContent?Filename-Publishers/Emera.Retrieved 11/12/2007).

UNESCO further set up a model public library in Enugu, Nigeria. This public library was a step in UNESCO's efforts to create educational and cultural institutions in Africa. The library was a teaching and learning center that functioned as a model for what good practices, facilities and services in a public library should be. These were to be emulated by other countries in Africa. The library was the designated venue for the second African public library development seminar in 1962. This Seminar reviewed the public library developments in Africa as they stood, and refocused the goals and development principles and directions that public libraries in Africa were to follow. Once again, key issues relating to public library development, such as the adoption of national legislation, establishment of centralized library services, emphasis on children's library services, education and training of professional librarians, establishment of national professional library associations, and production of suitable literature; were re-affirmed. By all appearances these seminars, particularly the Enugu Seminar, were a turning point for a number of countries. Public library development in regions such as East Africa moved faster and grew more focused – national legislation was adopted, centralized library services were launched, education and training of librarians initiated, etc.

HISTORICAL PERSPECTIVES AND ISSUES

Challenges and New Initiatives in the Provision of Public Libraries in Africa

It would not be possible to discuss the public library provision of each individual country in the entire continent of Africa. The approach adopted, therefore, is a blanket discussion of pertinent issues on the provision of public libraries taking East Africa (Kenya, Tanzania and Uganda), West Africa (Ghana and Nigeria) and Central and Southern Africa (Zambia and South Africa) as case studies.

The aspects discussed include: historical perspectives and issues on the provision of public libraries in Africa – the case studies; the challenges in the provision of public libraries in Africa; and ushering in the future – the new initiatives mooted as alternative approaches to the provision of public libraries in Africa.

The Public Library's Universal Mission, Objectives and Services

According to IFLA/UNESCO's Public Library Manifesto (1994), the public library is the local center of information, making all kinds of knowledge and information readily available to its users.

The services of the public library are provided on the basis of equal access to all, regardless of age, race, sex, religion, nationality, language or social status. Specific services and materials must be provided for those users who cannot, for whatever reason, use the regular services and materials, for example, linguistic minorities, people with disabilities, or people in hospitals or prisons.

All age groups must find material relevant to their needs. Collections and services have to include all types of appropriate media and modern technologies as well as traditional materials. High quality and relevance to local needs and conditions are fundamental.

Materials must also reflect current trends and the evolution of society, as well as the memory of human endeavorendeavors and imagination.

Collections and services should not be subject to any form of ideological, political and religious censorship, nor commercial pressures.

Mission of the Public Library

The following key missions, which relate to information, literacy, education and culture, should be at the core of public library services:

1. Creating and strengthening the reading habits in children from an early age;
2. Supporting both individual and self conducted education as well as formal education at all levels;
3. Providing opportunities for personal creative development;
4. Stimulating the imagination and creativity of children and young people;
5. Promoting an awareness of cultural heritage, appreciation of the arts, scientific achievements and innovations;
6. Providing access to cultural expressions of all performing arts;
7. Fostering inter-cultural dialogue and favoring cultural diversity;
8. Supporting the oral tradition;
9. Ensuring citizens have access to all sorts of community information;
10. Providing adequate information services to local enterprises, associations and interest groups;
11. Facilitating the development of information and computer literacy skills; and
12. Supporting and participating in literacy activities and programs for all age groups, and initiating such activities when necessary.

How has the real development of public libraries in Africa measured to the above specified ideals?

PROVISION OF PUBLIC LIBRARIES IN EAST AFRICA

East Africa, in this context, refers to the provision of public library services in Kenya, Tanganyika (Tanzania) and Uganda.

Until 1948, no real attempts had been made to provide public library services in East Africa. Most public libraries in the area had been founded by individuals or by trusts, and were initially only open to Europeans. Limited resources made it impossible to have trained personnel, and the stock often reflected the tastes of subscribing members. Services to elementary schools had been neglected, and where they existed (in secondary schools), stocks were inadequate and accommodation was poor.

At the time, the East African Literature Bureau, which originally had an ambitious programme for public library services throughout the territories, offered services such as the static branch library, book box and postal services. In 1959, S.W. Hockey was commissioned to conduct a study on the state of library services in the region and make proposals for their future development. The Hockey report was published in 1960 and made several recommendations that became the basis of library development in East Africa. Major recommendations include: the adoption of national library acts; the establishment of library Boards; centralized library services incorporating schools and public libraries; the establishment of library schools to educate and train librarians; and strong government financial support, among others.

Kenya, Uganda, and Tanzania adopted the National Library Services Act in 1963, 1964 and 1965 respectively. Kenya and Tanzania adopted centralized library services under the same boards, but Ugandan public library services were managed separately from other types of library services. The public libraries provided postal, book box, mobile and static branch library services. Since then, the development of libraries in general and of public libraries in particular has varied in success because of factors to be examined later.

PROVISION OF PUBLIC LIBRARIES IN UGANDA

In Uganda, the 1964 Public Libraries Act set up the Public Libraries Board, a body co-operate that aimed to establish, equip, manage and maintain libraries in the country. Libraries were interpreted to mean public libraries only. The services which had been transferred to Ugandan library services by the then East African Literature Bureau were taken over by the Public Libraries Board which was established by 1964 Public Libraries Act. The services were centralized and consisted of the headquarters where administration, selection, acquisition, processing and distribution of stock took place; the branch libraries; the postal services; and mobile and book box services.

In 1997 the Local Government Act was adopted, which decentralized public libraries under district, town and urban authorities. This in itself was a drawback because the new authorities appeared to have lower priorities about library development.

The Public Libraries Board was dissolved in 2003 and replaced with the National Library of Uganda Act, which set up the National Library of Uganda (NLU), which is under the Ministry of Gender and Community Development. NLU has some co-coordinating powers over other libraries – including public libraries – through the Ministry of Local Government. The mission of the National Library is to collect, preserve and disseminate Uganda's documented intellectual literature and culture, to give professional leadership in library and information delivery, and to promote the reading habit. The objectives of the NLU are:

1. To develop sound library services, plans and policies related to national development priorities and aspirations

2. To make library services accessible to all for the purposes of education, information, development and recreation

3. To promote and facilitate the provision of library services to all parts of Uganda, including rural areas where most people live and work

4. To acquire, preserve and make accessible documents of cultural, historical and educational value

5. To provide technical, professional and advisory services to local government and private sectors in the field of library services

6. To ensure that services are efficiently managed and that there is effective utilization of all material and human resources available

7. To support adult literacy and other continuing education programs by providing timely and relevant reading and information materials.

8. 8. To build institutional capacity for the promotion and delivery of library and information services

It is an ideal Act with very good intentions. However, some library authorities begrudge the Act for usurping their powers, creating a lot of duplication, and being a gigantic project not matched by the funding, staff, infrastructure and facilities required.

Despite the above complaints, NLU has supported public and community libraries by stocking them with the help of charity donations and purchases from donors under different projects, e.g. the Intra Africa Book Support Scheme and the Book Trade Project.

NLU also orients and trains staff from public and community libraries, giving them better library and marketing skills. Furthermore, library and community authorities are provided with guidelines on how to start and run libraries (http://www.nlu.go.ug/s2libs.htm Retrieved 11/6/2007).

NEW TRENDS IN PUBLIC LIBRARY PROVISION IN UGANDA

There are new trends in public library development, management and provision in Uganda today. First, though the Local Government Act, 1997, has its limitations its main provision namely the decentralization of public library development is commendable because it has brought public library service concerns down to grass roots level. The immediate effect of this policy has been the appreciation of library services in rural areas where the majority of Ugandans live and work. For example, this has resulted in the implementation of a rural library service project involving several districts in Uganda, including Mubende, Masaka, Mbarara, Kapchora and Luweero.

These operate on the same basis as community libraries, whereby accommodation, furniture and staff are provided by the community, but stock and supervision are the responsibility of the National Library.

Another timely development is the Multi Purpose Community centerTelecenter (MCT) at Luweero. It is funded by UNESCO, the International Telecommunications Union (ICU), and the International Development Research Center (IDRC). The Library at Nakaseke now has telephone, fax, Internet and e-mail connections and services, in addition to traditional library services.

The Acacia Initiative (Community and the Information Society in Africa) has introduced Telecenters in Uganda at Masaka, Kasangati, Zigoti, Kibaale, etc.

The National Library of Uganda's Reading Tents and the consolidation of books to school and children's libraries through Book Aid International are also new developments with great potential.

Public Library services in Uganda were and still are faced with a lot of problems, such as political interference, poor administration, lack of funding, poor staffing, etc These are discussed in detail in another section. New developments are expounded under New Initiatives.

PROVISION OF PUBLIC LIBRARIES IN KENYA

Kenya adopted the Hockey Report (1960) when it enacted the Kenya National Libraries' Services Board Act in 1965. The initial stock of 400,000 books was inherited from the East African Literature Bureau, which up to then was running public libraries through static, book box, postal and mobile library services. The first Kenya National Library Services Board commenced its functions in 1967, and the public library in Nairobi opened its doors to the public in 1969. The functions of the Board comprised of the establishment, equipment, management and maintenance of libraries in Kenya. The Board was particularly mandated to oversee the provision of public and school libraries in Kenya.

New Developments

Through the support and funding of the government of Kenya and donor agencies like the British Council, NORAD and UNESCO, KNLS has managed to put up a library in each of the eight provinces' headquarters in Kenya.

Currently, the services provided are managed from the KNLS headquarters – where the administration of the entire national library services is also based – and the Nairobi Provincial Library. The Public Library Network now embraces a total of 23 libraries in all provinces, districts and divisions. The total stock in all the services is up to 800.000 volumes. The total membership in the libraries network is 400,000, which excludes the [close to] million people who visit the libraries annually. These figures exclude the total figures of membership and use of other libraries (e.g. academic, special, etc.) in Kenya.

KNLS also provides community based libraries. This is an alternative to public library provision and requires the local community to contribute basic infrastructure such as land, buildings, furniture and equipment while the Board avails initial stock, staff and recurrent expenditure.

KNLS also provides the Camel Library Service (CLS), targeted at villages and settlements outside a 5 Km radius but within 10 Km of the regional library. The CLS works on the same basis as a mobile library service, except that the vehicles are camels. The advantage is that through the CLS, scattered populations are reached and served.

In order to ensure the sustainability of libraries and to enhance the funding of public libraries, the KNLS has instituted reasonable membership fees.

KNLS has also initiated innovative outreach approaches to public library provision. These involve the community in the administration of services that are appropriate to the community, and contribute towards service maintenance.

In the past those who wanted to establish public libraries anywhere in Kenya, were expected to provide a building. However, responding to the challenge of having a library building before public library services could be provided, today a book box service for farmers and children/students has been introduced by KNLS. The community contributes money to buy books, and KNLS processes and transports the books in boxes to the designated places. The set aim is for at least nine book boxes to be provided to each community, and for a student to have read at least 36 books a year. The book box service also includes the training of teacher-librarians to manage the services.

KNLS has also started two vital library services: the AIDS Awareness Service and Constitutional Information Services. Both services have played a role in educating the public. Through the support of the British Council, KNLS has also set up the Braille Unit to meet the reading needs of the blind.

Reacting to the problem that centers on the library being a foreign concept, KNLS has started a sensitization program to teach the relevance and importance of the public library for personal and community development. A public relations office has been established that publishes the Kenal Newsletter, which propagates the messages to the users wherever they are through and during exhibitions, such as agricultural shows, and National Book week.

The challenges that KNLS faces in the provision of public libraries will be discussed in a later section.

PROVISION OF PUBLIC LIBRARIES IN TANZANIA

Tanzania was the first in line to provide the public library services as proposed by Sydney W Hockey in 1960. The Tanzanian Libraries Services Board Act was enacted in 1963, followed by the Ugandan Public Libraries Board Act in 1964, and the Kenyan National Library Services Board Act in 1965. The Act empowered the

Tanzanian Libraries' Services Board to promote, establish, equip, manage, maintain and develop libraries in Tanzania (Dahlgren, C (1994). The 1963 Act was replaced with a new one in 1975 which extended the functions and powers of developing libraries under one umbrella, as per the NATIS concept. This concept was echoed by President Julius Nyerere in 1967 at the opening of the National Central Library in Dar es Salaam when he said: *"The real importance to our nation of this Central Library services is from the fact that this is the hub of a wheel, from which spokes will reach out to towns and villages throughout mainland Tanzania"*. The new act broadened the powers of the Tanzanian National Library Services Board by giving it the responsibility of supervising documentation services, training librarians, controlling and supervising public libraries, promoting literacy campaigns, stimulating interest in Tanzanian literature, promoting and developing indigenous literature, to libraries (Tanzania Library Services Act, 1975).

In order to fulfill this mandate, TNLS gives the following nation wide services:

1. Public Libraries
   This service includes the National Central Library in Dar es Salaam. Public libraries have reference and free lending services for both adults and children.
2. Rural library services
   According Sturges and Neille (1993), in 1989 Tanzania had over 3,000 village libraries with approximately 400 titles in each. These were and still are under the supervision of local staff, and are located in schools, clinics, courthouses or the offices of local authorities. The purpose of the libraries is to bring library services to rural areas.
3. School Libraries
   Tanzania has over 10, 000 primary schools and over 140 secondary schools. In order to begin to meet the needs of these institutions, six model secondary school libraries were developed, and a school mobile library service was initiated.
4. Government Libraries
   The Board has lent a hand in organizing government department libraries and in training the staff who work in these libraries in order to improve the provision of library services.
5. Special libraries
   The Board provides support and personnel in the running of these libraries.
6. Training/Staffing
   The Board conducts the National Library Assistants Certificate Course and organizes short continuing programs including seminars, workshops, etc.

7. The Board gives a supporting hand in the running of the Tanzanian Library Association; the current Chairperson of the Association is the Director of the TLS.

It may be safely stated that Tanzania has had a competitive edge in the provision of public libraries in East Africa. First, it had a very supportive President in the form of Julius Nyerere, who was always at the frontline of public library development. His support was instrumental, as was that of President Nkrumah in Ghana. This support continued in regimes that succeeded Nyerere. There was also the recruitment of a strong, knowledgeable and experienced Director, Max Broome, who equalled the appointment of Evans in Ghana. The Director implemented effective and coordinated library plans throughout the country. His good programs won government and foreign funding. A staff training program was also put in place.

Though public library provision has somewhat slowed down, new plans are underway to return Tanzania National Library Services to its former glory. These plans include: new procedures in recruitment membership in order to reduce congestion; the provision of rural public library services by reactivating the postal and mobile services; and the provision of rural public library services through community ventures with TNLS involvement. Also needing urgent beefing up is funding in order to meet the service costs.

Today, the recruitment of qualified and experienced staff, for example Dr. Ali Mcharazo, recently appointed Director of TNLS; practices such as allowing or sending staff to further their studies; and various continuous education initiatives have improved the quality and motivation of staff and consequently improved the library services. This needs to be enhanced.

Challenges will be discussed in a later section.

PROVISION OF PUBLIC LIBRARIES IN WEST AFRICA

In West Africa, Ghana (formerly referred to as the Gold Coast) and Nigeria were taken as the case studies.

Provision of Public Library Services in Ghana

The provision of public libraries in Ghana since 1951 is particularly associated with E. J. A. Evans for the fifteen years between 1951 and 1966. Other factors that contributed towards the provision of libraries, particularly public libraries, include the pioneering work of Bishop Anglionby, who was responsible for the early promotion of reading among Ghanaians (Cornelius, 1972); the British Council initiative, which helped lay the foundation for national library services (Dawuona-Hammond, 1963); considerable literacy; Ghana's healthy economic state, which assured the availability of capital and recurrent funds for library development; the need for public libraries by people seeking lifelong education, or by those who did not secure places in Universities, but were eager to pursue higher studies through private means; the UNESCO Seminar at Ibadan, 1953, during which issues regarding the organization and operation of public library services, selection and acquisition of suitable books, staff training, legislation, staff training, etc. were agreed upon; the progressive and supportive policy of Kwameh Nkrumah; the enthusiasm and hard work of the library staff; and a far-sighted and supportive Ghanaian Library Board.

The Act that established the Ghana (Gold Coast) Library Services Board was passed in 1949 and became operational in January 1950. It was one of the first library acts in Africa, and many countries took it as a model. The functions of the Act were to establish, maintain, equip and manage libraries in Ghana. At first the Act was interpreted to embrace all types of libraries. The ambiguity was settled in 1969/70 when a new act set up the Ghana Library Board and mandated it to establish, manage and maintain public libraries. Purposeful library buildings were constructed starting around 1953. Additionally, a postal library service for teachers, a mobile library service and branch libraries were started. With the support of government subvention and grants from town councils or local authorities, the Ghana Library Board services grew to include 18 branches, the Accra Central Library, three children's libraries in Accra, and regional libraries, all offering the services expected of public libraries.

In a nutshell, today public libraries provided by the Ghana Library Board comprise of the Headquarters, which advocates policy and carries out the administration of the whole system, provides central support and economic services, and also provides public library services over a wide geographic area to meet local needs (Almena, 1994). The Ghana Library Board now boasts ten administrative units in ten regions, and 43 service points for adults and 49 centers for children.

New Developments

The poor performance of public libraries in Ghana forced the Ministry of Education to set up a Community Libraries Project in order to improve the standard of education of pupils in the country. There are six such community libraries in Accra. The libraries are expected to serve the various communities, not only school children. Unfortunately, these services are facing problems similar to those of public libraries (discussed later, with new initiatives in a separate section).

Non-governmental organizations are making efforts to establish libraries for the public, particularly school children. One such NGO is the Ghana Book Trust, established by the Canadian Organization for Development through Education (CODE) in Ottawa, Canada. It has assisted by establishing libraries, providing books, and training library assistants throughout the country.

Provision of Public Libraries in Nigeria

The first public library in Nigeria was established in 1932 in Lagos via the financial assistance of the Carnegie Co-operation of New York and the Lagos Book Club. It was a subscription library. The colonial government did not take any active part in establishing public libraries in Nigeria. For example, on April 12th 1940, the colonial government objected to the Carnegie grant on the premise that it was of no practical value to Nigerians because African reading interests were limited.

The actual send off for public library development in Nigeria was UNESCO's initiative (with Nigerian governmental support), when the country hosted the Ibadan Seminar in 1953. The seminar focused on the development of public libraries in Africa. As already explained in the introduction, the Ibadan Seminar was instrumental in envisioning the nature, functions, pre- requisites and services of the public library. In fact, a public library was established at Enugu as a model to be emulated by the rest of Africa. Public library developments reflected the decisions made during the Ibadan Seminar. Some of these were national legislation, centralized services, free public library services, library services for all, stock embracing all manner of opinions, public funding, etc. Many librarians and administrators flocked to Enugu to see the model public library in action, and learnt much on how to establish public libraries in their own countries.

Ojo-Igbinoba (1995) stated that public libraries in Nigeria were primarily established by government to provide viable and relevant information to the entire public. Public libraries therefore are involved in the acquisition, selection, organization, and dissemination of information in the form of printed and non-printed materials for effective use. Patrons of the public library cut across all walks of life and include illiterates, pensioners, the disabled, children, adults, adolescents, farmers, etc. The public library is the main avenue through which the overall information resources in various areas of knowledge are made freely available to all members of society, irrespective of age, sex, race, educational level, or political and religious inclination.

Prior to the civil war, Nigeria's public library development was one of the best in Africa. It is unfortunate that the civil war had retrogressive impact on the Enugu Model Public Library and general public library development in Nigeria, as infrastructure, stock, staff and services were disrupted. Since then, public library development has never been the same. But all is not lost, because recent research showed commendable public library development, as explained below.

The study (Adebimpe, 1980) showed that 4 Public libraries were established between 1971 and 1975; 10 between 1976 and 1980; and 6 between 1981 and 1985. All these were established according to UNESCO's objectives. The study further revealed that despite the belief that Nigerians are not habitual readers; Nigerians were found to read if the libraries provided them with materials that are relevant to their needs. Another online source (http://emeraldinsight.com/InsightiewContent

Servelet?Filename=Published/Emera, retrieved 11/12/2007) established that public libraries in Nigeria are performing below expectation in terms of meeting their objectives. Virtually all the public libraries are poorly stocked and lack modern ICTs such as the Internet, and computer networks and communications.

Today, few public libraries operate in urban areas, and those that do have inadequate facilities. Mobile libraries, nicknamed public libraries on wheels, no longer pry isolated locations to supply public library services; and the postal library and book box services have been disbanded.

In view of the above, the following are recommended:

1. The Nigerian government should establish public libraries in various rural and urban communities
2. Public libraries should be adequately funded by government to ensure viable stocks, thereby enhancing services
3. Mobile library services should be re-energized in order to ensure effective public library service delivery to all parts of the country
4. There should be adequate and effective information technologies in all the various public libraries. Public libraries should be fully computerized, networked and have Internet access
5. Public libraries should embark on political and health awareness programs

New Developments

In order to instigate new trends in public library provision in Nigeria the following should be considered:

1. Needs assessment, because in order to scientifically establish the structure of a society, the information needs of this society and the ensuing services required to meet these information needs must be identified.
2. The creation of an administrative and managerial structure that delivers library and information services to where the majority of people are – the rural areas – so that the services are easily accessible.
3. The repackaging of library and information services in brands that are easily accessible, affordable and consumable (considering literacy levels, standards and affordability)
4. Enhancement of education and the training of information professionals to equip them with the appropriate language, marketing and PRO skills. This would allow them to penetrate rural areas where library and information services are badly needed
5. Ensuring that there are enough funds to run and maintain the services. Donor dependency should be substituted with adequate government funding

and/or the information professionals' fund generating initiatives, e.g. fund-raising or the sale of services and facilities at an affordable rate.

Provision of Public Libraries in Central Africa

Zambia was chosen as a case study in the provision of public libraries in Central Africa.The formal advent of public libraries in Zambia is associated with colonialism in the then Northern Rhodesia. However, history records that before colonialism, cultural traditions and beliefs of the various Zambian ethnic groups were preserved through memory, and reported from generation to generation. However, what is not certain is the degree of effective distortion, exaggeration or understatement contributing towards the authenticity of oral transactions overtime, and thus towards oral preservation and communication.

The shift from traditional (oral) to the written (reading and writing) mode of preservation and communication was ushered in with the arrival of missionaries, who introduced Western education. The first Missionary, David Livingstone, introduced the "tin-truck" portable library. It operated in Zambia between 1853 and 1873.

The Livingstone Subscription Library was established in 1908. A number of such libraries sprang up in the 1920's, but access was restricted to only the elite and rich in society, mainly the colonialists. Another landmark in the provision of public libraries was the establishment of the Northern Rhodesia Publications Bureau in 1947, which introduced a countrywide book box service scheme. In 1960, the Joint Publications Bureau received grant-aid from the Ford Foundation towards the development of a countrywide Public Library Service. In 1962 the Northern Rhodesia Library Service was established and subsequently became the Zambia Library Service (ZLS), which took over the responsibility of public library provision, among other functions.

ZLS is largely a rural library network providing a broad range of reading services, including agricultural information to support local farming, the mainstay of Zambia's economy.

New Developments

Currently, the public library services network comprises of the Headquarters based in Lusaka, 6 provincial libraries in the rural provinces and 18 branch libraries.

Some provincial libraries and branch libraries double as Centers of the National Library and Cultural Centers for the blind and provide Braille books, talking books and weekly news recorded on cassettes.

The Zambia Library Services also runs reading tent events, which take place throughout the year and fill in gaps wherever there are no library buildings.

In view of the level of illiteracy still found in Zambia, the concept of community information services has been implemented. This consists of the provision of information through alternative strategies, such as films, music, dance, drama, posters, and meetings, which diverge from the textual approach. This has afforded useful information to the rural and urban poor still living under the scourge of illiteracy and its implications.

Another service run by the ZLS is the school library service, which has set up over 1,000 library centers. The community holds responsibility for these centers, while the Zambia Library Services provides stock and trains the staff who work in them. These centers are often placed in schools, although others are located in refugee camps, forest stations and prisons

The training of teachers in Teacher Training Colleges and teachers already in the field is also carried out in order to ensure that teachers perpetuate the reading habit amongst their pupils/students (http://www.bookaid.org/cms.cgi/ste/whatwedo/countries/-zambia.htm).

Other information initiatives being implemented for the public include:

1. Improving ICT availability in rural areas and providing the assistance of United States Agency for International Development (USAID)
2. Developing the isolated information centers established by NGOs. These are targeted at professionals in various fields, such as: gender or the disadvantaged (for example, the visually handicapped).
3. The supply – by government ministries in conjunction with information providers – of information services through posters, films, leaflets etc.

Problems

Zambia Library Service is plagued with a litany of problems characteristic of National Library Services in Africa, including the lack of an institutionalized regular nationwide budget, made worse by the declining economy; the lack of functional library buildings; a shortage of educated and trained information professionals; a poor publishing and trade industry; ineffective government support; and dwindling international support. As Professor Lundu (2002) "Council libraries (public libraries) have lacked vision, leadership and funding and have depended heavily on donors ..."

The solutions to these problems are discussed in a later section.

Provision of Public Libraries in South Africa

Public libraries in South Africa were first introduced by the British colonizers. It is, therefore, small wonder that the libraries adopted the practices of the colonizing country. Judging by developments in the 1950s, public libraries were unevenly distributed, and access to them was granted based on racial lines, which meant that they were restricted to serving white people. It was only in the 1980s that libraries were opened to other South Africans.

Before 1994, the provision of public libraries was regarded as the responsibility of the local authorities, but governance and funding were complicated by the involvement of both provincial and municipal authorities. There were ten autonomous or non-affiliated public libraries in the city centers of Cape Town, Durban, East London, Germanton, Johannesburg, Pietermarizberg, Port Elizabeth, Pretoria, Roodepoort, and Springs. These derived their funding from municipal rates and revenues and were not attached to any provincial library services.

On the other hand, affiliated libraries were administered jointly by their local authority and the province to provide library materials mainly to the white population. The type of assistance rendered included financial grants, information resources, infrastructural support and professional service. The local authorities were responsible for the recruitment of human resources and for communication. Problems with public library provision during this period ranged from geographical and economical factors, to illiteracy, ignorance about public libraries and the lack of suitable reading material.

The 1980s saw the emergence of resource centers in South Africa as an alternative to the traditional public library. The resource centers became focal community centers that provided relevant information for study and other purposes. They were accommodated in single or multiple rooms where books, periodicals, newspapers and other information sources were kept and made available to the users. The demise of the resource center was as a result of dynamic changes in society and in economics, and resource centers were eventually integrated into public libraries.

After 1994, three surveys were commissioned to examine the state of public library provision and make appropriate recommendations. These were the Arts and Task Group (ACTAG, 1995), The Public and Community Libraries Inventory of South Africa (PaCLISA) – (Van Helden and Lor, 2002) and a survey by The Center of the Book (PICC, 2005), which focused on the public/community library sector.

The ACTAG made several recommendations, including that public libraries should be funded from the Reconstruction and Development Programme (RDP) to cater for literacy programs and materials, the promotion of a reading culture, and also the work for the disadvantaged, children and the youth.

The findings of PaCLISA indicated that public libraries were still serving the educated and the middle class, who are a small minority of the general public. Furthermore, in 2004 the number of libraries was not proportional to the population in the provinces. For example, Kwazulu-Natal with bigger population had 164 libraries, which was far less than 516 and 307 in the smaller provinces of Gauteng and Western Cape respectively.

The PICC report highlighted the challenges facing libraries, such as funding, change, alignment, governance, human resources, high illiteracy, poverty and unemployment (Nassimeni and May, 2006). Witbooi (2006), Leach (1998), and Aitcheson (2006) confirmed these challenges.

The biggest announcement came in 2005, when the South African Government pledged R 1,000,000,000, over three years for public library development provided that comprehensive research was carried out on the number and size of libraries in each municipality, the user statistics, human resources, the collections, and the demographics of each municipality.

Jacaranda Intellectual Property Business Consultants won the tender to develop a funding model for public and community libraries. Consequently, the following three recommendations were made, which have been turning points in the development of public and community libraries in South Africa:

1. Funding for the 2007/8 fiscal year is made available as a conditional grant to ensure that it is used for the intended purpose
2. R 15 million – 30 million gets allocated to each province, distributed from the total of R 2000 million.
3. Each province is provided with some direction on how to spend its allocation based on its unique circumstances, such as demographics, size and geographic area, separating structure, etc. (KPMG and Jacaranda, 2006)

These positive initiatives of central and provincial governments, together with the participation of communities and service providers and the goodwill of individuals, signal that book lovers, readers and concerned citizens are all joining hands to resurrect our public libraries. Amid all the doom and gloom, there does seem to be hope for the South African public library sector (Witbooi, 2007).

There are encouraging developments already in existence to testify to this. For example, The Western Cape Library Service boasts of being the most comprehensive library service in South Africa. It has a total of 305 library centers serving a population of 4, 465, 600 million people, with new facilities and upgrading in the pipeline for three district projects (The Western Cape Library Service, 2006).

Challenges Faced in The Provision of Public Libraries

Fifty-four years have elapsed since the launch of guidelines for model public library service provision at the Ibadan Seminar in 1953. Africa still struggles to meet the objectives of these guidelines. Challenges in this context are examined. This is not to disregard the remarkable standard of public library provision achieved in some countries in Africa.

Kay Raseroka (1997) pointed out that clearly, "*the general public library service conditions in Africa are in a depressed state*". This can be attributed to many factors, including: dependency on donor funds – inadequate in most cases and irreplaceable when terminated – which affect stock development and lead to uncompetitive staff salaries; unsatisfactory infrastructure development and maintenance; insensitivity towards local needs due to centralized services that often do not consult the grassroots population and consequently provide the wrong ser-

vices, which adults ignore but students sometimes embrace; lack of habitual readers – most read to achieve a purpose and no longer read when they are successful;
and low literacy rates that create dependency on oral or other alternative sources
of information. Furthermore, information professionals are sometimes not only inadequate in quantity, but are also short in quality, to the extent that they lack the
vision, commitment and creativity necessary to provide services that entice new
users and keep regular users interested.

Diana Rosenberg (2004) puts it bluntly:

"The early promise of libraries has not been fulfilled in Africa. Buildings and
other facilities have not been maintained, shelves are either empty or full of
out-of-date and irrelevant materials, and the percentage of the population using the services is negligible. This is more or less true, albeit at differing levels in different countries, for all libraries in the public sector, whether academic, public or special"

Another major problem already highlighted is the dependency on donor funding or
material donations. These are totally inadequate since they are no longer an alternative to a substantial institutional budget for public library service provision.

Perhaps the biggest obstacle is whether public library users, both current and
potential, are really convinced that the public library can make a difference in their
lives. Does my illiterate brother down in the remote rural village of Sakabusolo
know what difference using a public library would make to his health or that it
may result in more wealth? It is, after all, not possible for one to reach the peak of
a mountain without knowing the fundamentals of mountaineering.

Another burning question is whether the powers that be are committed to public
library provision and view it as a corner stone to community development. Are libraries politically rewarding? Would a local politician be voted to Parliament on
the premise that he/she would build a library as opposed to a hospital or school in
the constituency?

To conclude, it is generally important to take action on the following in order to
ensure faster and better provision of public libraries in Africa:

1. Explain the role of the public library in community development to the general population
2. Conduct research into what users need so that the appropriate services are
   provided
3. Alleviate illiteracy and create demand for public library use
4. Produce appropriate public library materials in adequate quantity and quality
5. Governments should pay more than lip-service commitment to funding and
   do all that is necessary for the development of library services (including library service legislation)

6. Prioritizing the education and training of information professionals as in any other professional association

7. Sharing experiences with those countries whose libraries and public libraries have succeeded in uplifting communities

Into the Future:
New Initiatives for the Provision of Public Libraries

Many now fear that the provision of public libraries failed to deliver what was expected. For example, it is clear that information poverty still haunts many of our communities. The term "information poverty" is used to describe the lack of the most basic survival information. The original concept and philosophy behind public libraries was to stop the spread of this scourge. The public library was meant to be the people's university, a source of knowledge that enabled the public to graduate from ignorance with the help of free (barrier-less) information facilities. The section that follows touches on new initiatives that intend to play a more realistic and meaningful role in providing information to the community.

Community libraries

Community libraries were conceived to provide survival information to the community; the kind of information necessary for full and equal participation in society. The Library Association (1980) defined community information services as:

"Services which assist individuals or groups with daily problem-solving and with participation to the democratic process. The service concentrates on the needs of those who do not have easy access to other sources of assistance and on the most important problems that people have to face, problems to do with their homes, their jobs and their rights".

Alemna (1995) explains that the rationale of community libraries lies in their essentially different sense of social purpose. They differ from traditional libraries in that they are proactive about their sense of social purpose. The primary stimulus is humanitarian, and its outcome is social intervention in support of positive prejudice.

Various studies (Obayade, 1984; Mchombu, 1984; and Durant, 1985; in Nigeria, Tanzania and Kenya respectively) have shown that rural people need information for their development in areas such as health, occupation, water supply, electricity, roads, education, religion and recreation. One immediate question arises: why have public libraries failed to supply such information to communities? One reason is that the public library is perceived as an organization for the elite, catering for fully literate members who can utilize all the reading materials in the library. Some staff members are also perceived as elitists – many of them are culturally disoriented and may not effectively communicate with the rural folk. Furthermore, much of the information resources in these libraries do not meet the real community's needs. Above all, the nature of the building, furniture and equipment is often imposing, and the community therefore perceives the entire enterprise as prohibitively expensive. The community library is a solution because it is conceived, born and nurtured by the community, and therefore naturally reflects the nature and interests of the community in its library services. It is also affordable and focused on providing relevant materials to the community, which controls and manages it.

Kay Raseroka (1997) believes that such initiatives are a radical departure from the traditional mould of librarianship, and notes that despite being gradually introduced, initiatives such as community libraries are steadily gaining momentum.

Rural Libraries and Resource Development Programme (RLRDP)

In Zimbabwe, the Rural Libraries and Resource Development Programme (RLRDP) uses drama, song and dance to disseminate information, substituting reading, lending and literacy support services. The RLRDP has formed alliances with existing community grassroots' groups, and non-governmental and government information programs.

The Village Reading Rooms programme (VRRP) – Botswana

This is another such initiative, although arguably not very successful. To date, the initiative has shown that it requires commitment from all its partners and a shared vision based on the good of the community it serves.

The Camel Library Service (CLS)

In Kenya, the Camel Library Service (CLS) is another classic example. This is a form of mobile community service that uses the Camel transport system. The Kenya National Library Services adopted the strategy of community participation and involvement to encourage local ownership. Community involvement and participation was enhanced through the formation of Local Committees that incorporate village elders, community opinion leaders and other local experts, and this has greatly contributed towards the success of the project (http://www.knls.or.ke/ history.htm).

The National Book Festival

The National Library of Uganda (NLU) is responsible for organizing up-country activities together with its partners – the local governments, NGOs, Trusts, etc. NLU organizes the National Book Festival, bringing together all the stakeholders in the Publishing and Book Industry under the Umbrella of the National Book Trust of Uganda. Various activities for primary pupils, secondary school students, women's groups, young adults and adult learners take place. Activities include reading marathons, book descriptions, story telling, book exhibitions and talks related to reading and literacy, among others. Such initiatives change perceptions about opportunities for development, and also cultivate a new culture intent on clarifying the needs of the community, thus rendering services sustainable.

Multipurpose Telecenters and Libraries

In 1997 the then Public Libraries Board, now the National Library of Uganda, in partnership with the International Telecommunication Union (ITU), the International Research Center, (IDRC), the British Council, the Ugandan Government and the Ugandan National Commission for UNESCO established the Nakaseke Multipurpose Telecenters and Libraries. The goal of the project was to stimulate rural development by facilitating access to information, learning resources and facilities, and ICTs, and also improving medical services through telemedicine. Reports from the field indicate that the telecenters are not being optimally used. Factors that could be causing this level of use range from lack of local literature, to computer phobia, poor funding, high maintenance costs, cultural taboos and power shading, among others. Similar developments have been witnessed in Mayuge, Kasangati and Buwama, etc, in Uganda.

CONCLUSION

Modern public library provision in Africa can be pinned down to the beginnings of philanthropy and colonialism on the continent. The former inadvertently spread literacy through reading and writing and initiated the need for storage, cataloguing etc., while the latter brought with it a culture in which libraries were a course of habit. Following the Second World War, UNESCO came to play a major role in establishing public libraries in Africa. Public library provision in Africa has reached different levels of development based on the level of commitment, government support, legislation, staff, and public response, among other concerns. Unfortunately, public library provision has declined to worrisome proportions in some countries. This is mainly due to the alien and elitist nature of the public library; the failure of the public library to identify community needs and therefore offer relevant services; inappropriate information materials; poor or inadequate staff; and the lack of committed institutional budgets, which creates dependency on donor funds. New initiatives, such as Reading Tents, multipurpose telecenters and villages libraries – Uganda; the Village Reading Rooms Programme (VRRP) – Botswana; Rural Libraries and Resource Development Programme (RLRDP) – Zimbabwe; and the Camel Library Service (CLS) in Kenya have been initiated, and there is hope that the involvement of communities will generate support and commitment to information service provision, leading to the development of more meaningful information services in Africa.

Internationally, initiatives such as the 2002 Millennium Development Goals (MDGs), the African Information Society Initiative (AISI) and New Partnership for African Development (NEPAD) are also hoping to catalyze the utilization of information within African communities.

References

1. A Short History of Carnegie Corporation's Library Program. Carnegie Reporter, Vol. 2 No. 3. [Online] Available: http://www.carnigie.org/reporter/07/library/shorthistory. html.
2. Aboyade, B.O (1984). "Communications potential of the library for non-literates, an experiment in providing information in a rural setting". *Libri*, Vol. 34 No. 3, pp 243-62.
3. Adimorah, E.N (1983). "An analysis of progress made by public libraries as social institutions in Nigeria." *UNESCO Journal of Information Services Libraries and Achieve Administration*. Vol. 5 No. 3, 167.
4. Alemna, A.A. (1994). "Community libraries: an alternative to public libraries in Africa. Library Review 44.7.
5. Atchison, J. (2005). Experiments in the provision of rural community libraries in South Africa: The Family Literacy Project's initiatives. *Innovation*, 32: 94-109, June.
6. Dahlgren, C (1994.). "The Tanzania Library Service: A Review of Recent Literature." Vol. 5, No. 1. [Online] Available: http://www.worlib.org/vol05mo1.
7. FLA/FAIFE World Report: Libraries and Intellectual Freedom. [Online] Available: http://www.ifla.org/faife/report/nigeria.htm.
8. Hockey, S.W (1960). "The Development of Library Services in East Africa." In: *Libraries in East Africa*, ed. by Anna Britta Wallenius, Uppsala Institute of African Studies.
9. IFLA/UNESCO Public Library Manifesto 1994. [Online] Available: http://www.ifla.org/ VIIs8/unesco/eng.htm.
10. Kenya National Library Service. [Online] Available: http:/www.knls.or.ke/history.htm.
11. Leach, A. (2006). Alternative funding and the public library sector: An exploratory overview with reference to South Africa. *Innovation*, 32: 125-155.
12. Leach, A. (1998). An overview of the public library sector in South Africa post-1994. *Innovation*. 16: 3-19.
13. Mchombu, K.J. (1984). "Development of library and information services in Tanzania". *Information Processing and Management*, Vol. 20 No. 4, 559-69.
14. Nassimbeni, M. & May, B. (2006). Adult education in South African public libraries: Enabling conditions and inhibiting factors. *Innovation*, 32: 29-40.
15. National Library of Uganda. [Online] Available: http://www.nlu.go.ug/g_info.htm
16. Perry-Widstrand, R. (1980). "Library Services – for Whom?" In: *Libraries in East Africa*, ed. by Anna Britta Wallenius, Uppsala Institute of African Studies.

17. Raseroka, H.K (1997). "Public libraries and life long learning – African perspectives. 63rd IFLA General Conference – Conference Program and Proceedings, August 31 – September 5.

18. Rosenberg D. (2004). *Current Issues in Library and Information Services in Africa.*<publisher?

19. South African National Committee for Co-operation between Public and School Libraries (2000). "A way forward for co-operation between school and public libraries: draft National Guidelines for the co-operation between school and public libraries in South Africa." 66th IFLA Council and General Conference, Jerusalem, Israel, 13-18 August [Online] Available: http://www.ifla.org/IV/ifla66/papers/ 151-133e.htm.

20. Sturges and Neille (1993). *The quiet struggle.* London, Mansell, 1993.

21. UNESCO Public Library Manifesto. [Online] Available: http:/www.unesco.org/webworld/libraies/manifestos/libraman.html.

22. Van Helden, P. & Lor, P.J. (2002). *Public and community libraries inventory of South Africa: PaCLISA final report.* Pretoria: National Library of South Africa.

23. Western Cape Provincial Library Service (2006). *Review*: 2005-2006. Cape Town: WCPLS.

24. Witbooi, M. (2006a). Mark's multi-million rural surprise for mayor. *Cape Argus.* 16 August, p. 4.

25. Witbooi, M (2006b). Setting up a point-use library facility: Testing and African model in Wesbank, Western Cape. *Innovation*, 32: 41-54, June.

26. (http://www.emeraldinsight.co/Unsught/ViewContent?Filename-Publishers/Emera. Retrieved 11/12/2made2007)

27. [Online] Available: http://www.nlu.go.ug/s2libs.htm. Retrieved 11/6/2007.

28. [Online] Available: http://emeraldinsight.com/InsightiewContentServelet? Filename=Published/Emera. Retrieved 11/12/2007.

29. (http://www.bookaid.org/cms.cgi/ste/whatwedo/countries/-zambia.htm).

30. [Online] Available: http://www.emeraldinsight.co/Unsught/ViewContent? Filename-Publishers/ Emera. Retrieved 11/12/2007.

31. [Online] Available: http://www.nlu.go.ug/s2libs.htm. Retrieved 11/6/2007.

32. [Online] Available: http://emeraldinsight.com/InsightiewContentServelet?Filename= Published/Emera. Retrieved 11/12/2007.

33. [Online] Available: http://www.knls.or.ke/history.htm. Retrieved 11/12/2007.

Bibliography

1. De Jager, K. & Nassimbeni, M. (2005). Towards measuring the performance of public libraries in South Africa. *South African Journal of Libraries and Information Science.* 71(1): 39-50.

2. Evans, J.A. Evelyn (1964). A Tropical Library Service: the story of Ghana's Libraries. London, Andre Deutsch, 174.

3. Gardner, F.M. (1966). "Unesco and Library and related services in Africa." *Unesco Bull. Libr.* Vol. XX, No. 5.

4. Guidelines for Public Libraries (1998). Section of Public Libraries Newsletter, Issue No. 20.

5. Hassner, K. "The model library project – a way to implement the UNESCO Public Library Manifesto."

6. Ikoja-Odongo, J.R. (2003). "Public library politics: The Ugandan perspective." World Library and Information Congress: 69th IFLA General Conference and Council. 1-9 August, Berlin.

7. Kaungamno, E.E. and Ilomo. C.S (1979). Books Build Nations. Vol. One – Library Services in West and East Africa. London, Tran Africa, 169.

8. Kigongo-Bukenya, I.M.N (1980). Public Libraries in Uganda. In: Libraries in East Africa, edited by Ann-Britta Wallenius. Uppsala, Institute of African Studies.

9. Kigongo-Bukenya, I.M.N. (1990). Combating Illiteracy through Public Library Services. In: Information and Libraries in the Developing World. Vol. One-Sub-Saharan Africa. London, the Library Association, 181.

10. KPMG & Jacaranda (2006). *Department of Arts and Culture Impact assessment study*. Unpublished report by KPMG Services (Pty) Ltd and Jacaranda Intellectual Property Business Consultants.

11. Library Association (1980). Community *Information: What Libraries Can Do.* Library Association, London, 1.

12. Sewell, P.H (1998). 'The evaluation of library services in depth." *Unesco Bull. Libr.* Vol. XXII, No. 6.

13. Wise, Michael and Olden Anthony (1990). Information and Libraries in the Developing World –Sub-Sahara Africa. Compiled and edited by Michael Wise and Anthony Olden. London, Library Association, 181.

ACADEMIC LIBRARIES

Reggie Raju and Jaya Raju

INTRODUCTION

A state-of-the-art well resourced and well-managed university library is a significant contributor to academic excellence – excellence in teaching, learning and research. The size of a university library's collection, it is argued by Kuh and Gonyea (2003:256), is an apparent indicator of academic quality. They also argue that
the library's central role in the academic community is beyond question. Therefore, it should be the norm that the university library consumes a reasonable percentage of a university's annual budget. This expenditure, as alluded to by Kavulya (2006:22), must be viewed as an ongoing annual investment in the development and growth of the institution. However, in Africa, university libraries are
"generally perceived to be inadequate and financial support of library development viewed as small in scale, piecemeal and lacking in coordination" (Kavulya,
2006:22). Cullen et al. (2004:330) corroborate the assertion by Kavulya when they
state that "Africa's [university] libraries, [are] under resourced and under utilized,
are facing a crisis that, though seemingly quiet, has the potential to affect the continent's intellectual capital for decades to come." The study undertaken by
Rosenberg (1997) confirms this bleak state of university libraries in Africa and
claims that university libraries have declined to a near total collapse. This decline,
according to Rosenberg, is characterized by low numbers of books per student, inadequate journal subscriptions and limited access to electronic information, which
has led to libraries being unable to adequately support teaching, learning and research activities in universities. These trends are exacerbated by limited space and
continuously declining budget levels adding to the inability of universities to satisfy the growing demand for education (Kavulya, 2006:22, Cullen et al. 2004:330;
Nawe, 2001:31).

The Carnegie report (*Carnegie challenge...*, 2000) argues that books and their
availability cannot be a priority in a continent ravaged by poverty, war, famine and
HIV/AIDS. However, in a global economy that is increasingly centered on access
to knowledge and information, books and information will always be a catalyst in
solving a nation's problems. The limited access to books and information will not
only retard Africa's capacity to solve its problems but will also negatively impact
on its full potential to contribute to the global information society. The Carnegie
report (*Carnegie challenge...*, 2000:1) cautions that Africa should make every effort to ensure that it is not left behind in the information revolution as it was in the
industrial revolution. Given that university libraries have the potential to ameliorate the state of the continent through teaching, learning and research, university
librarians have to redefine their traditional roles and make their contributions,
within given constraints, to teaching, learning and research. Further, there is a

need for librarians to seek alternative, but constant, sources of funding given that funding is the nerve center to efficient and effective library and information provision.

The discussion in this chapter on the current state of African university libraries builds on the findings of the work conducted by Rosenberg and colleagues (1997). The chapter briefly examines the findings of the Rosenberg study and then engages in discussion on critical issues currently impacting on the state of university libraries. The literature suggests that there are 'peaks' and 'valleys' in the development of university libraries in Africa (Ksibi, 2006; Ani, 2005; Mutula, 2004; Rosenberg, 1997). Countries such as South Africa, Botswana and Egypt are considered to be the 'peaks' while the vast majority of the countries in Africa are languishing way behind in library provision to its university communities. However, it must be noted that even in countries that are considered the 'peaks', development and levels of provisions, within those counties, are uneven (Raju, 2007; Rosenberg, 2005; Mutula, 2004). The focus of the chapter would be on that majority of African countries that are plagued by issues that prevent them from providing efficient and effective university library services.

The discussion of the critical issues referred to above include collection development and facilities, funding, staffing and status of librarians, resource sharing and the application of IT.

However, before engaging in a discussion on issues plaguing African university library services it is important to briefly make reference to the issue of standards for academic libraries. The Association of College and Research Libraries (2004) Board of Directors is of the view that standards should not be prescriptive but rather provide a comprehensive outline to methodically examine and analyze all library operations, services, and outcomes in the context of accreditation. Similarly, Lynch (1987:121), when commenting on standards for university libraries in developing countries, points out that "university libraries are encouraged to support national efforts at prescriptive standards and to develop various quantitative standards that reflect local, regional and national variations".

The Standing Committee for the Section on University Libraries and other General Research Libraries developed the IFLA Statement of standards for university libraries in developing countries (Lynch 1987:120). This Statement too takes cognizance of the fact that the roles and responsibilities of university libraries vary from country to country. At the same time the Statement provides a means by which the quality of the library serving a university can be assessed, offers guidance for improvements in the library and suggests a framework within which various countries or regions could develop their own statements of standards (Lynch 1987:121; Lynch 1982:39).

Lynch (1982:39) outlines six elements that are most common to academic library standards, which in the main, according to Pitman, Trahn and Wilson (2001), have not changed over the years. These six elements include: (1) the size of the collection, (2) the size *and* composition of staff and the balance between professional and support staff, (3) the percentage of the institution's total budget to be used to determine the library's budget, (4) the seating capacity of the library in ratio to the size of the student body, (5) library services, and (6) the library's administration. All standards for academic libraries emphasize that the primary objective of an academic library is to support teaching, learning and research (Lynch 1982:39), which is a core issue in this chapter.

To reiterate, the discussion in this chapter is centered on an examination of the critical issues referred to earlier that include collection development and facilities, funding, staffing and status of librarians, resource sharing, and the application of IT.

THE ROSENBERG REPORT

Rosenberg (1997) and a group of researchers conducted extensive research on the state and the future potential of university libraries in Africa. Rosenberg (1997) reports on, amongst others, critical issues such as collections and facilities, funding, IT and automation, resource sharing and staffing. According to the report (1997:14), the book and journal holdings of university libraries are poor. The poor collection has marginalized university libraries from its clientele. Olden (1998:491) points out that "academics no longer bother to visit" the library. Information for research purposes is acquired through the development of personal contacts with overseas colleagues who supply relevant information for teaching and research. Further, journeys abroad provide ideal opportunities to visit libraries and gather up-to-date information (Olden, 1998:491). The focus of the collection development policy, according to Rosenberg (1997:1, 17), is on the purchase of multiple copies of textbooks for Special Reserve or Short Loan collections. Olden (1998:491) provides the example of Makerere University (Uganda), which has set up book banks with multiple copies of textbooks which students borrow for the entire year. Given the fact that the collections are very poor, the university library is used primarily as a place for study rather than for its collection. Commensurate with this scenario, the improvement that the students demand is for more study space in libraries.

With regard to funding, university libraries are funded, via the parent body, by government (Rosenberg, 1997:25). However, a large percentage of this funding is allocated to cover staffing costs, which, in effect, leaves very little to nothing for the acquisition of books and journals. Rosenberg (1997:2, 25-27) reveals the dependence on external funding to build the resources budget: "In a number of libraries, outside support provides between 90% to 100% of acquisitions. In addition, virtually all new initiatives (e.g. IT) are the result of outside assistance" (Rosenberg, 1997:2).

Rosenberg (1997:28) submits that PCs, CD-ROM and email are becoming the norm rather than the exception. However, Rosenberg (1997:28) does indicate that "full-scale automation of library operations is rare." She goes on to caution that much of the innovation comes from donor support. However, the once-off cost is not a reality; IT software and hardware are expensive to maintain and update. Olden (1998:493) quite rightly points out that the future costs of technology are no different to the acquisition of books and journals which has already been seriously neglected due to the lack of funds – there is a need for continuity.

Resource sharing, according to Rosenberg (1997:31), was adopted by developed countries to compensate for the resource inadequacies of individual libraries and to cut costs. However, in Africa, resource sharing is limited to inter-library loans (ILL). However, even this limited form of sharing is under utilized. Rosenberg's (1997:31) research reveals very low use of ILL by university libraries either within a country, intra-Africa or internationally.

Olden (1998:494), in reviewing the Rosenberg report, comments that the lack of sufficient professionally trained staff is not a problem in the majority of African university libraries. However, the unnecessarily bloated number of "non-professional" staff detracts from efficient service provision (Olden, 1998:494; Rosenberg, 1997:34-35). Olden (1998: 494) explains that "non-professional" staff are not trained to help with queries and that they do not seem to value the library or fully understand its purpose. The conferring of full academic status to librarians in some African countries has enhanced the prestige of the profession. Hence the profession has increased its capacity to attract quality personnel to the LIS sector (Rosenberg, 1997:36).

As indicated, the Rosenberg report serves as a foundation for discussion in the rest of this chapter. The first issue to be discussed is the critical area of collection development and facilities.

COLLECTION DEVELOPMENT AND FACILITIES

In a survey conducted by Badu (2004:101), the physical resources that were identified as essential to achieving the desired goals of teaching, learning and research at a university were buildings, library equipment, furniture, and telecommunications infrastructure. The lack of space is seen as a problem resulting in poor access to library resources by researchers and students. According to Badu's (2004) study, the solutions to the inadequacies lay in constructing more library buildings, which ought to be designed to accommodate modern technology. However, Rosenberg (1998:5) points out that there is increasing dilapidation of library buildings as a direct result of dwindling allocation of funds. Given that the funding situation has not improved over the years, in fact it has worsened, one can assume that the buildings by now would have deteriorated even further than that described by Rosenberg. If there is a desperate need to expand the physical building facility, the popular option becomes the use of makeshift buildings. Agboola (2000:283), when describing the Nigerian situation, points out that 22 out of the 37 university library collections are housed in makeshift buildings.

The inadequacy in physical provisions does not augur well for meeting the desired objectives of teaching, learning and research. This hurdle to the fulfillment of the desired objectives of the university is compounded by the general agreement that the collections in African university libraries are inadequate (Ksibi, 2006:256; Badu, 2004:101; Cullen et al. 2004:330-331; Agboola, 2000:284; Rosenberg, 1998:12). The foremost contributor to the poor state of collections is inadequate funding. Ksibi (2006:256), when describing the Tunisian situation comments on the mediocrity and deterioration of the collections despite the increasing number of students and academics. Ksibi (2006:256) also states that, "Tunisian university libraries generally have between 2 to 30 titles per academic user, as compared to 250 in some developed countries, whereas according to the Tunisian standard it should be 50 titles per academic user". Agboola (2000) discusses the Nigerian situation using one of the premier universities in that country. The University of Ibadan's acquisitions rate dropped by 89.6% in just over a ten year period, from 17,000 volumes during the 1976/77 session to 1,770 volumes in 1989. Mechanisms were put into place through the World Bank to address the deteriorating book and journal collections. Agboola (2000:285) reports that the government in 1990 negotiated a World Bank Federal Universities Sector Adjustment Credit to inject $120 million (U.S.) into Nigerian federal universities in three installments:

The fund was for, *inter alia*, the supply of library books, journals and equipment. In recognition of the needs of the university libraries, 31% of the fund was earmarked for the supply of library materials and equipment. Unfortunately, only the first installment of the fund was drawn before the Nigerian political logjam of 1993 led to a premature conclusion. Notwithstanding, at the end of the exercise, the 20 universities that participated in the project had acquired some 178,978 volumes valued at US$7.723 million. A similar project to be funded by the European Union for state owned universities was also aborted because of the political situation in the country during the same period (Agboola 2000:285).

This Nigerian experience gives credence to the comments by Ksibi (2006:252) that the difficulties encountered in university libraries in developing countries are more political than anything else.

Kavulya (2006) presents a Kenyan experience. Kavulya's (2006:29) survey confirmed that funding of university library services in Kenya is inadequate. This is due, in the main, to diminished governmental fund allocations for universities and their libraries, which has resulted in low book acquisitions and limited journal subscriptions. Kavulya (2006:29) points out that this deterioration in the library collections is at odds with rapidly expanding student enrolment levels. Private universities in Kenya experience these problems too, but to a lesser extent (Kavulya 2006:29).

In a more recent publication, Kanyengo (2007) acknowledges that the funding crisis for books and journals is not restricted to one country – it is an "Africa problem." Kanyengo claims that "this scenario is repeated in countries from Kenya in the East to Zimbabwe in the South, as well as Nigeria in the West" and refers to Mutula's (2004) discussion on the lack of government support for university libraries in sixteen African countries. With specific reference to the premier university in Zambia, the University of Zambia, Kanyengo (2007) points out that inadequate funding from government has resulted in the cancellation of journal subscriptions. In these circumstances, one questions the contribution that a university library can make to the teaching, leaning and research objectives of a university without subscriptions to current journals.

Kanyengo (2007) also brings to the discussion the mutilation of library material and how such activities exacerbate the current situation of inadequate library resources. It is pointed out that the mutilation of information resources by library users has been increasing at an alarming rate. Such mutilation is attributed to inadequate photocopying facilities coupled with fewer current subscriptions. Kanyengo (2007) writes:

> Mutilation of articles in journals means that even if the library has permanent access to a particular journal, its content might not be complete. The resultant effect is frustration for the user who, after browsing through the catalog, was assured that the library has the journal and for the librarian who has been disappointed by not meeting the user's needs, especially as the library struggled to get access to the journal.

It must be accepted that the current state of university library collections in most African countries is inadequate, to say the least. Given such acceptance, Rosenberg (1998:12) suggested that there be some level of prioritization. Her suggestion was that priority must be given to multiple copies of textbooks. She also alluded to priority being given to the purchase of more journals and, more and newer books as there can never be a replacement for a basic book and journal collection. University libraries in Africa perform and continue to perform some level of support to the teaching, learning and the research program of the university, albeit at a significantly reduced level. Such support is as a result of the adoption of what Kanyengo (2007) refers to as survival strategies. The survival strategies referred to by Kanyengo (2007) are universal for the African continent and must be supplemented by the drive for additional funding to increase the acquisition of books and journals. The following strategies, to grow the book and journal collections, are proposed by Kanyengo (2007):

- Exchange programs;
- Donor funded print subscription;
- Donor funded electronic subscriptions; and
- Other complementary subscriptions.

All of these strategies have their merits and demerits. For example, the exchange program is an excellent alternative acquisition plan to supplement the library's journals collection. However, the assumption is that there is a locally produced title to exchange with and that the reciprocating institution would want that title. Kanyengo (2007) discusses in detail the benefits and problems of these survival strategies.

The publication by Kanyengo (2007) is concluded with a great sense of positivity demonstrating that a financial constraint is a hurdle that can be 'run-around' through resourcefulness. The forging of links and partnerships with different organizations can assist in circumventing huge cost implications for serials subscriptions:

> Libraries in resource-constrained environments must be selective when seeking partnerships so that they find ones that are necessary for their programs. These partnerships could also be formed with local institutions so that institutions can maximize their resources locally, although the local university libraries must themselves have enough resources to be able to share with other local institutions. In the final analysis, these programs are as vital in supplementing periodical subscriptions as they are in meeting the information needs of the local universities (Kanyengo 2007).

Adequate physical resources are essential to achieving the desired goals of teaching, learning and research of a university. However, physical resources in African university libraries are woefully inadequate with buildings being described as being in a state of dilapidation. This unfortunate situation is exacerbated by poor book and journal collections, which are due, in the main, to the lack of adequate funding. Further, as discussed above, the library is used more as a place to study rather than for its collections. It would seem that the dilapidated buildings is the 'preferred evil' for students. Unless there is massive injection of funding, physical resources are likely to continue to be inadequate and detract from efficient and effective library and information provision by African university libraries.

FUNDING

It is beyond debate that appropriate funding of university libraries is the bedrock upon which provision of a quality library service is based. Boadi (2006:64) supports this assertion:

It would be stating the obvious to say that adequate funding should be considered a basic necessity for the effective development of library and information services. But when such a fundamental consideration is often ignored or is not sufficiently appreciated by the sponsors of the services then it becomes necessary to reiterate even what is obvious as a means of driving the wedge in a little further.

However, as indicated by Kavulya (2006:24), university libraries in Africa exist in a paradoxical situation, where university authorities recognize the library's importance in supporting academic programs, but give them low funding priority. This low priority scenario is exacerbated by the diminishing value of African currencies. The purchasing power of the minimal funding is on a downward slide negatively impacting, *inter alia*, on collection development and the development of an adequate IT infrastructure. While it is easy to attribute the bleak state of university libraries in Africa to low allocation of funds by the national government, it is "criminal" when libraries do not utilize the meagermeager budget. Ubogu (2003) as cited by Mutula (2004:282) writes: "Despite decreased funding to libraries, some libraries in Africa do not exhaust their meager budgets that they are allocated and this becomes a reason for further cuts".

The survey conducted by Boadi (2006:65) reiterates the low levels of financial support with respondents using phrases such as "inadequate", "severely inadequate", "grossly inadequate" and … "[the] budget is not only inadequate; it is non-existent" to demonstrate the gravity of the situation. In the survey, one respondent indicated that, "for the past five consecutive years, the library has received no funding for books or periodicals" (Boadi 2006:65). Given the latter statement and the fact that budget allocations are small and that there has to be a five-year "catch-up," which is exacerbated by the declining value of the currency, African university libraries have to do something radical to remain effective information service providers. Boadi (2006) goes on to instill a greater sense of hopelessness when he points out that low levels of funding to African universities are the norm rather than the exception. However, there are some national governments that have developed strategies to overcome the drain on national coffers. For example, Jobbins (2001) in Mutula (2004:283) states that "in South Africa, many universities and technikons are being merged under a government strategy to reduce costs and enhance quality of education."

It is a given that funding of African universities, and subsequently of their university libraries, by national government is horribly insufficient to sustain an efficient library and information service. The national governments have remained unresponsive given that there is little or no change in governments' attitudes towards the funding of libraries (Boadi 2006:68). Therefore, it is imperative that librarians play a more significant role in acquiring funds that in some way would mean redefining some of their traditional roles as academic librarians. At present, there is heavy reliance on donations, gifts and exchange materials to compensate for poor funding from the national government. Rosenberg (1997) cautions about the level of donor-dependency as it does not engender sustainable growth and development. The Carnegie report (*Carnegie challenge...*, 2000:5) reiterates the need for university libraries to move from traditional reliance on government support and external funding, including donations, to self-generating funds and other alternative funding sources. Authors such as Boadi (2006), Cullen et al. (2004), Anyanwu and Akanwa (2001), Nawe (2001) and Ocholla (1998) propose different models for generating and sustaining a level of income that will impact positively on the level of service provided by university libraries. The more popular alternative is for librarians to engage in fund raising, which seems to be a common practice in Europe and America. However, African librarians have not shown any interest in fund-raising despite ever rising costs and shrinking budgets. Boadi (2006:71-72) suggests that the time has arrived for university librarians to positively consider fund-raising as one of the possible ways of averting total dependence on national governments. However, this would suggest developing staff with the necessary skills to engage in fund raising activities. It would also imply increasing the staffing quota to include personnel that will be devoted to fund-raising for the library (Boadi, 2006:71-72).

Again, given the significance of such a position (that of a fund raising officer) within the LIS sector in Africa, fund-raising and income-generating activities should be included in the curricula of LIS schools. Boadi (2006: 72) suggests that this will bring to the attention of future librarians issues such as the necessity to supplement the inadequate budgetary allocations, the fundamentals of fund-raising, strategies for the identification, cultivation and solicitation of potential funding sources and the role of effective communication in fund-raising activities:

> Courses like Infopreneurship, as is being taught in the Department of Library and Information Studies, University of Botswana, Gaborone, could be an indicator to the direction that library and information science schools should be going in this respect (Boadi 2006:72).

Anyanwu and Akanwa (2001) and Ocholla (1998) point out other ways to generate income to supplement inadequate national government funding. Anyanwu and Akanwa (2001:355), when discussing the Nigerian situation, propose the following ways of generating income:

- grants from oil companies and foreign donors;
- printing and binding services;
- establishment of bookshops;
- reprographic services;
- consultancy services; and
- friends of the library/patrons.

Ocholla (1998) acknowledges the skills of librarians and suggests the sale of their skills through information consultancy and brokerage to the private and public sectors. He indicates that there is a willingness from information consumers to pay for consultant services. The service would cover the offering of professional information or advice, or actually performing specified jobs for clients. Some of the areas identified to be in great need of consultancy services are:

- information management;
- information technology;
- information systems;
- archives and records management;
- research and data analysis;
- legal information;
- the establishment of libraries/documentation centers; and
- training of library and information personnel.

Librarians in African university libraries must accept that it is critical for them to use their skills to generate income to supplement the meager funding from government. They must accept responsibility for excellence in information provision and generating income will contribute to their endeavorendeavors to seek information provision excellence. Not engaging in such activities would contribute to the perpetuation of the current situation, which would lead to a collapse of LIS provision in Africa. Engaging in income generation would contribute to eliminating the frightening scenario outlined by Mutula (2004:282) where a university library had frozen the employment of staff and had engaged in student employment to do work of the professionals at nominal payment.

STAFFING AND STATUS OF LIBRARIANS

It is generally accepted that the largest concentration of well-qualified and experienced librarians and information scientists is found in university libraries. In countries such as Nigeria, librarians are granted academic status, which has contributed to the elevation of the LIS profession. The elevation of the profession has contributed to the ability to attract a better caliber of librarians to the university library sector. Given that these librarians have been granted academic status, there is an expectation for them to contribute to the body of knowledge in the discipline. Msuya (2002:252) discusses the focus areas of research that include information technology, staffing, finance and professional education. Such focus areas of research can only contribute to the identification of issues negatively impacting on the sector and the sourcing of resolutions thereof.

The Carnegie report (*Carnegie challenge...*, 2000:5) points out that there is no lack of professionally trained librarians in university libraries in Africa. However, there is concern over a scarcity of knowledge and skills in areas such as financial management, income generation and advocacy and, ICT. The focus areas of research identified by Msuya (2002), it is hoped, will contribute to addressing the concerns expressed in the Carnegie report. Further, there has to be some synergy between that which is being researched and the demands of the work place and that would include the acceptance and engagement of new technologies. Accordingly, Nawe (2001:32) points out that,

[T]here is a dire need to prepare people who can cope with the demands of managing transition from the old (library functions based) to the new (service based) set up that demands new and different ways of acquiring resources and facilities. Other demands include putting in place appropriate collection and human resource development policies to keep the libraries afloat as a minimum requirement, and at best to provide effective and efficient services commensurate with the academic needs and use of information. In a nutshell this means constantly remaining alert in drawing appropriate strategies that keep the profession on track.

African librarians are functioning in a paradoxical environment where on the one hand there is a shortage of information and on the other there is information overload. They have to come to terms with this paradoxical situation while in the throes of grappling with training or retraining issues necessitated by developments in information and communication technologies. They have to sharpen their information seeking skills and manipulate any opportunities that present themselves when searching for information.

There is a need for librarians to develop strategies to deal with this paradoxical situation. From a human resource perspective, Nawe (2001:32) suggests that employers engage in a four-step process to help their employees cope with the situation. Firstly, employers can nurture a culture of learning among employees; secondly, they can encourage individual employees to invest in their own development; thirdly, employers can inculcate an entrepreneurship attitude in employees. Lastly, there is a need to encourage managers to work with a wider range of activities. Nawe (2001:32) also suggests that employees make their own personal contribution to reducing the stress posed by this paradoxical situation by drawing up personal development plans, up-dating specialist skills, broadening experiences in the fastest selling skills in the information age, and generally improving their management skills. Ibegbulam and Olorunsola (2001:385) and Badu (2004:101) support the suggestions of Nawe (2001) by stating that there is a need for new skills for the new millennium, particularly skills to implement an IT strategy. Badu (2004:101) advises that, "service training and staff development in a more technologically developed country is the way to solving the human resource limitation".

Generally, library professionals in African university libraries are extremely well qualified in the LIS discipline. However, there is a need for them to become more active in the information revolution and to sharpen their skills in this new and exponentially advancing area of learning. This will help them embrace the challenges posed by the information technology revolution (Badu 2004:101; Nawe 2001:32).

RESOURCE SHARING

As indicated above, funding of university libraries in Africa is inadequate, to say the least. Therefore, it becomes imperative that librarians realign their thinking and embrace the paradigm shift from ownership to access. This would mean a move towards greater reliance on external sources for materials, that is, sharing of resources as a viable means of providing access to relevant and current information for their users (Adeogun 2005:152).

It is a given that access to information resources is paramount to the survival and success of any university in the current knowledge economy. Unfortunately, inadequate funding can only support the provision of very basic facilities and services. Thus, African university librarians would have to seriously apply their minds to efficient and cost-effective resource sharing cooperative agreements with other libraries. This will help improve the availability of and access to information resources that is important for teaching, learning and research (Adeogun, 2005:152). The availability of and access to information must be viewed against the backdrop of what Ani (2005:67) regards as a society that is experiencing a very real explosion of new information resources and formats. Further, there is the emergence of electronic information that has given birth to the electronic library or the virtual library. However, Africa is in an atypical situation in that "although information is more available worldwide today than in any other era of human history, most of it is inaccessible in the Africa countries" (Ani, 2005:67). Cullen et al. (2004:332) attribute this inaccessibility to lack of political will, as much as the lack of financial resources, management expertise and technology infrastructure. It is more important now than ever before to engage in cooperation and resource sharing among libraries. Badu (2004:99) points out that to date African university libraries have been engaging in traditional types of cooperative activities which includes cooperative acquisitions, union lists and inter-library loaning, common cataloguing and training in standard cataloguing practices.

In discussing resource sharing within the South African context, Raju (2007) cites Nfila and Darko-Ampen (2002:203) who point out that cooperation has now become a tenet of librarianship although it was confined, for many years, to inter-library lending. Libraries entered into reciprocal agreements for the borrowing and use of materials. This form of cooperation enabled libraries to borrow books and periodical articles that were not available in their libraries. In more recent decades, informal cooperative arrangements have been converted to formal agreements. Thomas (2007:81-82) and Molefe (2003) note that library cooperation within the South African context has become more and more formalized. They also note that, over the years, the South African LIS sector has been engaging in highly formalized collaborative activities. South Africa can now boast several well-developed structures similar to those found only in developed countries. These structures (or consortia) include, amongst others, the Cape Library Cooperative (CALICO), the Eastern Seaboard Association of Libraries (eSAL), and Gauteng and Environs Library Consortium (GAELIC). Nfila and Darko-Ampen (2002:205), in taking a closer examination of CALICO and GAELIC, comment on the very tight agreements to address issues such as electronic document delivery, shared library management systems, electronic journals and a variety of Web-based facilities.

Alemna and Antwi (2002:234-235) in supporting "consortiaism" point out thatincreasingly consortia building is placing emphasis on computerized, multi-library networks involving shared databases, telecommunication links, and common applications. However, in the case of Africa, they need not all be computer-based as slight modifications can be made to suit any particular situation. They go on to point out that currently there is a new focus on consortia building worldwide and for, *inter alia*, the following reasons:

• the quality of services is enhanced;
• the cost of service is reduced; and
• duplication of stock is minimized.

For the African university library scenario, the resource sharing process could include:

• interlibrary loan and document delivery;
• shared databases;
• sharing/exchange of staff;
• cooperative cataloguing;
• cooperative acquisitions;
• cooperation in the exchange of duplicate materials;
• sharing expertise in answering reference questions; and
• cooperative storage.

It is expected that each country will determine the best areas in which to function. A firmly articulated policy and plan can then be put in place (Alemna and Antwi, 2002:234).

Despite the inadequacies of university library collections, research conducted by Badu (2004:99) revealed that, in some African libraries, no forms of resource sharing takes place. This lack of sharing is confirmed by Adeogun (2005:158), who points out that many librarians in public or state libraries show no interest in getting into resource sharing relationships. It would seem that barriers to co-operation and resource sharing are both logistical and behavioral. With regard to logistical problems, there are literally inadequate resources to share, there are low levels of library services in general and often there is an absence of a national library to coordinate activities. The behavioral factors are: the lack of coordination and trust, problems with interdependence, and defective communications between cooperating libraries (Badu, 2004:99). Adeogun (2005:158) adds that cooperation is minimized as some librarians remain aloof from their colleagues in other libraries.

Alemna and Antwi (2002:237-238) in quoting Gorman and Cullen (2000) indicate that successful cooperation is characterized by:

- committed leadership;
- a formal governing structure;
- staff participation;
- staff training;
- adequate funds; and
- agreed collection description guidelines.

There is agreement (Raju (2007); Alemna and Antwi (2002:238); Nawe (2001:31) that for consortia to work in Africa there is a need for formalized rules and regulations and a signed agreement binding all parties within the consortia. Alemna and Antwi (2002:238) go on to say that,

> senior management, the governing body and the parent organization's executive must all be fully committed to the consortia. There should also be a central co-ordination point for the project. In this regard, one of the better-resourced university libraries would be the co-coordinating center. The governing structure must have the responsibility and authority to make and review policy, to review activities and to issue directives for management of the consortia.

It is abundantly clear that for university libraries to contribute to efficient teaching, learning and research, information must be made available. Resources are scarce within single holding libraries, however, cumulative resources could address the issue of meeting the information needs for teaching, learning and research. Therefore, avoidance of resource sharing and cooperation is immature, selfish and detrimental to the status of African scholarship.

APPLICATION OF IT

The primary role of university libraries is to support, through information provision, the university's mission of teaching, learning and research. For decades university libraries have been fulfilling this role in the context of paper based resources which called for explicit collection development policies, users' needs analysis, selection and acquisition in order to satisfy real and potential needs of users. Exponential developments in technology over the past three decades have brought to the fore a challenging and complex environment for libraries, and has called for a paradigm shift for collections, organization and provision of information services (Kiondo 2004:20). However, this paradigm shift demands technological developments that will support the move from paper-based resources to digital resources. Unfortunately, Ngimwa (2005) points out Africa is still struggling with fundamental technological challenges such as very limited bandwidth and inadequate IT infrastructure which are critical to the successfully exploitation of these educational resources. Ngimwa (2005) goes on to argue that if nothing is done, the digital gap will continue to widen and Africa will never be able to compete globally. This concern is shared by Cullen et al. (2004:330) and the Carnegie report (*Carnegie challenge...*, 2000) when it is argued that Africa should make every attempt to ensure that it is not left behind in the information revolution as it was in the industrial revolution.

The research conducted by Rosenberg (1998:7) revealed that African universities are embracing technology, at least, in the form of PCs, CD-ROM and e-mail. IT is becoming the norm rather than the exception in Africa. Unfortunately, in seizing this new technology, there is the impression that African university libraries can leapfrog to the electronic libraries phase and by-pass the book phase. La-Fond (2004:212) discusses the belief that

institutions can "trade infrastructure for information" and transform "from bricks to clicks to embrace disintermediation." The advantage for Africa? – less infrastructure to trade and more information to purchase, thereby leapfrogging ahead into virtual reality.

Ksibi (2006), Ngimwa (2005) and Rosenberg (1998) caution against such discourse as African university libraries are still beset with problems relating to poor IT infrastructure, which is exacerbated by poor funding.

Rosenberg (2005) claims that it is difficult to obtain a good overview of the status of electronic and digital initiatives in African higher education. She goes on to explain that evidence suggests that progress made by university libraries is very uneven, both between and within countries. Ani (2005:68) suggests that countries like South Africa, Botswana and Egypt boast high levels of automation and digitization. Ksibi (2006:252) corroborates this assertion and cautions that

[T]here is a risk of "infopoverty" due to the economic imbalance between the countries of the North and those of the South, which disqualifies the latter. The scientific excellence of the developed countries will have to be shared with the poorest countries.

The 'uneven African university library technology terrain' demonstrates that some university libraries have embraced the new mediums and have made them available to users while others do not have the necessary infrastructure to access those e-resources now available on countrywide licenses. Some libraries are fully automated while others remain manually organized. There are libraries that have automated some years ago but have still not yet been able to migrate or upgrade to new systems and so offer only limited services (Rosenberg 2005).

As indicated earlier, South Africa, Botswana and Egypt have achieved substantial progress with regard to technological developments. According to Kanyengo (2007) one of the major issues that have dogged Africa's march down the road of technology adoption is the high costs of bandwidth. It would seem that South Africa has come to grips with this problem and is therefore riding the crest of the technology wave. South Africa, in many instances, is compared to developed countries with regard to the utilization of technology at university libraries (Kanyengo, 2007; Ani, 2005; Mutula, 2004; Olden, 1998; Rosenberg, 1998). Agboola (2000:286), in describing the Nigerian situation, states that the application of IT is gradually taking firm root in Nigerian university libraries. It has become the norm for libraries to have personal computers. Some of the libraries have added CD-ROM drives to ensure that they can take advantage of published databases in that format. The University of Ibadan Library is the most advanced in the application of IT in the country. The University has fully automated its cataloguing and circulation processes using the network version of the TINLIB software capable of driving 20 workstations. It is argued by Agboola (2000:286) that as computers become cheaper and more librarians acquire computer literacy, it is anticipated that more of the manual processes in Nigerian university libraries will be automated.

Badu (2004), writing in the Ghanaian context, is not as optimistic as Agboola (2000) and paints a bleak picture of the state of IT at Ghanaian university libraries. Badu (2004:96) indicates that there is minimal use of computers in the university libraries and all housekeeping routines remain "unautomated." It is argued that technology has only influenced access to databases on the World Wide Web for a few faculty members through a DANIDA[1] project (Badu 2004:96).

Ksibi (2006) is more optimistic than Badu (2004) when describing the Tunisian IT scenario. According to Ksibi (2006:256), the Tunisian university library computerization project uses the most modern computer equipment. This modern equipment facilitates remote querying of libraries, which encourages sharing between libraries to promote quality services for education and research. Ksibi (2006:256) points out that,

> For virtual management of Tunisian university libraries, the powerful VIR-TUA (VTLS) software was acquired to introduce an online public access catalogue (OPAC)... The catalogue is especially important since the univer-

---

[1] Danish International Development Agency (DANIDA) is a Danish government organization set up to provide humanitarian help and assistance in developing countries.

sity libraries house collections that should include the most significant acquired knowledge in human intelligence (... Tunisian university libraries house nearly 1 million documents) and the most valuable products of Tunisian academic literature (100,000 theses and dissertations). Building a catalogue required standardization and historical conversion.

Ngimwa (2005) describes one of the more notable African achievements with regards to automation and digitization, that is, the African Virtual University. The African Virtual University (AVU) learning process is such that the leaner is independent and takes control of the learning process. The educator/lecturer takes the role of a facilitator. To achieve this high level of autonomy, the learner should have all the learning support at his/her disposal, and in particular, access to information resources. The role of the library is to support the learning process and therefore assumes a central role in the learning process. This role must recognize the various learning opportunities from different sources being available to the learner whenever he/she needs them, wherever he or she may be and however he/she is able to access them effectively. This learning process advocates appropriateness and flexibility in the way technology is used to support learning programs taking into consideration the diverse technological contexts across the African continent.

The AVU libraries make provision for the free-flow of information in digital format to the users of its facility. However, research has indicated that usage of the electronic library is still below par and this is due to poor connectivity. Ngimwa's (2005) research indicated that only 8% of the users had good connectivity. Connectivity, thus, is a major problem for the AVU library. Hence, there is an urgent need for a concerted effort to develop strategies to address the issue of connectivity, which the AVU has taken on. Ngimwa (2005) explains that the AVU is currently engaged in initiatives that attempt to overcome the bandwidth challenge on the continent. (The issue of bandwidth is discussed later.)

Over and above providing access to information to AVU students and addressing the issue of bandwidth, the library provides support to researchers in African universities via access to electronic information. This access supplements the provisions of existing libraries most of which have serious problems with scarcity of current research information. This gesture contributes towards raising the standard of learning and research in Africa. The AVU library holds over 4000 full-text journals and 8000 e-books in both English and French languages.

While IT is not the complete solution to the problems of accessibility to information in Africa it will, however, make a significant contribution to the accessibility of information to support teaching, learning and research despite the current problems. Badu (2004:96) cites a number of constraints regarding the use of IT.

These constraints include, *inter alia*:

[A] shortage of skilled personnel coupled with the lack of training culture in computer skills, lack of or inadequate IT infrastructure such as PCs and communication facilities, intermittent electric power cuts, [unsupportive] staff attitudes towards technology and the lack of permanent IT investment in all the libraries... [and a] lack of IT strategy integration in all the academic libraries.

These concerns raised by Badu (2004) are shared by Cullen et al. (2004:330). They point out that African university libraries are constrained by additional factors (to the above) such lack of computers, networks, bandwidth, and even vandalism in some areas (for example, the theft of copper telephone lines). This is exacerbated by low levels of co-operation between institutions and the propensity to develop own databases of local materials. As a result of this low level of co-operation digitization programs to increase African content on the Web is thwarted; the opportunity to share the different cultures and languages across the African continent is kept to a minimum.

However, the greatest constraint, as alluded to by Ngimwa (2005) is poor connectivity as a result of limited bandwidth. Ngimwa (2005) cites the ATICS survey of 2004 to determine the severity of the connectivity problem. The survey revealed that connectivity was too little, too expensive and poorly managed. The survey also revealed that,

an average African university has bandwidth capacity equivalent to a broadband residential connection in Europe, pays 50 times more for their bandwidth than their educational counterparts in the rest of the world and fails to monitor, let alone manage, the existing bandwidth (Ngimwa, 2005).

Further, the survey revealed that there was a

significant lack of knowledge about bandwidth quality and management. Most of the institutions surveyed (66%) did not have a Committed Information Rate (CIR) for their connectivity or did not even know what CIR is. Such ended up paying more for their bandwidth. The same goes for bandwidth management. Luckily some organizations such as the INASP [International Network for the Availability of Scientific Publications] have addressed this challenge by conducting bandwidth management and optimization workshops (Ngimwa, 2005).

It is evident that low connectivity is a significant barrier to access to e-resources, such as journals and other electronic information resources. Kanyengo (2007) points out that in Zambia, if users get access to a computer that is connected to the Internet, there is slow connectivity as a result of low bandwidth. Limited access to electronic resources has its root cause in insufficient funding to pay for additional bandwidth. As indicated above and confirmed by Kanyengo (2007), Internet connectivity is very expensive and unaffordable in most African countries (excluding South Africa) as compared to countries in Europe or the United States.

In direct response to the low connectivity problem and the negation of its objectives to make research information available to the research community in Africa, the AVU took the lead in consolidating bandwidth requirements through the formation of a bandwidth consortium. Aggregating the bandwidth demand would mean that it would be easy to negotiate for lower bandwidth costs and thus improve connectivity (Ngiwma, 2005). The AVU is the host institution for the Bandwidth Consortium consisting of 10 universities and two institutions and has managed to bring down the cost of bandwidth significantly. According to Ngimwa (2005) members of the consortium include:

- University of Dar es Salaam (Tanzania);
- Makerere University (Uganda);
- University of Ghana (Ghana);
- University of Education, Winneba (Ghana);
- University of Ibadan (Nigeria);
- Obafemi Awolowo University (Nigeria);
- Ahmadu Bello University (Nigeria);
- Bayero University (Nigeria);
- Port Harcourt University (Nigeria);
- University of Jos (Nigeria);
- Association of African Universities; and
- Kenya National Education Network.

Despite the fact that the consortium is dominated by Nigerian universities, it is a start and hopefully will grow to include other African countries. The growth of the consortium will increase the bargaining power with the distinct benefit of lowering bandwidth costs.

Kanyengo (2007) suggests that "storewidth" can contribute to increasing the speed of accessing material available electronically. Essentially it is the use of a large local information store on local area networks, that is, storing data on local devices. Kanyengo (2007) argues that this is a very cost-effective and reliable approach that is increasingly gaining popularity in large institutions such as universities. Bandwidth in local networks is free since the institutions own the equipment. Massive storage devices containing digital content can then be plugged into these networks and be shared simultaneously at high speeds. The AVU is currently piloting two such initiatives with the aim of supplementing the available bandwidth (Ngiwma 2005). It is evident from the above discussion that an increase in bandwidth would allow African librarians to engage new technology and positively contribute to information provision.

Rosenberg (1998:12) is of the view that not engaging new technologies would marginalize Africa from the mainstream of intellectual and scholarly life. However, technology must not be viewed as the ultimate solution to Africa's problem of 'information poverty' and, the 'bricks' library should not be neglected in the light of the availability of full text database: leapfrogging into the digital era is not the solution. However, it is important that Africa has access to research information so that it can make its contribution to the generation of new information, especially information on Africa. However, there are many hurdles that have to be negotiated including that of funding. Another significant problem that needs to be overcome so that Africa can actively participation in the global information world is that of bandwidth. There are solutions and alternatives to the bandwidth problem that are being investigated (for example, the AVU initiative) which will contribute to the resolution, albeit a partial resolution, to the much wider problem of scarcity of research information in the African context.

SUMMARY AND CONCLUSION

Rosenberg (1997) reported on the inadequacy of university libraries in Africa in the post-colonial era. The authors of this chapter argue that the remnants of colonialism propped-up university libraries in Africa during the immediate post-colonialism phase and helped in facilitating the exchange of information between African countries and the ex-colonial powers. However many African countries after a number of years of independence, have been ravaged by poverty, war, famine and HIV/AIDS. It would seem that many African governments lack the political will to invest in streams such as universities in order to develop adequate human resources for national development and to address issues of poverty eradication, illiteracy and disease. Priority with regard to funding is generally given to defense and to support military rule governments.

The direction of funding away from universities has catastrophically affected the functioning of African university libraries and information provision. African university library collections and facilities are described as woefully inadequate and deteriorating. Librarians may either accept the status quo and contribute to the degradation of academic librarianship in Africa or, alternatively, they may engage in what Kanyengo (2007) describes as survival strategies which include exchange programs, donor funded print and electronic subscriptions and, other complementary subscriptions. Resource sharing is also an immediate and viable method of "supplementing" individual university library collections. There has to be a paradigm shift from ownership to access. Furthermore, proactive African university librarians must accept fund raising as a core responsibility. There has to be a shift from traditional roles of academic librarians to include fund raising.

It is beyond debate that finance is a significant resource for an effective and efficient information provision service that supports the teaching, learning and research objectives of a university. It also influences the capacity to acquire the necessary IT infrastructure to support the library's mission. Despite the fact that African academic librarians are well-qualified academically, there is a void in their IT training and experience. This void is detrimental to information provision, which is already negated by poor IT infrastructure and low bandwidth. The African Virtual University (AVU) seems to be a consolidating factor in that it is currently developing a consortium to address the issue of bandwidth which would positively impact on information sharing given that it (the AVU) has over 4000 full-text journals and 8000 e-books to share with colleagues, students and researchers in Africa.

The authors would like to conclude by suggesting that African university librarians need to establish minimum benchmarks for information provision and to use these benchmarks to solicit necessary funding and expertise to meet these minimum benchmarks. African countries that are in stronger positions, or are the 'peaks', must display greater commitment to elevating the standard of academic librarianship in the rest of Africa, particularly with those institutions that are trapped in the 'valleys'. Further, there has to be a commitment to periodically review benchmarks and to continuously raise the 'benchmarks bar' until one arrives at the stage of information provision in African university libraries being effective and efficient and positively impacting on the teaching, learning and research objectives of universities. The consequence to any further deterioration will be the non-existence of university libraries – the alternative, is their exponential growth. The authors are currently engaging in research (refer to Appendix A) that would hopefully aid in determining such benchmarks for African university libraries. It is hoped that the data generated would be used as a source of information for the expansion of visions and the roles of university libraries and, for the development of strategic plans and other relevant policy development for African university libraries.

References

Adeogun, M. (2005). Resource sharing services and constraints in selected Seventh-Day Adventists university libraries in sub-Saharan Africa. *Information development*, 21(2): 152-160.

Agboola, A.T. (2000). Five decades of Nigerian university libraries *Libri,* 50: 280-289.

Alemna, A.A. and Antwi, I.K. (2002). A review of consortia building among university libraries in Africa. *Library management,* 23(4/5): 234-238.

Ani, O.E. (2005). Evolution of virtual libraries in Nigeria: myth or reality? *Journal of information science*, 31: 67-70.

Anyanwu, E.U. and Akanwa, P. (2001). Funding of libraries in Nigeria: the way forward. *International information and library review*, 33: 347-358.

Association of College and Research Libraries. (2004). Standards for libraries in higher education.
Available at http://www.ala.org/ala/acrl/acrlstandards/standardslibraries.cfm (Accessed on 22 January 2008).

Badu, E.E. (2004). Academic library development in Ghana: top managers' perspectives. *African journal of library, archives and information science*, 14(2): 93-107.

Boadi, B.Y. (2006). Income-generating activities: a viable financial source for African academic libraries? *Bottom line,* 19 (2): 64-77.

Carnegie challenge: revitalizing African libraries: the challenge of a quiet crisis. (2000). New York: Carnegie Corporation.

Cullen, R., Adeyoyin, S., Olorunsola, R. and Idada, D.A. (2004). Issues facing academic libraries in Nigeria. *Journal of academic librarianship*, 30(4): 330-332.

Ibegbulam, I.J. and Olorunsola, R. (2001). Restructuring academic libraries in Nigeria: issues to consider. *Library management*, 22(8/9): 381-386.

Kanyengo, C.W. (2007). Serials management in Africa: a review of survival strategies at the University of Zambia. *Serials Review*, 33(1): 33-39. Available at http:///www.sciencedirect.com (Accessed on 28 October 2007).

Kavulya, J.M. (2006). Trends in funding of university libraries in Kenya: a survey. *Bottom line*, 19(1): 22-30.

Kiondo, E. (2004). Around the world to: the University of Dar es Salaam Library: collection development in the electronic information environment. *Library hi tech news*, 21(6): 9-24.

Ksibi, A. (2006). University libraries in the South: from virtual to real. *Information development*, 22: 252- 262.

Kuh, G.D. and Gonyea, R.M. (2003). The role of the academic library in promoting student engagement in learning. *College and research libraries*, 64(4): 256-282.

LaFond, D.M. (2004). Library capacity building in Africa or the exportation of technolust?: discerning partnership models and revitalization efforts in the age of globalization. *The reference librarian*, 87/88: 209-272.

Lynch, B. (1987). Standards for university libraries. *IFLA journal*, 13(2): 120-125.

Lynch, B. (1982). University library standards. *Library trends*, 31(1): 33-47.

Molefe, C. (2003). Current developments in library cooperation among special libraries in Botswana. *South African journal of library and information science*, 69(1): 62-70.

Msuya, J. (2002). Developing a library research agenda at the University of Dar es Salaam. *Information development*, 18(1): 251-256.

Mutula, S. (2004). IT diffusion in Sub-Saharan Africa: implications for developing and managing digital libraries. *New library world*, 105(7/8): 281 – 289.

Nawe, J.M. (2001). Leadership challenges in higher education libraries in East Africa. *Information development*, 17(1): 29-34.

Nifla, R.B. and Darko-Ampen, K. (2002). Developments in academic library consortia from the 1960s through to 2000: a review of the literature. *Library management*, 23(4/5): 203-212.

Ngimwa, P. (2005). An African experience in providing a digital library service: the African Virtual University. Paper presented to the 4th Pan Commonwealth Forum on Open Learning. Available at http://ahero.uwc.ac.za. (Accessed on 2 November 2007).

Ocholla, D.N. (1998). Information consultancy and brokerage in Botswana. *Journal of information science*, 24(2): 83-95.

Olden, A. (1998). University libraries in Africa: book review article. *Journal of documentation*, 54(4): 489-498.

Pitman, L., Trahn, I. and Wilson, A. (2001). Working towards best practice in Australian university libraries: reflections on a national project. *Australian academic and research libraries*, 32(1). Available at http://www.alia.org.au/publishing/aarl/32.1/ptw.html. Accessed on 22 January 2008).

Raju, R. (2007). The need for academic libraries to graduate from co-operation to collaboration and beyond. Paper presented at a pre-WLIC meeting with SCONUL representatives hosted by the Durban University of Technology, KawZulu-Natal, South Africa, on 17 August 2007.

Rosenberg, D. (ed.) (1997). *University libraries in Africa: a review of their current state and future potential*. Three volumes. London: International African Institute.

Rosenberg, D. (1998). IT and university libraries in Africa. *Internet research: electronic networking applications and policy*, 8(1): 5-13.

Rosenberg, D. (2005). Towards the digital library: findings of an investigation to establish the current status of university libraries in Africa, International Network for the Availability of Scientific Publications (INASP), 1-29. Available at http://ahero.uwc.ac.za/index.php?module=cshe&action=viewtitlc&id=cshe_173. (Accessed on 2 November 2007).

Thomas, G. (2007). Academic libraries and the second decade of democracy: critical issues and challenges. In Bothma, T., Underwood, P. and Ngulube, P. (eds.). *Libraries for the future: progress and development of South African libraries*. World library and information congress: 73 IFLA general conference and council, 19-23 August 2007, Durban, South Africa, 71-87.

SPECIAL LIBRARIES

Janneke Mostert

1. INTRODUCTION

Within the knowledge society that has recently emerged, special libraries, as custodians and disseminators of subject specific information, have a very important role to play. The value of timely, accurate and relevant information has increasingly been acknowledged as providing a leading edge in the modern competitive world. Special libraries have thus been equipped to support their parent organizations by providing the information required to ensure the survival and continued existence of their parent bodies. However, not all special libraries are up to the task, as some are severely hampered by constraints that negatively impact on their ability to deliver the necessary services. This is especially true of special libraries in developing countries, especially those on the African continent.

This chapter will look at the development of special libraries on the African continent, and will provide an overview of noteworthy developments in specific countries. The challenges, issues and trends will also be discussed.

2. TYPOLOGY OF SPECIAL LIBRARIES

With the development of different types of libraries over the centuries, an effort was made to "typecast" or group together libraries with similar characteristics, qualities, elements, origins, functions or compositions (Ocholla 1993). Although numerous library typologies currently exist, there are some common approaches used in the grouping process. According to Ocholla (1993:27), these approaches include: *"functionality, territorial distribution, ownership, location, administrative convenience and the position in the social system"*. Special libraries, due to their unconventional nature, challenge library typologists in providing a clear-cut description that typifies all the libraries included in this group.

Libraries consisting of specialized collections date back to the clay library of the Babylonian king, Assurbanipal. Yet the term "special libraries" was only coined in 1908 when it was decided at a meeting of librarians to call the emerging libraries in America "special libraries" (Singh 2006). Despite the fact that these libraries have been around for many centuries, the concept has not yet been clearly defined and many opinions as to what exactly special libraries entail still prevail. As Poll (2007) points out: *"in most cases definitions indicate what it (special libraries) is not, rather than what it is, for example it is not a public, national, academic or school library"*. Adding to the confusion is the fact that these libraries cannot be typified by a single typology or specific set of characteristics because many types are included, such as news libraries, law libraries, libraries for the blind and deaf, museums, archives, corporate libraries and non-profit organization libraries. Additionally, these libraries are also not identified by a common name, for they are also known as Information centers, Information Analysis Centers, Documentation Centers, Information Resource Centers or Knowledge Management Centers. Ownership of the libraries also varies and includes role players such as governments and their departments, non-governmental agencies, commercial firms and news agencies.

Despite the above, consensus does exist about the fact that special libraries serve a very specific clientele, in most cases a very small group of users with very specific requirements, and have highly specialized collections concentrating on a specific subject, field or format. Staff complements are in most cases very small but highly specialized in terms of subject specific knowledge and library expertise (Bauer 2003; Lefebvre 1996; Poll 2007). Poll (2007) distinguishes between special libraries serving only their parent organizations, and those that are open to both the parent organization's staff and the general public.

The role of the special library is very closely related to its institutional activities, and is therefore mainly focused on making knowledge and expertise available to further the institution's goals.

The service delivery of these libraries is based on the following (Poll 2007:4):

- A collection that is tailored to suit the needs of the clientele
- Collections and services that consider current needs more than possible future needs
- The speed and accuracy of reference services
- Proactive delivery of relevant information to users
- Customized user services (personal profiles, alerting services, selective dissemination of information)
- Efficient background services
- Cost-efficiency of services

Collections within these institutions aim to serve the specific information needs of the organizations that they serve in order to increase the productivity and efficiency of the parent organization. This customization is achieved by reducing the time employees spend on data searching, and by providing information that can facilitate improved decision-making.

3. DEVELOPMENT OF SPECIAL LIBRARIES IN AFRICA

The growth and development of special libraries has been vital to library development in Africa. According to Sitzman (1988), the establishment of the first special libraries in Africa, with the exception of a few old repositories in Egypt, Mali and Ethiopia, dates back to the turn of the nineteenth century and was mainly due to the efforts of colonial governments. These libraries aimed mainly to assist colonial administrators in their governing duties, or were alternatively driven by the colonial government's interests in medicine, agriculture and geology. Most of these libraries started out without any real planning and on a very small scale, without too many information resources (a few publications, files and some journal and/or information service subscriptions), no qualified staff, and little or no funding. It was only at a later stage that funding, budgeting, and the employment of qualified staff became important issues (Sturges & Neil 1990).

Research institutes and surveyors concentrating on the mineral wealth of Africa showed the most prominent growth in terms of special libraries, with Sturges & Neil (1990) reporting that 20 libraries attached to national geological surveys already existed in 1967. Due to the lack of trained staff, qualified geologists acted as information officers that presided over collections consisting of a few books, plenty of reprints, pamphlets, maps, microforms and photographs. Currently, special libraries in the agricultural sector are the most prolific because most research institutes on the continent tend to concentrate on this field.

With the exception of a few countries, such as South Africa and Egypt, ownership of the majority of African special libraries rests with governments and their agencies; very few are in private or corporate/organizational hands. Huge disparities in their occurrence throughout the continent also exist, with South Africa and Egypt being the leaders in terms of numbers, Information and Communication Technology access and general development; meanwhile many countries such as Libya and Morocco are virtually void of any such libraries (Wertsman 1996). Closely related to the well-being of existing special libraries is the political and economic stability of a country, which in many African countries is precariously balanced. Ikoja-Odongo (2004) noted that peace was an essential element in the development and utilization of information services.

Collections range from being excellent to very poor, and from being relatively big to very small in source numbers. For example, the United Nations Economic Commission for Africa Library in Ethiopia contains 60,000 titles, while some special libraries in Sierra Leone only have about 500 (Wedgeworth 1993). Most of these collections are still print-based, but there is currently a drive towards providing access to digital documentation (Mutula, n.d.)

Donor funding from foreign countries has influenced many special library initiatives, sometimes resulting in insufficient planning and the establishment of a service environment insensitive to the needs of the African user (Baldwin & Varady 1989; Dimitroff 1993).

Despite many developments in the African special library sector, many authors still lament obstacles such as insufficient funding, collections, and buildings, and inadequate skills, training and services, which need to be addressed in order for these information providers to be seen as effective and efficient contributors to their parent organizations (Amonoo & Azubuike 2005; Chisenga 2006, Ikoja-Odongo 2004; Were 2006). Despite these shortcomings, Sturges and Neil (1990) advocate the important role that these libraries have played and are still playing in providing access to information resources to researchers and potentially being important instruments in the provision of information to target groups within their parent organizations.

4. SPECIAL LIBRARIES: A REGIONAL OVERSIGHT

The African continent is the second largest continent in the world, consisting of 53 countries. The continent is generally subdivided into four regions, i.e. Eastern, Western, Southern and Northern. Occasionally a fifth region, i.e. Central Africa, is used. For the purposes of this chapter, the Central and Eastern regions were combined.

In terms of the existence of special libraries, huge disparities abound between regions, and even between neighbouring countries. Many factors play a role in this, such as the importance attached by organizations to information access, the peace and stability of a country, and the leadership and skills offered by the library professionals.

4.1 Southern Africa

Countries falling within this region include: South Africa, Namibia, Botswana, Mozambique, Zimbabwe, Zambia, Swaziland and Lesotho.

This region boasts the country with the most prolific special library sector on the whole continent, i.e. South Africa, which has more than 600 such libraries. South Africa is also one of relatively few countries on the continent in which the government and its departments are not the major stakeholders of these libraries, with only 79 belonging to these institutions (Burger 2006/2007). The rest are all attached to private companies, especially those in the commercial and technological sector, mining houses, law firms, and financial institutions; and in private hands. Some of these libraries are also found in *parastatals* such as the Human Sciences Research Council (HSRC) and the Council for Scientific and Industrial Research (CSIR) (Stilwell 2007). These libraries are dispersed throughout the country's cities and towns.

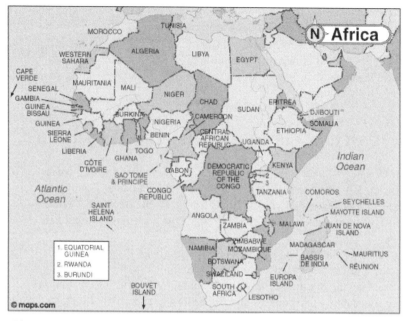

Figure 1: Map of Africa (Available from: http://www.infoplease.com/atlas/africa.html)

Special libraries within the other countries in the region are mainly found within major cities and are much fewer in number. Botswana's special libraries are mostly found within government agencies, within research institutes that are privately owned or belong to *parastatal* organizations, or within the financial sector, religious institutions, management consultancies, United Nations agencies, regional institutions such as the South African Development Community (SADC) and embassies (Nkanga 1999). Together with the South African libraries, automation is the best developed in this country. Zambian libraries specialize in fields such as the natural sciences, agriculture, law, education, baking and mining; and are in most cases financed and owned by government. To overcome the paucity of information sources in the country, a very good informal Interlibrary Loan scheme exists between these libraries and the University of Zambia (Wedgeworth 1993). Other than the government, many Zimbabwean special libraries are attached to Non-governmental organizations (NGO's). It also contributes towards the publication of important publications such as yearbooks and other regional publications (Mamvoto & Mutasa, 2007).

Swaziland's special libraries are found in most government ministries and international, private and Non-Governmental organizations, mainly to serve the needs of their parent organizations (Kunene n.d). Because it is a very small country with many pressing needs, Information Technology has not yet been fully introduced in all its special libraries, with the notable exception of libraries belonging to international organizations such as the United Nations Development Program, United States Information Service, British Council, and the United Nations Children's Fund, all of which have Internet access (Information Outlook Online, 2000). Lesotho, a country situated within South Africa, has very few special libraries, most of which are owned by government, but a few are also owned by research institutions and NGO's (Eifl.Net Lesotho, n.d.).

Namibian special libraries are mainly in the hands of government, organizations, churches and some private and foreign companies. The government's libraries, although found in all the departments, actually form one big library because the processing of all documents is done centrally and then dispersed to the mini-libraries. This is done to promote uniformity in all the mini-libraries within the organization. The computerization of services is also well advanced within the government's libraries, with services that allow internal and external networking (Morgentern 1993). The organization of *parastatal* and private special libraries ranges from well organized to disorganized, with many undocumented collections. The staff also ranges from being professionally trained to not having any training at all (Tötemeyer 1993).

4.2 Eastern and Central Africa

This region includes countries such as Tanzania, Uganda, Rwanda, Ethiopia, Malawi, Sudan, and Kenya.

The first special library in Kenya was founded in 1902 when a local newspaper, "The East African Standard", was established and required a library to support its reporting staff. Though prolific developments took place in the special library sector during the ensuing years, most such institutions, especially those affiliated with government departments, collapsed with the demise of the East African Community in 1967. Despite being in a rather neglected state, many of these libraries still have collections of grey literature, specifically government reports (IFLA/FAIFE World Report: Kenya, 1999). Some excellent libraries survived or were established in the period post-independence, some of which are currently seen as leaders in their fields of expertise in the region, such as the Kenya Agricultural Research Institute (KARI), the Kenya National Archives Library, and the Medical Training College Library. Libraries belonging to research institutions are in possession of the best collections and are also the best organized and serviced. However, most NGO's, religious institutions and cultural centers established by foreign missions and the United Nations also have well developed libraries, most of which have embraced Information Technology, thus enabling them to deliver computerised search and retrieval services (IFLA/FAIFE World Report: Kenya 1999).

Tanzanian special libraries vary in size and effectiveness. While the Library of Mineral Resources is one of the best in Africa, those belonging to the government departments are poorly developed and most are without professional staff (Dahlgren 1994). Some government departments, such as the Ministry of Agriculture, provide a centralized service, which means that acquisitioning is done centrally and then dispersed to branch libraries (MSN Encarta, 2007). Other than the government, NGO's and charity organizations are the major stakeholders of these libraries. Malawian special libraries date back to 1899, when the first agricultural library was established (Ranashinge 2006). Currently, central and branch libraries are maintained by the Ministry of Agriculture at research stations, training centers and divisional offices throughout the country. Resource acquisitions are performed at the central libraries, and materials are then sent to the branch libraries (MSN Encarta 2007). Though most of the special libraries are owned by government agencies, some belong to religious organizations, and a few can be found servicing hospitals throughout the country (Wertsman 1996).

The first special library in Uganda was set up in 1897 at Mulango Hospital, Kampala (Plumbe in Ranasinghe 2007). Currently, the country has a few special libraries mainly situated in Kampala or Entebbe, and owned by government, research institutions and commercial institutions such as the East African Development Bank (Akita, n.d.). In Rwanda, most ministries and public institutions have documentation centers of various sizes. There are also libraries belonging to religious organizations and dioceses (Wedgeworth, 1993).

Ethiopia has a relatively long history of special libraries, having for centuries housed old repositories in churches and monasteries of religious materials. Since the 1974 Revolution, many new special libraries have opened, and computers have been integrated into these libraries since the early 1980's. It was, however, only in the 1990's that automation was widely incorporated into the service delivery of these libraries. Currently, special libraries are serving government agencies, banks, the Institute for Public Administration, police, and the Air Force Colleges, as well as international organizations such as the Economic Commissions for Africa and the International Livestock Research Institute (Tsigemelak 2006).

4.3 Western Africa

Countries situated in this region are: Nigeria, Niger, Chad, Sierra Leone, Ivory Coast, Gambia, Gabon, Angola, Democratic Republic of Congo, Burkino Faso and Mali.

Within this region, the quality of special libraries ranges from poor to excellent. However, the libraries seem to function in isolation as not much is known about individual library holdings outside each institution.

Nigeria probably has the best developed special library system in this region, and the libraries are grouped into the following categories: private educational institutions, international organizations, foreign government, government and professional associations (Ajibero in Okiy, n.d.). The collections of these libraries range from grossly inadequate to excellent. The libraries falling under the auspices of the research institutions belonging to the Federal Ministry of Technology, as well as those belonging to foreign agencies such as the British Council and the

United States Information Service, are deemed as those best endowed (Wedgeworth 1993). Okiy (n.d.) places the blame of the poor state of the other research libraries on the shoulders of government, whose duty it is to fund these institutions. This state of affairs stems from the fact that the government is yet to see libraries and information as important commodities for commerce and industry.

Angola, despite still recovering from a crippling war, has got a sizable number of special libraries, most of which reside under the jurisdiction of the National Department of Libraries and are administratively linked to the ministries they serve. Although located throughout the country, (Notes: although?) the major libraries are found in Huambo, Luanda and Lubango, where they specialize in agriculture and animal husbandry (Wertsman, 1996). Even though the first special libraries date back to the period of colonial administration, the development of modern Ghanaian special libraries has been the direct result of the government's drive to embark on a modern economy. This occurred because the gathering of scientific data resulted in the establishment of many research institutes, and with them, libraries to support their research functions. Special libraries are currently found within research, financial, industrial, and commercial institutions, as well as within government ministries and departments and *parastatal* organizations (Alemna 1997).

Mali, together with Ethiopia, has a rich – though mainly undocumented – history concerning the storage of manuscripts in private collections (Diakite 1999). Special libraries stem from the period of colonization, during which they were only available to civil servants. Currently, there are about 64 special libraries in this country (Wertsman 1996).

Sierra Leone, which also only recently came out of a civil war, has a very small number (18) of special libraries concentrating on very limited subjects, but makes a very clear distinction between three major categories of special libraries, i.e.: special libraries, documentation centers, and information centers. Special libraries are associated with professional and learned societies, government departments, and research centers, while information centers are principally associated with government, research, and industrial establishments which require the provision of specific information (such as the Shell – Oil Refinery – library). Documentation Centers, such as the National Agricultural Documentation Center and the Development Center at the Ministry of Economic Development and Planning, process literature in their respective fields (Kargbo 2002).

Within the Democratic Republic of Congo, the Board of Libraries, Archives and Documentation is the central management, coordination and supervision organ of the library, archives and documentation centers. Their function is to oversee the planning and development of all documentary structures within the country and to set the standards that will ensure efficient performance by these structures. The Board is not seen as very effective, as it only supports services rendered by the

Peoples National Library, The National Documentation Center and the National Archives, while all other special libraries have to fend for themselves (Wedgeworth 1993).

Special libraries within Gabon, Gambia, Burkina Faso, the Ivory Coast and Niger are small in number and are mainly in the hands of government, research institutions, foreign institutions or religious institutions. Some of these libraries, for example those attached to research institutes in the Ivory Coast, contain only very small collections of less than 500 volumes, while others, such as the Center Regional de Recherche et de Documentation la Tradition Orale in Niger, are renowned for their collections. Untrained staff are a common problem within many of these libraries (Wedgeworth, 1993).

4.4 Northern Africa

Countries constituting the Northern regions include: Egypt, Liberia, Libya, Algeria, Morocco, and Mauritania.

Special library development in this region ranges from advanced (Egypt), to very poor (Liberia). Political and economic instability is a major deterrent to the development and maintenance of special libraries in the region. Donor-funding plays a major role in the establishment of the region's special libraries, often leading to ineffective and overpriced document delivery systems (Dimitroff 1993).

According to Dimitroff (1993), Egypt has the best developed information system in North Africa with approximately 380 special libraries in the region. These are found in government departments, semi-government institutions and learned societies. Very few are situated in the private sector. Although special libraries are normally allocated larger budgets than other library types, the amount is still paltry when compared to similar institutions abroad. The paucity of resources and the high costs associated with the printed medium have necessitated special librarians to form strong personal networks to gain access to other information resources. These networks utilize foreign supported libraries, such as the British Council Library or the American Center Library. A clear distinction is made between Information Centers and special libraries, with the services of the former seen as superior to the latter in terms of service delivery. Centers also provide indexing and abstracting services, translations, bibliographic activities, Current Awareness Services, and when access to digital networks are available, electronic searches (Wedgeworth 1993).

Algeria's special libraries are mostly affiliated to special schools and institutes, with some containing very good collections on commerce, the fine arts, agriculture, hydrography and engineering. Within countries such as Liberia, Libya, Morocco and Mauritania, only a few special libraries exist.

5. STATUS AND CHALLENGES FACING SPECIAL LIBRARIES

5.1 Status of special libraries/ librarians

The library and information systems of developing countries, specifically those from Africa, are generally backward and constrained (Kebede 1999). The inability of libraries to present any tangible evidence of their achievements, and librarians' failure to supply supporting evidence of their worth, often leads to disenchantment amongst employers, resulting in a low status being bestowed on the library profession and its services. Marginalization results in libraries being under-resourced, understaffed and underdeveloped, depriving them of the means to meet the demands of their constituencies, and thus being perceived as ineffective and therefore expendable. Special libraries, by nature of their ownership and functions, need to prove their worth and ability to contribute to the general productivity and efficiency of the parent organization, but literature reveals that their status is not much higher than that of other library types (Nwalo 2000; Okiy n.d.; Wedgeworth 1993).

5.2 Collections and local content

A collection's status is generally dependent on the status accorded to the library and the services it delivers by the parent organization, and therefore can range from being of a very high standard to extremely poor. Collection sizes also vary considerably, from tens of thousands of items to less than 500 (Tsigemelek 2006). A general trend amongst special libraries is to concentrate on collecting materials that reflect global content rather than local content – i.e. locally owned and adapted or relevant knowledge of the parent organization – thus providing material irrelevant to the needs of the local situation. This problem is enhanced by the limited use of local languages on the Internet, where English is predominantly used to convey information (Amonoo & Azibuike n.d.). Mchombu (2007) advocates the production and repackaging of information rich in local content rather than perpetuating various forms of intellectual and cultural dependence. Through the practice of repackaging/restructuring local information, specific client needs can be catered for, and information scattered across a large number of documents can be consolidated, leading to more efficient service delivery (Singh, 2006). Closely related to this is the development of local digital content. As Africa's technology moves into the 21st century, special libraries' clients have begun to demand access to information at all times, thus necessitating the existence of accessible online services. Mutula (n.d) views the development of local digital content as a huge opportunity for Africa, especially with governments becoming more aware of the capital outflow when purchasing foreign materials and services instead of providing their own local content. (Notes: revise. unclear)

5.3 Training of skilled information workers

Special library training has until recently been entrenched in a value system based on western principles which are alien to the African situation (Sturges & Neil 1990). Although reforms are currently underway in most African library schools, the Africanization of library training is still not adequate and schools have been unable to produce information professionals with relevant knowledge and competencies. According to Ikoja-Odongo (2004:3), the curricula are "*not inclusive of the information demands of the emerging African society*". The lack of practical, hands-on experience and the continued teaching of traditional library skills that focus primarily on the printed medium (i.e. classification, cataloguing and referencing) are factors contributing towards Africa's digital and information skills shortage.

In response to the lack of ICT competencies, many African library schools have recently introduced Information technology subjects, although these do not seem current and relevant enough to address the needs of the new e-environment. Additionally, most schools are still hampered by a lack of basic resources, such as enough computers to provide efficient training (Nwalo 2000; Ocholla and Bothma 2007; Rosenberg 2006). The lack of sufficient ICT training has had a direct impact on the ability of special librarians to perform effectively in their work environment, as they currently need both technological skills and subject specialization to provide the information required by their clientele.

The special librarian's work environment is characterized by continuous change, necessitating new skills and competencies to function in a volatile business environment. Technological advances require special librarians to redirect their traditional skills and functions to areas where they can add value to their organizations. Competencies that are currently required include: "*knowledge of relevant information sources, access, technology and management, and the ability to apply this knowledge to provide a high quality information service*" (Muller 2007). Skills issues are thus related to the development of management skills, the ability to understand the business principles on which their parent organizations are based, and the development of ICT skills (Kavulya 2007 and Muller 2007). Due to the total lack, or irrelevancy, of the continuous education programs meant to hone skills in African library schools, special librarians currently have to rely on their own initiatives to upgrade their skills and competencies, mostly through conferences and workshops, which in most cases do not cater for hands-on experience.

5.4 Library automation

To take advantage of the benefits that Information Technology offers in terms of information management, libraries have to automate their services. During the early '80's, African special libraries were among the first libraries automating their services. (Notes: paragraph requires better continuity/readability) This was done on a very small scale due to a lack of funds, and automation was introduced using local IT departments and programming experts (Mutula n.d.). Other automation initiatives came from organizations such as the United States Information Services and British Council media centers, which had access to significantly more funds. In the late 1980's, UNESCO provided software that was mostly free to libraries in the government, public and private sectors, enabling them to use CDS/ISIS software to develop in-house databases of local collections. Donor-funded CD-ROMS also influenced library automation (Mutula n.d). Countries such as Nigeria, Botswana, Egypt and South Africa have since taken a lead in library automation within special libraries, while other countries such as Ethiopia (Tsigemelek 2006) have implemented automation programs on a smaller scale. (Notes: varying degrees??) Although web-based systems have been the norm since the early 90's in many libraries worldwide, only a few libraries in Africa have created a web existence and web-services.

The shortage of skilled manpower needed to implement IT programs in African libraries is a major problem (Nwalo 2000). For example, special libraries in Botswana experienced a number of problems during implementation due to the lack of staff with computer experience. (Notes: what problems? Example insufficient) Lack of experience also influences the selection and acquisition of applicable software programs. In many cases, software selection is based on reports received from other users at conferences, and not based on thorough systems analysis (Adogbeji et al., n.d). Alternatively, librarians rely on the vendors of computer systems for both their hardware and software requirements (Tiamiyu in Adogbeji et al., n.d.). Nwalo (2000) expressed the hope that the implementation of Information Technology courses in African library schools would eventually overcome the current manpower shortage.

5.5 Information Communication Technologies

Modern Information and Communication Technologies (ICTs), specifically computers, information networks and software applications, enable special libraries to provide a variety of information services to their clients, faster and more efficiently than ever before in history. In Africa, libraries have adopted and are utilizing ICTs for various services, although huge disparities exist in the numbers available and the levels of utilization, not only between libraries, but also between countries within regions (Chisenga 2006). Were (2006) observed that even in institutions with high levels of ICT development, library units remained inadequately equipped.

Despite being the continent with the fastest growing telecommunications infrastructure, Africa's ICT diffusion is still lagging behind, and the digital divide between the continent and information-rich developed countries is increasing daily. Although Africa has 13% of the world's population, only 2% of the world's telephone lines and 1% of Internet connectivity (measured in terms of Internet hosts and users) can be found on the continent (Ongusola, 2005). Internet utilization is mainly centered in two countries, i.e. South Africa and Egypt, which respectively service 27.2% and 20.9% of approximately 12.9 million users (Were, 2006). Some of the factors responsible for these disparities are inadequate infrastructure; high tariff structures; strict regulatory structures; inappropriate or weak policy regimes; institutional weaknesses; limited economic resources; low tele-density; inadequate personal computers and internet hosts; insufficiently skilled technicians building ICT infrastructure; limited computer literacy; and the lack of available telecommunications networks (Mutula 2003:13; Oyelaran-Oyeyinka & Adeya 2004:2).

Chisenga (2006:16) identified six factors that prevent African libraries from taking full advantage of all the benefits offered by ICTs:

- Financing and sustainability of ICT infrastructure
- ICT technical infrastructure
- Using and managing ICT facilities
- Preservation of digital-based information resources
- Management of intellectual property rights
- Institutional policy and strategy

The implementation and utilization of ICTs requires funding for hardware, software, license fees, maintenance, upgrading of systems, telecommunications and subscriptions. With funding for special libraries being reduced worldwide, the ability of African special libraries to introduce and sustain ICT infrastructure in their institutions has been hugely diminished. In many cases, IT projects have been implemented and consequently disbanded or have failed to migrate to modern systems due to a shortage of funds. The constant change in the ICT industry and the lack of technically skilled library staff often results in inappropriate or outdated systems, or the operation of systems with insufficient bandwidth, leading to an increased amount of frustration with inefficient information systems (Chisenga 2006).

According to Chisenga (2006), many libraries in Africa introduced ICTs for the mere sake of having these technologies, without considering or creating a formal strategy for the acquisition, use and sustainability of the ICTs. Such a strategy could have assisted in aligning the introduction of ICTs with the institutional goals and missions of the parent organization, which in the case of special libraries is paramount to their continued existence.

5.6 Library networking and resource sharing

The paucity of information resources and dwindling funds necessitated African special libraries to form partnerships with other special libraries. Many formal and informal networks within countries exist; for example, in Egypt, Botswana and Zambia, libraries are cooperating in the fields of information sharing and the sharing of staff knowledge and expertise (Dimitroff 1993; Sekabembe 2002). Joining consortia which consist not only of special libraries but also other library types in order to share both print and digital based resources is becoming common for many special libraries (Mutula n.d; Eifl.Net n.d). Networks extending across country borders, e.g. the SABINET system in Southern Africa, also exist (Jalloh, 1999). Networking with special libraries affiliated to international organizations such as the British Council and the United Nations is also common, since these libraries have bigger budgets and better access to information resources from abroad. Sanni in Nwalo (2000) reports that several information networks exist in Africa. Most notable in terms of special libraries is PADISNET (Pan African Documentation Center Network), which aims to connect African centers performing research on development planning for data and information exchange. A major problem with most formal networks is that they are initiated and sustained by donor bodies from outside Africa, making them vulnerable should the bodies withdraw their support (Nwalo 2000).

6. TRENDS AND OPPORTUNITIES

6.1 Development of Consortia

Lack of funding impacts negatively on a number of aspects of library service delivery, making it difficult to access or acquire the required information resources, or negotiate competitive prices for IT hardware and software. Consortia provide a platform for collective bargaining with publishers, distributors or the vendors of library resources. This may result in access to a much wider range of resources at reduced costs. Consortia also allow access to sources available in other libraries at a very low cost to the user, enabling librarians to efficiently meet their information needs (Singh 2006). An added advantage is the fact that consortia allow library staff to exchange knowledge and expertise. Although Sekabembe (2002) reports that with the exception of South Africa, consortia development in Africa is still in its infancy and experiencing many operational challenges, librarians should keep seeking solutions, as the advantages of such a co-operative system for libraries in general, and special libraries in particular, outweighs any negatives.

6.2 Benchmarking and the measurement of value

The last decade was a period of upheaval and turmoil for special libraries, with many of them, especially those affiliated to the corporate sector, experiencing severe cuts or getting closed down or outsourced to external information vendors (Poll 2007). According to Henczel (2007), the environment within which special libraries exist is one of emerging technologies, evolving user expectations, diminishing budgets, changing cultural climates and competing organizationorganizational priorities. Chung (2007) therefore advocates that in order for special libraries to justify their continued existence and garner support and funding, the measurement of their economic value is necessary.

Two methods can be employed to calculate value, i.e. measuring the cost in terms of user time saved through the services offered by the library, or bench-marking. According to Chung (2007:2), the time-value evaluation method is used to *"measure and compare the relationships between time saved and costs avoided against the cost of library services"*.

In this respect, special libraries serving an institution or commercial firm can measure:

- whether library services save time and effort in finding relevant information
- the time it would have taken the user to find the information without assistance from the library
- what information literacy is gained through training provided by the library staff (Poll 2007 n.d.).

Special libraries servicing a general public could measure their importance in the region, society or culture by asking both users and non-users to rate the direct benefit they get from library use, or the potential benefit they can derive from the existence of the library.

Benchmarking is defined as: "a process for improving performance by constantly identifying, understanding and adapting best practices and processes followed inside and outside the company and implementing the results" (Jurow and Barnard in Nicholas 2007:n.p). According to Poll (2007), measuring the quality of special library services depends on the mission of each library. For example, measurements for institutional special libraries concentrate on the speed, actuality and accuracy of the reference and information delivery services. Also important is whether services and collections can be accessed via the user's desktop. Special libraries with long-range tasks and no specific population are measured by their specialized subject coverage, preservation and/or digitization activities, their engagement with cultural activities, and the comprehensiveness and speed with which bibliographies are prepared.

Poll (2007) identifies very specific performance indicators for special libraries. These indicators are based on the special tasks delivered by special libraries as outlined earlier in the chapter.

For libraries serving an undefined clientele, the immediate delivery of requested information is not as important as the quality of the collection for current and possible future demand.

Presently, very little benchmarking or value measuring activities are performed in African special libraries, providing them with little means to demonstrate that their work supports their institutional goals, and that ultimately the funds allocated to their service delivery will save costs for the institution. To demonstrate relevancy and worth, it is imperative that special libraries seize the opportunity to produce evidence-based measurements demonstrating their value in terms of strategic-level processes, i.e. by measuring what is needed to provide services and the impact of their information services on the business, geographic regions, strategic objectives, projects, and so on. The measurement and characterization of the user population in terms of size, location and needs is also necessary (Henczel 2007).

6.3 Information Communication Technologies

According to Muller (2007:118), users tend "*to measure libraries according to how they utilize information technology to fulfill their needs*". Relevancy and the success of services are also measured according to the newness of the technology used. Many special libraries in Africa are embracing technology as a way to create a presence outside their physical buildings; however, the issues of sufficient capacity and affordable broadband hamper digital service delivery and the creation and maintenance of a web presence. Additionally, Mutula (n.d) points out that IT is not currently effectively integrated in the development agenda of most African countries, as can be seen from the lack of ICT policies.

Mutula (n.d.) warns that if the "digital divide" – a situation where disparities exist between countries and communities in terms ICT access – is not addressed, information service delivery will suffer, resulting in the under-utilization of information resources and information sharing. Current national initiatives in many countries are aiming to bridge this divide, and it is therefore in each institution's (and this includes libraries') interest to develop programs that correspond with national initiatives in order to address the situation.

6.4 Designing demand driven information systems

According to Mchombu (2007), collections in most information centers reflect the subject profiles of the information collection developers and are thus not based on real needs and demands. Special librarians are also often surrounded by legacy collections, systems and processes that require a concerted effort to maintain, often resulting in information systems that are not supportive of the core functions of the library (Henczel 2007). Mchombu (2007) advocates the use of user studies to design information systems that are demand driven and accurately reflect the need for information. Given the paucity of information resources, African special librarians should seize every opportunity they can to build relevant collections or provide access to applicable sources, whether in print, digital or any other appropriate format. In this respect, information sharing could play an important role, as it ensures that information is made available beyond the boundaries of a physical building, thus adding value to society as a whole.

6.5 Acquiring new skills

The Internet has resulted in the increased independence of the user from an intermediary, threatening the existence of librarians as the custodians of information.

In order to turn this into an opportunity, special librarians need to reinvent their roles as "filters" of data. New skills, such as the ability to do web authoring, mapping and navigation of the digital information landscape, the ability to handle dynamic resources, and contributing towards knowledge management within the parent organization; should be obtained (Wittwer 2001). Communication has become an important skill, with special librarians having to move both the information and themselves outside physical boundaries by means of technology and through the development of informal information networks within their parent organizations. Librarians have to be able to determine what projects their clients are involved in, and to connect the client proactively to relevant information (Muller 2007). The librarian therefore needs to create awareness amongst end-users of the range of information available and the quickest and easiest way to access the required information. This means that the role of trainer must be assumed – training end-users in best practices in Internet searching, and/or exposing them to other relevant information tools or products. Special librarians should thus not only gain traditional skills, but also new skills that deal with IT -techniques or IT-knowledge (Wittwer 2001).

6.6 Marketing

Special libraries have many of the same marketing and promotional needs as other libraries. However, special libraries often have a more narrowly defined set of users and must often compete with other departments for funding and information resources (Berry, 1999).

A number of African corporate libraries have in recent years been downsized, closed or outsourced due to a lack of funding or managerial support, with management justifying their withdrawal by comparing the running cost of the library service to "free" information services offered through the Internet (Muller 2007). The diverse avenues available for information access today have become a critical challenge to the survival of the special library, as users may now be prompted to use electronic or commercial document delivery services, subscribe to databases, buy their own materials, or use abbreviated online abstracts instead of full-text documents for their research (Nkanga 1999). These myriad options available to the client are currently challenging the very survival of special libraries, more so within the African context where special libraries are securing less and less funding to ensure that their information sources remain relevant.

According to Singh (2006), the customer and satisfying his/her needs should be the main reason for marketing, requiring sensitivity from staff towards customer needs, and an understanding from staff that it is their responsibility to fulfill these needs.

7. CONCLUSION

Despite being the oldest library type established in Africa, African special libraries are probably the most challenged libraries on the continent in terms of their ability to provide relevant services and resources to their clientele. Since their very survival depends on their ability to provide tailor-made services to their clients, it is imperative that they move with the times.

In the quest for relevance, the biggest challenge faced by the special libraries is probably inadequate ICT infrastructure, hardware and software, as well as a shortage of trained staff and technicians. ICTs have revolutionized the way in which information is retrieved and disseminated and how services to clients are provided. Because the use of technology is an indicator to the client of the library's ability to deliver relevant information services, special libraries cannot afford to be found wanting. It will, however, take a concerted effort from many role-players in the information industry, such as governments, information service providers, IT technicians, managers of parent organizations, and library staff; to address all the issues and challenges related to information service delivery for Africa to be on par with the services delivered in developed countries.

Library schools need to address shortcomings in their training of library staff, specifically in the field of IT. It is no longer acceptable to concentrate the training of students on mainly theoretically based subjects when hands-on experience is paramount in providing them with a competitive edge in a fast moving, increasingly globalized world. The lack of continuous training facilities and courses have been identified as major shortcomings that need to be addressed by library schools, as the dynamic business environment necessitates the learning of new skills and the ability to adapt to existing systems. Currently, special librarians have to find their own way in order to try and keep their skills current.

The lack of benchmarking activities poses a serious problem to African special libraries, as it means that they have no measures in place to show their worth to their parent organizations. This provides them with no influence when negotiating for funding in order to obtain new services or the installation of ICTs within the library. This lack of tangible evidence often leads to special libraries being neglected, scaled down or even closed down.

On the positive side, it appears as if there is a growing consensus amongst special librarians that networking and resource sharing provides a workable solution to the paucity of information sources, and there is growing evidence that more libraries are forming both formal and informal networks of collaboration, not only amongst themselves, but also with other library types and even with libraries abroad.

Globalization necessitates that special libraries should become more aggressive market players, staying in the forefront of developments in their field of specialization, changes in their parent organizations, and innovations in the field of information delivery. African special libraries will have to find ways of overcoming their challenges in order to emerge as the suppliers of vibrant competitive services that add value to their employers.

8. RECOMMENDATIONS

1. Special librarians should make a concerted effort to market both themselves and the services that they offer. Users are not prone to use services just because a given facility is available in their organization. Proactive marketing alerts should prompt users to utilize that which is convenient, relevant and easily available.
2. All special libraries should embark on benchmarking activities, as this provides them with an insight into the value and productivity of their services, and also provides them with tangible evidence that can be used during negotiations with clients and the parent organizations. It can also indicate to staff where improvements need to be implemented.
3. Inadequate ICT infrastructure, hardware and software, training, and policies should be addressed at all levels, and librarians and their parent organizations should become actively involved in negotiations with their governments to find solutions to many of the problems still nagging the information industry in Africa. As governments are made more aware of the economic and social importance of information, they will possibly allocate more funds towards the improvement of infrastructure.
4. Training issues should be addressed, as the production of librarians with irrelevant skills is a bad reflection on the curricula of African library schools.

References

Adogbeji, O. B., et.al. (n.d.) Software selection and acquisition in Nigerian University and Special Libraries: The way forward. [Online] Available: http://cis.paisley.ac. uk/research/journal/V11/softwareselection.pdf. Retrieved on September 6, 2007.

Akita, J.M. n.d. Development of the National Archives and the National Documentation Center. [Online] Available: unesdoc.unesco.org/images/0003/000362/036237eo. pdf. Retrieved on October 16, 2007.

Alemna, A.A. (1997). A review of library provision in Ghana. *Library review*, 46(1): pp. 34 -44.

Amonoo, P. and Azubuike, (2005). A. Libraries and the Information Society in Africa. [Online]: Available http://www.uneca.org/aisi/docs/PolicyBriefs/Libra ries%20and%20the%20Information%20Society%20in%20Africa.pdf Retrieved on October 10, 2007.

Baldwin, C.M. & Varady, R.G. (1989). Information Access in Niger: Development of a West African special library. *Special libraries*, pp. 31 – 37. Winter.

Bauer, P. (2003). An overview of Special Libraries. [Online] Available: http://alia.org.au/ policies/special_libraries.html. Retrieved on September 6, 2007.

Berry, A. (1999). Promoting special library services. [Online] Available: http:// www.libsci.sc.edu/bob/class/clis724/SpecialLibrariesHandbook/promoting.htm. Retrieved on November 6, 2007.

Burger, D. ed. (2007). South African yearbook 2006/2007. [Online] Available: http://www. gcis.gov.za/docs/publications/yearbook/chapter5.pdf. Retrieved on September 11, 2007.

Chisenga, J. (2006). Information and Communication Technologies: opportunities and challenges for national and university libraries in Easter, Central and Southern Africa. [Online]: Chung, H. 2007. Measuring the economic value of special libraries. The bottom line: managing library finances, 20(1). [Online] Available: http://www.emeraldinsight.com/ViewContentServlet?Filename=//published/ emerald fulltextarticle/pdf/1700200104_ref.html. Retrieved on October 16, 2007.

Dahlgren, C. (1994). The Tanzanian Library service: a review of recent literature. World Libraries, 5(1). [Online] Available: www.worlib.org/vol05no1/dahlgren_ v05n1. shtml. (Retrieved on October 16, 2007.

Diakite, F. (1999). Services of libraries and reading in Mali. [Online] Available: http://www. ifla.org/IV/ifla65/papers/133-85e.htm. (Accessed 16 October 2007).

Dimitroff, A. (1993). Information access in a developing country: special libraries in Egypt. *Special libraries*, 25 – 29. Winter.

Eifl.Net Lesotho. n.d. [Online] Available: http://www.eifl.net/cps/sections/country/ lesotho. Retrieved on October 15, 2007.

Henczel, S. 2007. Special measures for special libraries: analyzing systems, needs and workflows. [Online] Available: http://www.ifla.org/IV/ifla73papers/152-Henczel-en. pdf. Retrieved on August 29, 2007.

IFLA/FAIFE World Report: Libraries and Intellectual freedom: Kenya. 1999. [Online] Available: http:// www.ifla.org/faife/report/kenya.htm. Retrieved on August 29, 2007.

Ikoja-Odongo, R. (2004). 16th Standing Conference of Eastern, Central and South Africa Library and Information Associations: a report. [Online] Available: http://www. scecsal.org/s2004report.pdf. Retrieved on October 10, 2007.

Information Outlook online. 2000. Internet in Swaziland. [Online] Available: http://www. sla.org/content/Shop/Information/infoonline/2000/mar00/edge.cfm. Retrieved on October 15, 2007.

Jalloh, B. 1999. Library Networking and Consortia Initiatives in Africa. *African Journal of library, Archives & Information Science*, 9(1):pp.1-15.

Kargbo, J.A. 2002. Effects of the Civil War and the Role of Librarians in Post–War Reconstruction in Sierra Leone. *World Libraries*, 12 (2) [Online] Available: http:// www.worlib.org/vol12no2/kargbo_v12n2.shtml. Retrieved on September 6, 2007.

Kavulya, J.M. 2007. Digital libraries and development in Sub-Saharan Africa: a review of challenges and strategies. The Electronic Library, 25(3):pp. 299-315. [Online] Available: http://emeraldinsight.com/ViewContentServlet?Filename=/published/emeraldfulltextarticle/pdf/2630250304_ref.html. Retrieved on October 15, 2007.

Kebede, G. 1999. Performance evaluation in Library and Information Systems of developing countries: a study of the literature. *Libri*, 49:106-119.

Kunene, D.J. n.d. Swaziland country report 1998 – 2000. [Online] Available: http://www. scecsal.org/sswalacr0.html.   Retrieved on October 15, 2007.

Levebre, L. 1996. The pecial library: what it is and what it can do for business and industry. Special libraries, pp.286 292. Fall.

Mamvoto, P. and Mutasa, M. 2007. The library as a tool for development: the case of Zimbabwe. [Online] Available: http://www.ifla.org/IVifla70/papers/083e-Mamvoto_ Mutasa.pdf. Retrieved on August 29, 2007.

Mchombu, K.J. 2007. Harnessing knowledge management for Africa's transition to the 21ˢᵗ Century, in Mcharazo, A and Koopman, S. Librarianship as a bridge to an Information and Knowledge Society in Africa. München: K.G. Saur.

Morgenstern, R. 1993. The special libraries of government and prospects of cooperation with libraries for *parastatal* and private information centers, in Tötemeyer, A.-J. ed. Coordination of Information Systems and services in Namibia. Papers of the seminar. Windhoek, Namibia. February 25 – March 5, 1993. [Online]   Available: http://www.eric.ed.gov/ERICDocs/data/ericdocs2sql/content_storage_ 01/0000019b/80/13/0b/99.pdf. (Retrieved on October 16, 2007.

Muller, B. 2007. Challenges facing special libraries in South Africa, in Bothma, T, Underwood, P and Ngulube, P. eds. *Libraries for the Future: Progress and development of South African Libraries*. Pretoria: Libraries and Information Association of South Africa (LIASA).

Mutula, S. n.d. IT diffusions in Sub-Saharan Africa: implications for developing and managing digital libraries. [Online] Available: http://aboutdisa.ukzn.ac.za/workshops/ Gabarone%20workshop/MutulaIFLAworkshop.pdf. Retrieved on August 31, 2007.

Mutala, S.M. 2003. Assessment of Africa's telematics, policy and regulatory infrastructure: potential for e-learning. [Online] Available: http://64.233.183.104/search?q=cache:lMLOPc6YjN0J:ahero.uwc.ac.za/index.php%3Fmodule%3Dcshe%26action%3Ddownloadfile%26fileid%3D81806115511890804686349+%22 Assessment+of+Africa%E2%80%99s+telematics,+policy+and+regulatory+infrastructure:+potential+for+e-learning%22&hl=en&ct=clnk&cd=1&gl=za.

Retrieved on October 3, 2007.Nicholas, P. 2007. Benchmarking: an imperative for special libraries in the Caribbean: the Jamaican case. [Online] Available: http://www.ifla.org/IV/ifla73/papers/152-Nicholas-en.pdf. Retrieved on August 29, 2007.

Nkanga, N.A. 1999. Strategy for marketing informaiton services in Botsewana special libaries and Information centers. *African Journal of Library, Archives and Information Science,* 9(1): 59-67.

Nwalo, K.I.N. 2000. Managing information for development in the 21st century: prospects for African libraries, challenges to the world. [Online] Available: http://www. ifla/IV/ifla66/papers/012-114e.htm. Retrieved August 29, 2007.

Ocholla, D.N. 1993. Typology of libraries. in Ocholla, D.N. and Ojiamb0. *Issues in Library and Information Studies.* Nairobi: The Jomo Kenyatta Foundation.

Ocholla, D and Bothma, T. 2007. Library and Information education and training in South Africa. , in Bothma, T, Underwood, P and Ngulube, P. eds. *Libraries for the Future: Progress and development of South African Libraries.* Pretoria: Libraries and Information Association of South Africa (LIASA).

Okiy, R.B. n.d. Using libraries in Nigeria as tools for education and national development in the 21st century. [Online] Available: http://libr.org/isc/articles/21/13.pdf. Retrieved on October 16, 2007.Ongusola, L.A. 2005. Information and Communication Technologies and the effects of globalization: twenty-first century "Digital slavery" for developing countries – Myth or reality, Electronic Journal of Academic and Special Librarianship, 6(1-2). [Online] Available: http://southernlibrarianship.icaap.org/content/ v06n01/ogunsola_101.htm. Retrieved on August 30, 2007.

Oyelaran-Oyeyinka, B. and Adeya, C.N. 2004. Internet access in Africa: empirical evidence from Kenya and Nigeria. Telematics and Informatics, 21(1). [Online] Available:
http://www.sciencedirect.com/science?_ob=ArticleURL&_udi=B6V1H-488NN KW-2&_user=1378591&_coverDate=02%2F29%2F2004&_rdoc-1&_fmt=&_ orig=search&_sort=d&view=c&_acct=C000052501&_version=1&_urlVersion =0&_userid=1378591&md5=0cbb388d665964bc7a5359a03b376908

Poll, R. 2007. Quality measures for special libraries. [Online] Available: http://www.ifla.org/ IVifla73/papers/152-Poll-en.pdf. Retrieved on August 29, 2007.

Ranasinghe, R.H.I.S. 2007. The factors which influenced the establishment and development of libraries in Sub-Saharan Africa. [Online] Available: http://www.ifla.org/ IV/ifla73/papers/144-Ranasinghe-en.pdf. Retrieved on September 6, 2007.

Rosenberg, D. 2006. Towards the digital library in Africa. The Electronic library, 24(3). [Online] Available: http://www.emeraldinsight.com/Insight/ViewContent

Servlet?Filename=Published/EmeraldFullTextArticle/Articles/2630240301.
html. Retrieved on October 9, 2007.

Sekabembe, B. 2002.Activities of existing and functioning library consortia in
East, Central and Southern Africa: a report of the case study done on behalf of
the International Network for the availability of Scientific Paper (INASP).
[Online] Available: http://ahero.uwc.ac.za/index.php?module=cshe&
action=downloadfile&fileid=81806115511851809254573. Retrieved on November 6, 2007.

Singh, S.P. 2006. Special libraries in India: some current trends. Library review,
55(8):520-530. [Online] Available: www.emeraldinsight.com/Insight?Vew
ContentServlet? Filename=Published/EmeraldFullTextArticle/Articles/
0350550806.html. Retrieved on October 16, 2007.

Sitzman, G. L. 1988. African libraries. Metuchen, N.J.: The Scarecrow Press.

Stillwell, C. 2007. Library and Information services in South Africa: an overview.
IFLA Journal, 33(2): 87-108.

Sturges, P and Neill, R. 1990. *The quiet struggle: libraries and information for Africa.* London: Mansell.

Tötemeyer, A.-J. 1993. 1993. Findings and recommendations of the University of
Namibia Department of Information Studies research report on school, public,
government, *parastatal*, private and training institution libraries and information services in Namibia,in Tötemeyer, A.-J. ed. Coordination of Information
Systems and services in Namibia. Papers of the seminar. Windhoek, Namibia.
February 25 – March 5, 1993. [Online] Available: http://www.eric.ed.gov/
ERICDocs/data/ericdocs2sql/content_storage_01/0000019b/80/13/0b/99.pdf. Retrieved on October 16, 2007.

Tsigemelak, D. 2006. Libraries and librarianship in Ethiopia: Status, prospects and
challenges. [Online]: http://units.sla.org/division/dpam/irc/demissew.pdf. (Accessed 29 Augustus 2007).

Wedgeworth, R. 1993. World Encyclopedia of Library and Information Services.
Chicago: American Library Association.

Were, J. 2006. Libraries as ICT and Information access points in Africa: success
cases and best practices. [Online] Available: http://www.uneca.org/disd/events/
2006/wsis-library/presentations/Libraries%20as%20ICT%20and%20
Information%20Access%20Points%20in%20Africa%20-%20Jacinta%20
Were%20-%20EN.ppt. Retrieved on October 10, 2007.Wertsman, V.F. 1996.
Librarian's companion: A handbook on libraries/librarians, books/newspapers,
publishers/booksales. 2nd ed.

Wittwer, R. 2001. Special libraries – how to survive the twenty-first century. The
Electronic library, 19(4): 221 – 225. [Online] Available:
http://www.emeraldinsight.com/Insight/html/Output/Published/EmeraldFullTextA
rticle/Pdf/2630190402.pdf . Retrieved on October 16, 2007.

SCHOOL LIBRARIES

Robert Ikoja Odongo

1. INTRODUCTION

This chapter examines school libraries in Africa by tracing their development, examining their state, and identifying the challenges facing them. School libraries in Africa cannot usefully be summarized on a continent-wide scale due to the region's general division into five different geographical units, each with widely varying cultures, distinct social forms and traditions, and different levels of development. The five units are as follows: the Arab world and the Maghreb countries of the north; the Anglophone west, east, central and southern Africa; the Francophone west and central Africa (and the Indian Ocean islands); the Lusophone Africa and South Africa. The chapter mainly focuses on school libraries in English-speaking Africa, although a few Arab countries are included. These libraries must be interpreted against the backdrop of a number of social and infrastructural concerns, including the impact of colonialism, the effects of growing populations, underdevelopment in the African publishing industry, the prevailing political situations on the continent (particularly military conflict in some countries like Chad, Congo Democratic Republic, Somalia etc, lack of resources, and profound social problems (Gill, 2001). Furthermore, factors such as the institutional preference of teachers as opposed to librarians in the running of libraries; reluctance of school-governing bodies in recognizing the importance of school libraries in the attainment of school objectives; library illiteracy amongst pupils; the role of donors; and the entry of computers into the school system; cannot be overlooked.

A school library is a learning center through which students and teachers alike further their educational programs (Otike, 1987:413). Wikipedia (updated Sept, 2007), defines a school library as "... *a library that serves the students, faculty, staff and parents of a public or private school.*" Essentially, the library's mission is to offer learning services, books and resources that enable the school community to use information effectively in various formats and media, and thus enhance critical thinking. A school library brings together four components, namely information resources, users, library staff and the environment. The first three elements must be operating in an environment that supports learning in order for a library to function effectively.

A school library is also alternatively referred to as a school library resource center (SLRC) in the United Kingdom or a library media center (LMC) in the USA. The major differences between the traditional school library and the SLRC or LMC are that the latter play a more integrative role in the learning and teaching done in a school, there is an emphasis on both print and non-print based materials, and there are facilities for recreation. The resource center/school media library center is therefore a place where there is a fusion of the skills of teachers, librarians, audiovisual experts and technicians. The school library/media center is a generic term for the different types of libraries identified by the level of education or grades, i.e. secondary (senior or junior, or high school), primary and elementary or kindergarten.

1.2 School library standards

In order to achieve the school library's objectives, schools are expected to either implement or to already have a school library policy. Besides the policy, standards have been set up by national departments of education, educational accrediting agencies, library associations and the International Federation of Library Associations and Institutions, and the United Nations Educational, Scientific and Cultural Organization (IFLA/UNESCO) to guide school managers. Standards are specific and quantitative statements that act as guidelines for institutions to follow in the establishment, maintenance and management of school libraries. For instance, schools in various enrolment brackets have requirements laid down to cover the number of books on shelves, seating capacity, technical organization and budgetary allocation. IFLA/UNESCO standards provide a general idea of what individual countries should have and do. These standards specify that the school library should provide information and ideas that allow individuals to function successfully in today's information and knowledge-based society. The school library should equip students with life-long learning skills and assist with the development of thought processes that will enable them to live as responsible citizens. It should link with other library and information networks in keeping with the principles found in the UNESCO Public Library Manifesto. Its staff should promote the use of books and other information resources, and its library services must be provided equally to all members of the school community, regardless of age, race, gender, religion, nationality, language, or professional or social status. Special services and materials must be provided for those who are unable to use mainstream library services and materials such as the blind pupils.

2. STATE OF SCHOOL LIBRARIES IN AFRICA

A review of literature has shown that school libraries appear to play a very limited role in Africa in the light of how many amount to no more than shelves of outdated and worn-out material, nominally supervised by teachers who are too busy, disinterested, or ill-paid to pay much attention (Olden, 1995:127). Rosenberg (2002) reinforced this, and argued that the early promise of libraries has not been fulfilled in Africa. For instance, the activities of libraries in countries such as Ghana, Tanzania, Kenya and Uganda have declined significantly from when they were first established. Through his study in Tanzania, Ilomo (1985) concluded that financial limitation was the main obstacle, although this reason is often used to disguise the existence of other crucial factors. He noted that the availability of financing did not necessarily mean that it would be channeled to the development

financing did not necessarily mean that it would be channeled to the development of school libraries. Nigeria in the 80s is an example, because despite being rich with oil money during that period, libraries in schools continued to decline. Buildings and other facilities were not maintained, shelves were either empty or, full of irrelevant materials; funding was inadequate, and the percentage of the population using the services was negligible. This is more or less still true – albeit at different levels in different countries such as Uganda for all libraries in the public sector. In her study focusing specifically on school libraries, Rosenberg (1998) found that the school library systems set up during independence are no longer active. The most immediate cause of this loss appears to be that libraries are no longer adequately financed by their parent bodies or institutions because the institutional budget covers only the cost of staff salaries and basic building maintenance. The libraries are therefore highly dependant on external assistance. Donations can provide between 90 percent and 100 percent of all acquisitions (Rosenberg, 2002:10). Rosenberg concluded that for young people who constitute the majority of Africa's population, this is nothing short of tragic.

Similarly in Ghana's case, Alemna (1990) found that school libraries still faced a myriad of problems and that they were not being solved by School and College Division (SCD) of the Ministry of Education. School libraries were deteriorating because of lack of government attention and low interest from administrators. In an unpublished paper (Alemna, 1996 in Rosenberg, 1998), the author argued on the overall lack of impact, saying that the official interest in libraries was "cool and casual", rather than active and sustained. This lack of commitment by government and lack of interest by school principals and heads had been the main reason behind why standards (neither those laid down in the 1972 *Manual for School Libraries in Ghana*, nor those proposed by Alemna in 1993) had still not been adopted, legislation had yet to be introduced, and why monies allocated to libraries were often diverted to meet other ends. There were no specific training requirements for school librarians in Ghana at least by 1996. The resulting use of unqualified staff led to poor services and libraries did not add to the quality of education offered in the schools. In 1994, Alemna lamented that no one appeared to be in a position to give any clear indication as to whether the growth of organized library services in schools had any impact on the poor reading habits of school leavers – which was the key reason for setting up SCD. He argued that even the introduction of a new educational system in Ghana in 1986 – one that demanded a greater use of books and libraries – did not result in more support for SCD and its role in developing school libraries. It is highly likely that the same status quo remains to this day taking into consideration that any change in the school library development would require massive capital inputs and commitment by school boards of governors and teachers. No spectacular change in this direction has been reported lately.

In this paragraph, I examine the Libyan school libraries. In Libya, the majority of school libraries are not entirely satisfactory. Lack of progress has been caused by a shortage of competent staff with adequate training, experience and/or knowledge. The lack of buildings specifically designed to serve as libraries is also a major obstacle blocking service delivery. Other reasons include lack of awareness on the part of the principals and administrators of the basic scientific and cultural role of the school library, and the lack of trained persons to select suitable books and other materials such as films, microfilms, slides etc. It is reported that there are also problems with cataloguing, classification and providing reader advice.

In the previous section the state of school libraries in Libya was described briefly. In this section school libraries in Mali are examined. The Malian state of school libraries, according to Sidibe (1998), is that the existing libraries are fairly equipped. The librarians (all teachers) manning them have all been through a training course. But the libraries struggle with the poverty of their collections, as books and reading materials require money. Lack of funds has resulted in: the libraries being almost totally dependent on external aid and gifts of books and materials; no suitable premises to house libraries are available as most books are stored in cupboards and in classrooms; and most importantly, the absence of a national documentation policy. Absence of policy means that problems libraries face cannot be effectively addressed because it is always in policy that power to raise and spend money or funds are included. In order to remedy these problems, Sidibe suggests that his government considers equipping each library with an autonomous budget; incorporating a library in the architectural design of every future school; ensuring the further training of librarians in general, and teacher-librarians in particular; and preparing a national documentation policy that should involve the population in its planning.

In this section I turn to East Africa beginning with Kenya. The state of school libraries in Kenya is almost similar to those in most other African countries. Kenya's government does not have any policy on school libraries although it is conscious of the value of school libraries (Otike, 1986). School libraries lack heightened recognition, suffer from inadequate funds, and lack qualified librarians. These libraries are mostly at the mercy of head teachers. The quality of library service is also dependent on the type of school it is serving. Primary schools generally have inadequate provision for libraries. And as for secondary schools, differences are bound to occur depending on the nature of those funding them. Old established schools have more superior collections than *harambee* (self-help) schools. Private schools run by international communities have sizeable collections run by professional staff, while those run as commercial enterprises generally offer the poor quality of service.

In Tanzania, the situation is as follows: government primary schools receive little or no grants for school libraries and are dependent on donations or on raising money locally; libraries are disorganized and normally in the hands of already overworked teachers who are usually unqualified for library work; few schools have purpose-built libraries, and the existing equipment and furniture is unsuitable for library use; and school libraries are not well used – except, perhaps, as study areas by senior pupils. Ilomo (1985) found that very few primary schools had libraries of any significance. In many cases, they were merely cupboards filled with purchased books, and many primary schools borrowed books from the National Library Center. According to him, much as the Ministry of Education would have liked to develop and modernize primary school libraries, implementation was, and still is, hampered by the lack of funds and the sheer numbers involved, and for this reason, priority is given to the improvement of secondary school libraries. Finance and staffing have both been limiting factors in the implementation of this service, although some development has taken place. Rosenberg's study (1998) summarized this position well, stating that school libraries in government-owned primary and secondary schools were dead. The few existing school libraries were run by private organizations. The situation in 1997 was much the same as it was thirty years earlier. The overriding problem the study unearthed was that schools did not even ask for libraries, let alone good ones. Rosenberg thought rightly that librarians have to be pro active and demand for libraries and recognize them as important. They have to want libraries, to recognize the need for libraries, and to realize that a well-stocked and well-organized library is essential for teaching and learning. Only then, according to Rosenberg and likeminded thinkers, would a part of the per capita grant given to each school be reserved for library expenditure. And only then would schools see the need to permanently appoint trained library staff and thus ensure control and continuity, rather than rely on teachers who are frequently transferred and, in any case, have other duties to perform. Rosenberg also attributed the problem to the school curriculum. According to the author, the education curriculum in Tanzania like in most African countries was biased towards formal instruction, and teachers only expected textbooks to be read – broad reading was discouraged. Therefore, unless there are changes in the attitude towards libraries, no lessons could be learnt from model libraries. Advice and training are generally of little use if they fell on deaf ears. Similar reasons were reiterated by those she interviewed in 1997. Funding or the lack of it was again cited as a reason for the failure of School Library Service (SLS) to maintain services, whether for the purchase of books, the running of mobile services or even for making transport available for librarians to visit schools. From Tanzania, examination of Uganda follows.

The White Paper on Education (1992) in Uganda recognizes that the state of libraries in educational institutions in the country is pathetic and has not changed since then. The facilities are either non-existent, or out of date. Although the government explicitly mentions the rehabilitation of existing libraries and the establishment of new school libraries as essential facilities in the construction of new schools, what is significant in the White Paper is the complete silence around libraries below secondary school level (Uganda, 1992). A further issue is the vicious circle of non-library use that is almost universal in Uganda. The teacher-training curriculum is non-library-oriented. The result is non-library-user teachers teaching a non-library-oriented curriculum to children of non-library-user parents (Kigongo-Bukenya in Nakabuye, 1996). Other reasons have also been advanced for the generally poor image of Ugandan school libraries. Some have blamed it on the lack of any clear and progressive ideology or commitment to library development. Others blame the education system and its lack of support for the school library as a teaching and learning resource that should be part of the curricula. Kibirige in Kigongo-Bukenya (1984) outlined the following factors as responsible for the predicament of Ugandan school libraries: the missionary influence; the British colonial influence (on schooling and the curriculum); the examination-oriented education system; attitudes of the educated (i.e. qualification and status achievement as the main aim of education); inadequate development (concentration of projects in or near urban areas); inadequate funding of education (as a result of an underdeveloped economic base); generally poor library services in public libraries without children's collections to serve as examples for schools; lack of defined national standards for libraries in general and school libraries in particular; the role and influence of external agencies and charity organizations on school library development (negative and positive effects); political disruptions; a laissez faire attitude towards the library by school administrators; the lack of a well-equipped indigenous book industry; inadequate and often out-of-date stock; and improper use, and in some cases, complete absence of library accommodation and facilities. Improvements in school libraries appear to result from individual head teachers' efforts and the work of school inspectors in their personal capacities, rather than consistent government policy.

In terms of the school library situation in Ghana, Alemna (1996) portrayed that the school libraries were not functioning well enough to take their proper place in the learning and teaching programs. The author found that existing school library facilities and services were mere collections of materials in space, with very little equipment for students to use. Few schools had special blocks or buildings for libraries, although a number of them had single rooms often attached to the classrooms that were used as school libraries. Book stocks were seriously inadequate, outdated and worn out, and therefore of very little use to students; and there were very few schools in Ghana with professional, full-time school librarians. All schools made use of library clerks and student-assistants. However, there were some good points about these libraries, such as the fact that the acquisition and processing of books was done by the Ghanaian Library Board, and the relationship with public libraries was very close.

In the neighboring Nigeria, Aguolu (1975) has revealed that, there was a general misconception that a library is a luxury that can be dispensed with, or that is not worth worrying about. The author found that school administrators were skeptical about the usefulness of a school library, or were not convinced that it could improve the quality of education given to pupils. Thus, primary school teachers saw no value in libraries, as they believed that the main aim of primary education is to teach the three Rs – reading, writing and arithmetic. Because of this mindset, the school library service was, and still is, the most neglected of all library services in Nigeria. Aina (1979:58) reinforced Aguolu's observations, noting that the development of school libraries was not encouraging because organized libraries did not feature in Nigerian primary schools, although library corners existed in many classrooms. The state of development in secondary school libraries wasn't any better. Aina (1979) found that it was only in Lagos that there was an effective school library service that assisted with the development of primary school libraries in the state.

For Lesotho, McGrath (1978) provides an overview of the development of school library services in that country. First of all Lesotho is a small country with less than two million people. It has primary and secondary schools managed by the Ministry of Education and by religious missions. While school library development commenced in many post-primary schools and in some high schools, there is almost no development at all in primary schools. The nation has not developed the school library policy. However, most schools have some space for a library collection but even while library spaces are available, they remain inadequate for the number of pupils enrolled in most schools. Many schools also lack sufficient shelves and have inadequate provision (i.e. tables, chairs, etc.) for a class of pupils to sit, read and write in. Few schools possess basic library equipment. The number, quality, and relevance of book stocks reveal marked variations from school to school. Collections in most schools do not meet the schools' educational needs. A few schools had started developing their libraries into multi-media resource centers and commenced in the acquisition of audiovisual materials and equipment. The dismal condition of most collections in schools is mainly due to the absence of a trained teacher-librarian with enough time to select materials, organize the collection and provide service. Only a very small number of schools have a teacher with enough scheduled time to serve as a Library Resource Teacher. The schools also suffer the absence of a regular, annual budget for the library to buy books. Many schools allocate no money from their funds for the purchase of library books. In the absence of the required funds, schools accept all donations without criticism and, as a matter of policy, generally never discard books, however unsuitable. Most of the organization within libraries is incomplete; some libraries exhibit no evidence of any organization. Organizational problems were a direct result of: (a) lack of trained teacher-librarians and, (b) lack of the time it would take for the available library teachers to organize and maintain the library's collection. Although some libraries provided pupils with adequate access to the library, most did not. Some instruction in book and library use was given in some schools, but there was little evidence of a planned sequential programme for the acquisition of the necessary book, library, and research skills over the years in secondary/high schooling. Current curricula did not encourage resource-based, re-search-oriented individual learning and small-group activity. The potential of most libraries to contribute to this development has scarcely been touched on.

In Zambia, Mukwato (1972) found the state of school libraries to be unimpressive, highlighting the lack of school library buildings within primary schools. Putting up buildings in thousands of primary schools was such an expensive business that authorities tended to argue that the classroom library, which already operated in nearly all primary schools, was the ideal solution. Mukwato acknowledged, however, that the Public Library Service in Zambia provided primary and secondary schools with books and that there was also a postal and mobile service. In another report on Zambia, Olden (1990) quoted Julie Carpenter and her colleagues in summing up the state of secondary school libraries as mainly responsive, passive elements within their institutions. The buildings were run down, the furniture was dilapidated, and the books were outdated and showing signs of intensive prolonged use. There were also a high proportion of largely irrelevant donated books taking up shelf space that would otherwise be empty. Olden cited a Zambian librarian who lamented that there are effectively no libraries in government schools in Kitwe, the second largest city. Mismanagement, vandalism, and dependency on book donations were among other problems that were reported. An IFLA report (2001) showed that while the educational infrastructure in Zambia is generally inadequate, there is also a great disparity between the resources that go to urban schools and the meager supplies available to rural schools. When a school or children's library exists within a community, it typically has fewer books and educational materials, or doesn't even have a library management system in place. The Ministry of Education (MOE) is struggling to promote a culture of reading amongst both adults and children.

Totemeyer (1996) described the Namibian school library scene prior to independence as a product of a century of colonialism, the last decades of which were dominated by its apartheid. Primary and secondary schools were fragmented to the point that eleven different ethnic authorities managed Namibian schools. The funding of schools was also arranged along ethnic lines. The result of this system was that a vast sum of money was made available to white schools, which were privileged with everything they required, including computers, books and other printed materials, and audio-visual software and hardware for their school libraries. The state of library provision for the schools designated for black students, on the other hand, was appalling. A study conducted in 1990 by the Department of Information Studies from the University of Namibia established that 77 percent of Namibian schools had no libraries or even book collections until recently when the Government of Namibia has began including a library room in each secondary school it builds. However, this room is often used for other purposes or stands empty without any furniture or stock (University of Namibia, 1990). There was no school library policy until the late 1990s. Obviously, the lack of school libraries in

Namibian schools was not the sole cause of this phenomenon. Other factors, such as poorly qualified teachers, the lack of classrooms and textbooks, and poor social environments within the home and community, were also responsible for this state of affairs. In the next paragraph school library development in Zimbabwe is described.

Made (2000) traced the development of library services in Zimbabwe to 1895-1927, when public/subscription libraries, school libraries and special libraries were established. School libraries were established as part of the rural library service by the National Library and Documentation Service. The aim of this arrangement was to enable students from schools with no static libraries to have access to reading material through this service. The operation of school libraries had been largely left to individual school authorities, with minimal central guidance and direction. At primary school level, there was virtually no library facility – not even one based on the class library. In schools where there were libraries books were stolen and abused and the library was likely to be locked up when the designated teacher-librarian was away. Only a limited number of titles, in English, were commensurate with the reading ability of African pupils.

A number of people have written about school libraries in South Africa. Dick (2007:13) for example found that there was a lot that had been written and published on the historical development of libraries in South Africa. He documented that as early as 1803, there were attempts to set up school libraries in mission stations, such as near Port Elizabeth. This was due to the missionaries' efforts to teach reading and writing that raised the literacy levels at these stations to the extent that they, the missionaries requested religious societies back at their places of origin, such as the Religious Tract Society, to supply schools with reading and religious materials. Other developments included the launching of reading rooms and library depots. Another author, Fourie (2007), who while discussing the library and information service structure in South Africa touched on the development of school libraries since the Carnegie survey in 1928 and the Interdependent Committee Report of 1937. He said there had been attempts to establish closer ties between libraries and education. The latest was based on Curriculum 2005, which was implemented in 1997 and was expected to raise the importance of school libraries – but did not. The National Education Act also comments on the provision of facilities such as libraries and their impact on schools. According to Le Roux (2002:16), the role of developing school libraries was assigned to the school governing bodies, which were expected to do their best to improve the quality of education in their schools and, therefore, to increase the budgets for their libraries.

Radebe (1996) also discussed school library development in South Africa within the framework of the historical development of its education. She cited policy discussions and how these attempted to inform the perspectives of the African National Congress (ANC) on education in general and on school library provision in particular. Policy proposals focused more on redressing past imbalances in favour of previously deprived black communities. On the whole, school libraries in South Africa have been marginalised and undervalued. Citing Lor (1992) and Stadler (1992), Radebe found that the general, across-the-board marginalisation of school librarians both within the school and in the library profession, the absence of a school library organization, a lack of realistic funding for these services and the low level of substantial policy research were issues that needed attention. Similarly, Hart (2006) identified key events and factors associated with school libraries. According to her, in order to understand the school library situation in South Africa, the following had to be taken into account: the legacy of apartheid; two government-sponsored surveys in 1997 and 1999; educational legislation since 1994; national norms and standards for school funding; Curriculum 2005 and the National Policy Framework for school library standards; increasing concerns over the poor reading abilities of South African learners; and the Technology-Enhanced Learning Initiative Policy Framework of 1996. Regarding apartheid, Hart highlighted the position of school libraries based on racial lines. The schools belonging to the white sector of education had libraries that were on par with those in the developed world, whereas libraries in black African schools were virtually non-existent. It was only in the 1980s that libraries in black schools began to improve with the appointment of school librarians and the addition of library materials' budgets. But the 1990s brought problems when government enforced national pupil/teacher ratios – in the interest of equity. This action saw a fresh wave of retrenchments of school librarians. The schools' governing boards paid those who remained. However in 1997, the Department of Education conducted a national audit of school facilities and found that less than 30 percent of South African schools had libraries. Another survey by the Human Sciences Research Council in 1999 revealed that during that period, 32 percent of South African schools had "on-site" libraries, and in terms of their distribution, there were huge provincial disparities. The report commented on the unavailability of many already existing libraries, which were often used as classrooms or shut for most of the day because the 'librarian' was also a fulltime teacher. A school Register of Needs audit of school facilities conducted by the Department of Education estimated that 8 million out of 12 million South African learners did not have access to libraries in their schools (Hart and Zinn, 2007:92). It should be remembered that South Africa held her first democratic election in 1994. This election brought about widespread changes in education. School libraries came to be recognized as the responsibility of three layers of government, i.e. national, provincial and school. In terms of the legislation passed following 1994, two are relevant – the national Education Policy Act of 1996, and the SA Schools Act of 1996. The National Education Policy Act spells out the responsibilities of the various layers, i.e. the central government retains policy building as its primary function, the provinces implement the policy, and the schools to run the libraries. The SA Schools Act aims to bring democratic management down to school level. It grants powers to governing bodies to appoint librarians. Curriculum 2005 emphasized outcomes-based learning, where libraries were meant to play a central role. Teachers were expected to move away from a *chalk-and-talk* format and reliance on textbooks towards *resource-based learning*. The result of this was no better. Citing Karlson, de Jager et al. (2007:143) stated that the adoption of outcomes-based education (OBE) by the department of Education was welcomed by school librarians, who saw a space in the education program for the inclusion of information literacy skills and consistent advocacy for the library and its role in learning. But this did not happen because of the dismal progress in finalizing the school library policy. Rather wittingly, the response had been that the Department of Education was still working on a policy framework that should have been completed in 2005. (Note: Improve links.) Teachers were overworked and there weren't enough books in the libraries. It was in 1997 that the government began the process of drawing up a national policy statement for school libraries. After wide consultations, the result came to be the *National Policy Framework for School Library Standards* (1998).

It should also be mentioned here that many policy provisions have been made that directly relate to school library service development in South Africa. These include: the ANC Policy Framework for Education and Training (1995); an NGO named Read, Educate and Develop (READ), an initiative that investigated the school library policy (1990); the 1992 National Policy Conference; and the National Education Policy Investigation (1992), renamed the National Education Coordinating Committee. In this document, Radebe (1996) highlighted a programme for the introduction of school libraries – particularly in disadvantaged black schools – and the sharing of resources. Radebe (1996) stated that in 1994, the ANC hired a research body, the CEPD, to develop a LIS policy and to translate policy proposals into implementation plans or strategies. This resulted in the Implementation Plan for Education and Training (IPET). The IPET document motivated the placing of LIS within the Ministry of Education, arguing that without libraries and information services, student-centered and resourced-based learning – designed to liberate students and teachers from authority and textbook-based learning – are doomed to failure. Radebe stated that almost all white schools had been provided with adequate school libraries or media centers. Citing Braude, Radebe (1996) conceded that school libraries in South Africa cannot be viewed through a single lens because of the existence of different and separate education departments. There are vast differences in the provision of libraries, ranging from a complete lack of services, to collections in small boxes, to fully equipped 'First World' media centers.

The South African results of a 2004 survey for the implementation of new a policy document makes for sober reading: 19 percent of the responding 5156 schools have a central library; 31 percent have a storeroom for a library; and 20 percent have no library at all (Hart & Zinn, 2007:93).

3. CHALLENGES OF SCHOOL LIBRARIES IN AFRICA

There is evidently a fundamental lack of appreciation amongst policy-makers and educators when viewing the role of the school library. Underpinning this thinking is the noted absence of school library policies and the lack of will on the part of governing bodies, both of which are important aspects of library management (Hart & Zinn, 2007:93). Educators across the board appear less than convinced that school libraries are beneficial. The reluctance of school governing bodies to recognize the need for school libraries is of particular concern. The marginalization of school libraries is an issue that stands out very clearly in the writings of Otike, Aina and Rosenberg. Through studies set in Nigeria, Carroll (1981) and Rosenberg (1998) reinforced the idea that commitment to school libraries is very low, partly due to the educational background of many administrators and teachers who rarely prioritize libraries at primary and secondary school levels. The present educational system is also very examination-oriented. The demands of the syllabus, lack of facilities, and the value attached to examinations all contribute to a system characterized by the provision of instruction by teachers, the study of a single textbook per subject, and copying of notes from a chalkboard. Library use seems to have little relevance in this system, even with the existence of an adequate school library, and this appears to be the norm throughout the continent. For this reason, many believe that advances in adequate accommodation and resources, insufficient commitment to school libraries, lack of materials, lack of trained librarians, and the weak state of school library provision are tied to larger issues of educational reform. Carroll stated that the challenges and obstacles facing school libraries in Africa include the lack of also local publishing. The author stated that accommodation is generally a serious problem for school libraries in Africa. Because of rapidly increasing school populations stemming from growing populations, classes are held in every available room or even outside. While a number of schools have a library the size of at least one classroom, a significant minority has no separate room. Those without such rooms have the library collection in the staffroom or head teacher's office. Where space is available, libraries often lack basic items such as tables, chairs and bookshelves. Funds available from governments are limited. This scarcity is compounded by the rapid expansion of education. Nigeria, for instance, introduced universal primary education (UPE) in 1976, and Uganda in 1996, and this has led to big surges in the primary school population. Linking this to an observation about the school libraries in Lesotho, it is found that a number of secondary schools had space for a library collection, but that the spaces were inadequate for the number of pupils enrolled. Even where a library existed, there was a constant temptation to transform the room into a classroom, especially if the library was poorly stocked or equipped and had no trained staff to run it. Sturges and Neill (1992:142) place the blame on librarians. They believe that African librarians are themselves less than convinced of the importance of librarianship for young people and do not generally place a high value on school libraries. Needless to say, I can also add that school administrators who consider librarians expensive are a likewise bottleneck.

The absence of library management tools such as classification schemes and cataloguing tools certainly diminish the effective use of a library – users simply cannot locate information. Lack of proper cataloguing and other bibliographic tools and failure to apply library standards in the methods of classification and cataloguing pose a problem in the organization and provision of library services, irrespective of how old the stock may be. In nearly all the countries surveyed, housekeeping jobs are reportedly performed manually and poorly. But through personal observation, I would add that the tools for library management are expensive and generally not available in African bookshops. The local publishing industry and book trade are also part of the failure of school libraries in Africa. African publishing is weak and underdeveloped, and few titles rooted in local situations are published. This situation is against the principle of effective library services, which requires relevant materials to be rooted in local culture. Research has shown that initial literacy skills are best acquired when taught in one's mother tongue.

Local books and a flourishing information sector are needed in order for local publications to become widely accessible, to promote local languages, culture and literature, and to underpin literacy and reading skills. Shelves mirror mostly foreign texts of little relevance to the African environment, and this is despite the feeling that primary schools would do better if the books available to them were published in the relevant local languages. Finally, rapid advances in information and communication technology offer exciting opportunities to address the challenges of the information divide. School libraries badly need computerization. However, the information infrastructure in Africa is not developed enough for computers to be roped in, and where computers exist, they are inadequate.

4. CONCLUSION AND RECOMMENDATIONS

School libraries in Africa as a whole are struggling in terms of budgets, value, and governmental support. The African publishing industry is developing, but not fast enough to get African books to school libraries. Preference for teachers to run libraries as opposed to librarians is a big handicap to school library development and progress. Current attempts at stressing learner-centered methodologies are largely theoretical; learning practices remain strongly teacher-centered. However, despite their relative lack of success in practice, school libraries remain a popular solution for ensuring access to reading materials (Rosenberg, 1998). This is because libraries have the capacity to acquire, organize and make reading materials available for use of teachers and school pupils. There is, therefore, need for all stakeholders to accept school libraries as essential institutions in schools; and their value (e.g. in improving examination results) has to be demonstrable. Thus, the support offered for a school library service has to stem from demand. Rosenberg contended correctly that libraries are bottom-up rather than top-down operations; they stem from community needs. Only upon fulfilling these needs would financial support be forthcoming. Generally, school libraries are there to provide supplementary reading materials. Some of the reading material may come from outside the country and through donations, and at the moment most of the material distributed in almost all the African countries consists of donations. But the core material, if it is to be relevant to school needs, must be published and available locally. This requires a vibrant local book industry, and if this is lacking (and it is), then the contribution of any school library to education will be drastically reduced (Rosenberg, 1998).

Having stated that the onus is for governments and other stakeholders to find urgent solutions to reverse the situation and improve the state of school libraries of the future, key elements of any program intended to bring school libraries back to a reasonable standard should include:

- *Developing and implementing a genuine school library policy in every country.* A school library policy is a necessary framework for the development of school libraries. The policy needs national and institutional support in order to contribute towards the attainment of the overall educational objectives. This would ensure that money, regulations, governance, procurements of information products and furniture, bibliographic tools and other requirements are made available, and infrastructure is improved or built and equipment brought in. Almost every other thing revolves around this.

- *Recognizing and employing a skilled professional.*
  School libraries need trained librarians in numbers that allow libraries to significantly contribute to their schools' objectives. The days of librarians as the sole 'gatekeepers' of information are long gone. Librarians today have the additional responsibility of ensuring that their clients are information-literate. Head teachers need to realize that school libraries without competent and motivated librarians are a liability. Library associations should work hard to support efforts or cause situations towards ensuring that there is a policy that recognizes employment of school librarians.

- *Space*
  Governments and schools should find ways to improve the infrastructure of their libraries. Using dysfunctional buildings, or having no room or space at all for a library, signifies that a school is struggling on a number of levels. Rehabilitating existing functional structures or extending them improves their value and impressions about their purpose. Governments should take lead in the process of building school libraries and furnishing them. Other stakeholders should not wait until government comes in. Initiatives should come from everybody to roll out development idea of library development.

- *Local language publishing program*
  Africa needs to develop the capacity to write, edit, illustrate and publish books in local languages and to get children to read these books. This requires research on what is needed by pupils in order to develop viable local language publishing programs, which would go a long way in developing the book trade in various countries and the stocking of school libraries. National Curriculum Development Centers have responsibility to participate in this endeavorendeavor. Indigenous publishers and authors are likewise encouraged to invest or engage in this virgin area of publishing.

- *Curriculum orientation*
  Rote-learning and single textbook dependence in teaching has destroyed the impetus to use school libraries. New methods of content delivery emphasizing self-directed learning using thematic curricula should be encouraged to make the use of school libraries a success. Education authorities particularly trainers must work towards making teachers understand the value of self-directed learning and the need to relate reading to the use of the school library.

References

Aguolu, C.C. (1975). The School Library as an Instrument of Education in Nigeria. *International Library Review* 7, 39-59.

Aina, L.O. (1979). Factors affecting development of Librarianship in Nigeria. In *International Library Review,* 11, 57-67.

Alemna, A.A. (1983). The Development of School libraries in Ghana. *International Library Review* 15, 217-223.

Alemna, A.A. (1993). The Development of School libraries in Ghana. *Library Management* 14 (4): 31-35.

Alemna, A.A. (1996). The future of school libraries in Ghana In Rosenberg, D. (1998). School library services: Ghana and Tanzania In *Getting books to school pupils in Africa – Education and research paper No. 26.* by Rosenberg, D. London: DFID.

Carroll, F.L. (1981). *Recent Advances in School Librarianship.* Oxford; New York: Pergamon Press.

De Jager, K., Mary Nassimbeni & P. Underwood (2007). Libraries, Literacies and learning: Retrospect and prospect In *Libraries of the future: Progress and development of South African libraries.* World Library and Information Congress 19-23 August 2007. Durban South Africa, 133-147.

Dick, A. (2007). The development of South African Libraries in the 19th and 20th centuries: Cultural and Political Influences In *Libraries of the future: Progress and development of South African libraries.* World Library and Information Congress 19-23 August 2007.Durban South Africa, 13-24.

Fourie, !. (2007). Library and information Service Structure in South Africa. In *Libraries of the future: Progress and development of South African libraries.* World Library and Information Congress 19-23 August 2007. Durban South Africa, 25-42.

Gallal, A.M. (1973). "Libraries in Libya" In *Unesco Bulletin for Libraries.* Vol. XXVII, no. 5, 257-261.

Hart, G. (2006). *School Libraries in South Africa: past, present and the future.* [Online] Available: http://www.sapartners.org/documents/School Libraries Accessed 9/6/2007.

Hart, G. & Sandy Zinn (2007). The Conundrum of School Libraries in South Africa. In *Libraries of the future: Progress and development of South African libraries.* World Library and Information Congress 19-23 August 2007. Durban South Africa, 89-106.

Ilomo, C.S. (1985). "The History and work of Tanzania library Service 1963-1980" In *Aspects of African Librarianship/* edited by Michael Wise. London: Mansel.

International Federation of Library Associations and Institutions (2001) Pan African/Pan Arab Conference on Public and School Libraries Rabat, Morocco 19-22 September, 2001 [Online] Available:http://www.ifla.org/index.htm. Accessed 21/11/07.

International Federation of Library Associations and Institutions (2006). IFLA/UNESCO School Library Manifesto. Retrieved from: IFLA-UNESCO School Library Manifesto. [Online] Available: http://www.ifla.org/VII/sII/ssl.htm#3d. Accessed 10/3/2007.

Kigongo-Bukenya, IMN (1984). *Provision of library services to children and the young adults. Lougborough.* (Unpublished M.Lib. Dissertation).

Le Roux, S. (2002) School library policy in South Africa: Where do we stand? In *South African Journal of Libraries and Information Science,* 68(2): 112-122.

Made, S.M. (2000). *Library and Information Services in Zimbabwe.* Harare: College press Publishers.

McGrath, L. (1978). *Development of School Library services in Lesotho.* Report prepared for the government of Lesotho by UNESCO. Paris: UNESCO.

Mukwato, L.E. (1972). School library service in Zambia: Present and future plans and the work of the Zambia Library Association. In *EALA Bulletin* No. 3 July, 97-112.

Namibia. University of Namibia. Dept of Library and Information Science. *State of school libraries in Namibia.* Namibia:UNAM.

Olden, A. *Information and Library in the developing world: 1 Sub Saharan Africa.* Edited by Wise, M & Olden, A. (1990) London: The Library Association.

Otike, J.N. (1987). The Role of a School Library: The Kenyan Experience. In *International Library Review,* 19, 413-421.

Radebe, Thuli (1996). Current trends in school Library development in Uganda *In School Libraries in Uganda*: Papers and proceedings of a DSE/EASLIS/MOES

Seminar held on the 20th-25th November 1995 in Kampala edited by Abidi Radebe (1996), S.A.H. Bonn and Kampala: DSE.

Rosenberg, D. (2002). "Library and Information Services in Africa" In *The Book Chain in Anglophone Africa: A Survey and Directory*. Edited by Roger Stringer. Oxford: INASP.

Rosenberg, D. (1998). School library services: Ghana and Tanzania In *Getting books to school pupils in Africa – Education and research paper No. 26*. London: DFID.

SIDIBE, A.B (1998). School libraries: Mali In *Getting books to school pupils in Africa – Education and research paper No. 26*. Ed. by Rosenberg, D. London: DFID.

Sturges, R.P. and Neill, R. (1992).*The Quiet Struggle: libraries and information in Africa*. London: Manzell.

Totemeyer, Andree-Jeanne (1996). School library development policy in Namibia. *In School Libraries in Uganda*: Paper of the proceedings of a DSE/EASLIS/MOES Seminar held on the 20th-25th November 1995 in Kampala edited by Abidi S.A.H. Bonn and Kampala: DSE.

Uganda. Ministry of Education (1992). *White Paper on Education Policy Review Commission*. Kampala.

Uganda. Public libraries Board (1976). *Report of the subcommittee set up to consider the relationship between the public libraries and libraries in schools and teachers training colleges*. Kampala: PLB.

UNESCO Expert (1970) *Meeting on national planning of documentation and Library Services in Africa*. Kampala Uganda. 5-7th Dec.

Wanda do Amaral (1998). Book box libraries: Mozambique In Getting *books to school pupils in Africa – Education and research paper No. 26*. edited by Rosenberg, D. London: DFID.

Wikipedia free encyclopedia School library, definition [Online] Available: http://en.wikipedia.org/wiki/School_Library. Accessed on 10/3/2007.

Wynter, J.H. (1979). Problems in Nigerian Library development since 1960. In *International Library Review, 11, 19-44*.

LIS EDUCATION

Omwoyo Bosire Onyancha and Mabel K. Minishi-Majanja

1. INTRODUCTION

The changing patterns of social-economic interaction in society often means that professions need to re-examine their premise and reorient themselves towards current trends and perspectives. Library and Information Science (LIS) education and training in Africa, having the responsibility of providing qualified staff for the library and information professions, is currently challenged to ensure that graduates have competencies that align the profession with current trends and perspectives. Many of the LIS schools in the continent recognize the fact that it is their responsibility to steer the profession towards new directions in response to changing information environment globally and locally. This chapter aims to examine the developments taking place within this specified context so as to provide not only a 'look-out' position for the sector, but also to establish a platform for mapping out future strategy.

Worldwide, LIS education is being transformed in accordance with its changing constituency – the changing LIS work place and visionary projection into the future. Studies conducted in the USA, Canada, the UK and other developed countries variously observe several identical changes that have taken place, the significant ones being change of name, broadening of aims, creation of new programs, review of curricula, new courses, distance education and fostering of closer liaison with industry. A *change of name* may reflect structural, strategic or cosmetic change. Some schools have dropped the word "library" from the name and brought in "communication" and/or "technology", while others have adopted what they consider more up-market names (Mangan 2000:3) without necessarily discarding the important tenets of the profession. In other cases, the change of name signifies a change towards creating professional information entrepreneurs rather than library functionaries. What has been more significant globally is the *broadening of the mission or aims* of the curricula so as to create opportunities for specialities that include high-tech or non-traditional library careers (Marcum 1997). Of equal significance has been the *creation of new programs* to accommodate the broadened aims, include new competencies and/or attract more students. *Revision/review of curricula* to adjust curricula to meet the demands of students, employment market and higher education sector is a challenge that has been necessitated not only by the evolutionary but also by the transformational changes in the profession. Stoker (2000) observes that the growth of information and communication technologies (ICTs) will continue to be the main reason behind the core curriculum's expanding to accommodate new significant areas such as systems analysis and design, and organizationorganizational theory. The same applies to the *creation/addition of new subjects/courses/modules*. It is important to note that as ICTs develop, some courses initially developed as separate ICT courses, have later been integrated in older core areas. The modern pressures of time and money, coupled with an increasing requirement for changing, job-specific skills, have resulted in the fading of the need to attend regular classes and given rise to the development of *web-based instruction and distance education* (Curry 2000). Stoker (2000) observes that alternative modes of delivery such as part-time, distance learning have arisen in the UK to alleviate the problem of cost. Stoker (2000) further states that full-time undergraduate programs in UK are losing market to distance education while there is potential for increasing postgraduate programs. LIS schools forge *closer liaison with industry* such as software companies, hardware manufacturers, telecommunications and broadcasting corporations (Curry 2000) in order to obtain free or subsidized hardware and software, while industry finds an opportunity for development or marketing of products. In response to the changes within the LIS profession as discussed above, many LIS schools in the developing world recognize the need to make a variety of alterations (Manmart 1997; Ocholla 2003). The common focus is the aim to produce professionals who can function effectively in the ICT-driven information environment and society transforming libraries into the 21st Century.

Mambo (2000) observes that not only has the demand for LIS professionals in Africa increased but so also has the number of education and training opportunities on the continent. This concurs with Ocholla's (2000) observation that the development of LIS education correlates with the growth of libraries. It is therefore imperative that the types and quality of LIS education graduates should reflect or be a reflection of the types of services provided in the libraries. Undoubtedly, trends in the development of ICTs in the world today are centrally significant to the trends in information services and hence LIS education and training. The term "LIS school" is used here to refer to an independent academic unit within (or without) a university, college, technikon/polytechnic or other tertiary institution that provides professional and/or paraprofessional programs in the broader field of information science. The authors are cognizant of the fact that institutions may name such a unit according to their specific, objectives, structure, job market influence, country framework and/or other preferences. According to Minishi-Majanja (2004:122), such units in Africa are designated as a school, institute, faculty, department or section and can also contain a combination of discipline-related nomenclature such as information, library, knowledge, science, studies or technology, etc.

2. DEVELOPMENT OF LIS SCHOOLS

In spite of the need for staff in libraries, archives and other information services, the development of education and training in Africa is a recent occurrence. The need for trained staff to work in libraries within the geographical continent of Africa can be said to have existed for as long as collections of information sources were first established. However, scholars who have researched and written about this topic have disregarded the ancient period o the Alexandrian Library and focused only from the 20th century period. This chapter does not aim to dispute their reasons for this. Neither does it aim to indulge in a philosophically historical discussion. We only point this out to provide a space for speculation or study. Suffice it that any attempt to provide a correct picture of current trends and perspectives, requires that we look back, albeit briefly, so as to put the present in perspective. Sometimes, when we look back on a clear day, the view extends further than previously surmised. But we would be remiss if we also failed to point out that published literature may not be available for us to provide an accurate picture of any phenomenon in Africa because of the long prevalence of the oral culture.

The establishment of 'modern' formal education for the library and information professionals in Africa can be traced back to 1938, when the first training of librarians began at the University of Pretoria (Raju (2003:74) in South Africa. University of Cape Town was the second in 1939, after which the next activity on record is in Ghana in 1944 at the Achimota Teachers' Training College (Gupta and Gupta 1997). The rest of sub-Saharan Africa started to establish LIS schools in the 1960s, coincidentally, but not surprisingly with liberation from colonial rule. However, the growth was slow in the 1960s and 1970s, with five and two schools being established in the sixties and seventies, respectively. A more significant increase in the number of new LIS schools was in the 1980s, when at least nine LIS schools were established, and in the 1990s when at least another eight new LIS schools were established. Ocholla (2000) observes that the development of LIS education, alongside of that of libraries in Africa, has tremendously depended on foreign governments, particularly Britain, France and USA. This is so, not only because of the colonial legacy in the case of Britain and France, but also due to the inadequate local economic resources. It is difficult to establish the exact number of LIS schools within sub-Saharan Africa at the moment. While it is estimated that there are approximately over 55 "LIS schools", most of which are located in the Anglophone countries, it is evident that there some new "schools' that have recently been established of which little is known. The demand for higher education in many countries of Sub-Saharan Africa has witnessed the emergence of many new private universities, some of which offer LIS education. Ikoja-Odongo (2006), for instance, mentions that apart from the longstanding LIS School at Makerere University, there are now three private universities that offer LIS education in Uganda. In Tanzania, there is a new player, i.e. Tumaini University College, in addition to the University of Dar es Salaam and Bagamoyo. In Zimbabwe, three polytechnics and one university offer LIS education (Hikwa 2006). In contrast, South African LIS schools have decreased in number because of the recent merging of HEIs and the rationalization of programs. Further, it is important to note that not all countries have established formal LIS education programs and hence depend on sending their people to other countries within the continent or overseas for LIS education.

3. NOMENCLATURE DEVELOPMENTS

Nomenclature of schools and programs is currently influenced by world trends as well as job market dictates. Apart from the qualification designation (e.g. BA, BS, Diploma, MPhil, MA, etc.) the general historical progression of the qualifying nomenclature in English can be summarized as follows:

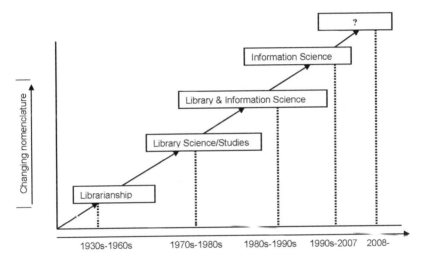

Fig 1: Change of nomenclature for LIS schools

Thus, many LIS schools in sub-Saharan Africa have had to change their name for different reasons. Initially in the 1970s and early 1980s, the names changed from "Librarianship" to "Library Science/Studies" (LS) so as to assert the fact that the discipline was scientific and professional as befitted university level disciplines. But the more significant change for the discipline happened in the 1980s and 1990s whereby LIS schools incorporated "information" science into their programs and thus changing names from "Library Science" to "Library and Information Science". This was the case at UNISA (1983), University of Zululand (1988), University of Natal (1989), Omdurman University (1995) and University of Cape

Town (1996). Bayero University made this change in 2002, and University of Botswana, University of Pretoria and Makerere University made similar changes although they did not indicate when this was done.

In most cases this change was made in order to accommodate the wider scope that had characterised LIS activities with the introduction of computers and other information technologies into the profession. Moahi (2006) also observes that the "traditional librarianship market" cannot absorb all graduates and hence many LIS schools have had to shift their education and focus to embrace a wider job market by offering programs that have broader scope. Thus, some LIS schools have added other terms to the LIS denotation so as to reflect the presence of other disciplines such as Communications and Information Technology. For instance at the University of Sierra Leone, the Institute of Library Studies has changed its name to the Institute of Library, Information and Communication Studies (INSLICS) and offers programs in Communication Studies. Currently, there is also much influence to include terms such as information systems, information technology, knowledge management (e.g. University of Johannesburg's Department of Information and Knowledge Management), etc. Apart from instructive naming, the positioning of LIS departments within the institutional "organograms" may have an effect on the nomenclature chosen because departments in universities are usually administered under a Faculty, School or Institute. This then requires that the name and discipline of the department be one that falls within the broader disciplinary area of the faculty/school/institute. Thus departments often adopt names that allow flexibility, such as "information science" which can fall under technology, applied sciences and/or engineering sciences, as is the case at the University of Pretoria in South Africa. While many LIS schools are invariably located in the Arts or Humanities Faculties, it is interesting to note that in Nigeria, some LIS schools are located in Education Faculties.

4. RANGE OF PROGRAMS AND CURRICULA

In general, LIS schools in sub-Saharan Africa offer three levels of undergraduate programs and four levels of postgraduate programs (Minishi-Majanja & Ocholla, 2004). Undergraduate qualifications include certificates, diplomas and bachelors degree, while postgraduate levels range from postgraduate diplomas to doctoral degrees. It is observable that the names and nature of programs are not uniform. Rosenberg (2000) observes that the lack of consistency in names of courses vis-à-vis standards of content and length is a historical accident that is often perpetuated by national or institutional structures and practices. Achieving some uniformity can be useful for equivalence and recognition of qualifications across institutions and across countries. Weech and Tammaro (2007) observe that "more librarians are seeking employment and further education outside their own countries, yet there are no clear guidelines for determining the equivalency of degrees and certificates. A learning outcomes / competencies approach could help with the communication between the stakeholders involved in lifelong learning of library and information professionals and those involved with the academic programs of education and training of library and information professionals." Following a survey, the IFLA Education and Training Section suggested a focus on three areas i.e. program orientation, educational process orientation and learning outcomes orientation (Tammaro 2005). Program orientation, according to the *Guidelines for professional L/IS educational programees-2000* (IFLA 2000), should provide both a broad general education as well as core LIS elements. Most of the university-based qualifications in sub-Saharan Africa have tried to incorporate both aspects. The educational process is much more difficult to implement uniformly because of varying levels of resources such as lecturers, ICT, library materials, etc.

While research and discussion on "equivalence and reciprocal recognition of academic qualifications" is still continuing at IFLA's Education and Training Section, it is fair to state that some of African countries are trying to find common ground within their borders. In South Africa for instance, the newly enacted Higher Education Qualification Framework (HEQF) addresses the issues of countrywide equivalence. However, the HEQF covers all tertiary institutions and is not prescriptive of any specific discipline. Thus LIS educators will still have the challenge of ensuring that their offerings and content is comparable without necessarily duplicating each other's programs. In Kenya, the situation is partially resolved by the involvement of the national curriculum body, the Kenya Institute of Education (KIE), which sets the curricula for all non-university programs and the Kenya National examinations Council (KNEC), which examines and certifies the qualifications. Thus there is a set of curricular for LIS ranging from the Craft (certificate) level to the Higher National Diploma level. However, the most notable LIS education is conducted in Universities, who do not use KIE curricula or KNEC examinations. Ikoja-Odongo (2006) observes that in Uganda, the new LIS schools inadvertently copy what Makerere is doing – however, not for uniformity's sake but for lack of expertise in curriculum design.

4.1 Curriculum development and core competencies

Many LIS schools are revamping and rationalising their offerings regularly so as to keep up with students' and market demands. Universities are demanding value for money as governments reduce subsidies to these institutions. However, it is true that in spite of curricula reviews (Ocholla 2000) many of the curricula still carry heavy leaning or patterns of LIS curricula from developed countries (Aina 1999) because these are considered "best" examples as they have been offered over long periods and, in a way, stood the test of time. Aina further highlights the dearth of local publications for use by students, the lack of which raises the issue of supporting literature that originates from other continents and hence contains a lot of content that African LIS students cannot easily relate to. There is always a general outcry over the neglect of local context and indigenous knowledge and practices in curricular. Part of the problem is the fact that most of the current LIS educators who are responsible for developing curricula are themselves either alumni of the foreign curricula and find it hard to come up with 'original' African curricula, or they lack expertise in curriculum development. However, it is important to remember that even the experienced LIS educators are careful not to provide too parochial an education that would render graduates restricted and unable to function outside their localities. This is an important consideration in the face of limited job markets on the one hand and the effect of globalization on the other. Thus, sub-Saharan LIS schools often aim to produce graduates whose core competencies including the ability to adapt to only different countries but also to the ever-changing job market needs. It is no wonder that the "core of LIS education and training is expressed in very generic terminology that embraces the broader information profession" (Raju 2003:232).

LIS education programs in sub-Saharan Africa provide basic knowledge that can be generally applied in an information service, including managing information collections, organization and retrieval of information, understanding information users and information needs, understanding information resources/products and providing service. Raju (2003) observes that the core of LIS education is elusive because of the constant/continuous evolution of the profession. There is a continued growth of a diversity of fields that are considered as core subjects, which when pitched against the need for market-ready graduates, make the task of preparing a curriculum difficult. The 10 *"core elements"* listed by IFLA (2000:2) are only the tip of the iceberg, not only because they are general enough not to be prescriptive, but also because by the same token, they are subject to interpretation (e.g. in areas of emphasis), often a subject to the knowledge and expertise of the curriculum designers. Raju's survey in South Africa produced a list of 25 possible subjects for the South African market alone (Raju 2003:235), a list that would get longer if the rest of the countries can be surveyed. In Africa, this situation is further exacerbated by the diversity of the continent in terms of the information environments, economies of scale, social development levels, ICT infrastructure and even literacy levels, which often make many of the LIS graduates seem unprepared for the workplace. Stoker (2000) warns of the adverse effect of an enlarging core i.e. the marginalization or elimination of some of the traditional mainstream/specialist courses, such as music librarianship, rare book librarianship and children's librarianship. But he observes that there is no clear-cut solution to the issue and recommends that educators respond to the employment market by, for instance, offering some of these specialisations as electives accordingly.

4.2   ICT curricula

Sub-Saharan Africa LIS schools offer a wide variety of ICT modules within their curricula. However, the curricula are not harmonized – either across the region or even within individual countries. Thus within one country, it is not unusual to find great diversity of offerings among the LIS schools, each attempting to offer what they believe to be key competencies for their graduates. But also underlying this diversity is the national and institutional ICT capacities (Ngulube 2006) because at national levels, some countries have made greater strides than others. For instance, the South African government recognises that ICT human resource capacity building is the key to the accomplishment of the ideals of the information age. To ensure that the country is well positioned for this society, not only is the infrastructure continually under scrutiny, but also higher education is expected to increase enrolments in the ICT fields of study (Ministry of Education, 2001). Another example is Uganda's liberalised telecommunications policy of 1996, which paved the way for private sector investment into, and hence greater and faster ICT penetration (Ikoja-Odongo 2006). The significance of governmental intervention is exhibited in the growth of the ICT infrastructure, which then provides a platform for institutions and LIS departments to increase their ICT diffusion. But this is not true of all African countries. Poor economies, political instability, large populations, bad leadership/governance and a myriad of other problems have not made it possible for many African countries to adequately address the subject of ICT infrastructure and education.

According to Minishi-Majanja and Ocholla (2004), the modules that generally top the list are of fundamental relevance to LIS practice. These include Operating Systems, Applications software, Hardware & Software selection, LANs and Intranets, Internet Facilities and Internet Tools. However, as mentioned before, what is taught in the above modules does not always translate into comparable knowledge and competencies. There is no uniform approach to what is taught, let alone how it is taught (Ngulube 2006). Additionally, even though sub-Saharan Africa LIS schools collectively offer what seems to be an adequately wide variety of ICT modules, research on ICT curricula reveals a preponderance of difficulties in the absence of African benchmarks and models (Ngulube 2006). Only few LIS schools offer what may be deemed as the full range of ICT competencies. In some of the individual institutions, the range of modules offered cannot even be deemed to be enough. For instance, Manda (2006:5) observes that the integration of ICT into paraprofessional training in Tanzania is limited in both modules and course content. He further observes that "as an independent subject, ICT is offered only as an optional course" in the MA Information studies curriculum at the University of Dar-es- Salaam (Manda 2006:5). However, and to emphasize the disparities among universities even within one country, Manda further observes that the BA-LIS programme at Tumaini University in Tanzania offers more ICT modules and content than the University of Dar-es-Salaam's MA programme, the basic deciding factor being resources (i.e. ICT and human).

Most ICT modules are offered as core and/or required within the LIS programs. In many cases, ICT content is said to be "integrated" in other modules that are core/required. Table 1 (*reproduced from Minishi-Majanja & Ocholla 2004:194*) shows the percentage of LIS schools, under each category, offering each module.

Table 1: Reflective of the relative importance of ICT Modules (2003 data) (N=29)

Module	% Core	% Elective	% Integrated	% Not Offered
Online Database Searching	55	0	35	10
Internet Facilities	55	3	28	14
Mgt of Library Automation	55	0	35	10
Gen. Applications Software	52	7	28	14
Library Software	52	0	38	10
Information Systems	48	10	28	14
Electronic Publishing	48	10	24	17
Internet Tools	48	0	24	28
Hard/Soft-ware Selection	45	10	35	10
Internet Hardware/Software	45	7	35	14
Hypertext	45	0	17	38
Operating Systems	41	7	35	17
Local Area Networks	41	0	41	17
Multi-/Hyper-Media	38	3	38	21
Intranets	38	0	38	24
Automatic Indexing/ Abstracting	35	7	38	21
Electronic Current Awareness	35	0	41	31
Programming	31	14	13	41
Electronic Document Delivery	31	0	38	31
Intelligent Gateways	31	0	24	45
Telecommunications	31	7	28	35
Data Communication	31	7	31	41
Computer Architecture	24	3	28	45
Text Digitization	24	3	21	52
Human-Computer Interaction	24	0	35	41
Artificial Intelligence	17	14	14	55
Distributed Systems	17	3	10	69
Broadcast Technologies	3	7	24	66
Software Engineering	3	10	17	69

4.3 Continuing education

The need for continuing LIS education in sub-Saharan Africa need no overemphasis considering that no amount of core is enough to last five years, leave alone a lifetime, in a fast-changing hi-tech world. Ocholla (2003) and Stoker (2000) rightly observe that no one skill will equip an individual at all stages of their career because technical skills quickly become outdated. Stoker (2000) further observes that professional education can no longer be delivered in one slice because of its diversity, and that knowledge and skills acquired in full time education now have limited span of relevance and hence need to be continuously updated. Thus there is obvious need for programs that specifically focus on continuing education. However, in planning continuous education programs, educators need to remember that the content of continuous education may not need to add up to complete programs of study because, in some cases, it may just be a module that is relevant to a new development. Additionally, employers and employees are no longer finding it affordable to allow for full time study leave.

Sadly, though, continuing professional education (CPE) for LIS workers in Sub-Saharan Africa is one of the LIS programs, which is underdeveloped in the region. Previous studies (e.g. Ocholla, 2000; Ocholla & Bothma, 2007) reveal that CPE programs in Africa are being offered through local professional bodies (e.g. Continuing Education and Professional Development [CEPD], the Library and Information Association of South Africa [LIASA], Namibian Workers Association, etc.) in collaboration with various LIS schools. Examples of the LIS schools that offer CPE include those that are affiliated with the following universities: University of Cape Town, University of KwaZulu Natal, University of Botswana, University of Johannesburg, Moi University (Kenya), Makerere University and the University of Namibia (Namibia) (Ocholla, 2000). It is worth noting, however, that this information is not current and therefore less is known about the status of CPE in LIS schools in Africa. Nevertheless, some LIS schools (e.g. the Department of Information Studies, University of Limpopo, South Africa) have joined the list of those that provide CPE. The University of Limpopo's department of information studies offers programs related to librarianship. Whereas most LIS trainers and educators concur that CPE is a very important component of LIS education and training, as a way of building capacity and re-energizing LIS workers especially in the ever-changing information and knowledge environment, they nevertheless note that the programme's implementation is challenging. The most challenging factor that was voiced by most Heads of Departments whose opinion was sought through emails is the staff capacity, which is said to be insufficient. The limited number of LIS staff members are said to be overloaded and therefore cannot support new programs such as CPE.

5. CRITICAL RESOURCES

Most studies on LIS education and training tend to focus on curricula and content, often neglecting the question of resources. At the recently concluded IFLA conference in Durban-South Africa (August 2007), a heated debate started regarding the relative importance (if possible, the ranking) of curriculum versus academic staff versus students as factors that influence the quality of LIS education. The debate came to specific conclusion but it was clear that each of the three components has significance towards the successful achievement of producing good quality LIS graduates. What did not feature strongly in the discussion was the role of resources (e.g. the library and ICTs), perhaps not because these are of lesser importance, but more because the three were sufficient variables to contend with. Thus, below we briefly discuss issues about the academic staff and ICT resources, two of the most influential resources in the quality of LIS education in sub-Saharan Africa.

5.1 Academic Staff

According to the findings of Minishi-Majanja (2004), the staff-student ratio in sub-Saharan LIS schools is 1:38. Most academic staff are qualified having satisfied stringent institutional standards for the appointment of academic staff. Nevertheless, many LIS schools cannot fill all their positions because of scarcity of qualified candidates vis-à-vis the uncompetitive salaries within the academic sector. Some LIS schools make use of temporary/contract or part-time staff, mainly consisting of practitioners who wish to earn extra money. Generally most LIS departments are small ranging from as few as three academics to the largest departments having about twenty-four, with an arithmetic mode of six academic staff (Minishi-Majanja 2004:148). The negative implication of these small departments is that often they are unable to earn enough personnel points for many senior positions such as professors or research fellows. Thus LIS professors who wish to ascend higher in their career have often had to leave the LIS department and join the university administration or leave the university altogether to research and other organizationorganizations.

5.2 ICT resources

At the institutional level, each university or college is able to muster substantial technological diffusion depending on its history, management (vision, policies, etc.), financial well-being (i.e. funding sources or innovativeness, etc.), and a host of other characteristics. In South Africa, the "historically black universities are much more badly resourced" while the "historically advantaged are well resourced and appear to do be doing better" in terms of ICT education and training (Ngulube 2006:4). In many African universities, the respective government is the main source of funding, with the result that many universities are poorly funded (Rosenberg, 2000) further resulting in inadequacies of resources. Moreover, long-term planning in such universities is often problematic since government funds are appropriated annually, without express assurance. A host of private universities have recently emerged in some countries such as Uganda (Ikoja-Odongo 2006) and Kenya, where the main source of university funding is the students' fees. While the fees are generally higher than those paid within the government-funded universities, the institutions are careful not to charge such high fees as to be prohibitive to the prospective students. Coupled with the fact that such universities aim to maximize profit, they tend not to invest heavily in expensive programs, infrastructure or equipment. The success of LIS schools in such universities depends on the 'viability' of LIS programs – often defined in terms of a greater number of students requiring minimum investment expenditure. This definitely compromises the level of ICT resources and education to be provided.

ICTs are a fund-intensive innovation, requiring not only careful budgeting, but also equally important, sustained funding. With the cost of computers falling dramatically, government interventions in lowering or abolishing levies on ICTs, and with systems becoming much easier to use and maintain, it is hoped that some of the prohibitive cost and infrastructural problems are being. Sub-Saharan LIS schools generally lack guiding policies for the development and use of ICTs. Where policies exist, usually within the parent institution, the policies are not comprehensive enough to take into consideration the needs of individual departments. Some LIS schools counter this state of affairs by formulating departmental policies to guide the procurement and use of ICT resources based on curricula needs. Such policies succeed if the LIS School has sufficient financial resources and autonomy, but in most cases, departmental ICT policies are difficult to effectively implement especially if there is institutional bureaucracy of approval, central financial management and centralized procurement and assets maintenance. Majority of LIS schools prefer to work within institutionally centralized ICT services that are properly funded and managed. Centralized ICT services have the advantage of institution-wide development and use, but it only works satisfactorily for the LIS department where the policy explicitly incorporates the goals and needs of all sectors, including those of the LIS School. In institutions where the political economy is slanted, coupled with the absence of such a policy, a LIS school may suffer from neglect and hence be unable to develop and use ICTs. In such a case, the LIS school may consider a decentralized system, as long as there is adequate autonomy, authority and financial innovativeness.

Hardware Availability

Although the number of computers has increased rapidly in some sub-Saharan countries, the process of computerization has not been as successful as it should be in the majority of these countries. This situation is reflected in the number of computers or the computer-student ratios in universities or LIS schools. The situation can be exacerbated when the inadequate computing facilities are centralized forcing students to scramble for the few facilities. Inevitably, LIS students may not get enough practice. Departmental LIS laboratories in a way ensure that LIS students have equal and relevant access to computers and it is noteworthy that 62% of LIS schools in sub-Saharan Africa have this set-up (Minishi-Majanja 2004).

Apart from computers, other components of hardware such as communications hardware, which are equally important, are usually not within the control of LIS schools. For training in optimal information handling, especially online services, the use of latest communication technologies such as the satellite range is important. Negotiating for network licenses with Internet Service Providers (ISPs) for telecommunication tariffs, and the procurement and maintenance of requisite hardware are perhaps best handled centrally in an institution. Minishi-Majanja (2004:208) observes that only 3% of LIS schools in sub-Saharan Africa use VSAT satellite communication system and 14% use fibre-optic careers. The Unshielded Twisted Pair (UTP), which is more widely (35%) used requires repeaters, every 1-2 miles, which is a difficult undertaking for remotely located institutions. Although most LIS schools in sub-Saharan Africa are in universities, which are in major cities, there are a growing number of geographically challenged institutions that would better utilize satellite communications. But with satellite communications, the challenge is on costs rather than logistics.

Software

The range of software used in LIS schools is a reflection of the general software market, which is teeming with variety and enhancement. In terms of operating systems, the Microsoft range of products rule the continent, with many institutions having one version or other of the MS Windows ranging from Windows 3.1 to Windows 2000. It is surprising that MS DOS is even still in the picture (Minish-Majanja 2004:209). Since additionally, the popular networking system is Novell, there is good basis for inter-networking among LIS schools as none would have to radically reconfigure their systems in case of inter-country or inter-institutional online collaboration. The variety of applications software is even wider and although the Microsoft applications are also prevalent, there are so many other software packages largely because most institutions take what they can get either as donations or with the hardware. The major obstacles in software procurement are the cost of software, which mounts due to the need for continuous updating/upgrading and/or license fees for software and networking.

Internet Access

Although Internet access is now widely available, efficiency is poor. LIS schools experience downtime, several times a week, the majority of downtime lasting for an hour or longer, but in some cases for more than five hours each time (which can be more than once a day). Telecommunication services are the root cause of these downtimes in terms of low bandwidth, technical faults, or other network configuration problems. Intra-African communications still leave much to be desired.

6. LIS RESEARCH IN SUB-SAHARAN AFRICA

This section traces the developments of LIS education and training by examining the subject content of LIS research conducted in Sub-Saharan Africa through a content analysis approach. According to Berelson in Palmquist (n.d.), content analysis is a "research technique for the objective, systematic, and quantitative description of manifest content of communications". The technique is used to determine the presence of certain words, concepts, themes, phrases, characters, or sentences within texts or sets of texts and to quantify this presence in an objective manner. Content analysis can be used to:

- Reveal international differences in communication content
- Detect the existence of propaganda
- Identify the intentions, focus or communication trends of an individual, group or institution
- Describe attitudinal and behavioral responses to communications
- Determine psychological or emotional state of persons or groups

A subject content analysis primarily focuses on the subject/topic terms used to index documents. Bierbaum & Brooks (1995) observe that through a subject content analysis one may be able to "track the introduction of new terms that reflect innovations and discoveries in [a] knowledge base" (Bierbaum & Brooks, 1995:533). The authors also argue that the 'rising and falling frequency" of the occurrence of the subject headings may assist when drawing inferences concerning the 'changing level of interest in a particular aspect' of a discipline. Consequently, appropriate decisions are made in respect to the patterns of research. A subject content analysis of a particular discipline would mirror not only the construction of a field by specific institutions, but also what happens to subject access as the knowledge base and environment of a discipline grow and change (Macias-Chapula, Sotolongo-Aguilar, Magde & Solorio-Lagunas (1999:565). Bierbaum & Brooks (1995), too, acknowledge that in order for one to make maximum usage of a database or have comprehensive access to the literature specific to a particular subject domain, he/she needs to be knowledgeable about the new terms and phrases used to index the said literature. It is also widely acknowledged that the growth of knowledge in a subject domain may be reflected in new and emerging research and/or study areas in that subject domain (Tague, Beheshti & Rees-Potter, 1981). Finally, knowledge of emerging areas of research may influence curriculum development in a given discipline.

This section is largely informed by data that was obtained from the online version of the Library, Information Science and Technology Abstracts (LISTA) database. Relevant research articles published between 1971 and 2007 were extracted from the database using country names as keywords. The search was conducted within the "Authors' Address" field using 'AF' field tag, where AF stands for Author Affiliation.

6.1 Growth in the number of subjects and articles, 1971-2007

The pattern of growth in the number of articles and subjects (see Table 2) partially reflects the development of LIS in Sub-Saharan Africa. It is worth noting that the growth of the number of research articles and subjects cannot be used as the only indicators of a discipline's growth. Other indicators may include the number of students graduating at any/or all levels of LIS education (i.e. National Certificate/Diploma and/or Undergraduate and Post-Graduate degrees) thereby influencing the number of LIS workers in a country. Table 1 show that the number of articles and subjects has continued to grow over time. From just ten subjects that were used to index 34 articles in 1971-1980, the number has exponentially grown to stand at 1300 subjects that were used to index a total of 723 articles that were published between 2001 and 2007. Similarly, the average number of subjects per article grew from just 0.29 to 5.40 within the same period of time, accounting for 1762% increase. Bierbaum & Brooks (1995) explains that such a pattern of growth may be associated with complexity of a subject being investigated, thus requiring more indexing terms to describe issues raised in a research article. Another factor that may have caused the type of growth pattern witnessed in Table 2 is the interdisciplinary or multi-disciplinary nature of LIS papers, which borrow various ideas, methodologies or theories from other disciplines and thereby necessitate the use of several indexing terms to describe them.

Table 2: Growth in the number of research areas and articles

	1971–1980	1981–1990	1991–2000	2001–2007
No of unique subjects	10	111	140	1300
Increase	–	101	29	1157
Percentage increase	–	1010	26.13	826.43
Cumulative increase	10	121	261	1558
Total no. of subjects [x]	10	219	406	3903
No. of articles [y]	34	106	217	723
Increase		72	111	506
Percentage increase		211.76	104.72	233.18
Cumulative increase	34	140	357	1080
Average no. of subjects/article [x/y]	0.29	2.07	1.87	5.40

6.2 Subject coverage of LIS articles, 1971–1980

Table 3 provides a total of 10 subject terms that were used to index LIS articles published between 1971 and 1980. It was noted that majority of the articles (i.e. 32 out of 34) did not contain subject terms within their 'subject' fields, which implies that only 2 articles provided subject terms. There was equal representation among the 10 subjects, each appearing in one article, which accounted for 2.94% of the total number of articles published in 1971–1980. Given that the number of subjects was very small during this period it would be premature for us to draw conclusions about the most used terms to index LIS articles since there was none. Nevertheless, it can be assumed that the subjects provided in Table 3 represent the subject areas of LIS research between 1971 and 1980. It is also worth mentioning that LIS education and training during this period was at the initial stages of development, having been introduced in the continent in the late 1930s (Raju, 2003).

Table 3: Research areas: 1971–1980 (*N = 34*)

No.	Subject	Articles	%
1	Academic Libraries	1	2.94
2	Documentation	1	2.94
3	Electronic Information Resource Searching	1	2.94
4	Indexing	1	2.94
5	Information Retrieval	1	2.94
6	Information Services	1	2.94
7	Libraries	1	2.94
8	Library Buildings	1	2.94
9	Research, Industrial	1	2.94
10	Technological Innovations	1	2.94

6.3 Subject coverage of LIS articles, 1981–1990

A clear indication of the most researched areas of LIS emerged between 1981 and 1990 as shown in Table 4, which presents the top 30 most commonly used terms. Leading is *information services,* which was used to describe a total of 17 (16.04%) articles followed by *academic libraries* (12, 11.32%), *libraries* (10, 9.43%), *information science* (7, 6.60%), and *librarians* (7,6.60%). Some of the terms that perhaps indicate the emerging areas of research in LIS in the 1980s and are worth mentioning include *information technology, libraries – automation, document delivery,* and *information retrieval.* These terms point to the use of the technology in enhancing information provision in LIS workplaces. This period, therefore, heralded a shift from the traditional methods of service provision in libraries (e.g. the use of card catalogues, manual check-outs and check-ins, etc) to the modern technologically driven service provision (e.g. use of Online Public Access Catalogues

[OPACs], automated check –ins and –outs, automatic generation of circulation reports, etc.).

It was also observed that *libraries* (i.e. the building, stock, staff, and services) were the most researched on areas of LIS as reflected in such terms as *academic libraries, libraries, librarians, library science, collection development (libraries), interlibrary loans, periodicals, libraries – automation, document delivery, documentation, books, information retrieval* and *occupations*. This pattern of LIS research may also be illustrative of the nature of training that was offered by LIS schools in Sub-Saharan Africa in the 1980s and/or before then. To a large extent, LIS education and training targeted library workers. This finding is in agreement with previous studies which state that the establishment of LIS schools in Sub-Saharan Africa prior to 1980 was for purposes of training library workers (see Aina, 1991, 1999; Gupta & Gupta, 1997; etc). One of the terms that was not previously used and that was introduced in 1981-1990 is *Information Science*. The term is currently widely used to refer to the science primarily concerned with the collection, classification, manipulation, storage, retrieval and dissemination of information. In addition, most LIS schools in Sub-Saharan Africa have adopted this term and made it the name of the schools as aforementioned under LIS nomenclature. A further notable observation is that at least one term that is not LIS-specific (i.e. agriculture) was noted during this study period.

Table 4: Research areas: 1981–1990 ($N = 106$)

No.	Rank	Subjects	Articles	%	No.	Rank	Subject	Articles	%
1	1	Information Services	17	16.04	16	8	Documentation	3	2.83
2	2	Academic Libraries	12	11.32	17	8	Management	3	2.83
3	3	Libraries	10	9.43	18	8	Mensuration	3	2.83
4	4	Information Science	7	6.60	19	8	Decision Making	3	2.83
5	4	Librarians	7	6.60	20	8	Marketing	3	2.83
6	5	Information Technology	6	5.66	21	8	Books	3	2.83
7	6	Library Science	5	4.72	22	8	Archives	3	2.83
8	6	Collection Development (Libraries)	5	4.72	23	9	Scientific Literature	2	1.89
9	7	Evaluation	4	3.77	24	9	Information Dissemination	2	1.89
10	7	Education	4	3.77	25	9	Associations, Institutions, Etc	2	1.89
11	7	Interlibrary Loans	4	3.77	26	9	Information Retrieval	2	1.89

No.	Rank	Subjects	Articles	%	No.	Rank	Subject	Articles	%
12	7	Political Science	4	3.77	27	9	Agriculture	2	1.89
13	7	Periodicals	4	3.77	28	9	Occupations	2	1.89
14	7	Libraries – Automation	4	3.77	29	9	Public Libraries	2	1.89
15	8	Document Delivery	3	2.83	30	9	Communication	2	1.89

6.4 Subject coverage of LIS articles, 1991–2000

The 1991–2000 year period ushered in an era in which several terms were introduced into the subject index, probably in line with the social and technological changes that greatly influenced LIS research during the said period. These new entrants include *library education, databases, library users, information literacy, information society, technology – information services, distance education, library orientation,* and *technology transfer.* The clamor for an information literate society in the 1990s perhaps compelled LIS researchers to conduct studies related to *information literacy* and *information society.* This may also explain the appearance in 1990-2000 of *library education* and *library orientation,* two of the methods through which *information literacy* can be attained.

Information technology-related terms (e.g. databases, information retrieval, information technology, libraries – automation, technology – information services, and technology transfer) together with the terms associated with the term library or libraries (e.g. academic libraries, library education, library science, library users, public libraries, libraries – automation, classification, librarians, collection development, library orientation and books) also dominated the period 1991-2000. It was also noted that the term archives, which was ranked 8th in the previous year period remained among the top ranked terms in 1991-2000. It should be borne in mind that Archives (sometimes classified together with records management) is one of the main courses that constitute LIS education. Other broad areas of LIS education and training include library studies (sometimes referred to as librarianship or library science), information science/studies, publishing and book trading, and information technology. An analysis of the ranking of terms in the two year-periods (i.e. 1981–1990 and 1991–2000) reveals that there have been shifts. For instance, information science moved from position 4 in the previous year period to become the top ranked term in indexing LIS articles in 1991-2000. Similarly, library science, information dissemination, and information retrieval improved on their rankings. Subject terms such as academic libraries, information services, libraries, information technology, librarians, collection development (libraries), archives, interlibrary loans and books were ranked poorer in 1991-2000. Some terms maintained the same ranking in both time periods. These include libraries – automation, evaluation, and education.

Table 5: Research areas: 1991–2000 (*N = 217*)

No.	Rank	Subjects	Articles	%	No.	Rank	Subject	Articles	%
1	1	Information Science	26	11.98	16	7	Information Society	7	3.23
2	2	Information Services	24	11.06	17	7	Education	7	3.23
3	3	Academic Libraries	20	9.22	18	8	Classification	6	2.76
4	4	Library Education	10	4.61	19	8	Librarians	6	2.76
5	5	Library Science	9	4.15	20	8	Technology – Information Services	6	2.76
6	5	Databases	9	4.15	21	9	Agriculture	5	2.30
7	5	Libraries	9	4.15	22	9	Collection Development (Libraries)	5	2.30
8	6	Information Dissemination	8	3.69	23	9	Archives	5	2.30
9	6	Library Users	8	3.69	24	10	Distance Education	4	1.84
10	6	Information Retrieval	8	3.69	25	10	Universities & Colleges	4	1.84
11	6	Information Technology	8	3.69	26	10	Library Orientation	4	1.84
12	6	Public Libraries	8	3.69	27	10	Interlibrary Loans	4	1.84
13	7	Libraries – Automation	7	3.23	28	10	Management	4	1.84
14	7	Evaluation	7	3.23	29	10	Technology Transfer	4	1.84
15	7	Information Literacy	7	3.23	30	10	Books	4	1.84

6.5 Subject coverage of LIS articles, 2001–2007

The following observations (based on findings in Table 6) were made concerning the subject content of LIS articles that were published between 2001 and 2007:

- Several subjects emerged to rank among the top 30 during this year period. They include: information resources, information resources management, knowledge management, Internet, communication & technology, publishers and publishing, information & communication technologies, research, Web sites, surveys, business enterprises, and information storage & retrieval systems.

- Again, as was the case in 1991-2000, information technology-related terms (e.g. Internet, communication & technology, information & communication technologies, library – automation, technology, Web sites, and information storage & retrieval systems) featured prominently. Of particular interest to us, in this category of terms, are the Internet, information communication & technologies, and Web sites. The study of the Internet and Web technology is increasingly becoming common in LIS schools in Sub-Saharan Africa. These studies revolve around the use of the Internet as an information resource, the use of the Web by libraries and other information centers for the provision of their services, webometric studies (e.g. link analysis, Web content analysis, etc), search engines, and email services, etc. Web design and networking are some of the common subjects that are taught in undergraduate programs in LIS schools, a situation that may explain the emergence of the aforementioned three subjects as research areas. Information & communication technologies (commonly abbreviated as ICTs), too, has gained recognition as one of the researchable areas in LIS in Sub-Saharan Africa. Studies on ICTs include the use of the technologies in information gathering, processing, storage and retrieval, and dissemination; facilitating public and private sector activities in areas such as public administration, transport, and urban and rural development; improving the quality of life for citizens such as health, social needs – for physically challenged, education, environment, and agriculture; sharing knowledge and improving access to information; and facilitating activities in the business sector such as travel and tourism, manufacturing, and electronic commerce.

- Another term that emerged between 2001 and 2007 and is worth mentioning is *knowledge management*. The term came from nowhere, so to speak, to take position number 8 in 2001-2007. It should be noted that although the practice of knowledge management has been going on for decades, the concept was born in mid-1990s. Its definition is elusive but is described as a "discipline that promotes an integrated approach to identifying, managing and sharing all of an organization's knowledge assets including unarticulated expertise and experience resident in individual workers ... it involves the identification and analysis of available and required knowledge, and the subsequent planning and control of actions to develop knowledge assets so as to fulfill organizational objectives" Kim (2000:3). Some of the terms that are closely associated with knowledge management and which similarly emerged during 2001-2007 are: *information resources management* and *business enterprises*.

- Although the term *libraries* has maintained a consistent presence throughout the years investigated, at no time has it performed as exceedingly well as in

2001–2007. For the first time, the term took the first position, having appeared 99 times. The implication of this pattern is that perhaps more library workers are undergoing further training (i.e. post-graduate level) which means that their researches would, to a large extent, focus on the library (i.e. services, stock, library automation, etc) or most post-graduate students find it convenient to conduct research/studies on libraries and their services because the libraries are within the vicinity of the LIS schools, which in turn means less time spent and costs incurred during research and more specially on data collection.

- As usual there were shifts in the ranking of most subject terms.

Table 6: Research areas: 2001-2007 (*N* = *723*)

No.	Rank	Subjects	Articles	%	No.	Rank	Subject	Articles	%
1	1	Libraries	99	13.69	16	15	Publishers & Publishing	22	3.04
2	2	Information Science	82	11.34	17	15	Archives	22	3.04
3	3	Information Resources	77	10.65	18	16	Information & Communication Technologies	21	2.90
4	4	Information Technology	74	10.24	19	16	Education	21	2.90
5	5	Information Resources Management	65	8.99	20	17	Libraries – Automation	20	2.77
6	6	Information Services	61	8.44	21	17	Information Dissemination	20	2.77
7	7	Library Science	53	7.33	22	17	Research	20	2.77
8	8	Knowledge Management	51	7.05	23	18	Technology	19	2.63
9	9	Academic Libraries	50	6.92	24	18	Information Literacy	19	2.63
10	9	Universities & Colleges	50	6.92	25	18	Web Sites	19	2.63
11	10	Information Retrieval	47	6.50	26	18	Surveys	18	2.49
12	11	Internet	38	5.26	27	18	Business Enterprises	18	2.49
13	12	Communication & Technology	34	4.70	28	18	Information Storage & Retrieval Systems	18	2.49
14	13	Librarians	32	4.43	29	19	Library Education	17	2.35
15	14	Agriculture	25	3.46	30	19	Public Libraries	17	2.35

7. CONCLUSIONS

Although LIS education and training in Sub-Saharan Africa is relatively a new venture in several countries in the region, it has nevertheless experienced remarkable growth and development. Worth mentioning too are the changes that LIS education and training has undergone, e.g. change of names of LIS schools, curricula development, staffing, adoption of modern ICTs, mergers (in the case of South Africa), closure (e.g. the department of Information Studies, University of Cape Town, South Africa), etc. Other developments include the proliferation of LIS schools in Sub-Saharan Africa while research – as reflected in the published literature – has recorded a tremendous growth rate in terms of the number of publications and subject terms that are used to index the LIS articles. Seemingly, LIS nomenclature (i.e. change of names for LIS schools) which is largely influenced by socio-cultural factors, has in turn, a direct influence on the areas of research as shown in Fig 1 vis-à-vis the trends of publication on different subject areas of LIS. There remain, however, a number of challenges and opportunities for LIS education and training in Sub-Saharan Africa. Some of these include the establishment of continuing professional education programs, whose main objective, as argued by Ocholla (2000:43) is to bridge 'the gap between the knowledge, skills and attitudes already held by the trainee and those that are required by the job".

Finally, we acknowledge the fact that there are a number of studies that have attempted to provide an overview of and/or trends in LIS education and training in Africa from a variety of perspectives, which we tried not to duplicate or reproduce here. These include: Aina (1991), Aina (1999), Gupta & Gupta (1997), Mambo (2000), Minishi-Majanja (2003; 2004), Minishi-Majanja & Ocholla (2004), Ocholla (2000), Ocholla & Bothma, 2007, Odini (1999), Raju (2003), Rugambwa (2001), Thapisa (1999a; 1999b), Many of these focus on sub-Saharan Africa, especially the Anglophone countries because data is easily available within this context. It is difficult to draw up a comprehensive and cohesive picture of the region, largely because of the availability of uniform data. Thus this chapter has tended to highlight and over generalize when in actual fact some of the situations are better or worse, truer or less true than depicted.

References

Aina, LO. 1991. Directions of the information professions in Africa as reflected in the literature. *International Information and Library Review* 23:365-380.

Aina, LO. 1999. The problems of tertiary publishing in Africa and implications for training and education of library and information professionals. *International Information and Library Review* 31:87-95.

Bierbaum, E. G., & Brooks, T.A. (1995). The literature of Acquired Immunodeficiency Syndrome (AIDS): Continuing changes in publication patterns and subject access. *Journal of the American Society for Information Science,* 46(7), 530-536.

Curry, A. 2000. Canadian library and information science education: trends and issues. *Education for Information,* 18 (4): 325-337.

Gupta, S & Gupta DK. 1997. Development of library and information science education in Africa. *International Information and Library Review* 25 (1):73-83.

Hikwa. L. 2006. Integrating information and communication technologies in LIS curriculum in Zimbabwe: A paper presented at the IFLA workshop on integrating ICTs in LIS curriculum in Africa. 21-23 November 2006 at Safari Court Hotel, Windhoek – Namibia.

IFLA. 2000. Guidelines for professional library/information educational programs – 2000. [Online] Available: http://www.ifla.org/VII/s23/bulletin/guidelines.htm.

Ikoja-Odongo. 2006. Integrating ICTs into LIS curriculum in Uganda. A paper presented at the IFLA workshop on integrating ICTs in LIS curriculum in Africa. 21-23 November 2006 at Safari Court Hotel, Windhoek – Namibia.

Kim, S. 2000. The roles of knowledge professionals for knowledge management: a paper presented at International Federation of Library Associations (IFLA), 65th IFLA Council and General Conference, Bangkok, Thailand, August 20th-28th, 1999. *INSPEL,* 34 (2000) 1:1-8

Macias-Chapula, C. A., Sotolongo-Aguilar, G. R., Magde, B., & Solorio-Lagunas, J. 1999. Subject analysis of AIDS literature, as produced in Latin America and the Caribbean. *Scientometrics,* 46(3):563-574.

Mambo, HL. 2000. Africa: focus on current library and information training needs and future patterns. *Library Review,* 49 (8):387-391.

Manda, PA. 2006. State of ICTs in LIS curriculum in Tanzania. A paper presented at the IFLA workshop on integrating ICTs in LIS curriculum in Africa. 21-23 November 2006 at Safari Court Hotel, Windhoek – Namibia.

Mangan, KS. 2000. In revamped library schools, information trumps books. *Chronicle of Higher Education.* 46 (31): A43-45.

Manmart, L. 2001. Impact of Internet on Schools of Library and Information Science in Thailand. *67th IFLA Council and General Conference, August 16-25, 2001.* [Online] Available: http://www.ifla.org. Retrieved May 13 2002.

Marcum, DB. 1997. Transforming the curriculum; transforming the profession. *American Libraries* 27 (1): 35-37.

Minishi-Majanja, MK. 2003. Mapping and auditing information and communication technologies in library and information science education in Africa: a review of the literature. *Education for Information,* 21:159-179.

Minishi-Majanja, MK. 2004. Mapping and auditing information and communication technologies in library and information science education in sub-Saharan Africa. (Unpublished thesis), University of Zululand.

Minishi-Majanja, MK & Ocholla, DN. 2004. Auditing information and communication technologies in library and information science education in Africa. *Education for Information,* 22:187-221.

Ministry of Education. 2001. *National plan for higher education in South Africa.* Government Printer: Pretoria.

Moahi, KH. 2006. The Integration of ICTs in the LIS curriculum: department of LIS, University of Botswana. A paper presented at the IFLA workshop on integrating ICTs in LIS curriculum in Africa. 21-23 November 2006 at Safari Court Hotel, Windhoek – Namibia.

Ngulube, P. 2006. The state of ICTs in LIS curriculum in South Africa. A paper presented at the IFLA workshop on integrating ICTs in LIS curriculum in Africa. 21-23 November 2006 at Safari Court Hotel, Windhoek – Namibia.

Ocholla, DN. 2000. Training for library and information studies: a comparative overview of LIS education in Africa. *Education for Information* 18:33-52.

Ocholla, DN. 2003. An overview of information and communication technologies (ICT) in the LIS schools of Eastern and Southern Africa. *Education for Information* 21 (2-3): 181-194.

Ocholla, DN & Bothma, T. 2007. Trends, challenges and opportunities for LIS education and training in Eastern and Southern Africa. *New Library World,* 108 (1/2):55-78.

Odini, C. 1999. Training and development of skills in a changing information environment. *Library Management* 20 (2), 100-104.

Palmquist, M. n.d. Content Analysis. [Online] Available: http://www.colostate. edu/Depts/WritingCenter/references/research/content/page2.htm.

Raju, J. 2003. The core in library and/or information science education and training. *Education for Information,* 21:229-242.

Raju, J. 2005. LIS education and training in South Africa: a historical review. *South African Journal of Libraries and Information Science,* 71(1):74-84.

Rosenberg, D. 2000. An Overview of education for librarianship in Anglophone sub-Saharan Africa. In Wise, M. (editor), 2000. *Education for Librarianship and Information Science in Africa.* Denver: International Academic Publishers, p 11-33.

Rugambwa, I. 2001. Information science education in sub-Saharan Africa: an analysis. *International Information and Library Review* 33:45-67.

Stoker, D. 2000. Persistence and change: issues for LIS educators in the first decade of the twenty-first century. *Education for Information.* 18 (2/3): 115- 123.

Tammaro, AM.2005. Report on quality assurance models in LIS programs. IFLA:Education and Training Section. [Online] Available: http://www.ifla.org/ VII/s23/index.htm.

Thapisa, A. 1999a. Developing lasting competencies for a twenty-first century information economy workforce in Africa. *Library Management* 20 (2), 90-99.

Thapisa, A. 1999b. Training for the real working world in the information economy. *Library Management.* 20 (2), 84-89.

Weech, TL & Tammaro AM. 2007. Feasibility of International Guidelines for Equivalency and Reciprocity of Qualifications for LIS Professionals. [Online] Available: http://www.ifla.org/VII/s23/projects/23-project-outlines.htm.

PART 2
ASIA:
INTRODUCTION

Abdus Sattar Chaudhry and Chihfeng P. Lin
Regional Editors

A great deal of diversity prevails in Asia, home of ancient civilization and focus of future socio-economic developments. This diversity is prevalent in area and population, languages and cultures, and levels of development. This perspective makes Asia more of a cultural concept incorporating a number of regions and people than a homogenous physical entity. While in the East, main countries, such as China, Japan, and Korea, are clearly considered part of the Asian region, on the Western side there seems to be quite a bit of overlap with the Middle East region. In the South, component parts of the region are better known by memberships of SAARC (South Asian Association for Regional Cooperation – Bangladesh, Bhutan, India, Maldives, Nepal, Pakistan, and Sri Lanka,) and ASEAN (Association of South-east Asian Nations – Brunei, Cambodia, Indonesia, Laos, Malaysia, Myanmar, Philippines, Singapore, Thailand, and Vietnam). The Central Asian region also overlaps with countries of the old Soviet block and Iran. For the purpose of this book, a more inclusive approach has been used.

While exhaustive coverage of all geographic territories of Asia is not the focus, peculiarities of sub-regions and unique LIS services and sectors in major Asian countries have been covered except the Arabic speaking nations. Chapters 4-7 cover academic, public, and special libraries and library and information science (LIS) education in Asian countries. Within the constraints of size, authors have tried to provide an overview of history and development and the current status of libraries in their respective areas of coverage and pointed to references and sources of information for further details. As a result of the diversity highlighted above, coverage for individual countries and sub-regions vary a great deal in terms of detail and style of presentation. But, the details given provide a good overview of the status of library and information services in the region of Asia.

ACADEMIC LIBRARIES

The Asian region is well known for old seats of learning such as Taxila and Nalanda Universities in India; Nanjing University in China; the Academy of Gundishpur in Persia; and Quoc Tu Giam University in Vietnam. The region is also well known for its world-class modern universities such as Peking and Jiao Tong universities in China, National University of Singapore, Hong Kong University of Science and Technology, and Indian Institutes of Technology, just to quote a few examples. These institutions of higher education are equipped with state-of-the-art libraries. In Chapter 6, Trishanjit Kaur has provided a good overview of academic libraries in more than 20 countries in different sub-regions of Asia. She highlighted recent developments in academic libraries in China and India that resulted in development of comprehensive automated library systems and provided glimpses of modern academic libraries in Hong Kong, Japan, Korean, Singapore, and Taiwan. While the well-known libraries are equipped with the state-of-the art technology and generous financial support, Kaur's overall conclusions indicate that the region's academic libraries in general face challenges of inadequate financial and other support and need to take steps to take full advantage of the treasures of information owned by their parent institutions.

PUBLIC LIBRARIES

Public libraries in Asia have developed along particular individuality of countries in different sub-regions. In Chapter 7, Mei-Hwa Yang has highlighted well-known libraries as examples of the public library scene and provided references for additional information on public libraries in different Asian countries. She pointed out that public libraries are very crucial for Asian countries as they play an important role in promoting literacy, economic development, life-long learning, and cross-functional approach to social inclusion. A unique feature of public libraries in Asia is that in some Asian countries the National Library plays a leading role in public library development. Public libraries in Asia are confronted with unprecedented challenges in terms of operations and management, such as the following: limited resources, expanding user demands, growing competition in the provision of information services and social networking, an enhanced focus on accountability for public sector organizations. But, it is encouraging to see that many innovative projects are being implemented in the Asian countries. Several countries have undertaken a variety of digital projects, such as China, Taiwan, Japan and South Korea. New devices include: RFID, which was first introduced in Singapore, and Palm Veins technology, which was first used for library-card holders in Japan. In addition, many e-learning practices are being implemented in Taiwan and some other countries. Yang concludes that a more pro-active approach in seeking out opportunities to deploy their unique skills, expertise, and resources public libraries can gain more support from the governments as well citizenry in Asian countries.

SPECIAL LIBRARIES

Like in other countries, special libraries in Asia differ from public, school, and academic libraries. They serve a fairly narrow clientele and emphasize on providing information that can help answer questions ("putting knowledge to work") instead of educating patrons on how to find information. In Chapter 9, Ferguson and

Lin, considering the diversity of special libraries, have taken a different approach. They have surveyed special libraries of Hong Kong and Taiwan, and used these as case studies to highlight the peculiarities of special libraries in Asia. They describe the similarities and differences where possible and guide the reader to look at the other materials in the bibliography to learn more about the situation in each country. Case studies from Hong Kong and Taiwan indicate that special librarians in Asian countries have many hats to wear all at the same time to get their collecting, acquisitions, cataloguing, public service, and collection management work completed and they have to this rather fast, especially for influential clients upon whose the success of the overall organization depends. These libraries were applying both "just in case" collecting strategies and the "just in time" collecting patterns. The need to collect and "mine" the work sponsoring organization was especially apparent within the more corporate libraries examined in the case studies. The authors conclude that special libraries in Asia face the challenges of lack of sufficient staff and funds, time to get all the work done, facilities in which to work, and opportunities to improve skills. Yet, most if not all of the special librarians interviewed seemed to be imbued with a passion for their jobs, putting knowledge to work.

LIS EDUCATION

Depending on the status of higher education and economies of individual countries in the region, Library and Information Science (LIS) education in Asia is at different levels of development. In Chapter 10 Khoo, Majid, and Lin trace the history of start of LIS education programs, provide a detailed list of sources of information on LIS education, and review the status of LIS education in Asia. While the earliest LIS education programs are traced back as early as 1915 in Pakistan and 1920 in China, authors report that most LIS programs in Asia began after the First World War. They also report that while some countries still do not have any LIS education programs (e.g., Cambodia, Laos, and Myanmar); some Asian countries are currently operating a large number of LIS programs (e.g., India, 167; Philippines, 69; China, 41; Thailand, 16; and Taiwan, 13). The authors conclude that as a result of globalization and other relevant developments, the trends in LIS education are similar to that of USA, UK, and Australia, while there is a deliberate effort to adopt the LIS education to local needs and culture. Currently, there is no formal accreditation program in place but some countries are governed by the guidelines set by the respective ministries of education and the various quality assurance programs introduced by higher education forums. Regional professional associations and conferences initiated as a result of collaboration among LIS programs in several Asia-Pacific countries are promoting quality improvement including a possible regional scheme of accreditation. As a result, an Asian brand of LIS is expected to emerge that, among other things, may also include an initiative of introducing 'I' Schools in Asia.

PUBLIC LIBRARIES

Mei-Hwa Yang

INTRODUCTION

The UNESCO Manifesto proclaims the belief in the public library as a living force for education, culture and information, and as an essential agent for the fostering of peace and spiritual welfare through the minds of men and women. The public libraries in cities, towns, and villages that serve as frontline libraries are the most important. These libraries may serve as a community-gathering place, as a reference center for local and world news, and as an educational facility promoting literacy and cultural diversity. These basic functions, though common to all libraries across the world, are nevertheless met in many different ways according to the particular needs of a community or a region. It can be said that public libraries are a microcosm of the world to which they belong. The pattern of public librarianship in Asia is not uniform, as each region has developed its own particular individuality. Since it is rather difficult to cover all countries in Asia, the author can only highlight some countries with familiarity. The countries below are arranged in alphabetical order. For additional information please check with *Encyclopedia of Library and Information Science, World Libraries Archive,* etc.

1. INDIVIDUAL COUNTRY

1.1 Bangladesh

According to 2003 Library Directory, there are 1603 Non-Government Public Libraries and 68 Government public libraries, including 1 Sufia Kamal National Central Public Library (Formerly Bangladesh Central Public Library), 3 Divisional Central Public Library, 60 District Library, and 4 Branch Library. Non-government public libraries movements started with the establishment of four public libraries in the year 1854. Most of the non-government public libraries open for3-5 hours in the evening. Very few library personnel are trained, most of them part time basis. These non-government public libraries are partly financed by subscription, partly by government grants and not fully by the local authorities (Shuva 2003).

The government public library started its journey with the opening of Bangladesh Central Public Library in 1958. Shuva (2003) pointed out that problems of public libraries in Bangladesh were: Lack of trained library personnel and training facilities, recognition of the necessity of libraries and library services in a social environment, funds, standards for public libraries, etc.

2.2 Cambodia

Like all other cultural institutions in Cambodia, libraries suffered greatly from neglect during the political, social and economic upheaval of the 1970s and have
largely been rebuilt from nothing in the period from 1980 onwards. Since the 1993
elections there has been a dramatic increase in the number of libraries, as well as
the number of young Cambodians using them regularly. In addition, technology is
now ensuring that even people in remote parts of Cambodia can have free access
to information. (Libraries, Cambodia Cultural Profile, 2006)

Libraries in Cambodia developed from two streams: the repositories of palm-
leaf manuscripts containing Buddhist scriptures and religious writings that were
preserved in the country's numerous wats, and the colonial-era document archives
that were established during the French protectorate in the late 19th and early 20th
centuries (Libraries, Cambodia Cultural Profile, 2006).

2.3 China

Since the 1980s, governments at all levels have attached great importance to the
construction of public libraries, regarding them as a significant element in the development of community culture (Wu 2005). By the end of 2004, there were 2,720
public libraries, including a national library, 37 provincial libraries, 2,240 municipal libraries, 85 juvenile/children's libraries, and 49,646 staff members.

In China, the size of the town and the amount of government investment determine the public library's condition and collection. (Wikipedia 2007) On average
460,000 people share a library. Public libraries are rarely found in the countryside.
About 90.3% of the populace never use public libraries, even though the national
standard states that within every 1.5 kilometers there should be a public library
and that a maximum of 20 thousand people should share a single public library.

The combined collections of all the public libraries total around 430 million
volumes. However, on average a person can get access only to 0.3 volumes. 9.43
million people hold public library cards, which means only 0.73% of the population do. by contrast,, two thirds of the population of the United States use public
libraries and 13,000 people share a library on average.

The Library Association of China set up "The appraisal standard regulation" for
all levels of public libraries, for which it serves as the principle for developing and
providing public library services. In addition, "The Professional Ethics Code for
Chinese Librarians" and "Standards for the Construction of Public Libraries" were
formulated for community of public libraries.

The past twenty years have seen unprecedented changes in library development
in China. Highlighted by the construction of the new buildings of such large libraries as the National Library of China, the Shanghai Library, the Fujian Provincial Library, and the Zhejiang Provincial Library, the library in China has experienced accelerated modernization. With rapid development in both quantity and

quality, Chinese libraries have become well-organized learning centers in small communities, and well-received cultural attractions in the urban areas (Wu 2005). With the on-going digital projects and increased implementation of high-tech equipment, such as RFID, the future of the public library in China is promising and impressive.

Shanghai Library, which covers 3.1 hectares of land, and has a floor space of 83,000 square meters, officially opened to the public on December 20th, 1996, is the largest public library in China and also one of the ten largest libraries in the world in terms of its rich collection and extensive floor space. Its holdings include 50.95 million items, ranging from the latest technical reports, patent and standard files, to ancient artifacts, and from paper copy, sound and video recordings, to digital databases (Shanghai Library website 2007).

2.3.1 Hong Kong

The Hong Kong Public Libraries consist of a network of 66 stationary libraries and 10 mobile libraries. They are evenly spread over the territory of Hong Kong and interconnected by an integrated automated library system to provide convenient access to a wide range of library services for the public. The library collection has 11.5 million items, including books, audio-visual materials, newspapers, periodicals, CD-ROM databases, microforms and maps (Hong Kong Public Libraries website 2007).

Hong Kong Central Library, the largest public library in Hong Kong with 2 million items in its collections, first opened its doors to the public on 17 May 2001. Equipped with advanced technologies and digital library facilities, it is also the administrative headquarters and the main library of the Hong Kong public library network as well as the major information center for Hong Kong. In addition to standard library facilities and services, it provides a central reference library of six subject departments, a toy library, a young adult library and hiring facilities comprising an exhibition gallery and a lecture theatre.

2.3.2 Macau

Under the Administration of Macao Culture, Macau Central Library (http://www.library.gov.mo/) was founded in 1895, and is composed of one main library and six branches. It has a total collection of approximately 550,000 volumes. Apart from a sizeable general interest collection, the Central Library is also a treasure trove for Macau local information, children's literature and Portuguese history in the Far East. The Civic and Municipal Library is a small and ancient library dated back to 1656. Ho Tung Library is a typical example of a private residence turned library. It was formerly the summer villa of Sir Robert Ho Tung who acquired it in 1918, and he actually lived here in the war years from 1941-1945. The 3-storey estate was bequeathed to the Macau Government in 1955. Being a garden library it has attracted many visitors.

2.4 India

The first landmark in the pre-independence history of the public library system in India is the enactment of delivery and registration of publications Act of Bombay government in May 1808. Calcutta Public Library was established in 1836 and was endowed with public donations. The first three decades of the 20th century can be marked as the golden period of Indian library system. On 31st Jan 1902 the Imperial Library Act was passed and Lord Curzon transformed the Calcutta Public Library into Imperial Library in 1906. The Department of Public Libraries came into existence from 1st November 1966 consequent upon the implementation of Mysore Public Libraries Act, 1965. The act provided for the establishment of the libraries. At present, the Karnataka public library system is one of the most popular and feasible systems, as compared to those in the other 28 states in India (Kumbar n.d.).

Established on March 22, 1890, Connemara Public Library is a repository of centuries-old publications, wherein lie some of the most respected works and collections in the country. It also serves as a depository library for the UN. A truly world class library with teak shelves and standard glass windows with a very tall ceiling reflecting colonial ambience was the idea of the H. Irvin the consulting architect of Madras Presidency. This large hall was set in a semi circle sandstone building constructed in Indo- sorcenic style that never seems to have aged even now. As a part of the centenary celebrations an additional three- storey building with a floor space of 21,235 square-foot opened on 24th June 1999. In 2005, it was selected as the best state central library in India (Connemara Public Library website).

Delhi Public Library was started as a UNESCO project in the year 1951 by the government of India. Delhi Public Library has a network of Zonal Libraries, Branches & Sub-branches, R.C. Libraries, Community Libraries, Deposit Stations, Sports Libraries, Mobile Library, Braille library, etc. spread all over Delhi. Some of the outstanding features of the library activities are services to Blind, Prisoners and offers Mobile Library service. Delhi Public Library is the biggest Public Library System in India and the busiest Public Library in South East Asia (Delhi Public Library website).

2.5 Indonesia

Indonesia, the fourth most populous country in the world after China, India and the US, occupies almost 2 million square metres of land area, is a vast country and has various degrees of development from one to another region. Compared to its neighbouring ASEAN countries, library development in Indonesia and specifically public libraries are still far behind. In terms of physical structures and number of librarians working in both public libraries and municipal libraries, Indonesia stands out among ASEAN countries. However, in terms of public services, like most public institutions in Indonesia, public libraries have been neglected and have not been placed on the government priority list (Kamil 2003).

The Sumatran province of Aceh was severely damaged by the earthquake and resulting tsunami. Of Aceh's eight public libraries, two were completely destroyed. These libraries were located in the hard-hit cities of Meulaboh and Sigli. The Aceh Provincial Library (BPD) was inundated with three meters of water. Twenty-three staff members were killed, including the library's director, Bachtiar Azis, who is listed as missing along with his family. In addition to loss of life, the BPD suffered physical damage and a near total loss of its collection. All library materials housed on the first floor were swept away by the waves, and the floor was covered in 30 cm.-thick mud. A collection of books received under legal deposit and housed on the second floor was left undisturbed and survived the disaster and looting intact. (Wikipedia)

2.6 Japan

The first public library in Japan was established in 1872 on the former site of Shoheiko (the Confucian Academy). It was later called Shojoakukan and run by the government. Its name has since been changed to Tokyo Library (Tokyo Toshokan), which was also the predecessor of the National Diet Library and modelled by local governments to public libraries in many regions during the Meiji period (Koizumi 2003).

It was with the enactment of the Library Law of 1950 that the public libraries in Japan changed to a modern form of public library and the number of public libraries increased. In 1963, the Japan Library Association published "Management of Public Libraries in Medium and Small Cities," which emphasized the importance of the relationship with the local community. This was an epoch-making report that revolutionized the concept of library service, the views of which spread to administrators of public libraries. In the 1970's, movements of local residents and increased budgets of local governments accelerated the rapid progress of public libraries (Koizumi, 2003).

Each city (over 50,000 population) has its own public library. It is a very popular establishment in Japanese society. However, 51.6 % of the towns in Japan have no public library (Statistics on Libraries in Japan 2006). In Japan, "library" (*toshokan*) usually means public library. High school students often use the public library as a place for preparing for the college entrance examination. In the 1980's, life-long learning came to be emphasized by local governments, which increased the use of the public library. In the 1990's, public libraries were more likely to be built along with other public cultural facilities, such as culture centers, museums, auditoriums, and so on.

There are no ministries or central government agencies that exclusively oversee the public libraries in Japan. In terms of national legislation, the Library Law was enacted in 1950 but no national policies have been established as laws.

As of 2006, there were 3,082 public libraries and 14,070 staff members. Benefited from the world's second largest economy, Japan spends 3.1 per cent of GNP on research and development. Budget for materials was 3,047,030 (in units of 10,000 yen) (Hosono 2006; updated by Statistics on Libraries in Japan 2006). The collection is 356,710,000 volumes. The total number of books borrowed each year is 618 million. Therefore, on average, 4.8 books are borrowed by each Japanese person. Parker (2005) indicates that comparative data from G7 countries put Japan slightly below average for the number of items borrowed per 100,000 people, but at the top of the scale in terms of books issued per library. The Mayor has much of the power in allocating resources in Japan, as in the USA. 62 per cent of people in Japan do not use the public library.

There are 1,030 libraries that offer Web-based OPACs, 606 libraries that provide Web-based functions for reservation services and 172 libraries with i-mode OPACs, 91 of them with reservation services. 97 libraries accept reference questions via e-mails (Japan Library Association 2007). During the last few decades, Japan has gone through a number of changes, ranging from high economic growth to the bubble economy and its burst, the advent of computerization, the shock of the Kobe earthquake, and the graying of its society, most Japan's public libraries face difficulties to cope with these socioeconomic changes.

Japan's public libraries emphasize the preservation of local literature and historical materials. Many libraries began to digitize these materials. In addition, Japan's public libraries make every endeavor to provide services for special readers. A barrier-free environment includes such features as braille paths and music signs. Public libraries provide an oral reading service and a mail loan service. Recently, Japan's public libraries began promoting mass health information to give readers useful health information. Tokyo Metropolitan Library, Tottori Prefectural Library (Hosono 2006) and Yokohama City Central Library (Ogawa 2007) are the leading libraries in this service.

Under partial amendment of the Local Autonomy Law enforced in 2003, the Shitei Kanrisha System (Designated Manager System) was established, which introduces appointed management to administer public institutions and facilities. A very complicated issue concerning public libraries is whether libraries operated under the Shitei Kanrisha System can function properly and provide professional services to the public (Hosono 2006).

As in many other countries in Asia, Japan's public libraries are also facing the challenges of budget cuts and professional librarianship. Reduction in funding is the problem all public libraries face. Most libraries have smaller budgets than they had the previous year. Since public libraries must cope with significant change, more professional librarians are needed to manage the libraries. The lack of a specialized authentication system remains a question in Japan (Hosono 2006).

In October 2006, Naka City became the world's first library system to use palm vein authentication technology. It relies on the unique pattern of veins inside each person's hand to identify users. The system offers a higher level of security than such biometric technologies as voice print, facial recognition, fingerprint recognition and iris scan (Fujitsu 2007).

2.7 South Korea

Korea set up its first Law Library in 1963. Its goal lies in the education, investigation, research, and training of body and mind. In 1987 the government comprehensively revised the Law Library. It replaced the body and mind training with information use and educational and cultural activities. The Library Promotion Act, written in 1991 to supersede the Library Act, emphasizes the "nurturing and promotion of libraries" and stipulates that "a library shall be managed by a library professional." The Library and Reading Promotion Action, legislated in 1994, incorporated the "promotion of reading" eventually obscuring its meaning as an "exclusive statute for governing libraries."

The aggregate nationwide public library holdings amount to 38.4 million books. That breaks down to 78,000 books per public library and 0.79 books per capita. The average full-time staff size per library is 12 employees. An estimated 2,000 professionally qualified librarians serve in public libraries, corresponding to 4.3 librarians per library and 38 percent of the total library workforce. Annual operating costs per library amount to 710 million won (US$760,000) on average, 12 percent of which is accounted for by acquisition of library materials. There are 5,129 staff and 30,544,742 collections at present. Since 2000, funds have been consistently increasing. Each library was allocated 4.5 hundred million Korea dollars in 2000, 5.4 hundred million Korea dollars in 2001, and 6.5 hundred million Korea dollars in 2002. Most big cities are allocated more than 100 hundred million dollars on average (Libraries in Korea 2006).

As stipulated by the library law, all Korean public libraries have established a single cooperative network to maximize the quantity and the quality of their services. The current cooperative network designates the National Library of Korea as the central organization and maintains 16 major Provincial Libraries, 35 Regional Libraries, and 514 Communities Libraries. As of the end of 2005, many public libraries adopted the RFID (Radio Frequency Identification) system based on ubiquitous technologies and provide e-books and e-journal services. Some public libraries also provide the search and receipt of audio or text messages through mobile phones (Libraries in Korea 2006).

Korean public libraries are managed under a dual system. At the central level, the Ministry of Government Administration and Home Affairs and the Ministry of Education and Human Resources Development are responsible for the management of public libraries; at the local level, public libraries are divided into those administered by provincial and city governments and those under provincial and municipal educational offices. This complicated system undermines cooperation and mutual support among libraries in many areas, including policy coordination, staff development and personnel assignments, collection development and cooperative preservation of materials, and interlibrary loans (Libraries in Korea 2006).

Library and information resources have been recognized as an essential part of the nation's resources and national information infrastructure. Therefore, systematic and up-dated strategies and policies on library and information resources are needed to assure the accessibility and usability of information to individual users (citizens). The execution of the Library & Information Policy has since been transferred from the Ministry of Culture and Tourism, and a reorganization of the Library was implemented in 2004.

The Korean Ministry of Culture set up "the Library Promotion Law" in 1991. In order to promote the dissemination of information, cultural activities and lifelong education, it expanded the original pure education concept to one of lifelong education. In 1994 the government set up "the Library and Study Promotion Law" which inherited the objectives of "the Library Promotion Law". Based on the Library Law, the goals of the Korean public library are the dissemination of information, cultural activities, and lifelong education. The digital library designed for children and juveniles is scheduled to open in 2008. IFLA held its 72nd annual conference in August 2006. All these things show that the vitality of Korea's library enterprise.

For future development, the Korean central and local governments have several plans to raise the scale and scope of public library services and to help the libraries function as centers for collecting and disseminating information and promoting community cultural activities in an age of knowledge. They plan to increase the number of public libraries to 750 by 2011 under the "Library Development Roadmap" announced by the Ministry of Culture and Tourism. This will translate into one public library for every 60,000 persons (Libraries in Korea, 2006).

2.8 Laos

The library system of Laos is not based on a common governmental law, and all public libraries in Laos are to be considered local branches under the National Library. Public libraries are presently found in Luang Prabang, Oudamsay and Pakse. Three bookmobiles are in Laos serving areas without a local public library. One of these being attached to the National Library as a donation from the Japanese government and serving the suburbs of Vientiane. Following a number of changed locations the National Library is now to be found in a stately building on Thanon Setthathirat in Vientiane. In 1990-92 UNESCO has sponsored three library volunteers from the West to help organizing the library techniques of the library. This impact is still to be felt in the library, but as the government's priorities presently are centered on the development of the school system, library budgets are limited (Evald 2004).

For further information, please see "National Library", Laos Cultural Profile. http://www.culturalprofiles.net/laos/Units/189.html.

2.9 Malaysia

Diversity of peoples characterizes the population of Malaysia. The multicultural nature of Malaysian society is mirrored in its multi-racial, multi-lingual and multi-religious makeup. The multi-ethnicity of Malaysia, has posed a great challenge to public libraries in providing services to meet the informational needs of one of the most culturally and linguistically diversified countries in the region. What poses a great challenge is the formulation of a strategic plan to enable the effectiveness of services, with the goal of creating a knowledge-based multicultural, multiracial, multilingual, and multi-faith society. This challenge is compounded by scenarios where problems occur in terms of varied literacy levels, a lack of mastering the languages, and low library literacy (Yaacob & Seman, 1998).

Up to the mid-1960s, the establishment of public libraries in Malaysia was hap-hazard and mostly without government funding. In 1968 the "Blueprint for Public Library Development in Malaysia" was published. The Blueprint attempted to draw up minimum national standards for Malaysian public libraries, which could be used to assess existing services and serve as guidelines for evaluation and action, and for setting new goals for future public libraries (Bates, n.d.). Since 1968 the National Library Committee has followed the recommendations of the Blueprint.

The National Library Act was passed in 1972. In reviewing the achievements and performance nearly a decade later, the Persatuan Perpustakaan Malaysia prepared its revised Standards for Public Libraries in Malaysia and subjected them to review by a wider audience at the Joint Conference of the Persatuan Perpustakaan Malaysia (PPM) and the Library Association of Singapore (LAS) in March 1977 (Mustafa & Wilkinson, 1977).

In 1981, the Persatuan Perpustakaan Malaysia issued its Library Building Standards for Malaysia4, which contained provisions for public libraries as well. These standards too were reviewed by a wider audience at the Seminar on Library Buildings in 1981.5 The major difference between Piawaian untuk Perpustakaan Awam di Malaysia and the Library Building Standards for Malaysia is that the former was never formally adopted or endorsed by any library, administrative or financial authority while the latter was adopted 'in principle' by the Costs and Standards Committee of the Government's Economic Planning Unit (Wijasuriya n.d.).

By 2006, there were 1,129 public libraries, including 14 state public libraries, 174 village libraries, 92 branch libraries, 6 regional/metropolitan libraries, 115 branch/district libraries, 60 town libraries, and 844 rural cyber information centers/libraries, 88 mobile libraries. Each state has developed an infrastructure for its public library system, with the aim of providing service to both the urban and rural regions. The main public libraries at the headquarters co-ordinate these functions with the branches in all districts while the mobile library systems try to reach regions not accessible to the public library system.

The National Library of Malaysia has developed an E-Library User Education Module funded by UNESCO. The E-Library User Education Module is an online self-tutorial or learning package aimed at educating the public to become skilled library users. This module is available in Malay and English and can be accessed at http://www.elib.gov.my. It is now being adapted for use in public libraries in Asia Pacific countries (Dato 2004).

2.10 Myanmar

The National Library in Yangon (Rangoon) founded in 1952 is administered by the Department of Cultural Institute, Ministry of Culture. The National Library has now collected about 618000 books and periodicals. It has a rare collection of materials on Myanmar and has a rich collection of rare and valuable Myanmar manuscripts about 15,800 in titles. This library was first free public library in Myanmar and it was known as "The Bernard Free Library", which was established on the 21st February 1883. The library has become a legal depository of Myanmar-Naing-Ngan, since the Printers and Publishers Registration Act promulgated in 1962 (Background History of the National Library of Myanmar). For further information, please see Online: Burma/Myanmar Library. http://www.burmalibrary. org/introduction.html, http://www.myanmar.com/Ministry/culture/text/P001.htm.

2.11 Pakistan

Pakistan has had a rich heritage. Some of today's leading libraries were founded in the nineteenth century: Karachi Metropolitan City Library (1851), Punjab Public Library, Lahore (1864), and the Civil Secretariat Library, Lahore (1885) (Khurshid 1990). As of 1989, there were 281 public libraries. With 215,000 volumes the Punjab Public Library is the largest of public libraries, and the country's third library in size. The next largest public library is the Dayal Singh Trust Library in Lahore, with 122,700 volumes; followed by the Liaquat Memorial Library in Karachi, with 120,900 volumes.

Public library development has been greatly enhanced through the establishment of the Punjab Public Library Foundation in 1985 (Khurshid, 1990). To provide a center for continuing education, information, enjoyment and positive use of leisure, the Ministry of Education, Government of Pakistan had decided to convert its existing Central Secretariat Library into a public library for the residents of Islamabad by the name of Islamabad Public Library on 1st July 1996. This Library has a collection of 34,000 Books (Islamabad Public Library 2002).

2.12 Philippines

There are a total of 949 public libraries from the northern province in Batanes to the southernmost province of Tawi-Tawi, including 1 Regional library, 1 Congressional library, 49 Provincial libraries, 79 City libraries, 507 Municipal libraries, and 312 Barangay libraries (Cruz 2002).

Republic Act 7743 is titled "An Act Providing for the Establishment of Congressional, City and Municipal Libraries and Barangay Reading Centers Throughout the Philippines, Appropriating the Necessary Funds Therefore and for Other Purposes." It was approved by both houses of Congress on June 1, 1994 and approved by then President Fidel V. Ramos on June 17, 1994. In consonance with the spirit of RA 7743, The National Library of the Philippines (NLP) annually provides the public libraries with book allocations. The Public Libraries Information Network launched in 1999, links the National Library and the public libraries in terms of sharing information and materials through the computer (Cruz 2002).

For 2001, the total collections of public libraries all over the Philippines have reached 1,004,707 volumes of books, 30,631 serial copies, and 49,929 other kinds of library materials. Because of such, the number of readers using these libraries had increased to 1,214,478 while cardholders numbered 44,180 (Cruz 2002).

Funded by the Commission on Information and Communications Technology (CICT) through the PHP4 billion eGovernment Fund, the Philippine eLib – the country's first public electronic library – boasts of a collection of more than 800,000 bibliographic records consisting of more than 25 million pages of local and international materials, 29,000 full text journals, and 15,000 theses and dissertations on diverse subject matters. The Philippine eLib was conceptualised in 2003 through the efforts of the Department of Science and Technology (DOST), led by Undersecretary Fortunato T. dela Peña, and four other government institutions. The Philippine eLib aims to enrich local content in digital format for community and global access. It also aims to promote and accelerate the exchange of knowledge resources among citizens, and international users (Rojales 2005).

2.13 Singapore

Driven by the desire to make Singapore a center of education and knowledge, the National Library Board (NLB) has one of the best public library systems in the world, one that strives to provide convenient access to knowledge resources. Public libraries are positioned as an integral part of the national learning infrastructure, actively supporting Singapore as a learning nation (National Library Board Singapore 2007).

From the outset, NLB has been directly responsible for both the national library and the public library functions. This responsibility was provided for by the first National Library Act (NLA) of 1958. In June 1992, the Library 2000 Review Committee undertook a review of library services to formulate a master plan for developing library services over the subsequent 10 years. Singapore's government endorsed the Library 2000 recommendations with a budget of $1 billion over eight years (Varaprasad & Kua 2006). The NLB was established on September 1, 1995 to spearhead the transformation of library services in the Information Age.

NLB's mission is to provide a trusted, accessible and globally connected library and information service so as to promote a knowledgeable and engaged society. It sees itself as an inspiring beacon of lifelong learning, bringing knowledge alive, sparking imagination and creating new possibilities for a vibrant and creative Singapore (National Library Board 2007).

The Library 2000 vision seeks to continuously expand the nation's capacity to learn through a network of libraries and information resource centers, which provide services and learning opportunities to support the advancement of Singapore. The Library 2010 Report sets out NLB's strategic direction for the next phase, which aims "to bring the world's knowledge to Singapore to create a positive social and economic impact". Library volunteers are seen as strategic community partners who actively play a part in value-adding and improving library services to the public. Active citizenry is encouraged as part of NLB's Library 2010 Blueprint to forge public libraries into social learning spaces (Siew 2007). There are currently 1 National Library, 3 Regional Libraries, 20 Community Libraries (10 co-located within shopping malls/ town councils), and 10 Community Children's Libraries.

Singapore was one of the first countries to apply RFID to its libraries. Its libraries provide self-service loans. NLB continues to project the image of an organizationorganization of excellence and innovation. The first public library blog in Singapore: library@orchard was launched on July 25, 2007. Public libraries in Singapore have become greatly integrated with the community and are seen as inviting and relaxing, places for meeting people and sharing with other book-lovers. Key challenges include building its professional capability, staying relevant to the society and the economy, making use of new available technology, etc. It is noteworthy that many parts of the world have replicated Singapore's efforts and success in their own countries.

2.14 Taiwan

There has been significant progress in various facets of libraries in Taiwan since the 1980s, such as library buildings, budgets, collections, services, library automation and networking and application of the Internet under government support. In general, libraries in Taiwan operated smoothly during the past two decades under cultural promotion programs, ICT development and national digitalized projects of the government, especially in the beginning of the new millennium.

The first private public library was established in January 1901 under the cooperative promotion of the officials and the public during the Japanese Occupation Era (Librarianship in Taiwan 2007). The Provincial Taipei Library was founded in August 1915. In l978, under the Government Cultural Construction Planning, public libraries advanced a big stride forward to a new milestone. The Library Development White Paper was issued in 1999. The Taiwan Library Law was enacted in 2001.

As of 2006, there were 562 public libraries (branches included) and the total collections in the public libraries reached nearly 27.6 million volumes in Taiwan. Loans total 39,055,813 volumes to date. According to statistics, 78,052 promotional activities were held and 4,393,450 people participated.

In 1992, Guidelines for the Management of Public Libraries was issued as a standard to evaluate library resources and services in Taiwan. The Public Library Information Service Network (PLISNET) was established in 1996 and completed in 1999 for the purpose of accessing bibliographic records and sharing library service systems via networking environment at the levels of provincial/municipal, and county/city public libraries. In addition, mobile library service enhanced the value and use of collections.

The Implementation of the Public Library Improvement Plan to enhance library space, buildings, facilities, and the library automation and networking infrastructure was hosted by the Ministry of Education and the Culture Commission in 2003. The total budget came up NT$ 317,641,666. In 2004, the new building of the National Central Library of Taiwan, which occupies an area of 59,000 square meters, was opened.

The Taipei Public Library (TPL) has formulated its "Strategic Plan 2005-2010" as a guideline for its operations and management development in the future. In 2005, by utilizing the RFID system, the Taipei Public Library inaugurated the world's first self-service library at an MRT station. It is noteworthy that the Taipei Public Library went through ISO 9002 TQM assurance in 2000 (Taipei Public Library web site 2005). The Beitou Branch of the Taipei Public Library is the first green building library in Taiwan. It opened to the public on 17 November 2006. In 2007, it was given the National Award for Architectural Excellence and the Outstanding Environment and Cultural Award. It embodies the principles of an ecological environment and serves as a multi-faceted learning center (Tseng 2007).

In 1996, the National Taichung Library hosted the "Public Library Information Network Guidance and Consultation Committee" which assisted 21 county and municipal libraries under their Bureaus of Culture and more than 400 town and village libraries to complete library automation projects. From 2003 to 2004, the National Taichung Library completed the "Improvement Plan of Public Library Space and Operations" and the "Public Library Automation and Network Project" in assisting more than 300 public libraries to complete software and hardware facilities improvements (National Taichung Library website 2007).

2.15 Thailand

"Public library" was developed from the "public reading room", which was firstly established in Bangkok in 1916 by the Education Department. In 1973, the public library was upgraded to an educational unit attached to the Adult Education Division of General Education Department. Later on, Non-Formal Education Department public library regulation 1992 to make public library be community information center for promotion of community learning and activities, as well as for development of community learning network. At present, there are altogether 850 public libraries over the country, which can be classified into 3 sizes: large-sized public library, middle-sized public library, and small-sized public library (Lerdsuriyakul 1999).

Public Library Section, Recreation Division, Department of Social Welfare, Bangkok Metropolitan Administration has provided only the bus mobile library services to serve the people in Bangkok Metropolitan Area. There are now nine buses. The first bus began in 1991, the second in 1995, the third in 1996, the fourth to the seventh in 1997, and the last two in 1999. The purpose of mobile libraries is to make libraries go into communities of the disadvantage including the children, to make them love books and reading which will be useful to themselves (Priwatrworawute 2000).

Mobile floating library began to provide service in January 1999 with intention to expand service to promote reading and learning of people living along the rivers and canals in terms of books, toys, videos, exhibitions and learning packages concerning reservation of water resources to make those people realize and participate in keeping their rivers and canals, as well as their environment clean. In addition, volunteers are provided to carry the book bags to the doors of those who are unable to travel conveniently from their homes to the floating library for service (Priwatrworawute 2000).

Besides 850 public libraries under the responsibility of the department of Non-Formal Education, there are still 13 public libraries attached to the Bangkok Metropolis Administration, 30 municipal public libraries, as well as 7 public libraries of Srinakorn Bank. Public library is considered as a significant knowledge source and learning center for population of all sexes and ages. They will have the opportunities in studying continuously. Thus, it is seen significant to improve public library to have more efficiency and ability response to the needs of learning of all target groups so that Thai society will finally turn to be a learning society (Nimsomboon 2003).

Thai Library Association (TLA) has initiated the presentation of awards for the "best libraries" of the year encourages the improvement of the public libraries and their activities in 1976, and set up "Standards for Public Libraries" in 1990. The Council of Education's Secretariat Office suggested in 2005, that public libraries should promote digitization, develop staff continually, and cultivate community relationships (Salaladyanant, 2006).

According to Sacchanand (2007), the status of public libraries in Thailand is still not satisfied. The evaluation of public libraries in Thailand, conducted by Sacchanand, Prommapun and Sajjanand (2006) and funded by the Educational Council of Thailand, showed that their performance was less than average. In regards to the passing criteria developed (X = 3.00), it was found that public libraries in Thailand as a whole and classified by types and regions did not pass the criteria. Most public libraries are substandard due to insufficient funding and staff. Budget and finance had the lowest average mean. Some 43 percent of the evaluated libraries, mostly in the Non-formal Education Department, receive an annual budget of less than Bt50,000.

2.16 Vietnam

When Vietnam achieved independence in 1945, there was just one library serving the entire country. Today under the overall guidance of the Ministry of Culture and Information's Library Department, the National Library of Vietnam oversees a network of 64 provincial and municipal libraries, 577 district libraries and some 7,000 commune and village libraries or book cabinets. A further 7,000 reading rooms are attached to Post Offices of Culture run by the Ministry of Posts and Telecommunications (MPT). Over 17,000 libraries and reading rooms operate under the guidance of the Ministry of Education and Training. However, Vietnam's library sector still faces a number of serious challenges, principally at local level where problems of inadequate premises equipment, collections and standards of service, lack of specialist training and standards of services, lack of training and limited application of information technology continue to hamper development (Vietnam Cultural Profile 2006).

While heavily used, Vietnamese public libraries are typically under-resourced and struggle with limited budget, facilities and resources to provide comprehensive information services to the community. According to statistics issued by the Vietnamese Government Ministry of Labour, Invalids and Social Welfare, there are an estimated 5.1 million people in Vietnam with some form of physical disability. Through the support of the Vietnamese government Ministry of Culture and Information, and the active assistance of organizations such as the Force Foundation, the General Sciences Library of Ho Chi Minh City has taken a leadership role in the provision of services to the visually impaired. Although for some time limited to Hanoi and Ho Chi Minh City, these services are now being expanded and delivered throughout the public library system of Vietnam (Bac 2005).

3. GENERAL DISCUSSION

Public libraries are deeply related to the functioning of a legitimate democracy. Governments should recognize the role that libraries have in promoting literacy, economic development, life-long learning and access to information. They should encourage a holistic, cross-functional approach to social inclusion, which includes the services public libraries provide. They should also ensure that public library services are funded appropriately and in a sustainable way to enable this complex and difficult work to be undertaken effectively. The patterns of evaluation of library services are complex and library systems should be devised to more clearly reflect the impact that libraries have in communities, which should not be limited to book borrowing.

Generally speaking, Asian countries share the same experience and confront the same challenges with each other in the following aspects:

3.1 Common Traits

The National Library plays a leading role in pubic library development. Some national libraries function both as a "public library" as well as a "research library." Due to a shortage of staff members, volunteers are heavily used. The use of volunteers can present challenges, but for those with limited resources, the opportunity to contribute to the library in a meaningful way should be perceived as a means of engaging with one's society.

3.2 Problems and Issues

In the twenty-first century public libraries in Asia are currently confronted with unprecedented challenges in terms of operations and management, such as the following: limited resources, expanding user demands, growing competition in the provision of information services and social networking, an enhanced focus on accountability for public sector organizations. In addition, they must come to grips with the following issues:

The learning abilities of children and youngsters are decreasing. They must come up with new ideas and areas of services to help meet the unique needs of Asian children and youth. In particular, they need to recruit children and adolescent librarians to help develop such services. Although there are library standards in Asian countries, they have limited relevance to the types of services offered. There is a lack of financial resources. Providing library services to the public usually requires substantial amounts of money and manpower. However, some local governments are reluctant to invest in libraries.

On the other hand, it is encouraging to see that many innovative projects are being implemented in the Asian countries.

3.3 Innovations

Several countries have undertaken a variety of digital projects, such as Mainland China, Taiwan, Japan and South Korea. New devices include: RFID, which was first introduced in Singapore, and Palm Veins technology, which was first used for library-card holders in Japan. In addition, many e-learning practices are being implemented in Taiwan and some other countries.

4. CONCLUSION AND RECOMMENDATIONS

In the future, public libraries need to demonstrate their value to those that establish and support them. Knowing how to develop a research agenda to support the value of libraries and library services is extremely important. Focus should be placed on the conditions that make for good learning environments, good environments for human relations and interaction, and good environments for promoting literature and reading. Libraries help in nurturing a society of life-long learners who can accelerate the creation of intellectual capital and create a new cycle of national innovation. This is an important factor of competition, one that is much needed for success in a competitive knowledge-based economy.

The problems of the public library are various and continuous. While some appropriate policy directives exist, the level of success in implementing such policies seems to depend on a combination of factors. These include favorable factors relating to organizational structure and resources, just as serious consideration of local concerns and structure contribute to successful implementation. A shift from collection orientation to user-behaviorbehavior orientation should be addressed.

The responsibility of the state and local governments for library management should be highlighted. Public libraries should not only provide a functional space, but create a welcoming social space as well. Effective ways must be devised to maintain community enthusiasm, interest, and involvement in the library project. Community empowerment is therefore recommended. Transforming strategies include: leadership training on topics that include participatory planning and decision making as well as collective actions; active mobilization of community participation in library activities; and the creation of a support system for local initiative and actions.

In addition, the formulation of national information policies should be undertaken. Public librarians need to take on a proactive role in providing appropriate library services for their communities. Librarians should have a thorough knowledge of their own communities in terms of both sociological and psychological aspects. Cooperating closely with other government authorities in the same community is highly recommended. In developing countries, personal relationships remain important and people are still friendly and optimistic. Public librarians should take advantage of this good point to take library services to the grassroots level (Nimsomboon 2003).

It is hoped that the public libraries in Asia would adopt a more pro-active approach in seeking out opportunities to deploy their unique skills, expertise and resources with those who have not traditionally used their services. They should be more vigorous in publicizing the nature and value of the services they provide. They should understand the nature and extent of excluded groups and the ways in which libraries can help them and recognize the potential to be derived from working in partnership with other groups and organizations. They should implement staff training and development programs to enable staff members to be confident in their roles as teachers and mentors in addition to those of information specialists and managers (Parker 2005).

References

Annual Report 2006/2007. National Library Board. Singapore, 2007.

Bac, N. T. (2005). Services for the blind in the public libraries of Vietnam: making Vietnamese public libraries more accessible to visually impaired people. [Online] Available: http://www.ifla.org/IV/ifla71/papers/084e-Nguyen.pdf. Retrieved February 8, 2008.

Background History of the National Library of Myanmar (n.d.) [Online] Available: http://www.myanmar.com/Ministry/culture/text/P002.htm. Retrieved February 11, 2008.

China, Libraries in the People's Republic of. (1968). In: Encyclopedia of Library and Information Science, Vol. 4, pp.627-646. New York: Marcel Dekker.

Connemara Public Library. [Online] Available: http://www. connemarapublic librarychennai.com/History.htm. Retrieved February 8, 2008.

Contemporary Libraries in the Far East. (1978). Encyclopedia of Library and Information Science, Vol. 24. New York: Marcel Dekker, 1978.

Cruz, Prudenciana. (2002). The National Library and the Public Library System in the Philippines. CDNLAO Newsletter, No. 45, November 2002. [Online] Available: http://www.ndl.go.jp/en/publication/cdnlao/045/453.html. Retrieved February 8, 2008.

Dato, Y. Bhg. Zawiyah Binti Baba. (2004). Annual Report to CDNL 2003 – 2004. [Online] Available: http://consorcio.bn.br/cdnl/2004/RTF% 20list/malaysia.rtf. Retrieved October 7, 2007.

Delpi Public Library. [Online] Available:http://www.dpl.gov.in/ welcome.html. Retrieved February 8, 2008.

Evald, Public. Libraries in Laos. [Online] Available: http://www2. db.dk/pe/laos. htm. Retrieved February 9, 2008.

Fujitsu Wins Contract for World's First Library System Using Palm Vein Authentication Technology (2005). [Online] Available: http://www. fujitsu.com/global/ news/pr/archives/month/2005/20051222-01.html. Retrieved October 21, 2007.

Hong Kong Public Libraries. (2006). [Online] Available: http://www.hkpl. gov.hk/english/aboutus/aboutus_intro/aboutus_intro.html. Retrieved October 21, 2007.

Hosono, Kimio. (2006). Changes in University and Public Libraries in Japan. IFLA Journal, 32, 119-130.

Islamabad Public Library. (2002). [Online] Available: http://www. nlp.gov.pk/ html/ipl.htm. Retrieved February 11, 2008.

Japan Library Association. (2005). Public Libraries. [Online] Available: http:// www.jla.or.jp/pub-statis-e.html. Retrieved August 19, 2007.

Japan Library Association. (2007). Service in websites at public libraries [Online] Available: http://www. soc.nii.ac.jp/jla/link/public2.html (in Japanese). Retrieved November 5, 2007.

Kamil, H. (2003) The Growth of Community-based Library Services in Indonesia to Support Education. [Online] Available: http://www.ifla.org/ IV/ifla69/papers/ 115e-Kamil.pdf. Retrieved February 8, 2008.

Khurshid, A. (1990). Library Resources in Pakistan: Progress, Problems, and Achievements. World Libraries Vol. 1, No. 1. [Online] Available: http://www. worlib.org/vol01no1/khurshid_v01n1.shtml. Retrieved February 8, 2008.

Kumbar, B.D. (n.d.) Growth and development of public library system in India with special reference to Karnataka. International workshop on "Democratization of Information: Focus on Libraries". [Online] Available: www.nigd.org/ libraries/mumbai/reports/article-4.pdf. Retrieved February 8, 2008.

Lerdsuriyakul, K. (1999). Public Library in Thailand. IFLA Conference Proceeding, 1999. [Online] Available: http://www.ifla.org/IV/ifla65/papers/106-79e. htm. Retrieved February 8, 2008.

Libraries, Cambodia Cultural Profile, 2006. [Online] Available: http://www. culturalprofiles.net/Cambodia/Directories/Cambodia_Cultural_Profile/- 1332.html. Retrieved February 8, 2008.

Librarianship in Taiwan, 2nd ed. (2007). Comp. by Library Association of the Republic of China & National Central Library. Taipei: National Central Library.

Libraries in Korea: Past, Present and Future. (2006). 2006 Seoul World Library and Information Congress, National Organizing Committee, Seoul, Korea.

Mustafa, Shahaneem & Wilkinson, Neil. (1977). Standards for Public Libraries in Malaysia in Keperluan mengetahui: Perkembangan perkhidmatan perpustaakaan awam bagi masyarakat; the need to know: Developing public library services for the community. Proceedings of a Joint Conference of the Persatuan Perpustakaan Malaysia and the Library Association of Singapore, Petaling Jaya 3-5 March 1977. Edited by D E K Wijasuriya in collaboration with Ch'ng Kim See, Khoo Slow Mun, Shahaneem Mustafa. Kuala Lumpur Persatuan Perpustakaan Malaysia, Library Association of Singapore.

National Library Board Singapore. (2007). [Online] Available: http://www.nlb. gov.sg/annualreport/fy05/01_mission.htm. Retrieved September 15, 2007.

National Taichung Library. (2007). [Online] Available: http://www. ntl.gov.tw/ English/. Retrieved October 21, 2007.

Nimsomboon, N. (2003). The Role of Public Library in Thailand as the Learning Center for Rural Communities. [Online] Available: http://www. kc.tsukuba.ac. jp/colloqium/030219a.pdf. Retrieved February 8, 2008.

NLB Overview. (2007). [Online] Available: http://www.nlb.gov.sg/ CPMS.portal; jsessionid=8jSyGH3MgsLW1PypVTC60MnQryTSs7hv1hJ6JSP67T9YGLgNT

96B!1623628394?_nfpb=true&_pageLabel=CPMS_book_AboutNLB. Retrieved August 19, 2007.

Ogawa, Keiichi. (2007). A New Midterm Program on Yokohama City Library – Advocacy Strategies for Its Innovation. International Conference on Public Library Management and Services Trends. Taipei: Taipei Public Library, October 24, 2007.

Parker, Sandra (2005). The performance measurement of public libraries in Japan and the UK. [Online] Available: http://www.emeraldinsight.com/Insight/View ContentServlet;jsessionid=56A5A64C4B50DF63DB9E8930CF8DE7A3?File name=Published/EmeraldFullTextArticle/Articles/2790070103.html. Retrieved October 21, 2007.

Parker, Sandra. (2005). Public libraries in Japan: a glimpse of the Far East. Update, 4, 33-35.

Priwatrworawute, P. (2000). Mobile libraries in Thailand. IFLA Conference Proceeding, 2000. [Online] Available: http://www.ifla.org/IV/ifla66/papers/ 092-175e.htm, 2007/8/19. Retrieved February 8, 2008.

Rojales, A. B. (2005). National Library of the Philippines creates public electronic library. Access. No.53. [Online] Available: http://www.aardvark net.info/ access/number53/monthnews.cfm?monthnews=05. Retrieved February 8, 2008.

Sacchanand, C. (2007). Status of Librarianship in Thailand. [Online] Available: http://www.tla.or.th/Status_Librarianship_Thailand.pdf. Retrieved February 8, 2008.

Sacchanand, C., Prommapun, B. & Sajjanand, S. (2006). Development of Indicators for Performance Evaluation of Public Libraries in Thailand. Bangkok: Education Council.

Salaladyanant, T. (2006). Digital libraries in Thailand. In C. Khoo, D. Singh & A.S. Chaudhry (Eds.), Proceedings of the Asia-Pacific Conference on Library & Information Education & Practice 2006 (A-LIEP 2006), Singapore, 3-6 April 2006 (pp. 148-155). Singapore: School of Communication & Information, Nanyang Technological University.Shanghai Library in brief. [Online] Available: http://www.library.sh.cn/english/guide/index1.htm. Retrieved February 8, 2008.

Shuva, N. Z. (2003) Public libraries in Bangladesh. [Online] Available: http:// www.pulmanweb.org/pulmanexpress/pulmanexpress_Oct2003.htm#_Toc538933 45. Retrieved February 9, 2008.

Siew, Wai Yeen Valerie. (2007). Engaging active citizenry among ingaporeans, young and old, at the Singapore public libraries. Library Management, 28, 17-26.

Taipei Public Library. (2005). [Online] Available: http://www.tpml. edu.tw/Taipei PublicLibrary/download/english/plan05-10.pdf. Retrieved October 23, 2007.

Toru Koizumi et al. (2003). Librarianship in Japan. In Encyclopedia of Library and Information Science (DOI: 10.1081/E-ELIS 120008590, pp. 1553-1560). New York: Marcel Dekker.

Tseng, Shu-hsien. (2007). The Planning, Construction, and POE of the Beitou Branch of the Taipei Public Library. International Conference on Public Library Management and Services Trends. Taipei: Taipei Public Library, October 24, 2007.

Varaprasad, N., Johnson, Paul, & Kua, Lena. (2006). Gaining Mindshare and Timeshare: Marketing Public Libraries in Singapore. April,19, 31-38.

Vietnam Cultural Profile. (2006). [Online] Available: http://www. culturalpro files.net/Viet_Nam/Directories/Vi_ACYAIw-7879_ADs-t_Nam_Cultural_ Profile/-562.html. Retrieved February 9, 2008.

Wijasuriya, Donald E. K. (n. d.) Performance measures for public libraries. [Online] Available: http://www.unesco.org/webworld/ramp/html/r8722e/ r8722e1e.htm. Retrieved August 19, 2007.

Wu, Jianzhong (2005). Library of the 21st Century. San Francisco: Long River Publishing, 235-242.

Yaacob, R. A. & Seman, N. A. (1998). Library and Information Services in a Multi-lingual and Multicultural Society in Malaysia. [Online] Available: http:// wason.library.cornell.edu/iaol/Vol.43/malaysia.HTM. Retrieved October 7, 2007.

The author would like to acknowledge the kind assistance of Dr. Keiichi Ogawa, Director, and Ms Yumiko Suzuki, Librarian, Yokohama City Central Library.

ACADEMIC LIBRARIES

Trishanjit Kaur

1. INTRODUCTION

The purpose of this chapter is to present a brief account of the history and development of academic libraries in Asia, and to provide an overview of academic libraries in this vast continent of Asia. Academic libraries include college and university libraries. Libraries have been called the "heart" of the university.

According to the United Nations, there are six sub-regions of Asia: Northern Asia, Central Asia, Western Asia, Southern Asia, Eastern Asia, and Southeastern Asia. Hence, the information in the chapter has been organized by region. Information about college libraries is not available for most of the countries, but wherever available it has been incorporated.

2. EARLIEST ACADEMIC LIBRARIES

2.1 Taxila and Nalanda Universities

Taxila University, which is oldest in the world, has been in existence since even before the time of the Buddha during 414 A.D. in the city of Gandhara in northwest India (now in Pakistan). It had an enrollment of 500 students, including princes and a few foreign students. The university had an excellent library. The library collection included works on Hinduism, political science, literature, medicine, and philosophy. The city of Gandhara, including the university and the library, was destroyed during the invasion of Hunas in the middle of the fifth century (Prasher 2002).

Another ancient university was the Nalanda; its name is derived from a Sanskrit term for "giver of knowledge." It was known as an ancient seat of learning. "For Nalanda, though a University was, nevertheless, a monastery."(Sankalia 1972). The university was located about 55 miles south east of Patna (in India) and was a Buddhist center of learning from 427 CE to 1197 CE partly under the Pala Empire. The university was at its peak of reputation and international glory in the ninth century A.D. The university had a splendid library with a collection of invaluable manuscripts and served over 2,000 teachers and 10, 000 students, including many from China, Tibet, Korea, etc. The library was known as Dharmaganja (Piety Mart) and had three buildings in it known as Ratnasagara (Sea of Gems), Ratnodadhi (Ocean of Gems), which was a nine-story building that specialized in rare sacred works, and Ratnaranjaka (Collection of Gems). Nalanda University's library was the biggest in Asia, and it was the first international residential university in the world. The university died a slow death about the time that some of the great European universities, including those in Oxford, England, and Bologna, Italy, were just getting started. Nalanda was destroyed and burnt by the Mohammedans in or about 1205 A.D. All the monks were butchered, and there was no one left to decipher any book from the vast and unique library. A number of ruined structures survive. The accounts of these and many other libraries can be found in the writings of the famous Chinese travellers Fa- Hein, Hiuen-Tsang, and I-Tsing, who visited India in 399 A.D., 629 A.D. and 672 A.D. respectively.

Medieval universities did not exist in Asia in the strict sense of the phrase. However, there were important centers of learning that can be compared to the universities of Europe. Nanjing University and Southeast University (Imperial Nanjing Institute) were founded in 258 in China. There were several other universities called Guozijian in ancient China. In Persia, one important institution was the Academy of Gundishapur. In the Near East, the Islamic Al-Azhar University in Cairo was founded in 988. In Vietnam, the Quoc Tu Giam functioned for more than 700 years from 1076 to 1779.

3. CENTRAL ASIA

Some of the world's earliest and most splendid libraries arose between the 2nd century B.C. and the 16th century along the fabled Silk Road, which linked China with Europe via Central Asia. The Central Asian republics have had much in common, in terms of their culture and history, from the age of nomadic tribes to independence in 1991. Barring Tajikistan, others have the largest number of private universities. Kazakhastan has 114 private and 50 state universities, and Mongolia has 29 private universities, while Tajikistan has only 2 (official) non-state universities. Although all countries of Central Asia have reformed their education system since the fall of the Soviet Union, some have apparently reformed more than others. There are some outstanding Academies of Science Libraries; among them are the library at the Academy of Kazakh (over 3,000,000 volumes), Kirghiz (602,000 volumes), Turkmen (500,000 volumes), and Uzbek (1,500,000 volumes). There is also the library at the Kazakh Polytechnic Institute (210,000 volumes). There are a few university libraries: Fundamental Library of the Kazakh, S.M. Kirov State University (750,000 volumes); Library of the Kirghiz State University (600,000 volumes); the Scientific Library of the Tadzhik, V.I. Lenin State University (300,000 volumes); and the Scientific Library of the Turkmen, A.M. Gorky State University (350,000 volumes).

But many libraries that the now independent states of Central Asia inherited after the collapse of the Soviet Union have over many years fallen victim to neglect, theft, and inadequate funding. Many libraries in Central Asia occupy buildings that are dilapidated and vulnerable to fire and flooding. The basement of the library of Tajikistan's Medical University was inundated during floods in Dushanbe. The University of Central Asia, the world's first internationally chartered institution was founded in 2000 by the governments of Kazakhstan, the Kyrgyz Republic and Tajikistan, and His Highness the Aga Khan.

4. EASTERN ASIA

4.1 China

"The founding of the Metropolitan University Library [now the Beijing University Library] in 1898 marked a new era in the history of Chinese librarianship. Although established under the auspices of the Qing imperial court (1644-1911), it was anything but an imperial library. Typically, Chinese imperial libraries were reserved exclusively for use by imperial rulers and the court. By contrast, as stated in the university regulations, the Metropolitan University Library was created to facilitate the growth of a modern program in higher education. So conceived, this new library would emerge as China's first modern academic library." (Liao 2004). Some scholars date the establishment of the Metropolitan University Library to 1902. This argument is based on the closing of the Metropolitan University, after only two years of its existence, with the Boxer uprising of 1900. Furthermore, although the library was given a name, there is no clear evidence that it was operational during this early period.

Modern academic libraries came into being in China at the start of the 20th century. Academic libraries established in this period were: St. John's University Library (1894), Tianjin West School Library (1895), Nanyang Normal College Library (1897), Peking University Library (1902), Nanjing University Library (1902), Southeast University Library (1902), Lanzhou University Library (1909), Tsinghua University Library (1912), Wuhan University Library (1917) and others. The oldest and biggest national academic library in China is the Peking University (PKU) library, which was founded in 1902 and celebrated its centennial anniversary on October 23, 2002. The university erected a new high-tech library building in 1998. With 6.5 million items, PKU owns the largest university library collection in Asia. The number of national university libraries rose to 20 (with an average collection of 87,426 volumes), while the number of missionary university libraries and private university libraries totalled 28. During the war against Japanese invasion from 1937-1945, many universities moved to the hinterland and carried a small number of collections. During this period many academic libraries were badly destroyed. In 1949, there were 132 academic libraries with a total of 7, 940, 000 volumes. From then on the development of libraries was steady and smooth. The National Plan for Library Coordination was introduced in 1957 by the State Council to promote resource sharing and encourage development of academic libraries. In 1957, the number of university libraries rose to 229 with collections of

14 million items. The Cultural Revolution (1966-1976) saw cuts in budgets for libraries as some university libraries stopped buying books, and subscriptions to periodicals were also discontinued. Construction of academic libraries almost ceased, and some were destroyed. The Reform and Opening–up Policy gave rise to renewed library development. The number of academic libraries was 670 in 1980, and in 1997 the number rose to 1162. China launched the "211 Project" in 1995 supported by the State Commission for Education. One of its two goals is to turn 101 universities into hubs for high –level research and specialization to aid national economic development in the 21st century in China. There are two service networks for helping 96 universities to exchange research information: the China Education and Research Network (CERNET) and China Academic Library and Information System (CALIS). CALIS is a nationwide academic library consortium with members throughout 27 provinces, cities and autonomous regions in China based on the Chinese Education and Research Network (CERNET).

Automation and networking in academic libraries can be divided in three stages. The first stage (late 1970s to mid 1980s) is a starting period towards library automation; the second stage (mid 1980s to early 1990s) is a period of integration of automation systems and local resource networks; and the third stage (from early 1990s on) is the period of networking and digitalization with an emphasis on nation-wide resource sharing. Several digital library projects were launched in September 1999, such as the Peking University Institute of Digital Library. The PKU library is providing digital reference service with Question Point, in addition to the traditional reference service, with the help of 20 reference librarians. Such online reference services are uncommon in China.

There are over 2000 universities and colleges with more than 6 million enrollments in total. Traditionally, academic libraries in China were small in terms of their collection and staff sizes. The libraries, in spite of facing several budget constraints, pay attention to resource sharing. They have formed local, regional, national, international, and speciality library networks to improve library cooperation, services, and resource sharing to meet a variety of needs from their users. The Shanghai Information Resource Network (SIRN) is well known for resource sharing among universities, research institutes, and public libraries in the city of Shanghai.

Academic libraries have more hours of operation than public libraries. Some academic libraries remain open even until midnight. Qualified staff is strengthening reference service. Some libraries are offering virtual reference to users on and off campus by email. Online navigation services to databases, electronic journals, and access to web resources are provided in academic libraries of China. Library orientation is organized for fresh students in the beginning of the session in most university libraries. Information literacy has become a nationwide issue in many educational institutions. Every university library offers an instructional course called "Literature searching and utilization." There are several programs of international exchange and cooperation among university libraries of China with foreign libraries. The academic libraries of China are facing the problems of uneven development, limited resources, management issues like networking, standardization, reengineering of organizations and processes, and integration of human and information resources. The quality of resources and services has been highly improved, libraries have been modernised, and they are playing an important role in teaching and research. "The trend of college and university mergers will continue in China in the next decade" (Huang 2000).

4.2 Japan

The history of academic libraries in Japan begins with the establishment by imperial edict of the Imperial University Library in 1886. The library was affiliated with the predecessor of the present-day Tokyo University, the oldest national university in Japan, founded in 1877. Keio University founded in 1858 and the oldest private university did not establish its library until 1890-four years after the Imperial University library because of a lack of financial support. From such modest beginnings in 1886, by the year 2002 there were 686 four-year universities and 541 colleges in Japan, almost 80% private. There are 1,257 university libraries and 324 college libraries. There are 260 million books and over 3,500 journal titles held in these libraries. Budget for library materials is about 74 billion yen, which accounts for 1.9% of total institutions cost. In most university libraries the bibliographic and holding data of the collection are input to the national database prepared by NII (National Institute of Informatics), which is called NACSIS-CAT. NII is also conducting the document delivery and inter-lending system, NACSIS – ILL. 90% of academic libraries have their own online public catalogue connected to the Internet, and larger university libraries often make available their rare books to the public with their homepage as the electronic library. An accreditation association evaluates universities. From 2002, the Association of the National Universities, contracting with some foreign publishes, is offering access to 2,600 e-journals. University libraries are becoming open until late evening and on holidays to allow working graduate school students and other researchers to access libraries, reflecting the needs of a lifelong education society. In 2003, the National University Corporation Law was enforced, and as a result of which all employees including library staff became non-officials, and the idea of private management policy was also introduced.

Prefectural University of Kumamoto has an impressive library, which consists of about 300,000 volumes (as of March 2006) in a wide variety of specialized fields. For more information visit http://www.pu-kumamoto.ac.jp/guide-e/facilities-e/library-e.htm

Library cooperative programs in Japan have not advanced much, unlike in the USA or European countries (Oshiro 2000).

4.3 Korea

The history of universities in Korea goes back to the Goguryeo Period. Modern university education was introduced in Korea toward the late 19th century. Yonhi College (1885, present-day Yonsei University) and Ewha College (1886, present-day Ewha Women's University), both private schools founded by American missionaries, were the oldest higher education institutions in Korea. By 1948, the year of the constitution of the Republic of Korea, the country had 42 total universities; the list has grown. At the end of 2004, the total number of universities and colleges in Korea was 438, comprised of 61 national and municipal universities and colleges, 200 private universities and colleges and 157 junior colleges offering two to three-year programs. Fourteen of these institutions, including Seoul National University, Yonsei University, the Korea University, and Ewha Women's University, have their own libraries with collections of 1 million volumes or more. The Seoul National University library has the largest collection, including close to 2,500,000 volumes, maintained by a staff of 107 (76 librarians). The next largest collection is 1,600,000 volumes at Kyungpook National University in Daegu. Automation, and it has quickly become a norm among university libraries. They are undergoing transition from traditional print-based resources to digital formats. The most notable change in Korea's university libraries is the composition of collections. The dwindling importance of humanities and social sciences in higher education in favour of scientific and technological fields has led to a diminishing share of printed books, eroded by academic journals, online databases and multimedia materials. Many universities are using RFID technology.

In the early 1960s, there were only two publicly funded institutions of higher education, namely the University of Hong Kong and the Chinese University of Hong Kong. By 1996-97 there were 8 universities and colleges all under the aegis of UGC. The individual library catalogues of the 8 UGC institutions are linked together with Z39.50 software to form a virtual union catalogue.

4.4 Taiwan

According to a survey in 1967, there were 64 college and university libraries in Taiwan. They had a combined holding of 3,281,069 volumes, serving 85, 346 students. During 2005-06, there were 60 general universities, 10 colleges and 29 technology universities, 46 colleges, and 17 Junior colleges bringing the total to 162. The National Taiwan University Library was established in 1928. It has two physically separate branches: the Law Library and the Medical Library, and also 33 divisional and departmental libraries. The library collection includes books, periodicals, pamphlet and audiovisual materials in a wide range of fields including the humanities, the sciences, law, medicine, engineering, agriculture, management, public health, electrical engineering and social sciences. The library collection presently includes more than 2,400,000 periodicals and 98 newspapers. It is the largest library collection in Taiwan. In addition, the library has over 50,000 rare books in Chinese and other languages, the largest such holding of any university library in Taiwan.

4.5 Macau

Macau, as a Portuguese colony in Asia, has been a bridge between the Western and Eastern cultures for more than 4,000 years. The College of St. Paul, the first western university in the Far East was founded here in 1594. People were generally not interested in higher education before the University of Macau was founded in 1992. The University of Macau library constructed in 1999 is the largest in the territory but also one of the most wired and technologically advanced library structures. It is a five-story building that has a working space area of 15,000 m^2 and a seating capacity of approximately 400. The print collection includes 210,000 volumes of monographs, 4000 periodical titles, and 12,000 volumes of old Chinese editions. There are also the historical archives, which mainly hold documents about Macau history. The university library has Internet connectivity and provides reference service and has an audio-video center, but it is struggling with the problem of a multilingual collection for different users belonging to different cultures.

5. WESTERN ASIA

The social and economic changes in Georgia, Armenia and Azerbaijan since the breakup of the Soviet Union have caused great upheaval in libraries there. Libraries are currently undergoing wide-ranging reforms intended to make their collections more accessible and to integrate themselves into the global information network (Gibradze 2001). The South Caucasian libraries are also automating, elaborating new national cataloguing rules and agreeing on standards for electronic data interchange. The most ancient manuscripts of the Azerbaijani language go back to the fourteenth and fifteenth centuries. The Ministry of Education administers 4,000 academic and school libraries. Libraries typically have closed stacks, and the collections themselves are not selected. The libraries also are rarely automated and make little use of technologies, which would connect them to other libraries around the world. Lack of necessary technology, computers, reliable telephone systems, and effective systems of international communication prevent the Azerbaijani librarians from accessing the global information network. Bahrain has two academic universities: Arabian Gulf University and University of Bahrain.

5.1 United Arab Emirates (UAE)

UAE University libraries were founded during 1977-78. In the beginning classification was done with the help of Dewey decimal classification. During 1988 automation of library services began. In 1990 the University was reorganized and the Libraries Administration became the University Libraries Deanship, which launched a major project to modernize its services in 1992. The university libraries include various locations for men and women separately. The resources available in the university libraries include books, periodicals, reports, electronic resources and microfiche. Books and periodicals are distributed to the branches according to the subjects covered at a specific branch, and the first copy of each book is available at Zayed Central Library. There are 300,202 volumes of Arabic books, 139,449 volumes of non-Arabic books, 17,634 titles of electronic journals and 345 manuscripts.

5.2 Kuwait

In 1966 Kuwait University (KU) established the central library on the Khalida Campus. The holdings included periodicals, the national heritage library, and a United Nations publications library. Since then eight libraries have been established at various other campuses of Kuwait University. The KUL's collection contains approximately 347,429 volumes of Arabic and non-Arabic monographs, and reference materials in different branches of knowledge. It provides access to 61 bibliographic and full-text databases.

5.3 Turkey

Although the history of the development of Turkish universities dates back to the 15th century, the development of modern university libraries occurred only in the 1950s when the Middle East Technical University (METU) was founded in 1956 in Ankara. METU Library was the first one that was based on the American campus system, thereby providing central library services for all students and faculty. There are 70 public and private universities in Turkey. The existing academic library services are not satisfactory. University library collections and budgets are rather limited, as the total number of items held in all university libraries is around five million, which is less than what an average American university library owns. Almost one third of university libraries own fewer than 500 periodical titles. There is a budget shortage, and universities spend between 0.2% and 3.8% with the average being 0.7%. In addition, there has been a great divide between libraries of developed and developing universities in terms of average expenditure per student. The funds are not sufficient even to purchase a core collection of books and periodicals let alone develop electronic information collections. Efforts are under way for interlibrary cooperation in Turkish university libraries to share electronic information resources by forming a consortium.

6. SOUTH EASTERN ASIA

More than half the universities in the Southeast Asian region have been established since World War II. When the war began, only one university in Indonesia had started functioning. In the 1960s, there were eight state universities and private universities. In the present territories of Cambodia and the Republic of Vietnam, there were no universities before the war. Three secular universities as well as a Buddhist and a small Catholic university were established later.

6.1 Brunei

Universiti Brunei Darussalam Library was established in 1985, after the taking over of the facilities of the then Sultan Hassanal Bolkiah Institute of Education (SHBIE) Library in Gadong. In 1994 when UBD moved to its new campus, the Library was endowed with a modern, large, functional and elegant building located on an elevated site overlooking the South China Sea. The library members have the privilege to access the eLibrary Portal, where more relevant information can be found. For further information, please see http://www.nla.gov.au/lap/2001brunei.html

6.2 Burma

In Burma, before 1920 there were only two college libraries belonging respectively to the Rangoon College and the Judson College, and then affiliated with the University of Calcutta (India). The University of Rangoon was founded in 1920; there was no separate university library until 1930. The two college libraries were managed by the respective colleges while the university library was placed under the direct control of University of Rangoon. To avoid overlapping of collections, a policy was chalked out in which it was defined which library is to procure what type of reading material according to the nature of the college and university. These three libraries were severely destroyed during the war. Later after the war, in 1946 when the university was restored, the two college libraries were not reopened, and only a single university library came into existence. In 1960 it held 60,000 volumes and nearly 500 titles of periodicals and newspapers including gifts received from the Asia Foundation, the Rockefeller Foundation, the British Council, USSR, and Peoples' Republic of China. For purposes of loan and reference, the library service was divided into two sections. The General Section rendered lending and general reference services, while the Research Section provided only reference services. The library had close access but not for teachers, honor students, and post-graduate students. Qualified library staff was limited. There were departmental libraries that managed their own collections, but books were acquired by the main library.

Burma's other university, the University of Mandalay, was founded in 1958 from the former College of Agriculture, a pre-war intermediate college of the University of Rangoon, which after the war had been giving degrees. In addition there is Moulmein College too.

The libraries of these two universities and the college have grown and improved over the years. The libraries conduct literature searches, maintain union catalogues of holdings on campus, and prepare and publish bibliographies. A notable activity is the library orientation program at Rangoon Institute of Technology, where library training has also been incorporated into the curriculum. Burma's academic libraries are decentralized, but during late 1970's decentralization appears to have given way to attempts at centralization.

The Online Burma/Myanmar Library launched in October 2001 is a database that functions as an annotated, classified and hyperlinked index to full texts of individual Burma documents on the Internet. It holds links to individual documents and websites. The library is using Greenstone digital library software to build the collection of documents housed on-site. This software allows full-text searching. The library's starting point was the Burma Peace Foundation's documentation of the human rights situation in Burma, and with the UN Burma material, this area still comprises about half the total number of items.

6.3 Cambodia

"From 1863 to 1954 Cambodia was a French colony" (Bywater 1997). In the colonial period Cambodia was amalgamated with Vietnam and Laos for most purposes, and the common university for the whole area was at Hanoi.

Royal University was founded in 1960; much of the teaching was done by foreign professors. While the renovation of the building was going on, the library operated from one small classroom. The new university library was completed at the end of 1996. Collection development for the central library (now the Hun Sen Library) began in 1992, and the first priority was to establish a sound Reference Library. Now the Hun Sen Library has the best reference collection as compared with any other library in Cambodia. Before the bulk collection of the university library was comprised of old, out-of-date material and typed or handwritten books known as "Cours." These "Cours" were course notes that had been prepared by teachers over the years. A collection as a gift was also received by the library, but the staff are not competent enough to handle it. Hun Sen Library currently has 2000 Khmer books, 10,000 English books and 400 French books with a staff of 12 librarians and 2 expatriate librarians. There are many every day hindrances to cope with like power failure and delay in shipments of reading material.

The Buddhist Institute was established in 1930 but had its origin in the Cambodian Library founded by King Sisowath in 1921, from 1925 known as the Royal Library. After being destroyed once, now the library has 3,240 volumes in Khmer and 2,852 mostly in English and some in French. The University of Cambodia renamed its library the Toshu Fukami Library on April 30, 2004. It is considered to be one of the best libraries in Cambodia with a collection of over 50,000 books, periodicals, magazines, and newspapers.

6.4 Indonesia

Indonesian university libraries show the continental European bias for highly decentralized and close access systems, while the university libraries in Malaysia and Singapore are patterned on British models (Huck-Tee 1982). More centralized university library services remain to be developed as many universities still maintain departmental libraries in the late 1970s. Most of the colleges and universities and their libraries in Indonesia are comparatively young, especially those outside Java. The implementation of digital libraries among Indonesian academic libraries is developing. Of 52 state universities, less than 50 per cent have been digitizing their documents. The use of digital libraries is restricted to a limited few, mainly situated on the island of Java. Academic libraries have printed collection, some are becoming hybrid, and a few are digitising their documents. More and more universities are becoming member of the Indonesian Digital Library Network.

6.5 Malaysia

In Malaysia there are technical colleges, colleges of further education, and teacher training colleges. Some of the university libraries are outstanding. These include the University of Malaya (established in 1959), Universiti Sains Malaysia (1969), Universiti Kebangsaan Malaysia (1970), Universiti Pertanian Malaysia (1971), and Universiti Teknoloji Malaysia (1972). Two recent universities are Universiti Utara Malaysia (1984) and the International Islamic University (1983), which is co-sponsored by a number of countries. On the whole university libraries are better funded than other libraries in the country.

6.6 Singapore

Nanyang University was established in 1955 with donations of people from all walks of life from Singapore and the region. In 1980, it merged with the University of Singapore to form the National University of Singapore. In 1991 Nanyang Technological Institute became Nanyang Technological University (NTU). During April 2006, NTU was incorporated as an autonomous university. The NTU library has more than half a million books and is growing at about 40,000 volumes per year. Students and staff can borrow up to 10 or 40 books. The electronic resources collection is comprised of 150 subscribed databases and 27,000 e-journal titles. It can be accessed from anywhere with only a password required. The library has state-of-the art facilities.

6.7 Vietnam

Vietnam's libraries have long endured conditions that in any developed country would be considered totally unacceptable. The oldest libraries were formed in the 11th century. Later the development of libraries was under French colonialism, the post-colonial period, the period of reconstruction (1975-1985), and the modern period (1985-1998). The academic library system consists of more than 250 colleges and universities in Vietnam. Some academic libraries have modernized their infrastructures (like Polytechnic University, the University of Hanoi, and the National Economic University). Two main factors that have influenced library development in Vietnam are the change in the national economy from a centralized to a market structure that has created new information requirements, and the collapse of communist nations like the Soviet Union that ended the flow of Russian language collections to Vietnam's libraries.

7. SOUTH ASIA

It is felt by some that higher education has expanded too fast in South Asian countries. It is practically nonexistent in Maldives and Bhutan. India has one of the largest education systems in the world, and its student population exceeds the total population of some of the countries of the world.

7.1 Afghanistan

As is well known, but perhaps little understood in its entirety, the last quarter century has been a catastrophe for Afghanistan at every level. The first College establishing Kabul University was instituted as early as 1932. During the 1950s and 1960s the Kabul University was one of the finest institutions of its kind in Asia, the intellectual heart of the country and pride of Afghanistan. But the entire system was gutted by 1994. By 1995, six universities were functioning with libraries that had outdated collections and no funds for acquisition. Trained librarians were not available. This university library was affected most disastrously as "50 percent of its once truly great collection was looted or burned by fires set by rockets. By some reports this amounted to 150,000 books and 6000 periodicals" (Dupree 1999).

According to Rawan (2005) there are 21 institutions of higher learning; four are located in Kabul and others throughout the country. There are 91 colleges and six regional universities in the country. Kabul University library received 60,000 new books, bookshelves, and other equipment from the Asia Foundation and other organizations. The library building was without cooling, heating, and an adequate lighting system. But now the main library of Kabul University is the best-equipped library in Afghanistan. It is equipped with computers, books, etc. donated by Iran. Iran has also helped in the training of library staff. There is a comparatively newer library facility at Afghanistan University of Education. This library is clean and attractive and has committed library employees and faculty. The Nangarhar University is one of the largest universities in Afghanistan. The library has about 18,000 books; most of these are in Arabic. In the past, exchange programs with international libraries, including the Library of Congress, Leningrad library, Tehran and others were generous. These programs no longer function. Replacement and updating of materials in all university libraries is an urgent requirement. Training of librarians is another challenge to be met.

University of Arizona (Tucson) librarian Atifa Rawan has been working in Afghanistan on library policy since 2002. Since then she has revamped four of the city's university libraries, and in 2005 outfitted Kabul University's agriculture library with a technology center and access to agricultural databases such as AGORA and TEEAL (Garner 2007:53).

7.2 Bangladesh

The history of establishment of colleges in Bangladesh goes back to 1841 when Dhaka College was established. Up to 1943, there were about 32 colleges in the country. According to a survey conducted by the Bangladesh Bureau of Educational Information and Statistics (BANBEISI) in 1995, there were 230 government colleges and 915 non-government general colleges in Bangladesh. The condition of libraries in almost all these institutions is unsatisfactory as required for the purpose of affiliation with the college only. There are also libraries with different professional colleges like Medical, Engineering, Agriculture and different training institutes. Except for the Engineering and Agriculture field, libraries in other institutions are poor in collection, organization and staff positions.

According to Chowdhury (1993:165) 95% of the colleges in the country do not have any separate library building. The library is housed in a damp room with scanty supply of light and air that is unsuitable for users. Most libraries do not have reading room facilities, they do not have sufficient furniture and equipment, and their books are in short supply. A few colleges have a large collection of books, but most of them are out dated, obsolete and dilapidated. Books written in English do not find any readers, and no college, irrespective of level and number of students, receives on average more than Taka 13,000 per year for the purchase of books from the government. Of 230 government colleges, only 17 have qualified professional librarians in them. The majority of the college libraries are run by either sub-professional or non-professional librarians.

The universities in Bangladesh are divided into four categories: general, special, open and affiliating. The history of university libraries in Bangladesh goes back to the establishment of Dhaka University in 1921. The Dhaka University library has 5,500,000 books and magazines. There are now 13 universities; in addition there are 15 non-government private universities approved by the University Grants Commission, of which only North-South University (with the best library where a Library of Congress Classification system is used) and Independent University have any mentionable libraries. The libraries in other private universities are yet to grow properly. Another modern university library is at Bangladesh University of

Engineering and Technology and has 320,000 volumes. It provides bibliographic and abstracting service, current awareness service, and document delivery service, photocopying service and a CD-ROM search service. As compared with public and other academic libraries, the condition of university libraries in Bangladesh is just satisfactory regarding their collections, manpower and services. Due to available resources, the deficiency of high calibre and skilled staff, poor modernization of the facilities and the lack of a union catalogue, the university libraries in Bangladesh fail to attract the potential library user into becoming a habitual one. On the other hand, Bangladesh has a National Policy on Information Communication Technology.

7.3 Bhutan

The Royal University of Bhutan's Sherbutse College has been an affiliate of the University of Delhi (India) since 1983. Sherubtse College library was inaugurated on April 26, 1989. It is the largest and the oldest academic library in the country. The Shercol library has 30,000 volumes of books and more than 100 journals and magazines. There are about ten newspaper subscriptions including three Bhutanese newspapers both in English and Dzongkha. The books are arranged according to the Dewey Decimal Classification System. The library is fully automated. The AUTOLIB software system from India is being used for this purpose. The search engine is used for simple as well as advanced searches with Boolean terms.

7.4 India

India could take pride in being one of the pioneers in higher education. From the original Nalanda (3rd-12th century A.D.) to the recent rebuilding of Nalanda, the journey has been rather long and tough for universities in India. In the medieval period, Muslim rulers established madrasahas (colleges). They had their own libraries, but access to the educational facilities was limited to only a few privileged people and scholars. The development of higher education in general and academic libraries in particular continued during the British period but at a slower rate. Many colleges during the early 1800s were without libraries, and no proper efforts were made to establish libraries in colleges with a few exceptions. Woods Education Despatch of 1854 is considered the *Magna Carta* of English education in India. On the recommendations of the Woods Education Commission, three modern universities in the cities of Bombay, Calcutta, and Madras were established on the model of London University. Libraries followed later. It was the leadership of Dr. S.R. Ranganathan that made India library conscious. To Indians, Dr. S.R. Ranganathan was what Melville Dewey was to Americans and James Brown to the English. UGC was established in 1953 to look after the development of higher education. There are four types of colleges: government, privately-managed, university colleges, and professional colleges. There are now 17,700 colleges in India. Most of the college libraries have inadequate library collections. There is both open and closed access. Only a lending service is provided, and there is hardly any reference service in college libraries. A few college libraries maintain a catalogue and provide user education.

The Indian universities are basically of two types: unitary and affiliating. There are about 350 universities in India at different stages of development. There is a mixture of universities, as there are traditional universities, and professional/technical institutions including forestry, dairy, fisheries, veterinary science, medicine, engineering and technology, information technology, journalism, law, and open universities. Specialization includes women's universities, popular sciences, regional languages, music and fine arts, statistics and yoga. In addition, there are "Deemed–to-be Universities" and "Institutions of National Importance.". Various commissions and committees were set up from time to time to find out how college and university libraries were doing, and valuable recommendations were suggested by them relating to finance, collection, staff, services, etc.

The UGC set up the Information Library Network (INFLIBNET) for networking, automation and modernizing the libraries of UGC-funded universities, colleges and institutions. INFLIBNET is funding and providing access to e-resources and conducting user orientation programs, training etc. About 35% university libraries are automated. Maintenance of libraries is affected due to lack of funds, insufficient space, lack of trained manpower, mind set of authorities, lack of infrastructure, and lack of latest resources.

The National Knowledge Commission set up by the Prime Minister on June 13, 2005 is a high level advisory body with the objective of transforming India into a knowledge society. It has recommended, in addition to other important recommendations, that by 2015 there will be 1500 universities and 50 central universities.

7.4.1 Re-building of Nalanda in India: a dream or a reality

Like the mythical phoenix, Nalanda University is all set to rise from the ruins. The idea for the university's revival was first mooted by former President of India A.P.J. Abdul Kalam, but it is likely to move as proposed gradually from being a US $1000,000 dream to becoming a reality. The proposed university will be situated 16 kilometres from the ruins of Nalanda. The Nalanda Mentor Group (NMG), which is headed by Nobel laureate Amartya Sen, is overseeing the revival project. The proposed university will be fully residential, like the ancient Nalanda seat of learning and will not be a monastic center. Its vision is based on a global philosophy while maintaining local relevance. The earliest year of functioning will probably be the academic year 2009-10, but it is yet to be sorted out and is not going to be smooth sailing for the new Nalanda.

7.5 Maldives

The Republic of Maldives is at a developing stage, and there is only a small body of supporting academic and professional literature about librarianship. UntilUntil 2001 there were no university-qualified librarians in the country. "However, the library system in the Maldives is still in a state of development and there are no libraries that are of 'world standard.' Most of the operations in the existing libraries are manual. Inadequate finance, shortage of qualified library staff, and poor professional status of library staff, are the major constraints on the growth, development, proper management and functioning of libraries in Maldives" (Gross and Riyaz 2004). The Maldives College of Higher Education is the only academic college and has the largest collection in the country. It was raised to the status of a university in 2007.

7.6 Nepal

A modern education system started in Nepal after the victory of the revolution of 1950 and the restoration of democracy. Campus libraries started with the establishment of the Trichandra campus library in 1918. This library was established with a collection of 15,000 volumes of books kept in locked cases. There are five universities at present in Nepal. Under Tribhuvan University (TU), there are 13 campus libraries in the eastern region, six in middle development region, 22 in Kathmandu valley, five in mid-western development region, and three in the far western region. In total there are 60 campus libraries in TU. Tribhuvan University Central Library (TUCL) established in 1959 is the largest library in Nepal in terms of space, collection, service, staff, library members, equipment and activities. It has over 3 00,000 volumes of books including 550 rare manuscripts, and 7,000 rare books and archival materials. There are OPAC, Internet, online journals, CD-ROMs, e-resources etc. The library is trying to modernize itself and develop into one of the best libraries in Nepal. It has also been compiling the Nepalese National Bibliography since 1981. It is also planning a network of university libraries with the financial support from UGC.

Kathmandu University is a private university and providing modern library services. It is using SOUL software for the automation of the library. Three other universities are providing basic library services but lack space, funds and staff.

7.7 Pakistan

The first university to be set up in Pakistan (before partition in 1947) was the Punjab University at Lahore in 1882. The University of Sindh, Jamshoro got its charter in April 1947. The growth of universities remained slow until 1968 as only 7 universities were established by then. "There are 55 universities and degree awarding institutions in the public sector, and 1,313 general and professional colleges throughout the country" (Mahmood, 2005). The National Education Policy (1998-2010) continues to place emphasis on higher education facilities.

The situation of university libraries in Pakistan is very dismal as a majority of the libraries in universities consist of a few hundred books and a few local popular magazines. Some even did not subscribe to a single standard journal. The criteria for the establishment of new universities were revised by Federal Cabinet on February 27, 2002. It recommended that before granting a charter to a university, both in the private and public sector, the library should have subscriptions to at least fifteen current journals of international repute, plus access to electronic journals. In addition, availability of at least 1500 books from major international publishers in relevant fields was made an essential condition. There are three organizational models of library service in universities of Pakistan: a strong central library, a decentralized library service, and a central library with department libraries. Like in India, the latter is the most popular organizational pattern in Pakistan. "University libraries in Pakistan are beset with an abundance of problems in almost every aspect of academic library development" (Haider 2004). The collection is inadequate in these university libraries. The oldest, Punjab University Library, has about 410,000 volumes; in other libraries the collection is half or less than half of this library. The number of journal subscriptions has fallen substantially. Readers' services are poorly developed, and often only reading room and lending services are given. A few libraries have organized reference sections but rarely other services like inter-library loan or the preparation of bibliographies are given. There are inadequate physical facilities, inadequate financial support, an absence of cooperative programs, and limited application of computer technology by libraries. Lately, a few universities have made efforts towards using information technology in libraries.

7.8 Sri Lanka

This country has one of the most literate populations amongst developing nations. There are no colleges in Sri Lanka, as secondary education is provided in schools only. University education is strictly controlled by the government; only a few institutes are truly autonomous. Most of the state universities depend on funds given by the UGC, as it is their primary and sometimes only source of funding. Sri Lanka has 16 large public universities, important ones being the University of Colombo, the University of Kelania, the University of Peradeniya, and the University of Jaffna to name a few. There is a lack of space in these institutions and an unwillingness to establish private universities. The University of Peradeniya is the heir to the oldest university tradition in Sri Lanka as the successor to the University of Ceylon, the first institution of its kind in the country. It was founded on July 1, 1942 as an autonomous corporation. From 30,000 volumes in 1942, the library collection has grown to 404,415 volumes by end of 2006.

"The use of computers in the libraries of Sri Lanka since the 1980s has resulted in the computerisation of collections and CD-ROM, internet, e-mail facilities etc.

have been made available in some libraries to varying extents. However, up to the present time there is no single library in the public sector, which is fully computerised. There is a need for university libraries to formulate a strategic plan for the automation specially taking into consideration their large collection of library material" (Illeperuma 2001).

8. CONCLUSION

After going through this chapter, it is clear that political, economic, religious, and educational factors have an impact on the growth and development of academic libraries and their services in different countries. University libraries all over are facing common problems of escalating prices and shrinking budgets, the application and integration of ICTs in libraries, problems arising due to instability of technology, preservation, lifelong learning of library personnel, resource sharing and networking, and copyright issues to name a few.

India and China, the two most populous countries in the world and falling in Asia, have the largest networks of education institutions. India expanded higher education at a relatively low cost but at a much faster rate. Chinese university libraries give great emphasis to establishing exchange and cooperative relationships with overseas libraries. The last two decades has seen a steady growth in Chinese academic libraries, at a pace coinciding with the overall development of society. The buildings have improved, and automation keeps pace with the changes all over. There are only a few academic libraries in Japan that have a collection development policy. Academic libraries were computerized earlier than the public or school libraries. Copyright is an important issue to be addressed caused by document delivery via telecommunications. Korea's university libraries rely heavily on foreign materials for information resources.

The high gender-inequality nations of South Asia, particularly Pakistan, Nepal and Bhutan, remain at the bottom in terms of socio-economic development. Religion is cited as the biggest hindrance in ensuring gender equalities. South Asian countries lag far behind the East Asian countries in the sphere of higher education. Sri Lanka has ignored higher education. But India and China will surely play a more important role in assisting educational modernization and globalization by not only just opening more colleges and universities, but also by addressing the issues hampering the growth of academic libraries in providing effective and efficient library services. Technology is definitely going to dominate in the organization of university libraries and disseminating information.

References

Bywater, Margaret A. (1997). Libraries in Cambodia: rebuilding a past and a future. 63rd IFLA General Conference- Conference Programme and Proceedings- August 31-September 5, 1997. [Online] Available: http://www.ifla.org/IV/ifla63/63bywm.htm. Retrieved January 17, 2008.

Chowdhury, Shafiqur Rahman (1993). *Importance and role of school and college libraries in Bangladesh.* Proceedings of Library Association of Bangladesh seminar on preparing the librarians and libraries of Bangladesh for the 21st century.

Dupree, Nancy (1999). "Libraries in Afghanistan". *International Preservation: A Newsletter of the IFLA Core Programme on Preservation and Conservation,* no. 19, July, 22.

Garner, Anne (2007). "Rebuilding Afghanistan...one book at a time". *American Libraries*, November.

Gibradze, Leila (2001). "Libraries in the South Caucasus". *Slavic & East European Information Resources,* vol.2, issue1.

Gross, Julia and Riyaz, Aminath (2004). "An academic library partnership in the Indian Ocean region". *Library Review*, vol.53, no.4, 220-227.

Haider, Syed Jalaluddin (2004). "Coping with change: issues facing university libraries in Pakistan". *The Journal of Academic Librarianship*, vol.30, no.3

Huck-Tee, L.(1982). Library education and the practitioner: university libraries. *In*: Library education programmes in developing countries with special reference to Asia. Ed by Russell Bowden. London: K.G.Saur, 43.

Huang, Hong-Wei (2000). "College and university mergers: impact on academic libraries in China". *College & Research Libraries*, March, 122.

Illeperuma, Sriyani (2001). "Sri Lankan university libraries in the new millennium". *Sri Lanka Library Review,* vol.14, no.2.

Illeperuma, Sriyani (2001). "Sri Lankan university libraries in the new millennium". *Sri Lanka Library Review,* vol. 15, no.1.

Liao, Jing.(2004) "The Genesis of the Modern Academic Library in China: Western Influences and the Chinese Response". *Libraries & Culture* Vol. 39, No. 2, Spring, pp. 161-174. [Online] Available: http://muse.jhu.edu/journals/libraries_ and_culture/v039/39.2liao.html. Retrieved February 12, 2008.

Mahmood, Khalid etc. (2005). "Library funding in Pakistan: a survey". *Libri*, vol. 55

Manzoor, Suhail (1985). "Academic libraries in Iraq." *International Library Review*, vol. 17.

Oshiro, Zensei (2000). "Cooperative programes and networking in Japanese academic libraries". *Library Review,* vol.49, no.8.

Prasher, R.G. (2002). *India's university libraries: organization, operation, and services.* Ludhiana: Medallion Press.

Rawan, Atifa (2005). Rebuilding the library infrastructure: Kabul University libraries assessment, implementation, and challenges and issues, February (via e-mail).

Sankalia, H. D. (1972). *The Nalanda university*. Delhi: Oriental, 26.

Silcock, T.H. (1964). *Southeast Asian university: a comparative account of some development problems*. Durham, North Carolina: Duke University Press.

Wu, Jianzhog and Huang, Ruhua (2003). "The academic library development in China". *The Journal of Academic Librarianship*, vol.29, no.4.

Additional reading

Akhtar, Hanif (1981). "University librarianship in Pakistan: problems and prospects". *Pakistan Library Bulletin*, vol.12, no.3-4.

Aman, Mohammed M. (1992). "Libraries and information systems in the Arab Gulf states: after the war". *Journal of Information Science*, vol.18, no.6

Ansari (Mohaghegh), N. (1974). *National planning and academic libraries in western Asia*. IFLA.

Blandy, Susan Griswold (1994). *Racial and ethnic diversity in academic libraries: multicultural issues*. Routledge.

Gorton, Tony (1979). "The development of academic libraries and librarianship in Thailand, 1950-1976." Journal of Librarianship and Information Science, vol.11, no.1.

Hasegawa, T. (1997). "Subscription trends of foreign journals at university libraries in Japan". *Asian Libraries*, vol.6, no.12.

Hitoshi, Kamada (2002). "East Asian collections and organizational transformation in academic libraries". *College & Research Libraries*, vol.63, no.2.

Hosono, Kimio (2006). "Changes in university and public libraries in Japan". *IFLA Journal*, vol.32, no.2.

Hussain, Imtiaz (1998). "Raping the libraries of Kabul". *Diplomat Magazine*, vol.8, no.6.

Kaser, David (1969). *Library development in eight Asian countries*. Metuchen, N.J.: Scarecrow Press.

Khalil, S. (2001). "On-line resource sharing in Pakistan". *Pakistan Library Bulletin,* vol. 32, no.3-4.

Khurshid, Anis (2000). *Planning and management of library and information services in Pakistan*. Karachi: Library and Information Services Group.

Kim, Y. (1960). *The role of the university in national development: four Asian case studies*. New Delhi: Vikas.

Mahmood, K. (1998). *Information technology in libraries: a Pakistani perspective*. Lahore: Pak Book Corporation.

Patel, Jashu (2004). *Libraries and librarianship in India*. Westport, Connecticut: Greenwood Press.

Ping, Ke (2002). "Toward continual reform: progress in academic libraries in China". *College & Research Libraries.*

Piyadasa, T. G. (1985). *Libraries in Sri Lanka: their origin and history from ancient times to the present times.* Delhi: Sri Satguru Publications.

Rahin, Abdul Rasoul (1998). "The situation of Kabul University library: its past and present". *World Libraries*, vol.8, no. 2.

Siddiqui, Moid A. (1997). "The use of information technology in academic libraries in Saudi Arabia". *Journal of Librarianship and Information Science*, vol.29, no.4.

Stoker, David (1992). "The development of academic libraries in Indonesia". *Journal of Librarianship and Information Science*, vol.24, no.1.

Tanake, H. (1973). "University libraries in Japan-present state and problems". *International Library Review*, vol.5, no.2.

Yasui, Yumiko (2005). Digital reference services of university libraries in Japan. [Online] Available:

http://iadlic.nul.nagoya-u.ac.jp/archives/IADLC 2005/yasui.pdf.

Retrieved February 12, 2008.

Welch, T.F. (1997). *Libraries and librarianship in Japan.* Westport, CT: Greenwood Press.

Wu, Jianzhong (2003). "The academic library development in China". *The Journal of Academic Librarianship*, vol.29, issue 4.

The author would like to acknowledge the valuable inputs of Dr. Kanwal Ameen, Mr. Royce Wiles, Mr. Jared Camins-Esakov, and Ms. Bina Vaidya.

SPECIAL LIBRARIES

Anthony W. Ferguson and Chihfeng P. Lin

1. WHAT IS A SPECIAL LIBRARY?

There are both narrow and broad definitions of a special library: Ellis Mount in a 1991 text published by the American Special Libraries Association defined them as "information organizations sponsored by private companies, government agencies, not-for profit organizations, or professional associations" (Mount 1991). On the other hand, the bylaws of the Special Libraries Association revised in 2005 provided a much broader perspective when it described special librarians as "information professionals dedicated to putting knowledge to work to attain the goals of their organizations ... employed most frequently by corporations, private businesses, government agencies, museums, colleges, hospitals, associations, and information management consulting firms." (What is a special librarian?) In any event, special libraries differ from public, school and academic libraries in that they serve a fairly narrow clientele and their emphasis is on providing answers to the questions ("putting knowledge to work") and not on educating their patrons on how to find the information as is usually the case in most other types of libraries.

The purpose of this chapter is not to deal with special libraries generally, but to look at them in the context of the Asian region. Asia, of course, can mean many things to many people. Because the authors live in Hong Kong and Taiwan, we will provide fairly detailed information about the condition of special libraries in these two parts of Asia, but we have also provided brief descriptions about the situations in a number of Asian countries to provide a broader picture of how these libraries are developing.

Are there many special libraries in Asia? While we have not done a country-by-country search of the literature to answer this question, the simple answer is "yes." For example, as early as 1992 when the *Directory of Southeast Asian Academic & Special Libraries* was published, there were 20 non-college/university special libraries listed for Hong Kong, 30 for Indonesia, etc. For Hong Kong this figure represents only a fraction of the number of special libraries that now exist. In the Hong Kong Library Association's Hong Kong Libraries Gateway online directory (Hong Kong Library Association) released in 2007. Hong Kong Libraries Gateway, http://dir.hkla.org/Browse_by_type.php) the following numbers were extracted as Table 9-1 (there is some overlap in the figures, e.g. hospital libraries and medical libraries.):

Table 9-1. Types and Numbers of Special Libraries in Hong Kong (2007)

Special Libraries Type	No. Libraries
Government	123
Hospital	104
Medical	84
Special	173
Theological	101

So, another characteristic of special libraries is their large number. In Hong Kong, for example, while there are hundreds of special libraries, there are only eight government sponsored university libraries and only a handful of independent college libraries.

Functionally, what is "special" about a special library? Like in all libraries, special libraries' staff members select, buy, arrange, preserve and provide help to clients. What's frequently different is the narrow focus of the information of interest to the special library's clientele, the likely possibility that the special librarian might need to do everything – the need to be a "one man band," and the lack of space and resources to collect broadly to have a broad range of information resources ready at hand just in case someone asks a question about them. These factors make the life of a special librarian stressful but on-the-job boredom is not a problem often encountered.

In the area of collection development and acquisitions, for example, there is generally a much greater emphasis on finding/acquiring needed information when it is needed, instead of trying to build up large collections just in case such information might be needed. The special librarian also has to develop a sense of who might have the kinds of information they might need in the fairly narrow subject scope of information needed by her/his clients. The special librarian then puts this network of possible sources to work when their client asks for some bit of information. This is not to say that no information is acquired in anticipation of need, but it is much less and what is acquired will include many more non commercial reports and documents dealing with the interests of the organization than an academic librarian, for example, would collect and the special librarian will also need to have great familiarity with the materials created by the organization itself.

The way all of this information is organized and accessed can also be quite different. While classification systems like Dewey Decimal or the Library of Congress might be ideal for patron browsing, for the special librarian with just a few minutes to find a needed fact or figure, such a system may be a hindrance. While special librarians might use one of these systems for some materials, it is likely they will need to arrange and index other materials much more intensively. Similarly, the integrated library system used by much larger public or academic libraries might provide too much of some elements and not enough of others, e.g., subject analysis.

Finally, and perhaps the most challenging of all the differences between special and other libraries is the need for the special librarian to be an expert in the body of literature of interest to the organization paying all the bills for its library. It is quite likely that they have had little or no formal training in their subject specialty – rather they have to learn by doing and to be successful they need to be fast learners.

2. CASE STUDIES OF HONG KONG AND TAIPEI

2.1 Special Libraries in Hong Kong

To test out the validity of the above generalizations in terms of special libraries in one part of Asia, four special librarians working in Hong Kong were interviewed. These included librarians working in a government sponsored library supporting the needs of the judiciary, a private law firm library, a hospital library, and a specialized library supporting the needs of students and teachers in a performing arts institute. A set of prearranged questions dealing with the basic functions performed by special librarians was posed: needs assessment, collection development, cataloguing, public services, organization, and professional development. They were also asked to talk about the special challenges with which they had to deal.

2.1.1 Assessing Needs

All of these special librarians confirmed that needs assessment was particularly important in an environment where they could not build large collections just in case some bit of information might some day be needed. An interesting finding was the degree to which special librarians need to pay attention to some users more than others. For example, the judicial unit librarian noted that not all of their users were equal and so they needed to pay special attention to the needs of the judges more than the other legal professionals using their library. This same sentiment was mentioned by the hospital librarian, but in this case it was the doctors who got the most attention, more than that given the nurses and hospital administrators. For the private law firm librarian it was the needs of the partners and senior lawyers that were most important. The performing arts librarian suggested that since most of her teachers were themselves performers and artists, a great deal of attention had to be given to understanding their needs. She felt performers were much more ego-centered that the other users with whom she had worked. All of this suggests that special librarians have to work on a more personal level with high powered professionals than school, public librarians or even academic librarians.

2.1.2 Collection Development

While special librarians do not have to collect as broadly as their colleagues in other kinds of libraries, they must work just as hard collecting at a greater depth than other librarians. The judicial agency librarian indicated that she needed to collect specialized materials on topics like the selection of judges internationally and the management of court buildings in addition to those on a broad range of legal issues. The medical librarian echoed this problem when he discussed the difficulties of collecting on surgery, dermatology, nursing, hospital administration, etc. The law firm librarian indicated that for a company like hers this was particularly difficult since the information needs of lawyers would change according to the cases they were working on. The importance of collecting Web resources was also detected. Special librarians, because of the limited size of their printed collections, utilize the Web to make up for these deficiencies and the special librarians interviewed in Hong Kong indicated this was the case for them. Another difference from other types of libraries is the importance of collecting information produced by members of their sponsoring organizations. The law firm librarian noted that often lawyers in one specialization make up for their deficiencies in another field by having their librarian "mine" their archives for work that can be reused and resold to their clients. The performing arts institute librarian indicated she felt she had to collect audio visual materials at a greater breadth and depth than other kinds of librarians.

2.1.3 Cataloguing and Bibliographic Control

In Hong Kong, this area seems to have remained fairly traditional and unchanged. All of the special libraries used internationally recognized classification schemes – although the hospital library employed the U.S. based National Library of Medicine scheme together with its MESH (Medical Subject headings) subject headings scheme, and the law firm employed the Moyes Classification scheme favored by libraries collecting both commonwealth and American law materials. However, providing non-traditional bibliographic access to information resources does happen. The court librarian indicated that their library maintained a database of local court judgments not appearing in the usual court reporters to which they subscribed and the performing arts librarian indicated that her library created a range of subject based Web resource pathfinders with links to useful documents of interest to their students and teachers.

2.1.4 Public Services

As noted in the Assessing Needs section above, two levels of public services are typically provided by special librarians. Some of their clients receive premium service where the librarian finds the information for them (judges, doctors, law partners, and performing arts teachers) while others (non judiciary legal professions, nurses, legal interns, and performing arts students) are taught how to find their own information. None of the librarians interviewed indicated that they routinely published reports designed to provide their users with regular reports focused on the topics of most interest to their clients, although the hospital librarian did indicate that he regularly monitored the websites of important medical research agencies and then would relay information about these reports to members of his user community. The need to search the firm's archives might also be seen as an atypical type of public service given by one of the special librarians.

2.1.5 Organization

All of the special libraries looked at in Hong Kong were organized along fairly traditional lines with staff, although few in number, working on collection development, bibliographic control, etc. Where they appeared in the organizations they served was a bit different from academic, public and school libraries. Whereas the latter sometimes enjoy a sort of separate "sacred cow" status in the eyes of their customers, special libraries are typically seen to be integral support services like personnel, housekeeping, etc. In terms of titles, the heads of these libraries are sometimes different from those in other libraries. For example, the judiciary library's head is called the Senior Judiciary Executive (Legal Reference and Library); the law firm librarian, the Library Manager. The head of the hospital library is called the Hospital Librarian and the head of the performing arts library is "The Librarian" following the British model of having a single Librarian although there might be many other librarians assisting that person.

2.1.6 Professional Development

All four special librarians spoke of the difficulties of keeping up with developments both in library science and their subject specialties. They indicated that they actively took advantage of training opportunities when they arose. The law firm librarian, who had also gone back to school to earn a bachelors degree in law, indicated she attended courses for legal professionals offered by her firm on a range of topics. The hospital librarian indicated that while there were funds available to attend conferences, since he was the only professional in his library it was quite difficult to be away from his library. The court librarian indicated he attended courses provided by the government and the performing arts librarian indicated that all of the professionals could apply for funding so that they could attend conferences related to their work and they were allowed to take courses on a non-credit basis at their institute.

2.1.7 Challenges

All of the special librarians identified as challenges the same issues common to all librarians: not enough funding support, not enough staff, not enough space, etc. For the hospital librarian, being the only professional librarian dealing with so many demanding medical practitioners certainly seemed to be the number one problem with which he had to deal. The law firm librarian within her own context echoed this sentiment but also added that the heavy emphasis on electronic forms of information brought with it the additional need to deal with difficult licensing and copyright issues. For the performing arts librarian, in addition to these issues, the technical and service related problems related to the equipment needed.

2.2 Special Libraries in Taiwan

According to *"Directory of Libraries and Information Centers in Taiwan"* (National Library of ROC, 2006), up to the year of its publication, there were 680 special libraries of various types shown as Table 9-2. The number of special libraries in Taiwan has continued to grow over the past two decades according to a brief description by Dr. Li-Hung Huang in the section of Special Library in the *Yearbook of Libraries in ROC 2007* (National Library of ROC 2007).

Table 9-2. Types and Numbers of Special Libraries in Taiwan Area (2006)

Types of Institution	No. of Libraries
Government/Parliament	196
Medical/Hospital	163
Theological	127
Private Industries	61
State-Run Industries	31
Research Institutions	30
Military Institutions	24
Associations	23
Mass Media Institutions	15
Others	10
Total	680

2.2.1 Personnel

A survey of special libraries in Taiwan, shown as Table 9-3, suggests that just over 40 percent of these libraries have full-time staff with Library and Information Science (LIS) background staff, 21 percent have part-time staff with a LIS background and 30 percent with full-time staff but without LIS background. The remainder have part time staff without the LIS (2.63%) or no special staff assigned at all (4.53%). Most of these libraries have one of two staff members working at a time.

Table 9-3. Human Resources Allocations of LIS Background in Special Libraries
in Taiwan Area (2006)

Staff Background	Libraries Answered Qs'	Total No. of staff	Percentage
FT and with LIS	175	345	41.77%
FT without LIS	126	221	30.07%
PT with LIS	88	015	21.00%
PT without LIS	11	113	2.63%
No staff member	19	0	4.53%

FT: Full-Time
PT: Part-Time
LIS: With Library and Information Science Education

2.2.2 Collections

Most of these libraries contain printed materials, although the number of print serials holding decreased by one-third as reported in 2006 over the numbers reported in 2005. On average, based upon figures by the libraries responding to a recent national survey for "*Statistics of Taiwan-Fukien Area 2005–2006*" (National Library of ROC 2006), a typical special library might contain around 23,000 volumes books; 400 periodicals titles; more than 1,000 electronic resources; and some of the respondents also contained thesis/dissertations, collections of materials relating to meetings held, and audio visual materials. Survey results further indicated that most special librarians were involved in providing special program or project support in addition to the normal sorts of functions/facilities provided by special libraries, e.g., circulation, reading areas, reference services, promotional activities, database searching, content services, electronic resources, inter-library loans, full-text duplication and delivery services, and selective dissemination information (SDI) services. Most special libraries in Taiwan are actively employing information technology. Most have websites (79%) and automated library systems (75%) employing a range of systems developed in-house or from national and international producers.

2.2.3 Major Challenges

Librarians responding to the survey identified the following major challenges: the lack of professional staff, financial support, facilities, status/recognition, and expertise in areas like cataloguing and classification. They feel overworked because they have to serve very demanding clientele, because of mergers, lay-offs, and an excessively transient workforce. They feel they need additional professional development opportunities including: 1) Information exchange, communication, and seminars with peer librarians; 2) workshops dealing with related and common issues; 3) on-the-job training and curriculum services, 4) information on how to solve their problems; 5) opportunities to visit of other special libraries, 6) opportunities to participate in professional organizations; 7) support for visits to special libraries in other countries; and 8) support for attendance at international conferences and workshops.

Case Studies. The approach taken by the writer in Taiwan differed from that employed to understand the needs of special libraries in Hong Kong. Here focused descriptions of two such libraries are presented to help the reader understand the nature of special libraries in this part of Asia. Many of the same themes observed in Hong Kong remain constant: Narrowly focused in-depth collections, small number of staff members, the goal is to provide at least a major portion of their clients with the information they need rather than to teach them how to find that information.

2.2.4 Foundation of Chinese Dietary Culture Library

Clients at this library are given access to a wide range of current and rare books journals, electronic databases, collections of thesis, A-V materials, photographs, pamphlets, cook books, dietary food promotion activity records, conference proceedings, and newspaper clippings dealing with most aspects of the topics of food and diet. The library is automated with an OPAC to help clients find the information they need. The Director indicated their users needed more non-book than regular book materials. This library serves various kinds of clients including academics and scholars who favor books, journals, electronic databases, and newspaper clippings. They also serve dietary practitioners who place more emphasis on the use of journals, photographs, and DVD on food decoration and designs. This library is both an information center for dietary research units but also provides a channel for professional development and training. Major clients include students, food service practitioners, and members of the public who are simply interested in food culture. The staff in this library, most of whom have LIS backgrounds but others with who had studied history and the liberal arts, spend time doing a wide range of duties including working in technical services (8 hours per week), collection development (6 hours per week); public service (10 hours per week), and even some time shelving books daily. Most clients work directly with the librarians on the staff. Self help tools like FAQ's are not employed. Library staff members, moreover, help clients find relevant web pages.

2.2.5 Taipei Medical University Library

While this library serves as an academic library, because of the nature of its clientele, it can also be considered as a special library as well. In addition to the more than 6,000 medical school faculty, staff, and students it serves; more than 2,400 medical doctors, their assistants, nurses, and the staff of affiliated hospitals rely upon this library for service and materials. Because the library is publicly funded, it must also serve the general public. Researchers and professors come mainly to access the library's databases and other sources of cutting edge medical technology information, while medical students spend their time using books and medical journals for their term papers.

Reference librarians spend most of their time providing current content services to medical doctors and their assistants. The library provides access to a wide array of audio-visual materials as well. Patrons personally visit the library but they also rely upon Internet-based reference services and electronic databases, e-journals, and e-books. Library staff members are also responsible for circulation, public services, information literacy programs, current content services, and for a Selective Information Dissemination (SDI) program. The library is open 84 hours a week and provides reference service until late in the evening as well. The head librarian is a full-professor and reports directly to the President of the University.

3. SPECIAL LIBRARIES IN OTHER PARTS OF ASIA

In addition to cases studies of Hong Kong and Taiwan, there are several evidences from other countries of the region, such as China, Japan, Singapore, Thailand, Pakistan, Vietnam. The development of special libraries in the area has similarities so as differences in terms of collection development, personnel, introduction of information technologies and challenges.

3.1 China

Special libraries are well established in modern China. J.P. Hu, in a 1996 article on "Special Libraries in China" noted that beginning in 1986 China had "promulgated more than 40 decrees and orders about the special libraries, defining their roles, usage, obligation and organization by law" and in 1994 issued a revised policy paper which outlined "the value of information and information services provided by special libraries to vitalize the economy and raise the living standards of people." (Hu, 1996) He indicated that there were four classes of special libraries, three of which were government sponsored at the national, provincial and local levels. The fourth class or type belong to non-governmental organizations but still focused their efforts on meeting the informational needs of their parent organizations. Zhou and Cai (1996) in another article the same year reported the results of a survey covering 30 different types of special libraries ranging from those in government agencies to hospitals to those associated with geological research groups. They indicated that there were a total of 36,401 such libraries but 30,000 of them were information agencies. If we ignore the news agencies, there were still another six thousand plus special libraries in China more than ten years ago including

1,432 hospitals or other health related special libraries. The number of staff working in China's special libraries appears to differ significantly from an average of 154 working in aircraft air craft industry libraries to only 4 in special libraries attached to profit making organizations. The size of these libraries also varies considerably from very small to very large although the Chinese practice of counting even issues of journals in surveys like that presented by Shou and Cai make those figure less than useful. There does not seem to be a more recent survey since a 2006 book on special libraries by Peng (Peng, 2006) referred to the same survey. Shih-Hu Chao and Quen-Qing Tsai (Chao & Tsai, 2006) stated that there are extreme differences among special libraries in China in terms of collections, human resources, some are more advanced in utilizing information technologies for modernize the libraries in many aspects. However, some are still under developed due to lack of financial support. The authors indicate the needs of inter-library networks are necessary for further development. The cooperation among special libraries needs leadership and planning for overall construction in order to avoid overlapped databases construction and repeated waste of limited resources. The education and training of professionals are in need to lead the profession.

3.2 Japan

Japan is a leading country among Asian's Four Dragons. Different types of specialized libraries are expected to have play have effective role in strengthened the information services and enhancing the growth of economy. Although a comprehensive description of special libraries of Japan could not be located, several articles provide brief descriptions of professional work including special libraries. These articles could be used as a source of information to find further details about special libraries in Japan (Tamura, 2004). A report on on-site visits to libraries (Miao, 2001) suggests that cultural exchange and enhancement were prioritized which included language specialized, and cultural preservation information services? One good example is the collection of Asia Economy Research Center where scholars and researchers of the country can utilize the services of a specialized library. There are also libraries specialized in languages and subjects. Some examples include the International Exchange Center Library, Foreign Language Libraries – International Exchange, British Cultural Exchange Center Library. The Social Science Classical Information Center collects materials for the library on topics such as interior design as author's life style that also preserve the "time" and "space" of the culture in 3D and museum-like environment.

3.3   Singapore

According to a 2000 survey conducted by the Library Association of Singapore, there were 24 private and 36 governmental special librarians in the year 2000 (Ramachandran 2001). This survey noted that most such private libraries contained 1,000 to 53,000 volumes with governmental libraries much larger at 2,000 to 158,000 volumes. At least one special librarian in Singapore has been concerned that with the advent of the Intranet the value of special libraries and their staff would be eroded: "some companies have disbanded their special libraries and information centers and replaced them with mere technological tools to help satisfy their information needs." This same librarian, however, suggested that to combat this possibility by doing more than just answering questions and instead by "getting involved in training, pro-active services, internet, intranet, content management, competitive intelligence, document management, knowledge management, project management, etc."

3.4 Thailand

Librarians in Thailand look to the establishment of the library of the Ministry of Education in 1887 as the first instance of a special library in their country. Today many are known as "information centers," the duties they perform are quite similar to those in other countries. In an article written in 1999 noted, "librarians and information specialists provide information services, such as preparing reports on specific topics required by corporate users, searching the on-line and CD-ROM databases and locating full-text documents, creating databases of organization's information, evaluating and purchasing software for the libraries and for database development, attending conferences and staff meetings, producing organization's publications and training staff to the know how of new information technology." (Siripan 1999) Special librarians in Thailand are expected to wear many hats including finding answers to questions, being the in-house WEB and computer expert, determining the information needs of the organization and arranging for the purchase of the required content, developing databases of relevant information, and many other duties. According to Siripan's article that Thai librarians face many of the same challenges as special librarians in other parts of the world including the lack of space and resources, and keeping up with subject and information science developments. At the same time there has been an attempt by university libraries to meet the needs of technology firms in technology parks in Thailand. They have found that they have to adopt the methods followed by special librarians to be relevant to their clients. (Premkamolnetr 1999)

3.5 Pakistan

Libraries overall in Pakistan have been characterized in one study as in a "gloomy state of affairs." (Mahmood 2006, p. 32). They lack funds, staffing, are negatively affected of the war next door in Afghanistan and Iraq, and they seem to be losing public confidence in an ever digital informational environment. The amount of recent information about special libraries in this country is a bit limited. A 1990 article by Khurshid provided statistics on the number of special libraries indicated that they grew from 178 in 1984 to 331 in 1989 (Khurshid 1990). While written some 18 years ago, given the barriers to development in Pakistan, perhaps this authors assessment still stands for many special libraries: "These libraries concentrate in the subject literatures of their respective organizations. They may have relatively few books, but considerable holdings in reports and journals. A good example is the Library of the Pakistan Institute of Nuclear Science and Technology, Nellore (founded 1968); it contains only 16,000 books, but has more than 330,000 technical reports and 275 current periodicals." (Khurshid, 1990) Location in Pakistan is apparently critical to a library's ability to employ modern technology. One special librarian in Kashmir noted that "sometimes it takes hours for me to send one e-mail. Sometimes it is easier for me to drive four hours to Islamabad to send e-mail." (Enright 2002). However, things may be improving rapidly. In this same article it was noted in 2002 that the Government had launched a Pakistan 2010 Program, part of which will help ramp up the amount of access to the Internet and the information found therein.

3.6 Vietnam

As noted by one author, "Vietnam's libraries have long endured conditions that in any developed country would be considered totally unacceptable. (Tran 1999: 5). The Communist Party has and continues to be in control of most aspects of daily life including how its libraries operate. However, the difference since 1985 has been that instead of the goal being to serve ideology, now the aim is increasingly to improve the economy. Special libraries, as such, are not seen as a separate category by the Vietnamese government. Rather they are scattered within other official categories like social science, health library, or agricultural library systems. A 2005 Conference of Directors of National Libraries in Asia and Oceania report on Vietnam, on the other hand, indicated in a section reporting the numbers of special libraries that there were "60 research libraries run by research institutes and 218 library and information centers under ministries and other governmental agencies." For the military it indicated that there were 1,000+ libraries and reading rooms (CDNLAO 2005). Nguyen Thien Can reporting conditions in the Saigon Times "Document Section" noted that while they have archival computer databases of articles from their own and other news sources, computers in organizations like this one are used largely for word processing purposes. (Nguyen) Moreover, when the computers have problems neither the librarians or the reporters are skilled in fixing them. Nguyen also indicated that there seemed to be a disconnect between the clients and the librarians and that so many problems were not being addressed. A visitor to the Southeast Asia Institute library in 1998 reviewed some of the challenges facing special libraries like this one but indicated how impressed he was with the devotion of the librarians he met to meeting the needs of their organization in the face of the problems with which they were faced (D'Amicantonio 1998).

4. CONCLUSIONS

There a strong current of "putting knowledge to work" instead of "knowledge for knowledge's sake" in terms of the service missions pursued by the of growing number of special libraries in Hong Kong and Taiwan. This seems to be particularly true in Hong Kong. With the growth in information brought about the WEB, there seems to be more and more employment opportunities for LIS professionals willing to devote themselves to making order out of this chaos. Other general themes include the view of these libraries being integral parts of these organizations, as opposed to being separate support systems.

The isolated nature of special librarianship is readily apparent within these libraries. The need for special librarians to find colleagues outside their own organizations was especially striking in Hong Kong. Special librarians in Hong Kong and Taiwan have many hats to wear all at the same time to get their collecting, acquisitions, cataloguing, public service, and collection management work completed. The challenges of keeping up with new developments in LIS and the subject focus of their sponsoring organizations are vividly apparent. In the case of the single professional hospital librarian in Hong Kong, attending a conference to learn new things and buying books while helping doctors gather information for immediate patient treatment means the need to be in multiple places all at the same time – the reality is it cannot all happen all the time. And so much of their work has to be done fast, especially for powerful clients upon whose success the success of the overall organization depends.

Both the more traditional "just in case" collecting strategies associated with educational support libraries, and the "just in time" collecting patterns of special libraries, were detected among the libraries examined for this chapter. Those with both students and practitioners as clients clearly need to pursue both roads to getting the information needed to meet the needs of their patrons. The need to collect and "mine" the work of those laboring in, or affiliated with, the sponsoring organization was especially apparent within the more corporate libraries examined here.

Finally, it is clear that while the lack of space given to many special libraries to store their collections greatly affects what can be collected and the nature of the service that can therefore be offered clients, the challenges faced by these librarians are all to common to librarians generally: the lack of sufficient staff and collection development funds, time to get all the work done, facilities in which to work, and opportunities to improve ones skills. Yet, most if not all of the special librarians interviewed seemed to be imbued with a passion for their jobs, putting knowledge to work.

References

CDNLAO (Conference of Directors of National Libraries in Asia and Oceania) Country Report 2005 (2005). [Online] Available: http://www.nla. gov.au/lap/ documents/vietnam06.pdf. Retrieved March 22, 2008.

Chao, Shih-Hu and Quen-Qing Tsai (1996) *Current development of special libraries in China,* China Academic Journal retrieved March 21, 2008 from http://www.cnki.net

D'Amicantonio, John (1998). Special library experience in Vietnam. Information Outlook 2 (12): 10. [Online] Available: http://findarticles.com/p/articles/mi_m0FWE/is_12_2/ai_53480030. Retrieved March 22, 2008.

Enright, Nikki (2006). Connecting in an Uncertain Environment. Information Outlook 6 (1). [Online] Available: http://www.sla.org/content/Shop/Information/infoonline/2002/oct02/chaudhary.cfm. Retrieved March 10, 2008.

Foundation of Chinese Dietary Culture Library. [Online] Available: http://www.fcdc.org.tw/html/esp1.htm. Retrieved January 31, 2008.

Hong Kong Library Association. Hong Kong Libraries Gateway. [Online] Available: http://dir.hkla.org/Browse_by_type.php. Retrieved September 29, 2007.

Hu, Junping (1996). Special Libraries in China: Present and Future. Chinese Librarianship: an International Electronic Journal. (1) 1: 1-7. [Online] Available: http://vnweb.hwwilsonweb.com/hww/jumpstart.jhtml?recid=0bc05f7a67b1790 e4878ce85ec6a66d7b53d4cc49a1627c9566a62f2b220bf4893926e553ddd6b0d &fmt=P. Retrieved March 8, 2008.

Khurshid, Anis (1990). Library Resources in Pakistan: Progress, Problems, and Achievements. World Libraries 1 (1). [Online] Available: http://www.worlib. org/vol01no1/khurshid_v01n1.shtml. Retrieved March 10, 2008.

Mahmood, Khalid, Hameed, Abdul, and Haider, Syed Jalaluddin (2005). Libraries in Pakistan: A Survey. Libri 55: 131-135. (quote 137). [Online] Available: http://72.14.235.104/search?q=cache:8hR8ON03ntIJ:www.librijournal.org/pdf/2005-2-3pp131-139.pdf+%22special+libraries%22+pakistan&hl=en&ct=cln k&c d=8. Retrieved March 12, 2008.

Mahmood, Khalid, Hameed, Abdul, and Haider, Syed Jalaluddin (2006). Libraries in Pakistan: A Systematic Study. Library Review (1) 55: 20-34.

Miao , Hua-Jien. (2001) *Report of on-site visiting ten libraries in Japan,* China Academic Journal. [Online] Available: http://www.cnki.net. Retrieved March 21, 2008.

Mount, Ellis (1991). *Special Libraries and Information Centers: An Introductory Text.* Second Edition. Washington, DC, 1991.

National Library of ROC (2006). *Directory of Libraries and Information Centers in Taiwan.* Taipei: National Library of ROC.

National Library of ROC (2006). *Statistics of Taiwan-Fukien Area 2005-2006 Taiwan,* Taipei: National Library of ROC.

National Library of ROC (2007). *Yearbook of Libraries in ROC 2007.* Taipei: National Library of ROC. Special Libraries: 107-114 (By Dr. Li-Hung Huang)

Peng, Jun-Ling (2006). Zhuanmen Tushuguan Yenjiu (Special Libraries Studies). Beijing: (Zhungguo Shuji Chubanshe (China Books Press).

Premkamolnetr, Nogyao, (1999). Collaboration between a Technological Universtiy Library and Tenant Park in Thailand. Asian Libraries (12) 8: 451-465.

Siripan, Praditta (1999). Special Libraries: As the libraries to the Year 2000. [Online] Available: http://tla.tiac.or.th/ifla/Ifla99_8.htm. Retrieved March 10, 2008.

Taipei Medical University Library. Retrieved January 31, 2008, from http://library.tmu.edu.tw/

Tran, Lan Anh (1999). Recent library developments in Vietnam. Asian Libraries 8 (1): 5-15. [Online] Available: http://chinesesites.library.ingentaconnect.com/content/mcb/173/1999/00000008/00000001/art00001. Retrieved March 22, 2008.

Tamura, Naoko (2004). National Food Research Institute Library. Pharmaceutical Library Bulletin (Yakugaku Toshokan); 49(3) 2004, pp. 215-216.

What is a special librarian? General Industry FAQs. [Online] Available: http://www.sla.org/content/membership/Genfaq.cfm. Retrieved September 28, 2007.

Zhou, Shi-hu and Cai, Chun-qing (1996). Zhungguo Zhuanmen- tushuguande Fazhan Xianzhuang (The status of special libraries development). Tushu Qingbao Gongzuo (Libraries and information Work) (3): 13-17.

LIS EDUCATION

Christopher S. G. Khoo, Shaheen Majid, Chihfeng P. Lin

1. INTRODUCTION

This chapter reviews the status of LIS education in Asia, except for the Middle East and Central Asia. The Middle Eastern region is covered in another chapter. There is little published information about LIS education in Central Asia. Hence, coverage of this region is deferred to a future version of this chapter. The chapter provides an overview of the history of LIS education in various countries, examines regional trends, especially in curriculum, quality assurance and regional cooperation, and discusses the challenges faced.

Asia is a vast area with diverse national histories, cultures, languages, political situations and levels of socio-economic development. The development of LIS education in a country depends to a large extent on the development of public library service in the country, higher education and academic libraries, and the country's economy and its need for information professionals. This chapter will first examine the situation in individual countries in Asia, and then attempt to identify major regional trends and challenges.

2. Sources of Information on LIS Education in Asia

Information on LIS education in Asia is widely dispersed, found mainly in regional conference papers and occasionally in LIS journals. The only attempt at an LIS journal for the region was Asian Libraries[1], published from 1991 to 1999 (with vol. 6-8, 1997-1999, published by Emerald). Some international LIS journals carry occasional articles on LIS education in particular Asian countries. They include:

- Journal of Education for Library and Information Science
- Education for Information
- Libri.

Recent journal special issues on LIS education in Asia are:

- Journal of Education for Library and Information Science, v. 45 no. 1 (Winter 2004) and v. 47 no. 3 (Summer 2006)
- Malaysian Journal of Library and Information Science, v. 8 no. 2 (December 2003)
- Singapore Journal of Library &Information Management, v. 29 (2000) and v. 32 (2003).

---

[1] Asian Libraries merged with New Library World in 1999.

A snapshot of the situation in the early 1990s can be found in *Asian Libraries*, v. 3 no. 4 (December 1993).

Many countries have their own national LIS journals, usually published by the national library association. Unfortunately, there is neither a comprehensive list of such journals nor a bibliography of articles on LIS education in these journals. Some national journals are, however, indexed by the *Library and Information Science Abstracts (LISA)*. A bibliography of articles on LIS education in Asia is being compiled for the LISEA (Library & Information Science Education in Asia) Web site (http://dis.sci.ntu.edu.sg/lisea/).

In addition to the IFLA annual conferences (http://www.ifla.org/IV/index.htm), regional conferences are good information sources on the developments of LIS education in different countries. Such conferences include:

- CONSAL (Congress of Southeast Asian Librarians, http://www.consal. org.sg/)
- A-LIEP (Asia-Pacific Conference on Library & Information Education & Practice, http://www.ntu.edu.sg/sci/a-liep)
- ICADL (International Conference on Asian Digital Libraries, http://www. icadl.org/, which usually includes a workshop or panel discussion on LIS education)
- ICLISE 2001 (International Conference for Library & Information Science Educators in the Asia Pacific Region, 2001, held in Malaysia, http://www. ifla.org/III/misc/iclise.htm)
- WISE workshop 2000 (Post-CONSAL Workshop on Information Studies Education, 2000, held in Singapore, http://dis.sci.ntu.edu.sg/wise/).

To provide a forum for LIS educators in Asia, the Asia-Pacific Conference on Library & Information Education & Practice (A-LIEP) was initiated in Singapore in 2006. The e-proceedings of A-LIEP 2006 (http://www.ntu.edu.sg/sci/a-liep/A-LIEP2006.e-proceedings.htm) have been archived on DLIST (http://dlist.sir. arizona.edu/). The e-proceedings carry some 31 papers on LIS education in Asian countries and provide an important snapshot of LIS education in the region. A-LIEP 2007 (http://course.shu.edu.tw/~aliep07/) was held in Taipei, and A-LIEP 2009 is scheduled to be held in Tsukuba, Japan.

The Web sites of LIS schools are potentially important sources of information about the history and curriculum of LIS programs. Unfortunately, many LIS schools in Asia are not represented on the Web, and many Web sites do not have detailed and up-to-date information in English. Directories of LIS schools and their Web sites can be found in:

- World List of Schools and Departments of Information Science, Information Management and Related Disciplines, maintained by Tom Wilson (http://informationr.net/wl/)
- World Guide to Library, Archive, and Information Science Education, 3rd ed. (Schniederjürgen, 2007)
- Directory of LIS Schools in Asia, maintained by the Wee Kim Wee School of Communication & Information, Nanyang Technological University, Singapore (http://dis.sci.ntu.edu.sg/lisea/schools/).

A survey of the state of LIS education in Southeast and East Asia was carried out by the LIPER (Library and Information Professions and Education Renewal) project of Japan (Miwa, 2006; Miwa et al., 2006; Ueda et al., 2005). As part of the review, a library educator from each of the following countries – China, South Korea, Taiwan, Thailand and Singapore – was invited to present a paper on LIS education in his or her country. The country reports are available on the LIPER Web site (http://www.soc.nii.ac.jp/jslis/liper/record.html).

3. HISTORY OF LIS EDUCATION IN ASIA

In many Asian countries, formal LIS education began around the middle of the twentieth century after the World War II, when many countries became independent and embarked on national development initiatives. Libraries were seen as playing an important role in supporting education, advancing literacy and enhancing the learning capacity of the citizens. LIS training programs were often initiated by the library associations of the countries. At institutions of higher learning, formal LIS education typically started with the university librarian as the program director or head of department, with practicing librarians as part-time faculty. Foreign LIS educators were engaged as consultants and examiners to provide a measure of quality assurance. Over time, the programs became more established, with full-time faculty and a full-time faculty member as department head.

In countries that are part of the British Commonwealth, such as India, formal LIS education often began as postgraduate diploma courses, following the British model, and were later upgraded to Master's programs with the addition of a Master's thesis. In other countries, LIS programs were offered at universities first at the undergraduate diploma or certificate level, and subsequently developed into Bachelor's and Master's programs. In addition, many teacher colleges and institutes of education started offering programs for training teacher librarians. LIS schools offering only a Bachelor's program are usually taught by instructors with Bachelor's and Master's degrees, while schools offering graduate programs have a number of faculty members with PhD degrees.

The development of LIS curricula in the region can be divided into three stages (Table 10-1). Most programs started as library science courses to train librarians for public and academic libraries (Stage 1). In Stage 2, the library science curriculum was expanded to include information science, with the addition of courses on library automation, applications of information technology, information retrieval, and online searching in bibliographic databases in the 1970s and 1980s. Courses on Internet technologies and the World Wide Web were added in the 1990s. During this stage of development, libraries, librarians and LIS schools were grappling with information and communication technologies.

With the burst of the dot.com bubble in the early 2000s and the arrival of a new generation of librarians and library educators who are comfortable with technology, LIS curriculum development has moved to Stage 3, where technology is not the main focus of attention. Rather, information and communication technologies (ICT) are viewed as enabling forces and tools, and the emphasis is on how to make effective use of technology to manage information and knowledge to serve the needs of users and organizations. LIS curriculum is expanding in two directions:

1. *information/knowledge management*: to prepare information professionals to manage information and knowledge in organizations, mainly in the corporate sector;
2. *digital information services*: to educate a new breed of librarians who can handle both print and digital resources and services, and can continuously adapt to the evolving online environment.

These three stages of curriculum development are reflected in the changing names of LIS programs: from *library science*, to *library and information science*, and more recently, to *information studies, information management, knowledge management*, and others. There is also a trend towards developing specializations in such areas as records management, archives, digital libraries, etc. In the more advanced Asian countries, many LIS schools are in Stage 3 of curriculum development, while LIS schools elsewhere in Asia are still grappling with a curriculum in Stage 1 or Stage 2.

The estimated number of LIS schools in various Asian countries is given in the Appendix. The numbers were obtained from several sources – country reports presented at conferences, the *World guide to library, archive, and information science education* (Schniederjürgen 2007), and the *Directory of LIS Schools in Asia*. The numbers are only indicative, since the counts depend on such factors as whether only departments or programs in full-fledged universities are included, and what is considered professional-level education in the country. Nevertheless, it can be seen that there is no lack of LIS education programs in Asia.

Table10-1. Stages in LIS curriculum development

Stage 1	Stage 2	Stage 3
Library Science	Expanded to include *Information Science* (with courses on library automation, online searching in bibliographic databases, information retrieval, and information technology, especially the Internet and World Wide Web)	Expanded to include *Information/Knowledge Management* (focusing on corporate information and management) Expanded to include *Digital Information Services* (incorporating digital libraries, e-resources, Web 2.0 and social computing)

For each Asian country below, we outline the history of LIS education, efforts to develop and reform the LIS education system, the system for accreditation and quality control, the information job market, and major challenges in the context of the country's economic and political situation.

3.1 East Asia

3.1.1 China

China has a long history of books, publishing and libraries. According to Wang (2006), China's history of book collections goes back at least 3,500 years. The first book on library science in China was written by Liu Xiang around 77B.C. during the Han Dynasty. It analyzed the national book collections of the time. Only a few chapters remain today. Since then, books on book-collecting and document science, as well as bibliographies of books, have appeared through the ages.

Modern library science, however, was introduced from the West in the early twentieth century. In 1913, American librarian Harry Clemens taught a course on library science at Nanjing University for the first time (Fan, 2006). In 1920, the first library science school, the Boone Library School, was founded in Wuhan by Mary Elizabeth Wood, Samuel Tsu Yung Seng and Thomas Ching Sen Hu, following the U.S. model (Fan 2006; Wang 2006). Within a decade, two other LIS departments were set up, at Shanghai Citizen University in 1925 and Nanjing University in 1927.

In the 1950s, Chinese library science education was influenced by the former Soviet Union. Many books of Soviet library science were translated into Chinese, and China sent students to study library science in the USSR.

Since the market-based economic reforms and opening-up of the country in 1978, China has looked to the U.S. and other countries for new ideas. LIS education developed rapidly after 1980, from 2 LIS schools to 52 in the period 1980 to

1990 (Wu, 2003; Ma 1993). At present, there are 44 LIS schools, offering a variety of Bachelor's, Master's and PhD programs.

LIS schools have changed their names to reflect the expanded scope of the field. For example, the department at Wuhan University was renamed *School of Library and Information Science* in 1984, while that at Peking University was renamed *Department of Information Management* in 1992.

Wang (2006) noted that LIS education in China has evolved into five areas of specialization:

- Library Science
- Information Science
- Information Management/Information System
- Archival Science
- Editing and Publishing Science.

The Chinese Ministry of Education regularly convenes national and international conferences to discuss the development of LIS education. In 1998, with the endorsement of the Ministry of Education, the LIS schools at Peking University, Wuhan University and Hebei University organized a seminar on national LIS education, which decided on the mandatory core courses for undergraduates majoring in information management: management science, economics, information management, data structure and database, information organization and retrieval, computer networks and management of information systems (Fan, 2006). In 2002, the Library Science Discipline Guiding Committee of the Ministry of Education held an inaugural meeting, in which it was agreed to hold a meeting on Library Science Education and Reform annually.

Since 1978, the Chinese government has invested more in libraries, and this has resulted in an increased need for librarians. The 15,500 libraries in mainland China, including 2,700 public libraries, 1,700 university libraries and 4,000 research institution libraries (Wang, 2006) represent a big job market for LIS graduates. However, LIS does not yet have a high status as an academic discipline in universities, and its public image also needs to be improved.

Some of the challenges facing LIS education in China that have been identified by Wang (2006) are:

- Lack of clarity about the core basic knowledge of the LIS field in the new environment, now that the field has expanded to include information science and information management
- Reconciling the two conflicting objectives of Master's programs – preparing graduates with practical skills for the job market versus inculcating research skills in students to prepare them for the PhD program
- Lack of academic preparation of graduates for rigorous research.

3.1.2 Japan

According to Kon (1993), library training workshops were run by the Japan Library Association as early as 1903. In 1921, the Ministry of Education established a librarianship training institute in the Imperial Library, which offered a 1-year program. The training institute was reorganized to become the National Junior College for Librarianship in 1964, and restructured into the University of Library and Information Science in 1980. It recently merged with the University of Tsukuba in 2002. This is currently the largest LIS school in Japan.

However, the first comprehensive LIS program at the university level was offered by the Japan Library School, established in 1951 at Keio University with the help of the American Library Association. The school added a Master's program in 1960, and introduced the first doctoral program in 1975.

The development of LIS education in Japan was influenced a great deal by the Japanese Library Law of 1950, which specifies a program of certification for public library professionals (Ueda et al., 2005). Two levels of public library professionals are specified – librarian (*Shisho*) and assistant librarian (*Shishoho*). According to the law, a person is qualified as a librarian if the person graduated from a polytechnic, college or university, and completed a training program specified by the law. The training program comprises 12 required courses and 2 elective courses (Miwa et al., 2006; Tsuji et al., 2006). The School Library Law, enacted in 1953, requires every school to have a school library and to employ a teacher-librarian (*Shisho-kyouyu*). There is no formal certification for academic or special librarians.

Shisho certification is popular among university students. 296 colleges and universities offer the program, and more than 10,000 students obtain this certification every year (Miwa et al., 2006)! However, less than 10% of these can get a full-time job in a public library. Currently, undergraduate LIS programs are offered by 10 colleges and universities, Master's programs by 8 colleges and universities, and PhD programs by 6 (Miwa et al., 2006).

In 2003, members of the Japan Society of Library & Information Science embarked on a major project called LIPER (Library and Information Professions and Education Renewal) to examine the status of LIS education in Japan, including curricula, employment trends, competencies needed and future prospects, with the goal of reforming Japanese LIS education (Miwa et al., 2006; Ueda et al., 2005). The study included questionnaire surveys, interviews and focus groups of the major stakeholders – faculty, students, graduates and professionals.

Miwa et al. (2006) pinpointed the following challenges facing LIS education in Japan:

- New employment opportunities for full-time librarians are decreasing due to an increase in outsourcing and part-time workers.
- The curriculum of *Shisho* certification programs is inflexible and out-of-date. The curriculum does not take into account the range of ability and experience

of students, and does not cover digital and multimedia information resources, human-information behavior, ICTs and knowledge management skills.

- LIS programs are not subject to quality assurance.

3.1.3 South Korea

The first library school was established in 1957 at Yonsei University, with both undergraduate and graduate programs (Kwon, 2003). This was followed soon after by programs at Ewha Womans' University in 1959, Chungang University in 1963, and Sungkyunkwan University in 1964. The first PhD program was introduced at Sungkyunkwan University in 1974.

In the 1980s, LIS department names were gradually changed to reflect the incorporation of information science, and a diversity of information science subjects were offered in the 1990s. With the Public Records Management Act coming into effect in 2000, LIS schools started offering courses in records management, to meet the demand for record management professionals.

There are currently 40 LIS schools at universities and teacher colleges, offering mainly graduate programs and 11 PhD programs. LIS schools in South Korea are grappling with the issue of the identity of the LIS field, and are reviewing their curricula and defining their research directions.

3.1.4 Taiwan

The first LIS program in Taiwan was an undergraduate library science program introduced in 1955 by the Department of Adult and Continuing Education at the National Taiwan Normal University (Lin, 2004). In 1961, another undergraduate program was introduced at the National Taiwan University, followed by a Master's program in 1980 and a PhD program in 1989. There are now 11 universities offering undergraduate and graduate programs, with most programs called *library and information science*. The exceptions are three programs with the names *information and communications, library, information and archival studies* and *digital library*. Lin characterized the recent trends in LIS curriculum in Taiwan as being related to the terms *digital, Internet* and *multimedia*. LIS education in Taiwan has particular strengths in digital libraries and digital content management.

Each LIS program in Taiwan is basically accredited by its parent university. However, librarians who wish to practice in public libraries have to pass a civil service examination for libraries. Since 90% of libraries are run by the government, most LIS graduates will attempt the examination. Nevertheless, there are increasing numbers of LIS graduates working as information specialists in the private sector.

Lin (2004) singled out the following challenges facing LIS education in Taiwan:

- The gap between undergraduate and graduate programs, and how to design programs for graduate students whose undergraduate education is in a different discipline
- LIS degrees not given any weight or recognition in the civil service examination, with the result that non-LIS graduates who pass the exam can assume librarian positions in the civil service
- The current emphasis on IT in the curricula producing graduates who are too system and technology oriented, lacking an orientation in the humanities, arts and education
- The need to strengthen communication skills in graduates.

3.2 Southeast Asia

3.2.1 Thailand

In 1951, a special program in library management was offered at Chulalongkorn University under a Fulbright program, where five American academics conducted six courses over a period of five years (Premsmit 1993 & 2004; Butdisuwan 2000). Subsequently, the Department of Library Science was set up at Chulalongkorn University in 1955, offering an undergraduate diploma course, followed by a Bachelor's program in 1959 and a Master's program in 1964. The curriculum was based on the U.S. model, with some adaptations to meet Thai needs. A one-year postgraduate Advanced Certificate in Library Science was offered in 1965 at the College of Education, Prasarnmit Campus (now Srinakharinwirot University) to train school librarians.

There are currently 16 universities and more than 36 Rajabhat Universities (former teacher colleges) offering undergraduate LIS programs, with the names *library and information science*, *information studies* or *information management*. Ten of these offer Master's programs, mostly MA in Library and Information Science. The first PhD program was introduced at Khon Kaen University in 2003.

Saladyanant (2006) reported that in Thai higher education, quality assessment is carried out at two levels:

- external assessment of the university as a whole by the Office of Education Standards and Evaluation (OESE)
- internal quality assessment at the department level.

The Ministry of Education requires each university department to set up its own quality assurance system, which must cover at least four elements: 1.) curriculum administration; 2.) resources for learning, teaching and research; 3.) student support and advising; 4.) needs of the job market and alumni feedback.

The main job market for librarians is in the government sector, especially in educational institutions (Premsmit 2004). However, many LIS schools are revising their curricula to include competencies needed in the private sector.

Problems in LIS education in Thailand include the following:

- Need for more faculty development, especially in emerging areas
- Strengthening research in LIS
- Need for textbooks in the Thai language since most of the teaching is in Thai
- Need to develop more PhD programs to educate LIS educators and researchers.

3.2.2 Malaysia

Lim (1970) and Wijasuriya, Lim and Radah (1975) traced the beginnings of LIS education in Malaysia to the formation of the Malayan Library Group in 1955, which organized classes in librarianship and prepared students to take the Library Association (U.K.) Associateship examination. A formal LIS program was introduced in 1968 at the MARA Institute of Technology (later restructured into the University of Technology MARA) (Jamaludin, Hussin & Mokhtar, 2006). The Institute started offering a three-year Diploma in Library Science program in 1973, followed by a Bachelor's, Master's and PhD program.

In 1987, a Master of Library and Information Science program was started at the University of Malaya. It was suspended after one run, but was revived in 1995. At present, there are four universities offering LIS professional education at various levels, including three PhD programs.

The names of schools and programs have evolved over time. For example, the school at the University of Technology MARA changed its name from the School of Library Science in 1973, to the School of Library and Information Science in 1980, to the Faculty of Information Studies, and finally to the Faculty of Information Management! The name changes reflected expansion of the programs and field of study, to include especially information management in the corporate sector. The undergraduate program has four areas of specialization:

- Library & Information Management
- Information Systems Management
- Records Management
- Information Resource Center Management (for school media management).

A major development in Malaysia is the establishment of an accreditation system for higher-education programs. The Malaysian government established the Malaysian Qualifications Agency to oversee all aspects of quality in higher education, including accrediting higher education programs and qualifications, and supervising and regulating the quality of higher education providers. Within this framework, a *Standards and Criteria for Programs in Library and Information Science* was formulated in 2007 by a committee comprised of representatives from the Malaysian Qualifications Agency, National Library, Librarian's Association of Malaysia, three established LIS schools, and potential employers (Singh 2007).

3.2.3 Indonesia

After Indonesia's independence was recognized by the Dutch in 1949, Indonesia began establishing public libraries in the 1950s in an effort to raise literacy levels. According to Sulistyo-Basuki (1993 & 2006), the first LIS program was a two-year "Training Course for Library Staff" established in 1952 by the Ministry of Education and Culture. It became the Library School in 1959, with the course extended to three years. In 1961, the program was moved to the Teacher's College at the University of Indonesia, and in 1963 the Department of Library Science came under the Faculty of Letters at the same university.

In 1982, the education system in Indonesia was restructured. Tertiary education was organized broadly into Diploma, Bachelor's, Master's and Doctoral programs, which is still the system in use today. Currently, 15 universities offer a Bachelor's LIS program and at least 2 offer a Master's program.

Indonesia has gone through tremendous political changes in recent years, and this has had a major impact on LIS education. President Soeharto, who was in power for 32 years until 1998, applied a strong central government policy to standardize the education system in Indonesia through the Ministry of National Education. The Directorate General of Higher Education (DGHE) supervised all tertiary education, including LIS education. DGHE established various committees, called consortia, which determined the curriculum for each discipline, including library science. The Consortium for Philosophy and Literature covered the area of library science. A nation-wide curriculum for LIS education was issued in 1986, and revised in 1992 and 1996. The DGHE also granted approval for the opening of new LIS schools after reviewing submitted proposals. The programs were thus accredited by DGHE.

Things changed drastically after Soeharto stepped down in 1998 in the face of student demonstrations and unrest (Sulistyo-Basuki, 2006). In the post-Soeharto era, known as the Reformation Era, more autonomy was granted to regions and cities. Now the DGHE specifies only 52 credits or 40% of the 144 credits for undergraduate programs, leaving each institution to decide what courses to offer for the remaining credit hours. Because of a lack of experienced faculty, professional literature and IT facilities, the LIS schools have difficulty filling the remaining credits. Further, the DGHE curriculum states just the course titles and the number of credits, leaving it to the schools to flesh out the course content. Unfortunately, there are not many LIS books in the Indonesian language, and some good books by left-leaning authors had earlier been banned.

In the new era, any university can initiate undergraduate and graduate programs in LIS without DGHE permission. However, the LIS school must be supervised for two years by the National Accreditation Agency set up by the Ministry of Education, comprised of DGHE officers, academics, and representatives of the Indonesian Library Association. This laxity has given rise to new programs without adequate resources. Many LIS schools do not have good library resources, or access to online databases, or good IT laboratories. Also, many graduate programs do not have faculty with PhD qualifications.

Since most LIS graduates are employed by special and academic libraries, LIS schools tend to tailor their curriculum accordingly, thus neglecting school and public libraries, which are generally in poor condition (Sulistyo-Basuki 2006). Furthermore, the majority of LIS schools are in Java and Western Indonesia, with only three schools situated in the less developed Eastern Indonesia. LIS graduates are reluctant to work in Eastern Indonesia, where libraries are in a poor shape, the infrastructure is poor, and there are few opportunities for career development.

3.2.4 Philippines

According to Vallejo (1993), the first courses on "library economy" were offered at the University of the Philippines in 1914. In 1916, the program was raised to a four-year program leading to a BSc in Library Science. In 1917, courses for school librarians were offered at the Philippine Normal School. In 1961, an Institute of Library Science was set up at the University of the Philippines, and a Master's program was finally introduced. There are currently some 72 universities and colleges offering LIS programs, but many of these programs are LIS majors within a Bachelor of Education program.

The most significant feature of the LIS profession in the Philippines is the licensing of professional librarians by the state. The practice of librarianship is regulated by The Philippine Librarianship Act of 2003, which updates the earlier Act of 1990 (David & Perez, 2006). To practice as a librarian, one needs to hold a *Certificate of Registration* and a *Professional Identification Card* issued by the Professional Regulatory Board for Librarians of the Philippine Regulations Commission. The Act, in effect, recognized the essential role of librarians and libraries in national development and in developing the intellectual capacity of the citizens (Nera 2006; Santos 2003).

The Act defines the scope of the licensure examination and the content of the LIS curriculum. Only graduates with a Bachelor's or Master's degree in LIS are allowed to take the exam. Such a regulation enables the Board for Librarians to recommend to the Commission the closing of a library school when a substantial proportion of the graduates do not pass the licensure examination.

There is a big job market in public, academic and school libraries. A professional librarian is required to be employed in every school, college or university – having a professional librarian in the institution is a basic requirement for school or university programs to be accredited by the various professional associations and accreditation bodies. As less than 50% of the candidates pass the exam on average, there is a high demand for licensed librarians. There are about 4000 licensed librarians, which is 10% of the total number of libraries in the Philippines

(David & Perez, 2006)! The image of professional librarians is good and the salaries of librarians are competitive, in some cases comparable to that of deans.

There are, however, some challenges facing LIS education in the Philippines (David & Perez, 2006):

1. A gap between theory and practice, partly due to a lack of materials on theories relevant to the Philippine situation
2. Lack of information materials and learning resources to support the curriculum, and consequently lack of hands-on experience
3. Lack of IT software and hardware
4. Instructors' lack of up-to-date knowledge of current trends, issues and practice of librarianship.

3.2.5 Singapore

LIS professional training in Singapore started as a postgraduate diploma program conducted by the Library Association of Singapore, from 1982 to 1992 (Thuraisingham 1984 & 1989). The instructors were a mix of faculty engaged from library schools in the U.K. and Australia, and local practising librarians. In 1993, a Division of Information Studies was established at the Nanyang Technological University's School of Applied Science to offer an MSc program in Information Studies (Khoo 2004 & 2005). The School of Applied Science later became the School of Computer Engineering. Being situated in an engineering school, the Division developed a particular strength in information technology and digital libraries. The Division merged with the School of Communication Studies to form the School of Communication & Information in 2002.

The Master's of Science (Msc) program has developed rapidly in its 15 years of existence. The curriculum was restructured in 2002 to offer the following areas of concentration:

- Archival Informatics
- Knowledge Management
- Information Systems
- Library and Information Science
- School Media Resource Management.

The overwhelming popularity of the Information Systems and the Knowledge Management concentrations persuaded the school to offer a separate MSc program in Knowledge Management in 2002, and an MSc in Information Systems program in 2005 in collaboration with the School of Computer Engineering. The Knowledge Management program was the first in Asia and one of the earliest in the world. In addition to the MSc programs, the Division also offers a research Master's program and a PhD program.

There is currently no accreditation system for LIS education in Singapore. Since the program at the Nanyang Technological University is the only LIS program in

Singapore, it is seeking to develop a regional accreditation system through collaboration with LIS schools in the region.

The main challenge facing the school is the difficulty of attracting local students to the PhD program and recruiting PhDs in the library science area. The problem of attracting local PhD students is common across all the faculties, due to the pragmatic Singaporean mindset. Most local graduates prefer to enter the industry and secure a remunerative position, rather than devote a few years to PhD research. Of the 15 full-time faculty members in the Division, almost all have PhDs. However, only 4 of the PhDs are in the LIS field and only one of these is a Singaporean. The other faculty members have PhDs in computer science or management.

3.3 South Asia

3.3.1 India

LIS education in India is nearly 100 years old. W.A. Borden from the U.S. started the first training program for library workers at the Central Library in Baroda in 1911 (Sarkhel 2006; Singh, 2003b). In 1929, S.R. Ranganathan introduced a certificate course at the Madras Library Association, which later moved to the University of Madras. In 1937, the course was converted to a one-year postgraduate diploma program (Mahapatra 2006; Mangla 1993). The first department of library science was established at the University of Delhi in 1946. It offered a postgraduate diploma in 1947 and a Master of Library Science in 1951, which was renamed Master of Library and Information Science in 1972.

There were only five universities that offered postgraduate diploma courses before India's independence in 1947. The number increased to 42 in the 1970s. Today, there are some 167 universities offering various kinds of LIS programs (Mahapatra 2006; Singh 2003a & 2003b). An estimated 120 universities offer Bachelor's degrees, 78 Master's degrees, 21 two-year integrated Master's degrees, 16 Master's of Philosophy (M.Phil.). degrees and 63 Ph.D. degrees. However, there is wide variation in the quality, ranging from strong programs at the cutting edge to weak programs with little resources.There is thus an urgent need for internal quality assurance and accreditation of LIS education in India (Sarkhel 2006; Singh 2003b).

To improve the quality of LIS education in Indian universities University Grants Commission (UGC) since its inception in 1956 has convened several Committees to review and make recommendations on various aspects of LIS education (Sarkhel 2006; Rath 2006;):

1. Ranganathan Committee on the Development of University and College Libraries, 1959
2. Ranganathan Committee on Library Science in Indian Universities, 1965

3. Kaula Committee on Curriculum Development in Library and Information Science, 1993
4. Karisiddappa Committee on Curriculum Development in Library and Information Science, 2001 (University Grants Commission, 2001).

The Committees make recommendations for standardization of curriculum, enrolment, infrastructure, quality of teachers, teaching and evaluation methodology, and research programs. However, implementation of the recommendations at the various universities is voluntary.

The UGC also set up the National Assessment and Accreditation Council (NAAC) to strengthen the quality of higher education in India (Sarkhel, 2006). The NAAC can carry out institutional accreditation and departmental accreditation. To date, no quality assessment has been carried out on an LIS department.

Varalakshmi (2006) reported that the traditional library job market is stagnant, with the development of public libraries and school libraries being neglected. Promising job markets are in university libraries and corporate libraries in technology companies. Raghavan and Agrawal (2006) noted the emergence of the corporate sector as a growing job market. This is because of the increasing number of multinationals establishing offices and various kinds of centers in India, and the modernization and globalization of Indian companies. More companies have come to realize that there is a need to hire information specialists to handle information management and knowledge management. Raghavan and Agrawal considered knowledge management to be one of the most promising emerging job markets for LIS professionals. They identified another emerging job market as that of the information product/service industry, including e-content creation, e-learning, cataloging and library automation.

Problems facing LIS education in India include (Mahapatra 2006; Mangla 1998; Sarkhel 2006; Singh 2003a & 2003b):

- Unplanned proliferation of LIS schools
- Wide variations in syllabi, teaching methods, evaluation methods and course content
- Inadequate number of faculty members, leading to high student-teacher ratio
- Inadequate resources and infrastructure in terms of classroom space, IT facilities and teaching aids
- Libraries with inadequate collections and resources
- Inadequate opportunities for faculty development
- Lack of internal quality assurance and accreditation system.

3.3.2 Pakistan

A one-year postgraduate certificate program was launched in 1915 by American library pioneer Asa Don Dickinson at the University of the Punjab, Lahore (Anwar 1992; Kaser 1992). This was the first formal program in Asia and the second in the world after Columbia University. The certificate program was suspended after the foundation of Pakistan in 1947 due to small student enrollment, but was revived in 1950 (Anis 1992).

The first postgraduate diploma program was established at the University of Karachi in 1956, followed by the University of the Punjab in 1959. The first Master's program was introduced in 1962 at the University of Karachi. Currently, seven universities in Pakistan offer two-year Master's degree programs, and an open university offers various distance-learning library science degrees.

The first PhD program was started at the University of Karachi in 1967, followed by several other universities. Recently, concern was expressed regarding the quality of these PhD programs, resulting in the Higher Education Commission (HEC) of Pakistan intervening and suspending some of them in 2006. However, programs with qualified academic staff and adequate resources were allowed to continue with a new "M.Phil. leading to PhD." scheme.

The HEC plays an important role in enhancing the quality of LIS education in Pakistan. To maintain minimum standards and consistency in LIS education, it developed a model curriculum in 2002 that all LIS programs are expected to follow. The model curriculum gives LIS programs the flexibility to adapt it according to their specific needs, resources and available faculty.

Currently, there is no professional accreditation body for LIS programs. However, Ameen (2007) reported that the HEC is developing a comprehensive multi-level mechanism of accreditation, both at the program and institution levels. All universities are expected to establish a "Quality Enhancement Cell" to introduce and implement the procedures in the Self-assessment Manual. LIS programs are also required to participate in this self-assessment scheme, which is expected to improve the overall quality of LIS education in Pakistan.

3.3.3 Bangladesh

Bangladesh has about 50 years of history in LIS education. Islam and Chowdhury (2006) reported that a certificate course in librarianship was offered by the Dhaka University Library in 1952, but it ran for only one session. A Department of Library Science was established in 1959 at the University of Dhaka with a post-graduate diploma program modeled on a similar program of the University of London. A B.A. (Hons) program was introduced in 1987, together with a name change to Department of Library and Information Science. A PhD program in library science was approved by the University of Dhaka in 1978. Currently, 2 public universities offer B.A. and M.A. in LIS, and 12 private institutes offer postgraduate diploma courses.

Islam and Chowdhury (2006) noted that the public library system is poor, so job opportunities in public libraries are limited. It is also rare to find a library run by an LIS professional in a corporate organization. Most LIS professionals work in educational institutions and special libraries, though the government does not require every school or college to have a librarian. Consequently, remuneration for LIS professionals remains low and career development opportunities are poor.

The following problems are found in the LIS education system in Bangladesh (Islam & Chowdhury, 2006):

- Lack of infrastructural facilities, including classrooms and laboratories
- Inadequate reading materials, including textbooks, classification and cataloging tools, and LIS journals.
- Inadequate full-time faculty
- Insufficient research and resources to support research
- Lack of faculty members with PhD degrees from Western countries
- Lack of job and career prospects, and low social status of librarians
- Lack of national policies relating to LIS professionals and LIS education.

4. TRENDS AND ISSUES

From the above description of the state of LIS education in various Asian countries, it is clear that LIS education is at different stages of development across countries and even across different regions in particular countries. Nevertheless, it is still possible to identify some regional trends, as LIS education appears to be moving in the same general direction due to increasing globalization, advances in information and communication technologies, the growth of the World Wide Web, and the influence of LIS developments in the U.S., U.K. and Australia. These three countries continue to educate a significant number of Asian librarians and library educators, and publish the bulk of LIS literature.

4.1 LIS Programs and Curriculum

Based on the country reports of LIS educators from five Southeast and East Asian countries in 2003 and 2004, Miwa (2006) identified the following trends in LIS education in the region:

1. elimination of the word "library" from the names of LIS programs in order to attract students
2. shift in the educational level from undergraduate to graduate
3. changes in core subject areas from an emphasis on manual-based collection development to ICT-based information/knowledge management
4. depreciation of LIS education for school librarians (except in Thailand)
5. decreasing opportunities for new employment in library markets due to over production of LIS graduates and economic recession
6. low interest among well-educated graduates in seeking employment opportunities in the public library market, which is characterized as offering relatively low social status and wage levels compared to national and academic libraries

7. lack of understanding among employers in accepting LIS graduates as capable knowledge workers
8. increase in the number of faculty with doctoral degrees, who prefer to teach cutting-edge courses rather than traditional library oriented courses.

These trends are true of the more developed countries in the region, which are developing what we consider Stage 3 LIS curricula. There is a further trend to educate information professionals for knowledge management roles in corporate organizations. LIS curriculum has also expanded to include management of digital and Internet resources, and development of new types of information services.

LIS schools are grappling with the following issues in the curriculum:

- defining the Information field and determining the core competencies
- rapid development in information-communication technology, especially Web and mobile technologies, and their implications for the LIS profession and LIS education
- determining what new competencies are needed in libraries as well as corporate environments
- determining how to impart these new competencies to LIS graduates and what resources are needed.

The required new competencies appear to be focused in the following areas:
- application of new information and communication technologies
- handling of digital, multimedia and Web-based information resources
- information/knowledge management in organizations
- soft skills, including communication skills.

However, many parts of Asia are still underdeveloped, with poor communication infrastructure, poor public library systems, and limited access to information technology. As some countries in Southeast Asia (especially Indo-China and Indonesia) have emerged from political turmoil relatively recently, they are still in the early stages of national and economic development, with a poorly developed public library system. Some countries, such as Cambodia and Laos, have no LIS schools. In the poor or undeveloped regions, LIS schools are struggling even to offer Stage 1 library science programs to prepare librarians for public and academic libraries. They have inadequate resources to incorporate information and communication technology into their programs. Within large countries like Indonesia, India and Thailand, there are wide disparities in economic development, library and information infrastructure, and LIS education programs – across the country as well as between urban and rural areas. The situation is exacerbated by the proliferation of LIS programs in institutions of higher learning, without thought for adequate resources and quality assurance.

A major exception is the Philippines, where the library association succeeded in its effort to have the government recognize librarianship as a profession that is essential to national development. State licensing of librarians was established, and the status of librarians and, consequently, the remuneration have improved. Nevertheless, because the country is still struggling with economic development, many LIS programs suffer from inadequate resources.

There is a substantial interest in the region in distance and online LIS programs, and in e-learning. Singh (2003) listed 27 institutions in India offering distance programs. Wang (2007) discussed the need for online LIS programs in Taiwan and the issue of quality assurance. Sacchanand (1998) surveyed LIS distance programs in the Asia-Pacific region. An update to this survey is urgently needed to determine the state of distance and online LIS programs in Asia.

4.2 Accreditation, Quality Control and Reform

None of the Asian countries has an accreditation system for LIS programs that is administered by the national library association, as in the U.S., U.K. and Australia. In most cases, the LIS program can be said to be accredited by the parent university. However, some indirect system of quality assurance has been established by the governments in the various countries.

In India, Pakistan, China and Indonesia, the Ministries of Education have set up national bodies to work with university departments, including LIS schools, to periodically deliberate and publish a model curriculum for LIS programs to follow or adapt to their situation. The model curriculum may be non-binding recommendations as in India and China, specify minimum requirements as in Indonesia, or prescribe a curriculum to be followed but with sufficient flexibility for local adaptations as in Pakistan. Malaysia is implementing a new accreditation system that involves representatives from the government, library association, library schools and employers.

In the Philippines, Japan and Taiwan, the focus is on licensing librarians, rather than accrediting the LIS programs. In the Philippines and Taiwan, aspiring librarians have to pass a licensure exam to work in public libraries. However, this raises the issues of who sets the examination questions and whether the questions are biased toward any particular LIS program. The examination also presupposes a certain set of competencies to be examined, and this has to be reviewed and revised regularly. One advantage of such a system is that it can be used to identify programs whose graduates have low passing rates. The Japanese system mandates a certain minimum curriculum, and all students who complete the curriculum are considered qualified to practice in public libraries.

The issue of accreditation of LIS professional programs has been discussed in regional LIS education conferences and workshops for a number of years. Several LIS educators have expressed the need for a Western-style accreditation system, with a panel of library educators and LIS professionals as assessors. The recent A-

LIEP 2007 conference in Taipei had a whole session devoted to discussing accreditation issues.

In 2000, Majid et al. (2003) carried out a questionnaire survey of LIS schools in Southeast Asia about a regional accreditation scheme. Most of the schools surveyed agreed on the need for such a scheme for LIS degrees in the region, and expressed interest in participating in one. Surveys in other parts of Asia have also found support for regional accreditation schemes (e.g. Rehman 2007). Khoo, Majid and Chaudhry (2003) discussed the issues involved in a regional accreditation system, including identifying an appropriate regional body to administer the accreditation system, problem of determining a framework and set of standards that takes into consideration the needs and situations in each country and still maintain minimum common standards to allow librarians to qualify for employment in other countries in the region.

4.3 Research and Literature

Substantial, high quality research is badly needed to advance library and information service in Asia. Unfortunately there is a dearth of high-quality research in LIS partly because of the lack of trained researchers and PhDs in the region. At the same time, good researchers often choose to work in emerging or theoretical areas, especially in the areas of IT, digital libraries and the Web, that are often not relevant to practical library and information services. There is thus an urgent need to focus the limited research talent on advancing the theory and practice of library and information service in various environments, and on the issues and problems faced in the region.

There is also severe lack of LIS textbooks written in the local languages. Faculty members often have to devote a substantial amount of time writing or translating textbooks in the local language. Fortunately, in many Asian countries, students are able to read textbooks in English, even if they are not comfortable writing or speaking in the language. English language textbooks however do not address the particular issues and situations in Asian countries.

4.4 Faculty Development

LIS faculty development is a challenging issue in Asian countries. The less developed countries have very few PhD holders and very few PhD programs to train researchers and educators. LIS professionals also have difficulty enrolling in PhD programs overseas because of inadequate command of English. There are also insufficient continuing education opportunities for LIS educators to learn about new developments and acquire new knowledge in emerging areas. There is limited funding for overseas travel to attend conferences and workshops.

4.5 Regional Collaborations

Traditionally, the region has looked to the U.S., U.K. and Australia for leadership in the LIS field. There is however a recent trend in higher education in general, and LIS education in particular, to develop collaborations and cooperatives in Asian countries, as many Asian countries are developing rapidly and their universities are developing into world class institutions. Collaborations in LIS can be seen in the joint organization and participation in regional conferences, such as A-LIEP, LIPER Workshops, and ICADL conferences, and in student and staff exchanges and visits. Some LIS schools have also set up programs for funding visiting fellows (such as the ACRC fellowships at the Nanyang Technological University, Singapore), and providing PhD scholarships for international students. Research collaborations are also taking place, mainly as a by-product of staff exchanges and visits. At the ICADL 2007 conference, Dr Shigeo Sugimoto and Dr Shalini R. Urs put forward a proposal to form a *Consortium of I-schools in Asia-Pacific* (CISAP) to provide a framework for closer cooperation in the region.

5. CONCLUSION

Most countries in the Asian region have had more than 50 years of history in LIS education. However, LIS education is at different levels of development in different countries because of their different historical backgrounds and level of economic development. However, because of globalization and increasing regional networking and dialog, LIS education in the region is moving in the same direction. It is expected that with the increasing collaboration in the region, an Asian brand of LIS will eventually emerge. Meanwhile, it is important to improve the training and continuing education of LIS faculty, and improve the resources of LIS schools.

ACKNOWLEDGEMENTS

The authors acknowledge with grateful thanks the editorial assistance of Ms. Liew Soon Kah, and the assistance of Ms. Shizuko Miyahara with translation of Japanese articles.

References

Ameen, K. (2007). Issues of quality assurance in LIS higher education in Pakistan. In *World Library and Information Congress: 73rd IFLA General Conference and Council*. [Online] Available: http://www.ifla.org/IV/ifla73/Programme2007. htm. Retrieved March 1, 2008.

Anis, K. (1992). Library education in Pakistan: Concerns, issues and practices. In S. Rehma, A.S. Chaudhry, & A.H. Qarshi (Eds.), *Library education in Pakistan: Past, present and future*. Lahore: PULSAA.

Anwar, M. A. (1992). State of the library profession in Pakistan: From celebration to reality. In S. Rehma, A.S. Chaudhry, & A.H. Qarshi (Eds.), *Library education in Pakistan: Past, present and future*. Lahore: PULSAA.

Butdisuwan, S. (2000). Library and information science education in Thailand: General scenario. *Singapore Journal of Library & Information Management*, *29*, 44-49.

David, L. T., & Perez, D.R. (2006). An assessment of the perception of licensed librarians about their aca-demic preparation and satisfaction in their job as librarians. In *Proceedings of the Asia-Pacific Conference on Library & Information Education & Practice 2006 (A-LIEP 2006)* (pp. 416-422). Singapore: School of Communication & Information, Nanyang Technological University. [Online] Available: http://www.ntu.edu.sg/sci/a-liep/A-LIEP2006. e-proceedings.htm. Retrieved March 1, 2008.

Fan, F. (2006). Collaboration and resource sharing among LIS schools in China. In *Proceedings of the Asia-Pacific Conference on Library & Information Education & Practice 2006 (A-LIEP 2006)* (pp. 284-287). Singapore: School of Communication & Information, Nanyang Technological University. [Online] Available: http://www.ntu.edu.sg/sci/a-liep/A-LIEP2006.e-pro ceedings.htm. Retrieved March 1, 2008.

Islam, M. S., & Chowdhury, M. A. K. (2006). Library and information science education system in Bangladesh: An overall situation. In *Proceedings of the Asia-Pacific Conference on Library & Information Education & Practice 2006 (A-LIEP 2006)* (pp. 358-363). Singapore: School of Communication & Information, Nanyang Technological University. [Online] Available: http://www.ntu. edu.sg/sci/a-liep/A-LIEP2006.e-proceedings.htm. Retrieved March 1, 2008.

Jamaludin, A., Hussin, N., & Mokhtar, W. N. H. W. (2006). Library and information career in Malaysia: Aspirations of educators and the reality of the industry. In *Proceedings of the Asia-Pacific Conference on Library & Information Education & Practice 2006 (A-LIEP 2006)* (pp. 423-426). Singapore: School of Communication & Information, Nanyang Technological University. [Online] Available: http://www.ntu.edu.sg/sci/a-liep/A-LIEP2006.e-proceedings. htm. Retrieved March 1, 2008.

Kaser, D. (1992). Asa Don Dickinson: A librarian of his times. In S. Rehma, A.S. Chaudhry, & A.H. Qarshi (Eds.), *Library education in Pakistan: Past, present and future* (pp. 3-10). Lahore: PULSAA.

Khoo, C. (2005). Educating LIS professionals for Singapore and beyond. In J. Tan et al. (Eds.), *Celebrating 50 years of librarianship in Malaysia and Singapore* (pp. 26-37). Singapore: Library Association of Singapore; Kuala Lumpur: Persatuan Pustakawan Malaysia.

Khoo, C., Majid, S., & Chaudhry, A.S. (2003). Developing an accreditation system for LIS professional education programs in Southeast Asia: Issues and perspectives. *Malaysian Journal of Library & Information Science, 8*(2), 131-150.

Khoo, C.S.G. (2004, November). Trends in LIS education in Singapore. Paper presented at the *1st LIPER International Seminar on November 13, 2004, at Keio University Mita Campus, Tokyo, Japan.* [Online] Available: http://www soc.nii.ac.jp/jslis/liper/record/singapore-e.pdf. Retrieved January 15, 2006.

Kon, M. (1993). Education for librarianship in Japan. *Asian Libraries, 3*(4), 73-77.

Kwon, E.-K. (2003). Current situation of library and information science education in Korea (in Japanese). Paper presented at the *2nd LIPER Seminar on December 6, 2003, at Tokyo University Hongo Campus, Tokyo, Japan.* [Online] Available: http://wwwsoc.nii.ac.jp/jslis/liper/record/resume031206. pdf. Retrieved January 9, 2006.

Lim, H.T. (1970). *Libraries in West Malaysia & Singapore.* Kuala Lumpur: Art Printing Works. (As quoted in Abdoulaye, 2003)

Lin, C. (2004). Library and information science (LIS) education in Taiwan: The development, current situation, and future perspectives. Paper presented at the *1st LIPER International Seminar on November 13, 2004, at Keio University Mita Campus, Tokyo, Japan.* [Online] Available: http://wwwsoc. nii.ac.jp/jslis/ liper/record/taiwan-e.pdf. Retrieved January 15, 2006.

Ma, F. (1993). Library and information science education in China. *Asian Libraries, 3*(4), 58-67.

Mahapatra, G. (2006). LIS education in India: Emerging paradigms, challenges and propositions in the digital era. In *Proceedings of the Asia-Pacific Conference on Library & Information Education & Practice 2006 (A-LIEP 2006)* (pp. 634-637). Singapore: School of Communication & Information, Nanyang Technological University. [Online] Available: http://www.ntu.edu. sg/sci/a-liep/A-LIEP2006. e-proceedings.htm. Retrieved March 1, 2008.

Majid, S., Chaudhry, A.S., Foo, S., & Logan, E. (2003). Accreditation of library and information studies programs in Southeast Asia: A proposed model. *Singapore Journal of Library & Information Management, 32*, 58-69.

Mangla, P. B. (1998). Library and information science education: Trends and issues. In M. K. Jain (Ed.), *Fifty years of library and information services in India* (283-293). New Delhi: Shipra.

Mangla, P.B. (1993). Library and information science education in South Asia: India, Pakistan, Bangladesh, and Sri Lanka. *Asian Libraries, 3*, 23-40.

Miwa, M. (2006). Trends and issues in LIS education in Asia. *Journal of Education for Library and Information Science, 47*(3), 167-180.

Miwa, M., Ueda, S., Nemoto, A., Oda, M., Nagata, H., & Horikawa, T. (2006). Final results of LIPER (Library and Information Professions and Education Renewal) 1 project in Japan. In *World Library and Information Congress: 72nd IFLA General Conference and Council.* [Online] Available: http://www.ifla. org/IV/ifla72/index.htm. Retrieved March 1, 2008.

Nera, C.M. (2006). The professionalization of Filipino librarians. In *Congress of Southeast Asian Librarians (CONSAL): 13th General Conference.*

Premsmit, P. (1993). Library and information science education in Thailand: A summary. *Asian Libraries, 3*(4), 87-88.

Premsmit, P. (2004). Library and information science education in Thailand. Paper presented at the *2nd LIPER International Seminar on December 18, 2004, at Keio University Mita Campus, Tokyo, Japan.* [Online] Available: http://wwwsoc.nii.ac.jp/jslis/liper/record/thailand-e.pdf. Retrieved January 15, 2006.

Raghavan, K. S., & Agrawal, N. (2006). Has the market place for information professionals changed? In *Proceedings of the Asia-Pacific Conference on Library & Infor-mation Education & Practice 2006 (A-LIEP 2006)* (pp. 409-415). Singapore: School of Communication & Information, Nanyang Technological University. [Online] Available: http://www.ntu.edu.sg/sci/a-liep/A-LIEP2006.e-proceedings.htm. Retrieved March 1, 2008.

Rath, P. (2006). Preparing library and information professionals for the 21st century: Issue and challenges for library and information science educators in India. In *Proceedings of the Asia-Pacific Conference on Library & Information Education & Practice 2006 (A-LIEP 2006)* (pp. 35-40). Singapore: School of Communication & Information, Nanyang Technological University. [Online] Available: http://www.ntu.edu.sg/sci/a-liep/A-LIEP2006.e-proceed ings.htm. Retrieved March 1, 2008.

Rehman, S. (2007). Accreditation of LIS programs in the Arabian Gulf region. In *Proceedings of the Asia-Pacific Conference on Library & Information Education & Practice 2007 (2nd A-LIEP 2007)* (pp. 70-86). Taipei: Department of Information & Communications, Shih-Hsin University.

Sacchanand, C. (1998). Distance education in library and information science in Asia and the Pacific Region. In *World Library and Information Congress: 64th IFLA General Conference and Council.* Retrieved March 1, 2008, from http://www.ifla.org/IV/ifla64/64cp.htm

Saladyanant, T. (2006). Quality assurance of information science program: Chiang Mai University. In *Proceedings of the Asia-Pacific Conference on Library & Infor-mation Education & Practice 2006 (A-LIEP 2006)* (pp. 432-435). Singapore: School of Communication & Information, Nanyang Technological University. [Online] Available: http://www.ntu.edu.sg/sci/a-liep/A-LIEP2006.e-proceedings.htm. Retrieved March 1, 2008.

Santos, A.M. (2003). The professionalization of librarians in the Philippines: The role of library associations. In World Library and Information Congress: 69th IFLA General Conference and Council. [Online] Available: http:// www.ifla.org/ IV/ifla69/papers/134e-Santos.pdf. Retrieved March 1, 2008.

Sarkhel, J. K. (2006). Quality assurance and accreditation of LIS education in Indian Universities: Issues and perspectives. In *Proceedings of the Asia-Pacific Con-ference on Library & Information Education & Practice 2006 (A-LIEP 2006)* (pp. 427-431). Singapore: School of Communication & Information, Nanyang Technological University. [Online] Available: http://www.ntu.edu.sg/ sci/a-liep/A-LIEP2006.e-proceedings.htm. Retrieved March 1, 2008.

Schniederjürgen, A. (Ed.). (2007). *World guide to library, archive, and information science education* (3rd ed.). München : K.G. Saur.

Singh, D. (2007). Accreditation of library and information science education programs: The Malaysian experience. In *Proceedings of the Asia-Pacific Conference on Library & Information Education & Practice 2007 (2nd A-LIEP 2007)* (pp. 87-112). Taipei: Department of Information & Communications, Shih-Hsin University.

Singh, S. P. (2003a). Are we really ready to face challenges of the LIS profession? In *Knowledge Management in Special Libraries in Digital Environment: Papers presented at the 24th All India Conference of IASLIC* (pp.449-456). Calcutta: IASLIC.

Singh, S.P. (2003b). Library and information science education in India: Issues and trends. *Malaysian Journal of Library & Information Science, 8*(2), 1-18.

Sulistyo-Basuki, L. (1993). Library education and training in Indonesia. *Asian Libraries, 3*(4), 41-48.

Sulistyo-Basuki, L. (2006). Political reformation and its impact on Library and Information Science education and practice: A case study of Indonesia during and post-president-Soeharto administration. In *Proceedings of the Asia-Pacific Conference on Library & In-formation Education & Practice 2006 (A-LIEP 2006)* (pp. 172-179). Singapore: School of Communication & Information, Nanyang Technological University. [Online] Available: http://www. ntu.edu.sg/ sci/a-liep/A-LIEP2006.e-proceedings.htm. Retrieved March 1, 2008.

Thuraisingham, A. (1984). The part-time post-graduate diploma course in library and information science – The Singapore experience. *Singapore Libraries, 14*, 63-66.

Thuraisingham, A. (1989). Education for librarianship and information studies in Singapore. In *The need to read: Essays in honour of Hedwig Anuar.* Singapore: Festival of Books Singapore Pte Ltd.

Tsuji, K., Yoshida, Y., Miwa, M., Takeuchi, H., Muranushi, T., & Shibata, M. (2006). Library and information science education in Japan: Results of a 2005 survey of shisho certification. *Journal of Education for Library and Information Science, 47*(3), 238-255.

Uddin, M.H., & Rahman, M.A. (2003). Library development and education in Bangladesh: An overview. *Singapore Journal of Library & Information Management, 32*, 49-57.

Ueda, S., Nemoto, A., Miwa, M., Oda, M., Nagata, H., & Horikawa, T. (2005). LIPER (Library and Information Professionals and Education Renewal) Project in Japan. In *World Library and Information Congress: 71st IFLA General Conference and Council*. [Online] Available: http://www.ifla. org/IV/ifla71/ Programme. htm. Retrieved March 1, 2008.

University Grants Commission. (2001). *UGC model curriculum: Library and information science*. New Delhi: UGC.

Vallejo, R.M. (1993). Library and information science education in the Philippines: A summary. *Asian Libraries, 3*(4), 81-82.

Varalakshmi, R.S.R. (2006). Educating 21st century LIS professionals – Needs and expectations: A survey Indian LIS professionals and alumni. *Journal of Education for Library and Information Science, 47*(3), 181-199.

Wang, M.L. (2007). The impact of e-learning quality assurance on LIS education in Taiwan. In *Proceedings of the Asia-Pacific Conference on Library & Information Education & Practice 2007 (2nd A-LIEP 2007)* (pp. 15-28). Taipei: Department of Information & Communications, Shih-Hsin University.

Wang, Y. (2006). Trends of LIS education in China. Presented at the *Asia-Pacific Conference on Library & Information Education & Practice 2006 (A-LIEP 2006)*. [Online] Available: http://www.ntu.edu.sg/sci/a-liep/A-LIEP2006.e-pro ceedings.htm. Retrieved March 1, 2008.

Wijasuriya, D.E.K., Lim, H.T., & Radah, N. (1975). The barefoot librarian: Library development in Southeast Asia with special reference to Malaysia. London: Clive Bingley. (As quoted in Abdoulaye, 2003)

Wu, W. C. (2003). The reformation and development of LIS in China [in Chinese]. *Library Work and Study, 2003*(5), 2-5.

APPENDIX. NUMBER OF LIS SCHOOLS IN ASIAN COUNTRIES

Country	No. of LIS schools/depts
East Asia	
China	44
Japan	8
Mongolia	1
South Korea	5
Taiwan	13
Hong Kong (China SAR)	1

Country	No. of LIS schools/depts
Southeast Asia	
Indonesia	15
Malaysia	4
Philippines	72 (including many teacher colleges)
Singapore	1
Thailand	16
Vietnam	10
Myanmar	1
South Asia	
Bangladesh	3
India	167
Pakistan	8
Sri Lanka	1

PART 3
AUSTRALIA:
INTRODUCTION

Stuart Ferguson
Regional Editor

Library development is affected by a number of factors, such as geopolitics, socio-economic factors, demographics, climate and environment. Library development in Australia and New Zealand has been colored by the British colonial past of each country, particularly that of Australia, which was formed out of separate British colonies in 1901, each with its own capital city and unique library history. Both countries have been strongly influenced by library movements in Britain and have on occasion attempted to emulate leading British institutions, such as the Bodleian Library in Oxford, but both have also had to deal with factors that differentiate them from the British experience: for instance, the distance of both from the main sources of books, for so long the life-blood of libraries, and, in the case of Australia, the sheer internal distances and state and territory divisions, which have affected the development of educational systems and institutions. In recent years, too, the library and information professions in both countries have given greater attention to the needs of indigenous populations – an area in which New Zealand has a clearer national focus than Australia.

The library and information professions in both countries are well developed, with largely graduate professions. The situation differs from other English-speaking countries, most notably the USA, in that both professional associations – the Australian Library and Information Association (ALIA) and the Library and Information Association of New Zealand Aotearoa (LIANZA) – allow undergraduate as well as postgraduate pathways to professional membership. Postgraduate pathways differ too from those in other countries, with the Graduate Diploma (often embedded within a Masters program) recognized as a professional qualification. There is also a healthy body paraprofessionals, with Library Technician programs offered by colleges of Technical and Further Education. As the following chapters demonstrate, there are also significant differences between the two countries, with school systems in Australia mirroring the US model, with dual-qualified teacher librarians the norm, and the New Zealand sector resembling the British model, with school librarians and media specialists who do not have teaching qualifications (or teachers' salaries).

As is in many other countries, libraries in Australia and New Zealand are undergoing substantial change as a result of factors such as globalization, financial crises, developments in information and communication technologies (ICT) and the changes in the publishing industries. Many of the leading libraries in both countries have embraced the technological changes and have been at the forefront, or close, of digital library development. Both national libraries, for instance, have used ICTs to become more 'national' in terms of service delivery and presence than they were in the days of print, and the National Library of Australia's Online Web Archive, Pandora, marks a world-leading effort to collect Australian Web resources. As for other countries, however, development is patchy, with public (government) schools, for instance, generally lagging behind private schools in terms of technology and resources. Significant changes are taking place, with the traditional special library disappearing from some organizationorganizations, especially in the corporate sector. Library and Information Science education, which has always enjoyed 'fruitful tensions', has some important issues to resolve, with professional associations, educational institutions and employers liaising on workforce planning. The following chapters attempt to capture the main strands in these fascinating developments.

PUBLIC LIBRARIES

Chris Jones, Philip Calvert and Stuart Ferguson

In Australia and New Zealand, the term, "public library," is generally taken to refer to the range of community libraries that provide free library and information services within their local government jurisdictions. Both countries also have national libraries, funded by the national government and dedicated to the collection and preservation of their country's documentary heritage. The system of publicly funded libraries is complicated in Australia by its federal system of government, inherited in 1901, when the independent Commonwealth of Australia was formed from previously separate British colonies. Each of Australia's states – New South Wales, Victoria, Tasmania, South Australia, Western Australia and Queensland – has its own state library, most of which developed out of the early public libraries. These have close links with public libraries in their respective states and perform a similar collecting role to national libraries. The two "territories" in Australia – Northern Territory and the Australian Capital Territory – also have their own well-established library services.

NATIONAL, STATE AND TERRITORY LIBRARIES

The National Library of Australia, the National Library of New Zealand (Te Puna Mātauranga o Aotearoa) and Australia's eight state and territory government are legal deposit libraries. Each, therefore, plays a key role in collecting and preserving the documentary heritage within its respective political jurisdiction. The other main role of these deposit libraries is to provide leadership on key issues within the relevant jurisdiction (Missingham & Cameron 2007; 73). There is considerable cooperation amongst them, much of it through their joint membership of National and State Libraries Australasia (NSLA; previously Council of Australian State Libraries but renamed in 2005 to reflect its expanded membership, which includes the National Library of New Zealand). One of the benefits of collaboration has been increased public access to information, such as the AskNow! service, established in 2002, which uses chat software and internet and library resources to provide a 24/7 information service, and involved all the Australian state and territory libraries, the national libraries of Australia, New Zealand and Singapore, and fifteen public libraries (Missingham & Cameron 2007: 79).

The National Library of Australia began life in 1901 as the Commonwealth Parliamentary Library and was initially based in Melbourne, where the federal government was sited, not moving to Canberra until 1927. It was unofficially renamed the Commonwealth National Library in 1923 but it was not until the passing of the National Library of Australia Act in 1960 that it acquired its statutory title, and in 1961 its parliamentary and archival functions were reassigned to the newly created

Commonwealth Parliamentary Library and the Commonwealth Archives Office (Biskup & Goodman 1994: 145). At the time of the influential Munn-Pitt Report of 1935, *Australian Libraries: A Survey of Conditions and Suggestions for Their Improvement*, the National Library was the sixth largest library in Australia (Biskup & Goodman 1994: 145), but it is now the largest, with 5.4 million items listed for 2007 (Ferguson 2007: 345). From early on, the Library has acquired some significant Australiana collections and items, such as the Petherick collection of Australian and Pacific materials (1911).

Over the years, collecting institutions such as the National Library of Australia have harnessed information and communication technologies to create institutions that are far more 'national' in terms of service delivery and presence than ever their print-based predecessors could be. The National Library promotes the view that legal deposit principles should be applied to digital resources as rigorously as they are to the print publication environment. In 1995 it established Pandora: Australia's Online Web Archive, which, in collaboration with state and territory libraries, supports the development of a digital collection for the Australian public. By 2005, the Archive held copies of more than 10,000 Australian digital resources, more than twenty per cent of which no longer exist in the public domain of the internet (Missingham & Cameron, 2007: 77). In 2005, the National Library began the first of its 'whole-of-domain' harvests of Australian websites, and collected and archived more than 185 million unique documents from 811,000 sites (Missingham & Cameron, 2007:. 78). Other initiatives include the formation of the National Coalition on Maintaining Access to Australia's Digital Information Resources; the development of a national Information Access Plan, through the NSLA; Libraries Australia (replaced the Kinetica service in late 2005), which provides a free search interface to forty million resources held by over a thousand Australian libraries and other collecting institutions, and an online interlibrary loans system; PictureAustralia (piloted in 1998), which is a digital image service that involves all state and territory libraries and (since 2006) a collaboration with Flickr; and MusicAustralia (2005), which provides access to online and print music resources in the national, state and territory libraries.

The National Library of New Zealand was established in 1965. Its statutory responsibilities are laid out in the National Library of New Zealand (Te Puna Mātauranga o Aotearoa) Act of 2003. In 2007 it had over two million items in its collection. Like its Australian counterpart, it has enjoyed an active acquisitions program, most notably with the bequest of the Alexander Turnbull collections as long ago as 1918, which includes photographs, drawings and prints, oral histories, manuscripts and archives and a range of printed materials (Missingham & Cameron 2007:. 77). Perhaps rather unexpectedly, the Alexander Turnbull Library (the research collection within the National Library of New Zealand) is the home of an internationally renowned collection of works by John Milton and his contemporaries. It also has a fine collection of South Pacific materials, often collected in person from the island nations of the Pacific by Turnbull Library staff.

The National Library of New Zealand is a government department, and in that capacity offers policy advice to the Minister Responsible for the National Library on library and information issues. This covers a fairly broad area, including matters such as electronic publishing, copyright legislation and the development of a knowledge economy through greater access to information resources. The Library has been a leader in digitization in New Zealand, and over the years has launched a variety of digital projects designed not only to increase access to the Library's resources for all the people of New Zealand, but also as a learning tool for the librarians themselves. The Library has its own Digital Strategy (National Library of New Zealand 2003), and it plays a significant part in the wider national Digital Strategy which aims to create a digital future for all New Zealanders, using the power of information and communications technology (ICT) to enhance all aspects of people's lives (http://www.digitalstrategy.govt.nz/).

State libraries in Australia are primarily public libraries that focus on research and reference services and in this resemble the German state libraries. Whereas state libraries in the USA serve state legislatures, Australian parliaments have developed their own libraries independently of the state libraries (Biskup & Goodman 1994:. 41). Australian state libraries originate in either public libraries or local subscription libraries, although all eventually included 'public' in their names until most exchanged 'public' for 'state' in 1943 – New South Wales was the exception, calling its state library the Library of New South Wales between 1969 and 1975 (Biskup & Goodman 1994: 41). Each of the state libraries is a legal deposit library for its state and therefore resembles a national library in its mission to collect and preserve the documentary heritage within its geopolitical territory. Each has valuable historical collections: for instance, the State Library of New South Wales's Mitchell Library collection, based on over 67,000 items that were bequeathed to the Library in 1907.

Both Australia's territories are now self-governing and, although not full states, have 'state like' library services. Northern Territory Library is a well-established library service, with earlier institutions going as far back as 1877 (the Palmerston Institute), and has an extensive collection of Northern Territoriana. It is treated by publishers and government departments as a legal deposit library. Since 1935, residents of the national capital, Canberra, had a library lending service, run by the National Library, but self government in 1989 for the Australian Capital Territory (ACT) led to the establishment of a territorial library.

ROLE OF AUSTRALIAN STATE AND TERRITORY LIBRARIES IN PUBLIC LIBRARY PROVISION

Unlike the National Library, Australia's state and territory libraries have close ties with public libraries. The ACT Library Service and State Library of Tasmania deliver services through largely centralised systems. In Northern Territory too public libraries are integrated with the territory system, with delivery of public library services a partnership involving the Department of Education, Employment and Training, communities and local government. The Northern Territory Library provides support, including services to remote communities through a series of Libraries and Knowledge Centers (Missingham & Cameron 2007: 81-82).

Outside Tasmania, state libraries do not actually manage public libraries but provide support for them through cooperative arrangements. Western Australia does have a relatively centralized system, with provision of collections and a range of information services through the state's public libraries, but these are managed at a local level. In Queensland, those public libraries serving populations greater than 20,000 provide their own services, funded largely by local government, with the State Library of Queensland providing some support, including specialist services such as Indigenous Services. In smaller local government areas, however, library services are provided centrally through the Country Lending Scheme (CLS), with local government providing staff and buildings. The State Library of South Australia supports public libraries through Public Library Services (previously Public Library Automated Information Network), with collection support, a state-based catalogue, a range of grants and services for smaller communities. New South Wales and Victoria have similar cooperative models, with largely independent library services run by a single local government authorities or regional library services and support from the state libraries in the form of subsidies and library development grants.

It is worth noting that state libraries provide far more than just funding – amongst other things, they can lobby on behalf of public libraries, develop cooperative arrangements, provide professional advice, provide subsidized access to the Internet and online databases, offer access to major collections and act as important library training organizationorganizations: for instance, in 2002, State Library of New South Wales established its Public Library Network Research Program, which provides quality research and evaluation to support the promotion, planning, development and review of the NSW Public Library Network (Missingham & Cameron 2007, p. 82). In 2004 Victoria's public library services, the Library Board of Victoria and the State Library of Victoria agreed on a new framework, which 'proposes a new focus for collaboration in order to achieve increased community and government understanding of and engagement with libraries and greater efficiency and effectiveness of library services' (Missingham & Cameron 2007, p. 82). This may provide a model for other states.

THE MISSION OF PUBLIC LIBRARIES

… no other agency in society has the breadth of role, the user range and diversity and the potential impact. In an age of specialization and community silos, public libraries are unique. (*Alan Bundy, 2003, p. 6*)

The public library is there for everyone, and in general the services it provides are free of charge. In Australia, this freedom of access is encapsulated in various State legislations and is embedded in the philosophies of national industry bodies like Public Libraries Australia (PLA) and the Australian Library and Information Association (ALIA).

The Library and Information Association of New Zealand Aotearoa has made this statement (LIANZA, n.d.).

Services are funded from the public purse for two reasons:

1. They are not commercially viable even if essential to the public good.
2. They fulfill an accepted individual right, which would only be available to the privileged if not available free of charge.

LIANZA believes that public libraries satisfy both these criteria. Recognising that in times of economic stringency there is a tendency to look for ways of raising funds for public services other than by taxation, the Association asserts that it is essential that a basic level of public library provision be retained in accordance with its Standards for Public Library Service, adopted in 1980.

1. Public libraries should be free and universally available.
2. Public library services should be available free of charge, except such charges as defined in the Standards.
3. Public library collections should reflect the interests, immediate and potential, of the community and should cater for individuals as well as popular requirements.
4. All users should be able to borrow and have access to all services from public libraries.
5. Public libraries should be an integral part of local government.
6. Financing of public libraries should be the combined responsibility of local and central government.

Such a broad scope with such a low price tag means that people from all ages, all levels of ability, all ethnicity, all educational needs and with differing demands are walking through the doors of a public library somewhere.

So what is the shape of the community that public libraries are striving to serve? Table 1 features selected key Australian demographics taken from the 2001 and 2006 Census.

Table 1: Key Statistics from the 2001 and 2006 Census of Australia

	2001	% of Total Persons	2006	% of Total Persons
Population	18,769,249	N/A	19,855,288	N/A
Median age	35	N/A	37	N/A
0-4 years	1,243,969	6.6	1,260,405	6.3
65 years and over	2,370,878	12.6	2,644,374	13.3
Never married	4,691,609	31.6	5,278,600	33.2
Separated or divorced	1,609,314	10.8	1,801,979	11.3
Couple families without children	1,764,167	35.7	1,943,643	37.2
One parent families	762,632	15.4	823,254	15.8

Overall the population has grown 5.7% but it is the nature of the growth that has implications for public libraries. The population is aging and it will continue to do so as baby boomers (those born between 1946 and 1965) move through their life cycle. Moreover, the nature of the family unit is changing. More people are alone at home or are in a relationship without children, whilst children are increasingly being raised in single-parent families.

Overlaying these trends within the population is the geographic reality of Australia. The twenty million people living there are spread across 7.8 million km^2, but this spread is far from even. There are centers of dense and multicultural population surrounded by large regions of low population density where infrastructure such as roads and broadband communications are a sought-after resource.

PUBLIC LIBRARIES IN NEW ZEALAND

Unlike Australia, there is no organization that provides official coordination of the public libraries in New Zealand. The Library Association of New Zealand Aotearoa (LIANZA) facilitates voluntary cooperation, especially through PUB-SIG, one of its most active special interest groups, which states that its purpose is 'To promote and support the development of public library services and the librarians who work in them' (PUB-SIG, n.d.). The SIG collects and publishes annual statistics of public library financial data, outputs and performance measures. It also regularly updates national standards for public libraries (LIANZA, 2004). The latest revision includes sections on information literacy, services to people with languages other than English or Maori, and library technology.

In the absence of any official coordination in New Zealand, public libraries serving a population of more than 50,000 people joined together in Metronet (2005). Nineteen libraries are members at the start of 2008. This organization is funded by the member libraries, so its activities are inevitably limited, but it has attempted some interesting projects. In 2005 the Metronet libraries funded a national promotional campaign. Fifteen-second advertisements were shown on national television during a ten week period. They also paid for posters featuring national celebrities from the worlds of sport, music, fashion and so on, celebrating the benefits of libraries.

HISTORY OF PUBLIC LIBRARIES

The first successful libraries in Australia were established in Sydney during the 1820s, developing largely out of private collections and operating on a subscription basis. At this time the School of Arts movement was being established in Britain and the concept of a community based library soon took hold in Australia. The first of these schools of art, more commonly called mechanics institutes, was established in Tasmania in 1827. These institutes flourished across Australia and by 1900 there were around a thousand institutes in operation. Throughout the 1850s and 1860s several free library services were established.

Although public libraries were clearly becoming a part of many communities, the 1932 Munn-Pitt Report, mentioned above, presented scathing findings on the quality of library service and the facilities in which they were housed. As a result of this the Free Library Movement was established and championed by a number of key figures. The Free Library Movement gained slowly but steady support, and by the mid-1940s the state and territories had all established some form of free, public library service. The reality, however, was that the level of commitment by each State, particularly in regards to funding, meant that decades would pass before the modern library systems of today arrived. Each state and territory has developed a model for public libraries services best suited to its own demographic and geographic factors. In some states, consequently, local government is the main provider of public libraries, whereas in others the state government plays a more prominent role in centrally coordinating services (see above).

Public library history follows a similar pattern in New Zealand to that in Australia. The public libraries were established by British colonists in imitation of the civic institutions in the old country. The earliest New Zealand public library was the Port Nicholson Exchange and Public Library (in others words, Wellington), established in 1841.

THE FACTS AND THE FUNDING

The Australian Bureau of Statistics conducted a nation-wide survey of public libraries in 2004. This revealed that there are 532 local government library organizationorganizations operating from 1,716 locations. They employ 10,606 staff and utilize 6,315 volunteers. They cost $545.2 million to operate, with $521.9 million coming from government sources. Public libraries hold forty-two million items, which are lent out 176 million times to around 100 million visitors each year. Every single figure provided above has increased since a similar survey conducted in 1999/2000.

There is no direct federal funding of public libraries in Australia, although the Commonwealth Government does support the National Library of Australia. This organizationorganization provides public libraries with access to an excellent collection of resources and it also maintains the nation's bibliographic databases, Libraries Australia, but this remains the extent of the relationship. Any other funding is incidental and non-recurrent. Consequently, the day-to-day running of the public library networks is maintained largely through a mixture of state and local government funding (see above).

Public libraries in New Zealand are funded by the local government authority (generally known as the Council), which in turn raises revenue from local taxation called rates. Commonly in large authorities there are several library buildings with one central and several branch libraries, but all are part of the same library system. This is not uniform, however – indeed nothing in New Zealand's public libraries appears to be – so the number of separate library authorities seems to vary with each count, but a number of about seventy-two is accurate enough. The largest in Auckland and Christchurch serve populations of around 400,000, although at the other end of the scale there are at least ten libraries serving fewer than 10,000 people. Naturally the largest libraries have been able to develop many new products and services over the years, but the smallest libraries have just a few staff and are unable to provide more than book collections of about 20,000 items.

The National Library of New Zealand used to provide some assistance to public libraries, especially the smaller ones, but this service was closed in the 1990s. It assists in formulating policy but has no further powers. Together with the national library association (LIANZA) and Local Government New Zealand, the National Library developed a strategy that sets out the roles that public libraries can play in delivering desired community outcomes. The main audience was local government representatives who can allocate the needed resources to achieve the aims set out in the strategy. As well as some expected roles, the policy described libraries as public spaces, and the parts they play in supporting lifelong learning and good citizenship (*Public Libraries of New Zealand*, 2006).

FORCES SHAPING PUBLIC LIBRARIES

There are many forces that shape the modern public library in Australia and New Zealand, and these must be identified if one is to understand the emerging role that public libraries will continue to play in their communities:

Social inclusion: the aging of the population and changes in family structure mean that people are seeking safe places where they can connect with others. This connection may be physical or virtual.

Technology and information boom: in these countries, the Internet is now present in one shape or form in the lives of most people. This presence brings with it technology, training and telecommunications challenges as well as the problem of the sheer magnitude of data that the average seeker of knowledge confronts. It is also becoming a major distribution channel for the entertainment industry.

Client Expectations: anyone who has worked in a public library for any length of time will know how much the staff-client relationship has changed. The emphasis now is on providing a library service, not just a collection and the client certainly has higher expectations than ever before. Nor will this diminish, as Joseph (2006) notes: '...the aging of the baby boomers may herald much higher expectations and demands of library services.'

Competition: public libraries face competition on a wide range of fronts. State and local governments are increasingly under financial pressure to provide all the services the community demands. The marketplace is now abundant with alternative forms of entertainment and the Internet has opened opportunities for individuals or other organizationorganizations/companies to undertake information seeking alternatives. On all these fronts the library must compete and be willing to market its services and expertise, increasingly to non-traditional funding bodies.

Catering for the aging: the population is getting older and this has broad-reaching implications for public libraries. Collection formats (e.g., talking books) for this age-group are not cheap, there are genuine accessibility issues and there are training needs.

Lifelong learning: education from cradle to grave is becoming an expectation. The term lifelong learning is prevalent and is having an impact on public libraries, especially at both ends of the age spectrum.

THE EMERGING ROLE OF PUBLIC LIBRARIES

This changing world, influenced by demographics and social and technological forces, has led to much soul-searching as to the role the public library must play in the community. Perhaps the most notable analysis in Australia in recent times led to the research report *Libraries/building/communities* commissioned by the Library Board of Victoria and the Victorian Public Library Network. This report found that public libraries contributed to the community on four fronts: 1) overcoming the digital divide 2) creating informed communities 3) convenient and comfortable places of learning and 4) building social capital. These essentially capture all the implications of our modern society for public libraries.

Clearly the provision of information is still the bread-and-butter of the public library service. Such provision builds community capacity through an informed public. The modern public library, however, needs to do much more than this. A strong expectation is now placed on public libraries to meet the leisure needs of the community, and recent times have seen a growing trend with libraries becoming a place of social inclusion. They are the modern "village square'." A survey of library clients conducted by Cox (2000) identified the role the library plays as a safe, shared community space where residents and newcomers can gain a sense of connection.

As in Australia, reading has always been a popular leisure activity in New Zealand. Perhaps related to this, visits to the public library also figure highly in the lives of the average New Zealander. A Cultural Experiences Survey (CES) conducted by Statistics New Zealand (2003) showed that using libraries was one of the country's most popular cultural activities. It was the second most popular activity during the four-week reference period, after book purchasing, reflecting New Zealanders' enthusiasm for literature. The survey showed that an estimated 1,100,000 people (39% of all adults) used public library services in the four weeks of the survey period. Women were more likely than men to use the library (45% compared with 33%). The data showed that older people had a high level of library usage, 46% of those in the '65 and over' age group having visited a public library in the four week period. Other groups with relatively high rates of library use include 35–44 year olds (41%) and 15–24 year olds (40%). The former group may be more likely than others to use libraries because they take young children with them, while the latter group may be involved in study.

In addition to taking on the traditional role of the village square, the public library must also be at the forefront of modern telecommunications. This means providing access to broadband communications and online databases to those who, for whatever reason, lack such access, and to offer training and/or assistance in mastering these telecommunications channels.

Underpinning of all of this is a profound assumption of equity of access. For this reason public libraries provide free access to information. This also largely means free access to the Internet, though some public libraries charge for the use of e-mail and accessing non-preferred Web sites.

THE CHANGING NATURE OF THE PUBLIC LIBRARY

It comes as no surprise that the changing role of public libraries in such a changing world has had a significant impact on the way the library operates. Bearing this in mind, it is appropriate to look at how public library services are evolving.

The collection

The traditional role of lending stock is still the cornerstone of library service. Total loans for public libraries in NSW have risen steadily and reached over forty-seven million in 2005/06 (State Library of NSW 2007:x). A key component of the collection still remains the book. Certainly new formats and means of information delivery have had an impact on public libraries, but the lending of books remains largely unaffected. There has even been the emergence of a new form of collection (or an old one upgraded) – the graphic novel. As public libraries seek to maintain a place in the leisure industry and remain engaged with youth, the appealing format of the graphic novel has seen collections being established across Australia and New Zealand.

All this means that public libraries find themselves having to maintain the traditional collection as well as embracing the new. Typically public libraries now hold material in talking book, magazine, music CD, CD-Rom, DVD and large print formats. Talking books and large print are particularly relevant in an aging community that presents real challenges to the library budget as they are a more expensive format, particularly the talking book.

In relation to the audiovisual environment the challenges are also substantial as the ground is constantly changing. It is likely that the DVD is the highest turnover format in every public library system in Australia and New Zealand, but it would be a brave library professional who could confidently say what will be the format of choice for audiovisual material in two or three years time. Clearly, the online delivery of such material is growing day by day, and public libraries need to be considering how to incorporate this into their collection and service. One should expect public libraries to provide download stations for music, DVDs and talking books. At this stage, such provision, with associated licensing issues remains largely uncharted waters for public libraries in Australia, although this is certain to change: in New South Wales, for example, the Macular Degeneration Foundation has recently entered into a joint undertaking with public libraries (called the Navigator Library Access Project) to distribute hand-held Navigator readers to their clients. These readers contain a number of electronic book titles. The distribution of readers and the uploading of new titles will be managed through the public library system.

Public libraries are digitizing some of their materials, although generally on a small-scale. Often libraries have started with collections of older photographs, usually of the local area and its people. This helps the libraries to meet the usually high level of interest amongst clients in local history and genealogy. Digitization of rare materials, such as those held by Auckland City Libraries, also helps preserve the materials while making images of them more widely available. Public libraries like to take their part in the National Digital Strategy (New Zealand. Ministry of Economic Development, n.d.) and the subsequent Digital Content Strategy, and this is a trend that is likely to gather momentum.

Client service

The emphasis of the modern public library has shifted from the collection to the client. This is not to say that the principles of good collection management and development have been abandoned but rather that the client now features prominently in these practices. Increasingly we see client input being taken into account. Most libraries now use client suggestions as an important selection tool and some libraries even hold regular client selection activities. Public libraries still strive to provide what the client needs but they are also catering for what the client *wants*.

A key feature of good client service is the timeliness with which a request is met and this has seen libraries reviewing their selection, cataloguing and processing structures to reduce the time it takes for an item to reach the shelves. The nature of client service is also evolving, and it is no coincidence that public library staff is regularly trained in good client service practices. This is being embraced as library staff generally prides themselves on such quality service.

The layout of collections is also being shaped by client needs. Many public libraries have now adopted bookstore practices and are grouping fiction works by genre. This concept is even filtering into the hallowed domain of the non-fiction collection. The time of the Dewey Decimal Classification system is not yet over, but increasingly non-fiction material is being grouped in like areas to form smaller sub-collections. Interestingly, some public libraries in New Zealand are abandoning the 'living room' concept and reverting to a more traditional classified approach, usually because it is more cost-efficient.

The growing importance being given to the role of the library as a place of social interaction has seen more and more consideration being given to relaxation space as well as the provision of meeting rooms.

Reference services

Traditional reference work has also been affected by developments in client service. It is now often the case in public libraries that all library staff will provide some level of first-point-of-contact reference service and in numerous cases the traditional Reference Desk has completely disappeared, giving way to floor-walking staff.

The reference service is also experiencing the growth of reader's advisory (RA) work. Public library staff may now be expected to recommend a good title to read and libraries are developing RA tools, such as genre pamphlets and Web pages containing reader's advisory sites. In conjunction with this there has been strong interest in supporting local book clubs, which appear to be going through a renaissance. Some libraries offer their own book clubs while others support clubs within the community.

Buildings and mobile libraries

Already many communities are meeting the challenge and forging new models for both the physical design of public libraries and the delivery of public library services to the community.

This quote comes from *People Places* (2005), a publication of the State Library of NSW. It demonstrates the importance of intelligent design in developing the modern library and the attention such design is receiving in the public library industry.

There are growing signs that local government is aware of the increasing role that public libraries play in their community and this has led to the availability of funds to construct client-friendly new buildings. At any given time there are around fifty new public libraries at a significant planning or construction phase in New South Wales alone. Alongside buildings there are developments occurring with mobile libraries. Mobile libraries are going through a transition from a book drop facility to a library on wheels. With modern technology and telecommunications these new mobile libraries play an important role in rural remote areas.

For those councils with limited funds – and this applies to many rural local government areas – there are opportunities to co-locate with other services. Increasingly public libraries are co-located with other council services, tourism, community centers and even schools. Such an arrangement requires a cooperative and clearly understood relationship between all parties involved if it is to work effectively.

Accessibility

"Build it and they will come" bears fruit only if the client can gain access on arrival. For this reason public libraries seek, with varying success, to ensure there is adequate car-parking for clients. Greater consideration is now being given to adequate space within the library. In part this is for client comfort but it is also driven by the need to cater for varying levels of mobility and the increasing occurrence of personal motorized scooters. For many library clients the problem lies not with the library layout but with accessing it in the first place. To meet the needs of homebound residents many public libraries provide a home delivery service. The increasing age of the community would indicate this service will gain increasing prominence in future years.

The modern public library also has to provide access to the virtual library user. It is likely that all public libraries have some form of web presence and that most provide access to the library catalogue online. It is increasingly typical that items can be reserved, extended and even requested by inter-library loan online. Reference inquiries are being received online and responded to in kind, although not necessarily in a live, synchronous environment.

In addition to providing online access to services public libraries are finding a role in the provision of clients with free access to fee-paying databases. This has seen the development of state-wide consortia arrangements such as Gulliver in Victoria and NSW.net in NSW. With the costs of subscribing to online databases proving to be a deterrent to some of the smaller public libraries extending their services to include online content, New Zealand's public libraries successfully negotiated a nationwide deal with some online database vendors. This means that medium and small-sized public libraries can now offer access to information that simply would not have been possible if they had negotiated with the vendors independently. Currently (2008) databases available include some from EBSCO, ProQuest and Thomson Gale. The consortium is always looking for more suitable content, especially if it is relevant to New Zealand.

The EPIC (Electronic Purchasing in Collaboration) initiative is the result of a development process partly funded by the National Library of New Zealand. Participants in the consortium pay according their place in a set of "bands" that put schools in Band A, the smallest public libraries in band B, and so on, with largest public libraries in Band F and the National Library in the last category, band J. EPIC is also funded by the Ministry of Education so that all schools can have access. Some tertiary and special libraries have joined the consortium. There are remaining issues with which to be dealt. There are librarians who feel that this resource is under-used in public libraries and they need to know why. It could be a lack of training – both from staff and clients – it could be reluctance on the part of library clients to use electronic resources, or it could be simply that the databases do not contain the sort of information that most people go to a library to find.

There are other examples of innovative ways by which libraries provide access to their clients. The Broken Hill City Library provides a book mail-out, called the Outback Letterbox Library Service while in a metropolitan environment, Gosford City Library offers a Book Express service at key railway stations for busy commuters.

The pressure to increase client access has led to many libraries reviewing their opening hours. Weekend opening times have been extended, budget permitting, and some libraries have even established drive-through arrangements.

Marketing, promotion and outreach

The competitive and client-driven environment has led to significant advancements in the marketing and promotion of library services. It is not uncommon for libraries to have designated marketing or outreach staff, and much thought and innovation is being put into the interior design and feel of the library. Marketing practices from the commercial world are being adopted, including more effective and attractive use of signage. Image has become an important issue and there are even publications offering advice to public libraries on how to best achieve 'the look' (Hennah 2005). Incorporated into this image makeover are good client service principles designed to make access to the collection faster and simpler. This marketing approach has also generated improvements in promotional and information material and library pamphlets are generally more professional in appearance than they once were.

In conjunction with improvements in presentation public libraries are now more likely than ever to tap into local media to promote services and events. This is particularly the case in rural areas where access to such media is often readily available.

Promotion has also entered the online world. The emergence of Web 2.0 tools such as blogs, wikis and RSS feeds has seen the advent of Library 2.0. Library 2.0 represents, essentially, the embracing of these new means of communication by libraries. This presents great opportunities for libraries in the development of their web sites and services but there is the associated challenge of providing library staff with the knowledge and willingness to implement such technologies. To overcome this, a number of library services have developed staff training programs in Library 2.0. The constantly evolving nature of all things web based means such training needs to expand and evolve to stay abreast of client needs. The fact that by the time this chapter is published the world will be up to Library 2.x or even Library 3.0 is testament to this need.

This new promotional environment has seen libraries willing to venture into outreach events and services. Involvement with such events is not new (for instance, children's story-time) but the extent of involvement and the innovation demonstrated is impressive. Recent times have seen the growing take-up of programs such as Bookstart (aimed at new-born children), lapsit programs (aimed at very young children), summer reading programs for school children, the hosting of concerts and the Living Library program (where residents borrow people for a set period of time).

This events/outreach environment also has educational opportunities. A number of public libraries hold study workshops for secondary school students, and many are embracing homework help arrangements that may occur within the library or online, through commercial services. The Auckland model is based upon cooperation between Auckland City Libraries, local schools and the Ministry of Education (Auckland City Libraries, 2007), and as well as access to information resources and expert help, this homework center provides a snack!

Not only do these events demonstrate the importance outreach plays, but they also reveal the extent to which the public library has become a part of the lifelong learning experience.

Technology

Technology is now a key feature of every public library service. The demand for public access Internet terminals appears insatiable and this has resulted in greater provision of such facilities, though at a cost. There are budgetary and staffing implications, and many public library staff find it challenging and discomforting when dealing with client problems with the technology. On top of this, staff will have an increasing need to be familiar with Web-based products and delivery mechanisms.

New Zealand's public libraries provide access to electronic resources as well as print, and do so by several means. Many libraries have public access computers available for a variety of purposes, including simple word processing for study or work, but the greatest use of the computers is for access to remote electronic sites via the Internet. Typically, libraries charge clients for surfing the Web and using email accounts, but provide access to a selected range of Web sites for no charge. A challenge now being faced is how (and indeed, *if*) the libraries meet client demand for access to social networking sites such as Facebook and Bebo. Somewhat related to this, some libraries have Playstation machines to attract the teens (especially teen males) to the library.

All libraries have a web presence, although some smaller libraries only have pages that are part of the parent body's site. The CES mentioned earlier said many people use the library via the Internet. In the twelve months before the survey, an estimated 400,000 people, or 15% of adults, visited library Web sites. Younger people were more likely to have done this than older people, particularly those over fifty-five, with 19% of 15–24 year olds using library sites during the twelve months, compared with just 3% of people of sixty-five and over. A combined activity by Datacom, Auckland City Libraries and Manukau Libraries produced a portal (nzlibraries.com) to make it easier to find the Web sites of public libraries around New Zealand.

Radio-Frequency Identification (RFID) is one of the most rapidly developing technologies and has the potential to provide great benefits to public libraries. RFID offers client self-check opportunities, stocktaking solutions and even item return and sorting capabilities. At present the costs make the implementation of RFID daunting but it is certain to feature strongly in new library developments, and has done so already in Manukau and Tauranga libraries in New Zealand.

Cataloguing, stock processing and collection management

Despite the possibilities of cooperative cataloguing, public library services have typically employed specialized cataloguing staff. This practice is changing. Library suppliers are now providing cataloguing and processing services, and many libraries are taking up the offer. A significant benefit of such an undertaking is that it results in books and other items getting to the shelves faster, making for a more positive client experience. In order for this arrangement to be effective and consistent it is necessary for the library to draw up detailed specifications. As more libraries pursue this option there has been an industry-wide tendency towards uniform specifications.

Some libraries have taken the matter a step further and have fully profiled their collection needs, thus enabling them to transfer the selection process to the supplier. Obviously this requires great detail and is dependent on good feedback mechanisms.

Staff

All of these changes within the library environment are having a direct and profound impact on staff. Maintenance of technology and any attendant training requires staffing. Outreach and marketing requires staffing, particularly if community sectors such as children, youth and the elderly require targeted services. RFID and self-check has staffing implications as does the outsourcing of processing and cataloguing.

Public libraries are moving from a staff structure based on recognized positions that had been stable for many decades to a new and evolving world. How things will end, if they ever do, is not easy to predict, but it is reasonable to say that specialist cataloguing positions are likely to be more strategic in nature – taking on a collection management role. In conjunction with this evolution, stock processing positions will either disappear to pay for outsourcing, or take on an outreach role. Similarly, developments in RFID may result in either the reduction of circulation staff (to pay for the cost of RFID) or their redeployment to other areas. All this points to staff roles changing from being process-driven to being client-driven.

Securing adequate funding

All these trends and demographic changes bring with them major budgetary implications. Rising staff costs, increased client expectations, new technologies, expanded formats, more sophisticated library buildings, provision of relaxation space, even the aging of the community all place pressure on library budgets. This is occurring at a time when local and even state governments are reining in expenses, making the funding environment even more competitive.

One approach to dealing with this situation has been to reduce expenses in one area to offset increases in another. For example, the costs associated with outsourced cataloguing may have been absorbed by a reduction in the staff budget. Consortial purchasing arrangements are also becoming prevalent as libraries seek to minimize costs without negatively affecting service.

As well as reducing costs, public libraries have become more active at pursuing greater government funding. This has led to the emergence of Public Libraries Australia (PLA). In the past public libraries were solely represented by the Australian Library and Information Association (ALIA) but as they represented *all* libraries their resources were so stretched that it made the lobbying required for public libraries at a federal level difficult. PLA is now pressing for funded partnerships that integrate with government policy and advance the capacity and provision of public library services, amongst other things. There is scope for projects such as Bookstart and online tutoring programs to be funded nationally and distributed through all public libraries. The greatest challenge PLA and ALIA face is to make the Federal Government truly aware of the relevance and potential of public libraries.

In addition to federal funding there remains a need for public libraries to be taken more seriously by state governments. There have been some positive moves but in New South Wales the level of state funding has dropped to only around 7% of overall operating costs.

Recognizing the difficult funding environment Australasian public libraries have been innovative in seeking alternative funding solutions. Some libraries have secured grant funding from government departments not normally associated with public libraries by offering new programs or repackaging existing ones to demonstrate their wider benefits to the community. Others have entered into partnerships to establish joint-use facilities.

Philanthropy has not been a strong feature of Australian society, but some public libraries have successfully sought business sponsorship to conduct various programs. Even the 'Pandora's Box' of merchandising has been opened and a number of libraries now provide drink and snack machines as well as selling a range of products. Some are outlets for booksellers and there are several libraries (especially in New Zealand) with coffee shops. This latter arrangement not only has the potential to raise a small amount of income, butit also enhances the client experience and encourages them to stay longer in the library.

An emerging and useful source of income for libraries has been the hiring out of facilities. New libraries are being designed so that meeting space is accessible after hours (or even during normal business hours) and many community and business organizationorganizations are taking up the opportunity. Another development has been the formation of 'Friends of the Library' groups, with support ranging from voluntary work, for instance, participation in homebound services, to the raising of funds through book sales and drink machines for specific projects such as microfilming of local historical documentary resources.

Underlying all of this has been the fundamental principle that basic library services should be provided free of charge and, to date, public libraries have staunchly resisted the option of charging for these services. The modern library should be positioned as one the cornerstones of the community. To do this it must acknowledge the evolving nature of its environment, embrace new opportunities and developments but it should not lose sight of the traditional strengths that make it such a fundamental part of life in Australia and New Zealand.

References

Auckland City Libraries (2007). *Akozone homework centers.* Auckland: The Libraries. [Online] Available: http://www.aucklandcitylibraries.com/kids/ akozone homework Retrieved on January 8, 2008.

Australian Bureau of Statistics (2007). *Basic Community Profile: Australia* Cat. No. 2001.0

Australian Bureau of Statistics (2005). *Public Libraries: 2003-04,* Cat. No. 8561.0. [Online] Available: http://www.abs.gov.au/Ausstats/abs@.nsf/0/08CD EAE368A2A931C A256A780001D4DB?Open.

Biskup, P. & Goodman, D. (1994). *Libraries in Australia.* Wagga Wagga, NSW: Center for Information Studies.

Bundy, A. (2003). 'Vision, mission, trumpets: public libraries as social capita' *NSW Country Public Libraries Association conference 2003: Public libraries light up lives,* Tweed Heads, NSW – 3 July 2003. [Online] Available: http://www.lga.sa.gov.au/webdata/resources/Files/Conference_Paper_on_librari es_in_Australia___Dr_Alan_Bundy_2003_pdf1.pdf.

Cox, E. (2000). *A safe place to go: Libraries and Social Capital,* University of Technology, Sydney.

Ferguson, S. (Ed.). (2007). *Libraries in the twenty-first century: Mapping future directions in information services.* Wagga Wagga, NSW: Center for Information Studies.

Hennah, K. (2005). *Public libraries image handbook,* State Library of Victoria, Melbourne.

Hopkins, S. (2007). Decimating Dewey: introducing a bookshop arrangement for shelving the nonfiction collection, *APLIS,* vol. 20, no.1, 8-11

Joseph, M. (2006). *Active engage valued: older people and NSW public libraries,* State Library of NSW

LIANZA (n.d.) *Free public library service.* Wellington: LIANZA. [Online] Available: http://www.lianza.org.nz/about/governance/statements/freepublic. html. Retrieved on January 12, 2008.

LIANZA. (2004). *Standards for New Zealand public libraries.* 6th ed. edited by Jill Best. Wellington, LIANZA.

Metronet. (2005). *"Inspire me" campaign.* [Online] Available: http://www. nzlibraries. com/promo.html (accessed October 19, 2007).

Metronet. (2005). *New Zealand's libraries band together.* Available at: http:// www.metronet.org.nz/Documents/NZLibrariesBand_Together.pdf. Retrieved on September 21, 2007.

Missingham, R. & Cameron, J. (2007). National, state and territory libraries: Information for the nation. In Ferguson, S. (Ed.). (2007). *Libraries in the twenty-first century: Mapping future directions in information services,* pp. 73-87 Wagga Wagga, NSW: Center for Information Studies.

National Library of New Zealand. (2003). *A digital strategy for the National Library of New Zealand.* Wellington: The Library.

New Zealand. Ministry of Economic Development. (n.d.) *Digital strategy.* [Online] Available: http://www.digitalstrategy.govt.nz/ (accessed December 21, 2007).

PUB-SIG. (n.d.). *Purpose.* [Online] Available: http://www.lianza.org.nz/com munity/pub-sig/. Retrieved on November 8, 2007.

Public libraries of New Zealand: a strategic framework 2006 to 2016. (2006). Wellington: Local Government New Zealand, LIANZA, National Library of New Zealand. [Online] Available: http://www.lianza.org.nz/library/files/ store_011/ StrategicFramework2006.pdf. Retrieved on July 21, 2007.

State Library of New South Wales. (2005). *People places: a gide for public library buildings in New south Wales,* State Library of New South Wales, Sydney

State Library of New South Wales. (2007). *Public Library Statistics 2005/06,* State Library of New South Wales, Sydney

State Library of Victoria. (2005). *Libraries/building/communities,* State Library of Victoria, Melbourne.

Statistics New Zealand. (2003). *Measure of culture: cultural experiences and cultural spending in New Zealand.* Wellington: Statistics New Zealand.

ACADEMIC LIBRARIES

Anne Horn, Philip Calvert and Stuart Ferguson

Academic libraries are taken to refer here to two particular types of library: university libraries and those libraries which serve the vocational education and training (VET) sector through colleges or institutes of technical and further education (TAFE). (School libraries are dealt with in a separate chapter.) Universities cover undergraduate programs, principally Bachelors degrees, and postgraduate programs such as the Graduate Certificate, Graduate Diploma, Masters degrees and doctoral programs. The main TAFE awards are Certificate, Diploma and Advanced Diploma. Universities are largely funded by national government – the federal Commonwealth Government in Australia's case – although, as elsewhere, an increasing amount of university funding needs to come from non-government sources, particularly research funding. In Australia institutes of TAFE are funded by state and territory governments, although from 2005 the Federal Government began providing funding for the development of technical colleges outside the TAFE sector that would provide vocational education for secondary school age students. This latter development may well be affected by the change in federal government in late 2007.

The mission for academic libraries globally is to support the teaching, learning and (where appropriate) research activities of their parent institutions. In Australia and New Zealand, universities and their libraries have also had a long tradition of reaching out to the community, contributing to the cultural and intellectual life of the nation. Australia has thirty-nine universities; of which thirty-seven are public institutions and two are private. New Zealand has eight universities. The libraries supporting these institutions are diverse, of high quality and innovative. Based on 2005 figures, there are sixty-eight institutions in Australia's VET sector, with over 1,100 campuses, 1.7 million students and some eleven per cent of Australia's working age population accessing TAFE (Oakley & Vaugha 2007: 43).

AUSTRALIAN UNIVERSITY HISTORY

The diversity of university libraries in Australia and New Zealand is characterised by size, location, mode of study undertaken, programs supported, research intensity, collections, organizational structures, and partnerships with other educational providers and industry. Around forty per cent of Australian university libraries support large student cohorts of 30,000 and over. Most operate multiple branch libraries. Twenty-five percent provide services through rural and regional campus libraries.

To understand this diversity, it is worth briefly looking at the history of universities in Australia and the diversity of the student population, which together will provide a helicopter view of the Australian higher education landscape. A history of Australia's higher education sector is available in a national report published in 1993, known as the "blue book." Depicted in the blue book are the different phases of growth and expansion, which have led to a marked variance between different groups of universities in terms of the age of the university, its student population and level of funding.

The first university in Australia was Sydney University, taking its first students in colonial times in 1852. By 1979 there were nineteen universities. At this time, the states' capital cities were home to large institutions, with enrolments between 13,500 and 18,500 (Queensland, New South Wales, Sydney, Melbourne and Monash). There were six universities of medium size (Macquarie, Western Australia, Adelaide, La Trobe, New England and the Australian National University) and eight of the smaller, more recent foundations (Newcastle, Deakin, Flinders, Tasmania, Wollongong, Murdoch, James Cook and Griffith) (DEET 1993).

During the same period, the advanced education sector, consisting of colleges of advanced education (CAEs) and institutes of technology, was growing rapidly. Both universities and CAEs were struggling to satisfy unmet demand for higher education. The years 1987 to 1990 saw the establishment of a 'Unified National System', established by the federal government of the day and characterized by mergers and rationalization of institutions and campuses, conversion of CAEs to universities, and increased cooperation with the Technical and Further Education (TAFE) sector (DEST 2004). The Western Australian Institute of Technology, for instance, was converted to Curtin University of Technology. At the completion of this phase of development there were the current thirty-nine universities.

From 1990 onwards, there has been dramatic expansion in the number of students studying in higher education, reaching 984,146 in 2006. Of these, 75% were domestic students and 25% international students (DEST 2007). Students studying undergraduate programs comprised the largest cohort of enrolments at 69%, with 22% of students in postgraduate coursework programs and 5% undertaking higher degrees by research. Only 3% were enrolled in non-degree programs. Students' selected mode of study was still predominantly on campus, with 80% of students, even though it is commonly known that students spend less time physically attending lectures and tutorials. External student numbers have been steadily decreasing to 13%. Multi-modal options are commonly recognized as offering greater flexibility for students yet accounted for only 7% of enrolments in 2006.

The geographical distribution of students closely matches the demographics of the country, where 24.3% of the population lives in rural Australia and 16.9% of students are from rural backgrounds (Griffith University).

NEW ZEALAND UNIVERSITY HISTORY

The first university in New Zealand was the University of Otago, founded in 1869. As other universities were established it was decided that they would be stronger if combined, hence the establishment of the University of New Zealand in 1870. When it was dissolved in 1961 there were six constituent colleges, which have all since then become universities, and subsequently two more have been created, the most recent being in 2000 when the Auckland Institute of Technology became the Auckland University of Technology. The figures for 2006 show 238,039 domestic equivalent full-time students (EFTS) in formal tertiary education, and 32,457 international students, although it should be noted that these figures are for tertiary education, not higher education as they are in Australia. This was the first fall in the participation rate after several years of growth. Participation was highest amongst eighteen to nineteen-year-old females, of whom 27.1% were enrolled at a university (New Zealand Ministry of Education 2008).

AUSTRALIAN COLLEGES OF TECHNICAL AND FURTHER EDUCATION (TAFE)

Australian colleges of TAFE have long been the 'poor relations' of the Australian higher education sector. In 1965, following the so-called Martin Report, *Tertiary Education in Australia* (1964-65), those technical colleges which provided tertiary programs were upgraded to colleges of advanced education or institutes of technology, a new area of tertiary education, and, in the following years, these received significant federal funding. In the same period, however, the remaining technical colleges, those, for instance, offering programs in trade, commercial and further (continuing) education, did not benefit from the extra federal funding and remained reliant on the relatively low levels of state funding.

In 1973, the Federal Labor Government established the Australian Committee of Technical and Further Education, which was followed in 1974 by the Kangan Report, *TAFE in Australia: Report on Needs in Technical and Further Education*, which promoted open access to the VET sector for people of all ages and enunciated the now familiar philosophy of lifelong learning. Libraries came in for criticism and were re-envisioned in the Report as 'learning resource centers', which were seen as centers for student-centered teaching and learning and as an integral part of TAFE educational programs (Biskup & Goodman 1994:. 253). The change in terminology gained currency for many years although the term "library" reappeared in time. The following years saw the establishment of the Tertiary Education Commission (1977) and a temporary influx of federal funding, which saw TAFE book stocks double (Biskup & Goodman 1994: 253). By 1980, however,

the federal Commonwealth Government had begun to cut back on its TAFE funding and TAFE libraries returned to relying largely on state government for support.

In 1992 the Australian National Training Authority (ANTA) was established,
which, combined with the Australian National Qualification Framework (see below), marked a national approach to VET. The role of ANTA was to develop and
implement 'a national vocational education and training system with agreed goals
and priorities':

- close interaction between industry and vocational education and training providers;
- an effective training market;
- an efficient and productive network of publicly funded providers;
- increased opportunities and improved outcomes; and
- improved cross-sectoral links between schools, higher education and vocational education and training (*Australian National Training Authority*).

From 2005, the Federal Government put measures in place to transfer the ANTA
functions to the Department of Education, Science and Training (DEST 2005).

LIBRARY SERVICES

Library services are provided to students regardless of location, program or mode
of study. It is common for students to have access to library services and resources
on campus and online. A cooperative national borrowing scheme (University Library Australia), complimented by various state-based schemes, allows students
and staff to borrow from any other university library electing to participate. This
borrowing scheme is a cooperative arrangement amongst member universities of
Universities Australia, the industry peak body, which represents thirty-eight universities. University Library Australia was developed and is overseen by the
Council of Australian University Librarians (CAUL). This may well be a product
of, and is certainly suited to, delivery of educational programs to a geographically
dispersed population. Seven of the eight university libraries in New Zealand established a similar scheme in 2005: University Library Aotearoa New Zealand
(ULANZ).

A number of university libraries continue to offer distance education services.
Deakin University Library has been recognized for its services to students studying off campus and at a distance through its Australian Award for University
Teaching, received in 2005. For Massey University, service to distance students is
a core business activity, as it is for distance learning providers like Charles Stuart
University and University of New England. Library services to international students studying off shore are commonly an extension of off-campus and online services. A relatively small number of universities have invested in building a physi-

cal library presence off shore. Examples include Monash University's Clinical School Library in Johor Bahru, Malaysia, and RMIT International University Vietnam's new learning center.

Library collections reflect the teaching and research priorities of the institution. Libraries supporting research-intensive universities, not surprisingly, have a greater depth to their collections, providing a valuable resource for the nation. These are often referred to as the "sandstone" or "Group of Eight" universities, and include the Australian National University, Monash University and the universities of Sydney, Melbourne, Queensland, Adelaide, Western Australia, and New South Wales. Multi-campus libraries invest proportionally more in circulating collections, coupled with responsive inter-campus loans and document delivery services. Libraries operating full library services across multiple city campuses include the University of Western Sydney, Queensland University of Technology, RMIT and the University of South Australia (all Australian) and Massey University in New Zealand. Some also have a regional and rural presence; for example Deakin University, Charles Sturt University, LaTrobe University, the University of Newcastle and Central Queensland University.

There is also considerable diversity in Australia and New Zealand in the way libraries as organizational units within the university are managed. Libraries most commonly fall under the purview of the Deputy Vice-Chancellor, Academic, or Deputy Vice-Chancellor, Academic Services. In some instances, the organizational boundaries dividing the university library, information technology services and/or learning support services have been traversed, bringing together responsibilities for information and education services, systems and technologies. The University of Melbourne, Griffith University and the Queensland University of Technology have organizational systems of this nature.

The diversity of the higher education landscape has not presented an impediment to collaboration. The Council of Australian University Librarians (CAUL) provides a forum for discussion and collaboration, allowing opportunities for its members to pursue common interests; especially in the provision of access to scholarly information, the library's leadership role in the management of information and the library's contribution to the university experience. The Council of New Zealand University Librarians (CONZUL) provides a similar forum across the Tasman: their strategic plan states, "CONZUL's key functions reflect the members" desire to provide leadership in a knowledge society by strengthening the strategic capacity of university libraries' (Conzul 2007). The CAUL Electronic Information Resources Committee (CEIRC) and its program benefit Australian and New Zealand university and research libraries through the collaborative purchasing of electronic resources.

There is similar collaboration in the VET sector, with support from ANTA since 2002 for the consortial purchase of electronic databases for the benefit of Australian TAFE staff and students.

Organization of TAFE libraries varies. New South Wales and Queensland developed more centralized library systems than the other states and territories, with functions such as acquisitions, cataloguing and systems development being conducted by a central agency – although Queensland dismantled its Library Network in Brisbane, the state capital, in the 1990s and moved to a less centralized model that was based around regional clusters. The TAFE libraries sector has its own peak body, TAFE Libraries Australia (TLA). The vision enunciated in the Kangan Report of TAFE libraries as "learning resource centers" catering for student-centered teaching and learning has been realised (although many of the resource centers have reverted to being known as libraries), with a strong emphasis on the need to promote lifelong learning and information literacy – a key aim of the Australian Library and Information Association (ALIA). Both the TLA and CAUL support the information literacy framework developed by the Australian and New Zealand Institute for Information Literacy (Bund 2004), which 'aims to embed information literacy within the total educational process' (Oakley & Vaughan, 2007: 47).

QUALITY

The quality of universities in Australia and New Zealand is evident in the generally high level of student satisfaction with library and information services; the benchmarking activities undertaken within Australia and New Zealand libraries, extending to overseas benchmarking activities in some instances; and the international recognition of leading developments in electronic resources management, digital library services and repositories, and library building design.

The Insync (Rodski) *University Library Client Survey* is undertaken widely throughout Australia and New Zealand. A number of libraries also evaluate their performance with overseas libraries using the Association of Research Libraries' LibQUAL+ ™. Similarly, CAUL statistics provide universities and their libraries with standardized data for longitudinal and comparative data. New Zealand university libraries contribute data both to CAUL and to the CONZUL statistics. The University of Wollongong Library has been recognised by the Australian Universities Quality Agency (AUQA) for its leadership in embedding quality improvement processes in its operations.

Australian TAFE programs are accredited by the appropriate state or territory bodies using national standards and competencies documented in the Australian Quality Training Framework (AQTF), under the Australian Qualifications Framework (AQF). Each state and territory jurisdiction is responsible for registering TAFE colleges and institutes as Registered Training OrganizationOrganizations

(RTOs), which are required to comply with both national standards and the relevant state and territory laws and regulations.

INNOVATION

For over twenty years, Australian university libraries have been amongst the world leaders in the adoption of new technologies. Most university libraries are on their third or fourth generation of library management systems. Where Australian university libraries differ from the rest of the world is that all of them, not just a few, are making sophisticated use of technological *innovations.* Similarly, the organizationorganizational structures have been adapted to reflect the integration of new technologies in all aspects of library services. Libraries are continuing to review their workforce, identifying the skills necessary to adapt readily to new technologies, changes in client behaviorbehaviors and organizationorganizational imperatives.

Australian libraries recognized early the advantages to be gained by delivering web access to information resources, given the country's distance from the major publishing and distribution centers of the world. Academic staffs have integrated new technologies and electronic resources into their course development and teaching. Carol Tenopir's studies comparing journal reading in the U.S.A. and Australia are worthy of note (http://web.utk.edu/~tenopir/speeches/index.html). Libraries have supported students and staff through virtual reference services of various forms for some years, with SMS and instant messaging services more recently joining the suite of communication channels available for clients. Digital library services are also being influenced by Web 2.0 applications. There are recent examples of innovative approaches to the web catalogue, subject guides and, more generally, how the library connects with clients through the use of social networking software.

The introduction of digital repositories, the testing and development of standards and processes, and the evaluation of use are receiving a greater focus. The Australian Federal Government has supported initiatives in the areas of open access repositories and e-research. National research assessment exercises in Australia and New Zealand have provided the impetus for developing repositories of research output, even if the detail of the Australian scheme remains unclear at present, with a change of federal government in late 2007. University libraries have generally assumed responsibility for creating and maintaining research repositories, including the development of metadata schemes to promote access. The aim of the Australian Digital Theses Program Learning is to establish a database of digital copies of theses produced by postgraduate students at various Australian and New Zealand universities. Learning repositories are also part of the Australian higher education landscape, although there is quite a variance between institutions in the management of these.

Innovative learning spaces are increasingly a feature of library buildings and the wider campus development. The redevelopment of library spaces is happening within the context of developing "away from the class room" places that support new approaches to teaching and learning, improve student learning outcomes and enhance the holistic student campus experience. The benefits of bringing together student support services in one place, or the "one-stop-shop" information service, are also driving these developments. The concept of the 'information commons' has been implemented in several universities, with the library either running or participating in the facility: for example, the University of Auckland operates an information commons at three locations. It states that " the Information Commons is an integrated learning environment where all students will have access to electronic information resources, electronic learning materials and productivity software, allowing them to integrate information in to course work" (University of Auckland Library 2008; see also the Auchmuty Information Common, University of Newcastle 2007).

Learning spaces that are now part of library building design are flexible in their configuration. They support peer-to-peer learning and individual study in a variety of study environments, from the casual and social to the more formal and reflective (see University of Queensland. Ipswich and Biological Sciences Libraries). Information technologies and multi-media are integrated throughout the spaces, taking advantage of wireless networks: for instance, WirelessVic (Victoria University of Wellington 2006). Students also consider cafes and extended hours to be essential elements supporting their learning.

CONCLUSION

The challenges facing academic libraries in Australia and New Zealand are not dissimilar to those facing academic libraries around the globe. Scholarly communication and new models of publishing, accompanied by the issues of copyright and intellectual property, are core business concerns. Control of information, affordability and access will continue to generate debate in the higher education sector and with publishers and providers of information.

The performance of academic institutions is increasingly evaluated in the same way as any other large business enterprise. The library's contribution to the institution's performance is assessed at the institutional level in terms of its contribution to the mission and goals of its 'enterprise'. The Australian Universities Quality Agency (AUQA) and the New Zealand Vice-Chancellors' Committee (NZVCC) assure the academic quality of universities and the library's performance, while the Australian Qualifications Framework (AQF) fulfills a similar function in the VET sector. The library's role in supporting teaching, learning and research, and its contribution to the student experience are key indicators of the value the library brings to the academic institution, evident in the strategic plans of academic libraries in this part of the world and world wide.

References

Australian National Training Authority (ANTA), http://www.mceetya.edu.au/ mceetya/australian_national_training_authority_(anta),11941.html

Biskup, P. & Goodman, D. (1994). *Libraries in Australia.* Wagga Wagga, NSW: Center for Information Studies.

Bundy, A. (ed.) (2004). *Australian and New Zealand Information Literacy Framework: Principles, standards and practice.* 2nd ed. Adelaide: Australian and New Zealand Institute for Information Literacy. [Online] Available: http://www.anziil.org/ resources/Info%20lit%202nd%20edition.pdf.

CONZUL (2007). *Strategic directions 2008.* [Online] Available: http://www. conzul.ac.nz/strategic_plan.htm. Retrieved February 1, 2008.

Department of Employment, Education and Training. Higher Education Division.(1993). *National report on Australia's Higher Education sector.* Canberra: Australian Government Publishing Service.

Department of Education, Science and Training. (2004). *Rationalising responsibility for Higher Education in Australia.* Issues paper. [Online] Available: http://www.dest.gov.au/NR/rdonlyres/C593AB29-F984-4FD4-8CDA-7D6F09 65C01C/4046/ rationalising_responsibilities.pdf. Retrieved March 14, 2008.

Department of Education, Science and Training. (2005). *Outcomes of consultations on the new national vocational education and training (VET) arrangements.* [Online] Available: http://www.dest.gov.au/sectors/training_skills/policy_ issues_reviews/key_ issues/ anta/information.htm. Retrieved March 18, 2008.

Department of Education, Science and Training. (2007). Students [full year] selected higher education statistics. [Online] Available: http://www.dest. gov.au/NR/rdonlyres/ECADEDDB-C358-4B97-9244-7A74D9974061/18815/ 2006FullYearStudentdata_shortanalysis3.pdf. Retrieved March 14, 2008.

Griffith University. Australian Tertiary Education. Student demographics. [Online] Available: http://www.griffith.edu.au/vc/ate/content_he_student demogs. Html. Retrieved March 14, 2008.

Oakley, S & Vaughan, J. (2007). Higher education libraries. In S. Ferguson (Ed.), *Libraries in the twenty-first century: Mapping future directions in information services* (pp. 43-57). Wagga Wagga, NSW: Center for Information Studies.

New Zealand. Ministry of Education. (2008). *Education counts.* [Online] Available: http://www.educationcounts.govt.nz/home.

University of Auckland. Library. The Information Commons. [Online] Available: http:// www.information-commons.auckland.ac.nz. Retrieved January 12, 2008.

Victoria University of Wellington. (2006). *WirelessVic.* [Online] Available: http://www. vuw.ac.nz/wireless/.

SPECIAL LIBRARIES

Sue Henczel, Gillian Ralph and Julie Sibthorpe

In Australia and New Zealand, the term "special library" refers to libraries that provide resources and services to employees of an organization or industry. The majority have collections and/or services supporting a specific subject area. These include, but are not limited to, libraries in government departments, law firms, private companies, banking and finance institutions, research organizations, religious groups and professional associations.

STATISTICS

Globally, statistics for special libraries are hard to obtain. Spiller (1998:1) considers that this may be because there is a huge variation in "size, subject matter and type of the different special libraries and information centers – not to mention a natural unwillingness of commercial organizationorganizations to make information about their activities publicly available." In Australia and New Zealand a contributing factor is the demise of the traditional special library with physical collections in favor of electronic collections and virtual services. Many special librarians are operating in non-traditional environments through mergers with others such as records management, knowledge management and information technology. Consequently the library is no longer a discrete unit within the organization, and tends not to be counted as such.

The exact number of special libraries in Australia and New Zealand is therefore not known. The most current *Directory of Special Libraries in Australia* at the time of writing was published in 1999 and lists 1,125 special libraries. Anecdotal evidence suggests that there has been a decline in the number of special libraries since 1999; however, the Australian Libraries Gateway, provided by the National Library of Australia, lists well over 2,000 libraries that would be considered "special." A count of those listed on the Australian Libraries Gateway totals 2,425 special libraries in December 2007. This includes multiple libraries within large organizations where libraries are established in a number of locations.

Statistics New Zealand (2006) lists more than two hundred specialist libraries and information centers serving government departments, business and other organizations in New Zealand. In *Informing New Zealand* (Fields 2007: 141), Paddy Plunket states, "There is no exact data available on the number of special libraries in New Zealand in 2007," but estimates around 250. However, 292 special libraries are listed in the 2006 edition of *New Zealand Contacts in Libraries* (Contacts Unlimited 2006) compared with 290 in 2000.

TYPES OF SPECIAL LIBRARIES

Special libraries in Australia and New Zealand can be categorized according to their industry, using *New Zealand contacts in libraries*, (Contacts Unlimited, 2006), the *Directory of special libraries in New Zealand 2007* (National Library of New Zealand, 2007), the *Australian Libraries Gateway* (National Library of Australia) and data provided by the Australian Library and Information Association (ALIA). In New Zealand the authors have also categorized them according to whether they are within commercial or non-commercial organizations. Unfortunately the categories used in Australia and New Zealand differ, which makes it difficult to compare directly the numbers and types of libraries in each country.

New Zealand

Table 1: Special libraries in New Zealand by category (Ralph and Sibthorpe 2007)

Commercial organizations	*No. of libraries*	*% of total*
Agriculture/primary produce	9	3.0%
Pharmaceutical/food /chemical, plastics and building materials	2	0.8%
Energy	9	3.0%
Manufacturing, engineering and architects	18	6.0%
Financial	13	4.5%
Legal	29	10.0%
Information consultants	8	2.7%
Media/publishing	17	5.8%
Tourism/ telecommunications	2	0.8%
Lotteries/Standards	3	1.0%
Science/Environment	24	8.2%
Total commercial organizations	**134**	
Non commercial organizations		
Central government	52	17.8%
Local government	6	2.0%
Health and medical	51	17.6%
Theology	13	4.5%
Museums and galleries	19	6.5%
Industry and professional organizations	3	1.0%
Other organizations including embassy, fire, military and voluntary	14	4.8%
Total non-commercial organizations	**158**	
Total special libraries	**292**	100%

In New Zealand there has been a definite decline in commercial sector special libraries in recent years, both in the number of libraries and in the number of people staffing them. The decline may reflect the restructuring and movement of companies endeavoring to survive in the current economic climate, as these small libraries are very vulnerable in times of economic constraints.

At the same time there has been growth in the non-commercial governmental sector in New Zealand. The majority of these are in the departmental head offices that are usually situated in Wellington, the capital of New Zealand and the center for government.

Australia

Table 2: Special libraries in Australia by category (Henczel 2007)

Category	No. of libraries	% of total
Agriculture	17	1%
Business / Corporate	411	17%
Cultural Organizations	309	13%
Government	561	22%
Health / Medical	408	17%
Legal	171	7%
Local History and Genealogy	217	9%
Media / Publishing	53	2%
Religious	141	6%
Special Interest	137	6%

In Australia, government libraries constitute the largest group of special libraries (22%), with health/medical and business/corporate slightly smaller at 17% each. The number of cultural organizations that maintain libraries is increasing, as is the number of local history and genealogy libraries.

Over 80% of special libraries in Australia and New Zealand are in non-commercial settings. The largest group is made up of government libraries – central and local government in New Zealand, and state/territory government, federal government and other government entities in Australia. Government libraries also include the parliamentary libraries. In Australia government department libraries at both federal and state level are at the mercy of election cycles and budgetary restraints, and over recent years have experienced considerable mergers, restructures and closures. Other significant groups are those in the health sector, which include those serving the health industry and those attached to hospitals and serving medical needs. An interesting area of growth in both countries is the increasing number of libraries in the cultural sector, such as museum and art gallery libraries.

All these libraries serve the objectives of their parent organizations and are funded directly by them. Their clientele consists of diverse groups, often with different information needs, usage behaviors and delivery preferences.

A significant proportion of the material in these special libraries is electronic which enables it to be networked for users in different locations. Other libraries offer a mixture of many formats in their collections including DVD and CD collections. The library catalogue is generally accessed through organizational intranets or websites.

Corporate/Business Libraries

In Australia, corporate/business libraries make up 17% and in New Zealand, about 20% of the total of all special libraries. Corporate/business libraries are the most vulnerable sector of special libraries and quickly experience the direct impact of changes in corporate structure, takeover and merger activity and cost cutting.

As noted already, funding for corporate libraries is obtained from the parent organizations served. In some cases the costs incurred in running the library operation are passed on to users, either within the organization or through its clients, as is often the case with law library clients. The fact that corporate libraries are often unable to return income adds to their vulnerability, with the risk that they can be seen as overhead charges to their parent organization, therefore it is seen as very important to promote the services of the library to the parent organization proactively and to make sure that the costs needed to run it are transformed into measurable benefits to the company.

In Australia and New Zealand the financial services industry and professional groups such as lawyers, engineers and architects, host the largest number of special libraries, after government and health libraries.

Law Libraries

The largest group of libraries in the commercial sector in New Zealand is law libraries. In New Zealand in 2007 there were around twenty commercial law firms with libraries, four libraries attached to the District law societies, four court libraries, the Auckland High Court Judges Library, the Court of Appeal Library, Crown Law Office Library and the Law Commission Library.

In New Zealand District Law libraries exist to support the needs of lawyers in all firms especially those that do not have their own in-house resources. District Law Society libraries were funded by compulsory Law Society membership fees, however this funding base has been changed by the *Lawyers and Conveyancers Act 2006* (due to be enacted in 2008) by which District law societies will become incorporated societies with voluntary membership. A national committee of the Law Society has been set up to advise on the running of the District law libraries, which already have a culture of resource sharing and jointly produce the legal journals database, LINX.

In Australia there are 171 law libraries crossing commercial and non-commercial sectors. Over ninety are commercial law firms with some firms having up to six libraries in different states and territories. Law libraries are also found in commercial organizations and banking and finance institutions. Non-commercial law libraries include those in state and federal government departments, university law faculties and state and federal law courts and professional associations.

Law librarians in commercial firms require specialist knowledge of legal material, much of which is not available electronically. Law libraries in Australia and New Zealand contain specialist legal materials for their jurisdictions, notably case law, legislation, indices and finding aids, legal encyclopedias, texts and commentaries, and legal journals. Another significant service offered in legal libraries is business research, reflecting the need for lawyers to understand their clients' business environments. Law librarians are also responsible for training new staff in the use of legal materials.

As in other corporate libraries, law librarians also need to involve themselves in the wider activities of the company, so they have developed skills such as website content management, knowledge management, including storage and access of opinions and precedents of the firm, and sometimes records and archive activity.

Law librarians are supported by professional associations in both Australia and New Zealand. The New Zealand Law Librarians' Association (NZLLA) was established in 1989. Until 2000, the New Zealand Law Librarians' Group (as it then was) operated as a Special Interest Group (SIG) of LIANZA. In 2001 it separated from LIANZA and became the New Zealand Law Librarians' Association. The group has had an important lobbying role, promoting issues of public access to information, on behalf of the profession, librarians and the public, as well as producing publications for use with legal materials. A notable publication from this group is their *Principles of Professional Conduct* (http://www.nzlla.org.nz/principlesof professionalconduct.cfm).

The Australian Law Librarians' Association (ALLA) grew from an informal special interest group in 1969 to an incorporated national association in 2006, with divisions in Australian Capital Territory, New South Wales, Northern Territory, Queensland, South Australia, Tasmania, Victoria and Western Australia. ALLA represents librarians and information professionals working in courts, universities, government departments, law firms and professional associations.

Parliamentary libraries

In Australia and New Zealand parliamentary libraries exist to support members of parliament (MPs). They produce publications, including *Bills Digest* (containing summaries of legislation before the house), *Background Papers*, *Current Issues Briefs*, *Research Notes*, *Research Papers*, electorate profiles and media monitors to keep MPs up to date. Each parliamentary library has large specialized and historic collections to serve the immediacy of questions that come in. Staff are also responsible for the parliamentary library website, which provides access to a range of online library resources, key Internet links and links to other sources of parliamentary information and seminars.

The parliamentary library matches its opening hours to those of the parliament's sitting hours, and tailors services to the specific and usually urgent needs of their user group of MPs. In New Zealand the Parliamentary Library is the largest special library. Australia has ten parliamentary libraries, one supporting the Federal Government, based in Canberra, and nine state or territory parliamentary libraries supporting their respective governments.

Health and medical libraries

Those libraries that support the health and medical sector represent a large group of non-commercial special libraries. In New Zealand there are fifty-one health/medical libraries, twenty-two of which serve not-for-profit health organizations such as the Accident Rehabilitation and Compensation Insurance Corporation (ACC) and the Alcohol Advisory Council (ALAC). The rest are medical libraries, which are "set up in hospitals to support the work of the employed medical, nursing and allied health professionals" (Fields 2007:153). There are twenty-four medical libraries at hospitals including twenty-one district health boards in New Zealand, and two medical libraries attached to university libraries. (Philson Library at University of Auckland and the University of Otago Medical Libraries). This includes two special libraries focusing on Pacific health, based in Whakatane and Tauranga Hospitals, and the Ministry of Health Information Center.

Medical libraries are subject to the *Minimum Standards for New Zealand Health Libraries* (Library and Information Association of New Zealand Aotearoa 2005), which contain requirements for planning, development, organization and administration, resources and service provision in health libraries. These standards are enforced by Quality Health New Zealand, the accreditation body for teaching hospitals. Inspections are carried out to ensure compliance. As well as the special interest group (SIG) for special librarians there is also a special interest group for health, which provides a forum for health sector library and information professionals. There is a Health-Info discussion list that is the email discussion group for issues concerning health information in New Zealand.

Australia has 408 health/medical libraries. These include hospital libraries, libraries supporting regional health services, professional associations supporting those employed in the health sector and a diverse range of miscellaneous health libraries supporting medical research, education and alternative medical practices. This category also includes those libraries established within federal, state and territory government departments, institutes and authorities that operate within the health sector.

ALIA offers institutional membership for health/medical libraries and individual membership for those employed within health/medical libraries. Health libraries are supported by ALIA's Health Libraries Australia, which provides professional support, professional development and networking.

Galleries, museums and archives

In both Australia and New Zealand the number of libraries within museums and galleries is increasing, as is the number of librarians and information professionals employed by museums and galleries. Librarians in this sector are using a wide range of skills to manage budgets, organize volunteer staff, and maintain collections of print and electronic material as well as physical objects and artifacts from collections. Some museum librarians have important, large-scale digitization projects underway, carry out user education functions and take part in the curation of collections. One of the key related roles is managing archives and records.

In New Zealand there is a professional group for museum and gallery staff called AHLAG – Auckland Heritage Librarians and Archivists Group (http://ahlag. auckland.ac.nz), which is not affiliated to LIANZA. There are approximately twenty member organizations in this group, which is restricted to the Auckland region. Galleries, libraries and museums special librarians formed this informal group, which has been meeting in Auckland since 1997.

This sector represents a growing opportunity for special librarians, requiring a mixture of skills, but it also offers an important dimension for New Zealand special librarianship, in that it attracts Maori and Pasifika librarians and staff to work closely with their cultural heritage materials.

Local history and genealogy

In Australia the number of libraries supporting regional historical societies and trusts, genealogical and family history societies, and migrant and indigenous groups is increasing. There are currently over two hundred, some of which are co-located with branches of public libraries and others that are independent. State libraries also provide significant specialist genealogical and local history services.

EDUCATION FOR SPECIAL LIBRARIANSHIP

The ALIA and LIANZA websites list the providers for library and information qualifications. LIANZA's *Library qualifications: a summary of New Zealand library qualifications* can be found at http://www.lianza.org.nz/development/education/qualifications.html. Formal library qualifications from an accredited national provider or from relevant institutions overseas are generally regarded as a minimum requirement. Other experience that is considered valuable includes special library experience, knowledge of the subject matter and knowledge of sources of information relevant to the industry in which the library operates. Skills that are sought include research skills and specific and general information technology skills. Increasingly a strong client focus or customer service orientation is required, which encompasses personal characteristics such as good communication skills, the ability to deal with a diverse range of people at all levels of the organization, the ability to work both independently and as a team member as well as well-developed organizational skills.

EMPLOYMENT IN SPECIAL LIBRARIES

According to the 2001 New Zealand Census publication, *Employment in the Cultural Sector*, there were 3,627 librarians in total, 78% of whom were women. Business services and government administration employed 15% of the librarians (Statistics New Zealand, 2006, p. 23). In the 2006 Census the total number of employees working in libraries was 4,410, an increase of 17.76% (correspondence with Sue McGeough, Statistics New Zealand, November 2007).

The Australian 2006 census data group the library workforce under *Culture and Leisure Occupations* and indicates that it employs 24,849 people. Of these, 10,085 are librarians, 6,510 library technicians and 8,254 library assistants. Just over 83% of Australian library workers are female, which shows only a slight movement in the gender breakdown over recent years. Geographically, New South Wales has 29% of the workforce, Victoria 24%, Queensland 16%, Western Australia 13%, South Australia 9%, the Australian Capital Territory 7%, and Tasmania and the Northern Territory have 2% (ALIA 2007).

Positions in special libraries are being advertised under an increasingly diverse range of titles including Librarian (and variations such as reference librarian, library assistant, research librarian, liaison librarian, reading services librarian), Records Manager (including records librarian, knowledge manager, records officer), Information Analyst (information specialist, information advisor, information and advice coordinator, research consultant, document and knowledge management analyst, strategic research analyst) and those that require specific skills such as oral historian, systems librarian, online content publisher, law librarian and interlibrary loan document delivery librarian.

Most positions are currently advertised directly by the employer, and others through consultants and employment agents.

THE AGING WORKFORCE

People aged forty-five and over will 'account for 42% of the labor force in 2011, against 35% in 2001 and the 27% it was in 1991' (Drake, 2003, p. 1). This report from Drake International "uncovered lots of Australian government policy on these issues but highlighted a lack of corresponding policy and guidance in New Zealand around the impacts of an aging labor force."

The age of librarians in the 2001 Census publication *Employment in the cultural sector* indicated that '7 out of every 10 female librarians (70%) were over 40 years old' (Statistics New Zealand, 2006:24). The situation is similar in Australia with 2006 Census data indicating that 65% of librarians are over forty-five years of age and only 12% are aged under thirty-five years.

The impact of this on special libraries is that those with specialist subject expertise will soon leave the workforce, or may have done so already and many of them will not be able to be replaced. Many special libraries are one-person libraries, and the opportunities for knowledge sharing, knowledge capture and so on are minimal. This situation is exacerbated by difficulties in attracting suitable candidates to the profession and specifically to special libraries, which are often perceived as being less secure career choices than academic or public libraries. There is some leakage as qualified professionals move to other professions for higher salaries and as organizations replace traditional libraries (including physical collections and in many cases staff) with 'just-in-time' information provision by paying for what they need when they need it.

PROFESSIONAL REPRESENTATION

There is no consolidated approach to supporting or representing special libraries in Australia. Many remain under the umbrella of the *Australian Library and Information Association* (ALIA) while others have formed consortia, collectives or associations. ALIA provides individual and institutional membership options and has a number of discipline-based and state-based groups that support special libraries including those in the health/medical, legal, business/corporate and education/research sectors. ALIA also provides a number of state-based groups that support one- person libraries (OPALs), many of which are special libraries.

The major professional library organization in New Zealand is *Library and Information Association of New Zealand Aotearoa : Te Rau Herenga O Aotearoa*, (LIANZA) formed in 1910, which has a special interest group (SIG) for special librarians.

Not all special librarians are ALIA or LIANZA members. In New Zealand 13% of librarians who belong to LIANZA work in special libraries, the majority of whom are based in Wellington (62%). In Australia there are currently 814 individual ALIA members who are employed in special libraries (18% of total individual membership) and 453 institutional memberships (49% of total institutional memberships) that would fall into the category of special libraries.

In order to support special librarians in Australia and New Zealand further, a local chapter of the Special Libraries Association (SLA) was established in June 2004. The Australia and New Zealand Chapter of the Special Libraries Association (CANZ) currently has eighty-five institutional and individual members. SLA has a huge membership globally and offers worldwide networking, education and training opportunities for special librarians in Australia and New Zealand. The Association has twenty-six subject divisions, which cater for specialized interests such as Business & Finance Division, Engineering, Chemistry, Knowledge Management, Legal and Science and Technology. LIANZA and the SLA have a signed Memorandum of Understanding to benefit members of both associations and it is expected that ALIA and SLA will have a similar agreement in place by the end of 2008.

Special libraries in Australia are collaborative both within and beyond their sectors and/or disciplines. State and federal government, law and health libraries have all formed well-organized professional associations to provide support through networking, communication, resource sharing, professional development and training and collaborative purchasing. The Australian Law Librarians Association (ALLA) is a national association with state and territory divisions. The Australian Government Libraries Information Network (AGLIN) supports libraries within federal government departments, the Government Libraries Information Network in NSW (GLINN) supports New South Wales State Government libraries and the Government Agencies Information Network (GAIN) supports State Government libraries in Tasmania. Health Libraries Inc. (HLI) is based in Victoria and provides support to health libraries. There are many other formal and informal consortia that represent special libraries at local, state and/or national level.

Until 2003 the Australian Library and Information Association (ALIA) conducted biennial conferences for Special, Law and Health Libraries with the 10th conference being held in Adelaide in August, 2003. There was a one-day special libraries symposium held in Melbourne in 2005. Annual conferences are held by AGLIN, ALLA, HLI and other groups representing special libraries.

New Zealand special librarians are a small group but do work closely to maximize their resources and expertise. In addition to holding an annual conference, LIANZA provides important special interest groups, which include Special Libraries and Information Services Group (SLIS) and Health SIG for health sector library and information professionals. The BIC (Bicultural SIG) and Te Ropu Whakahau (TRW): Maori in Libraries and Information Management, formed in 1991 and affiliated to LIANZA, contribute to furthering the spirit of the Treaty of Waitangi. The New Zealand Law Librarians' Association (NZLLA) was established in 1989.

Other associations and professional groups that support specific aspects of special librarianship are the School Library Association of New Zealand Aotearoa : Te Puna Whare Matauranga a Kura (SLANZ), which was launched in 2000. Local

Government New Zealand (LGNZ), established in 2004, involves all those working in the local government library sector.

The Archives and Records Association of New Zealand (ARANZ) was established in 1976, and the Auckland Heritage Librarians and Archives Group (AHLAG) is a network that meets quarterly to discuss a standing agenda of common issues. These include storage; preservation; digitization; disaster management; events, including training opportunities; exhibitions and cooperative initiatives. Membership is open to librarians and archivists working in the heritage field in the wider Auckland region. Records Management Association of Australasia (RMAA), New Zealand Branch, was established in 2002. Galleries, Libraries and Museums (GLAM), formed in 2007, is an informal group of people who work in galleries, libraries and museums with an interest in preservation. They are not necessarily formally trained and meet irregularly in Auckland.

Special librarians in New Zealand are aware of LIANZA's current development of a professional registration scheme (discussed in another chapter), which will focus attention on the need for more formal processes of training and quality control. It is extremely important that support is given by special groups (SLANZA, NZLLA, SLIZ, RMAA, ARANZ) to promote skills and professional identity, especially for people who work in isolated situations. Under the scheme each qualified individual librarian has a responsibility to ensure that his or her skills and competencies develop and grow through experience and a program of ongoing training. ALIA has a similar Professional Development (PD) registration scheme, which is offered to its members on a voluntary basis.

ISSUES FACING SPECIAL LIBRARIES IN AUSTRALIA AND NEW ZEALAND

The following factors have a significant impact on the structure, growth, viability and profile of special libraries in Australia and New Zealand.

Technology

Technological systems are used to acquire and manage resources – online ordering and integrated library management systems are the norm. Communication and outreach activities include mailing lists, new books lists, database access provision, library websites, RSS feeds and blogs. Providing access to databases and subject guides is a vital part of providing an integrated service. Current awareness is also useful in order to direct information to the desktop of interested clients, either through the library or directly from the databases.

Training users to work effectively with the tools available is a demonstration of the special librarian's skill. Training informally, either as one-on-one training when it is required, or in more formal group training sessions, provides the user with the skills and confidence to use the databases effectively. When the special librarian creates guides to databases to assist users, this adds value to the information. A working knowledge of the metadata, indexing, structuring of information in databases, Web 2.0 applications, social software and IT networks is required. Librarians in special libraries are inherently early adopters of new technologies. Web 2.0 applications have been integrated into service provision, access points and communication processes.

The technological systems required by special libraries are often separate from the technical infrastructure, which is integrated throughout the organization. This creates issues related to service and support, funding and training.

User expectations

For reference and research work there is a prevailing perception that users no longer require an information intermediary – the literature increasingly refers to a process of "disintermediation." This is particularly true for the emerging generations of information users who are independent and efficient web and database searchers. Google and other search engine technologies have brought many people into the age of Boolean search techniques, and taught them limiting and field searching without their being aware of it. Many end-user databases are user friendly, too. Clients expect instant provision of information to their desktops and in many cases they will find it themselves rather than seek the assistance of a librarian.

Seamless integration of electronic information

Related to the electronic provision of information to the desktop is the issue of the 'invisibility' of the library's role in the provision of information. As databases, electronic journals and books and other electronic resources are provided seamlessly through intranets and library websites, the role of the library is not always evident.

Marketing

Special library staff use many methods to market their services to their clientele and are proactive at leveraging new technologies to do this. Communication is increasingly through websites and intranets, blogs and wikis, RSS feeds and emailed alerts. Traditional methods such as branding and outreach provide a strong identity and style. Each interaction with clients within the company or organization is another chance to market the services and resources on offer, and this is one reason why the personal skills advertised for in job advertisements are so critical to the success of a special library.

Author interviews with special librarians from both commercial and non-commercial sectors in New Zealand have so far shown that they possess a strong service ethic, which makes them move naturally towards marketing to niches, in the realization that different user groups need different services and that it is important to create the services to match the need. They understand diverse client groups and are well aware of the need to spend time networking with individuals, socially or professionally, all the time intent on raising the profile of the library's services within the organization. Most present a corporate look in their dress, and possess a high level of organizational knowledge.

Measuring and communicating the value of special libraries

Special libraries typically do not generate income so a monetary measure of the value of the library to the parent organization is inappropriate. Various studies during the 1990s have provided both quantitative and qualitative methods for assessing the benefits of the special library's contribution in corporate settings; however, anecdotal evidence suggests that, despite these studies, few organizations fully appreciate the strategic contribution of their special library. As efforts continue to quantify benefit, special librarians continue to provide critical information to enable the organizations to function. Measuring and evaluating the library's performance and particularly in how it supports the parent organization strategically is a critical component of the role of the special librarian. Processes must be in place to capture data about how the library is perceived by its clients and how the resources provided for library services are being used, always in the context of how the organization is benefiting in a business sense by having a library that provides efficient information provision to support business processes.

Special libraries use a variety of effectiveness measures; for example, assessing the value of research undertaken in terms of the amount of time and resources a member of staff might have expended in locating the material themselves. Communicating value and impact to management is critical so that they are aware of the impact of the library's effectiveness in saving time and money and producing tangible results in the form of good research for decision-making.

Current business conditions

Both the Australian and New Zealand economies are currently decelerating after a number of years of strong economic growth of around 4% on average per year. Statistics and anecdotal evidence indicate that there has been a loss of libraries and library staff in the commercial sector, due to a number of economic and commercial factors.

Globalization in particular is having a strong effect on the companies and organizations employing special librarians. New Zealand has become a branch office nation with high tech and manufacturing companies moving offshore because of high tax rates, high exchange rates and particularly the high US dollar, a net outflow of skilled workers to Australia and the UK, and corporate strategies and rationalizations (restructures, mergers and so on). Consequently the New Zealand commercial sector has lost at least nine libraries in organizations and one in the non-commercial sector in the last five years.

By contrast, growth is currently being experienced in the government sector, with a higher increase in employee numbers than in the private sector. Government spending has increased and attempts are being made to improve efficiencies. The expansion of this sector is reflected in an increase in the overall numbers of non-commercial special libraries. Despite this increase there have been some rationalizations, resulting in the loss of libraries and positions.

SPECIAL LIBRARIES IN TRANSITION

There is a wide range of special libraries in Australia and New Zealand serving business, industries and the professions. While only 20% of all special libraries are in the corporate sector, it is here that job losses and library closures are occurring. Meanwhile there is growth in the number of libraries and staff in the government sector, and it is encouraging to see the stability of legal, health and medical library numbers.

New Zealand

As noted above, there is an increase in library staff now working in museums, galleries and archives, an area that is also attracting numbers of Maori and Pacific Island staff in New Zealand. The majority of special librarians are based in Wellington, as a direct result of government sector growth and policies of centralizing government functions. Another feature of the workforce is that it is highly trained but, in line with other library sectors, it is definitely aging, with two-thirds of qualified librarians now over forty years old.

The special libraries sector in New Zealand is made up of a well-trained body of librarians, with excellent qualifications and up to date training, along with good personal skills. Maintaining high standards in special libraries and marketing to employers the value of a special library and the skills of its staff is important. There is a strong demand from employers for new skills. Traditional skills are required in addition to newer ones, including greater information technology expertise, knowledge management, and records and archives management. Realizing the importance of keeping the library workforce up to speed with new developments and skills, LIANZA is offering a professional registration process and offering some of the necessary training to keep librarians competitive.

Challenges faced in special libraries in New Zealand are much the same as those faced in other countries. The changing requirements of employers combined with an aging workforce require a serious look at immediate training needs. Current global business conditions challenge companies all over the world during the current credit crunch.

Growth in the non-commercial sector is encouraging; however, this situation might change with a possible change of government in the current election year, 2008. Although special librarians have been early adopters of Web 2.0 technologies, to advance their services and their image to clients, the self-help mentality fostered by Google and other user-friendly products threatens the traditional information intermediary role of the special librarian.

Australia

Special libraries in Australia are diverse in scope and structure. Their collections reflect the strategic and operational priorities of the organization or industry they support. The importance of the collections from a national perspective is related to the age of the library, the collection development and management expertise of the librarian, and the resource budgets over the years. The size and structure of the library and its positioning within the organization or industry can vary according to factors such as perceived value and budget. Many are one-person libraries while others have significant numbers of staff. Some are considered to be strategically vital to their organizations while others are seen as "support" services. In many organizations the special library is no longer a discrete unit but part of a larger information or knowledge management operation. It may be combined with records management, archives, information technology or research, or it may operate in a "virtual" space using technology to provide resources and services to those who need them.

Current trends

Current trends include repositioning, space reduction and collaboration. Many special librarians are now playing key strategic roles in delivering resources and services to their organizations. This is a significant shift from the traditional library service, which was regarded as a 'support' service. While many special librarians remain members of ALIA, LIANZA and SLA, it is becoming increasingly common for special librarians to join non-library professional associations to support their broadening roles and their alignment with the key players in their organizations. Second, reduction of special libraries' physical space and a consequent reduction of their physical collections is becoming increasingly common. Many operate without a physical collection at all. Finally, networks, partnerships and consortia enable special libraries to deliver a broader range of resources and services than they could individually.

Over recent years all libraries have experienced significant changes resulting from new technologies and economic factors. The changes have brought both challenges and opportunities for special libraries, with new roles emerging for special librarians. Titles such as strategic information manager, information consultant, web/intranet manager and knowledge manager have become commonplace. As Schachter puts it (2007), "The age of the information intermediary may be over, but the role of special librarian is merely evolving."

References

AHLAG –Auckland Heritage Librarians and Archives Group (2008). Auckland. Auckland Heritage Librarians and Archives Group. [Online] Available: http://ahlag.auckland.ac. nz.

Australian Libraries Gateway: Find a library. (2008). Canberra, ACT. National Library of Australia. [Online] Available: http://www.nla.gov.au/apps/libraries.

Australian Libraries and Information Association (ALIA). (2008). Australian Libraries and Information Association. [Online] Available: http://www.alia.org. au/.

ContactsUnlimited (Ed.). (2006). *Contacts in New Zealand libraries*. Wellington: Contacts Unlimited.

Directory of special libraries in New Zealand (2007), National Library of New Zealand.

Drake. (2003). The Age chasm ; successfully managing age in your organisation. Drake whitepaper, l.

Eames B. (Ed.) (1999). *Directory of special libraries in Australia* (10th edition). Kingston, ACT. Australian Library and Information Association, Special Libraries section.

Fields, A. & Rebecca, Y. (Ed.). (2007). *Informing New Zealand : libraries, archives and records* (5th ed.). Wellington: The Open Polytechnic of New Zealand. (p. 141, 153).

Henczel, S. (2007). Special libraries in Australia. Canberra, ACT. Australian Gateway. [Online] Available: http://www.nla.gov.au/apps/libraries.

LIANZA (Library and Information Association of New Zealand Aotearoa). (2008). *Library qualifications: a summary of New Zealand library qualifications*. Wellington. [Online] Available: http://www.lianza.org.nz/development/education/qualifications.html.

McGeough, S. (2007). Correspondence. Wellington. Statistics New Zealand.

Minimum Standards for New Zealand Health Libraries. (2005). Wellington: Library and Information Association of New Zealand Aotearoa.

New Zealand Law Librarians Association. (2008). *Principles of professional conduct.* Auckland. New Zealand Law Librarians Association. [Online] Available: http://www.nzlla.org. nz/principlesofprofessionalconduct.cfm.

Ralph, G. and Sibthorpe, J. (2007). Emerging trends in New Zealand special libraries. Auckland.

Schachter, D. (2007). Special libraries in transition: what to do if the axe is falling. *Information outlook, 11*(7), 42 – 43.

Spiller, D. (1998). UK special library statistics : the challenge of collecting and analysing data from libraries in the workplace, 1 – 8.

Statistics NewZealand. (2006). Employment in the cultural sector. Wellington: Statistics New Zealand.

Statistics NewZealand. (2006). New Zealand official yearbook 2006. Wellington: Statistics New Zealand, 23.

SCHOOL LIBRARIES

James E. Herring

Teacher librarians in Australia and school library teams in New Zealand make up a sizeable percentage of qualified librarians in their respective countries because of the large numbers of schools in those countries, thus school libraries have an important role to play in the overall provision of library services to the populations of these countries and in particular to the children of school age. The importance of school libraries and their staff in developing adult citizens who have the requisite information literacy skills to play an active part in the democracy of the two countries is often underestimated. This is not to say that school libraries only exist to fulfill a utilitarian role of helping to producing the nation's workforce because teacher librarians and school library teams seek to engage their students in the world – both print and digital – of information. School libraries in Australia and New Zealand have moved away from their traditional roles of providing books – often mainly fiction – to school students and their focus is now firmly related to the school curriculum and to how and what students learn in and out of school. This chapter will examine:

- The role of the school library
- School library standards
- School library staffing and the role of the teacher librarian and school library team
- Information literacy in schools
- School library collections
- The use of ICT in school libraries

and will highlight the similarities and differences between school libraries in Australia and New Zealand.

THE ROLE OF THE SCHOOL LIBRARY

School libraries across the world exist to play an active part in developing learning amongst students in the school, and in Australia and New Zealand the role of the school library is defined in relation to the learning and teaching context within which the school library exists. In Australia, the Australian School Library Association (ASLA) states that the "School library and information programs and services are integral to the goals of the school and the aims of the school curriculum" (ASLA 2004a, paragraph 1). Since the goals of all schools will be to develop student learning, the school library will have this as its dominant role. In New Zealand, the Ministry of Education and the National Library of New Zealand (2002:4) hold that "The school library or information center is at the center of school life and learning programs in both primary and secondary schools." The role of the school library will thus be central to the development of learning in the school.

In both countries, it can be seen that the key role of the school library outlined above is centered on *learning* i.e. not on the provision of information resources. School libraries have moved on from having a primarily *support* role in the school to having a more active and central role, and this new and much more education-orientated role for the school library will also have an effect on the role of the teacher librarian or school library team. The key aspect of this role is the development of information literacy amongst students in the school and this role is expanded on in the section on information literacy below.

All other roles of the school library will therefore be subservient to the main role of actively developing learning and information literacy in the school. School libraries have a clear role in providing learning resources in schools but in a different sense from other libraries such as children's libraries in the public library sector. While school libraries provide students with fiction, the *main* aim of the fiction collection will not be for leisure but to improve the students' literacy and appreciation of literature. ASLA (2004a, paragraph 1) argues that excellent resource provision will ensure that

- every student has access to a variety of quality, relevant, accurate and current information resources;
- students' personal growth is supported by resources which meet their developmental needs and interests;
- teachers' effectiveness is enhanced by access to recent curriculum and professional development material.

The ASLA (2004a) policy statement also states that effective resource provision must include learning resources, which are professionally organized, and that access to these resources is suitably provided. The school library in Australia also has a role to provide access to resources outside the school and this will include access to other libraries and organization in the local community as well as on a wider scale. With the present ubiquity of the Internet, providing access to the web is now a key role for the school library. The ASLA (2004a) statement identifies key roles for the teacher librarian in managing funds to provide relevant resources and in drawing up a school collection management policy.

In New Zealand, the Ministry of Education and National Library of New Zealand (2002:13) states that the library's role in resource provision includes

- coordinating the management of the school's information and learning resources and making them accessible to the school community and beyond;
- ensuring effective access to all of the school's learning resources through an automated library system.

It also recommends that the school library play a leading role in providing web access for students and identifying key sites as learning resources. Another significant role identified by the Ministry of Education and National Library of New Zealand (2002:11) is in relation to inclusivity and argues that "The library should be for everyone in the school community – for people of all ages, levels, and backgrounds."

SCHOOL LIBRARY STANDARDS

In Australia, the most recently published standards for school libraries are in relation to 'the professional knowledge, skills and commitment demonstrated by teacher librarians working at a level of excellence' and the standards (ASLA 2004b:1) examine the levels of excellence which Australian teacher librarians should aim for in order to provide a high standard of teaching and library practice. The standards (ASLA 2004b:1) define a teacher librarian as a dually qualified member of the school staff who will "support and implement the vision of their school communities through advocating and building effective library and information services and programs that contribute to the development of lifelong learners".

The standards also examine what excellent teacher librarians will know, including an understanding of the school curriculum and learning and teaching within curricular subjects but also across the curriculum, as well as the management of the library and its resources, including extensive use of ICT. The standards (ASLA 2004b:2-3) indicate that excellent teacher librarians "are well-informed about information literacy theory and practice" and that in practice, they "collaborate with teachers to plan and implement information literacy and literature programs that result in positive student learning outcomes." The standards are recognized as being valuable for the development of teacher librarians as excellent school professionals, but there is (anecdotal) concern that the standards might be used by school principals as actual expectations of all teacher librarians rather than as goals towards which teacher librarians might aim.

Although in New Zealand, there are no formally entitled school library standards, the Ministry of Education and National Library of New Zealand (2002) document is viewed as a set of standards that can be updated. These standards identify "six guiding principles, which together provide a flexible framework to guide all New Zealand schools in developing and improving their libraries" (p. 14). The principles relate to

- information literacy in which 'The school library is a *learning environment* central to the development of an information-literate school community' (p.14);
- reading, where the school library is seen as a key factor in developing reading habits in students;

- access, in which "The school library is a *hub and interface* with organized systems for accessing and managing information and resources" (p.14);
- information resources, in which the school library is seen as collecting and managing relevant learning resources for the school; and
- place, in which "The school library is a student-centered *facility* designed to play a key role in the intellectual, educational, and cultural life of the school" (p.14).

Thus, the New Zealand standards, like their Australian counterparts, set high goals for schools and school library staff, and it is in the area of staffing that the key differences lie between the Australian and New Zealand school libraries.

SCHOOL LIBRARY STAFFING AND THE ROLE OF THE TEACHER LIBRARIAN OR SCHOOL LIBRARY TEAM

In Australia, in most primary and secondary schools, the teacher librarian is a person who is a qualified teacher who is also a professional librarian. ASLA (2004b:1) states that 'A teacher librarian holds recognized teaching qualifications and qualifications in librarianship, defined as eligibility for Associate (i.e. professional) membership for the Australian Library and Information Association [ALIA].' An important to make here is that Australian teacher librarians are *paid* on teacher scales and their level of salary is related to their status in the school, e.g., some teacher librarians are recognized as heads of department. There is no definitive level of staffing in Australian schools although it is clear that independent schools often have much higher levels of staffing than government schools. For most secondary schools, either in the public or private sector, the minimum staffing is likely to be one teacher librarian plus clerical staffing and the level of clerical staffing usually relates to the size of school in relation to student numbers. As in other parts of the developed world, the teacher librarian profession is an aging one and there is a shortage of teacher librarians. This is reflected, for example, in the policy of the New South Wales Department of Education to sponsor students undertaking the Postgraduate Diploma in Teacher Librarianship at Charles Sturt University. (New South Wales, Department of Education and Training 2008 and Charles Sturt University 2008).

In New Zealand, school libraries are staffed mainly by professional librarians who are part of a library team. As was found by the Education Review Office (ERO) (2005) report, there is a wide variation in staffing across the country. Professional librarians are, with very few exceptions, only found in secondary schools, and not all secondary schools have professional librarians. A key difference with Australian teacher librarians is that professional librarians in New Zealand (i.e., those holding a recognized librarianship qualification but not a teaching qualification) are *paid* at local government salary levels, which are well below teaching salary levels. This system is the same as that pertaining in UK schools, and New Zealand schools have similar problems to the UK in retaining professional staff, who are often attracted away by higher salaries in the private sector or in university libraries. The ERO (2005, Secondary – Less effective practice) reported that thirty per cent of secondary schools did not have adequate library resources and that "In many schools, the library was not adequately staffed, library staff were untrained and the roles of some staff were not clear." The report stressed, however, that schools with professional staffing were more likely to meet the needs of students and staff and that many school library teams provided an excellent range of services.

The debate over whether school librarians across the world should be qualified as both teachers and librarians continues today. While it is clear that some school librarians without teacher qualifications can and do provide better services and leadership, e.g., in ICT in their schools, than dually qualified teacher librarians in other schools, it is generally accepted that the ideal staffing for a school library is that it should be led by a dually qualified teacher librarian.

The role of the teacher librarian is outlined in the ASLA (2004b) standards cited above, and a number of school library and teacher associations in Australia have statements about the role of the teacher librarian, including the New South Wales Teachers' Federation (2000). A very clear and comprehensive outline is provided by the School Library Association of South Australia (2003), which identifies the following aspects of the teacher librarian's role:

- teaching and learning, including meeting the aims of the school curriculum and providing students with information literacy skills
- leadership, including taking on leadership roles in the school in relation to information literacy and resource provision
- curriculum involvement, including working collaboratively with teachers in developing information literacy across the school curriculum and advocating the use of ICT in the school curriculum
- management, including effective management of the school library staff and learning resources and contributing to the development of the school intranet
- services, including selecting and organizing the learning resources of the library and promoting services and resources across the school
- literature promotion, including making students aware of the wide range of literature available, including non-fiction and working collaboratively with teachers to promote reading.

It is likely that if this role statement were revised for 2008, then there would be a greater emphasis on the use of ICT in the school library and on the mediation of digital resources for students. Herring (2005) states that increased use of the web in schools, the development of school intranets, including school produced learning websites for students can be seen as a threat and an opportunity in relation to the role of the teacher librarian. Herring (2005) also argues that teacher librarians who do not move with the ICT times are likely to find that their role in the school is diminished.

In New Zealand, the role of the school librarian is more often incorporated into statements about the role of the school library team. The National Library of New Zealand (2007) provides guidelines for potential job descriptions for school library staff, including teacher librarian and library manager/librarian, although as noted above, most professionals who work in school libraries in New Zealand are school librarians, i.e., fit into the library manager/librarian category. The role of the teacher librarian, according the National Library of New Zealand (2007:10) includes a responsibility to 'Promote information literacy across all year levels and curriculum areas'; manage the library staff, budget, resources and ICT in the library; and liaise with external bodies such as the national school library association. For the library manager/librarian, the National Library of New Zealand (2007 p.13) identifies the role as including providing 'Support the development of information literacy' in the school; effectively managing the school library systems and procedures; ensuring the 'Provision of high quality resources, including online, that meet the reading and information needs of the school community' (p.14); and liaising with external agencies.

In comparison with the role cited for the Australian teacher librarian, the National Library of New Zealand (2007) appears to have a restricted view of what might be achieved by a teacher librarian in particular, although the report does indicate that each school will identify key roles and responsibilities. The role of the library manager/librarian does seem rather limited and it is certain that most secondary schools in New Zealand would want a greater contribution from someone holding that position.

INFORMATION LITERACY IN SCHOOLS

In both Australia and New Zealand, information literacy has been the dominant theme in school librarianship in recent years, as with school libraries across the world. The increased use of the web as the main resource used by students and teachers to find information (despite the best efforts of some teacher librarians) has highlighted the need for students, teachers and teacher librarians to be information literate, although there is debate about the precise meaning of the phrase 'information literacy'. The most cited definition of information literacy tends to be that of Doyle (1994: 40) who defines information literacy as "the ability to access, evaluate, and use information from a variety of sources, to recognize when information is needed, and to know how to learn" and indicates some of the attributes that an information literate student might have. Doyle's (1994) definition would, in this author's opinion, be improved by starting with the ability to recognize and define the information need, since finding, evaluating and using information must follow from the premise that an information need has not only been recognized but has been defined and explored, e.g., via a written or mental concept map, so that the information seeker has a clear *purpose*.

In Australia, there has been a plethora of literature on information literacy. In an often cited (and republished) article, Langford (1998:1) posed a number of questions relating to the term "information literacy" including: "Is it a concept or a process? Is it an embodiment of essential skills that have only had name changes over the decades?" More recently, ASLA (2006:8) states that "Information literacy means being information smart', reflecting some of the new terminology of 'smart information users" (Hay and Eyre 2005). One of the most common models of information literacy used in Australian schools is Ryan and Capra's (2001: 3) ILPO model, which has the following elements:

- *Defining*: The stage of formulating questions, analyzing and clarifying the requirements of the problem or task…
- *Locating*: Following the defining stage, the student identifies potential sources of information and is able to locate and access a variety of resources using multiple formats.
- Selecting/Analyzing: The student analyses, selects, and rejects information appropriate to the problem or task from the located resources…
- Organizing/Synthesizing: In this stage, the student critically analyzes and organizes the gathered information, synthesizes new learning incorporating prior knowledge, and develops original solutions to a problem or task.
- Creating/Presenting: The student creates an original response to the problem or task, presenting the solution to an appropriate audience.
- Evaluation: In this final stage, the student critically evaluates the effectiveness of his or her ability to complete the requirements of the task and identifies future learning needs.

This model has similar elements to other recognized models of information literacy such as *The Big Six* (Eisenberg & Berkowitz 1990) and *PLUS* (Herring 1996 and 2004).

Examples of how teacher librarians in Australia have developed information literacy programs in their school can be found in most recent editions of the journals *Access* (http://www.asla.org.au/pubs/access), *SCAN* (http://www.curriculum support.education.nsw.gov.au/schoollibraries/scan/index.htm) and *Synergy* (http://www.slav.schools.net.au/synergy.html). but two examples are provided here.

Ryan and Hudson's (2003) work on developing an effective and evaluated information literacy skills program in a Melbourne school demonstrates how teacher librarians can have an impact on student learning and the school curriculum. A key feature of Ryan and Hudson's (2003) program was to integrate information literacy development *within*, and not separate from, the school curriculum. The Year 7 (first year high school) students used a series of scaffolds developed by the teacher librarians who collaborated closely with teachers and this enabled the students to have a focal point for planning their assignments, i.e., defining purpose, finding relevant information, reading for information, taking meaningful notes and avoiding plagiarism, and writing or presenting the assignment. Ryan and Hudson's (2003) approach was to give students a series of questionnaires which evaluated how well students were able to take a holistic view of their assignments and they found that students who were in the early stages of Year 7 did not do this but focused too much on finding information. As students progressed through the year, the subsequent questionnaires showed that most students' understanding of their information literacy skills had improved, particularly in relation to the way in which students could examine their initial purpose and relate finding and using information to that purpose.

Fitzgerald (2007) worked with teachers in her school to examine the impact of a 'guided inquiry' approach to developing information literacy skills with Year 7 students. The approach is based on the work of Todd and Kuhlthau (2005), and Fitzgerald (2007, p. 30) notes that guided inquiry involves 'targeted instructional interventions of a school librarian and classroom teacher teams that guide students through curriculum based inquiry units'. The aims of the project were to identify which interventions were most appropriate and included asking students to identify their own strengths and weaknesses in their use of information literacy skills. Students were also encouraged to develop their own personal approaches to completing the stages of doing an assignment. Fitzgerald (2007, p. 33) outlines the findings of the study and states that students were 'relatively unaware and inarticulate about their process of doing research' and that, with the support given, students demonstrated "high interest and a move towards deep knowledge of their topic." Fitzgerald (2007:35) sums up the guidance that might be given to other teacher librarian/teacher teams by stating "Provide students with an engaging research task...Teach them how to build deep knowledge and understanding, and guide them at every stage of the process." This last piece of advice is perhaps the most important in that there is much anecdotal evidence that students are supported very well at the *early* stages of completing an assignment but that guidance often falls away when students have to read, evaluate, understand and *use* the information they find.

The published research and literature on information literacy in New Zealand is less in quantity but not in quality. The early work of Gawith (1987) led the way to subsequent research and the development of Gawith's (2000, paragraph 1) "3 doors to information literacy" model has been influential in the development of information literacy in New Zealand schools. Gawith (2000) describes her model as "a complex learning/teaching model covering emotional, social and cognitive dimensions of learning and embracing many skills and strategies. It has been extensively and successfully trialed over five years of research." The work of Moore (2001 and 2002) has been particularly influential in how information literacy has been highlighted as a key educational concept in the school sector, and her work is regularly cited in later publications.

The National Library of New Zealand (2005:2) identifies a range of "critical factors" for schools wishing to develop information literacy and these include:

- school's staff share an educational philosophy of and a commitment to a school-wide information literacy program in which the library plays a critical role.
- Library staff have information literacy expertise and work collaboratively with all teaching staff in the information literacy program.
- All school staff practice and model information literacy skills and behaviors.

The third point here is a crucial one since across the world one of the key limiters to the success of information literacy programs in schools has been the lack of emphasis on information literacy skills *in the classroom* as opposed to in the school library.

The School Library Association of New Zealand (SLANZA) (2006, p.1) reviewed a range of literature and models in information literacy from around the world and decided to create its own model for New Zealand, with the aim 'To create and publish an information processing model that can be used by all sectors of the compulsory education sector'. The SLANZA (2006, p.3) model is similar to other models in that its elements are:

Defining
Locating
Selecting Processing
Organizing
Creating/ Sharing
Evaluating.

One of the advantages of the SLANZA (2006) model is that is has incorporated some topical concerns that have not been highlighted so prominently in previous models, such as plagiarism.

Probert (2006) reports on a study undertaken in New Zealand schools that highlighted a lack of understanding on the part of teachers in relation to the concept of information literacy, and Probert (2006) states that many teachers viewed the concept as relating to ICT. The outcomes of the study, according to Probert (2006) demonstrate the need for teachers to have a greater understanding of the concept as well as the practice of information literacy in schools. This reflects a similar need in many countries across the world.

SCHOOL LIBRARY COLLECTIONS

School library collections could once be identified as what was held in the school library, i.e., what could be *seen* on entering the library plus what had been borrowed and what the teacher librarian held in separate storage, such as newspaper clippings files. The advent of digital resources has transformed that model and in today's school libraries in Australia and New Zealand, as elsewhere, what is *not seen* on entering the library can be of more educational value than what is seen. The challenges for teacher librarians and school library teams are to identify the needs of their community of users, develop a collection development policy, evaluate then select materials, and organize these materials for access.

In Australia, the book by Dillon et al (2001) was influential in gathering together a coherent set of chapters on aspects of collection development and stressed the need for teacher librarians to be aware of their community's needs *before* developing print and digital collections. This emphasis on user needs is very important and Kerstjens (2006, Book end, paragraph 1) argues that teacher librarians are key to developing learning resource collections in school libraries because "They understand the resource needs of teachers". If school library collections are not to be seen as the province only of the teacher librarian, it is important for the teacher librarian to publicize the availability of learning resources amongst school staff and involve the staff in the selection of these resources. This is reflected by Queensland Government Library Services (2006, paragraph 1) that states that "A well-developed school resource centre collection is achieved if selection is a collaborative operation involving the teacher-librarian, key staff members and where appropriate, students and parents."

Developing a collection development policy is seen as key element in providing a school library collection that meets the needs of the school community and the development of such a policy is emphasized in a number of Australian states and territories by the relevant department of education. For example, in Western Australia, the Department of Education and Training states that a collection development policy should be based on the school philosophy and be part of the overall school development plan, and should contain statements of policy on:

- introduction: scope and role of the collection, source of funds;
- selection policy;
- weeding policy;
- challenged material policy, and
- donated material policy (2008, paragraph 2).

Two of the most recognized examples of collection development policies in schools are those of Braxton (2004) and Horton (2004). While collection development policies for Australian school libraries have been developed in recent years, it is clear that guidelines provided by various departments of education are out of date in that they fail to take enough account of the development of *digital* collections in school libraries. In particular, new sets of guidelines are needed for teacher librarians who develop mediated collections of websites on particular curricular topics. This in-school development of learning resources is not often catered for in school library development policies.

The key to successful school library collection development lies in selecting the appropriate resources and while this aspect is emphasized in collection development policies, it is often underdeveloped or appears to be less important than the more administrative aspects of acquisition, weeding or challenged materials. Tanner states that the selection of learning resources for the school library should follow established selection principles but should also include:

- ensuring the selection of relevant and high quality digital resources that are tailored to the library's specific mission, goals priorities and user needs.
- applying equivalent evaluation standards in digital resource selection" (2001, Collection management issues, paragraph 1).

The Tasmania Department of Education (2007, Selection criteria) identify a range of selection criteria including 'purpose', 'suitability', 'production', 'value for money', and 'equal opportunities', and similar guidelines can be found in other department of education guidelines across Australia as well as in individual school library policies. While these criteria are generally useful and fit well with print collections, they do not reflect the increasing use of digital learning resources in schools. Spry and Hayman (2008) emphasize this point by posing the questions: "How can a school library build the best possible collection of learning resources, taking advantage of user contributions while maintaining the integrity and educational value of the collection? How can we develop collection policies for this new environment and what is the most effective way to manage a collaboratively built collection?"

In New Zealand, the issues relating to collection development are very similar to those in Australia. The National Library of New Zealand (2007:3) has produced guidelines for school library teams and identify the process as shown in Figure 1 below.

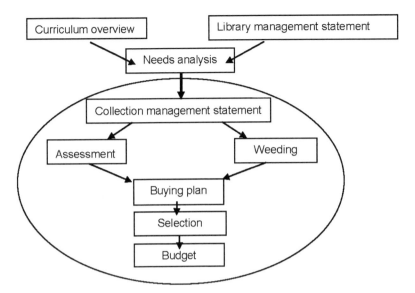

Figure 1 Collection management process

It is clear that there is a commendable emphasis on assessing user needs in the National Library of New Zealand's (2007) recommendations. One aspect of collection development, in terms of *access* to information in New Zealand schools is the availability to all schools of the EPIC databases. The National Library of New Zealand (2008) notes that "EPIC (Electronic Purchasing In Collaboration) is a venture between New Zealand libraries and the Ministry of Education. EPIC provides schools with access to an unparalleled range of electronic resources from the following database providers: EBSCO, Encyclopedia Britannica, Oxford Online, Proquest, Thomson Gale. The EPIC databases are available to all New Zealand schools and this is one area in which resource provision in New Zealand is better than that in Australian state schools although many independent Australian schools purchase some of the databases included in the EPIC package.

There is debate in the global world of librarianship as to whether the organization of school library resources should be included in the area of collection development but this author takes the view that a collection can only be developed if it is easily accessible in both physical and virtual form, so that users can easily find and select by accessing or borrowing resources relevant to their needs. In both Australia and New Zealand, the key service used by schools for cataloguing and classifying school library resources is the Schools Cataloguing Information Service (SCIS). The Curriculum Corporation (2007, paragraph 2) states that SCIS 'manages a database of catalogue records producing services and products specifically for the needs of school and school libraries throughout Australia, New Zealand and overseas. Our customers access the catalogue records over the Internet via SCISWEB'. The advantages for teacher librarians and school library teams is that professional staff no longer have to spend much time in cataloguing and classifying learning resources, and this time can be more productively spent supporting students and staff in their use of learning resources.

THE USE OF ICT IN SCHOOL LIBRARIES

As was noted above, the use of ICT has transformed the school library. The increasing use of web technologies has widened the range of services that can be offered to students and other members of the school community and has enabled teacher librarians and school library teams to become ICT experts in their schools, often leading to innovative ways of connecting students to the learning resources they need. Teaching students how to use the web effectively has been highlighted above as a key part of information literacy teaching in schools in Australia and New Zealand. In both countries, it is important that school library staff are themselves effective web searchers in order to gather together relevant resources for particular curricular topics that students may be studying. One of the key ways in which school library staff have been able to increase student access to relevant and mediated learning resources is through the in-school creation of tools that students can access, and these include school library websites, learning websites, wikis and blogs.

In Australia, Braxton provides a comprehensive guide for teacher librarians wishing to build their own website and notes that a school library website can provide:

- an introduction to and information about your school
- access to materials which help your parent body understand how their children develop and learn
- a virtual staffroom to help your staff develop their professional expertise
- support for the implementation and delivery of the classroom curriculum
- access to a virtual library of selected online resources
- opportunities for students to participate in national and international online learning projects
- opportunities for students to celebrate their learning and share it with the world (2005, Introduction, paragraph 3).

School library websites are less developed in New Zealand schools but an interesting example of involving students in the design of the school library websites is provided by Wellington Girls' College (Techangels 2008).

Designing resources for students to use in school can result in tailored resources for students, in other words, based on the needs of a particular class of students or a particular assignment in which the students are engaged. Spence (2005) notes that "In my last 3 schools, I have developed a virtual library of pathfinders, hotlists and online assignments with embedded weblinks." Grantham (2007) discusses the advantage of a virtual library at her school and states that students can be provided with curriculum-relevant links to online resources when undertaking assignments. Grantham (2007) gives a further example of an in-school resource by describing an online discussion group for Year 12 biology students. Herring (2005) notes that the creation of learning websites for students by the teacher librarian and teaching staff can enhance collaboration between school staff, as well as producing neatly packaged learning resources for students.

The advent of Web 2.0 has further increased the opportunities for teacher librarians to create new learning resources for students and school staff. In Australia, O'Connell (2006 and 2007) has been one of the leading advocates of Web 2.0 in the school library community and argues (2006:46) that "We need to look for new ideas and new ways of working with literacy, information literacy, and digital fluency for teaching and learning." O'Connell's *Heyjude* blog is a popular source of Web 2.0 learning for teacher librarians in Australia and elsewhere, and O'Connell (2007) notes the possibilities of using blogs, wikis and social networking sites to enhance learning in the school. Wall (2006:30) also promotes the use of Web 2.0 tools in schools and concludes that "Podcasts, blogs and wikis are examples of technologies that are relatively feely available and can be included in a school library as other resources to allow for a variety of learning styles."

Examples of wikis created by teacher librarianship students at Charles Sturt University in a subject taught by this author can be found at a wiki created by Butson (2007), which is an example of how one student can bring together the work of other students. The use of a wiki in this way is very possible in the school context. Wikis also present teacher librarians who do not have web design skills to create learning websites for their students which can combine curricular material (what the students are taught), mediated online materials (what the students learn for themselves), information literacy advice (how the students can improve their own learning) and assignment information and advice (what the students will create).

The National Library of New Zealand (2008, paragraph 1) has been active in promoting in-service courses for school library teams, aiming 'To take advantage of emerging technologies that enable school libraries to guide learners effectively through the rich, changing information landscape. Participants will feel increasingly confident and capable incorporating Web 2.0 into school library practice.' An example of a school using Web 2.0 is Wellington College's (2008) *The Girvan Library Blog*, which contains book reviews but also student work.

In both countries, the use of ICT in school libraries will continue to develop and school library staff will be able to contribute in particular to growth of online learning in schools as well as increased use of mobile technologies by students and staff in schools. ICT continues to be a learning journey for school library staff.

CONCLUSION

This chapter has highlighted some key aspects of school librarianship in Australia and New Zealand but it is not possible to cover all aspects of the topic in such a short space. Thus aspects of management such as budgeting and staff management; of systems management such as the use of integrated library systems; and the social and community role of teacher librarians and school library teams, have not been covered. What is clear is that school librarianship is alive and well in both countries. Australia leads the world of school librarianship in some areas such as staffing and ICT use although there is not an even spread between independent and government schools. Although New Zealand school libraries are generally less well staffed and resourced (apart from EPIC databases), there are some excellent examples of vibrant and innovative practices here. The future of school libraries in both countries will depend, as ever, on government policy and on in-school decisions on funding, but the increased focus on the development of students' information literacy, both within and outside the school, will mean that school libraries, both virtual and physical, will play an important part in the education of both nations' children.

References

Australian School Library Association (2004), ALIA / ASLA joint statement on library and information services in schools. [Online] Available: http://www. asla.org.au/policy/p_services_in_schools.htm. Retrieved January 31, 2008.

Australian School Library Association (2004a), Policy statement – resource provision. [Online] Available: http://www.asla.org.au/policy/p_rp.htm. Retrieved January 31, 2008.

Australian School Library Association (2004b), Standards of professional excellence for teacher librarians, Australian School Library Association/Australian Library and Information Association, Zillmere, Queensland.

Australian School Library Association (2006), A teacher librarian advocate's guide to building information literate school communities, Australian School Library Association, Zillmere, Queensland.

Braxton, B (2004), Collection development. [Online] Available: http://palmdps. act.edu.au/resource_centre/policies/collection_dvpt.htm. Retrieved January 31, 2008.

Braxton, B (2005), Inside out: from inside to online. [Online] Available:, http:// palmdps.act.edu.au/resource_centre/inside_out/index.htm. Retrieved January 31, 2008.

Butson, E (2007), ETL 501 pathfinders and hotlists. [Online] Available: http://501pathfinders.wetpaint.com. Retrieved January 31, 2008.

Charles Sturt University (2008), Graduate certificate in teacher librarianship [Online] Available: http://www.csu.edu.au/courses/postgraduate/teacher_ librarianship_gc/. Retrieved January 31, 2008.

Curriculum Corporation (2007), About SCIS. [Online] Available: http://www1. curriculum.edu.au/scis/about/about.htm. Retrieved January 31, 2008.

Education Review Office (2005), Student learning in the information landscape. [Online] Available: http://ero.govt.nz/ero/publishing.nsf/3e9bdcd6b9de8 edaca2 5692100069835/039bf184f04614edcc25712d00133365?OpenDocument#Appen dix%201%3A%20Related%20information. Retrieved January 31, 2008.

Eisenberg M and Berkowitz R (1990), Information problem-solving: The big six skills approach to library and information skills instruction. Ablex, Norwood, NJ.

Fitzgerald, L (2007), Investigating guided inquiry: a beginning, *SCAN*, vol. 26, no. 2, 30-37.

Gawith, G (1987), *Information alive.* Auckland: Longman Paul.

Gawith, G (2000), 3 doors to information literacy. [Online] Available: http:// infolit.unitecnology.ac.nz/3doors/home.php. Retrieved January 31, 2008.

Grantham, C (2007), Virtual library: e-ssential, *Access,* vol. 21, no.3, 5-8.

Hay, L and Eyre, G (2005), Smart information use: an exploration of research and practice, *Access*, vol. 19, no. 2, 27-33.

Herring, J (2005), The end of the teacher librarian, *Teacher Librarian,* vol. 33, no. 1, pp. 26-29.

Herring, J (2005a), The instructional website as a focus for teacher librarian and teacher collaboration: a research study, *Synergy*, vol. 3, no. 1, 29-38.

Herring, J (1996), *Teaching information skills in schools.* Library Association Publishing, London.

Herring, J (2004), *The internet and information skills.* Facet Publishing, London.

Horton, R (2004), Policy for P.L. Duffy Resource Centre, Trinity College. [Online] Available: http://www.trinity.wa.edu.au/plduffyrc/library/lib/phil.htm.

Kerstjens, C (2006), No time to gather dust, Connections 57. [Online] Available: http://www1.curriculum.edu.au/SCIS/connections/cnetw06/57gatherdust.htm. Retrieved January 31, 2008.

Langford, L (1998), Information literacy: a clarification, *School Libraries World-wide*, vol. 4, no.1, 59-72.

Ministry of Education and National Library of New Zealand (2002), *The school library and learning in the information landscape.* Wellington, Learning Media Limited.

Moore, P. (2002), An analysis of information literacy education worldwide. [On-line] Available: http://www.nclis.gov/libinter/infolitconf&meet/papers/moore-fullpaper.pdf. Retrieved January 31, 2008.

Moore, P (2001), Learning inspired connections', Keynote paper at the 2001 IASL conference, Auckland. [Online] Available: http://www.iasl-online.org/events/conf/keynote-moore2001.html. Retrieved January 31, 2008.

National Library of New Zealand (2007), Information guide: job descriptions and performance appraisals, Wellington, National Library of New Zealand.

National Library of New Zealand (2008), School libraries 2.0: designing and managing 21st century school library services. [Online] Available: http://www.natlib.govt.nz/about-us/events/full-courses-details?course_id_pk=25. Retrieved January 31, 2008.

New South Wales, Department of Education (2008), Teacher librarian retraining program information. [Online] Available: https://www.det.nsw.edu.au/employment/teachnsw/retrain/lib_info.htm. Retrieved January 31, 2008.

New South Wales Teachers' Federation (2000), The role of the Teacher-Librarian in the school community. [Online] Available: http://www.nswtf.org.au/TeacherLibrarians/role.html. Retrieved January 31, 2008.

O'Connell, J (2006), Engaging the Google generation through Web 2.0 : part 1, *Scan,* vol.25, no.3, 46-50.

Oconnell, J (2007), Judy's web 2.0 notes: Transforming learning. [Online] Available: http://judyoconnell.wordpress.com. Retrieved January 31, 2008.

Queensland Government Library Services (2006), Learning resource selection guidelines for schools. [Online] Available: http://education.qld.gov.au/library/resource/eval/evalg-guide.html. Retrieved January 31, 2008.

Ryan, S & Capra, J (2001), Information literacy planning for educators: the ILPO approach, *School Libraries Worldwide*, vol.7, no. 1, 1-10.

Ryan S & Hudson V (2003), Evidence–based practice, transformational leadership and information literacy at Santa Maria College, *Synergy,* vol. 1, no. 1, 29-41.

School Library Association of South Australia (2003), Teacher librarian role statement. [Online] Available: http://www.slasa.asn.au/rolestatement. Html. Retrieved January 31, 2008.

School Library Association of New Zealand (2006), i2k Information to knowledge: a model for guided inquiry learning for New Zealand schools. Wellington, School Library Association of New Zealand.

Spry, B and Hayman, S (2008), Collections 2.0: Including users in library collection policy and management in a read/write world, Digital Environments Abstracts, ASLA Online III Virtual Conference – May 2008. [Online] Available: http://www.asla.org.au/pd/online2008/environments.htm. Retrieved January 31, 2008.

Tasmania, Department of Education (2007), Section 3, 3.3 Criteria for selection. [Online] Available: http://www.education.tas.gov.au/school/educators/ resources/schoollibraries/guidelines/section3-3. Retrieved January 31, 2008.

Techangels (2008), Students work on real-world projects. [Online] Available: http://www.techangels.org.nz/Documents/Acrobat%20PDFs/Real%20 World%20Projects.pdf. Retrieved January 31, 2008.

Wall, J (2006), Emerging technologies : what do they mean for libraries?, *Access,* vol. 20, no.4, 29-30.

Western Australia, Department of Education and Training (2008), Collection development. [Online] Available: http://www.det.wa.edu.au/education/cmis/eval/ library/selection/sel1.htm. Retrieved January 31, 2008.

LIS EDUCATION

Gillian Hallam[1] and Philip Calvert

The topic of library and information science (LIS) education has been under the spotlight in the professional literature in Australia and New Zealand for a number of years. Critical issues of discussion encompass the apparent lack of a core curriculum for the discipline, the perceived gulf between LIS education and LIS practice, and the pressing need for career-long learning and development. One of the central points of debate that emerges repeatedly is the long-standing question about the positioning of the profession: is LIS a graduate profession of highly skilled individuals valued for their expertise and professionalism or is it a profession of anyone who works in a library, regardless of their qualifications (LIANZA, 2005)?

While Australia and New Zealand do not stand alone in this debate – similar issues are echoed in many other countries – there are inevitably some local characteristics that warrant exploration. The discussion presented here highlights the historical background to professional training, the specific professional policies and standards that guide LIS education and some of the challenges facing professional and paraprofessional education, given the changing environment of education in Australia as a whole, with some comparisons made with the New Zealand situation. While all too often library practitioners point the finger at the library educators to 'right the wrongs', the authors wish to reinforce the idea that the future of effective and relevant LIS education is a matter for all stakeholders in the profession: practitioners and educators, students and staff, employers and employees, with cohesion potentially offered by the professional body.

THE LIS EDUCATION JOURNEY IN AUSTRALIA

While formal professional education for librarians was introduced by the Library Association in the United Kingdom in 1885 and by the American Library Association in the United States in 1887, the situation in Australia was more complex. It has been argued that the 'establishment of a professional association is an essential step in the crystallization of professional ideals and aims, and it was the inability of librarians in Australia to found a permanent professional organization which for a long time retarded the development of a system of education for Australian librarians' (Bramley, 1969:109). The challenges to the establishment of a professional association included the geographical and political realities of Australia

---

[1] Gill Hallam's text is based largely on an earlier work, Education for library and information service', in Ferguson, S. (ed.) (2007), *Libraries in the twenty-first century: Mapping future directions in information services*, pp. 310-336 (Wagga Wagga, NSW: Centre for Information Studies) and is reproduced in part and in adapted form with the kind permission of the Centre for Information Studies.

with its federated system of states and territories covering an extensive land mass, as well as the difficulties in realizing the true professional status of librarianship. First attempts at tuition for library staff were introduced at the Public Library of New South Wales by the Librarian, H.C.L. Anderson. Having attended the Second International Library Conference in London in 1897, Anderson aspired to see a process like the one introduced in the United Kingdom, with library training and an examination leading to the qualification of a diploma. He introduced classes at the Public Library, initially for staff of the Library, but later also for other interested students.

The Munn-Pitt report, published in 1934, highlighted the pressing need for a single professional body that could encourage and support library education in Australia. This report ultimately led to the foundation of the Australian Institute of Librarians (AIL) in 1937, with the express goals of establishing professional unity to raise the standards and status of librarianship in Australia. Membership of the Institute was restricted to "professional librarians." Initial steps to formalizing the education and training of librarians in Australia were delayed by the Second World War, but eventually took place in 1944 when the AIL introduced a 'qualifying examination'. The Australian Institute of Librarians became the Library Association of Australia (LAA) in 1949, open to a broader spectrum of members, and with the acceptance of elective specialist papers in the examination. The LAA examination was renamed the 'registration examination' and formed the main career pathway for librarians until 1980. The registration exam comprised nine papers, with three foundation topics, four core subjects and two elective subjects (Bramley 1969).

The first academic qualification was introduced by the University of New South Wales in 1960 as a Graduate Diploma of Librarianship with the university both teaching and examining its students. The award was deemed equivalent to the Association's registration exam. In 1963 the General Council of the LAA adopted the formal position that librarians should hold a postgraduate qualification. However, in 1965, the Australian government introduced colleges of advanced education and institutes of technology as a new area of tertiary education. Library education fitted into this domain, with a number of courses emerging at the undergraduate level. Since 1968, the professional association in Australia has accepted both undergraduate and graduate qualifications as first award courses for librarians. The Library Association of Australia became the Australian Library and Information Association in 2000.

PROFESSIONAL EDUCATION POLICIES AND STANDARDS IN AUSTRALIA

In their study of standards of LIS education across the world, Dalton and Levinson (2000) identified three models that aim to establish and maintain the standards for library and information science (LIS) education: governmental monitoring; formalized LIS accreditation/approval processes; individual course/departmental standards. The processes in place in Australia represent the second model, that of formalized LIS accreditation/ approval, as is also the case in the United Kingdom and in the United States, although each is distinctive (Hallam, Partridge & McAllister 2004). The Australian Library and Information Association (ALIA) acts as the standards body for the library and information profession. ALIA holds responsibility for the recognition of courses that provide a library and information studies qualification, both the professional programs offered by universities and the paraprofessional programs offered by colleges of technical and further education (TAFE). ALIA's course recognition process is directly linked to the categories of membership of the Association, specifically in terms of the Associate membership, which requires members to hold an ALIA-recognised LIS qualification at undergraduate or graduate levels, and the Library Technician membership, with members holding an ALIA-recognised library technician qualification. Other categories of ALIA membership include General Member, Student, Associate Fellow and Fellow, as well as Institutional Member.

Under the education standards process, ALIA currently recognizes eighteen courses leading to library technician qualifications (ALIA 2006a), the majority at the level of the Diploma in Library and Information Services. One university offers the paraprofessional qualification as an Associate Degree in Science (Library Technology) and another as a Bachelor of Science (Library Technology). At the professional level, ten universities offer ALIA-recognised LIS courses at undergraduate and graduate levels (ALIA 2006b). This compares with sixteen library schools in 1990. Five of the ten institutions offer courses at both undergraduate and postgraduate levels; one university limits its offering to an undergraduate program; four universities offer only postgraduate programs (Graduate Diploma or Masters); one university offers only a Masters course, either as a general professional program (Master of Information Management) or teacher librarianship (Master of Learning Innovation). Harvey (2001) has noted that "librarianship has perhaps always had an identity crisis in that it can be argued that it encompasses every field of endeavor." The multidisciplinary nature of librarianship today requires knowledge and skills that cut across information technology, management, psychology, education, communications, law and human services. A response to this situation can be found in the diverse intellectual emphases in different institutions in terms of faculty or discipline affiliation for the LIS school: courses can be found in schools or faculties of information technology, business, management, education, humanities and social sciences, media and information, or law, business and the arts.

In recognizing courses at the professional level and the library technician level, ALIA draws on its core education policies: *ALIA's Role in Education of Library and Information Professionals* (ALIA, 2005a), *Courses in Library and Information Management* (ALIA, 2005b) and *Library and Information Sector: Core Knowledge, Skills and Attributes* (ALIA, 2005c). Seven key criteria are taken into consideration: course design, curriculum content, student assessment, staffing, resourcing, quality assurance mechanisms and infrastructure. As courses may be offered, of course, in diverse ways – for instance, face-to-face, online or as a hybrid of both – ALIA seeks to ensure that learning outcomes will be consistent across the various delivery modes (ALIA 2006c). Institutions planning to offer an LIS course are required to submit documentation to respond to the seven criteria and to be open to scrutiny through a site visit by a panel of LIS educators and industry practitioners. The courses are monitored through the submission of an Annual Course Return (ACR). The ACR is a mechanism to capture information at the micro-level about the individual courses and at the macro-level about general trends in LIS education, from the dual perspectives of the student cohorts and staffing levels.

ALIA has adopted a conceptual approach in terms of articulating the core knowledge, skills and attributes (2005c) of the LIS profession. The key characteristics of the LIS workforce are presented as: promoting and defending the core values of the profession; understanding and responding to people's information and learning needs; managing the storage, organization, access, retrieval, dissemination, preservation and use of information; developing, delivering and evaluating information facilities, services, sources and products; envisioning and planning future directions for the library and information sector; and advancing library and information science and its application to information services (ALIA 2005c). The core knowledge and skills encompass the knowledge of the broad context of the information environment; an understanding of information seeking, information infrastructure, information organization, information access, information services, sources and products; information literacy education; and the generation of knowledge, to foster a culture of research and evidence-based practice (ALIA 2005c). In addition, value is placed on the generic skills and attributes that are an essential dimension of an effective profession: communication skills; ethical standards and social responsibility; critical, reflective and creative thinking; problem-solving; skills in the areas of ICT application, project management and business acumen; team relationship skills; and self-management. ALIA stresses that "as all areas of library and information practice will continue to evolve and develop over time, the overall framework of knowledge, skills and attributes needs to be able to encompass the changing nature of the discipline to ensure a flexible, adaptable and innovative profession" (ALIA 2005c). This provides a descriptive, rather than pre-scriptive framework for the curriculum. The goal of contemporary LIS education in Australia might be described as having the potential "to give students a broad education in the field that will serve as a foundation for any related career path they may choose" (Stoffle & Leeder 2005:317), rather than providing specialized training to prepare students for specific positions. This inevitably results in concerns amongst the "specialists," such as cataloguers, law librarians or archivists, about the adequacy of the education programs available.

THE COMPLEXITIES OF PROFESSIONAL LIS EDUCATION IN AUSTRALIA

It cannot be denied that the ongoing process of reform in higher education in Australia in recent years has had specific implications for LIS education. As universities strive to achieve greater efficiencies, the principles of economic rationalism inevitably apply. The bulk of the available funding will go towards the bigger and stronger (and more influential) disciplines where high numbers of students are guaranteed, such as medicine, law and business. Smaller niche disciplines like library and information science have found their autonomy and their identity threatened. In general, independent "library schools" have progressively been subsumed into LIS departments, to ultimately become nothing more than a discipline stream, or even just a single course, within a school within a faculty. In many cases this means that the LIS schools "have been forced into alliances with other disciplines, and it is unlikely that any school now teaches courses over which they have full control" (Genoni 2005a). This in turn has implications within the framework of course recognition by ALIA, as local conditions in individual universities may make it increasingly difficult to compare "apples with apples" in terms of the content of the curriculum. It also makes it difficult to accurately determine the actual number of graduates who will seek to enter a library career.

When international comparisons are made, there is an apparent imbalance between the total population and the number of institutions offering LIS courses in this country. Current figures are presented in Table 1.

This imbalance means that not only are the Australian LIS schools competing for graduate enrolments within their own institutions, to encourage students to study towards the Graduate Diploma in Library and Information Studies rather than, say, a Graduate Diploma in Justice Studies, but also there are arguably too many institutions competing nationally for the small number of students who do in fact wish to pursue a LIS career. In contrast to the United States (usnews.com 2006), no formal data is published in Australia to assist students in assessing the quality of LIS schools and their staff.

Table 1: Comparative data for LIS schools (2005)

Country	LIS schools	Population	Ratio of LIS schools: population
Australia	10	20 million	1:2 million
Canada	7	33 million	1:4.7 million
United Kingdom	14	60 million	1:4.3 million
United States	50	295 million	1:5.9 million

The relatively small numbers of LIS students at individual universities increases the vulnerability of the courses themselves. It is immensely challenging for an academic unit with perhaps four academic staff and less than a hundred students to be influential and respected, when there are programs with thousands of students and hundreds of faculty staff, in the overall pool of tens of thousands of students enrolled at a university. In 2001 Schauder estimated that it took 31.43 full fee paying Australian students to cover the employment costs of one academic staff member. If the course requirements are eight academic subjects for a Graduate Diploma, with the worst case scenario of two academics running four units each, the minimum enrolment just to cover salaries is 62.86 full time students. Harvey (2001) and Bundy (2001) both proposed that Australian LIS courses should have a minimum of 6 academic staff dedicated to the LIS discipline. They have calculated that this model would require an annual full-time graduate student enrolment of 188.57 students, which given the multiplicity of library schools in Australia is unsustainable. What are the implications of students having, for example, only two teaching staff for the whole course? Surely it is critical to have a balance of staff with diverse professional experience to provide the opportunity for a range of views to be presented?

There is some evidence that the market for LIS qualifications may currently be moving towards a postgraduate entry model, ironically as was first proposed by the Library Association of Australia in the early 1960s. The International Federation of Library Associations and Institutions (IFLA) has stressed the importance of an undergraduate degree as the foundation to the graduate qualification: 'Students should acquire a broad general education (topics from other disciplines) as a significant preparatory component of the total education program for the library/information professional' (IFLA, 2000). Indeed, the overall trend in student numbers in Australia indicate that proportionally fewer students are interested in the undergraduate qualification, dropping from 47% in 1997 to 34% in 2005.

Myburgh (2003) has commented on the problems of offering LIS programs at the undergraduate level, with falling enrolments and the perceived poor quality of students resulting in a number of institutions closing down their bachelor courses.

As a matter of contrast, in the United States, Master's courses are the only accredited programs. The Graduate Diploma as a qualification survives only in Australia and South Africa, with an ever increasing number of universities internationally offering Master's courses. Myburgh highlights the underlying pedagogic reasons: "A post-bachelor Master's degree should become the basic pre-professional training. The Graduate Diploma is not enough. It is not possible to meet the needs of the profession within this framework. We don't need more superficialists, who train within a one-year time frame, and have a smattering of bits and pieces of knowledge across a discipline area that is too wide to capture within one year" (2003). There have long been questions as to how well a twelve month course can prepare graduates for the workplace. Genoni (2005a) points out that the issue is becoming more critical as the ever-increasing need for new and more complex professional skills and knowledge places further tensions on the curriculum.

Harvey and Higgins, on the other hand, highlight the problems of industry recognition of the higher degree: "Professionally-recognised bachelor's qualifications… are accorded the same professional status as graduate diplomas or masters degrees. Holding a masters qualification in Australia is not usually linked to higher levels of pay; pay scales are theoretically the same for all first professional qualifications. There is, therefore, no financial incentive to pay the extra costs incurred in studying at the masters level" (2003:151). Student fees are a thorny issue in the context of Australian university education, where funding, rather than pedagogic principles, tend to drive many of the educational decisions. In 2005, Dr Brendan Nelson, then Minister of Education, Science and Training and responsible for recent higher education reforms, stated that 75% of undergraduate study costs are funded by government, with the student responsible for 25% of the costs, either payable upfront, or deferred as a student loan (Nelson 2005). Graduate programs, however, are full fee paying – so with no government subsidy – with fees ranging for Graduate Diploma programs from about $7,500 to $12,000, depending on the institution. Masters programs range from $12,000 to $24,000. Student loan schemes are available for graduate students. At the same time, it can also be argued that the undergraduate degrees provide a career pathway for aspiring library technicians who wish to upgrade from a vocational diploma to a professional qualification (Harvey & Higgins 2003). Given the emerging skills shortage in Australia, which will result in strong competition amongst industry sectors for well-qualified professional staff, career progression through upgrading from paraprofessional to professional qualifications is a valuable strategy to meet the demand for workers.

ISSUES FACING PARAPROFESSIONAL LIS EDUCATION IN AUSTRALIA

In 1970, in response to the changing dynamics of the workforce and a shortage of professional librarians, the first library technician course was introduced by Whitehorse Technical College in Box Hill, a suburb of Melbourne, with a curriculum that focused on vocational, practical skills as opposed to the theoretical knowledge covered in professional curriculum. The new course covered 'library procedures, display techniques, audiovisual techniques, business procedures, together with subjects such as sociology and staff supervision' (Rochester 1997:52). The Library Association of Australia (LAA) moved to accept the course recognition criteria for library technician courses in 1977, subsequently introducing a new category of membership for library technicians in 1978. Gradually, each state and territory introduced its own vocational library courses.

In 1999 significant changes were made in the area of education for library technicians and library assistants, with the development of a new national training package, the Museums and Library/Information Services Training Package. The agency responsible for the formulation of the Museums and Library/Information Services package was CREATE (Cultural Research Education and Training Enterprises Australia), with considerable industry consultation. In 2004, advice on training for the cultural sector was transferred to Innovation and Business Skills Australia (IBSA) as the relevant industry skills council. The training package currently comprises three specific components: the Competency Standards, in other words, units of competency which reflect discrete workplace outcomes; the Assessment Guidelines, which describe the industry requirements for assessment; and the Qualifications Framework, which details how the units of competency are packaged into nationally recognised qualifications (IBSA, 2005). The Australian Qualifications Framework (AQF) qualifications for the cultural sector include Certificates II-IV, Diploma and Advanced Diploma. There is currently some discussion in the Vocational Education and Training (VET) sector about the feasibility of some TAFE institutions introducing a Vocational Graduate Diploma in Library and Information Services. These days, some library technicians choose to progress their careers by undertaking a university course in LIS studies, while, on the other hand, it has also been noted that library technician courses also attract a number of students who already have tertiary qualifications (Carroll 2005), reflecting the complexity of the qualifications within the LIS sector.

The original goals of library technician education were to offer a complementary, but distinct, career path to that of librarians. It was not envisaged to be a pre-professional program. Carroll (2002) has noted, however, that the structure of the national qualifications framework and the competency standards now sees the educational outcomes at the higher levels of vocational education dovetailing with

university learning outcomes. This situation presents employer with specific challenges when recruiting. It appears that not all employers acknowledge the professional status of new graduates, meaning that too many new librarians find themselves "functioning in that grey area inhabited by both the professional and paraprofessional" (Carroll 2002). Employers do need to consider how best to accommodate this convergence of qualifications, so that the profession continues to attract people with strong analytical, evaluative and critical thinking skills and the
potential to become future leaders.

LIS EDUCATOR ISSUES

It has been frequently stated that practitioners and educators inhabit two different
worlds, with insufficient interplay and interaction between them. "Many librarians
have little firsthand experience with library education after they graduate. They
don't go back to the schools for alumni functions, and often their knowledge of
what is happening in the schools comes to them second- or third-hand" (Moran
2001:54). It may also be argued that many library educators, working in their academic worlds, may be totally out of touch with current industry practice. In Australia, as in many other countries, there are today significant tensions between the
demands placed on academic staff, on the one hand to secure funded research projects and on the other hand to provide relevant educational outcomes for the LIS
profession.

   The push for educators to "publish or perish" further adds to the inherent tensions, especially when the high impact academic journals are not the regular reading material for practitioners. Equally well, however, there has been some degree
of criticism about the lack of professional reading undertaken by practitioners – or
at least that "researchers and practitioners do not read each others' literature"
(Haddow & Klobas 2004). This means that "as academics relentlessly push the
profession towards theory and abstraction, practitioners pull with equal might toward day-to-day relevance" (Mulvaney & O'Connor 2006:38). There are inevita-
ble tensions between the dimensions of theory and practice in the academic arena,
and indeed Grogan (1983) raised this as a persistent issue in the education of librarians. While, in principle, research and practice should enjoy a mutually beneficial relationship to create "a strong theoretical framework within which a practitioner community can develop" (Haddow & Klobas 2004), it has been argued that
practitioners have long felt that educators were out of touch with practice.

   Beyond this, however, there is a major concern in Australia about the progressive decline in numbers of academic staff members in the LIS discipline. Over the
period 1996-2005, the number of staff decreased literally by 50%, from 130 to 64.
Over the same period, the VET sector has experienced a similar decline, dropping
43% from 79.2 full time equivalent (FTE) staff to 45. The problem is compounded
by the fact that not only are the numbers dropping, but the educators themselves

are "greying." "Library education in Australia expanded rapidly in the late 1970s and 1980s, and a number of those who joined the teaching departments in their early period of growth still remain" (Genoni 2005b). This situation raises serious issues in terms of the currency and relevance of the curriculum in such a dynamic field as LIS. It is essential that the curriculum itself is dynamic, providing graduates with the knowledge and skills they will need as soon as they join the workforce. Libraries and information centers are very different places in 2008, compared with twenty or even ten years ago. Staff development for existing academic staff is therefore crucial.

At the same time, there is anecdotal evidence that the LIS departments in Australia are finding it very difficult to attract new staff. In the light of higher education reforms, there are growing expectations that a PhD is one of the essential selection criteria for a career as an academic. Durrance (2003) has reported that in the United States in the 1990s, more than 90% of LIS faculty held a PhD. This situation contrasts starkly with the LIS sector in Australia, where the PhD remains a relatively scarce commodity. Macauley (2004) provides some interesting insights into the role of the doctorate amongst LIS professionals, reporting that in 2002-2003, only 1.3% of the personal membership of ALIA held the title "Dr." He argues, however, that "credential creep" should result in a growing number of doctoral graduates. Nevertheless, it is pertinent to ask questions of the practitioners:

> How many practising librarians recognise there is a problem [in recruiting librarians into the faculty ranks]? How many have thought about getting a doctorate? How many administrators have encouraged some bright young librarian to venture into a doctoral program? How many administrators provide time off for working librarians to do homework, attend class, and do all the other things necessary to pursue and advanced degree? (Seavey 2005:56).

Thus, at this point in time, it would appear that there are few incentives to become an educator. It is rare for library and information professionals to be willing to invest several years of their life to obtain a higher degree, when the remuneration they will be finally be offered as a lecturer, with little or no teaching experience, is going to be substantially less than the remuneration they would receive by remaining in the workforce and potentially winning promotion to the senior ranks as an industry practitioner (Genoni 2005b). Within the academic institutions, the funding to employ casual academic staff, to help individuals gain experience in the classroom, is also becoming harder to acquire. Inevitably, without effective succession planning, LIS departments become increasingly vulnerable.

THE SITUATION IN NEW ZEALAND

The main focus of the discussion has been LIS education in Australia. It should be noted, however, that LIS education in New Zealand exhibits many similarities to the structures found in Australia. Postgraduate library and information management programs are offered at a university, while an undergraduate degree program and non-graduate programs are available from a polytechnic. It took some time for the division of responsibilities to appear, however, and the history of library education, which will be described later, shows some variation to its cross-Tasman counterpart.

Currently (early 2008) the key issue in career and professional development for library and information managers is professional registration, which has considerable implications for library education. This scheme is organised by the national library association, the Library and Information Association of New Zealand Aotearoa (LIANZA), and has commonalities with similar schemes run by other national library associations, e.g. CILIP in the United Kingdom. The scheme is intended to boost the status and reimbursement of librarians by recognising suitably qualified people as "professionals." It is a mixture of recognition for educational qualifications passed and the application in a workplace of the knowledge learned during study. Two of the objectives of the registration scheme are closely connected to library education:

- an assurance for future employers, both in New Zealand and overseas, that a registered member meets professional standards of competency in the body of knowledge and ethics required for professional library and information work;
- international benchmarking and recognition of professional library qualifications for New Zealanders wishing to work overseas. (LIANZA, 2007)

In order to ensure that national qualifications are adequate for a professional scheme, LIANZA is developing an eleven-point Body of Knowledge based upon the ten point IFLA guidelines (2000), with the addition of one extra point: "Awareness of indigenous knowledge paradigms, which in the New Zealand context refers to Māori." LIANZA's statements, so far, have indicated that the Body of Knowledge must be studied on a graduate level for Registration.

This is a considerable change from the situation that has pertained before Registration, with nobody taking responsibility for accreditation of LIS programs. Naturally the university and polytechnic that offer LIS programs have their own internal quality control processes, but there was none specific to the LIS sector such as the accreditation schemes run by the ALA. In a specific sense there still will not be accreditation even with Registration, but LIANZA will call on an external assessor to determine if the Body of Knowledge is adequately represented within core courses of all the LIS programs.

New Zealand has a population of just over four million people, which is only the same size as one of Australia's largest two cities, therefore it make no sense to have several different providers. It is the market that has largely decided that there should be only one provider at postgraduate level and one at undergraduate and non-graduate level. Under current government rules for tertiary level education, it is possible for other institutions to offer LIS programs, but their viability would have to be questioned. The outcome of this is that the two providers with LIS programs have to act as de facto national institutions. This came about through a process starting in 1945 with the establishment of the New Zealand Library School, which was set up within the National Library Service (later to become the National Library of New Zealand), offering a non-graduate certificate and a postgraduate diploma in librarianship. In the 1970s, as library education around the world was moving into academic institutions, it was hoped that the same would happen in New Zealand with the Victoria University of Wellington (VUW) becoming the host, but the problem was that the university did not want the non-graduate Certificate program. This was finally resolved in 1980 when the postgraduate Diploma became a VUW program and the Certificate became a program offered by the Wellington College of Education. The latter moved to the Open Polytechnic in the 1990s so that it could offer distance courses, and this institution has expanded the offering to include an undergraduate degree. In 1996 the postgraduate Diploma program ceased and a Master of Library and Information Studies program commenced at VUW. In 2004 archives and records management qualifications were introduced at VUW.

A significant review of library education conducted in the late 1980s pointed to the need for distance learning methods to be introduced in New Zealand because of the difficulties experienced by some students having to move to Wellington for full-time study (Saunders 1987), and both the university and polytechnic have been diligent in the development of distance learning methods so that now all LIM programs can be completed at a distance.

THE NEED FOR CAREER-LONG LEARNING FOR LIS PROFESSIONALS

In both Australia and New Zealand, it is argued strongly that that entry-level qualifications are the starting point, not the end point: "A first professional course should be acknowledged to be simply an important first step in the career, supplemented by continuing education as an essential ongoing process to gain the knowledge and skills needed to support a successful career" (Middleton & Hallam 2001:193). While the universities can adopt a proactive stance to incorporate new areas of knowledge and skills into the LIS curriculum, new developments in practice require existing staff to grow and develop. It has become imperative for practitioners to keep their skills and knowledge current and relevant.

In Australia, ALIA launched its Professional Development (PD) program in 2000 to encourage members to engage with career-long learning: "Professional development demonstrates the individual practitioner's personal commitment of time and effort to ensure excellence in performance throughout his or her career. The dynamic and changing library and information environment demands that library and information professionals maintain and continue to develop their knowledge and skills so that they can anticipate and serve the information needs of society and their individual clients" (ALIA, 2005d). Significantly, the distinction is made in the PD program between the necessity of developing both LIS specific areas (for instance, information resources, resources acquisition and management) and generic areas (teamwork, effective communication, critical and evaluative thinking).

Career-long learning is therefore integral to professional success and individual professional development needs to be supported through a combination of education, personal achievement and work-based opportunities. Education for the profession should not be considered the sole responsibility of the LIS educator, but must be viewed as a career-long learning process that involves the individual, universities, training providers, employers and professional associations: 'Library schools don't operate in a vacuum… LIS education needs a healthy infrastructure involving faculty, students, alumni, and practitioners' (Ling Hwey Jeng 2005:3). In Australia, ALIA seeks to foster the collaboration of the diverse stakeholders, by working with the universities and TAFE colleges to ensure the quality of the LIS programs recognised by the Association (ALIA 2005a; ALIA 2005b; ALIA 2005c; ALIA 2006c), by encouraging and supporting practitioners to participate in the professional development scheme (ALIA 2005d) and by encouraging employers to work with the library educators in the provision of formal LIS programs, and to support professional development and workplace learning for their staff (ALIA 2006d). LIS education is a critical issue for the professional association, but beyond this it is also a critical issue for the profession in its entirety. It requires concern, cooperation and collaboration – today, tomorrow and into the future.

References

Australian Library and Information Association (ALIA) (2005a). ALIA's role in education of library and information professionals. [Online] Available: http://www.alia.org.au/policies/education.role.html. Retrieved February 15, 2008.

Australian Library and Information Association (ALIA) (2005b). Courses in library and information management. [Online] Available: http://www.alia.org.au/policies/courses.html. Retrieved February 15, 2008.

Australian Library and Information Association (ALIA) (2005c). Library and information sector: core knowledge, skills and attributes. [Online] Available: http://www.alia.org.au/policies/core.knowledge.html. Retrieved February 15, 2008.

Australian Library and Information Association (ALIA) (2005d). Professional development for library and information professionals. [Online] Available: http://www.alia.org.au/policies/professional.development.html. Retrieved February 15, 2008.

Australian Library and Information Association (ALIA) (2006a). ALIA-recognised library technician courses. [Online] Available: http://www.alia.org.au/edu cation/courses/library.technician.html. Retrieved February 15, 2008.

Australian Library and Information Association (ALIA) (2006b). ALIA-recognised librarianship courses. [Online] Available: http://www.alia.org.au/education/ courses/librarianship.html. Retrieved February 15, 2008.

Australian Library and Information Association (ALIA) (2006c). ALIA recognition of courses: Criteria for recognition of first award courses in library and information management at librarian and library technician level. [Online] Available: http://www.alia.org.au/education/courses/criteria.html. Retrieved February 15, 2008.

Australian Library and Information Association (ALIA) (2006d). Employer roles and responsibilities in education and professional development. [Online] Available: http://www.alia.org.au/policies/information.centres.html. Retrieved February 15, 2008.

Bramley, G. (1969). *A history of library education.* London: Clive Bingley.

Bundy, A. (2001). Education, education, education. *InCite* (June, 4).

Carroll, M. (2002). The well-worn path. *Australian Library Journal, 51*(2), 117-125.

Carroll, M. (2005). Profile of Australian library technician students. *LIBRES, 15*(2). Retrieved on February 15, 2008 from http://libres.curtin.edu.au/libres15n2. Retrieved February 15, 2008.

Dalton, P. and Levinson, K. (2000). An investigation of LIS qualifications throughout the world. 66th IFLA Council and General Conference, Jerusalem, Israel, 13-18 August 2000. [Online] Available: http://www. ifla.org/IV/ifla66/ papers/061-161e.htm. Retrieved February 15, 2008.

Genoni, P. (2005a). The changing face of LIS higher education in Australia. Part 1. *InCite 26* (July, 18).

Genoni, P. (2005b). The changing face of LIS higher education in Australia. Part 2. *InCite 26* (August, 18).

Haddow, G., and Klobas, J. E. (2004). Communication of research to practice in library and information science: Closing the gap. *Library and Information Science Research, 26*(1), 29-43.

Hallam, G., Partridge, H. and McAllister, L. (2004). LIS education in changing times. *Australian Law Librarian, 12*(2), 11-32.

Harvey, R. (2001). Losing the quality battle in Australian education for librarianship. *Australian Library Journal, 50*(1), 15-22

Harvey, R. and Higgins, S. (2003). Defining fundamentals and meeting expectations. Trends in LIS education in Australia. *Education for Information, 21*(2/3) 149-157.

Innovation and Business Skills Australia (IBSA) (2005). *General information on Training Packages: frequently asked questions(FAQs).* [Online] Available: http://www.ibsa.org.au/downloads/FAQs_General_Trng_Pkgs_FINAL.pdf. Retrieved February 15, 2008.

International Federation of Library Associations and Institutions (IFLA) (2000). *Guidelines for professional library/information education programs – 2000.* [Online] Available: http://www.ifla.org/VII/s23/bulletin/guidelines.htm. Retrieved February 15, 2008.

Library and Information Association of New Zealand Aotearoa (LIANZA). Taskforce on Professional Registration (2005). *Professional future for the New Zealand Library and Information Association: Discussion document.* [Online] Available: http://www.lianza.org.nz/library/files/store_009/ prof_reg_discussion _doc.pdf. Retrieved February 15, 2008.

Library and Information Association of New Zealand Aotearoa (LIANZA) (2007). *Library and information profession registration scheme.* [Online] Available: http://www.lianza.org.nz/registration/. Retrieved February 15, 2008.

Ling Hwey Jeng (2005). The points of ALA Task Force on Library School Closing. *PRISM, 13*(2). [Online] Available: http://www.ala.org/ala/accreditation/ prp/prism/prismarchive/FA05v13i2.pdf. Retrieved February 15, 2008.

Macauley, P (2004). Challenging librarians: The relevance of the doctorate in professional practice. *Challenging ideas. ALIA 2004 Biennial Conference*, Gold Coast, 21-24 September 2004.

Middleton, M. and Hallam, G. (2001). Generic education for specialist information professionals. *Australian Law Librarian, 9*(3), 181-194.

Moran, B. (2001). Practitioners vs LIS educators: Time to reconnect. *Library Journal, 126*(18), 52-55.

Mulvaney, J.P. and O'Connor, D. (2006). The crux of our crisis. *American Libraries, 37*(6), 38-40.

Myburgh, S. (2003). Education directions for NIPs (new Information Professionals). Paper presented at the 11th Information Online Exhibition and Conference, Sydney, 21-23 January 2003. [Online] Available: http://con ferences.alia.org.au/online2003/papers/myburgh.html. Retrieved February 15, 2008.

Nelson, B. (2005). Interview: Dr Brendan Nelson, Minister for Education, Science and Training. ABC Four Corners. [Online] Available: http://www.abc.net. au/4corners/content/2005/s1399260.htm. Retrieved February 15, 2008.

Rochester, M.K. (1997). *Education for librarianship in Australia.* London: Mansell.

Saunders, W.L. (1987). *An evaluation of education for librarianship in New Zealand: a report to the Joint Advisory Committee on Librarianship.* Wellington: Published for the Joint Advisory Committee by the Dept. of Librarianship, Victoria University of Wellington.

Seavey, C.A. (2005). The coming crisis in LIS education. *American Libraries, 36*(9), 54-56.

Stoffle, C.J. and Leeder, K. (2005). Practitioners and library education: a crisis of understanding. *Journal of Education for Library and Information Science, 46*(4), 313-320.

Usnews.com (2006). Best graduate schools: library *science*. [Online] Available: http://www.usnews.com/usnews/edu/grad/rankings/lib/libindex_ brief.php. Retrieved February 15, 2008.

PART 4
EUROPE:
INTRODUCTION

Leif Kajberg and Marian Koren
Regional Editors

Readers are travelers, that is, travelers in the mind, exploring unknown worlds, encountering different cultures, listening to unheard languages. Those who have become known in history, famous scholars and scientists, authors and artists, started their development by traveling through Europe. Travelers through Europe will notice the enormous diversity from country to country; not only in terms of landscapes but also especially in culture, buildings, language and customs. Within a few hundreds of kilometers, the whole scenery changes; one has to adapt and get accustomed again to new ways of life. This enormous diversity and variety, this historic intermingle of expressions, relations, struggles and neighborhood is hardly understandable. Is there really a kind of unity called Europe? In his explanation of the *Idea of Europe*, Georg Steiner gives some characteristics for Europe: Europe is made up of coffeehouses or cafés; the landscape is on a traversable and human scale; its history has been one of long marches. Street signs reveal and memorize its history of statesmen, scientists, artists, writers of the past; the twofold descent from Athens and Jerusalem, and lastly, the apprehension of a closing chapter, e.g. Oswald Spengler's *Untergang des Abendlandes* (Steiner 2004). Europe received its name by an outsider. Europe is an Asian princess abducted by a powerful god in the shape of a white bull. As a scant comfort, Aphrodite told the orphaned princess that this part of the world would from now on bear her name: Europa. Does this Greek myth pay a disguised tribute to the much older Asian cultures? Does it mean, that only coming from another part of the world, say the Americas or Asia, one really perceives this part of the world as a whole, as Europe? Those who have been traveling to the outskirts of the world, will notice, that only returning home, made them realize what Europe is and means to them. Confrontation with other cultures, outside Europe, has caused European intellectuals to doubt about the values propagated through European culture. Cultural relativism, however, can be seen as expression of one of the main European values: to doubt and remain critical even about oneself. This might be a basic value which should be and, in fact, is reflected by (public) libraries in a European context.

In more concrete terms, tracking Europe in all its diversity is not that easy. Europe is a complex entity and presents a definitional problem. One way of tackling this problem is to resort to geographical labeling: Europe is a "geographical name" denoting the continent of the eastern hemisphere between Asia & the Atlantic with an *area* of 3,997,929 *square miles* (10,354,636 *square kilometers*) and a *population* of 498,000,000 (Merriam-Webster OnLine 2008). For more details about the processes of European integration, see the European Navigator website.[1] About 230 different languages are spoken in Europe, but according to the Unesco Red book on endangered languages at least a hundred others spoken in Europe are about to disappear (UNESCO 2003). Within the European Union, 23 official languages are used (listen to a sample at: http://europa.eu/abc/european_ countries/languages/index_en.htm) (The European Union 2008). The European Parliament holds a language policy for Europe (European Parliament 2008). The 2006 Special Eurobarometer survey 64.3 *Europeans and Languages*, which considers the language skills of European citizens and their attitudes towards language learning, shows a clear support to language learning (European Commission 2006). 56 % of citizens in the EU Member States say that they are able to hold a conversation in one language apart from their mother tongue and 28 % of the respondents state that they speak two foreign languages well enough to have a conversation. English remains the most widely spoken foreign language throughout Europe, German being the most widely spoken mother tongue. 2001 was designated the European Year of Languages by the European Union and the Council of Europe. Forty-five countries participated in the European Year of Languages with the general aim of encouraging language learning throughout Europe (European Commission 2001). Learning of other languages is also encouraged through a European Day of Languages (26 September) with the additional purpose of celebrating linguistic diversity, "plurilingualism" and lifelong language learning.

Seen from outside Europe, this part of the world is in quite a few cases considered synonymous with the European Union (EU), but Europe is more than the EU, and several European countries are not members of the Union. As the situation is now, the EU numbers 27 member states, but they do not represent all European countries (OECD 2007). The 27 EU member countries are the following: Austria, Belgium, Bulgaria, Cyprus, Czech Republic, Denmark, Estonia, Finland, France, Germany, Greece, Hungary, Ireland, Italy, Latvia, Lithuania, Luxembourg, Malta, the Netherlands, Poland, Portugal, Romania, Slovak Republic, Slovenia, Spain, Sweden and the United Kingdom.

On the other hand, some non-member countries are firmly heading towards EU membership. Similarly, the EU – a leading international economic power with some features of a federation – is not the only European-level organization of European countries. Another important organization with a pan-European dimension is the Council of Europe with 47 member countries. The Council of Europe does not have the legislative powers of the EU; it is especially concerned with

---

[1]   Available at http://www.ena.lu. The European Navigator is "a multilingual, multi-source and multi-media knowledge base that contains more than 15,000 documents on the historical and institutional development of a united Europe from 1945 to the present day", established and maintained by the Centre Virtuel de la Connaissance sur l'Europe (Virtual Resource Centre for Knowledge about Europe – CVCE), which aims at creating and disseminating, through ICT, reliable content on the history of European integration.

human rights and principles of democracy and such issues as social cohesion, education, culture and heritage in a European perspective.

But, as already indicated, Europe is also a mosaic of cultures, ethnicities and languages represented by formal nation states and a rich mix of regions and minorities with their own distinctive mark in several respects. In quite a few cases, regions and minority populations have been allowed a self-governing status within the formal framework of a nation state. Hence, in the range of sub-chapters on Europe's libraries and the education of information professionals presented here, this specific part of the world is considered from a broader cultural and historical perspective, beyond borders and definitional limitations. Europe is a greying continent, which needs talents and manpower imported from outside. Through the EU, ambitious agendas have been set for economic growth, research production and expansion of higher education and aspirations are high in other areas including climate protection. At the same time, Europe is faced with the challenge and opportunities of cultural diversity and those of the multi-cultural society and immigration.

Up to 1989, the fall of the Berlin Wall, and 1991, which marks the collapse of the Soviet Union, Europe was divided into an Eastern part and a Western part representing two different political and economic systems. Communist ideology in the Eastern part markedly influenced the mission and functions of library systems. Thus, the change of political regimes and the transition into market-driven economies also meant reorientation and paradigm shifts in the library sector and in LIS education.

In providing an overview of European libraries and explaining the nature of library developments in Europe, there is a need for good-quality and comprehensive statistics. Actually, the LibEcon project conducted within the framework of the European Union was successful in collecting and bringing together basic statistical information for all types of libraries covering all European countries. In 2001, in the enlarged EU (covering EU plus countries joining the Union on 1 May 2004), basic statistical details for *all* libraries (National, Academic and research libraries, Public, School and Other) looked as follows:

- Registered users: more than 138 million, 30% of the population
- Spending on libraries: 14,271,412,575 Euros
- Full-time equivalent staff: 336,673
- Number of service points 186,826
- Number of visits – 3,171,215,882
- Number of visits per head – 7.0
- Number of loans – 3,324,238,175
- Number of loans per head – 7.3

Unfortunately, due to lack of European funds, the LibEcon database could not be continued, but the above statistical details at least gives an idea of the size and financial volume of libraries along with library use in Europe. The last LibEcon Newsletter from 2004 made a ranking of the top 10 best performing library countries: Finland, Denmark, Estonia, Iceland, UK, Norway, Slovenia, Sweden, Lithuania, and Ireland/Netherlands, based on 2001-produced data. In the meantime significant changes have taken place, especially for the better in the Baltic States, in a number of East-European countries and in Spain.

In the European region, the challenges facing libraries are similar to those at the international level, but with some peculiarities. Until now, the political and legislative framework of the European Union has not produced one coherent European advocacy plan or pan-European library associations. Several actors fulfill a part of this role without explicitly saying so. An explicit division of tasks is not discussed at present and this makes true strategic cooperation at the European level quite difficult. In Europe there is no such thing as a European Library Association, at least for the time being. Thus, the concept of an all-embracing umbrella organization spanning all sectors of libraries and librarianship and acting as a united voice and a collective advocate of libraries on the continent does not translate to Europe and European conditions. A construction like this would simply not make sense in today's Europe of nation states with individual library history development and with individual library traditions, administrative and legislative structures and culture. Or put in a less sweeping manner: the time for it has not come yet. EBLIDA (the European Bureau of Library, Information and Documentation Associations), which is very small and young compared to the ALA Washington Office (USA) working since 1945 to represent libraries at Capitol Hill (Congress) (ALA 2008), looks after the interests of the European library, archives and information sectors and those of information professionals broadly. EBLIDA lobbies for libraries at European level, undertakes information communication and conference activities with focus on library-related issues of a European nature and seeks involvement in European projects. The idea of creating a European region within IFLA has sometimes been raised in the corridors, but has mostly been considered a duplication of efforts, tiresome (because of the IFLA regulations) and a weakening of IFLA.

In setting out to study library systems and library developments in Europe, a striking difficulty is that of coming to grips with the comparative, cross-country and inter-cultural perspective. A fairly large body of professional and academic literature exists on the systems, state of the art, role and history, etc. of libraries in *individual* European countries, but there is a remarkable dearth of comparative research approaches and studies within the sectors of libraries and the universe of LIS education and research in Europe. In brief, comparative, contrasting and overarching research studies that look at European libraries and librarianship from the broader perspective of a region or continent are difficult to identify. Meeting this challenge and filling this need implies the implementation of fact-finding studies and well-defined research projects that are truly comparative and cross-country in scope and so designed that they cover problem areas, issues, developments, challenges, etc. as they have manifested themselves or are appearing in the various parts of Europe.

The four sub-chapters that are included on Europe's academic, public and school libraries along with LIS education are meant as a consolidated collective interim effort to at least partially cover the above lacuna. In the meantime, however, alternative ways of mapping and describing *Library Europe* should be considered. In this respect we should turn our attention to LIS students, the scholars of tomorrow, who are travelers. Thus, LIS students from outside Europe should be encouraged to explore the world of libraries and librarianship in Europe. They should come to Europe within the context of international exchange and fieldwork projects and study abroad programs to do personal observations and report on their impressions. They should be given the opportunity of gathering information from interviews and fact-finding exercises as a basis for the preparation of state-of-the-art and more analytic papers. They should see for themselves and reflect on their observations on library structures and library practice and the extent to which these differ or appear similar across national boundaries. Obviously, the reverse approach can be imagined as well: students would make a report on the historic and current developments of their own region and have this discussed with students in another region of the world.

References

ALA American Library Association Washington Office. [Online] Available: http://www. ala.org/ala/washoff/washingtonoffice.cfm. Retrieved August 6, 2008.

European Commission: (2006) Special Eurobarometer survey 64.3 Europeans and Languages. [Online] Available: http://ec.europa.eu/education/policies/lang/languages/eurobarometer06_en.html. Retrieved August 6, 2008.

European Commission: European Year of Languages (2001). [Online] Available: http://ec.europa.eu/education/policies/lang/awareness/year2001_en.html. Retrieved August 6, 2008.

The European Parliament 4.16.3 Language policy. [Online] Available: www. europarl.europa.eu/facts/4_16_3_en.htm. Retrieved August 6, 2008.

The European Union, Europa portal: Languages in the EU. [Online] Available: http://europa.eu/abc/european_countries/languages/index_en.htm. Retrieved August 6, 2008.

Merriam-Webster OnLine (2008). [Online] Available: http://www.merriam-webster.com/ dictionary/europe. Retrieved August 6, 2008.

OECD Glossary of statistical terms. [Online] Available: http://stats.oecd. org/glossary/detail.asp?ID=871. Retrieved August 6, 2008.

Steiner, George (2004). The Idea of Europe/Het idee van Europa. Tilburg: Nexus Institute. University of Tilburg.

UNESCO: Red Book of Endangered Languages (2003). [Online] Available: http://www.tooyoo.l.u-tokyo. ac.jp/archive/RedBook/index.html. Retrieved August 6, 2008.

PUBLIC LIBRARIES

Marian Koren

1. INTRODUCTION

The chapter outlines the developments of public libraries in Europe. Some historic aspects and current issues are addressed. The purpose of this chapter is to give an overview of public library services as developed in European countries and to present joint efforts at the European level. In addressing this topic, the chapter treats the following sub-questions:

1. What are the basic concepts underlying public libraries in Europe?
2. What role do public libraries play in national and European development?
3. How are public libraries cooperating at the European level?
4. What currents trends and future challenges are public libraries in Europe facing?
5. In addition to these introductory remarks, this paper has five other sections exploring these questions.

2. EXPLORING THE EUROPEAN PUBLIC LIBRARY LANDSCAPE

A European history of public libraries has not yet been written. Even a recent thorough overview is missing. (Danset 2003; Pors 2002; Poulain 1992) This is quite understandable as public libraries in Europe are closely related to public governance of each nation state with its own history and culture, and follow the enormous variety and intricate structures of administration and initiatives of citizens. In the meantime, public libraries started about 100-200 years ago, as centers for reading and information for middle class members and for the working class. Libraries were the places that especially the poor and the poorly educated could come to. Public libraries focused on what we now term as lifelong learning, and provided a variety of ways in which people could improve the quality of their lives. As 'street corner universities' they gradually became the place for everyone and included all members of the society, from the new born babies to the newcomers from other countries, within or outside Europe. What strikes every traveling observer is the enormous diversity in the spread and shape of public libraries throughout Europe. They can be a tiny local library on the outskirts of Ireland with an exhibition on education in the Irish language, or a glass palace in Malmö, Sweden. They can have the atmosphere of professional fairy tale telling in Portugal or intensive youth and Europe information corners in Slovenia. But all these public libraries have much in common; they form a unity in diversity – as is the character of Europe.

In the present state of the art of public libraries in Europe, some fundamental characteristics unite them: basic trust, credibility, democracy, information, education, culture, communication, all related to developed and acknowledged human rights. Public libraries form part of the European civilizations, reflect the human values and the human rights based upon them. Ultimately, the national state is responsible for guaranteeing freedom of expression and free access to information, the cornerstones of public library services. Library services are based on trust: libraries trust their users that they will care for the books and other materials they are borrowing or consulting. Users trust their libraries, that they will provide materials from a variety of sources, unbiased in its choice of materials. Public libraries are acknowledged as basic public service and trusted by politicians (from all parties) to perform their tasks professionally. Libraries have to work on continuous credibility, when it comes to providing digital library services. Living in a diversified Europe, with a multitude of languages, cultures and customs, libraries reflect the European tradition of critical reflection, doubts about its identity and achievements, and a critical notion of Europe's role in the world. Creating awareness and understanding of the riches of ideas, concepts and views on human life and its expressions in literature, art, monuments, etc., as developed in Europe, is part of the library's task to preserve relevant documents and facilitate education about their content. Preserved national heritage should be made available Europe-wide, to increase mutual access and understanding: intercultural dialogue.

3. THE ROLE OF PUBLIC LIBRARIES IN NATIONAL AND EUROPEAN DEVELOPMENT

3.1 National development

Initiatives of community groups, churches and liberal or charity institutions have played a substantive role in building up the social-democratic welfare states in many European countries. Public libraries were set up by these groups and gradually received funding from the state and local government. In most countries public libraries are a responsibility of the local government with some incentives at the national level. In France and Germany for example, public libraries are part of local government; in The Netherlands (16 million inhabitants), public libraries still are mainly private non-profit foundations and receive local subsidies. Dutch public libraries have maintained the roots of a readers' association including a subscription fee, at least for adults. Nevertheless, a large network of public libraries has been established, nowadays with around 4 million members, and counting 90 million visits a year. Here, after World War II, provincial library centers (PBCs) were created as service organizations for setting up public libraries in rural areas. In other countries, such as Sweden, the region is just an administrative and not a politically elected level of government: the regional library services (*länsbibliotek*) include mainly consultancy, training, innovation and promotion. In France, the *Bibliothèques Departementales de Prêts (BDP)* deliver practical services (collections, mobiles, reading and cultural programs) to smaller libraries. In some countries the regional services are provided by a larger city library or county library, e.g. in the United Kingdom. In order to understand the public library system, one has to know the system of political responsibilities and the public administration. Public libraries mainly follow the set-up of the public administrative system: unitary (e.g. Czech Republic) or federal (e.g. Belgium, Germany); centralized or more decentralized. The variety of administrative structures, sometimes with each having its own level of libraries, e.g. in France, make comparison between public library systems within Europe a difficult undertaking. Various attempts to make a typology of some sort, or based on geographic proximity of public library systems in Europe, have failed, due to the enormous diversity and differences in stages of development, structures and approaches to public library service.

Consolidation of the first public library establishments in legislation or other regulation took place first in the United Kingdom and Ireland (1840, 1855); in the 1920s followed by the Czech Republic, Denmark, the Netherlands, Slovakia, Latvia, Estonia and Finland. Between 1995 and 2000 most countries have updated their library legislation, which does not exist in Austria, Germany, Luxemburg, Malta and Spain. Changes were necessary because of decentralization of responsibilities for public libraries to local governments, local authority reforms, upcoming new information technology and infrastructure, consolidating of the public domain, and library professionalism.

In the Netherlands, in the late nineties, a concentration of local government (economy of scale) was undertaken resulting in a smaller number of local authorities. After this local government reform, a decentralization of national responsibility for public libraries took place and has effected quite some differences in library services all over the country: differences in access, user fees, quality and variety of services and facilities. In the early new millennium, a process of restructuring the library organizations into larger units to provide the necessary scale for the new information infrastructure and a strong innovation policy and program have supported improved professionalism and specialization. Similar processes (merging of municipalities, merging of library organizations, review of division of tasks and infrastructure) are taking place in other countries at different paces.

To provide an example of a public library structure: based on these developments, the Public Library system in the Netherlands consists of three layers of library services related to three levels of government serving the population of which 10-20 % inhabitants have an immigrant background. At the local level about 1,100 public libraries are financially supported by local authorities, in average up to 80%. In addition, 15% of the income is obtained through users (membership and overdue fees) and 5% through other paid activities like room rent, courses and lectures. Most of the communities operate a library or mobile service (60 buses in total). Local libraries can have a service contract with a provincial library service organization. There are 12 provinces (ranging from 400,000 to 2.5 million inhabitants). At the provincial level, the provincial government subsidizes regional library infrastructure, programs and projects executed through provincial service organizations and some libraries with regional tasks. At the national level, the state (Ministry of Education, Culture and Science) subsidizes the Netherlands Public Library Association as a sector institute (in other countries this is a national agency for (public) libraries, such as in Belgium (Flanders), Denmark, Ireland, Norway and Portugal) for maintaining and improving the public library network, including tasks for professional quality, innovation, IT, promotion of reading and maintenance of a central lending collection facility for foreign languages. A major task has been added in 2007: cooperation with services for the visually impaired is included. The Association receives membership income from all public libraries. Other income is received through national grants for major IT projects, especially so as to build further on the digital library: www.bibliotheek.nl.

Central library supply services are offered by NBD/Biblion Ltd (a merger of a former department of the Association and Netherlands Library Service, NBD), a partly non-profit library-supply foundation established by public libraries, booksellers and publishers in 1970. Through the set up of a central/national library supplier a high quality of presenting – library-fit materials; bindings lasting at least 12 years – has been achieved even for smaller libraries. The quick introduction of RFIDs in Dutch public libraries was made possible because NBD/Biblion inserted the new chips in all items, regardless of whether a library had decided to start self- service yet. Similar (profit) supplier services are active in the Nordic countries and in the German-speaking countries (Germany, Switzerland and Austria).

3.2 European development

There are over 40,000 public libraries in Europe. The main roles of public libraries are the following: giving access to published information, to offer lifelong learning opportunities, to safeguard cultural identity in a changing world and to ensure that citizens can cope with information technology and have access to the equipment and systems they need. Prolongation of the traditional, democratic values for public libraries, enlightenment, learning and access are the basis, according to the Public Libraries in the Information Society-study (PLIS-study 1996), which also discusses and analyses the future roles of public libraries.

One of the needs of public library development in Europe is to provide an overview and have access to good-quality statistics. Unfortunately, because of lack of European funds, the LibEcon-database could not be continued. Its last Newsletter issued in 2004 ranked the 10 best performing library countries in the following order: Finland, Denmark, Estonia, Iceland, UK, Norway, Slovenia, Sweden, Lithuania, Ireland/Netherlands (based on 2001 data). In the meantime significant changes have taken place, especially for the better in the Baltic States and a number of East European countries and Spain. The results of a questionnaire-based survey performed by the NAPLE Forum (National Authorities on Public Libraries in Europe) in 2001 revealed a similar distribution on the part of *public* library organizations. Findings showed that Finland is on top regarding user reach (60%), followed by other Nordic countries (50+%) and Estonia and the Netherlands (29%). In the Netherlands this percentage refers to memberships, not to users without a library card (40-50%). Finland also tops the loan per capita list (20 items), followed by the other Nordic countries (except Norway), Estonia and the Netherlands (9-15 items per capita) with lower levels for the Baltic states and even lower for Southern Europe (Pors 2002).

Around the year 2000 public libraries in a number of countries worked hard to become included in a national strategy for the Knowledge Society demanding that the state and its agencies express commitment to the role of the public library system in relation to digital services for the citizens. This commitment is demonstrated in reports and visions for the future and may also include real financial support. According to Pors (2002) strong support and visions were presented in Belgium (Flanders), Denmark, Estonia, Finland, Ireland, Netherlands, Norway, Portugal, Spain, Sweden; with some state support and vision found in Austria, Croatia, Cyprus, Czech Republic, Greece, Latvia, Lithuania, Slovakia, Slovenia; and a low degree of commitment in Germany, Luxemburg and Malta. In the meantime, especially Germany is on the move to develop visions at least at the regional level (*Bundesländer*), and the East European countries have very dedicated policies for the transformation of society. In most countries, the general policy is e.g. that public libraries have to provide Internet access to the users. This positive picture is a major step forward (within just five years) compared to the state-of-the-art as presented in the PLIS study (1996). The implications of the active public library role in the information society are realized step by step: a broader range of Internet services; a faster digital infrastructure; coordination in acquisition of digital content (consortia and licensing) and delivery of services; and increasing staff competencies. In most countries, rather impressive efforts have been made in relation to staff upgrading and the establishment of systems of continuing education. Especially the Baltic States have implemented sound structures within a very short time. Equal access to information is the driving force to work for a complete network and adapted services for all citizens.

3.3 Lifelong learning

When the European Commission launched the concept of Lifelong Learning, and stressed the need for local learning centers, librarians were skeptical because of the strong stress laid on the economic motives and because the EC was apparently forgetting that libraries have always been centers for non-formal and informal learning. As is shown in Portuguese research (Calixto 1999), libraries can fulfill roles, which for citizens in a European context will lead up to a European CV and more mobility[1]; visibility of learning opportunities and possibilities to learn in other countries. Libraries throughout Europe have responded to the Lifelong learning paradigm, creating "second chances" to update basic skills and also offering learning opportunities at more advanced levels. Formal systems of library provision need to become much more open and flexible so that they are tailored to the needs of the learner. These services, especially distant learning, have been well developed in the United Kingdom and Ireland. In the Netherlands, libraries are very visible in the Week of Learning, the Learning Festival; national and local partnerships with the regional educational centers (ROC) and "folk universities."

3.4 On public library buildings in Europe

On the occasion of the Netherlands presidency of the Council of Europe, a conference named "Creating Public Paradise" and focusing on the building of public libraries in the 21st century was organised in The Hague in March 2004. One of the few European surveys on public library buildings was undertaken in preparation of this conference (Koren 2004). In Greece and East European countries purpose-built libraries do hardly exist or date from a long time ago. A funding scheme and (inter)national standards are lacking. There are, however, examples of modern public libraries in these countries and more library construction projects can be expected in the years to come. During the last decade improvements have been made in e.g. Spain and Slovenia. In most European countries, public library buildings can be qualified as 'traditional' or 'lending' libraries, but this picture is rapidly changing already demonstrating more modern, qualitative ideas or concepts in almost every country. Libraries are no longer mere book-lending institutions but have translated cultural, educational and/or communal functions into their architecture. Buildings are developed according to these functions. The concept of the library as a community and information center, providing materials and working places for *lifelong learning,* makes libraries restyle and design for presenting combined media collections, internet-access and working places. Meeting, interacting and communicating are literally gaining ground with some examples to be mentioned here: the Public Library of Amsterdam (opened 2007) or Kolding, Denmark (opened 2006). Partnerships are expressed in the combined or collocated library: libraries share one roof with other cultural, educational or communal institutions like theatres, museums, schools or university libraries. Examples: Viiki in Finland, Härnosand *sambiblioteket* in Sweden, CODA, Apeldoorn in the Netherlands. Also, there are many examples of libraries being located in shopping cen-

---

[1] EU standardized format for presenting one's CV and applicable throughout Europe, see: http://myeurocv.com/

ters and malls, which serves to increase their accessibility and visibility to many citizens. A number of states upgrading the level of public library services make use of references to the IFLA Public Library Manifesto to set up a scheme and create guidelines for public library construction; this is, for instance, the case of Portugal. The state institute co-funds 50% of the initial investment, and this covers the following areas: the project studies, construction, furniture and equipment, collections (print and multimedia) and services automation. Especially the children's departments are equipped with spaces for storytelling and art workshops. More recently, some libraries have started offering community information and self-learning services and implemented information and communication technologies; access to the Internet is free as are the rest of the services available. Examples of new/restyled public libraries can be found in cities like Santa Maria da Feira, Oporto, Loures, Sintra, Cascais and Albufeira.

Attempts to set up a database with library buildings in Europe are made. In the meantime DOK Delft (Netherlands) may serve as an example of library innovation through redesign of building and services. Being the most modern library of the world is the mission and challenge the public library in Delft (95,000 inhabitants) wants to take up – and it is already listed among the 25 Most Modern Libraries in the World (Laun 2008). The special merging with an art center (DOK) and a disco center has created an innovative and inviting space to explore and live a modern lifestyle. DOK Library Concept Center is the bold title at the entrance of the glass 4-store façade. It offers access to a world of information, inspiration and entertainment in a dynamic communication and surprising environment. The large building from the seventies has radically been rebuilt and redesigned by architect Aat Vos of Aequo Architects and Liesbeth van der Pol of Dok Architecten transforming it into a multicultural center of 4,300 m2.

3.5 Public Libraries on the Internet

The challenge for libraries is whether they will successfully not only apply, but also successfully integrate new technology into their services. A number of European countries have developed national strategies to work for one coherent library service. People's Network is a well-known example from England for the basic infrastructure. The strategies, often following a general National Action Plan, aim to bring the nation to the top in the global competitive economy. In a decentralized situation, library associations taking the initiative for new services have to balance between local initiatives and practices and the need for a nationwide scale to implement and fund digital infrastructure, coordination and services. In most European countries, a national library portal has been designed or is under construction (e.g. in Slovenia). Sometimes it is an extensive portal also including the digital school library and the virtual children's library, completed with request and order services, solely organized by the public libraries (in the Netherlands: Bibliotheek.nl). In other cases the similar name of the portal (bibliotek.dk in Denmark) started mainly as a request and order facility and is extended with other services like Ask a librarian. In the longstanding tradition of working for efficiency through cooperation and networking, such as interlibrary loan, which also includes international services, new facilities have been developed to serve the interests of the user communities.

The national library portal for accessing the virtual public library of a country is the product of the joint efforts of public libraries coordinated by the Library Association (Netherlands), the Norwegian Archive, Library and Museum Authority (Norway) or the National Library (Slovenia) acting on behalf of the Ministry. It provides access to a user-friendly, digital library collection. The information can be geared to individual user requirements by means of user profiles (*my library*). In this way, for instance bibliotheek.nl combines not only the know-how and expertise of many Dutch public libraries, but also that of a number of selected partners. Public libraries also join forces by purchasing of digital content, such as newspaper and historic archive material, consumer information, databases on literature information, etc. The virtual network of librarians working in teams and groups to propose and select content (such as health, history, literature, economy, Europe), to answer queries on advanced levels (Al@din, virtual reference service), assists in the editing of various parts of the library portal. Aquabrowser is the specially designed convenient browsing applied in the Dutch digital library (and now also used in for instance the USA.). It is based on associative connections and frequency of search terms. Another service is the Seek&Book service, a request and delivery service, executed in the Netherlands and in Denmark (bibliotek.dk).

Dedicated sites often correspond with larger (library) policies such as lifelong learning, cultural diversity, social inclusion, services to visually impaired and print handicapped, or simply: another area such as health or music. Public libraries are cooperating with education centers to create attractive learning offers. In cooperation with educational television and professional educational institutions libraries are organizing information and support for people looking for a(nother) job. They can, supported by TV sessions, get local advice by a coach and group training and a special infopoint (WerkPlek, *Workplace*) in the library, which is supplemented by a dedicated website (Werkzat). Since many modern courses make use of digital programs, people can test and improve their competences in a special public e-learning course presented by the public libraries. Newcomers to many European countries are supported by dedicated services to learn the main language and understand the new country's culture. Such national services have practical information organized around major subjects, with which immigrants are confronted: housing, finances, education, health, legislation etc. and they can be found in the Netherlands and in the Nordic countries following the example of Finfo in Denmark: multilingual information for ethnic minorities.

3.6 Providing information about Europe

One special task for public libraries is related to the provision of information about Europe, not only about its institutions, the European Parliamentarians etc, but also about new EU-directives, upcoming policies in the field of employability, agriculture etc. Public libraries presented themselves as the basic network for European information in the same way as they provide citizens with national government information. Some subjects include: general public information (through EU-Information relays: Europe Direct and Documentations Centers); Youth information on exchange, studies, travel, subsidies; Employability, Mobility of people, students, workers, professionals (including legal and other aspects) as well as Elections and Enlargement (about daily life and the culture of 'new' EU-member states.) The European Commission never fully acknowledged the role of public libraries in these services, and continued its own individualized contract model. But the public library network in Croatia, Denmark, Finland, Germany (some), the Netherlands, Slovenia and Sweden performs a major task for the EU citizens' information service. The European Parliament wishes to extend the rights related to citizenship of the European Union. For informed European citizens an adequate information service is necessary.

4. HOW ARE PUBLIC LIBRARIES COOPERATING AT THE EUROPEAN LEVEL?

In the preceding paragraphs we discussed public libraries in Europe and European public libraries. There is a third dimension: the European level of public library policies, strategies, and structures. If we speak about policy making, does it then mean: all that is done at a national level is also executed at the European level or does it mean that public libraries develop policies at the European level, which cannot be formulated at the national level? What is the "extra" that the European context and perspective offer (Dittrich 2003)?

One of the earliest specific studies on public libraries in Europe was devoted to the implementation of new technologies and a paradigm shift in services: the updated library. The Telematics/PLIS study (1996) already indicated the need for actions at the European level: actions within areas such as concerted actions and studies on policies and planning, initiatives to improve skills and competence (training and distance learning for librarians); studies on organizational structures, charges, service levels, and solutions for small libraries) and projects developing new tools such as user instruction as well as digital reference services and marketing. According to the report generated by the Telematics/PLIS study 'A European source for funding is highly desirable and would be helpful in accelerating change in public libraries.' (Public Libraries and the Information Society: a study. Telematics for Libraries ARCHIVE, 1997)

4.1 European projects

With the advent of new information technology and the information society, the European Commission, especially DGXIII, initiated a dedicated public libraries programme in the nineties and sponsored related cultural and heritage projects to which libraries also applied. At a later stage this public library-centered funding initiative was integrated with the more general EU Framework Programs (FP). In general, public libraries are more locally orientated than e.g. national libraries and therefore experienced more difficulties in fulfilling EU project requirements (e.g. cooperation with libraries in at least three countries) and international project management. But they managed very well in projects such as exploring multimedia for children (CHILIAS) or information skills for young people (VERITY) along with a number of projects on telematics, distant learning and service to people with a handicap.

Real cooperation at the European level started when a number of public library directors (cooperating in the PUBLICA project) exchanged experience on new technology-driven services and discussed the need for larger investments, which were to be achieved through strategic action (the Leuven Communique). Other public library projects followed such as PULMAN and CALIMERA, which produced manuals and guidelines for policy making and implementation of new technology in traditional and new public library services, management, target groups and other aspects of the libraries in the information society. In the same way as public libraries attempted to acquire a place in the national formulation of the information society, they also had to demonstrate their role in the development of the European society. The Copenhagen Declaration (1999), the outcome of a high level European conference stated:

We support the following roles for public libraries, highlighted in the Leuven Communique:

Democracy and citizenship – Public libraries have a strategic opportunity to increase quality of life and democratic possibilities for citizens of the Information Societies by providing free and equal access to high-quality information.

Economic and social development – Public libraries support the growth of communities through the provision of information services designed to meet local needs. They are important tools for reducing disparity between the information rich and the information poor citizens of Europe.

Lifelong learning – Public libraries provide, through their widespread distribution across Europe, a cost-effective infrastructure for lifelong learning and easy access to the content of the virtual networks. They also support students at all levels of formal education.

Cultural and linguistic diversity – Public libraries are cultural institutions in accordance with the cultural dimension of the EU Treaty with a great responsibility for cultural heritage, literature and literacy.

The Declaration was founded on and referred to the one and only Report on 'the Role of Libraries in the Modern World' of the Committee on Culture, Youth, Education and the Media of the European Parliament (the Ryynänen Report) – a major study commissioned by the European Commission on Public Libraries and the Information Society (PLIS study) – and a Council of Europe Cultural Committee report on Library Legislation and Policy in Europe. With these building bricks, a common basis for national and European policies regarding public libraries was formed on which action by the European Commission was requested to stress the key role of public libraries in the emerging Information Society and the need for a European level information policy.

National and federal governments were requested to prepare a national information policy recognizing the vital and unique role of public libraries as access points for the majority of citizens and supported by suitable library legislation. Furthermore, a suitable networking infrastructure was required, drawing together all information creating agencies and traditional memory institutions (libraries, museums and archives) so as to encourage information and resource sharing and practical co-operation between public libraries. The main request was a development program for public libraries to ensure minimum standards of access to every citizen, including new facilities, and placing public libraries high on the social agenda defending an equitable copyright.

It was clear that action was necessary for public libraries covering the following issues: re-assessment of roles to respond to changing social needs; long-term co-operation and partnerships for cultural and community education; and effective marketing of services to all sectors of the community.

4.2 Advocacy

When EBLIDA, the European Library Lobby Bureau, was set up (1992), it was clear that resources would be limited and focus on advocacy, especially in the field of copyright and related issues, would be its first and foremost rationale. Other policies of the European Union and developments in Europe are considered less threatening and therefore mainly monitored, with incidental actions: information policy, lifelong learning, cultural heritage, professional mobility and trade agreements. The EBLIDA actions in the field of copyright, public lending right, public information access and its information and training support in Eastern Europe have proved that this focus as successful, but not enough for all national association members. A newly elected Executive Committee and President (2007) may try other strategies thus moving towards more development policies, e.g. digital libraries and culture. Another focus on advocacy and development is coming from NAPLE, a forum of national authorities responsible for public library policies and development in Europe. Sometimes this responsible authority is found in the ministry (Finland) or located in a separate agency (Denmark) or in a hybrid organization as with the Netherlands Public Library Association, which is both a national association and an agency for performing national library tasks. The variety of national structures makes it difficult to create a coherent group, but the felt need to create a forum for supporting national public library policy making and have a say in European library developments, e.g. the European Digital Library, is easily understood. In general, one has to note, that the executive powers of all these organizations are very limited. An office with 1-2 paid staff members at the most. In fact, this is a situation in which national associations very often find themselves. For the professional development, IFLA remains the main association, also for European librarians. The good plans and projects libraries have been able to undertake in a European setting have been funded and encouraged mainly through the European Union's Information Society Programme. A number of libraries has also discovered the Grundtvig programme, which is an easily accessible programme for professional projects and exchanges, e.g. on evaluation of library involvement in National Learning Weeks.

To conclude on this part: European advocacy and cooperation is still in the making. A Europe of libraries is still hard to find. The scattered activities of individual librarians, libraries and associations need to be backed up by more coherence and focus. Professional associations are gradually changing strategy and focus, turning professional development issues into effective advocacy.

5. CURRENT PUBLIC LIBRARY TRENDS AND FUTURE CHALLENGES IN EUROPE

The European Union has formulated its ambitions in the Lisbon Declaration: becoming the most competitive knowledge region in the world by 2010. And so the Netherlands government has agreed to it and is working on it, partly with the help of libraries. In fact, this is true for many European countries. Nevertheless, The European Union has not formulated a library policy, apart from the report by Mirjam Ryynanen, the Finnish Member of the European Parliament. But libraries are affected by EU regulations, especially in the field of copyright and lending right. Furthermore, they can profit from ICT programs, although for the most part only national and research libraries have staff to develop EU projects.

5.1 Public library trends

In general, libraries boast a strong tradition in Europe with stronger accents on social democracy and self-learning in the northern hemisphere. A number of tendencies which public libraries face in most European countries can be discerned: in the field of legislation/policies: decentralization. The process of decentralization brings policy making on a level closer to the community, but at the same time this process involves the risk of loosing the coherence of a public library network that is especially necessary for major IT investments. Furthermore, the acquired knowledge on the identity and role of public libraries might not be present to the same extent on a local level. Another issue is the struggle for maintaining the public domain: an increasing number of (digital) sources are not published in the traditional sense. Closed networks and expensive licenses form a threat to publicly available information. In the same sense, some information created with public funds is privatized, without any exception for libraries to make public information available for citizens. Rights of right holders may form a threat and should be balanced with users' rights in the public domain. Libraries collaborate in EU lobbying through EBLIDA, the European Bureau for Library, Information and Documentation Associations (www.eblida.org) (based in the Netherlands, in the premises of the Netherlands Public Library Association). A European Library Agenda is a basis for development policy and lobby. One can easily add other issues to the EBLIDA work, where the EU increasingly takes a position and library associations all over Europe should cooperate to play their part in it: World Summit on the Information Society, Cultural Diversity, Open Access, Anti Terrorist legislation, World Trade Agreements, etc.

Most libraries are struggling for getting necessary investments covering such areas as IT, buildings, media and staff. No service or business can survive or flourish without necessary investments. Libraries need to be restyled, and new technology requires allocations of funds but also continuous investments to meet the needs of demanding users. Most countries like the United Kingdom (Peoples Network) and Netherlands (National Action Plan) have formulated IT investment plans for libraries, but this is not enough for restructuring the whole sector. In a number of European countries, library networks are reorganized to find a better economy of scale and division of (national) tasks. The regional level seems to be the crucial factor in keeping the network and maintaining its strength by facilitating and adding value to local developments. For example, Denmark and the Netherlands exhibit substantial changes in the library landscape. Another difficult issue is the recruitment of future-oriented staff (from various backgrounds). A number of European countries are faced with the challenge of having a percentage of older staff members, who will leave their jobs in the coming years. New staff must meet different requirements that are not always addressed by the current Library and Information Science education courses. Increased focus is placed on the effects and added value (performance measurement). The credibility of libraries takes a new shape in the need for describing library results in other terms than just the number of loans. Qualitative research tries to present a variety of outcomes from library activities. Many countries are working on benchmarking of libraries, e.g. the United Kingdom, Denmark, and the Netherlands. A number of these issues are discussed at the European conference organized by the Forum of National Public Library Authorities: NAPLE (www.naple.info).

5.2 TRANSFORMATION OF THE LIBRARIES: SERVING CITIZENS OF EUROPE

The shift of paradigm from lending libraries to hybrid libraries due to the presence and impact of new media, new user groups, and new demands in communities is the major incentive for library transformations. But user-orientation and marketing are paramount. In fact, the users are directing the new services into guided facilities.

One of the main questions to be confronted by public libraries in Europe is whether they can see themselves as forming one network serving the citizens in Europe by common efforts. Part of the libraries' common tasks is:

1. Recognizing the needs of immigrants, as immigrants of various nationalities and languages spread over Europe, libraries must make efforts to provide materials in those languages. Cooperation should improve these services.
2. Accessibility of public information services. The strongest feature of public libraries remains their basic information service. Efforts have to be made to integrate digital services in order to make public services transparent and accessible to all citizens.
3. Facilitating cultural orientation and mobility. An increasing number of people live in a culture, which is not their traditional culture. Others see a growing number of "minority cultures." Libraries can help to give background information and create a setting for orientation, getting to know the diversity of the modern communities and creating a place for understanding different customs. A recent example is the Human Library where citizens can have a chat with a member of a minority or other group in society with whom they are not familiar and might have prejudices about: refugee, handicapped, homosexual, Muslim, student, politician. A mobile library stops near a festival and offers human sources to learn from.
4. Cross-border services; in an increasingly united Europe, library service need not be restricted by national borders. Services can be extended to neighboring communities, which often form an extended cultural community. Learning languages and literature from various European countries can form part of library services and be included in training for librarians.

5.3 Strengthening the European library network: learning from each other

Public libraries have not yet clearly initiated a strategy of becoming more visible in Europe. They need a strong legislative framework. They can strengthen their networks by various means: especially the exchange and development of concepts and knowledge; views and policies; research and staff training programs. To give an example of the benefit of exchanging concepts: Dutch librarians visited Sweden and Finland in 1986 and discovered the concept of *Kulturhus* (a combination of library, museum, music school, local archive etc.). They also appreciated the UK services of Community Information and the shop in the shop formula of various info-points in the library. Now, the first Dutch versions of the *Kulturhus* have been introduced, in which possible profit services as banking, health insurance and office hours for the notary, social services etc. are included under the same roof. Another example is the application of the Children's Book Jury, a reading promotion concept, in which children are invited to read and list their personal Top Five and send their votes to be counted nationally thus resulting in a big national TV-covered Children's Jury Award program. This Dutch invention is now applied in Sweden and Iceland and it also works similarly in Austria.

5.4 European agenda setting

Public libraries can be instrumental in a number of European policies, but they are also unique institutions and public services with intrinsic value. Their basic identity is closely related to democracy and access to information makes them different from schools, museums, theatres and community centers. This basic feature should be acknowledged and form part of a European Library Agenda and policy making entity. The development part of Public Libraries should build on the Ryynänen report (Ryynänen, 1998), which gives an excellent description of basic element of libraries and a necessary policy to support libraries as the most important networks that organize access to knowledge. After the appearance of this report the European Commission has been silent about libraries, but the Commission turns up in many projects (e.g. training), services and even consultations. The German Library Association responded to the European Communication: *Challenges for the European Information Society beyond 2005*. Here one finds arguments for the role of libraries as a support structure for the digital knowledge based society in Europe: political and social benefits in the form of high-quality information, information literacy and media competence, lifelong learning, informed citizenry, democratic access and evaluation of media, cultural promotion and education, etc. "European libraries have much potential. When provided with a clear mission, a supportive framework and sufficient funding, they can multiply their contribution to the necessary achievement oriented education infrastructure" (Ruppelt 2005:2).

The European Library is a test case in many respects. The cooperation between the network of public libraries and the national library (and academic libraries) is a delicate issue. In some southern and central European countries the national library is at the same time a university library (Croatia, Denmark, Estonia and Slovenia), but the relationship to public libraries is often weak. In other countries, such as Belgium, Netherlands, Portugal and some of the Scandinavian countries, national libraries mainly operate on their own with public libraries constituting a separate network. This traditional division of types of libraries is no longer adequate in a knowledge society. The idea of a European Library is bringing together or collecting sources of European heritage (from libraries, museums and archives) and offering digital access to them. So the name has been changed into *Europeana*. Launched June 2007, 6 million works should be digitised between 2007 and 2012. A separate foundation (EDL Foundation) has been set up (2007) to encourage all types of institutions to become members and share their sources. Some national and European organizations are advocating for a stronger focus on the relationship with public libraries and through them with the larger European public. Cultural heritage in digital form will only be successful if included in cultural and reading programs inviting to active participation and experience – such as public libraries are used to organise.

References

Astbury, R. (1998) Public Libraries. In: Line, M., Mackenzie, G. and Sturges, R.P., 1998 (eds), Librarianship and Information Work Worldwide 1998, London: Bowker Saur, 81-103.

Die Bibliothek der Zukunft: Visionen: Prognosen und Utopien (2008). *Forum Bibliothek und Information*, Vol. 1, 40-69.

Bohrer, Chr. (ed.) (2000) *Library Legislation in Europe*. Discussion Papers and Country Papers, Council of Europe/Goethe-Institute Munchen, Bad Honnef: Bock+Herchen .

Brophy, P. (2000). *The library in the twenty-first century. New services for the information age.* London: Library Association Publishing.

Budzyńska M., Jezierska M. *Biblioteki powiatowe 1999-2003*. [Online] Available: http://ebib.oss.wroc.pl/raporty/powiat3/.

Calixto, J-A. (1999). As bibliotecas públicas portuguesas face aos desafios da sociedade da informação. Portuguese public libraries facing the challenge of the information society, in: *Liberpolis-:-Revista-das-Bibliotecas-Publicas*. (2), 3-7.

Calimera EU Project: Coordinating IST for Europe's local cultural institutions. [Online] Available: www.calimera.org.

Council of Europe/EBLIDA, Guidelines for library legislation [Online] Available: http://www.coe.int/t/e/cultural_co-operation/culture/resources/texts/DECS_ CULT_ POL_book(2000)1_EN.pfd.

Danset, F. (2003). 'L'Europe des bibliothèques, ABF Congrès Aubagne, ABF, Paris

Davies, R. (ed.) (2003) Public Libraries, Museums and Archives : the eEurope Agenda for Local Services. Final Report of the PULMAN Network of Excellence, European Commission.

Dittrich, K. (2003) Europe, quo vadis? Introduction to Cultural Components: Literature and Culture in Europe, Studium Generale, organised by Vereniging van Openbare Bibliotheken, in cooperation with Goethe-Institut Amsterdam and supported by the European Cultural Foundation, Amsterdam. [Online] Available: www.eurocult. Org.

European Commission Education and Culture, TUNE project: Training of Library Users in a New Europe: www.tune.eu.com (Culture 2000).

European Commission DG XIII Libraries Programme. Telematics Applications Programme. [Online] Available: www.LibEcon2000.org.

European Commission. DG XIII Telematics for Libraries Archive. [Online] Available: http://cordis.europa.eu/libraries/en/publib.html.

European Commission: Preparing Europe's digital future i2010 – Mid-term review. [Online] Available: http://ec.europa.eu/information_society/eeurope/i2010/index_en.htm.

Goulding, A. (2006). *Public Libraries in the 21ˢᵗ century. Defining Services and Debating the Future.* Ashgate: Aldershot.

Marshall, T. (1950). *Citizenship and social class and other essays*, Cambridge: Cambridge University Press

Koren, M. (ed.) (2008). *Working for Five Star Libraries. International perspectives on a century of public library advocacy and development.* The Hague: Netherlands Public Library Association.

Koren, M. (1996). *Tell me! The right of the child to information.* The Hague: NBLC. [Ph.D dissertation, University of Amsterdam]

Koren, M. (2002). European Public Libraries – in Development. Lecture at the NAPLE conference 3-4 October 2002, Copenhagen.

Koren, M. and J. Krol, H. Roos (2008). *New library buildings in the Netherlands.* Den Haag, Netherlands Public Library Association [volume 4 in series; vol. 2= Creating Public Paradise, European conference, 2003].

Koren, M. (2007) Kulturhus, a Scandinavian concept on the move. A view from experiences in the Netherlands, in: *Scandinavian Public Library Quarterly*, 2.

Laun, C. (2008) The 25 Most Modern Libraries in the World. [Online] Available: www.best collegesonline.com/blog/2008/07/02/the-25-most-modern-libraries-in-the-world.

Middelveld, H. (2002) *Kulturhus*, Concept voor een lokaal netwerk, Den Haag: NBLC.

Niegaard, H., J. Lauridsen and K. Schulz (eds.) (2008). *Biblioteksrummet*. Inspiration til bygning och inretning. Danmarks Biblioteksforening: Copenhagen.

Pors, N.O. (2002) The Public Library in the Electronic World. [Online] Available: http://www.bs.dk/publikationer/andre/naple/index.htm
http://www.bs.dk/publikationer/english/naple/index.htm.

Poulain, M. (1992) Les bibliothèques en Europe. Paris: Editions du Cercle de la Librairie.

PUBLICA: A concerted action for Public Libraries; ICT project. [Online] Available: http://cordis.europa.eu/libraries/en/publica.html.

Public Libraries and the Information Society: a study. Telematics for Libraries ARCHIVE (1997). [Online] Available: http://cordis.europa.eu/libraries/en/ plis/study. html. Retrieved on August 5, 2008.

PULMANweb: Public Libraries Mobilising Advanced Networks: www.pulman web.org

Ruppelt, G., Libraries as Important Component of the European Information Society, Statement of the Federal Union of German Library and Information Associations (BID) on 12 January 2005. [Online] Available: http://www.bideutsch land.de/ download/file/politik_europa/EuropInformationsgesellschaft.pdf.

Ryynänen, M. Report on the Green Paper on the role of libraries in the modern world. Committee on Culture, Youth, Education and the Media. Report A4-0248/98 25 June 1998 and Report 23 October 1998. [Online] Available: http:// www. cordis.lu/libraries/en/reportrole.html.

Steiner, George (2000). Speech on knowledge economy, 11 September. [Online] Available: http:// www.opengov.uk.

Thorhauge, J., G. Larsen, H.-P. Thun, H. Albrechtsen, M. Segbert (ed.) (1997) *Public libraries and the Information Society*. Office for Official Publications of the European Communities: Luxembourg. [PLIS study]. [Online] Available: http://cordis.europa.eu/ libraries/en/plis/homeplis.html.

Websites

CALIMERA archive: www.calimera.org

EBLIDA: European Bureau of Library, Information and Documentation Associations: www.eblida.org

EUROPEAN LIBRARY: Www.theeuropeanlibrary.org and www.europeana.eu

LIBECON: International Library Economics Research: www.libecon.org

NAPLE FORUM: National Authorities on Public Libraries in Europe: www.naple. info

PUBLICA archive: www.cordis.lu/libraries/en/publica.html

UNESCO Library Portal, Public Libraries in Europe: http://www.unesco.org/ webworld/portal_bib/pages/Libraries/Public/Europe/index.shtml

About Regional Editor/author:

Dr. Marian Koren is Head of Research and International Affairs at the Netherlands Public Library Association, and secretary of FOBID Netherlands Library Forum, The Hague, The Netherlands

ACADEMIC LIBRARIES

Frédéric Blin

INTRODUCTION

Europe is a continent, not very big compared to other continents but still very diverse with its over 40 countries and quite as many political and economic realities, higher education and research systems. Drawing a portrait of European academic libraries that would reflect the exact reality of all the different countries is not to be achieved in the frame of a short chapter. I will therefore focus on the main projects and programs put up in European academic libraries, and on the political decisions and orientations taken in order to enhance their development and their adequacy to the new challenges raised by the digital age. In my point of view, these are the sign of a fundamental trend accompanying a fast evolution of European academic libraries, and more largely, of the scientific communities' relationship towards scientific documentation and information.

1. WHAT IS AN "ACADEMIC LIBRARY" IN EUROPE?

Higher education and research organizations in Europe are most often very complex: there are universities, "high" schools, research agencies, learned societies, and so on. Therefore, "academic and research libraries" is a difficult concept to apprehend, if we consider that they are libraries serving students, academics and researchers. In fact, this definition could apply to national libraries as well, and we actually find, in relatively small countries, several "national and university libraries" or national libraries with an organizational link to a university, for instance in Bosnia-Herzegovina[1], Croatia[2], Denmark[3], Finland[4], Iceland[5], Macedonia[6] or Slovenia[7]. Furthermore, historically important libraries such as the *Staatsbibliothek zu Berlin – Preussischer Kulturbesitz* in Germany or the *Bibliothèque nationale et universitaire de Strasbourg* in France, which are neither genuinely "national" (they are not the *Deutsche Nationalbibliothek* and the *Bibliothèque nationale de France*) nor authentically "academic" (they do not belong to a higher education and research institution), must be considered as "academic and research libraries"

---

[1] Nacionalna i univerzitetska biblioteka Bosne i Hercegovine: http://www.nub.ba/.
[2] Nacionalna i sveucilišna knjižnica u Zagrebu: http://www.nsk.hr/.
[3] The Københavns Universitetsbibliotek is a department of Det Kongelige Bibliothek: http://www.kb.dk/.
[4] Kansalliskirjasto: http://www.kansalliskirjasto.fi/index.html.
[5] Landsbokasafn Island – Haskolabokasavn: http://www.bok.hi.is/.
[6] Nacionalna i univerzitetska biblioteka Sv. Kliment Ohridski – Skopje: http://www.nubsk.edu.mk/.
[7] Narodna in univerzitetna knjižnica: http://www.nuk.uni-lj.si/.

because of their essential mission which is to serve the academic community in the broader sense of the term.

It is this mission that has to be taken into account above any other consideration when trying to define an academic and research library. Therefore, unless they are "university libraries" as well, we will not consider national libraries here, because their core mission is to preserve a national heritage and not to serve this specific community of users.

2. NETWORKING: AT THE HEART OF EUROPEAN ACADEMIC LIBRARIES

Networking is at the heart of libraries' functioning throughout the world, but it is perhaps nowhere as important as it is in Europe. Like in other parts of the world, most European libraries have to face limited budgets, a problem which has been even more critical in the last 10 years due to the continually growing costs of electronic resources. Networks have been established as one solution to counterbalance this situation. They can take on different forms; among others: national bibliographical services and tools; collaborative collection management policies; consortia; national digital scientific libraries; associations; multinational and European projects.

The main networks have been established through bibliographical services like national catalogues. The vast majority of European countries seem to now have a national catalogue for their academic libraries' resources (for instance the Estonian catalogue *ESTER*[8], or the French *SUDOC*[9]). Now appear catalogues and tools dedicated to specific kinds of resources, or resulting from international cooperation, like: the British Union Catalogue of Serials *SUNCAT*[10]; the Nordic / Baltic Union Catalogue of Serials[11]; the portal "Medieval Manuscripts in Dutch Collections"[12]; the European Virtual Opac for Chinese Studies[13]; national portals for theses and dissertations in Austria[14], francophone Belgium[15], Germany[16], Lithuania[17], the Netherlands[18], Portugal[19], Spain[20] or the United Kingdom[21]; national portals

---

[8]   ESTER: http://ester.nlib.ee/search.
[9]   SUDOC: http://www.sudoc.abes.fr.
[10] SUNCAT: http://www.suncat.ac.uk/.
[11] http://www.nb.no/nosp/english.html.
[12] http://www.mmdc.nl/static/site/index.html.
[13] http://www.sino.uni-heidelberg.de/evocs/.
[14] Österreichische Dissertationsdatenbank: http://media.obvsg.at/dissdb.
[15] BICTEL/e: http://www.bib.ulb.ac.be/fr/bibliotheque-electronique/theses-bictele/index.html.
[16] DissOnline: http://www.dissonline.de/.
[17] Elektronines tezes ir disertacijos (ETD): http://aleph.library.lt/F?func=find-b-0&local_base=ETD04.
[18] DareNet – Promise of Science: http://www.darenet.nl/en/page/page.view/promise.page.
[19] Depósito de Dissertações e Teses Digitais: http://dited.bn.pt/.
[20] Base de datos de tesis doctorales (TESEO): http://teseo.mec.es/teseo/jsp/teseo.jsp.
[21] ETHOS: http://www.ethos.ac.uk/.

for digitized journals in Germany[22], Switzerland[23] or the United Kingdom[24]; the digital library of the Library Network of Western Switzerland[25].

These tools can be produced either through the additional efforts of all libraries in the country, or thanks to a central structure with national missions. In some countries, this role is played by the national library acting as head of the academic libraries' network; it can be the case especially in countries where the national library is also a university library. Other countries have other solutions. In France, the *Agence bibliographique de l'enseignement supérieur* (national bibliographical agency, financed by the Ministry for Higher Education and Research) is in charge of maintaining the *SUDOC*[26] and *CALAMES*, a new catalogue dedicated to manuscripts and archives[27]. In Germany, the *Deutsche Forschungsgemeinschaft* (DFG – German Science Foundation)[28] financed the creation of two national digitization centers, by the *Bayerische Bibliothek* in Munich[29] and the *Niedersächsische Staats- und Universitätsbibliothek* in Göttingen[30], in order to overcome the federal structure of the country, permit the development of national digitization projects, and establish a national registry of works digitized in Germany[31].

Few countries seem to have a national collaborative collection management policy, aiming at sharing between the main libraries in the country the responsibility of excellence in the various academic disciplines. That is the case in Germany, with the network of the *Sondersammelgebietsbibliotheken*[32], which have recently been given the additional mission of building thematic digital libraries named *Virtuelle Fachbibliotheken* (ViFAs)[33], or in France with the *Centres d'acquisition et de diffusion de l'information et technique* (CADIST)[34]. Sweden, with the *Bibsam* network coordinated by the Royal Library[35], and Estonia, are other countries with similar or approaching networks. In the United Kingdom, it seems that the *Consortium of Research Libraries in the British Isles* (CURL)[36], along with the *Research Information Network (RIN)*[37], has been thinking[38] about establishing such a national collaborative collection management policy.

---

[22] Digizeitschriften: http://www.digizeitschriften.de/.
[23] SEALS: http://retro.seals.ch/digbib/collectionsHome2.
[24] Medical Journals Backfiles Digitisation Project: http://library.wellcome.ac.uk/node280.html.
[25] RERO: http://www.rero.ch/. RERODOC: http://doc.rero.ch/.
[26] ABES: http://www.abes.fr/.
[27] http://www.calames.abes.fr/pub/.
[28] DFG: http://www.dfg.de.
[29] http://mdz1.bib-bvb.de/~mdz/.
[30] http://www.gdz-cms.de/.
[31] Zentrales Verzeichnis Digitalisierter Drucke: http://www.zvdd.de/sammlungen.html.
[32] http://webis.sub.uni-hamburg.de/.
[33] http://www.vascoda.de.
[34] http://www.sup.adc.education.fr/bib/intro/Cadist.htm.
[35] http://www.kb.se/bibsam/.
[36] http://www.curl.ac.uk/.
[37] http://www.rin.ac.uk/.

Parallel to this reflection in the UK, the question emerged of a possible collabo-rative storage of library collections, especially of less-used journal collections, in order to overcome the shortage of storage place in libraries[39]. Such structures al-ready exist in Scotland, with the *Collaborative Academic Store for Scotland*[40]; in France with the *Centre technique du livre de l'enseignement supérieur*[41] serving the academic libraries of Paris and the region of Ile-de-France; in Switzerland with the *Coopération en archivage des périodiques imprimés*[42]; or are in planning like in Spain, with the GEPA – *Garantia d'Espai per a la Perpetuïtat de l'Accés*[43] built by the Catalonian academic library consortium[44]. Still, similar initiatives seem to be relatively rare in Europe.

The financial benefits of such solutions are obvious and, like the development of consortia, help libraries face the costs of electronic resources for which the VAT rate is in many European countries a critical issue[45]. Library consortia which fundamental mission is to negotiate the acquisition of electronic resources, now exist in all European countries thanks in part to the European conferences of ICOLC (*International Coalition of Library Consortia*)[46] and the action of the eIFL (*Electronic Information for Libraries*) foundation which helped to build such con-sortia in as many as 20 European countries[47]. According to a study conducted in 2002[48], there are three main types of consortia in Europe: a national centralized one, like in Finland with *FinElib* which is led by the National library with the co-operation of the academic libraries[49]; a national decentralized one, like in France with *Couperin,* which is an association of higher education and research institu-tions[50]; and a regional one like in Spain or Belgium. Several types of consortia can be found in a same country, for instance in the United Kingdom where the JISC (*Joint information Systems Committee*)[51], a national agency negotiating – like a

---

[38] http://www.rin.ac.uk/ccm-menu.

[39] http://www.rin.ac.uk/collaborative-storage.

[40] http://cass.nls.uk/.

[41] http://www.ctles.fr/.

[42] http://www.kub-cbu.ch/navi.cfm?st1=400&st2=150&st3=&st4=&w=2300&status=2.

[43] http://www.cbuc.es/cbuc/programes_i_serveis/gepa.

[44] Consorci de Biblioteques Universitàries de Catalunya (CBUC): http://www.cbuc.es/.

[45] See the report of the « Frankfurt Group », *Survey on the impact of VAT on libraries and the scientific publication markets*, 2006: http://www.sub.uni-goettingen.de/frankfurtgroup/vat/EndberichtVAT210 906.pdf.

[46] http://www.library.yale.edu/consortia/.

[47] http://www.eifl.net/. European member countries of eIFL are: Albania, Armenia, Azerbaijan, Belarus, Bosnia-Herzegovina, Bulgaria, Croatia, Estonia, Georgia, Kosovo, Latvia, Lithuania, Macedonia, Moldavia, Poland, Russia, Serbia, Slovakia, Slovenia, Ukraine.

[48] GIORDANO Tommaso. "Library consortium models in Europe: a comparative analysis", *Alexandria*, n°14 (2002), 1, p 41-52. This typology is only one possible model: another model is described by HORMIA-POUTANEN Kristiina; et al. *Consortia in Europe: Describing the Various Solutions Through Four Country Example* – http://www.redorbit.com/news/display/?id=448194.

[49] http://www.kansalliskirjasto.fi/kirjastoala/finelib/.

[50] www.couperin.org/.

[51] http://www.jisc-collections.ac.uk/.

consortium – electronic resources for the whole country, is next to NoWAL (*Northwest Academic Libraries Consortium*)[52].

In some countries, these evolutions have led to the creation of online portals dedicated to academic and scientific resources, which are or can be considered as real national digital scientific libraries. Examples can be found in Denmark (*Danmarks Elektroniske Fag- og Forskningsbibliotek*)[53], Finland (*Tieteen linkkitalo – Science Linkhouse*[54] and *Nelli*[55]), Hungary (*Magyar Elektronikus Könyvtar*)[56], Italy (*Polar CNR*)[57], Iceland (*Hvar*)[58], Ireland (*Irish Research eLibrary*)[59], Lithuania (*Lietuvos akademinių bibliotekų tinklas*)[60], or in a lesser degree Russia (*eLibrary*)[61]. The Swiss project *E-Lib (Swiss Electronic Library)*, whose "strategic objective is to set up E-lib.ch as the leading and central national gateway in terms of a single point of access for academic information provision and information research in Switzerland and to establish it as a long-term entity"[62] must as well be seen as such an answer to create one unique access point to academic and scientific resources on a national scale.

Library networks involving several European countries are very active as well. Nordic countries have a long tradition in this regard, and have organised a number of common programs, associations or structures like: *DIVA*, institutional repository for Norwegian, Swedish and Danish universities, housed by the Swedish university library of Uppsala[63]; *NordInfolit*, an expert network in the field of information literacy[64]; *ARLIS/Norden*, an association of art libraries[65]; or more recently the *Nordbib* program, whose final objective is to establish a common Nordic infrastructure for access to scientific information[66]. These countries have in parallel encouraged and developed close working relations with libraries and library networks in the three Baltic States since they became independent in the early 1990s, for instance on educational libraries, art libraries, and on library and information science education.

---

[52] http://www.nowal.ac.uk/.
[53] http://www.deff.dk/.
[54] http://www.linkkitalo.fi/.
[55] http://www.nationallibrary.fi/libraries/nelli.html.
[56] http://mek.oszk.hu/.
[57] http://polarcnr.area.ge.cnr.it/.
[58] http://www.hvar.is/.
[59] http://www.ul.ie/~library/irel/irelnews.htm.
[60] http://www.labt.lt/.
[61] http://www.elibrary.ru/defaultx.asp.
[62] http://www.e-lib.ch/.
[63] http://www.diva-portal.org/about.xsql.
[64] http://www.nordinfolit.org/.
[65] http://www.arlisnorden.org/index.html.
[66] Nordic Research Library Programme for the Development of Access to Scientific Information in the Nordic countries: http://www.nordbib.net/.

Some of these European networks are working as associations. With over 350 members from 30 countries, the main European research library association is the *Ligue des Bibliothèques Européennes de Recherche* (LIBER)[67]. LIBER is active in many fields of interest to academic and research libraries: collection development, library management, licensing and VAT on digital resources, Open access, digitisation and preservation of cultural material, library buildings and architecture, among others. LIBER is working closely with other European library associations, like EBLIDA (*European Bureau of Library, Information and Documentation Associations*)[68] and CERL (*Consortium of European Research Libraries*)[69], or structures like SPARC Europe (*Scholarly Publishing and Academic Resources Coalition*)[70], to promote and defend academic and research libraries' interests and activities in front of national and European governments, or of scientific communities. Academic libraries in southern Europe have in parallel organized their own association, SELL (*Southern European Libraries Link*)[71], for exchange and collaboration on matters relative to electronic resources, and around common historical background and cultural identities.

More thematically oriented or specialized associations exist as well, like EAHIL (*European Association for Health Information and Libraries*)[72], BETH (European Theological Libraries)[73] or EURASLIC (European Association of Aquatic Sciences Libraries and Information Centres)[74]. Associations are very active and have largely contributed to the evolution of the academic and research libraries' landscape in Europe.

Finally, European funds have for years been incentives for collaboration between European libraries on specific projects involving several countries. For the last three years, such initiatives have emerged from the *E-Content +* program[75] and the *I2010: Digital Libraries* strategy[76] of the European Commission. Furthermore, many European research projects dealing with scientific information are benefiting from an active contribution from librarians, working along with researchers. Most of European projects have both a prospective dimension and an

---

[67] http://www.libereurope.eu/.

[68] http://www.eblida.org/. EBLIDA concentrates on "European information society issues, including copyright & licensing, culture & education and EU enlargement. EBLIDA promotes unhindered access to information in the digital age and the role of archives and libraries in achieving this goal".

[69] http://www.cerl.org/web/. CERL "seeks to share resources and expertise between research libraries with a view to improving access to, as well as exploitation and preservation of the European printed heritage in the hand-press period (up to *c.* 1830). The Consortium was formed in 1992 on the initiative of research libraries in many European countries and legally came into being in June 1994".

[70] http://www.sparceurope.org/. SPARC "advocates change in the scholarly communications market, supports competition, and encourages new publishing models (in particular, open access models) that better serve the international researcher community".

[71] http://www.heal-link.gr/SELL/index.html.

[72] http://www.eahil.net/.

[73] http://theo.kuleuven.be/beth/index.htm.

[74] http://www.euraslic.org/.

[75] http://ec.europa.eu/information_society/activities/econtentplus/index_en.htm.

[76] http://ec.europa.eu/information_society/activities/digital_libraries/index_en.htm.

operational objective. That's the case for the following projects, in which academic and research libraries are particularly involved in 2007–2008:

- DRIVER (Digital Repository Infrastructure Vision for European Research), a "project to build a large-scale public infrastructure for research information across Europe" with which LIBER signed an agreement77;
- DART-Europe E-Theses portal, "exploring the use of a more focused metadata standard for European e-theses" 78 (DART-Europe is endorsed by LIBER);
- eBooks on Demand (EOD), project involving 14 European libraries and co-ordinated by the library of the Innsbruck university in Austria, about digitising books existing in the libraries' catalogues on the request of users[79].

It has to be mentioned that academic libraries are not the target audience of *Europeana*, the European digital library, which is in the first stage of its development dedicated to the cultural heritage of European countries[80]; still, they are represented by both LIBER and CERL in this very symbolic project.

Networks and collaborations between academic libraries in Europe have existed for a long time, and have developed themselves even more for the last 20 years. However important this reality is, it may not be the most significant evolution that presently occurs in Europe, as well as in other parts of the world. The most exciting challenge faced by academic and research libraries today is to find or reaffirm their place in the new academic and scholarly environment that issued from the digital revolution.

3. ACADEMIC LIBRARIES IN THE SCHOLARLY ENVIRONMENT: A EUROPEAN RESPONSE?

A first view of the importance of this challenge can be obtained from the international open archives in Library and Information sciences. On E-LIS[81], 8 from the 10 most represented categories are in connection with academic libraries and their role in the scholarly communication process: Repositories (426); Information dissemination and diffusion (426); Academic libraries (412); Bibliometric methods (335); Use and impact of information (283); Intellectual property (266); E-journals (263); E-resources (253). User training (216) and Electronic publishing (198) are

---

77 http://www.driver-repository.eu/.
78 http://www.dart-europe.eu/.
79 http://www.books2ebooks.eu/index.php5.
80 http://www.europeana.eu/.
81 http://eprints.rclis.org/.

not far behind[82]. Academic and research libraries are subject to intense professional and scientific thoughts, dealing essentially with their role in the acquisition,
evaluation and dissemination of scientific information, as well as in the training of
their patrons to this scientific information.

European academic and research libraries are actively involved in institutional
repositories programs and projects. A very recent study comparing 56 institutional
repositories from 11 countries all over the world (including France, Germany, the
Netherlands, Sweden and the United Kingdom) showed that nearly 95% of the total time required to run those institutional repositories came from the library[83].
This very high percentage can be an explanation as to why the scientific responsibility of the European project DRIVER has been given to the director of the Goet-
tingen university library (Germany); the same person is, by the way, head of the
German national portal dedicated to information on Open Access[84] as well. And
on this last point, it is furthermore very significant that the international reference
portal for Open Access Journals, the *Directory of Open Access Journals* (DOAJ),
is an initiative of the Lund University library (Sweden)[85].

Those two relatively new questions (open archives and institutional repositories,
and open access to information) have permitted closer working relationships between librarians and scholars. The latter, becoming more aware of the issues at
stake in the field of scientific information, are involving themselves more and
more into projects directly or indirectly connected to libraries' field of competencies and, vice versa, librarians are more often invited to take part in projects or reflections dealing with science, its evaluation, its dissemination and its preservation. The involvement of libraries in an academic network like *Nereus*, the network of European economists[86], is a first example of these closer relationships between the two communities, and their collaboration alongside public and private
editors on portals for scientific journals, like the ones existing in Croatia[87] or in
France[88], is another.

This evolution has in many countries institutional consequences. Funding for
academic and research libraries is coming more and more from research agencies,
not only for research projects on library collections, but for the most essential missions of libraries – like acquisition of scientific literature – as well. It is particularly obvious in the field of negotiating the acquisition of scholarly electronic resources: the agencies SURF in the Netherlands[89] and JISC in the United King-

[82] Statistics as on April 28th, 2008.
[83] Primary Research Group, *The International Survey of Institutional Digital Repositories,* November
      2007, 121 p., http://www.primaryresearch.com/content-200711071-Information-Science.html.
[84] http://open-access.net/.
[85] http://www.doaj.org/.
[86] http://www.nereus4economics.info/.
[87] Hrčak, Portal znanstvenih časopisa Republike Hrvatske: http://hrcak.srce.hr/index.php?lang=en.
[88] PERSEE: http://www.persee.fr.
[89] www.surfdiensten.nl/.

dom[90] have set up specific departments for this particular mission. Of course, library consortia are very active in this field as well, but a national coordination policy can be given by such a national research agency. In Germany, the DFG has been for decades financing scientific projects on library collections, like cataloguing of medieval manuscripts, or digitization programs. Since 2005, it also finances a "national licenses" (*Nationallizenzen*) program, where the main German academic and research libraries are given the responsibility of negotiating with the editors and publishers, and for the whole German academic and research community throughout the country, the acquisition of the most important electronic scientific resources[91]. An analogue initiative exists for instance in Ireland as well with the Irish Research eLibrary[92], launched in 2004, which is an integral part of the national research strategy. Moreover, negotiating licences for electronic resources has now become a multinational issue: within the Knowledge Exchange network, SURF, JISC and the DFG, along with the Danish Electronic Research library DEFF, are working "towards a European approach to licensing e-resources," through exploring "with publishers the possibility of cross-border licensing arrangements,"[93]

Another core mission of libraries is being more and more taken over by research institutions: the preservation of documents. This phenomenon applies essentially to digital documents and resources, because of the very complex technological and very expensive financial[94] aspects of long-term preservation of digital information. Important research structures have been set up in many countries, in Germany[95], the United Kingdom[96], on European level[97]. National libraries are very active in this field as well, often benefiting from their experience in web archiving. On the contrary, the responsibility of academic and research libraries needs to be evaluated and perhaps strengthened, maybe especially for the digital data produced by their institution. The Swiss *E-Archiving* project led by the Consortium of Swiss Academic Libraries[98] could serve as an example for similar initiatives in other European countries.

Academic libraries are in fact very concerned by an approaching cause of concern, which is the archiving of electronic resources. This concept, which has a

[90] http://www.jisc-collections.ac.uk/.

[91] http://www.nationallizenzen.de.

[92] http://www.ul.ie/~library/irel/irelnews.htm.

[93] http://www.knowledge-exchange.info/.

[94] The british project LIFE is dedicated to analysing the costs of long-term preservation of digital information: http://www.life.ac.uk/.

[95] KOPAL: http://kopal.langzeitarchivierung.de/.

[96] Digital Curation Centre: http://www.dcc.ac.uk/. Digital Preservation Coalition: http://www.dpconline.org/graphics/index.html.

[97] Projects CASPAR, http://www.casparpreserves.eu/ and Digital Preservation Europe, http://www.digitalpreservationeurope.eu/.

[98] http://lib.consortium.ch/index.php?lang=2.

more "documentary" dimension, refers to "hosting" the electronic files of the e-resources produced by editors and publishers. Must these files be hosted only by theirs producers, libraries buying only access to them and not the e-resources themselves, or can libraries buy those files and, therefore, assume the responsibility for their archiving? Three main solutions co-exist at present in Europe:

- The direct negotiation with editors and publishers for the transmission of those files to the national library (this system is adopted in the Netherlands with the e-depot of the Koninklijke Bibliotheek99);
- A distributed architecture, where e-resources are archived by several libraries throughout the country (in the United Kingdom with the LOCKSS UK network100);
- The adoption of the Portico solution, a "not-for profit service that provides [editors and libraries] with a permanent archive of scholarly literature published in electronic form". This American initiative is still not very widespread in Europe: only some libraries in Cyprus, Greece (the most represented country outside the United States), Ireland, Sweden and the United Kingdom are members of the Portico program101.

Open Access to scientific information and long-term preservation of digital data are at the heart of the considerations for a common European research policy debated since the beginning of the decade. The Berlin Declaration on Open Access to Knowledge in Sciences and the Humanities signed on October 2003[102] initiated a movement which most recent result is the launch of the Ljubljana Process in April 2008, to revive the European research area[103]. Meanwhile, the role of the European Commission was absolutely fundamental: it commissioned a *Survey on the economic and technical evolution of the scientific publication markets in Europe*[104] in 2005; launched a "i2010: Digital Libraries initiative"[105] in 2006; issued a *Communication on scientific information in the digital age: access, dissemination and preservation*[106] in February 2007; published a green paper entitled *The European Research Area: New Perspectives* in 2007[107] followed by a public consultation on its conclusions. In this process, both the information professionals and scholarly communities met and defended the interests of a scientific communication that would be open and preserve the digital contents. And in fact, the most essential contribution of the European Commission "has been to emphasise

---

[99] http://www.kb.nl/dnp/e-depot/e-depot-en.html.
[100] http://www.jisc.ac.uk/whatwedo/programmes/programme_preservation/programme_lockss.aspx.
[101] http://www.portico.org/index.html.
[102] http://oa.mpg.de/.
[103] http://www.eu2008.si/en/News_and Documents/Press_Releases/April/0415MVZT_COMPET.html.
[104] http://ec.europa.eu/research/science-society/pdf/scientific-publication-study_en.pdf
[105] http://ec.europa.eu/information_society/activities/digital_libraries/index_en.htm.
[106] http://ec.europa.eu/information_society/activities/digital_libraries/doc/scientific_information/communication_en.pdf.
[107] http://ec.europa.eu/research/era/consultation-era_en.html#greenpaper.

how digital access to scientific information is related to the digital preservation of the record of scientific publications and data."[108]

Commenting on this process, Chris Armbruster, Research Associate by the Max Planck Digital Library[109] (Germany), proposed in March 2008 "A European Model for the Digital Publishing of Scientific Information"[110], where the "key functions of registration, certification, dissemination, archiving and navigation" are redistributed between publishers, libraries and repositories. In this model, libraries have the responsibility of archiving the "certified and published version of scientific information (publications and data), guaranteeing long-term preservation and open access."[111] The role of libraries is fundamental here and, as Chris Armbruster writes, "the age-old tradition of the deposit library may be revitalised by designating digital deposit libraries." If his model proposes that dissemination of the resources and "navigation services targeted at specific audiences" could be of the responsibility of publishers, who can for those two key functions provide a commercial and fee-based service, they should also be non-exclusive and allow a multitude of service providers to propose their own solutions.[112] That lets the door open for academic libraries to continue their first mission, which is to serve their public in the most appropriate ways, including digital libraries or thematic portals.

4. THE NEED FOR A NEW POSITIONING?

All those recent evolutions emphasized another need, felt – by both academics and librarians – to be more essential than ever: the information literacy competencies of students and scholars. European academic libraries have organised information literacy instruction courses for many years, either in the frame of disciplinary courses or through targeted actions. Information literacy instruction has become one of the main missions of academic libraries, in the same way as acquiring scientific literature. Networks of competencies on this particular matter have even been set up in some countries: Czech Republic[113], France[114], Germany[115], Scandinavia[116], Scotland[117], Spain[118], United Kingdom[119], and on the European level as well.[120]

---

[108] ARMBRUSTER Chris, "A European Model for the Digital Publishing of Scientific Information?", 2008, 20 p., p. 3. Available at SSRN: http://ssrn.com/abstract=1106162.

[109] http://www.mpdl.mpg.de/.

[110] ARMBRUSTER Chris, *Op. cit.*

[111] Ibid., p. 18.

[112] Ibid., p. 18-19.

[113] IVIG: http://knihovny.cvut.cz/ivig/index.html.

[114] FORMIST: http://formist.enssib.fr/.

[115] Informationskompetenz: http://www.informationskompetenz.de/index.htm.

[116] NordInfoLIT: http://www.nordinfolit.org/.

[117] Scottish Information Literacy Project: http://www.caledonian.ac.uk/ils/index.html.

[118] Alfamedia: http://www.mariapinto.es/alfamedia/index.htm.

In a way, this new mission epitomizes the strengthened position of librarians in their institutions' programs dealing with, on the one hand, students' education, and on the other hand, research activities. In a time when the library as a physical place is being questioned and information is now dematerialized, some analyses have concluded that merging within a same structure a certain number of complementary activities would be useful: working spaces for students, access to physical and electronic information, information literacy instruction, information and communication technologies instruction, distance learning. Such structures are usually named "learning centers" and built upon the existing library, which is active in the educational field of teaching information literacy and traditional place where information can be found and students can learn in a convivial atmosphere. Such learning centers can be found essentially in the United Kingdom[121] and Spain where there are called *Centro de Recursos para el Aprendizaje e Investigación (CRAI)*[122], but also in Finland[123] or Switzerland[124]. In universities where they exist, those learning centers are at the heart of the academic social life.

A dichotomy between education-oriented libraries and research-oriented libraries seems to be at present either burgeoning or growing, depending on the country, the higher education and research infrastructures, and the national culture. Is this evolution going to break up academic libraries into two separated and independent services, one being an educational service dedicated to answering the students' needs, and the other being a center for scholarly publication and electronic resources? In fact, this question must be analyzed in reference to the growing specialisation of the institutions themselves, which can either refocus on educating the students' masses or completely devote themselves to scholarly research. In the first option, enlarged opening hours of libraries are a necessity: the students of the university of Dortmund (Germany) were therefore enthusiastic when their library decided to open 24/24 and 6/7.[125] In the second, long-term preservation of scholarly information, either on physical or digital format (including digital primary data issued from research activities), and management of institutional repositories

---

[119] The Information Literacy website: http://www.informationliteracy.org.uk/.

[120] European network for Information Literacy : http://www.ceris.cnr.it/Basili/EnIL/index.html.

[121] For instance at the Hallam University in Sheffield: http://www.shu.ac.uk/services/lits/libraries.html.

[122] For instance at the University of Barcelona (http://www.bib.ub.edu/). For information on the CRAI, see: Ministerio de Educacion y Ciencia, *De la biblioteca universitaria al. Elaboración de una guía sobre la organización y gestión de un CRAI en el contexto de las universidades españolas, 2004.* Available on : http://wwwn.mec.es/univ/html/informes/estudios_analisis/resultados_2004/ea0072/crai.pdf.
See also: MARTÍNEZ Dídac, *El Centro de Recursos para el Aprendizaje CRAI. El nuevo modelo de biblioteca universitaria.* Available at: http://www.aab.es/pdfs/gtbu_crai.pdf.

[123] The library of the university of Kuppio is one of the 3 services of the *Centre for Information and Learning Resource Services*: http://www.uku.fi/wwwdata/pulu/Departments/130.shtml.

[124] The *Centre de connaissance* of the *Ecole polytechnique fédérale de Lausanne:* http://learningcenter.epfl.ch/page29889-fr.html.

[125] http://www.ub.uni-dortmund.de/ubblog/rund-um-die-uhr: it is however interesting to see that some comments on this decision left on the library's blog would have preferred an opening on Sundays rather than opening after midnight.

are considered by British scholars as the future core missions of librarians five years from now.[126]

These different views of libraries' missions, often solicited by librarians themselves[127], are enriching the debates on evaluation of library services. Giving the better service at an efficient cost is becoming more challenging than ever, and measuring libraries' activities was seen as sufficiently important by the European Commission that it financed a project on international library statistics, the Libecon Study, which gives data on libraries in 37 countries throughout the world (including 29 European countries) for the years 1997–2001[128]. A majority of European countries now establish more or less complete statistics for their academic and research libraries[129], and LIBER is as well involving very actively in this field, having organised a seminar on "Measuring quality in libraries" in March 2007.[130] This seminar dealt with the adoption in European countries of the American program LibQUAL+, which aims at giving libraries "a suite of services that libraries use to solicit, track, understand, and act upon users' opinions of service quality"[131]. So far, only some libraries in Denmark, Finland, France, Norway, Switzerland and the United Kingdom – as well as the European Parliament – have adopted LibQUAL+ and conducted surveys according to its methodology. Similarly, some European libraries and consortia are members of the COUNTER initiative, which deals with measuring the online usage of networked electronic resources.[132]

Evaluation of libraries is becoming more fundamental than ever, due to the conjunction of two essential realities: the growing costs of academic and scholarly literature, especially in digital form; and the influence of international competition not only for scholarly research but for attracting the best students as well. An efficient library is becoming an important asset for higher education institutions in the international competition.

---

[126] Research Information Network and Consortium of Research Libraries, *Researchers' Use of Academic Libraries and their Services*, 2007: http://www.rin.ac.uk/files/libraries-report-2007.pdf.

[127] See for instance the satisfaction survey conducted in Germany, of users of academic libraries specialised in social sciences and humanities: http://www.che.de/downloads/IIB_Bibliotheken.pdf.

[128] http://www.libecon.org/.

[129] For instance: Austria, http://www.statistik.at/web_de/statistiken/bildung_und_kultur/kultur/bibliotheken/index.html; Denmark, http://www.bs.dk/showfile.aspx?IdGuid={5F52DB69-A2CE-457E-A59C-006 C95ADAB8F}; Estonia, http://pub.stat.ee/px-web.2001/I_Databas/Social_life/01Culture/10Libraries/10Libraries.asp; Finland, https://yhteistilasto.lib.helsinki.fi/language.do?action=change&choose_ language=3; France, http://www.sup.adc.education.fr/asibu/; Germany, http://www.bibliotheksstatistik.de/; Norway, http://www.ssb.no/english/subjects/07/01/40/ffbibl_en/;
Spain, http://www.rebiun.org/cuestionarios/indicadores/indicadores_main.asp#;
Sweden, http://www.scb.se/Templates/PlanerPublicerat/Default.aspx?produkt=KU0102&type=PUB;
Switzerland, http://www.bfs.admin.ch/bfs/portal/fr/index/themen/16/02/02/key/02.html;
United Kingdom, http://www.lboro.ac.uk/departments/dis/lisu/.

[130] http://www.libereurope.eu/node/228.

[131] http://www.libqual.org/.

[132] http://www.projectcounter.org/index.html.

FINAL CONSIDERATIONS

Although very diverse, higher education and research libraries in Europe are, mainly because of the increasing importance of electronic resources, undergoing noticeable change. Active networking and cooperation, both on a national and European scale, where associations and funding from the European Commission play big roles, are characteristic of the European academic libraries' landscape. Furthermore, libraries and research communities are working in closer collaboration on the notion of scientific information and other common concerns: open archives and institutional repositories, scholarly publication, archiving of electronic resources and long-term preservation of digital data, information literacy needs. These evolutions prompt libraries to question their place within the academic structure, while at the same time reaffirming their importance for the competitiveness of their institution in the global academic and scholarly competition.

Libraries are now considered more and more essential to efficient scientific policies in Europe, being sometimes at the heart of national strategies that have been established in last years in the fields of access, dissemination and preservation of scientific data and production. Are we, therefore, heading in European countries towards the implementation of national documentary policies for the acquisition of resources of national and international interest, and niche documentary policies for each of the individual academic libraries[133]? This is not unlikely.

Considering all these evolutions, what could be the ideal profile of an academic library's director today? An "inspired and visionary librarian, with strong leadership and managerial skills, with knowledge and (international) experience of the latest developments in the area of scholarly information and a close affinity with research and higher education, who orchestrates the scholarly information strategy of the university, serves and promotes the interests of the institution in relevant national and international networks" were some of the qualities required for the position of Director of the University of Maastricht Library (Netherlands), as published in the corresponding job advertisement in early 2007. This advertisement, open to international candidates, is symbolic of the new orientation of European academic libraries. It also questions the initial training of library professionals, and the recruitment procedures of those who will be administrating them. The employment market for academic library directors will be more and more open to competition, as concerns the professional profile of the candidates as well as their nationality.

Paris, May 5th, 2008

---

[133] This assumption has been developed by David Aymonin, head of the Library of the Ecole fédérale de Lausanne (Switzerland), during the Annual Congress of the French Academic Libraries Directors' association (ADBU) 2007, http://www.adbu.fr/IMG/pdf/aymonin_adbu_dunkerque_20070921.pdf.

LIS EDUCATION

Leif Kajberg, Aleksandra Horvat and Esin Sultan Oğuz

1. INTRODUCTION

Providing a decent description of the patchwork of academic traditions, structural specifics and course profiles characterising Library and Information Science (henceforward LIS) in Europe presents a formidable task to those embarking on such a project. Explaining features of the past of LIS education along with current trends in curriculum development and educational reorientation within the space of ten pages or so seems almost impossible. Therefore, rather than intending to provide a more or less sketchy coverage of Europe's national LIS educational systems and practices for the sake of completeness, we decided to draw a picture that singles out LIS education scenes in a few larger areas in Europe for more detailed treatment. The depiction of LIS educational structures and developments in selected nation states produced by this selective approach is rounded out in this chapter by an outline and discussion of some key issues and activities of a transverse and cross-country nature. Within the LIS academic community, education is frequently intertwined with research efforts and LIS educators have a major role in LIS-specific research and knowledge production. However, the research dimension of LIS schools is not addressed in the sub-chapter.

1.1 European LIS Education: Diversity Prevails

Given the range of differing LIS academic levels from country to country and the multiplicity of national degrees, diplomas and vocational/professional qualifications, the project of delineating the "topography" of European LIS education is an unenviable one. Ample evidence on the mix of degrees and qualifications can be found in the recent edition of *World Guide to Library, Archive and Information Science Education* (Schniederjürgen 2007). The variety of curricular approaches, thematic orientations, subject emphasises and "paradigms" represented by LIS academic programs throughout Europe is conspicuous. Thus, the thematic profiles of courses and LIS programs in European countries range from archives/libraries/ museums, book science/bibliology, business and management, cultural librarianship, digital libraries and librarianship, documentation, engineering-oriented information studies, information and communication technology-specific, information science pure, literacy, learning and educational support orientation, LIS "mainstream" to traditional/classic librarianship. Just to give an illustration of the diversity of programme profiles that can be found.

No less motley is the picture of academic quality assurance practices and accreditation of LIS programs. Most of the European LIS schools rely on national-level accreditation bodies and mechanisms with national governments or specific government-funded agencies overseeing matters of quality assurance. In some national contexts combined solutions involving internal quality audit are the norm. Some LIS academic institutions also use external assessors such as employers and international panels of experts (Kajberg and Lørrin 200:28). As the situation looks now, formally established European-level accreditation and quality assurance procedures for LIS educational programs are non-existing.

A bird's-eye view of the European LIS education scene reveals an array of credit point systems, academic traditions, program structures and lengths, course levels, placement structures, curricular emphases, forms of teaching and assessment, etc. Nevertheless, convergence of educational structures and trends towards increased transparency in the field of LIS education are clearly discernible, not least because of the active involvement of governments and higher education institutions in Europe in the Bologna Process, which has as its aim to establish a European Area of Higher Education (EHEA) by 2010. The overall intention is to harmonise the European higher education system architecture and within this framework efforts are made to achieve comparability between degree qualifications while at the same time acknowledging and respecting the differing national educational traditions. So far the main focus has been on degree systems, quality assurance and study periods and it is essential to point out that the Bologna Process essentially considers systems, not curricular contents. However, in LIS, there are examples of initiatives involving the introduction of joint modules educational institutions located in two or more countries. Also reported are studies on the comparability and equivalence of course themes in different national contexts and the prospects for tuning specific curricular topics (Vilar, Zumer and Bates 2007).

In many European countries, there is a well-established and long-standing tradition of university-based LIS education and on the whole the tendency goes towards offering university-level LIS programs. Hence, in some countries the pattern is that formal academic preparation has gradually replaced vocational training schemes and sandwich courses, etc. provided by institutions outside the university sector. A concrete example of this transformation can be found in Hungary, where the Berzsenyi College in Szombathely has become a part of the University of West Hungary and is now called the University of West Hungary Savaria University Center. As a consequence, the LIS Department of the former College now operates in conjunction with the Institute of Social, International and European Studies at the new university. However, in a few countries, it is still possible to locate "profession schools" and very practice-oriented courses by and large modelled on the apprenticeship approach. Most European LIS schools provide practical training of some sort, but the time students spend on fieldwork placement seems to be on the decline (Borup Larsen 2005: 233-234).

The number of LIS schools in Europe is estimated at 200-250 (Borup Larsen 2005:232; Wilson, 2008) with the number of schools included in the above *World Guide to Library, Archive and Information Science Education* being somewhat larger. A count reveals that there are 346 entries in the book covering LIS schools in European countries. In looking at the organizational contexts, in which European LIS educational institutions operate, we find that the very large majority of institutions function as a unit or department within a specific faculty or as a programme within a particular department. There are extremely few mono-faculty universities or stand-alone academic institutions with the Royal School of Library and Information Science (Denmark) and Enssib (École national supérieure des sciences de l'information et des bibliothèques (France) as notable examples. In universities, LIS educational units are typically located within such host faculties as Arts and Humanities, Social Sciences, Communication and Media, Business Studies and Computer Science. The size of the student body of LIS schools varies from less than 50 students to more than 1,000 enrolled students with approximately two thirds of the schools having student populations in the range of 51-400. It is not unusual for a LIS department to have less than 200 students and LIS schools generally tend to be very small (Borup Larsen 2005:239). This is also illustrated by the number of full-time staff members in LIS departments: more than half (64%) have fewer than 20 staff members and more than a quarter (27%) had fewer than 10. Typically, the size of the academic staff is 11-20 (Borup Larsen 2005:239-240).

1.2 Subject Emphases of European LIS Curricula: Some Characteristics and Trends

As stated above, LIS education in Europe boasts a rich diversity of curricular traditions and domain-specific orientations. Traceable in Italian LIS education, for instance, is the prominence and historical significance of cultural heritage as a discipline and many universities offer archival studies and provide courses on palaeography and preservation of cultural goods. *Book science* or *bibliology* has for many years occupied a firm curricular place in some of Europe's LIS schools. "Bibliology" is the umbrella term for the scholarly disciplines studying the phenomena related to the book world and the book as an entity. In the former Soviet Union and in the Eastern and central European countries, library schools and institutes of culture, etc. tended to include the study of books from a variety of aspects in their programs. However, during the last decades, the prominence of book science and its sub-disciplines has diminished in LIS curricula throughout Europe. Today, scholarship and education of specialists in the field of book science enjoy a strong position in LIS education in the Baltic countries, and LIS schools in such countries as Croatia, the Czech Republic, Poland, Portugal, Romania, Slovakia and Ukraine offer courses in the field (Reimo 2007).

Looking at the approaches to teaching the historical aspects and developments within LIS, there seems to be a dividing line between West European and Scandinavian LIS schools with their emphasis on library/information history and the institutions in Central and Eastern Europe where there is a continued strong coverage of book science/book history (Reimo, 2007, p. 7). Thus, for instance, the postgraduate degree programs on offer at the Institute of Information Studies and Librarianship at the Charles University in Prague also include a 2-year master's degree in book studies. Further, the Kharkiv State Academy of Culture in Ukraine offers a Master in Book Studies (Sheyko 2005:117). The emergence of *digitization of cultural heritage* as a curricular area in LIS schools has brought new relevance to the treatment of the historical dimension in LIS curricula. Thus, the point is made that specialists involved in digitization projects must master not only the technological skills, but must also be knowledgeable about manuscripts and printed materials so as to make the right decisions in selecting materials for digitisation (Reimo 2007:12).

A prevailing feature of some LIS curricula – for instance those of some of the Scandinavian schools – is their inclusion of a cultural and literary knowledge base as part of the LIS curriculum. Thus, subjects such as culture and media studies, adult fiction and children's books have for many years occupied a firm place in LIS-specific curricula (Audunson 2005a). As in other parts of the world, the interface and interaction between archives and libraries and records management increasingly find their way into the curricula of some LIS schools, e.g. in Germany and Portugal. In other schools, e.g. in Scandinavia, museums and the keeping, "processing," conservation, digitisation and mediation of the objects of "memory institutions" are increasingly gaining ground in LIS course offerings. On the whole there is an increasing awareness of the response to be provided to the interrelated educational needs existing within the European Archives Libraries Museums (ALM) community. A study on university programs and educational institutions preparing future professionals in the ALM field identified three European academic institutions devoted to the entire ALM field (Dragija-Ivanović, Faletar, Pehar, and Aparac-Jelušić 2005:49).

In many European countries, schools in the LIS field have undergone processes of transformation and curricular restructuring directed towards resolving the dichotomy between librarianship and information science. But in France, there are academic institutions that traditionally orient themselves strongly towards the concepts of *document* and *documentation science* in the theoretical underpinning of librarianship and information systems and services. Similarly, the Department of Documentation Studies at the University of Tromsø, Norway sees itself as an academic unit concerned with *documentation science* emphasizing the scholarly concern with the entity of the *document*. More trendy labels such as knowledge management, information sciences, business information systems, or information and communication studies have been adopted by other schools, and the inspiration from the business school environments is discernible in some places. This seems to be the case in countries such as the Netherlands and the United Kingdom.

The last few years have seen a growing interest in *information literacy* as a field of research and analysis, as a policy area and as a curriculum subject. Thus, many conferences and seminars on information literacy have been held and networking initiatives and European projects have been started. European-scale initiatives include the European network on Information Literacy (EnIL) with the maintenance of the European Observatory on IL (Information Literacy) Policies and Research as one of its three action lines.[1] The concern for information literacy has spread to the European LIS education community and some LIS educators are currently engrossed in conceptualising the field while at the same time contributing to the discussion of its integration into LIS curricula (Koltay 2007; Corradini 2007:25).

2. SELECTED EUROPEAN LIS EDUCATION LANDSCAPES

2.1 Eastern and Central Europe

In many Eastern European countries, there was a need to reform national educational systems and to shift away from structures and ideological values rooted in the regime of the former Soviet Union. As a consequence, in the years after the fall of the Berlin Wall, new higher education structures were established, outdated tertiary educational elements were eradicated and new curricula, and teaching and learning materials were created while at the same time links and partnerships with western academic colleagues were initiated. At the same time the epistemological outlook was broadened and extensive use of textbooks and study materials published abroad began (Virkus 2007:11). In Poland, changes in higher education led to the establishment of four models of LIS education at accredited universities:

1. Two-stage, bachelor/master, studies in information science and library/ or book studies;
2. Librarianship specialisation in non-LIS departments running MA programs;
3. Postgraduate studies in LIS and
4. Doctoral studies (Woźniczka-Paruzel 2005:165).

In Estonia, three academic institutions provide LIS education with the Department of Information Studies at the Tallinn University being the only institution offering LIS programs at all three academic levels and with coverage of information science, information management and records management. In Russia, the system of LIS education is being constantly transformed. LIS education in the Post-Soviet Era reflects the complicated period of social and economic transition characterising the Russian society, reforms in higher education in general as well as the dynamic developments in libraries. In 2007, there were 26 higher education institutions in Russia providing LIS education. These include state universities and higher specialised institutions of culture. In 2002, the library faculties were transformed into LIS faculties and new State-approved standards for qualifications in LIS were created. A general LIS-specific syllabus has been issued, which includes

---

[1] http://www.ceris.cnr.it/Basili/EnIL/index.html (accessed 15 March, 2008)

both a federal and a national and regional part. A look at the subjects and sub-disciplines covered by the prescribed syllabus reveals the emphasis on liberal arts and social science fields (e.g. foreign languages, political science and Russian language and speech culture). The considerable weight given to bibliographic studies in the library-related components of the syllabus is reminiscent of library courses and library professional activities in the Soviet epoch (Donchenko and Kerzum 2006).

2.2 Croatia and Neighbouring South-East European Countries

Croatia may be taken as an epitome for the neighbouring countries in the South-East of Europe; from 1919 until the dissolution of Yugoslavia in 1991, its educational and library systems were developed along more or less the same lines as with Slovenia, Bosnia and Herzegovina, Serbia, Macedonia, Montenegro and Kosovo, which today are all independent countries.

Until the 1960s, there was no formal schooling at the university level available to librarians, and professional knowledge was acquired by passing a state examination for librarians. The obligation to pass the examination was first prescribed by regulation in 1928 for librarians of the National Library in Belgrade and the University Library in Zagreb; in 1931 it was extended to include all librarians in state libraries (Hanz 1971). Soon after the end of World War II the obligation to pass the professional examination was reintroduced for civil servants in libraries and archives.

The first programme of postgraduate studies in librarianship, documentation and information sciences, open to graduates from any discipline, was introduced at the University of Zagreb in 1961. The programme significantly contributed to professionalizing librarianship and helped create a core group of formally educated librarians for all types of libraries, yet mostly for university libraries. Until its closure in the end of the 1980s it attracted numerous students from all parts of the then Yugoslavia.

In the early 1960s, programs in librarianship were introduced in teacher training academies in Croatia, Bosnia and Herzegovina and Slovenia. In the 1970s, they were mostly replaced by university studies. New programs were opened for graduate students at the Faculty of Philosophy, University of Sarajevo (1972), Faculty of Philosophy, University of Zagreb (1976), and Faculty of Philology, University of Belgrade (1978).[2] The Zagreb and Belgrade programs were characterised by their interdisciplinary approach to library studies, i.e. students of any academic discipline were allowed to enrol. Reliance on information technology was another characteristic they shared, what normally meant that traditional core courses, such as library management, cataloguing, classification, bibliography, and history of book and libraries, albeit under slightly different names, were enriched

---

[2]   Faculty of Philosophy has been a traditional name for faculties offering study programs in social sciences and humanities.

by courses in database organization, theory of information science, etc. The Sarajevo programme differed in that it was opened at the Department of Comparative Literature and Librarianship for students of comparative literature only and offered a combination of literature courses and courses in librarianship.

Graduate library studies at the Faculty of Philosophy, University of Zagreb were established in 1976/77, first as a two-year supplementary study programme, open to students of any academic field, and from 1986 also as a four-year programme in Information Sciences for librarians, archivists, museum documentalists and information science experts. The programme was based on the assumption that information sciences comprise several disciplines, e.g. librarianship, archival studies, museum studies (ALM studies) and information science pure and that the latter provides a common basis upon which the other disciplines can develop. All students attended the same courses in the first two years and in the 3rd year they could choose among librarianship, archival studies, museum studies or information science. Each year around 100 students enrolled in all programs, around 40 chose librarianship. Since its establishment, more than 650 students of librarianship had graduated. The last generation enrolled in that programme in 2006.

The Bologna reform, introduced in 2005, proved to be a difficult task for LIS educators not only because the programme had to be revised in order to follow the 3+2 cycle, but also because of the trend to merge previously more or less independent programs for different categories of information sciences experts into a single programme. Taking into account a relatively wide scope of the information sciences field, the establishment of a single LIS programme is likely to result in a less specific and less practice-oriented curriculum. The first Bachelor's of Information Sciences will graduate in 2008. Master's programs for librarians, archivists, museum documentalists and information science experts will be offered for the first time in 2008/2009. Students with Bachelor degree in any discipline will be allowed to enrol into Master's programme, but they will have to meet additional requirements as compared to Bachelors of Information Sciences.

All programs are carried out by the faculty of 25 persons with either a doctoral or a Master's degree.

New LIS graduate programs were introduced in 1999 at the University of Osijek and in 2003 at the University of Zadar. The two LIS departments collaborate closely relying on the same staff and offer some joint programs. The curriculum is rich in courses on the book, reading, and information literacy. A new Master's program for publishers has also been envisaged.

At present the only doctoral program in information sciences has been organized by the University of Zagreb. It has replaced the earlier postgraduate programme in information sciences with the streams librarianship, archival studies, museum studies and information science (1994 – 2006).

All university programs must be reviewed and approved by the National Council for Higher Education.

Bosnia and Hercegovina

Since 1972 librarianship could be studied at the Department of Comparative Literature and Librarianship, Faculty of Philosophy, University of Sarajevo as a 4-year programme in comparative literature and librarianship. Bosnia and Hercegovina joined the Bologna Process in 2003 and the first revised programs were introduced in 2006/2007 allowing students to choose LIS as an independent study programme leading to the Bachelor degree (3 years) and Master's degree (two more years). In 2006, an agreement on co-operation was concluded with the University of Zagreb and teachers from Zagreb help the Sarajevo staff of 3 full-time teachers deliver the programme. The new curriculum has been modelled partly in accordance with the curriculum taught at the Zagreb University. 50 students are enrolled in the library programme each year. A doctoral programme is not available at present.

Librarianship can also be studied at the new University of East Sarajevo, founded in 1993. Since 1997, the programme in librarianship combined with literature has been offered by the Department of Literature and Librarianship. The four-year programme leads to the Bachelor degree and is executed by 25 full time teachers who teach ca 100 students.

Slovenia

Since 1987, LIS studies are taught at the Department of Librarianship, Information Science and Book Science, Faculty of Philosophy, University of Ljubljana. The program was harmonized with the Bologna process in 2006. A teaching staff of ten full-time academics and one part-time lecturer take care of about 200 students. Besides the traditional library courses, the curriculum offers courses on production and distribution of books, electronic publishing, records management, documentation, and information science. Students can choose elective courses in psychology and literature.

Serbia

An LIS curriculum is taught at the Department of Librarianship and Informatics of the University of Belgrade as a four-year program. In addition to the traditional library courses in library management, cataloguing and classification, bibliography and history of libraries, courses on database management, Internet and Web, and multimedia have been introduced into the curriculum as well as courses in records management and museum documentation.

There is no formal training provided as of yet for librarians in *Macedonia* and *Kosovo*, although specific courses have been organised for them by the universities in the neighbouring countries.

2.3 Turkey

The Republic of Turkey was established in 1923, and the need for qualified human resources employed in libraries was stressed in expert reports produced in the early years of the New Republic (Ersoy and Yurdadoğ 1963:206; Baysal 1992:56). From 1925 to 1952, along the lines of the proposals contained in those reports, a number of courses were designed and provided aiming to develop librarian skills, knowledge and techniques as well as promoting choice of librarianship as a profession (Ötüken 1957:20). Particularly those courses run between 1942 and 1952, being the first continuous training on library science, by Adnan Ötüken at Ankara University provided suitable conditions for the foundation of an institute that would offer for the first time library science studies within a university (Ötüken 1957:14-15). The first library science studies at BA level started in 1954 at Ankara University. This was followed in 1964 by Istanbul University as well as by Hacettepe University in 1972 with post-graduate studies. Witnessing the success in post-graduate studies, Hacettepe University launched its undergraduate studies in the discipline of library science in 1974 (Çakın 2005:14).

Until 1988, the academic studies were continued as a single discipline within an organizational framework called the Department of Library Science; however, the discipline was later divided into further branches on the grounds that the existing body of studies was not sufficient to train such workforce as needed in archives as well as in documentation and information centers. The studies were grouped under the Department of Library Science into three disciplines (discipline of library science, discipline of archiving, and discipline of documentation and information) were continued until 2002. This practice, which was based on the notion that the said disciplines were different in content, became less efficient in time in the face of progress in information technologies. The characteristics of the sectors employing a workforce trained in this field made clear that all the relevant professional skills, knowledge and techniques should be taught in a holistic approach (Çakın 2005: 16-18). Based on this understanding, the names of Departments of Library Science were changed in 2002 into Departments of Information Management, and all the related disciplines were brought together under this name. With the change of name, the study program was also revised, which now stresses the notion that information management underlies all those disciplines. The aim here was to emphasize that actually professionals provide information services but are called by different titles (Çakın 2005:19). Underlining that the label "information management" is an umbrella term, Çakın, the architect of the reconstruction process in librarianship and information science studies in Turkey, has pointed out that the graduates of the departments will continue performing their tasks in libraries, archives and documentation centers in their capacities as librarian or archivist. He has added that the title "information manager," on the other hand, will be a sort of higher identity for information professionals to be employed at information centers and in new service areas requiring information and documentation man-

centers and in new service areas requiring information and documentation management (Çakın 2002:6).

There are six study programs in the discipline of library science and information science offered by universities in Turkey. One of these programs had not started to admit students as of this writing.

Since the beginning of studies on library science and information science in Turkey, the greatest international influence has possibly been exerted by student and staff exchanges within the Erasmus program besides the influence of the American line of library science studies on the foundation of departments. Mutual visits at student and faculty level have been continuing in departments that made exchange agreements with European universities. It is considered that incorporating the notion of cultural diversity and an international perspective in study programs would enable the students to adapt themselves more easily to the changing global conditions, and that the experience gained by the faculty members would contribute to the improvement of study programs designed for international students at national universities (Oğuz 2007:286).

2.4 Northern Europe (Germany and the United Kingdom)

Germany

Typical of German (and previously West German) LIS education has for many years been the differentiated and sector-oriented/specific system of courses, which mirrors the multifarious and very hierarchically structured employment market for higher and medium-level library and information professionals and semi-professionals. Moreover, course offerings, bodies of knowledge transmitted to students, qualifications and job titles still reflect the traditional dichotomy between *documentation* and *librarianship*. As a consequence, in Germany, the somewhat compartmentalised LIS workforce includes *documentalists*/information specialists (university degree in a subject discipline degree topped by a documentation/information-related speciality course), diploma documentalists (4-year specialized program covering information retrieval, information systems, information service, information management, etc.), media documentalists, medical documentalists and documentation assistants. In the library field, primarily university libraries and large special libraries have for many years offered positions as academic or scholar librarians that are open to university graduates in various subject disciplines and which requires a complementing library-related programme. In addition, there are diploma librarians possessing a full library qualification (awarded after three or four years of undergraduate study) and library assistants in both public libraries and academic libraries. Finally, some universities have launched degree programs with a clear business profile leading to the qualification of corporate information manager. Also offered by a few universities are degree programs with an information science focus. However, during recent years the winds of change have began to influence existing LIS educational structures and routes to professional qualification in Germany. Preceding this process is the adoption of the revised Framework Act for Higher Education in 1988, which led to university reforms in the federal states of Germany (*Bundesländer*). The key elements of the university reforms are improved student mobility for students, introduction of the two-tiered Bachelor/Master degree system, greater transparency in teaching and course structures, reduced course lengths and promotion of lifelong learning (Krauss-Leichert, 2003, p. 301). As part of the implementation of the structural changes of higher education, a system of credit points was implemented (Krauss-Leichert 2002). Paralleling the structural reforms in higher education in general and in LIS education in particular are efforts within LIS academic contexts to re-examine librarianship and LIS as a discipline. The Bologna Process-inspired reorganization of LIS education implies the introduction of a 3-year Bachelor's degree, which will replace the traditional librarianship diploma course and a Master of Arts (MA) programme of typically 2 year's duration. The MA is offered partly as a consecutive course that builds on, and expands what has been taught in the bachelor context, and partly as a an additional qualification in LIS that can be taken by graduates from other disciplines (non-consecutive Master). An exciting feature of the MA degree programme is that it provides room for specialisation, absorption and even students' research. In 2007, the Humboldt-University, Berlin and seven universities of applied sciences (the so-called *Fachhochschulen*) offered degree programs designed in harmony with the new model of delivery (Bachelor/Master). MA programme designations include Information Science & Engineering/Information Science, Information Science and Management and Library and Information Management. However, MA opportunities are not yet available in all places and two schools in Bavaria concentrate on traditional librarianship courses (Hellmich and Schleh 2007).

The United Kingdom

In the UK, LIS education has for many years been available at undergraduate and postgraduate level. The two principal routes to professional qualification – an undergraduate LIS degree as the one route and a postgraduate LIS qualification coupled with a first degree in another discipline as the second route – still exist, but the way in which schools present and label their course offerings has changed along with the actual course content. In the 1990s, the "librarianship" or "library studies" gradually disappeared from the names of schools in the field. Alliances with other university disciplines left their stamp on the profile of some LIS departments, which became more blurred. At the same time Bachelor's programs with a LIS orientation came under pressure because of insufficient intake of qualified applicants. These programs were either abandoned or fundamentally revised. Problems in attracting applicants also affected the postgraduate LIS courses. Thus, recent years have seen an erosion and redefinition of traditional LIS and a diversification of LIS qualifications. A shift away from LIS in a more classic sense has been observable and information management has increasingly been seen as the core element in LIS education and typically combined with business-oriented subject component and business studies. Further, degree programs mirror close relations with computer science and information technology. The Chartered Institute of Library and Information Professionals (CILIP), which accredits LIS programs, had its role in LIS education redefined, developed a new Framework of Qualifications and started devoting more energy to quality assurance and benchmarking in the field. Paralleling this effort was the publishing of a Subject Benchmark for Librarianship and Information Management in 2000 (Um and Feather 2007). As the situation is now, 16 universities have programs that consider the LIS domain broadly and which have been accredited by CILIP. However, the number of universities offering information-related degrees covering for instance information systems or information management is considerably larger (Feather 2007:1). Overall, there is a marked shift towards Master's programs and Um and Feather conclude that "there is thus some evidence that the orientation of LIS in the UK has tended to shift from its traditional base in the humanities and social sciences to science and technology" (Um and Feather 2007).

3. CONTINUING EDUCATION FOR LIS PROFESSIONALS

In some European countries, LIS schools arrange continuing professional activities targeted to practitioners in the field. Thus, for instance, systematic continuing education is provided by the Continuing Education Centre for Librarians at the Department of Library Science and Information Science, Faculty of Social Science, University of Latvia (Gudakovska and Holma 2005). In Denmark, the Royal School of Library and Information Science provides a large-scale continuing education programme targeted to the library and information sector at large. The School has an in-house unit that plans and develops continuing education activities and annually around 200 short courses, seminars and theme days are offered to all kinds of library staff. Training courses, seminars, workshops or presentations tailored to the needs of individual libraries, organizations or interest groups are organised as well (Larsen 2005).

In quite a few countries continuing professional education for LIS staff is conducted by national players and providers such as national professional associations, national libraries, specialised national (training) centers as well as national agencies and focal points. A few illustrative examples are given in the following.[3] In Bulgaria, there is a Centre for Continuing Education for Librarians and in Norway the Norwegian Archive, Library and Museum Authority organises short

---

[3]   http://www.calimera.org/Lists/Resources%20Library/Dissemination,%20networking%20and%20trai ning/Training%20Guideline%20-%20Version%202.pdf (access date 15.3.2008).

courses, seminars, workshops, etc. pertinent to LIS professionals. In Croatia in 2002, the National and University Library, the Libraries of the City of Zagreb, the Department of Information Sciences of the Faculty of Philosophy in Zagreb, and the Croatian Library Association founded the Center for Continuing Training of Librarians. Annually it organises an average of 60 one-day courses for more than 1,000 librarians.[4] The Center collects a small fee from the participants but is mostly funded by the Ministry of Culture. In Bosnia and Herzegovina, there is a Center for continuing education of librarians located in the National and University Library in Sarajevo. In Sweden, BIBSAM, the Royal Library's Department for National Co-ordination and Development arranges seminars and conferences for library staff. In Poland, the Bibweb Project serves as a distance training tool enabling library staff to acquire and develop competencies and skills related to the offering of innovative services to library users. In Slovenia, the Institute of Information Sciences organises professional training and counselling in the fields covered by the national shared bibliographic system COBISS. In the UK, the Chartered Institute of Library and Information Professionals (CILIP) is a larger-scale provider of continuing professional education for LIS professionals. In France, l'Association des professionnels de l'information et de la documentation (ADBS, the Association of Professionals of Information-Documentation) has for long taken an active role in maintaining and updating the skills of information professionals. Thus, provision of continuing education is one of the Association's major objectives. In co-operation with the National Academy of Arts and Trades and with the National Institute of Documentary Techniques, ADBS offers a range of distance learning courses (Lamouroux 2007). In Russia, in-service refresher courses for library staff are available as a formalised promotion and career improvement opportunity. In addition, the State Library Policy has as its priority and pursues the creation of a continuing education system for members of the library workforce. Thus work is in progress on building an all-Russia continuing education system of refresher courses and library staff skills updating activities. In the Czech Republic continuing education schemes supported by the central government (the Ministry of Culture and the Ministry of Education, Youth and Sports) are available to librarians and other information professionals.

4. CO-OPERATION, CONVERGENCE AND JOINT PROJECTS

A significant part of the day-to-day collaboration between Europe's LIS schools encompasses the exchange of teachers and students and in this respect many European LIS schools rely on joint schemes such as ERASMUS, a component of

---

[4] http://www.nsk.hr/CSSU/ (access date 15.3.2008).

the European Union's multi-dimensional SOCRATES programme. The broadly-based SOCRATES programme, now the Lifelong Learning programme (LLP), has for some years funded different kinds of cross-country activities in the broad area of education. But there is a veritable family of EU higher education programs and they are mainly directed towards other parts of the world intended as they are to foster co-operation and create links and joint degree courses between universities in EU countries and universities in other continents. For instance, the highly pro-filed Erasmus Mundus programme supports European top-quality master's courses and intends enhancing the visibility and attractiveness of European higher educa-tion in third countries. Erasmus Mundus provides an additional opportunity of networking and collaboration in European LIS education and thanks to grant money from Erasmus Mundus, Oslo University College (Norway), Parma Univer-sity (Italy) and Tallinn University (Estonia) have been able to join forces to design and offer a joint Masters programme on Digital Library Learning (DILL) that started in autumn 2007. The course leads to a joint Master's degree equivalent to 120 ECTS (Virkus 2007: 9). Also, there is an increasing awareness of distance learning in LIS education and several domestic and transborder projects and ac-tivities have been implemented.

In 2003, the Department of Information Studies at the Tallinn University launched an online-delivered MA course in information management and three current projects at the Department focus on virtual mobility (Virkus 200:13). In Aberdeen, Great Britain, the Department of Information Management at the Robert Gordon University, has built up an extensive body of experience in provid-ing education on the Web. Thus, the Department relies on the Virtual Campus at the University for delivering distance learning to domestic students as well as to a diverse population of international students (Johnson and Reid 2007). Today EUCLID (the European Association for Library and Information Education and Research) can be regarded the major player in European LIS education. Set up as a joint forum for European LIS schools in 1991, the Association has been active promoting links, co-operation and joint initiatives between LIS schools and LIS educators in Europe. Within EUCLID there has for some years been a growing in-terest in discussions on the comparability and equivalency of LIS qualifications throughout Europe and the Association has organised seminars on issues in cur-riculum development and internationalisation. EUCLID's concern with the con-vergence of LIS educational programs and the contents of LIS curricula in Euro-pean countries culminated in the completion in 2005 of the *LIS Education in Europe* project.

The major visible long-term product of the European LIS curriculum project is the electronic book that was published in December 2005 (Kajberg and Lørring 2005). The project was conceived as a collective Europe-wide effort with clear reference to the Bologna Process. In these years, LIS education is undergoing transformation in many European countries and the traces of the Bologna Process is increasingly visible in the restructured systems and course offerings (Feather,

2007, p. 4, 5). Thus, in some European countries, the 3 + 2 + 3 overarching academic cycle representing the levels of undergraduate, graduate and Ph.D. studies has gradually replaced a more conventional practice-oriented and profession-centered LIS education prototype with elements of practical training.

The BOBCATSSS conferences organised every year in January under the auspices of EUCLID stand out as a successful, innovative and very visible collaborative effort in European LIS education. The aim of the BOBCATSSS, which was first arranged in 1993, is to enhance cooperation between LIS students and professionals in Eastern and Western Europe. The special thing about this symposium is that student groups from LIS institutions located in Eastern/Central Europe and from Western Europe join forces in organising the event. However, there are other groups and fora, typically more specialised in nature, where European LIS educators meet, network, exchange ideas and agree on joint initiatives and projects. Examples of this include the European Network for Information Literacy (ENIL), the Nordic-Baltic Research School in Library and Information Science (NORSLIS) and HIBOLIRE, the Nordic-Baltic-Russian Network on the History of Books, Libraries and Reading.[5] In a couple of countries, there are national-level associations of LIS schools such as Konferenz der Informatorischen und Bibliothekarischen Ausbildungseinrichtungen (KIBA), an umbrella forum for German LIS academic institutions, and the British Association for Information and Library Education and Research (BAILER). Moreover, EBLIDA (European Bureau of Library, Information and Documentation Associations) takes an increasing interest in issues related to LIS programs and LIS qualifications. EBLIDA also underscores the pertinence of bridging the gap between the LIS school sector and the field of practice when discussing the future of European LIS education, the LIS profession and the services it provides.

5. CURRENT TRENDS AND FUTURE CHALLENGES IN LIS EDUCATION IN EUROPE

In taking European LIS education forward, more attention needs to be devoted to academic quality assurance mechanisms. Since promotion of European cooperation in quality assurance is a key item on the agenda of the Bologna Declaration, the Bologna Process provides an obvious opportunity for bringing about tangible and substantial quality enhancement and transparency in European LIS education (Audunson 2005b). On the other hand, aiming at a unified or standardised European-level process of accreditation for LIS programs does not appear realistic. Instead of centralized bureaucratic procedures, a more appropriate strategy would be

---

[5] The homepage of the Network is accessible at: http://www.helsinki.fi/historia/hibolire/

to "europeanize' national evaluation measures and accreditation processes by developing a pool of joint European expertise than can be drawn upon by national accreditation bodies (Audunson 2005b: 5). Quality assessment in LIS education needs to be confronted not least from the perspective of equivalency and reciprocity of LIS professional qualifications.

A current IFLA study looks at the feasibility of establishing guidelines for equivalency and reciprocity of LIS professional qualifications to facilitate the exchange and cross-border mobility of LIS professionals in Europe (Tammaro and Weech 2007). The curricular discussion continues and there are new and upcoming issues to be addressed including the educational implications of digital librarianship. Capitalizing on current trends in digital library development in Europe and the emerging conceptual frameworks in this field, some European LIS educators show an increasing interest in discussing and defining the role and professional competences of the digital librarian. Also addressed are models for designing curricula for digital librarianship and the level and delivery formats of courses aimed at educating digital librarians (Tammaro 2007).

In addition, continued efforts are required to enhance educational convergence and formal cooperation and networking among Europe's LIS academic institutions. For this purpose, formalised collaborative structures and communication mechanisms such as thematic networks of institutions across boundaries, technical communication infrastructures, collaboratories and regular meetings, physical or virtual, would seem required and obvious. In the student mobility area, new opportunities are coming up including the notion of *the virtual campus* and schemes for *virtual mobility*. Virtual mobility refers to agreements set up between two or more higher education institutions that allow their students to acquire a number of ECTS points at one of the foreign partner universities or through participation in a joint activity between the partners. The ECTS points resulting from this international experience will then be transferred to the student's diploma records at his/her home university. Virtual mobility takes place in a virtual learning environment: students study in their domestic academic environment, and, as a consequence, they need not travel outside their home countries.

Hence, accelerating the use of IT solutions and making the most of ICT-based course delivery and learning opportunities present a constant challenge to European LIS schools. A variety of tools are now available including networked collaborative software and web-based communication packages furthering the interpersonal communication. One of the valuable features of distance education and e-learning is the possibility of resource sharing between LIS schools in different countries and the increased feasibility of teaching modules and options that are more narrow in scope and likely to attract relatively limited numbers of students. In this way, elective courses can be shared through collaborative e-learning across countries (Bawden 2007). However, in addition to reliance on virtual conferences and other web-based communication packages furthering the interpersonal communication, formal or informal, between LIS school academics, consideration should be given to more ambitious and far-reaching solutions.

Another major challenge is to develop a set of common goals and joint policies for European LIS school activities and their collaborative structures. In this area, there is work to be done, within EUCLID and at the national level. On the whole, LIS schools in Europe are faced with common challenges emanating from the growth and diversification of higher education systems, the increased significance of lifelong learning, the shortage of skills and expertise in key areas, the employability of graduates produced along with the expanding market share of private and transnational education providers. Other challenges include the introduction of innovative delivery formats and tackling the apparent problems of inconsistent terminology in curricular contexts and within the LIS discipline as such.

A peculiar problem is the existence of very small LIS departments. In the European LIS education landscape, it is not unusual to find departments with only 2-4 permanent teaching staff members. For departments of that small size, it seems like an overwhelming burden to maintain and transmit a body of knowledge to students that fairly accurately and believably portrays the contents of the LIS domain in all its broadness and complexity. Besides, the robustness of the very small departments is fairly questionable because of their invisibility and the risks of financial contingencies and organizational turbulence caused by external factors and policy decisions in the broader university environment. Maybe it is time to consider more unconventional modes of course provision in the LIS area and to aim at organizational structures for provision of LIS programs that go beyond the familiar institutional frameworks known as LIS schools. The 4-year undergraduate degree course in information science jointly provided by the Faculty of Arts and Humanities and the Faculty of Engineering at the University of Porto, Portugal, serves as a concrete illustration of this type of approach. As a result of this cross-faculty collaborative model, an information science curriculum has been tied together, which displays a high degree of interdisciplinarity. Thus, modules are offered within the course framework that cover such complementary and auxiliary disciplines as the history of cultural practices, logic and epistemology, linguistics, cognitive psychology, computer systems, operating software, accounting and administrative law (Ribeiro 2007).

As shown by this somewhat compact portrayal, LIS education in Europe presents a mixed bag with its miscellany of language contexts, historical distinctiveness, academic cultures, epistemological traditions and structural intricacies. But rather than dwelling too much on perceived structural barriers and academic complexity, one may see the prevailing cultural and academic diversity within what one calls "LIS Europe" as a strength and an asset. So from this perspective, there is reason to praise the variety of disciplinary conceptions, curricular approaches and "cultural flavours" reflected by today's European LIS academic community.

References

Audunson, Ragnar (2005a) Library and information science education: is there a Nordic perspective. Paper presented at the "World Library and Information Congress: 71th IFLA General Conference and Council", August 14-18, 2005. Oslo, Norway. [Online] Available: http://www.ifla.org/IV/ifla71/papers/061e-Audunson.pdf. Retrieved March 9, 2008. Audunson, Ragnar (2005b). LIS and the Creation of a European Educational Space: Lecture, Lisbon September, 30, 2005. [Online] Available: http://euclid.hio.no/files/pdf/lisbon-lecture.pdf. Retrieved March 9, 2008.

Bawden, David (2007). "Facing the educational future". Information Research vol. 12, no. 4. [Online] Available: http://InformationR.net/ir/12-4/colis/colise01 (access date 9.3.2008)

Baysal, J. (1992). "Kitap ve kütüphane tarihine giriş. İstanbul". TKD İstanbul Şubesi, 56.

Borup Larsen, Jeannie (2005). A Survey of Library & Information Science Schools in Europe. In: European Curriculum Reflections on Library and Information Science Education. [Online] Available: http://biblis.db.dk/uhtbin/hyperion.exe/ db.leikaj05. Retrieved March 15, 2008.

Çakın, İ. (2002). "Kütüphanecilik bölümleri: yeniden biçimlenirken". Düşünceler, vol. 58, Kasım, 3-9.

Çakın, İ. (2005). Cumhuriyet'ten günümüze bilgi profesyonellerinin eğitiminde başlıca yönelişler, Türk Kütüphaneciliği, vol. 19, no. 1, 7-24.

Corradini, Elena (2007). "Competencies and curriculum for information literacy, International Round Table at Milan, Palazzo delle Stelline, 16 March 2007". IFLA SET Bulletin, vol. 8, no. 2, [Online] Available: http://www.ifla.org/ VII/s23/bulletin/ SET_Bulletin-July2007.pdf. Retrieved March 15, 2008.

Donchenko, Natalia and Kerzum, Irina (2006). "Between slump and hope: Library and information science education in Russia". The International Information & Library Review, vol. 38, 181-184.

Dragija-Ivanović, Martina, Faletar, Sanjica, Pehar, Franjo and Aparac-Jelušić, Tatjana (2005). LIS programs reflecting the needs of the archives, libraries and museums community: a preliminary research report. In: Coping with continual change – change management in SLIS. Proceedings of the European Association for Library and Information Education and Research (EUCLID) and the Association for Library and Information Science Education (ALISE) Joint conference, Potsdam, Germany, 31 July – 1 August 2003.

Ersoy, O. and Yurdadoğ, B.U. (1963). "Education for librarianship abroad in selected countries: Turkey". Library Trends, vol. 12, no. 2, 205-210.

Feather, John (2007). LIS Education in the New Europe. Bologna and beyond. Paper presented at the "60th Anniversary International Conference PERSONALITY. INFORMATION SPACE". University of Latvia, Faculty of Social Sciences,

Department of Information and Library Studies, 11-12 October 2007. In: Personality. Information Space / Personîba. Informâcijas Telpa [CD-ROM].

Gudakovska Iveta and Holma, Baiba (2005). The educational situation for library and information science in Latvia: some considerations before embarking on the development of new academic programs. In: Coping with continual change – change management in SLIS. Proceedings of the European Association for Library and Information Education and Research (EUCLID) and the Association for Library and Information Science Education (ALISE) Joint conference, Potsdam, Germany, 31 July – 1 August 2003.

Hanz, B. (1971). "Library education in Yugoslavia". International Library Review, vol. 3, 113-120.

Hellmich, Julia and Schleh, Bernd (2007). "Bachelor und Master zwischen allen Stühlen? (Bachelor, Master und Berufsstart)". Buch und Bibliothek, vol. 59, 706-712.

Johnson, Ian M. and Reid, Peter H. (2007). "Distance Learning and International Students". Focus on International Library and Information Work, vol. 38, 63-66.

Kajberg, Leif and Lørring, Leif (Eds.) (2005) European curriculum reflections on Library and Information Science education. Copenhagen: Royal School of Library and Information Science.

Koltay, Tibor (2007). "A new direction of library and information science: the communication aspect of information literacy". Information Research, vol. 12, no. 4. [Online] Available: http://informationr.net/ir/12-4/colis/colise06.html. Retrieved March 15, 2008.

Krauss-Leichert, Ute (2002). "Quo vadis Deutschland? Internationale Studienabschlüsse und Credit Point Systems". Buch und Bibliothek, vol. 54, 471-475.

Krauss-Leichert, Ute (2003). "The case of Germany: a report on the status of international degrees and credit point systems". New Library World, vol. 104, 300-306(7).

Lamouroux, Mireille (2007). Continuous training with the ADBS, the Association of Professionals of Information-Documentation: a new positioning. Paper presented at "Librarian@2010 Educating for the Future". Lisbon 19th, 20th, 21st September 2007. [Online] Available: http://www.apbad.pt/Librarian@2010/Abstract_12.pdf. Retrieved March 15, 2008.

Larsen, Gitte (2005). Continuing professional development: trends and perspectives in a Nordic context. Paper presented at the "World Library and Information Congress: 71th IFLA General Conference and Council", August 14-18 2005. Oslo, Norway. [Online] Available: http://www.ifla.org/IV/ifla71/papers/143e-Larsen.pdf. Retrieved March 15, 2008.

Oğuz, E. S. (2007). Kütüphanecilik ve Bilgibilim Eğitiminde Uluslararası İşbirliği: Avrupa Birliği Faaliyetleri. In S. Kurbanoğlu, Y. Tonta ve U.Al. (Eds.) *Değişen*

Dünyada Bilgi Yönetimi Sempozyumu, Ankara, October 24-26, 2007 (p. 284-287). Ankara: H.Ü. Bilgi ve Belge Yönetimi Bölümü.

Ötüken, A. (1957). Türkiye'de kütüphanecilik öğretiminin tarihçesi. Türk Kütüphaneciler Derneği Bülteni, vol. 6, no. 1-2, 20.

Reimo, Tiiu (2007). The place of book science in library and information science (LIS) education. Paper presented at the "60th Anniversary International Conference PERSONALITY. INFORMATION SPACE". University of Latvia, Faculty of Social Sciences, Department of Information and Library Studies, 11-12 October 2007. In: Personality. Information Space / Personîba. Informâcijas Telpa [CD-ROM].

Ribeiro, Fernanda (2007). LIS education in Portugal between academic and practice. Paper presented at "Librarian@2010 Educating for the Future". Lisbon 19th, 20th, 21th September 2007. [Online] Available: http://www.apbad.pt/Librarian@2010/Abstract_01.pdf. Retrieved March 15, 2008.

Schniederjürgen, Axel (Ed.) (2007) World guide to library, archive and information science education, 3rd new and completely revised edition, Munich: K.G. Saur.

Sheyko, Vasyl (2005). Curricular changes in restructuring library and information science education in Ukraine. In: Coping with continual change – change management in SLIS. Proceedings of the European Association for Library and Information Education and Research (EUCLID) and the Association for Library and Information Science Education (ALISE) Joint conference, Potsdam, Germany, 31 July – 1 August 2003.

Tammaro, Anna Maria and Weech, Terry L. (2007). The IFLA Feasibility Study of Guidelines for Equivalency and reciprocity of qualifications for LIS professionals – A progress report with a focus on the needs of European LIS academia and practitioners. paper presented at "Librarian@2010 Educating for the Future". Lisbon 19th, 20th, 21th September 2007. [Online] Available: http://www.apbad.pt/Librarian@2010/Abstract_07.pdf. Retrieved March 15, 2008.

Tammaro, Anna Maria (2007). "A Curriculum for Digital Librarians: a Reflection on the European Debate". New Library World, vol. 108,. 229-246.

Um Ai Young and Feather, John (2007). "Education for information professionals in the UK", The International Information & Library Review, vol. 39, 260-268.

Vilar, Polona, Zumer, Maja and Bates, Jessica (2007). "Information seeking and information retrieval curricula development for modules taught in two library and information science schools: the cases of Ljubljana and Dublin". Information Research, vol. 12, no. 4. [Online] Available: http://InformationR.net/ir/12-4/colis/colise03.htlm. Retrieved March 15, 2008.

Virkus, Sirje (2007). Cooperation and international aspects of LIS education. Paper presented at the "60th Anniversary International Conference PERSONALITY. INFORMATION SPACE". University of Latvia, Faculty of Social Sciences, Department of Information and Library Studies, 11-12 October 2007. In: Personality. Information Space / Personîba. Informâcijas Telpa [CD-ROM].

World List of schools and departments of information science, information management and related disciplines, maintained by T.D. Wilson. [Online] Available: http://informationr. net/wl/ Retrieved March 15, 2008.

Woźniczka-Paruzel, Bronisława (2005). Transformation of library and information science studies in Poland and its sources. In: Coping with continual change – change management in SLIS. Proceedings of the European Association for Library and Information Education and Research (EUCLID) and the Association for Library and Information Science Education (ALISE) Joint conference, Potsdam, Germany, 31 July – 1 August 2003.

PART 5
LATIN AMERICA:
INTRODUCTION

Filiberto Felipe Martínez-Arellano

The rich and appreciation of the situation of libraries in Latin America and the Caribbean necessarily requires, in the first instance, an understanding of the region's features. Morales Llanos, Correa Cortez and Torres Cruz (1997), in their description of Latin America, point out that the region is made up of twenty-one countries spread over an area of 20 million square miles. The region, while divided by the equator, extends further to the south than to the north. Argentina, Bolivia, Brazil, Colombia, Costa Rica, Cuba, Chile, Dominican Republic, Ecuador, Guatemala, Haiti, Honduras, Mexico, Nicaragua, Panama, Paraguay, Peru, Puerto Rico, El Salvador, Uruguay and Venezuela are the countries that make up the region. After 1960, four new countries, Jamaica, Barbados, Trinidad y Tobago, and Guyana, came into existence and these have been grouped in a sub-region denominated the Caribbean and Antilles.

The aforementioned authors continue their characterization of the region by stressing that each of the region country exhibits a wide variety of living conditions that are a function of their climate, geography and the customs and traditions derived thereof. This is why each country has its own a life style, which is a distinctive social adaptation. This complex set of circumstances in countries of Latin-America and the Caribbean exhibits areas of overlap in terms of music, celebration and beliefs, but deep diversity from nation to nation also is in evidence.

Likewise, they add, that the Latin-American and the Caribbean Region have suffered a generally deficient educational history, which has left its trace on almost everyone. On one hand, the State has encountered many difficulties, including crushing poverty, as it strives to reform the educational system, leaving the population disenfranchised from educational opportunities.

At the present time in Latin-America and the Caribbean, there is a palpable social barrier that in many cases restricts access to educational opportunity, as it reserves these opportunities for urban populations enjoying above average incomes. In contrast, rural populations face limitations in terms of the low quality of the educational institutions, the dearth of qualified teachers and the need to travel long distances to attend school.

Additionally, they point out that the middle and lower classes are currently exhibiting a drop in school attendance, forced to meet immediate economic needs rather than continuing in school. This drop in attendance is evident in students from 13 to 24 years old. Even though the market for education is expanding (especially at the elementary level), the Region's illiteracy rate for ages 15 through 64 is 13.2%.

Finally, it is pointed out that in the Latin-American and the Caribbean Region, 75% of the population lives in urban areas, while 25% make their living in the agricultural sector in rural areas. Among urban dwellers, the average rate of unemployment is 11%. Unfortunately, owing to conditions already described, the vast majority of the employed population (38.9% of the general population) work in low paying manufacturing jobs and lead lives of relative scarcity.

Indubitably, the development of libraries in Latin-American and the Caribbean is linked to the features of these regions, some of which have been mentioned above. In the field of libraries, there is an evident dearth of consolidated school libraries throughout the region; while efforts are afoot to ameliorate this deficiency by having public libraries in varying degree of development do double duty. Public libraries of this kind, grouped in systems or networks, are most evident in Colombia and Mexico. University libraries, organized in library systems have achieved a considerable degree of development. Among the distinct types of libraries, those operated by universities are clearly the high developed in Latin-America and the Caribbean. Moreover, specialized libraries in the region exhibit a high degree of development. The impetus provided to libraries in Latin-America and the Caribbean is a product, among other factors, of the efforts to expand the ranks of professional librarians in many of the region's countries.

The purpose of papers that make up this chapter is to present a general overview of the current status of the diverse kinds of libraries that can be found in Latin America and the Caribbean, as well the challenges and pending tasks to be carried out in order to promote their improvement and development. Likewise, this chapter includes a contribution describing the status of LIS education in the region. Without a doubt, the brief presentation of the features of diverse libraries in the region, with their peculiarities and varying degrees of development, is no small feat; nonetheless, we hope to contribute to the understanding of Latin-America and the Caribbean libraries. Moreover, our intention, reflected in this series of articles, is to contribute to a global understanding of Library and Information Science, which hopefully can further the germination of comparative studies.

Reference

Morales Llanos, Catalina, Correa Córtez, Andrés Julián y Torres Cruz, Juan Camilo (1997). *América Latina*. [Online] Available: http://www.monografias.com/trabajos7/amla/ amla.shtml. Retrieved March 23, 2008.

PUBLIC LIBRARIES

Elsa M. Ramírez Leyva
Translation by Filiberto F. Martínez-Arellano

PUBLIC LIBRARY BIRTH FOR THE PEOPLE ENLIGHTENMENT

Since their inception, in early twilight of the colonial period, public libraries in Latin America have had complicated periods, times of confidence strides and other ones of dire precariousness; however, they have never ceased to undergo changes. In 1646, still under the colonial regime, the first proposals to open public libraries in the region appeared. Noteworthy among these proposals is the *Biblioteca Palafoxiana,* in Puebla, Mexico, considered the first one in Latin America; and the *Biblioteca Turriana.* Collections of both of these libraries reflected the needs and interests of religious scholarship, while their regulations expressed innovative ideas regarding public access. In Colombia, the proposal is put forth asserting that learning should be wrested from the control of religious orders and books should serve all society, not only elite groups of scholars.

During the eighteenth century in the Latin American colonies, as it was so in the old continent, access to books was restricted to a reduced group, notwithstanding the growth of both literary and scientific activity. At the same time, a minority of literate elites began to break away from dogmatic texts and to write texts that broke with moral and political cannons. Little by little, individuals from the great illiterate masses began to learn to read and write, thereby creating new and diverse reading publics. Simultaneously, three historical watersheds, the Industrial Revolution, the Enlightenment and the rise of France and England – at the expense of Spain and Portugal – encouraged the emancipation of overseas colonies resulting in profound political, economic and cultural transformations. These circumstances established the foundations for a transformation in the education and writing orientation, which eventually provided the underpinning for the rise of public libraries in Latin America.

During the nineteenth century, Latin American countries that had achieved their independence incorporated progressive ideals of modernization from industrial and literate societies, which had influence in educational projects that impelled literacy and reading habits. At the same time, there was present the consolidation of diverse printing processes and a strengthening of the publishing industry (in terms of production and commercialization); and, of course, library services were transformed to support people education, especially for adults. As a result, new habits and customs regarding to delivery, access, and consumption of texts arose.

Certainly, the public library assumed a new paradigm according to the ideals of justice, public education and freedom of expression. This conception was totally opposed to traditional and normative concepts about collection development and access only for an elite, based on arguments of learned privilege and the perceived danger of exposing ignorant and inexpert minds to advanced ideas. In this way, the "public library" and the "public school" constituted the means of "the spreading of the light" through "edifying letters."

Most of the proposals regarding the establishment of national public libraries in Latin American and Caribbean nations arose from conferences that saw the need for bringing people greater access to education and reading.[1] The term "public" identified these institutions created by liberal governments, while the term "national" was a testimony of identity and showed the capability of preserving and exhibiting its own culture.[2] The maturation of this library gradually displaced the conservative positions that considered a risky to provide books without oversight them, which at that time would not have a broad social impact since the literate population was still a small minority. Moreover, this tendency sustained a liberal ethos of the library's "generosity" in the project of enlightening the peoples' mind.[3] In this first stage, library collections reflected the interests of learned and religious scholars rather than the population needs in its early tentative steps toward literacy and education. At the same time, libraries belong to education institutions broadened access to their collections in order to offer reading to all the people. Similarly, small public libraries, notably popular libraries and reading stands whose collections consisted of confiscated and donated materials containing both books and administrative documents, were created in urban areas.

Among the countries that after 1814 promoted libraries establishment, the following can be mentioned: **Argentina**, where the first popular libraries were opened to foster culture dissemination, popular education, and reading promotion;[4] **Bolivia**, where by a decree, public libraries were established in provincial departments to "promote the progress of enlightenment and uniformity of educational standards"; **Brazil,** where the Royal Portuguese Library with 60,000 books, one of largest collections in South America, was opened to the public, although for the first sixty years, it was only used by a literate elite. In Bahia, then the Brazil Capital, the first public library was founded with the stated mission of promoting peo-

---

[1] Ramírez Leyva, Elsa M. "Introducción". In *Historia de las bibliotecas nacionales de Iberoamérica: pasado y presente*. ABINIA / coords. José Moreno de Alba y Elsa M. Ramírez Leyva. México: UNAM; Instituto de Investigaciones Bibliográficas, Centro Universitario de Investigaciones Bibliotecológicas, 1995. p. xxi

[2] Acevedo, Hugo. "Biblioteca nacional de Argentina". In *Historia de las bibliotecas nacionales de Iberoamérica: pasado y presente*. ABINIA / coords. José Moreno de Alba y Elsa M. Ramírez Leyva. México: UNAM; Instituto de Investigaciones Bibliográficas, Centro Universitario de Investigaciones Bibliotecológicas, 1995. p. 3

[3] Lafuente, Ramiro. *Un mundo poco visible: imprenta y bibliotecas en México durante el siglo XIX*. México: UNAM, CUIB, 1992. p. 25

[4] Impeled by the Presidente Domingo Faustino Sarmiento (www.corrientes.gov.ar/sauce/bibliotecas/default.asp) accessed: 23/04/08.

ple instruction. Thereafter, other libraries arose in other states.[5] In **Colombia**, the first public library was founded in the State of Medellin; later, other public libraries, directly related to the public education policies, were established in several of the country municipalities. Likewise, at the end of the century, more than one hundred mobile libraries and reading rooms were established. In **Chile**, the Santiago Severin Library arose thanks to the philanthropy of its founder and for a long time was the only "regional" public library in the country. It became, nonetheless, the basis for opening small libraries throughout the country.[6] In **Costa Rica**, the first public library was created in the *Intituto de Alajuela,* which later became the National library. Also, the first public library regulations governing the operations of the four existing public libraries were drafted. Likewise, in 1899 it was opened in a women's section in the National Library, so that the library would no longer be a private men's club.[7] In **Cuba**, the public library arose from an initiative of the *Sociedad Económica de Amigos del País* [Economic Society of Country Friends] of the Havana in order to impel development of public instruction, as well as to promote reading for all the people through schemes that included a writing requirement to go to the library to read books that interested them.[8] In **Ecuador**, bibliographic holdings of the University of Santo Tomas became the foundations of the National library. Later on, the public and the university library were merged for a period of fourteen years. **El Salvador** founded its National Library to which the popular culture libraries that emerged were ascribed. In **Mexico**, during the thirties, a debate arose regarding the creation of the National Public Library, but the fears of some conservative legislators blocked its inception. Nonetheless, during the nineteenth century, public libraries and those from education intuitions continued their expansion. Toward the end of that century, there were 150 libraries in Mexico. Moreover, the National Library, inaugurated in 1882, opened a nocturnal annex for workers that was opened to the public until 1976.[9] In **Nicaragua**, the National Library was founded as evidence of the State's commitment to bringing

---

[5] Arze Aguirre, René. "Biblioteca Nacional de Bolivia". In *Historia de las bibliotecas nacionales de Iberoamérica: pasado y presente.* ABINIA / coords. José Moreno de Alba y Elsa M. Ramírez Leyva. México: UNAM; Instituto de Investigaciones Bibliográficas, Centro Universitario de Investigaciones Bibliotecológicas, 1995. p. 35

[6] López Muñoz, Ricardo. "Bibliotecas públicas chilenas: ¿centros de participación ciudadana y de inclusión social?". (www.cerlalc.org/revista_noviembre/pdf/n_art03.pdf) accessed:24/04/08

[7] Solano Murillo, Rosario. "Biblioteca Nacional de Costa Rica". En *Historia de las bibliotecas nacionales de Iberoamérica: pasado y presente.* ABINIA / coords. José Moreno de Alba y Elsa M. Ramírez Leyva. México: UNAM; Instituto de Investigaciones Bibliográficas, Centro Universitario de Investigaciones Bibliotecológicas, 1995. p. 101

[8] Viciedo Valdés, Miguel. *Breve reseña sobre la biblioteca pública en Cuba antes de 1959.* [en línea] (http://bvs.sld.cu/revistas/aci/vol11_06/aci10106.htm) accessed:24/04/08

[9] Vázquez Mantecón, Carmen, Alfonso Flamenco Ramírez y Carlos Herrero Bervera. *Las bibliotecas mexicanas en el siglo XIX.* México: SEP, Dirección General de Bibliotecas, 1987. p. 227

culture to the people.[10] **Panama** saw an animated library movement, which included the establishment of a popular library that lasted only three years. In 1916, the popular library reappeared. In **Peru**, the public library arose with the creation of the National Library, which was considered a basic institution for guaranteeing human being freedom and an authentic democracy. In Uruguay, in 1815 arose the idea of creating a public library for young students by bringing together diverse private collections. In **Venezuela**, the proposal regarding the foundation of the National Library arose to meet the need to promote social well being by means of the public enlightenment, and access to statesmen of the doctrines needed to learn how to govern and legislate. Other libraries that formed later became part of it.

Public libraries for education

Economic, political and technological transformations in the twentieth century propelled public education and literacy campaigns whose purpose was to reach goals for modernization of diverse social aspects of Latin American nations. At the same time, the conception of library public service also began to change, under the strong influence of the North American library model. This was reflected in the conformation of collections and public services that were distinct from those required by the scholarly elites of the nineteenth century. Upon reorganization, some public libraries remained within the national library organization, while other ones gravitated to educational and cultural institutions as internal library departments or directions. Likewise, public libraries were established within private educational institutions. The taxonomy of libraries gradually became a function of their users and goals; however, in most places of our region, the public library assumed the school library function in response to the expansion of educational centers without library facilities. With financial support of the United States of America, diverse "Benjamin Franklin" public libraries were founded in several countries, including Mexico in 1947. Within an atmosphere of greater freedom, publishing activity increased, diversified and expanded its markets.

In the first half of the century, important changes occurred. Between 1908 and 1948, in **Argentina**, popular libraries suffered at the hands of government authorities who viewed them as nuclei of opposition capable of promoting values of solidarity and social movements, in addition to buy and lend books considered as of inconvenient nature. Later, these libraries were once again promoted, although during the time of the dictatorship, they went through difficult times. Argentina stands out for having a robust publishing industry. In **Colombia**, the Act no. 24 established in 1921 public libraries in every municipality with a population of more than 10,000 inhabitants. Its stated purpose was the popularization of universal knowledge and the dissemination of works from diverse knowledge subjects. In

---

[10] Coloma González, Fidel. "Notas sobre el desarrollo histórico de la biblioteca nacional de Nicaragua". En *Historia de las bibliotecas nacionales de Iberoamérica: pasado y presente*. ABINIA / coords. José Moreno de Alba y Elsa M. Ramírez Leyva. México: UNAM; Instituto de Investigaciones Bibliográficas, Centro Universitario de Investigaciones Bibliotecológicas, 1995. p. 367-8

Chile, in 1921, the State created the General Direction for Libraries to be responsible for organizing the country's existing libraries. It was not until 1929, however, that these libraries were open to all persons. Later this Direction became the *Dirección de Bibliotecas, Archivos y Museos (DIBAM)* [Direction for Libraries, Archives and Museums], charged with the tasks of organizing the country's libraries and drafting the organizational standards for all libraries open to the public. In 1907, in **Costa Rica**, the National Library established a circulation section specialized in Pedagogy for elementary schools. From 1920 to 1936 a children's room was also in operation. A decree of 1941 declared as a matter of public interest, having a public library in every province, and the National Library is charged with the duty of providing books. In 1907, in **El Salvador**, public libraries were founded in several provincial capitals, and in 1923, under the authority of the National Library, a system of "circulantes," popular, and free libraries were set up. In **Mexico**, upon the creation of the Secretariat of Public Education,[11] the Department of Public Libraries was formed in order to guarantee student and the general population access to books for their education. By 1923, there were 671 libraries in operation in Mexico and this intense activity brought with it the first courses in Library Science and the first scholarships for studying in the United States. Moreover, the first professional associations and fellowships in the library field also arose, as well as the first Library Science journal, *El libro y el pueblo* [The book and the people], including articles addressing library issues.

Along the years, diverse library services were created, including services for workers, children, and mobile libraries in public parks; however, some of these libraries did not always prosper because a lack of funding. It was during that time the first building designed expressly as a library was built. It had been common to adapt existing buildings, some of them colonial structures, into libraries. The publishing industry continued its expansion and was further impelled by the influence of Spanish exiles.

In 1931, in **Nicaragua**, a children's section was opened in the National Library. In 1924, **Panama** established its National Library and a public library in every provincial capital. In 1943, the National Public Library Service Regulations were instituted under the authority of the National Library. In 1922, **Peru** created, by a decree, the first popular libraries in every provincial capital. In **Puerto Rico**, in 1902, the municipal public libraries were open. After decades of instability in the library settings, Venezuela issued a proposal to create a national library network with the collaboration of diverse levels of government and the various library projects headed by the Librarian Blanca Alvarez. Because of certain conditions, however, these efforts bore little fruit. Meanwhile, the Book Bank, a sort of experimental nucleus, was established with the purpose of promoting steps to set up pub-

---

[11] José Vasconcelos was a great promoter of public libraries, considering them as one of the most important institutions. His ideal was the U.S. library model, with which he had contact in his childhood.

lic libraries and publish children's books. During the breadth of the twentieth century in Uruguay, public municipal libraries arose, which now form the backbone for information access.

The public library: manifestation of democracy and culture access

By the middle of the twentieth century, the recently created UNESCO (1945) began a crusade to eradicate illiteracy, extend education and promote information freedom. UNESCO raised the public library as a blazon symbolizing democracy. In 1949, it drafted the Public Library Manifesto, whose purpose was to promote democracy and persuade governments to legislate in favor of library projects and guarantee their maintenance. Additionally, this manifesto sought to orient librarians in the duties of providing without distinction free access to books for all the people. The effect of this manifesto in Latin America was relative and uneven, because the priorities and limited budgets in many countries were oriented toward existing literacy programs and school construction projects. In 1970, the International Federation of Libraries and Institutions promoted the inclusion of libraries into library networks, which produced substantial changes in countries throughout the region. Another important initiative was the UNESCO Conference on the Current State and Development of Strategies for Public Libraries in Latin American and the Caribbean, celebrated in 1982 with the collaboration of the *Centro Regional para el Fomento del Libro en América Latina y el Caribe* (CERLALC) [Regional Center for the Book Promotion in Latin America and the Caribbean] and the Venezuelan Autonomous National Library Institute. The analysis of the public libraries situation, from a regional perspective, produced the "Caracas Declaration"[12] – which has been a landmark because it both described the state of libraries and their central problems with that movement, and set a direction for their future.

In the second half of the twentieth century, the most common characteristic of Latin American public libraries was the support diversity; but despite this often unfavorable situation, public libraries scored some notable advances in terms of their structure, growth and diversification of resources and services offered. An important innovation in this period was the opened access to collections and the automatized loan service. There was also advancement in the technological infrastructure to automate processes and library management. Equipment and infrastructure for public access to the Internet in urban areas saw a gradual expansion. Likewise, some countries funded extension projects in order to create new loan service modalities beyond library walls. There was also a trend to strengthen participation in activities to support reading habits. As part of the responsibilities for

---

[12] Basic documento "La biblioteca pública en América Latina, su estado actual y reflexiones en torno a su desarrollo futuro". En *Reunión Regional sobre el estado actual y estrategias de desarrollo de la biblioteca pública en América Latina y el Caribe*, 1982. (www.fundaciongsr.es/documentos/manifiestos/caracas.htm – 19k) accessed: 25/04/08

coordination offices, library personnel received training in diverse systems. These changes occurring over the decades can be appreciated in several countries.

In 1986, in **Argentina**, the *Comisión Nacional Protectora de Bibliotecas Populares* (CONABIP) [National Commission for Popular Libraries Protection] was reborn. With an emphasis in infrastructure and training, the Special Fund for Popular Libraries was created to support and develop the 2000 popular libraries making up the national library network. Among the plans and programs contemplated can be mentioned: the reading and book promotion of reading and books, citizen information services, services for persons with disabilities, and the *MY PC Program* that consists in implementing computer teaching and learning centers to reduce computer illiteracy.

In **Bolivia**, in 1945, control over the state libraries and institutions and private cultural societies was established by the Supreme Decree. The concept of a library system structure appears in a government declaration. At the same time, the collection grew, and the National Library and the National Archive were improved. Furthermore, new popular and public libraries were created. The Book Bank creation, to provide texts to low income students and to promote reading habits to broad sectors of the population, was also proposed.

Between 1970 and 2005 a wide library network based upon the Book Bank was achieved. In 1992, in **Brazil**, by a Presidential Decree, the *Sistema Nacional de Bibliotecas Públicas* (SNBP) [National Public Library System], an agency of the National Library, was created to strengthen the country's public libraries and to create a democratic society armed with the critical awareness for the full exercise of citizenship. The *Plan Nacional del Libro y la Lectura* (PNLL) [Reading and Book National Plan] proposed the strengthening of the public and school library systems, so that each state would be supplied with at least one library. Currently there are 5,385 public libraries.

In 1952, **Colombia** promoted the design of a model public library and the UNESCO and the Colombian government installed the Pilot Public Library of Medellin for Latin America, which was based on a North American model that sought to promote cultural expression, access to books and reading habits. Separately, 1969 saw the launch of a library network consisting of libraries administered by the government through the Colombian Culture Institute. In 1973, the National Information System was created, and in 1974, the first network belonging to a private institution, the public libraries of the *Cajas de Compensación Familiar* (COMENFALCO) [Family Compensation Fund]. In 1978, the National Library System became the National Public Libraries Network ruled since 1998 by the Ministry of Culture. Currently, 1601 libraries are involved in developing intense activities.

Since 1996, in **Chile**, Clara Budnick has been renewing the library system through the General Directorship for Libraries, Archives and Museums, wherein the Public Library Coordination Office, which oversees the administration, coordination and standards in the 378 existing public libraries, is setting the foundations for a national system. It also established the organization structure, a National Coordination Office, Regional Coordination Office, and municipal public libraries. Likewise, it started the project "*Mecanismos de Gestión Participativa*" (MGP) [Participative Management Mechanisms] consisting of building and implementing a methodology to promote cultural programs based upon a national census about kinds of contacts established between libraries and their communities. During this period, it also started the installation of library modules in subway stations and markets, among other sites, and computer equipment for Internet access in public libraries.

In **Costa Rica**, in 1950, popular libraries arose, and by 1971 – with the creation of the Ministry of Culture, Youth and Sports, there were ascribed eighteen public libraries. Three years later, the Department of Libraries was established in order to coordinate them. In 1991, the *Sistema Nacional de Bibliotecas* (SINABI) [National Library System] is formalized and charged with the task of contributing to the general development of citizens by means of the free access to information. Today there are a total of fifty-four libraries.

In **Cuba**, in 1958, the National Library assumed the duties of a public library not only to correct deficiencies in this kind of services, but also to function as a laboratory and methodological center for the network. The year 1960 saw the establishment of the General Directorship of Libraries devoted to extend and strengthen the services of 379 public libraries. Later, the National Library was ascribed to the Ministry of Culture, under the Library Directorate, as an entity for directing and coordinating the 413 public libraries existing at the time and in charge of the duties for promoting reading habits and books.

In **El Salvador**, in 1968, an executive decree established the National Library and Archives Administration, grouping itinerate libraries and the General National Archive under one umbrella. The year 1974 saw the name change of itinerate libraries to public and school libraries. The National Library that had operated as a public library formed a collection of books and activities for children, including story time.

Currently, the Network made up of fifteen public libraries is a dependency of the *Consejo Nacional para la Cultura y el Arte* (CONCULTURA) [National Council for the Culture and Arts]. By 1983, in **Mexico**, there were 351 public libraries under the Public Secretariat. In that year, led by the prominent librarian Ana Maria Magaloni, one of the most important library projects in Mexico was launched. Under her leadership, the Directorate was promoted to the rank of General Direction for Libraries, and the resources of three government levels were brought to bear in its development plan. She also established standards for library buildings and furniture, a collection development program, holdings organization, and automation processes. Likewise, she modernized and implemented diverse programs, among which are those to promote reading, free computer classes for children, and professional development training as well as annual update seminars for personnel. She provided support for the publications and research program focused on community studies and library history, among other subjects. She also promoted the General Law on Libraries and created a network of public libraries made up of thirty-two state coordinating offices. By the end of her administration, in the year 2000, 5,700 libraries were in operation throughout the country under the aegis of the *Consejo Nacional para la Cultura y las Artes* (Conaculta) [National Council for the Arts and Culture]. Currently, there are 7210 public libraries. The last few years have seen the celebration of biannual national meetings where participants from the libraries making up the network read papers, share experiences and discuss library issues.

In **Nicaragua**, around 1979, the *Frente Sandinista de LIberación Nacional* [Sandinista Front for National Liberation], with support of the Organization of American States and the UNESCO, developed forty-eight public libraries in support for popular education. From 1984 to 1988, the Ministry of Culture created the General Directorship for Libraries and Archives to coordinate the national library system and the network of forty-one public libraries throughout the country.

In 1924, **Panama** established public libraries in each provincial capital. The National Coordination Office for the Public Libraries Network of the National Library was in charge of their development and strengthening to fulfill their mission of offering access to print media and information services to the broad general public – without distinctions of any kind – in order to open opportunities for their individual and collective development. Additionally, since 1984, national campaigns to promote reading habits were begun.

In **Peru**, by 1986, the National Library, in charge of public libraries, oversaw 680 libraries, but from1987 to 1991, economic downturns and political turmoil eroded these gains until 1992 when a process of recovery began. That was signaled by the approval of a new structural organization of the *Sistema Nacional de Bibliotecas* (SNB) [National Library System], later the National Coordination Center, made up of public, school, university and specialized libraries. By the year 2005, the National Library System began activities and projects aimed at implementing and propelling services to municipalities and providing the resources needed for the development of national library policy, which currently places emphasis on the management of 2127 public libraries nationwide.

In **Uruguay**, the municipal public libraries are an agency of the *Servicio de Bibliotecas y Casas de Cultura* [Library and Cultural Services Centers]. Each library enjoys the grade of an Administrative Unit within the Municipal Government.[13] In 2007, the National Library launched the National Coordination System for Popular

---

[13] Basile, Claudia y Magdalena Reyes. "Situación de las Bibliotecas Públicas Municipales de Montevideo". Montevideo: Asociación de Bibliotecólogos del Uruguay, 2005. (http://www.febab.org.br/apresentacao/Textos/Seminario%20IFLA%20Uruguai.doc) accessed:25/04/08

and Penitentiaries Libraries. At this time, the need to formalize a National Library System is discussed. While several local libraries are associated independently, remaining under the authority of their natural superiors, there are voluntarily relationships for cooperation, coordination and exchange.

In **Venezuela**, in 1957, arose the idea to establish a library on the basis of the Medellin pilot library model. At that time there were 300 libraries. In 1974, Virginia Betancourt became Director of the National Library and she is credited with overseeing its flowering. She improved its structure and modernized its library and information services in support of educational, social and cultural development of communities. Under her leadership, models, standards and procedures were established throughout the Public Library System, including the use of automation in order to make information and books more accessible to broader segments of the population. Additionally, a program involving itinerate boxes of books was launched to reach remote populations. The professional training for personnel area was reinforced with funds from the UNESCO. During this period, the Libraries Act was approved and the Book Promotion Foundation and the National Reading Commission were founded. By 1993, there were 261 public libraries and another 413 related sites divided between reading rooms, loan stands, bookmobiles, and community information points.[14] By 1982, the second stage of the system was launched in order to improve infrastructure, develop collections and ensure the delivery of services in accord with quality standards. Today, there are 727 libraries in operation throughout the country.[15]

The preceding data allows us to summarize that during the twentieth century, the *UNESCO Manifesto for Public Libraries* did not have the expected effect in the region because of political and economic issues in each country. Likewise, the libraries did not have a sustained development because important initiatives are of a rather circumstantial nature. Nevertheless, libraries in Latina America exhibit significant progress and, despite the difficulties experienced, it could be said that they have survived and, indeed, have prospered in the later half of the century. They have achieved highly structured organizations and have opened new settings in terms of both quality and quantity of services. Some libraries promoted project aimed at attracting diverse publics, beyond the traditional student public. Special emphasis was afforded to programs aimed at creating a taste for reading in children. Cultural extension activities carried out beyond the library walls have constitute innovative approaches for disseminating library services. National associations and libraries themselves have promoted conferences that address themes of interest. Meanwhile, libraries began to be included in the agendas of regional

---

[14] Fierro Bustillos, Lourdes. "Biblioteca Nacional de Venezuela (1810 -1994)". En *Historia de las bibliotecas nacionales de Iberoamérica: pasado y presente*. ABINIA / coords. José Moreno de Alba y Elsa M. Ramírez Leyva. México: UNAM; Instituto de Investigaciones Bibliográficas, Centro Universitario de Investigaciones Bibliotecológicas, 1995. p. 227

[15] Lovera de Mantellini, Graciela. "El Sistema Nacional de Bibliotecas Públicas en Venezuela". *Revista Interamericana de Bibliotecología* 1987, vol. 10, no. 1, p. 55–7

summits, including those under the aegis of the Organization of American States in cooperation with the CERLALC. These conferences have been the source of policies and project initiatives and the creation of groups such as the Ibero-American Public Library Head Librarians Forum.[16]

The public library in the Information Society

Since the year 2000, the greater part of public libraries in the region fell under the national systems or networks as either agencies of the national library or the federal education and culture infrastructure. Others belonged to the private sector or NGOs. Moreover, the quantitative growth tended to reach stability in several countries, which has helped to reorient efforts to optimize collections, personnel, and resources, including infrastructure, buildings, furniture and electronic technology installations. As a result, a gradual growth has been evident in the incorporation of electronic resources and technological infrastructure aimed at offering Internet access and orientation for its use. Several libraries have seen the launch of projects aimed at development of information literacy. Likewise, as part of high priority programs, reading habits and activities promoting books receive special attention. Some libraries have instituted novel programs that incorporate new promotional spaces beyond the library walls in markets, subways stations, parks, mobile collections and more.

Library services and the rescue of indigenous culture in local indigenous communities receive special attention. Citizenship information services and community cultural programs are instituted to create links among diverse social sectors. Worthy of note is the strong push to provide professional development for personnel. In some cases, job descriptions call for professional studies. More and more countries launch reading and book promotion programs in which libraries, schools and the family stand as pillars to support efforts to create a community of readers, and help to reduce digital divide.

Contribution of the IFLA in the public libraries development in Latina America and the Caribbean

The International Congress on Libraries and Documentation Centers, held in Brussels in 1955, approved as its declaration of principles and objectives, a memorandum prepared by the IFLA Public Libraries Section, which emphasizes the public library mission, In the 1970s, international organizations, including the IFLA, sought to inscribe the thrust of library development into a model of systems and networks, an approach that has influenced public libraries in the region ever since.

---

[16] Fundación Biblioteca Nacional de Panamá. Biblioteca Nacional Ernesto J. Castillero R. *Red nacional de bibliotecas públicas: directrices para el desarrollo de las bibliotecas públicas panameñas,* 2004 (http://www.picbip.org/index.jsp) accessed:25/04/08

At the same time, the IFLA has collaborated with UNESCO in the review and updating of the third version of the *IFLA/UNESCO Manifesto on Public Libraries*, which has been translated into more than twenty languages and it has been considered as an important statement of fundamental principles for public libraries. The *IFLA/UNESCO Guidelines for Public Libraries* published in 2001 (in substitution of the 1986 Guidelines) were updated. These have been highly useful for librarians, helping them to find solutions to issues arising in public libraries as they enter in the Information Age. On another track, the IFLA, through the aegis of its Latin America and Caribbean Section, the support from the ALP Program,[17] and the efforts of the IFLA Regional Office, headed by Elizabet Ramos de Carvalho, have carried out projectss aimed at the expansion and reinforcement of libraries in the region. Currently, in collaboration with FAIFE, several workshops have been organized with the purpose to orient librarians in the adoption of the *IFLA/UNESCO Manifesto on the internet and its Guidelines*.

CONCLUSIONS

For over two centuries, public libraries in Latin America and the Caribbean have had many ups and downs. This unstable trajectory, notwithstanding, they have been able to adapt to changes and challenges. It would be difficult to corroborate all of its social effects, but it is undeniable that its services have been gradually extended so that reading and access to books and information, and now to the Internet have been made easier for an ever growing segment of the population. Such is the case of libraries pioneering the creation of services devoted to children, young people and adults, rural and indigenous communities, workers and marginalized populations, and visually challenged persons, or recluses. Moreover, there have been efforts for the creation of specific administrative structures to organize and coordinate public libraries, as well as the drafting of relevant legislation and the design of library buildings.

Likewise, these libraries have contributed to the Library Science development in their respective countries, and the most import matter has been the formation of human resources that began with courses in Library Management and later bloomed in establishment of Library Science schools to professionalize the personnel required for the specialized activities in the field. Also, the creation of fellowships and associations was the start point for analysis and debates of relevant issues, to provide forums for sharing experiences, and the promotion and defense of libraries. The first professional journals in the field also find their origins in the creation of these libraries.

---

[17] Several Nordic development agencies, as well as some libraries and librarian associations have provided generous support for carrying out several projects. Funds have been donated by diverse organizations that support library development, being one of them the Swedish International Development Agency.

There is still much to be done in order to guarantee, through supervised policies and actions, that public libraries in Latin America and the Caribbean would not be impacted by the uncertainty of fickle circumstances. These would help us to solve one of the main problems of Latin America and the Caribbean libraries, the unequal distribution of quality and quantity in library and information services. The twenty-first century seems to provide a propitious opportunity for rectifying the errors that have undermined library efforts in the region. We should to seek their revaluation as the ideal medium for achieving social transformation in the road toward the Information Society. Moreover, we must insist that is essential to guarantee a sustained development of the wide access to library and information services and literacy for all.

Bibliography

Asociación de Bibliotecas Nacionales de Iberoamérica (1995) *Historia de las bibliotecas nacionales de Iberoamérica: pasado y presente.* ABINIA / coords. José Moreno de Alba y Elsa M. Ramírez Leyva. México: UNAM; Instituto de Investigaciones Bibliográficas, Centro Universitario de Investigaciones Bibliotecológicas.

Agudo Guevara, Álvaro. (1982). *La biblioteca pública en América Latina, su estado actual y reflexiones en torno a su desarrollo.* París: UNESCO, PGI, UNISIST. (Reunión Regional sobre el estado actual y estratégias de desarrollo de la biblioteca pública en América Latina y el Caribe).

Bailón Albizu, Anahí (1999). *Las bibliotecas públicas de Piura: experiencia y perspectivas.* Lima: Pontificia Universidad Católica del Perú, Departamento de Humanidades. (Bibliotecología e Información; 5).

Bernard, Marie-Annick (1989). *Apuntes sobre la organización y el funcionamiento de las bibliotecas públicas peruanas.* Lima: CONCYTEC; Ausonia.

Campbell Jerez, James. (2007). "El rol de las bibliotecas públicas comunitarias en el desarrollo socio-económico de Nicaragua". *Biblios,* vol. 8, no. 2. [Online] Available: http://eprints.rclis.org/archive/00013224/01/28_00.pdf. Retrieved April 25, 2008.

Castro Aliaga, César (2002). *La biblioteca pública municipal en el Perú: avances y perspectivas.* Lima: Colegio de bibliotecólogos del Perú.

Chávez Campomanes, María Teresa (1969). "La biblioteca pública y la biblioteca escolar". *Anuario de Bibliotecología y Archivología,* vol. 1, 31-43

Checa de Silva, Carmen. (1986). "Las bibliotecas públicas en el Perú". *RIDECAB. Revista de Información y Documentación Educacional,* vol. 7, no. 14, 47-71

Cruzado, Manuel (1890). *Discurso sobre el origen de las bibliotecas públicas existentes en la República Mexicana.* México: Oficina Tip. de la Secretaria de Fomento.

Escamilla G., Gloria. (1969) "La biblioteca pública y sus departamentales". *Anuario de Bibliotecología y Archivología*, vol. 1, 13-29

Espinosa Borges, I. A. (1968). *Problemas bibliotecarios del Uruguay*. Montevideo: Fuentes de Información Uruguaya.

Fernández, Stella Maris (1998). *Situación del sistema bibliotecario argentino: sus falencias, sus aciertos, sus necesidades. Propuestas para solucionar la situación*. Buenos Aires: Sociedad de Investigaciones Bibliotecológicas.

Fernández de Zamora, Rosa María (2001). *Las bibliotecas públicas en México: historia, concepto y realidad*. In: *Memoria del primer Encuentro Internacional sobre Bibliotecas Públicas. Perspectivas en México para el siglo XXI*. México: CONACULTA.

Jaramillo, Orlanda (2005). *La biblioteca pública: una mirada desde su génesis y desarrollo* (2005). Medellín: Universidad de Antioquia, Escuela Interamericana de Bibliotecología.

Jaramillo, Orlanda, Montoya Rios, Monica & Gómez L., Biviana (2004). *Presencia de las bibliotecas públicas en Medellín durante el siglo XX*. Medellín: Universidad de Antioquia, Escuela Interamericana de Bibliotecología.

Lafuente López, Ramiro (1992). *Un mundo poco visible: imprenta y bibliotecas en México durante el siglo XIX*. México: UNAM, CUIB. (Monografías; 14)

Levi, Nadia. (1969). "El servicio de extensión bibliotecaria en la biblioteca pública y la educación de adultos". *Anuario de Bibliotecología y Archivología*, Época 2, vol. 1, 45-58 50

Lovera de Mantellini, Graciela (1987). "El sistema nacional de bibliotecas públicas en Venezuela". *Revista Interamericana de Bibliotecología*, vol. 10, no. 1, 47-63

McCarthy, Cavan M. (1975). *Developing libraries in Brazil*. Metuchen, N.J.: Scarecrow.

Mettini, I.J.L. (1974). *Plan para el desarrollo de las bibliotecas públicas y escolares*. Tucumán: Universidad Nacional de Tucumán: Biblioteca Central.

Miranda, Alice. (2007) *Acerca de la bibliotecología en Costa Rica*. In: *Bibliotecas y Bibliotecología en América Latina y el Caribe: un acercamiento*. México: UNAM, CUIB.

Naveillan Fernández, Teresa (1990). *Sistema Nacional de Bibliotecas Públicas de Chile*. Chile: IFLA.

Oporto Ordóñez, Luis (en prensa). *La biblioteca y archivo histórico del Congreso Nacional de Bolivia. Las bibliotecas a través de la historia*. Bolivia: Fondo Editorial de la Biblioteca y Archivo Histórico del H. Congreso Nacional.

Osorio Romero, Ignacio (1986). *Historia de las bibliotecas novohispanas*. México: SEP, DGB. (Historia de las bibliotecas en México; 1).

Parada, Alejandro E. (2002). *De la biblioteca particular a la biblioteca pública*. Buenos Aires: Instituto de Investigaciones Bibliotecológicas, Facultad de Filosofía y Letras, UBA; Errejotapé.

Parada, Alejandro E (2002) "Crisis en la Argentina: una respuesta desde la historia de las bibliotecas públicas". *Información, cultura y sociedad. Revista del IIB,* no. 6, 7-13.

Quintana Pali, Guadalupe (1988). *Las bibliotecas públicas en México: 1910–1940.* México: SEP, DGB. (Historia de las bibliotecas en México; 3).

Reipert, Herman José (1972). *Historia da biblioteca publica municipal Mario de Andrade.* Sao Paulo: Secretaria de Educacao e Cultura, Departamento de Cultura, Divisao de Bibliotecas.

Rodríguez Gallardo, Adolfo. (2001) *El trabajo de IFLA y ALP en América Latina y el Caribe.* México: IFLA.

Sena Correa, Emilce Noemí. *Las bibliotecas públicas y escolares como espacios de desarrollo de la cultura y la educación. Estudio de caso de Paraguay.* [en línea] Documento, 16. [Online] Available: http://www.febab.org.br/apresen tacao/Textos/Semina rio%20Trabalho%20Emilce%20Sena.doc. Retrieved April 25, 2008.

Servicios bibliotecarios para todos. Conferencia General IFLA (1985) [Chicago]: Hildamar de Rengifo; IFLA.

Suaiden, Emir José. (1987). "Biblioteca publica e comunidade". *Revista Interamericana de Bibliotecología,* vol. 10, no. 1, 33-46.

Suaiden, Emir José. (1980). *Biblioteca publica brasileira: desempenho e perspectivas.* Sao Paulo: LISA, Instituto Nacional do Livro.

Valderrama G. Lucila. (1971). "Cronología esquemática de la Biblioteca Nacional". *Fénix. Revista de la Biblioteca Nacional,* no. 21, 5-16.

Vázquez Mantecón, Carmen. (1987). *Las bibliotecas mexicanas en el siglo XIX.* México: SEP, DGB. (Historia de las bibliotecas en México; 2).

Viciedo Valdés, Miguel. Breve reseña sobre la biblioteca pública en Cuba antes de 1959. [Online] Available: http://bvs.sld.cu/revistas/aci/vol14_1_06/aci10106. htm Retrieved April 24, 2008.

UNIVERSITY LIBRARIES

Filiberto Felipe Martínez-Arellano

Latin-American and the Caribbean university libraries show diverse degrees of development. While it is undeniable that university libraries are the best funded and consequently have better infrastructure and staff than otherlibraries, there are dissimilarities among university libraries in the region. These differences can be ascribed to the diverse university models that have been adopted by countries in the region.

The development of Latin American and Caribbean university libraries occurred according with the colonizer models. Then, there are library systems on several English or Dutch speaking Caribbean islands that followed the organizational and service models of their Anglo-Saxon ancestors, which, in spite of the socio-economics of the region, show greater structural congruence than their Latin American counterparts. Likewise, despite the obvious cultural parallels among Latin-American countries, it is evident that their circumstances vary widely; indeed there are vast differences within the national borders of Latin American and the Caribbean nations. Consequently, one can assert that there is no one library model followed by all countries in the region.

UNIVERSITY LIBRARIES IN LATIN AMERICA AND THE CARIBBEAN

Didriksson (2002) describes the prevailing model of university in Latin America and the Caribbean, which denominates as the "macro-university." He also mentions that despite national and institutional differences between countries in the region, these macro-universities are generally, and from stance of numerous features and indicators, very similar.

Didriksson (2002) points out these similarities can be summarized in five core features as follows:

1. **Size.** These universities have enrollments that often exceed 60 thousand students, an enrollment figure which stands in notable contrast to most any university around the world. Within the region there are several universities of this size, indeed there are universities with enrollments of over 100 thousand or 200 thousand (See table 1). Such is the case, to mention only two, of the *Universidad Nacional Autónoma de Mexico* (UNAM) and the *Universidad de Buenos Aires* (UBA). While, short of the 60 thousand student threshold for "macro" status, there are universities in the region boasting enrollments of 30 to 40 thousand students that fulfill the other following four criteria.

2. **Complexity**: These universities are complex in nature; that is, they uphold an organizational structure that covers the entire gamut of modern knowledge, includ-

ing a wealth of disciplines, majors and specializations at the graduate and under-graduate levels.

3. **Research**: Most of the research of great impact and quality generated in Latin America occurs in these macro-universities.

4. **Public financing**: For the reasons explained above and other ones, they are allocated the bulk of monies budgeted for higher education in their respective countries and are, therefore, public universities in nature.

5. **Historical and cultural role**: These universities hold in their charge important historical and cultural assets, both tangible and intangible, which makes them unique in the regional panorama with respect to their responsibilities in upholding and conserving their respective nations' identity, monuments and symbols, serving as builders of a unique social ethos.

This model, present in most universities in Latin America and the Caribbean, makes university libraries are jointed in *library system* and a *central library*. The university library system centralizes and coordinates processes and services of branch libraries that exist in different faculties and schools along the campus. Additionally, university libraries in Latin America and the Caribbean play an important role in academic activities of students and professors, while also providing a fundamental support for research.

LIBRARY SYSTEMS

The UNAM, one of the most representative universities in the region with the highest enrollments as well, boasts a highly developed library system, being perhaps, unique in Latin America. Its context and features include:

Higher education in Mexico is provided by scholarly universities, technological institutes and universities, and teachers' training colleges. Currently, Mexico has nearly 4,000 higher education institutions, of which 341 are federal, 521 are state institutions, 1,789 are private, and 1, 170 are autonomous. Revealing a decidedly centralized tendency, 25% of these public and private universities are in the Mexico City metropolitan area. Universities such as the UNAM, the *Colegio de México*, the *Instituto Tecnológico de Estudios Tecnológicos de Monterrey (ITESM)*, and the *Instituto Tecnológico Autónomo de México (ITAM)* are among the most prestigious in the country (Saenz Domingo 2008a).

The UNAM offers 73 undergraduate degrees to 259,000 students and carries out more than 50% of the research occurring in this country. In support of its substantial teaching, research, and cultural extension activities, the university enjoys the most highly developed library system in Latin America.

UNAM Library System consists of more than 140 libraries, most of which are on the main university campus, *Ciudad Universitaria,* in Mexico City. Other ones are located at UNAM campuses along the country, and even some ones in foreign countries. The purpose of these libraries is to provide high quality, timely and efficient library and information services to support the UNAM substantive activities: teaching, research, and cultural extension.

The UNAM Library System is coordinated by the General Direction for Libraries, which sets library policies, emits recommendations and impels information products and services to support the development of library branch collections. Additionally, the Direction provides guidelines and oversees collection development and catalog creation, including data base design and management, as well as implementation and maintenance of automated library services. These diverse activities are carried out for the purpose of providing the university community with high quality, efficient library services by means of up-to-date technology.

The staff of the UNAM Library System consist of 2,283 employees, of which 293 (13%) has academic status. The remaining personnel are either administrative or support staff.

Its collection includes 6,106,010 books and 7,438 professional journals. It also contains a collection of 717, 000 dissertations submitted at UNAM schools.

The UNAM Library System is equipped with a set of online catalogues. LIBRUNAM, it is made up of the records of books purchased or donated to the UNAM; SERIUNAM, containing the collection of scientific journals belonging to the UNAM Library System, and other research institutes and higher educations institutions of this country; TESIUNAM, containing the records of UNAM theses, submitted by undergraduate and graduate students, which have been donated to the Central Library. The UNAM library system also has developed the following databases: HELA, a data base of periodicals belonging to the Latin American Periodicals Collection, created in the UNAM in 1975. This data base includes 3,000 titles of periodicals published in Latin America and the Caribbean, as well as journals published by international organizations (Pan-American and Ibero-American); CLASE y PERIODICA, offer summaries of articles, essays, book reviews, bibliographical reviews, briefs, editorials, interviews, statistics and other information published in 1,500 humanities, social science, and science and technology journals in Latin-American and the Caribbean; MAPAMEX, containing the records of map collections from seven libraries within the UNAM Library System and six from other external higher education and research institutions.

Moreover, the UNAM library system has developed a *Digital Library (BIDI UNAM),* whose collection consists of 7,300 online journals, 162 international databases, over 41,000 full text dissertations and approximately 6,000 electronic books. This collection is made up of resources produced by the UNAM, specialized provider resources, and donated and free access resources.

It can be also mentioned that UNAM library system publishes a journal titled, *Biblioteca Universitaria, Revista de la Dirección General de Bibliotecas de la UNAM,* [The University Library, Journal of the UNAM General Direction for Libraries], which serves as a forum for disseminating professional experiences of UNAM librarians. The Direction also leads a program of academic events and another for continuing education that provides courses, as well as training and update activities in the diverse areas of Library and Information Science.

Another important example is the University of Sao Paulo Library System, in Brazil, Rodríguez Gallardo and Amaral (2002) have said that it exhibits a level of development similar to that of the UNAM Library System. Their holdings are considerable and important. In addition to traditional information support media, both library systems boast databases and vast online resources, as well as full-text collections of periodicals, a situation that is more the exception than the rule at libraries throughout the region. In practical terms, these two libraries own all the scientific journals that are relevant to scholarly communities. Each university library system holds a collection of 6,000 title journals, which is not common to find in university libraries, even in developed countries. Additionally, Brazil has developed a national network that allows access to online resources. This network is funded by the federal government through the *Coordenação de Aperfeiçoamento de Pessoal de Ensino Superior (CAPES) do Ministério da Educação* (Coordination Office for the Improvement of Higher Education Personnel of the Ministry of Education).

Notwithstanding the aforementioned features of these university library systems, it is also important to point out that libraries in Latin America and the Caribbean cannot be separated from their respective contexts. These university libraries are not the rule but the exception and they are necessarily manifestations of the particular economic, political, educational and cultural milieus in each Latin American country.

COLLECTIONS AND PERSONNEL

Certainly, the development of university libraries in the region is directly related to the prevailing conditions in each country, which, of course, have influences on the funding these libraries can hope to have allocated to develop their collections and hire personnel. These issues have been among the dominant topics presented and discussed in several forums and papers studying university libraries in the region.

As already discussed, the region has libraries with magnificent collections. In many universities, the number of libraries and the total volumes in the collections that form the library systems are truly impressive (See table 1). However, a critical issue arises with the problem of updating them, which impairs the services designed to support research and teaching. Moreover, the annual increase in the cost of items acquisitions, particularly the cost of scientific journals, restricts many libraries to maintain their collections and to stay abreast of the times by acquiring the latest titles.

As a result, in terms of enrollment numbers, many of the region university libraries are often under-funded and exhibit collections that are behind the times. Likewise, on occasions, the ratio of student/collections is far from the ratios recommended in international standards. Notwithstanding these issues, in recent years, universities have sought alternative sources of funding for improving their library collections, such as fees for entrance exams and donations to cover infrastructure needs. Likewise, it is important to point out that some universities have developed virtual library projects that include electronic resources and full text journals to support research and teaching functions. These virtual libraries are often directly linked into the university web page (Sanz Domingo, 2008).

On another track of ideas, some university libraries are staffed with sufficient and qualified personnel, while there are others that run with minimal operational staff. In several countries, the lack of qualified personnel in LIS working in university libraries is also evident. Moreover, in some universities, administrators place little importance on the need for hiring qualified professionals in LIS.

On the other hand, the number of LIS professionals trained in the region does not meet the demand of these libraries. Rodríguez, Gallardo and Amaral (2002) mention that only in the most developed countries in the region, Brazil and perhaps Colombia, professional librarians staff libraries. In Mexico, the recent trend has been to hire professional librarians, particularly in management positions. Nevertheless, and even when Mexico's university libraries are highly developed, there is a need in many of them to bring professional librarians into their staff.

TECHNICAL SERVICES

In order to provide efficient, effective and high quality library services, libraries have seen the need to organize, classify and catalog their collections. University libraries in Latin America and the Caribbean have been influenced by the cataloging and classification standards of the U.S. Library of Congress. These libraries have found support for their cataloging efforts in the cards distributed by the Library of Congress, the records from its catalogue, the National Union Catalog (NUC), and at the present time, catalog records available online.

In order to avoid the duplication of efforts and costs, cataloging and classification tasks, in most of the university library systems, are carried out by a central office in charge of technical services. Currently, in most university libraries, the Anglo-American Cataloging Rules and Marc format are in use. Likewise, the classification system most commonly used by university libraries in Latin-America and the Caribbean is the Library of Congress Classification. Moreover, the assignment of subject headings has required a process of translation and adaptation of the Library of Congress Subject Headings (LCSH). These translations and adaptations are present in the *Lista de Encabezamientos de Materia de la Biblioteca Nacional de México* (1978) (Subject Heading List for Material of the Mexican National Library); and in the *Lista de Encabezamientos de Materia para Bibliotecas* (LEMB) (Subject Heading List for Library Material), whose first version was published by the OAS in 1967, later republished by the *Instituto Colombiano para el Fomento de la Educación Superior* [Colombian Institute for the Promotion of Higher Education] (1985), and once again by the Luis Arango Library, in Colombia (1998).

Like many other libraries around the world, university libraries in Latin America and the Caribbean carry out cataloging and classification activities using both commercial and locally developed automation systems.

Saenz Domingo (2008a) enumerates the most commonly utilized automation systems used in the university libraries of Mexico, which of course are also used in Latin American and the Caribbean libraries: SIABUC, Aleph, Unicorn/Web CAT, Logicat – Grifos, Alexandria and Altair. According to the information provided by the SIABUC website, this system, which was developed at the University of Colima, is in use in more than 1,500 institutions in Mexico and Latin America. Aleph is in use in ten countries of Latin America. Moreover, Zavala Barrios (2004) mentions that several library catalogues are supported by one of the following systems, Micro Isis or Winisis in its updated versions, Calco System, Aleph, Unicornio, Absys, or Sabini.

Additionally, the use of technology in university library has led to the creation of union catalogues in order to offer information on available resources, both in print and digital formats, which are in a set of libraries. In Argentina, the *Base de Datos Unificada* [Unified Data Base] (http://www.siu.cdu.ai/servicios/bdu/), a prime example of this trend, is a collective catalogue that groups the catalogue records of university and other libraries type across Argentina. This catalogue was created with a collaboration of university libraries and constitutes a qualitative and quantitative improvement in their service.

The website on this database includes the following information: The Unified Data Base is the result of a collective effort of diverse Argentine universities, which saw the benefit of interconnecting their respective catalogues. To date, this database contains almost one million records derived from forty universities and other institutions.

The Unified Data Base resides in the web site of the SIU (http://puelche.siu.edu.ar). It allows users to locate an individual item in any of the member libraries and process the interlibrary loan, if it is a remote library. Searches can be carried out by title, author, ISBN and other access points. Furthermore, these searches can be made in all the libraries registered in the database or restricted to certain individual libraries. At the same time, this system helps to save money, since it allows importation of records generated by the member libraries, using the process known as copy cataloging.

The project was originated in 1998, when the SIU gathered a group of university Rectors who expressed interest in forming such a shared system. A pilot project that included the libraries of the National Universities of Córdoba, Cuyo, Quilmes, Río Cuarto, Sur and the National Teachers' Library was launched. Other universities were incorporated thereafter.

The outlook for the project, on one hand, is to make the Unified Data Base available in MARC on the web site, and on the other, bring it up to date with the collaboration of the member libraries using this format. At the same time, the SIU has developed a distance-training package for the purpose of promoting cataloging in this format. The UNESCO has also collaborated in the development of Isis Marc, a shareware tool used in MARC cataloging.

From its beginnings, the project strove to encourage collaboration and access to information in Argentine universities, while improving library practices and standards. Moreover, the changeover from traditional cataloging systems to the MARC system in the country constitutes clear and concrete progress.

INFORMATION TECHNOLOGIES

University libraries are service entities whose main objective is to support teaching and research programs. Because of the vast amount of information generated at unprecedented rates in every kind of media, in recent years, a new responsibility has been added to the traditional library role, that of information transfer and filtering (Saenz Domingo, 2008). Without a doubt, new information technologies, telecommunications, the use of networks and the computer have also transformed university libraries in Latin America and the Caribbean. The use of information technologies has contributed to the automation of libraries. Moreover as these technologies developed hardware and software costs became increasingly accessible. This transformation process has been so striking that libraries are moving to a concept of "libraries without walls," offering more and more services beyond the library's premises. By way of the Internet, researchers can use online reference resources and the catalogues twenty-four hours a day and from anywhere on the world. Similarly, these technologies have made new library models possible, such as electronic libraries, virtual libraries and digital libraries (Zavala Barrios, 2004).

The web site "Libraries on the Web: Mexican, Central and South American, and Caribbean Libraries" (http://lists.webjunction.org/libweb/CSA_main.html) provides a listing of some of the virtual libraries developed in Latin America and the Caribbean. The following is the mentioned list of countries with the number of virtual libraries as listed on said web site.

Antigua and Barbuda	2
Argentina	15
Bahamas	3
Barbados	1
Bermuda	1
Brazil	15
Chile	11
Colombia	16
Costa Rica	1
Cuba	2
Dominican Republic	2
Ecuador	3
El Salvador	1
Guadeloupe	1
Guatemala	1
Guyana	1
Jamaica	3
Mexico	29
Nicaragua	2
Panama	1
Paraguay	1
Peru	19
Puerto Rico	10
Trinidad and Tobago	4
US Virgin Islands	1
Uruguay	1
Venezuela	3

Furthermore, the web site titled "BIBLIOTECAS DE LAS UNIVERSIDADES LATINOAMERICANAS" (Libraries of Latin-American Universities) (http://www.universia.com.ar/contenidos/bibliotecas/biblatinoamericanas.htm) provides links to the virtual libraries developed in Latin America and the Caribbean universities, including the following:

> Biblioteca Universidad de Sao Paulo
> Sistema de Bibliotecas de la Universidad de Campinas
> Bibliotecas de Brasil – Paraná
> Hemeroteca de la Universidad National de Colombia

Biblioteca Luis Angel Arango
Universidad Nacional de Colombia
Universidad del Valle
Universidad Nacional de Costa Rica
Universidad de Concepción
University of Nuevo Leon
Universidad Regiomontana
Universidad de las Américas – Puebla
Biblioteca de la Universidad Americana
Universidad de Lima
Universidad de Arturo Prat de Iquique
Universidad de Atacama
Universidad de Chile
Universidad de Talca
Fundación Universitaria Luis Amigó
Universidad Nacional de Colombia
Universidad Nacional de Colombia. Sede Medellín
Universidad Nacional de Colombia. Sede Palmira
Corporación Universitaria de Ibagué – CORUNIVERSITARIA
Universidad de los Andes

Additionally, information and communication technologies have been keys to the creation of university library networks. The *Red Interamericana de Conectividad de Bibliotecas Universitarias* (RICBLU) (Inter-American Network of University Libraries Connectivity) is a prime example of these efforts. This network is formed by four universities in four countries from the four regions of the Organización Interamericana Universitaria (OIU) Inter-American University Organization. The main participant members are as follows: Université de Montreal, Canada; Universidad Veracruzana, Mexico; Universidad de Costa Rica; Universidad Nacional de Cuyo Cono Sur, Argentina. The web site of this network provides the following information:

In order to carry out its duties, the RICBLU groups the collaborative resources of 158 libraries from 134 universities in twenty countries distributed over eight regions (Canada, Mexico, Central America, the Caribbean, Colombia, the Andean Region, the Southern Cone and Brazil) of the Inter-Americana University Organization.

The objective of RICBLU is to encourage interconnectivity of the region libraries by creating an inter-American platform to support an electronic network of library documents and information. The construction of a network of this kind will contribute not only to improving teaching and research in regional institutions of higher learning, but also it will allow a more rational use of national and regional resources. The project strives also to facilitate the mechanisms of cooperation between libraries as they confront the challenges imposed by the tasks of automation of processes and digitalization of their respective collections. Additionally, the establishment of this networks aims to strengthen the process of professional development of librarians, administrators and technicians, while broadening the library's ability to provide technical assistance. In both connectivity and training, the RICBLU program targets university library professionals and technicians, head librarians and university administrators, as well as professors, researchers and graduate students from LIS programs.

While there are library systems that offer services by means of cutting edge, automated technology, there are still many in which library services are quite limited. However, Rodriguez Gallardo (1996) points out that, despite the problem they face, in Latin-America the best equipped information management institutions are, in fact, university libraries, largely because they are embedded in an academic context where information is afforded high value. However, in order to offer high quality information storage and retrieval for users, computing equipment is the key. Likewise, an expandable remote-accessed network for transmitting data is also necessary. Above all, libraries must be staffed with duly trained professionals, who can adapt to change and act efficiently as they manage information gathering and delivering.

INFORMATION LITERACY

With reference to the limitations of university libraries at Latin America and the Caribbean, Lau y Cortes Vera (1995) points out the traditional objectives of libraries are to train users and disseminate information by means of the reference services. Unfortunately, as is the case in Mexico, these objectives are only really reached in the large academic libraries. Until recent times, the scarce human resources of libraries were occupied in information processing and circulation tasks, and few at all had robust reference service departments. Currently, many libraries continue to devote much of their staffs to these activities, and even when having reference service personnel on staff, these individuals are often not fully qualified for this work, which implies an educational role.

The university library continues to be a passive cloister where materials in print and electronic supports are accumulated with the hope that self-motivated, interested users will arrive to consult them. In the Mexican sphere, this situation has become a vicious cycle in which the library awaits the client who is unprepared to take advantage of the services and products available. What is even worse, the client is unaware of how to use the information once it has been acquired. The user generally is unaware of the services he can demand in a library, because his teachers are almost as clueless as he or she. If the library does not train users and dis-seminate its services among them, it runs the risk of becoming sorely under-exploited to such a degree that its very existence might be questioned. Confronted with these limitations, the university library has few alternatives in its battle to break out of this vicious cycle characterized by the libraries wealth of information versus the low demand of users. Among the alternatives available is the use of new information technologies and computer networks in order to educate users.

FINAL CONSIDERATIONS

Despite their uneven development, university libraries in Latin American and the Caribbean have become central motors in the information provision and services to students, professors and researchers. While it is true that these libraries exhibit important differences because of their respective socio-economic milieus, all of them are taking strides to improve their collections, services and personnel, as they adopt new information and communication technologies and put these to op-timal use.

REFERENCES

Didriksson T., Axel (2002). *Las macrouniversidades de América Latina y el Caribe.* (http://www.iesalc.unesco.org.ve/pruebaobservatorio/documentos%20pdf/muniv_al_didriksson.pdf) Accessed 23/3/2008.

Lau, Jeús y Cortes Vera, Jesús (1995). *La agenda rezagada: la formación de usuarios de sistemas de información.* Presentada en el Coloquio de Automati-zación de Colima, Noviembre de 1995. (http://www.uacj.mx/dia/Cursos/dhi/docs/doc16.htm) Accessed 23/3/2008.

Rodríguez Gallardo, Adolfo (1996). *La biblioteca universitaria: factor clave de la globalización informativa en América Latina.* In 62nd IFLA General Confer-ence – Conference Proceedings – August 25-31, 1996. (http://www.ifla.org/IV/ifla62/62-roda.htm) Accessed 23/3/2008.

Rodríguez Gallardo, Adolfo & Amaral, Suelí Angelica do (2002). *The role of uni-versity libraries in Latin America in the promotion of democracy and diversity. In 68th IFLA Council and General Conference, August 18-24, 2002* (http://www.ifla.org/IV/ifla68/papers/132-147e.pdf) Accessed 23/3/2008.

Sanz Domingo, Pedro (2008). *Bibliotecas en Iberoamérica.* (http://www.absysnet.com/tema/tema14.html) Accessed, 23/3/2008.

Sanz Domingo, Pedro (2008a). *Bibliotecas universitarias en México.* (http://www.absysnet.com/tema/tema27.html) Accessed 23/3/2008.

Zavala Barrios, Catalina (2004). *Las bibliotecas nacionales de América Latina y su rol en las políticas de información, a través de los avances tecnológicos.* (http://www.inforosocial.net/ponencias/eje01/37.pdf) Accessed 23/3/2008.

Table 1. Libraries of Latin America and the Caribbean

University	Students Number	Year	Libraries	Collection (Volumes number)	Web site
Universidad de Buenos Aires	297,639	2004	18	1,000,000	http://www.sisbi.uba.ar/
Universidad Nacional de Córdoba	114,918	2006	21	150,000	http://www.unc.edu.ar/modules/seccion_portal/index.php?id=272&idsec=14
Universidad Mayor de San Andrés	37,109	2006	25	121,000	http://www.umsa.bo/umsa/app?service=page/Ac0300
Universidad Federal de Río de Janeiro	5,643	2000		1,000,000	http://www.ufrj.br/pr/conteudo_pr.php?sigla=BIBLIOTECA
Universidad de Sao Paulo	65,564	2001	42	6,007,946	http://www.usp.br/sibi/biblioteca/bases_frm.htm
Universidad Nacional de Colombia	243,159	2006	23	800,000	http://www.sinab.unal.edu.co/
Universidad de la Habana	15,980	2006	24	945,000	http://www.dict.uh.cu/historia.asp
Universidad Central del Ecuador	31,663	2006	15	170,000	http://www.uce.edu.ec/biblioteca.php
Universidad de San Carlos de Guatemala	114,000	2006	10	82,881	http://biblos.usac.edu.gt/
Universidad Nacional Autónoma de Honduras	56,077	2006	8	200,000	http://afehc-historia-centroamericana.org/index.php?action=fi_aff&oldid=58&module=enlaces
Universidad Nacional	269,000	2006	142	574,700	http://www.dgbiblio.unam.mx/

University	Students Number	Year	Libraries	Collection (Volumes number)	Web site
Autónoma de México					
Universidad de Panamá	65,225	2006	32	198,064	http://www.sibiup.up.ac.pa/
Universidad Nacional Mayor de San Marcos	34,223	2006	21	450,000	http://sisbib.unmsm.edu.pe/BibVirtual/bi bvirtual.asp
Universidad Autónoma de Santo Domingo	26,040	2006	7	104,441	http://www.uasd.edu.do/html/biblioteca. html
Universidad de la República del Uruguay	59,436	2006	30	100,000	http://www.rau.edu.uy/universidad/bibu ni/
Universidad Central de Venezuela	45,000	2006	84	280,000	http://www.sicht.ucv.ve:8080/bvirtual/
Universidad de Puerto Rico	69,567	2006	14	250,000	http://biblioteca.uprrp.edu/
Universidad de Chile	24,822	2006	19	1,000,200	http://bibliotecas.uchile.cl/

Sources

Didriksson T., Axel. *Las macrouniversidades de América Latina y el Caribe.* Available [Online] Available: http://www.iesalc.unesco.org.ve/pruebaobserva torio/documentos%20pdf/muniv_al_didriksson.pdf) Retrieved April 34, 2008.

The Europa World of Learning 2007. 57th edition. London: Routledge, Taylor & Francis Group, 2006.

SCHOOL LIBRARIES

Mary Giraldo Rengifo
Translation by Filiberto F. Martínez-Arellano

1. INTRODUCTION

The purpose of this document is to offer a panoramic vision of school libraries evolution in Latin America, their trends, the main elements that characterize them, and their development perspectives. The region's most consolidated programs provide the analytical framework for this study. In order to identify the variables involved in adopting a model, studies about the origins of this kind of libraries and European models have been undertaken.

The lack of a national diagnosis on school libraries in the region and time limitations constitute the main obstacles to the analysis and validation of the information obtained. As a result, this chapter should be understood as a starting point to develop future studies about this subject.

2. THE SCHOOL LIBRARY

2.1 Origin of school libraries and current models

In 1749, Benjamin Franklin provided his vision for the Philadelphia Youth Education Academy, asserting that:

> ...must be equipped with a library, with several maps of all countries, globes, mathematical instruments and laboratory equipment for experiments in natural philosophy and mechanics, printing presses of all kinds, prospects, buildings, machines, etc. (Franklin, quoted by Lerner, 1999, p. 198)

That vision originated the concept of school library as different from the public library. Franklin's proposal, however, could not be put into practice because of the political, economic, pedagogic and ideological conditions prevailing in his time, which, moreover, were reflected in the pedagogical model based on the school textbook.

During a great part of the nineteenth century, illiteracy in the United States and Europe was more the rule than the exception. Literacy had not yet been recognized as a universal right.[1] When educational programs were diversified, the interests of students were also awakened to different kinds of works. This new educa-

---

[1] Education as an univerasl right falls under the category of economic, social and cultural rights known as Third Generation Rights. These rights were adopted and presented for signature, ratification and adhesion many years later on December 16 1966 in the United Nations General Assembly, as part of the *International Pact on Economic, Social and Cultural Rights* (Resolution 2200 A (XXI), Articles 13 and 14; according with Article 27, entered in force on January 3 1976)

tional policy contributed to the creation of school libraries that served as an alternative to the sectarian services and reading material offered in Sunday religious schools. With respect to this matter, Henry Barnard, Secretary of Education in Connecticut, stated:

> The school building is the proper place for housing a district library. A library, containing select books, open to teachers, children and adults from the district in general, for reference and reading, complementing the educational resources of schools…Without these books, the instruction provided in schools is useless in practice, and the art of printing is not made available either to the poor or the rich. (Long, quoted by Lerner, 1999, p. 196)

To meet the new demands, services for schools in the United States and Great Britain were provided by public library branches or by means of books loans to teachers to support their use in classes. Gradually, a few school libraries began to appear. The first school librarian was designated in Brooklyn, New York, in 1900, and four years later, the State created the School Library Division in order to promote and supervise library services in elementary schools.

At the end of the World War II, European countries and the United States adopted a new model for the reconstruction that became the social-economic model known as the *Society of Well-Being Model,* based on the consolidation of social capital, equal opportunities, universal literacy and guaranteed access to elementary education. According to this framework, educational institutions in the Great Britain and the United States created their own libraries in order to offer books and other media needed to complement and diversify reading materials that had been limited to textbooks. [2]

With the adoption of didactic approaches espoused by Bruner, the comprehensive educational model based on meaningful learning and the student's construction of knowledge, the Anglo-American school library model, as a *resource center for learning*, gained preeminence in the United Kingdom.

Another European model for school libraries arose in France. An analysis of the school libraries history in France shows that before World War I, libraries were more concerned with preserving books than lending them out or allowing users to consult them. After World War II, as it happened in the United States and the United Kingdom, France moved to renovate and modernize public education. By the 1960s and through the 70s, France was in a position to implement its library models denominated *Library-documentation Centers* for elementary schools, and *Documentation and Information Centers* for secondary schools. These models

---

[2]   In 1749, Benjamin Franklin conceived the idea of a school library with a collection books and other media such as maps and instruments, etc. This vision was complemented by Henry Barnard who advocated greater diversity in book collections. It was not until this period that his ideas were generally materialized.

were based upon the Freinet pedagogical theories, including the student's autonomy as a learner, the diversity of media and information resources, as well as other modern education statements. The most important achievements of the French library model were:

> The formation of a well rounded reader and the utilization of diverse media and formats, didactic approaches and designs to work with students in libraries, though admittedly too concerned with the formation of users without regard for didactic specialties and, because of this, valid only in elementary schools, without incidence on pedagogical uses of libraries in the curricular planning of teachers. (Jordí, 1998, Couet, 1990, quoted by Castán, 2002, p.41).

Other European countries with decentralized systems formulated a third model of library known as the *hybrid model of public and school library.* For example, a small segment of colleges and schools in Germany equipped with adequate libraries has a two-fold function, both as school library and as a branch of the municipal public library. In other cases, the school library offers services to several schools. In Sweden, a country with a long tradition of libraries, there are as many of these hybrid libraries as there are in Germany as well.

According to the results of several diagnosis indicators from 2002, 2004 and 2005, schools in Spain are not equipped with genuine school libraries. These libraries, when they exist, rely on volunteers from the teachers or personnel with reduced hours for operation. The lack of a genuine integration of the library with curricular objectives and a lack of recognition of their pedagogical role by teaching staff are two of the major obstacles that characterize Spain's school libraries. Classroom and departmental libraries have provided scant contributions to the pedagogical project.

> Without a plan or a centralized management model, the services offered by libraries in the classroom are fragmentary and uncoordinated. For these reasons, the educational community has been unable to use resources on activities in the field of reading, and information and learning. (Mechesi 2005: 304)

In contrast to what happened in the United Kingdom, the comprehensive educational model implemented in Spain in the decade of the 1990s did not produce similar effects, and libraries were not able to become strategic pedagogical resources.[3] Over the last few years, however, to comply with the European Union Directive, Spain has intensified strategies to accelerate socio-cultural and educational changes. In this context, education policy strives to bring into line the dis-

---

[3] Spain's dictatorship created structural changes that were difficult to overcome in the short term.

tinct approaches that vary from region to region. Moreover, it attempts to establish a legal framework that guarantees the inclusion of school libraries in the educational system, and as part of the broader vision of the Spanish Library System. Furthermore, the mandatory existence of these libraries in all school centers gives them a prominent role in the curricular planning.

In other regions of the world, as in the Soviet Union, the establishment of school libraries, and the improvement of the existing ones, was carried out in 1957 according to political ideology that supports citizen formation within the new social order.

In most of the African, Asian and Latin-American nations, school library services have been sorely deficient because of structural issues. Education in these nations had been reserved for social elites, and, recently, efforts have been done to broaden the reach of education although they have not yet achieved the impact hoped for, due to political, economic, cultural and social obstacles.

To sum up, this historical overview allows us to infer that it is not enough to simply adopt a pedagogical model in order to implement school libraries as a strategic pedagogical resource. Structural factors arising from the political, ideological, cultural, and socio-economic settings can exercise considerable sway in the definition of a particular library model.

With regard to the adoption of models, Europe has seen wide acceptance of the Anglo-American model among librarians and teachers. However, this is not a universal model. The hybrid model, adopted as an intermediate step when resources are limited, led to issues regarding the respective identities, duties and missions of public libraries versus school libraries, which has resulted in its rejection by teachers.

2.2. Trends in school libraries in Latin America

The development of libraries in Latin America has followed a pattern similar to the one followed in Europe. Early on, during the conservative governments that followed independence until the middle of the nineteenth century, education was the responsibility of the family and the church. Schools, using a single textbook, were reserved for the elite. Religious orders from Europe founded the first universities or "colleges," many of which had libraries.

As a consequence of the political changes occurring at the turn of the century, governments with a liberal orientation, so called "radicals," began to found the first public or popular libraries. For example, in the nineteenth century in Colombia, General Francisco de Paula Santander founded the first public libraries, and in Argentina, Domingo Faustino Sarmiento established the Comisión Nacional de Bibliotecas Públicas (CONABIP) National Popular Libraries Commission to promote the creation and development of popular libraries constituted by private associations.

In Mexico, the first references to school libraries in Latin America are found in 1921, when the Education Minister, José Vasconcelos, created the Directorate for Popular Libraries and – within the framework of a campaign to eradicate illiteracy – promoted the founding of diverse types of libraries: popular and itinerant libraries, worker associations and unions libraries, as well as school libraries.

As a national information policy strategy and in response to UNESCO initiatives and those from other international and regional organizations, the 1970s saw the formation of the National Information System. These became regional nodes of the Unisit Program and the UNESCO General Information Program. The OAS, the CERLALC, and the education ministers contributed to the creation of national and regional school library networks. This is especially evident in Venezuela, Colombia, Costa Rica, Chile and Peru, where collaboration resulted in the constitution of the *Proyecto Multinacional de Bibliotecas Escolares* (1979-1981) [Multinational School Libraries Project], which was sponsored by the OAS. This and other projects, such as the *Modelo flexible para un Sistema Nacional de Bibliotecas escolares* [Flexible Model for a National School Library System], focused on the development of methodologies and cooperative strategies, regional cooperation, training programs and support materials for school libraries.

The decade of the 1980s saw the implementation of school, departmental and municipal libraries networks in various countries, including Venezuela and Colombia, in accord with the *hybrid model of the school-public library.* In international conferences in the 1990s, Venezuela and Chile continued to lead the discussions surrounding the issues of school libraries. In Colombia, the neo-liberal political currents promoted reforms of the concept of the State, which led directly to the establishment of school libraries and the position of school librarian.

The year 2004 saw the emergence of *Plan Iberoamericano de Lectura – Ilimita* [Ibero-American Reading Plan – Unlimited] from an Ibero-American Summit, under the CERLALC and the OIS coordination. The objective of this plan was to promote the creation of reading societies by means of diverse strategies and alliances of private, civic and public spheres. One of its central achievements was the elaboration and publication of the *Agenda de Políticas Públicas de Lectura* [Agenda of Public Policy on Reading], which can serve as a guide for LatinAmerican governments in the drafting of public policy regarding reading. The Agenda posits ten priorities, among which are the creation and update of public and school libraries.

In recent years, CERLALC has continued carrying out diverse actions to promote the creation of school libraries, including virtual forums, meetings, and surveys of school librarians and education ministers of several Latin-American countries. These activities help to complete the picture about the status of school libraries in Argentina, Chile, Colombia, Costa Rica, Mexico, Brazil and Spain.

Among the findings of these surveys, it is the identification of important developments in the consolidation of national programs for school libraries in Argentina and Chile. In the first country, their coordination is overseen by the Teacher's National Library, which has made considerable progress in the field of standards. The 2006 Education Law compels education institutions to implement school libraries staffed by either teachers or professional librarians. Likewise, novel strategies, such as learning communities, have been developed. In Chile, the program coordinated by the Ministry of Education has consolidated a resource center learning model and developed a modular instruction package for the formation of students in the optimal use of information and the library itself. The library is managed by interdisciplinary work teams made up of teachers and librarians, an operative model that has allowed for greater articulation with educational projects and curricular goals. Other countries, notably Mexico through its Secretariat of Public Education and Brazil by the way of the Education Ministry, have taken important strides as well, especially with regard to providing collections to schools.

Other local initiatives include the *Red Distrital de Bibliotecas Escolares de Bogotá* (Colombia) [District Network of School Libraries in Bogotá], coordinated by the Secretariat of Education, which is posited as a collaborative strategy to implement the district's reading and writing policy. To this end, programs have been developed to train administrators, teachers, librarians and students.

In many countries of the region, education is no longer a monopoly of the state. Many private educational institutions have school libraries with quality services matched to the curricula. These libraries often promote collaborative activities involving students, teachers, administrators, librarians and parents. In the remaining school libraries, where they exist, the hybrid model prevails. These libraries often resemble children or youth libraries with story time and other animated activities as their central activity, and are, therefore, not exploited by teachers for pedagogical ends, suggesting that they are unaware of this library potential, or because they are entrenched in traditional teaching models based upon the textbook. This situation creates a disconnection between the work carried out by classroom teacher to promote learning skills and the mission of the library.

A very narrow idea regarding reading continues to plague the region. Despite the efforts of libraries to promote critical thinking and reading skills, other abilities, such as search and research skills, and evaluation and critical uses of information derived from diverse supports, media and formats seem to be completely absent. It is not enough, therefore, to have diverse current collections. The training of teachers and school librarians in the pedagogical uses of information in meaningful contexts poses a great challenge to libraries.

2.3. The school library in the education system context in Latin-America

In many of the Latin America countries, the education system is in a disarticulated stage, in which vacuums, insufficiencies and deficiencies in one part of the systems have repercussions in others.

In practical terms, the ideal of universal education is an unfulfilled promise in many countries, even when speaking of the elementary grades.[4] Indeed, data on illiteracy and functional illiteracy show that the educational gap continues to widen through out Latin-America.[5]

A comparison of higher education policy with school system policy brings several important differences into relief. The most significant is the distinct social value afforded to the library in each vision. In the university sphere, it plays a central role in the university accreditation and the quality of education offered. The university community values the library as an educational asset where plurality and diversity are possible. Likewise, it is considered as an important element of the Center for Learning and Research Resources. On the other hand, school libraries play only a marginal role in the classroom, and, therefore, receive scant attention in national curriculum policy, official education standards and institutional planning. These disparities are evident in the inadequate budgets allocated to school libraries, the lack of qualified librarians, and other material or equipment that encumber the library mission.

Within the new context of the Information Society, the distinct value afforded to reading and knowledge at each level of the educational system can serve as a working hypothesis for understanding without denying their interdependency and the growing gap between the components of the education system. That is, the media is confused with the ends, although it is understood that skills must be de-

---

[4] The *Committee on Economic, Social y Cultural Rights*, approved the *General Observation N° 11 of the* Resolution 2200 A (XXI), of December 16 1966 known as the *International Pact on Economic, Social and Cultural Rights*, with regard to Article 14, which addresses elementary education. *The Committee knows that for millions of people throughout the world, the enjoyment of the right to an education is still a remote objective. Moreover, in many cases, this objective is less and less real. The Committee is also aware of the extraordinary structural obstacles and impediments of other nature that stand in the way of the full application of Article 13 in many signatory States.*

[5] According with the OIS, there are 34 million persons who are totally illiterate and 110 million who are functionally illiterate among young people and adults in Ibero-America, which is to say that 40% of the population has not finished the sixth grade. With regard to total illiteracy, Cuba, Venezuela, Spain, Argentina and Uruguay have the lowest incidence of illiteracy, at levels below 3%; Chile, Paraguay and Costa Rica fall between 4 and 5.13%; Panama, Mexico and Colombia stand at between 7.6% and 8.5%, while the rest of the region's countries stand over 8.5%. With regard to functional illiteracy, only Cuba stand below 3% (2.96%); Panama , Peru , Uruguay, Argentina, Mexico and Colombia are below 15%; the Dominican Republic, Costa Rica, Guatemala, Ecuador and Chile fall between 15 and 21%; Brazil and Paraguay stand between el 21 and 30%; Bolivia, Nicaragua and El Salvador fall between 35 and 42 %, y and Honduras exhibits 58%. These data allow the conclusion that functional illiteracy is dramatic in most countries including those of the Southern Cone which tally level above 10% of the population.

veloped in stages during the school years, from the early laying of foundations exploiting the child innate curiosity, through the creation of study habits, research and critical thinking skills, to the unfolding of critical reflection, all of which are intimately tied to the development of reading skills.

2.4 Perspectives for school libraries in Latin-America

The Information and Knowledge Society offers vast opportunities for school libraries, but only if they are recognized as strategic educational resources in education policy and budget planning efforts, as well as a social space for education integrated in a curricular project. It is vital that school leadership develop a vision of the library role in the formation of autonomous life-long learners who are capable of using critically information derived from diverse media and supports. In this new learning model, the processes of analysis and reflection are vital.

The teacher, therefore, must become a planner in the education process and a facilitator of the learning process that rests on interactive and cooperative methodologies. The school librarian also must assume a new role as and "educational agent. Then, it is not only enough to rely merely on more resources, whether these are technological in nature or relayed to the library's physical installations, to carry out his/her mission. Changes in attitude, skills and knowledge are the keys to adapting to the new educational settings. Collaboration with other professionals is fundamental in planning and implementation of reading-based curricular projects and information activities. These new competences shall require a two-fold approach to the formation of librarians, who must be both teacher and librarian, engaged in constant professional development in order to face the changes to come in the twenty-first century. Also, in order to upgrade, library and information services will require considerable investments in library and information services improvement

The ideological orientation underlying educational policy can pose both threats and challenges to school libraries. An idealized vision of information and communication technologies, seeing them as a panacea for all the educational system's current woes, might lead to a replacement of librarians and libraries with the tutor and digital libraries. This scenario appeals to the cyber-myth of an educational utopia. On the other hand, the defenders of the humanist approach see schools as a space for edifying citizens, a place where knowledge and culture are transmitted from generation to generation, in which the school role is as an instrument of democratization of knowledge and the development of critical and reflexive thinking with regard to reality. For these proponents, the school as a social system must reform from within, innovating both methods and organization. Under this view, the library can be seen as pure potentiality, provided it assumes the great challenge of transforming its practices in order to adapt to this new environment characterized by incertitude. The task is not an easy one.

Which model is the one for Latin America? Should all Latin-American nations adopt the same model? Do these nations offer the conditions for making a choice? There are no easy answers. From, the international panorama, one can infer that there is no one model of the school library to fit all countries. The model put forth must be a function of underlying political, ideological, social, cultural, technological and economic factors that determine the promotion or suppression of school library projects. Furthermore, one must take into account the relative coherence of public policy orientation regarding education and the pedagogical model of the respective school systems.

A pedagogical resource is not a magic wand; even the best of libraries cannot change the nature, functions and traditions of the school. (Castán, 2002, p.42)

Diagnostic studies of the current conditions of school libraries are the logical starting points. These studies can help reveal the distinct socio-cultural, political and educational issues of our respective countries and lead ultimately to an informed designation of a model. As far as possible, these diagnostics must examine the diverse players who intervene in the creation and operational dynamics of libraries, notably administrators, librarians, students and teachers. New criteria must be brought to bear in assessment, especially with regard to identifying library practices that are effective in promoting the fulfillment of the library mission as a pedagogical resource, including evaluations of the use of information technology by students and teachers.

These results might invite us to explore and reinvent hybrid model that may be valid in certain situations.

Bibliography

Area Moreira, Manuel (2005). *La educación en el laberinto tecnológico.* Barcelona: Ediciones Octaedro, 219.

Camacho Espinosa, José Antonio (2004). *La biblioteca escolar en España: pasado, presente.. y un modelo para el futuro.* Madrid: Ediciones de La Torre, 252 p.

Castán, Guillermo (2002). *Las bibliotecas escolares: Soñar, pensar, hacer.* Sevilla: Diada Editorial, 189.

Castrillón, Silvia (1982). *Modelo flexible para un sistema nacional de bibliotecas escolares.* Bogotá: Ministerio de Educación: OEA, 1982.

Cerlalc – OEI 2004). *Agenda de políticas públicas de lectura.* Bogotá: Cerlalc, 89 p.

Cerlalc 20078). *Por las bibliotecas escolares de Iberoamérica.* Bogotá: Cerlalc, 56 p.

Coloquio Internacional de Bibliotecarios (12°. 2005, Guadalajara) (2006). *La biblioteca: centro de recursos para el aprendizaje y la investigación. Memorias.* Guadalajara: Universidad de Guadalajara, 289.

Lerner, Fred (1999). *Historia de las bibliotecas del mundo: desde la invención de la escritura hasta la era de la computación.* Tr. Inés Frid. Buenos Aires: Ed. Troquel, 283.

Naciones Unidas (1999). *Aplicación del Pacto Internacional de Derechos Económicos, Sociales y Culturales.* [Online] Available: http://www.unhchr.ch/tbs/doc.nsf/(Symbol)/E.C.12.1999.10.Sp?OpenDocument. Retrieved April 25, 2008.

Zuluaga Garcés, Olga Lucía (2004). *Modernización de lo sistemas educativos iberoamericanos Siglo XX.* Bogotá: Cooperativa Editorial Magisterio, 357.

LIS EDUCATION

Adolfo Rodríguez Gallardo

EDUCATIONAL SYSTEM IN LATIN AMERICA

Educational systems of most of the countries included in this chapter are different from the ones of Puerto Rico and Jamaica. In almost all Hispanic-Portuguese countries, the system includes an elementary school of six years, a secondary school of three years, and post-secondary or high school studies preceding college, also of three years.

The next level is professional or tertiary-undergraduate studies. These schools do not provide general studies, unlike Anglo-Saxon countries. Furthermore, our professional schools focus on technical training, and their structure mirrors Spanish and Portuguese schools. Thus, educational systems in Latin America differ from other places, since the first professional educational level are tertiary-undergraduate studies, which takes four or five years, at a tertiary or higher level. Professional practitioners of library science are trained at this level. Next in the system is the level of tertiary-graduate studies, which may take one or, most frequently, two years. As for tertiary-undergraduate studies, this level requires the elaboration of a final work or dissertation to obtain the degree.

INSTITUTIONS AND PROGRAMS

Let's begin by comparing the first and second edition of the directory compiled by Fang and Nauta (1985) and Fang, Stueart and Tuamsuk (1995), with the help of Figure 1.

Figure 1. Comparison Between the First and Second Edition of the Works published by Josephine Riss Fang (1985, 1995)

Country	1985 Schools (A)	1985 Schools with Known Programs (X)	1995 Schools (B)	1995 Schools with Known Programs (Y)	Difference Between Schools (B-A)	Difference Between Schools Having Known Programs (Y-X)
Argentina	13	13	9	9	-4	-4
Bolivia	1	1	1	1		
Brazil	31	31	13	13	-18	-18
Chile	1	1	1	1		
Colombia	4	4	3	3	-1	-1
Costa Rica	1	1	2	1	1	
Cuba	1	1	1	1		
Ecuador			2		2	
El Salvador	1	1	1	1		

	1985	1985	1995	1995		
Country	Schools (A)	Schools with Known Programs (X)	Schools (B)	Schools with Known Programs (Y)	Difference Between Schools (B-A)	Difference Between Schools Having Known Programs (Y-X)
Guatemala	1	1	1	1		
Jamaica	1	1	1	1		
Mexico	7	5	4	4	-3	-1
Nicaragua	1	1			-1	-1
Panama	1	1	1	1		
Paraguay	1	1	1	1		
Peru	2	2	1	1	-1	-1
Puerto Rico	1	1	1	1		
Uruguay	1	1	1	1		
Venezuela	2	2	3	2	1	
Total	**71**	**69**	**47**	**43**	**-24**	**-26**

Source: Josephine Riss Fang and Paul Nauta, *International guide to library and information science education*, (München ; New York : K. G. Saur, 1985). Josephine Riss Fang, Robert D. Stueart and Kulthida Tuamsuk, *World guide to library archive and information science education,* 2nd rev. and enlarged edition (München ; New Providence : K. G. Saur, 1995).

At a first glance, there is a reduction of the number of schools, in only one decade of both schools (34%) and schools with known programs (38%) is striking; at a second glance, we find the case of Ecuador, a country that was not included in the first edition, we note the closing of the only school existing in Nicaragua and that Costa Rica opened a new one whose program is unknown. In general, this comparison suggests that out of 71 schools in 1985 only 47 were working in 1995, and that the 69 schools with known programs were reduced to 43 in the same period. Also, it should be noted that the countries with most schools and programs are Argentina and Brazil and that, from all the countries in Latin America and the Caribbean, only 18 do provide formal study programs in library science.

Taking into consideration the extent of the work performed by the editors of the above-mentioned study, as well as the difficulties and disadvantages inherent in its conformation, we deemed it reasonable to analyze the data provided by Maris and Giunti on study plans in Iberoamerica on Figure 2.

Figure 2 Schools and Schools with Known Programs by Maris y Giunti (1999)

Country	Schools	Schools with Known Programs
Argentina	26	26
Bolivia	1	1
Brazil	31	18
Chile	2	2
Colombia	4	4
Costa Rica	3	3
El Salvador	1	1
Guatemala	1	1
Mexico	8	8
Panama	1	1
Paraguay	1	1
Peru	2	2
Puerto Rico	2	2
Dominican Republic	2	2
Uruguay	1	1
Venezuela	2	2
Total	**88**	**75**

Source: Estella Maris Fernández and Graciela María Giunti, *Planes de estudio de las escuelas de bibliotecología, archivología y museología de Iberoamérica* (Buenos Aires: Sociedad de Investigaciones Bibliotecológicas ; IFLA, Programa Avance para el Desarrollo de la Bibliotecología en el Tercer Mundo, 1999).

Although the work is limited to Iberoamerica, Maris and Giunti provide data on 16 countries, with a total of 88 institutions, from which 75 have known study programs; the difference observed between schools and programs in the case of Brazil results from the lack of information about the programs for 13 schools, although it is known that they offer some kind of teaching regarding library science. However, this confirms that most of the programs do concentrate in Argentina and Brazil.

According to the data gathered by Maris, at the end of the last century Latin America had 88 institutions teaching library science (17 and 41 additional institutions to the ones identified in the first and second edition, respectively, of Fang's directory). In addition to the differences regarding the number of schools, we must point out that this source does not provide information related to Cuba, Ecuador y Jamaica, but it does so for Dominican Republic.

Regarding programs, information was available for 75 schools (6 and 32 additional schools in Fang and Nauta (1985) and Fang, Stueart and Tuamsuk (1995)).

To identify the variables implicated in Fang's and Maris' results regarding the number of schools and programs is an enormous task. However, if we take a chronological approach considering the establishment date of schools, we may determine whether differences are due to a recent change in educational systems.

Almost all schools have been established starting from the decade of seventies and in general after the Second World War. Thus, the influence of the UNESCO may have played an important role, as well as its programs to promote libraries and library science teaching.

Although the data identified so far is illustrative in nature, it does not provide an answer to our concern of knowing with at least some certitude the number of library science schools in Latin America and the Caribbean. We therefore deemed pertinent to use directories of schools available in Internet.

As it can be seen, the data related to the number of schools operating in Latin America and the Caribbean widely differs from one source to another. However, Maris and Giunti (1999) are outstanding since they have identified 88 schools, followed by the Associaçao Brasileira de Educaçao em Ciencia da Informaçao with a total of 79 schools, the Fang and Nauta's *International Guide to Library and Information Science Education* (1985) with 71, and the Directory on Institutions on Library and Information Science in Iberoamerica and the Caribbean (INFO LAC) with 51 schools. Because there was not enough information about the programs' levels on the Web's directories, we consider appropriate to establish that kind of comparison only between Fang Fang and Nauta (1985) and Fang, Stueart and Tuamsuk (1995), and Maris and Giunti (1999).

Later we will detail the available data to better understand the characteristics of library science teaching in Latin America and the Caribbean. It must be noted that when I refer only to Latin America and not to the Caribbean, I am talking about the nations with a Hispanic-Portuguese heritage.

Since it is difficult to establish equivalences without previously considering common parameters, to better classify and understand educational systems, in this work we will use the division established by the UNESCO and used by Josephine Riss Fang and Paul Nauta in their work *International Guide to Library and Information Science Education* (1985). In that work they state that elementary school takes six years and that in most Latin-American countries it is known as educación *primaria (elementary school)*, which is followed by a higher level of three years referred to as *secundaria (secondary school)*, which is in turn followed by a level of three years called *bachillerato* (post-secondary studies) or high-school.

The next level is *licenciatura* (tertiary-undergraduate studies), which takes between four and five years. In some cases, a degree is granted after three years in this level, which certifies the student as technician or "Bachiller in Library Science", but these cases are not acknowledged as professionals of Library Science, and they cannot continue to postgraduate levels, which are *maestría* (tertiary-graduate studies) which takes from one to two years and, finally, *doctorado* (terti-ary-postgraduate studies), which may take from three to five years.

We have used two grades for short programs for which we have information: One refers to a level of *capacitación* (training) which corresponds to programs that take less than one year, while the other refers to the level of *técnico* (techni-cian), for those programs that last two years and often do not require post-secondary studies.

The depth of library science training activities varies to a great extent. There are courses from few hours to the postgraduate levels: Tertiary-graduate studies and tertiary-postgraduate studies, including also intermediate options. The most popu-lar level is tertiary-undergraduate studies, which covers from 40 to 69% of all teaching activities. The highest levels of tertiary-graduate studies and tertiary-postgraduate studies are the ones with the smallest number of programs. There are only five institutions providing tertiary-postgraduate studies in all Latin America and none in the Caribbean. This may explain the low production of books and pa-pers on basic or methodological topics, since most of the production in Latin America and the Caribbean refers to experiences related to the improvement of li-brary services and organization.

Teaching levels

The library education begins in the twentieth century, and although these efforts did not mature in some countries, in others they found fertile ground. Anyhow, the oldest school of Latin America is the *Federaçao das Escolas Federais Isoladas do Estado de Rio de Janeiro (FEFIER) Centro de Ciencias de Informaçao, Curso de Biblioteconomia e Documentaçao* founded in 1910 (Riss 1985:76-77), currently Universidade do Rio de Janeiro, which since then has been working regularly. At the beginning of the last century, the European trend could be perceived more than that of any other region, because the Bibliographic Institute of Brussels summoned many of the empiric librarians of the continent to its meetings reaching a sensitive influence on them. When these librarians went back to their countries, they pro-moted the preparation of national bibliographies, fostering the establishment of li-brary science schools, and started efforts or programs, although sometimes not permanently, trying to train personnel working in libraries.

The level of professional education is not the only one being performed on Latin America. It is highly frequent that the educational efforts are made at lower levels, like these courses in a few training, or programs covering less than two years and for which it is not necessary to have finished post-secondary school (12 years of schooling).

Possibly, the best known and most complete source to date regarding the educa-tion levels is the work of Maris and Giunti, so we analyzed this information by means of Figure 3.

Figure 3. Level of library science studies according to Maris and Giaunti (1999)

Country	Total programs	Technical (Less than 3 years)	Post-secondary	Tertiary undergraduate	Tertiary graduate	Tertiary (post-graduate)
Argentina	56	16	28	7	3	2
Bolivia	2		1	1		
Brazil	24			17	5	2
Chile	4			2	2	
Colombia	5	1		4		
Costa Rica	6	1		4	1	
Dominican Republic	3	2		1		
El Salvador	1		1			
Guatemala	1			1		
Mexico	13	2		7	3	1
Panama	1			1		
Paraguay	2	1		1		
Peru	5		2	2	1	
Puerto Rico	2				2	
Uruguay	1			1		
Venezuela	2			2		
Total	**128** **(100%)**	**23** **(18%)**	**32** **(25%)**	**51** **(40%)**	**17** **(13%)**	**5** **(4%)**

Source: Estella Maris Fernández and Graciela María Giunti, *Planes de estudio de las Escuelas de Bibliotecología, Archivología y Museología de Iberoamérica* (Buenos Aires : Sociedad de Investigaciones Bibliotecológicas; Progreso de la Bibliotecología en el Tercer Mundo ALP/IFLA, 1999.)

Now, we are going to analyze the characteristics of the different library science education levels, as well as some factors conditioning them. The elements are of different origin and nature, but its analysis would allows us to understand the characteristics of each level on which specialty studies are offered.

Training

As it may be seen with this classification of the programs by levels, 18% corresponds to the technical level, although it is impossible to clearly define if they are after 12 years of schooling or included in them. These studies do not grant a university title but offer a diploma at the conclusion of courses. In some countries it is possible to continue up to a higher level, the Bachelor's degree, after having concluded technical post-secondary school, in others this is a terminal level and the student is expected to be trained as a specialized technician in the field of library science.

These courses have remedial character, because they pretend to train people working in libraries and do not have the knowledge required for an appropriate performance. The interest is focused on the work performed by the personnel is efficient, but it does not pretend to offer disciplinary bases to students, only practical knowledge helping them to improve their work.

Technical post-secondary school

This level is characterized by covering three years of study; we do not know if previous post-secondary school (twelve years) is required in all cases, or if at the same time of studying library science, preparatory studies of higher education are carried out. It is possible that in some countries, the studies are equivalent to a professional level, but it is almost impossible to know it given the variety of differences that have been established between the teaching systems in Latin America. For practical purposes and in order to explain congruently and bases on the number of schooling years, we decided to qualify this level of studies that includes three years dedicated to library science as post-secondary school.

There still has to be offered an explanation why this level of studies is so popular on the continent, and based on which reasons the countries and educational institutions promote them, instead of struggling why the library science education is made on professional level, as it happens with many other disciplines.

A possible explanation why there are so many programs at this level, 25% of the programs last for three years, is that Latin America continues having a serious problem regarding the social acknowledgement of professionals in library science. Maybe it is considered that the librarian activity requires personnel trained in a certain way, but not necessary at professional level.

Another possible explanation is that teachers and students are satisfied with this level of studies and do not feel the need to continuing at a professional level, since this would imply another years of study, thus extending post-secondary school. Likewise, the fact that in some countries it has been fostered that certain kind of studies not necessarily conduce to professional studies, but that medium technicians shall be trained to become included early on the labor market, may have an influence.

Whichever is the right explanation, what is important is that 43 % of all programs is among training programs and those we called post-secondary school. While, as we will see later, the highest levels of the educational pyramid include very little programs.

It has to be pointed out that the country with the major number of technical and post-secondary school programs is Argentina, having 44 of a total of 55; that is, 80% of the studies performed on these levels on the continent are made in that country.

Tertiary undergraduate

This level is the one with the most programs and the most common of the Latin American professional studies since it includes a total of 51 programs throughout Latin America (40% of all efforts); that is, the main part of the professional education. The studies of Bachelor's degree require 12 years of previous studies, what implies the conclusion of post-secondary school. The studies usually have a duration of four years, but in some cases they extend to five. It is common that a research paper or a thesis are demanded in order to conclude the education, although in some schools they have replaced it with upper level courses, reports and others. The country with the major number of programs at that level is Brazil offering almost a third of all programs with Bachelor's degree; Argentina and Mexico with seven programs each sum up to 28% of the total. Within the scheme of higher education in Latin America, the Bachelor's degree level is the first professionalizing degree or that conduces to professional exercise of a discipline, from this point of view it is equivalent to the Master's degree which is usual in Anglo-Saxon countries, where the student, after reaching this level, is ready for professional service.

A great influence on the library science education at Bachelor's degree level was represented by the holding of the so-called Mesas de Medellín, Colombia, which in several occasions assembled educating expert groups in Latin America sponsored by the Organización de Estados Americanos (OEA), who discussed and formulated a course of study ideal for the continent. Although not all schools followed faithfully the recommendations, the major part of the study programs reflected the Medellín recommendations. What made them abandon that scheme, slightly conventional, was possibly the incorporation of technology in the study plans and programs. With this incorporation, the influence of Anglo-Saxon library science increased and the library science schools have followed, particularly, the US teaching schemes. What has characterized schools on the continent is having kept the library science heritage of previous years, but even though it is true that the course contents have changed, very few library science schools have undergone a change as dramatic as the one that occurred in US schools, in which even the name library and library science have disappeared in order to give rise to the name Information Science.

Post-graduate Master's degree

This educational level is relatively new in Latin America and the Caribbean. In the latter, it appeared in Puerto Rico in 1969 and in Jamaica in 1971. In the rest of Latin America, it opened on different dates, but all of them at the end of the sixties or at the beginning of the seventies. This level requires 16 or 17 years of previous schooling. The Master's degree is concluded, in Puerto Rico and Jamaica, after two years and in Latin American countries it may be somewhat longer, but while education has a mainly professional character in the first two countries, in the others it is an initiation to research and to methodological and epistemological studies. Thus, for graduation purposes a more profound and better-documented and founded research product than the one presented in the Bachelor's degree is expected. It may be affirmed that all education made on the area is part time, because the students have to work and the possibility to obtain a scholarship allowing them to dedicate full time to their studies is remote; relatives are almost always those who have to sustain the studies.

In some library science schools, it is possible that students get enrolled coming from other fields, but the majority are graduates in the specialty. When students from different fields are accepted, they are requested to course a series of courses considered as pre-requirement to enter the Master's degree level. These subjects may vary from one single course up to several.

According to data available to us, in Latin America and the Caribbean there are 17 programs representing 13% of the total of programs in the area. Almost all of these programs require a research showing the disciplinary education of the student for graduation.

Post-graduate Doctorate

This level is the one with less programs of all study levels imparted in Latin America and the Caribbean, representing only 4% of the total. Of the whole of these programs, two of them are imparted in Brazil, two more in Argentina (although the degree is not exactly in library science but in education, because the schools are an integral part of a higher instance in the education area) and, the most recent of all, in Mexico. The number of students is small and of teachers too, because in order to give classes at this level a doctor's degree is required, which in most of the cases was obtained abroad or in other subjects in the own country by means of thesis papers related to library science and information.

On Latin America, this level of education is very new, some of the doctors who recently obtained their degree, and reside and work in Latin America, have received their degree at foreign universities in the US, Great Britain and, more recently, in Spain where a Master's degree is not required in order to study and obtain the Doctorate.

There are two options to obtain the doctorate degree: one in which the student takes several subjects and which may take up to two years, and has to be concluded with a thesis showing education and ability to perform research work independently. The other, the one applied in Mexico, allows the student to be admitted to perform research with the help of a tutorial committee, dedicating himself for at least three years and not more than five years to the completion of his research. In this modality, the student only has to take and pass some subjects if the main tutor considers it necessary for the thesis.

In both cases, the student has to submit a paper that implies an advance in the subject, or a novel methodology for better comprehension of a topic.

Archival science

In Latin America, archival science is separated from the studies of library science. These two subjects, even though close, are studied and taught as if there were no connection between them. Most of the time, archival science studies are even performed in institutions or schools totally different from those of library science. The duration of the studies also varies, but in this case there are only three levels, the one of courses of less than three years, the one of those with a duration of exactly three years and the one that requires more than three years to be concluded, that is, the Bachelor's degree.

Possibly in Puerto Rico and Jamaica, archival science and library science are taught in the same schools, following the Anglo-Saxon tradition, but there is neither any certainty about it, nor evidence of them being performed separately.

It has also to be pointed out that the most part of the programs and schools of this specialty are in Argentina.

CONCLUSIONS

The educational system in Latin America has marked the main features of teaching in library science, which is different from the educational system of Anglo-Saxon countries and constitutes a factor that impedes making generalizations.

Due to the information previously presented, we may conclude that Latin America has followed the patterns, both European and American, in the education of library science. Although at the beginning of the century the major influence was the European, at the mid-twentieth century the influence of North American library science is perceived more intensely, especially with the introduction of information and communication technology.

It is also important to point out that the information about the number of schools and study programs varies largely, depending on the consulted source, and that among these, there is no agreement regarding the number of schools and programs.

In Latin America there are several teaching levels from those taking care of auxiliaries to the Doctorate. The most common educational level is the Bachelor's degree, accounting for 20 years of study.

The area that has to make the largest effort in order to have professional teaching programs is the one corresponding to the Non-Latin Caribbean, which, except for Jamaica, does not have any library science college.

It is necessary to take a census in the schools in Latin America, with normalized information, in order to learn more exactly about the teaching situation in library science are in the area.

Sources Consulted

Associçao Brasileira de Educaçao em Ciencia da Informaçao. "Escolas da área de CI Iberoámerica, Caribe e México". [Online] Available: http://www.abecin.org. br/Escolasal.htm. Retrieved June 4, 2004.

Centro de Servicios y Recursos para Bibliotecas y Bibliotecari@s. *@bsysnet.com* <http://absysnet.com/> Retrieved June 9, 2004.

"Escuelas y departamentos de bibliotecología." [Online] Available: http://www.geo cities.com/crachilecl/asociac.htm. Retrieved June 8, 2004.

Fang, Josephine Riss and Paul Nauta eds. *International guide to library and information science education.* (München: K. G, Saur, 1985).

Fang, Josephine Riss, Robert D. Stueart and Kulthida Tuamsuk eds. *World guide to library archive and information science education.* 2nd revised. and enlarged ed. (München; New Providence : K. G. Saur, 1995).

INFO LAC. "Directorio de instituciones sobre el área de bibliotecología y ciencia de la información en Iberoámerica y el Caribe". October 1999. [Online] Available: http://infolac. ucol.mx/directorio/escuelas.html. Retrieved June 9, 2004.

Maris Fernández, Stella and Graciela María Giuti. *Planes de estudio de las escuelas de bibliotecología, archivología y museografía de Iberoamérica.* (Buenos Aires: Sociedad de Investigaciones bibliotecológicas. Progreso de la Bibliotecología en el Tercer Mundo, ALP/IFLA, 1999.)

UNESCO. "Archives portal." [Online] Available: http://www.unesco.org/web world/portal_archives/pages/Education_and_Training/Institutions/Latin_America /index.shtml. Retrieved June 10, 2004.

UNESCO. "Libraries portal." [Online] Available: http://www.unesco.org/web world/portal_bib/Training/Institutions/Latin_America/index.shtml. Retrieved June 9, 2004.

Wilson, Thom. "World list of departments and schools of information studies, information management, information systems, etc. – other countries of the world." [Online] Available: http://informationr.net/wl/wlist7.html. Retrieved June 9, 2004.

PART 6
MIDDLE EAST:
INTRODUCTION

Sajjad ur-Rehman
Regional editor

This section deals with library and information situation in the Asian Arab nations. We are not using the terms such as Middle East, Arab countries or Arabian Peninsula as these are either too general or too specific. Arab countries are located in two parts of Africa and in the Western Asia. Middle East covers non-Arab nations of Turkey, Iran and Afghanistan. We had to confine ourselves to a naturally homogenous geographic unit. Turkey and Iran present altogether different contexts and scenarios in all the aspects of linguistic, socio-cultural, and politico-economic domains. Likewise North African nations have a peculiar context. Egypt and Sudan can also be identified in the African context, as these are two leading nations of the African union. This leaves us with the twelve nations of the Asian Arab world that include the six-nation entity of the Gulf Cooperation Council (GCC) and six other nations. The GCC has the membership of Saudi Arabia, United Arab Emirates, Qatar, Oman, Bahrain and Kuwait, also termed as Arabian Gulf or Arabian Peninsula. However, these terms would imply inclusion of Iraq that has been politically detached from the rest of the region during the last couple of decades. The other six nations include the states of Lebanon, Syria, Jordan, and Iraq. The Palestinian territory is also part of the same region, sharing a whole lot with the remaining countries. The last nation included in this grouping is Yemen, located on the south of Saudi Arabia. Keeping in view the natural makeup of this region, we have treated these twelve nations in this section as Asian Arab nations.

During the last many decades, the region of the Asian Arab nations has been a victim of an unrelenting turmoil. Since the creation of Israel in 1948, Palestinian exodus and the resulting regional tension caused three wars in 1948, 1967 and 1973. Lebanon's civil war brought destruction to all its civil institutions. Saddam's Iraq was engaged in a decade-long war of attrition with Iran during 1980s. In 1990, after Kuwaiti occupation, another yearlong armed struggle had a far-reaching effect on the socio-political dynamic of the region. Engagement of the US and allied forces in Iraq in 2002 has yet not ceased, leaving a lasting mark on the socio-cultural fabric of this community of nations. This seemingly never-ending turmoil has had a devastating effect on educational, scientific, technological and cultural infrastructure of this region. Indeed some nations have suffered more than others during these tragic times. Iraqi, Syrian and Palestinian lands have preserved civilization's cradle of humanity. Earliest libraries were found in Sumeria, Babylonia and the valley of Euphrates. Immensely valuable treasures of human scholarship and legacy of Islamic glories are found in this region. Most of these treasures have now been abandoned with horrifying apathy and neglect. This situation has affected library and information situation in the region.

This region has also been marked by another distinct feature. Six of these twelve nations have world's largest reserves of petroleum and natural gas. The other six nations in the region do not have these natural reserves. The six nations are extremely affluent while the other six have had struggling economies. Consequently, we have witnessed that some of the oil-rich nations have built their infrastructures in an amazingly short period. Educational systems and institutions in these countries have been developed from almost a point of non-existence. Their universities have all been developed during the last 40-50 years. They have tried to develop academic, school, public and special libraries in the context where there were few institutions of modern learning and scholarship. On the other hand, other six countries have been trying to develop these institutions without adequate financial support. Their growth could not be as dramatic or impressive as we find in the neighboring nations. We find a clear line between haves and have-nots in the area of library and information services. It is reflected in the quality and quantity of information resources in these countries. Some Saudi universities take pride that they are reaching the one million figure in their collection. During the same period, Syrian university libraries might have not added even one tenth of the collection to their library resources. Some Saudi university libraries are amongst the leaders of library automation and IT consumption while a neighboring country is still struggling with having an automated system for its century old university library.

Many Gulf countries were in a rush to develop and these had abundant financial and physical resources. They had to rely on expatriate workforce for managing the human aspect of these initiatives. Hundreds of librarians, library technicians and support staff thronged these countries to benefit from the lucrative employment opportunities. However, within a couple of decades, they felt the need of having indigenous professionals. This led to the establishment of library education programs in the region. This was the time when thousands of Egyptians filled the academic and professional positions in the GCC nations. They brought their Egyptian models of organizational bureaucracy and educational practices to these countries. They served as primary consultants, along with some Western experts, who designed the first library education programs in this region. Since Egypt had adopted a model of bachelor degree in library science for entry into the profession, all the schools developed in the region were based on the same notion that a bachelor in library science was the professional degree the LIS professionals needed to have. As a result, we find that during the last 30-40 years, thousands of library science degree holders have entered the LIS profession with a bachelor degree. For Master's and Ph.D. studies, they were encouraged to go overseas. Lately some programs of graduate studies have been developed, but these are not as vigorous and developed. Today we find that professional leadership is reserved for those who have graduate degrees and there are no clear tracks of career advancement for the large number of professionals. They do not appear to be active in professional activities. This has also reflected in having a poor image of LIS profession and professionals in the country. It is worth noting that civil service organizations in these countries have a salary structure based on an undergraduate degree. Those with a graduate degree do not get the incentives in terms of remunerations or promotion.

We also note that Jordanian Library Association has been the most dynamic professional forum in the region. Since its founding, it has organized hundreds of training programs for thousands of working staff members. Lebanese Library Association has also been active. Concurrently the GCC nations did not have any professional associations. In countries like Saudi Arabia and Kuwait, founding of professional societies was not allowed. Lately there have been some changes in the relevant laws and we find that professional societies are being organized in these countries. In Kuwait, a professional society was formally instituted a couple of years back. In the absence of professional organizations, these countries have lagged behind in organizing continuing education programs, professional publishing outlets, and viable positions on the policy issues facing the LIS community. Around mid-80s, professional leadership of some university libraries organized the Arabian Gulf Chapter of Special Libraries Association as a substitute forum of national professional societies. It has been conducting an annual conference and also conducting a couple of training program every year. It seems that in the absence of professional organizations in these nations, the LIS profession has not reached the point of maturity.

Most libraries in the region have resources in Arabic and English languages. The medium of instruction in almost all the LIS education programs is Arabic. There is a serious paucity of textbooks and reading materials in Arabic language. Whatever is available is not current and qualitative. Most faculty members in the region are not active in research and publishing; producing little in English and Arabic. This is not a desirable situation for LIS education in the region. Whatever is being produced is mostly descriptive and narrative in nature. There is a need that graduate studies are strengthened in LIS programs and the faculty members pay more attention to research and publishing.

It has been three decades and despite a number of initiatives, there has been no agreement on Arabic MARC. As a result, no sizable bibliographic database in Arabic language has been developed. Libraries have developed bilingual automation systems. Now some leading bilingual systems such as Horizon and VTLS are available for bilingual processing. Lack of progress in this area has deprived the cataloguers from using any credible source of authority. They have also been unable to network their resources. During the last decades, a number of major initiatives like OCLC have been taken to remedy this situation. There is a huge market of Arabic bibliographic data, and there is a need that professional work with adequate quality control is managed in this area.

Large libraries are building electronic resources and services to satisfy the needs of their new clientele. In this sense, there is a need for the large libraries to initiate digitization projects for Arabic resources. Indigenous Arabic information sources have not been indexed. Digitization projects should be well conceived and these must provide for metadata control, searching capability, and effective retrieval.

There has been a tremendous progress in the development of libraries, LIS infrastructure, and information services in this region, yet a great deal needs to be accomplished. Affluence in this region provides a promise, but there is a big challenge ahead for the profession and professionals to mature fast and pursue strategic vision with foresight and farsightedness.

PUBLIC LIBRARIES

Hayat Alyaqou

1. INTRODUCTION

Investing in public libraries is investing in the potential of the community in the information age where a well-informed society is the need of the day. Public libraries represent the equal right of every member of the community to find information for their education and development.

This chapter looks at the status of public libraries in the Asian Arab world (total of 12 countries), an area known for its deep respect to knowledge and reading which are interwoven in the teaching of the Holy Qura'n.

The main areas covered in the chapter are: history, development, and organizational setup of public libraries; resources and services and an investigation of the availability of OPACS; staff and building, and the main challenges that face public libraries in the region. It is noteworthy that the literature found about the 12 countries varies is amount, depth, and recentness. So, all the aspects could not be covered for all the countries covered in this chapter.

2. HISTORY, DEVELOPMENT, AND ORGANIZATIONAL SETUP

The genesis of most public libraries in the Asian Arab world was through the efforts of individuals and also through mosques, which traditionally housed books especially religious ones.

The practices of organizational setup or governance in this region vary from one nation to another. But the general trend is for the Ministries of Education or Culture to provide legal and administrative setups for public libraries. Below are the details of the historical development of public libraries and the practices of public library governance in each country.

2.1 Bahrain

Public libraries in Bahrain are supervised by the Directorate of Public Libraries in the Ministry of Education. There are nine public libraries. The largest public library is Manama Public Library that was established in 1946 and it is the depository for the United Nations Publications since 1975 and is also the national depository library of Bahrain (Ministry of Education in Bahrain n.d.). The situation where a public library serves the needs of the national library is not common. The decision was based on a recommendation made in 1982 by W.G. Alison, the past president of the UK Library Association who was invited by the Ministry of Education in Bahrain. He recommended that the public library should function as the national library since the population in Bahrain is small. (Young & Ali1992)

The second largest library in Bahrain – Muharraq Public Library (renamed in 1997 to Bahrain National Bank Library) – was established in 1969. It includes several special collections including a special collection for the blind (Ibraheem 2006).

Other public libraries are: Isa Town Public Library (established in 1972), Sitra, Riffa, Hidd, and Jidhafs public libraries (established in 1976), Arad Public Library (established in 1979), and Salmanya Medical Center branch of public library (established in 1979) (Ministry of Education in Bahrain n.d.).

2.2 Iraq

In his book about the history of libraries in Iraq, Kazanchi (2000) points out that the first public library was Alsalam Library, which was established in 1920 with the efforts of the citizens. In 1926, after the library ceased providing its services, its collection was taken over by the Ministry of Education. In 1929 the Ministry opened its first library with the command of King Faisal of Iraq. Another library followed in 1930. In 1956 it was legislated to establish local administrations in the 14 governorates of Iraq, and these administrations started to establish public libraries. In the 60s, the Ministry of Interior Affairs, responsible for managing the governorates, decided to solve this duality by taking care of public libraries but keeping the technical supervision at the Ministry of Education. After the revolution of July 1968, the National Library took over the supervision of public libraries. A national conference was held in the same year and it recommended that either the Ministry of Interior Affairs or the Ministry of Local Government might supervise public libraries. Eventually the practice has been that the parent ministry of public libraries is taking care of these public libraries. In 1998, there were 127 public libraries (Kazanchi 2000).

According to Johnson (2005), there are 144 public libraries in Iraq now. Many of these libraries were damaged or looted due to the political circumstances. Recovery and reconstruction efforts are undergoing though. Arnoult (2004) stresses that the reconstruction agenda should include: working on finding suitable premises since many libraries were totally burnt, and efforts should be made to preserve what is left of the old collections. The second thing should be rebuilding catalogues. Computerisation is necessary, yet a prude decision has to ensure that the choices of libraries are compatible with each other.

Mosque libraries and private/public libraries are also common in Iraq. There are 33 public libraries in the mosques, supervised by the Ministry of Endowments.

As far as private/public library are concerned. Abdulqadir Aljeelany Library has 1700 manuscripts and 41,000 volumes (Kazanchi, 2000).

2.3 Jordan

Public libraries in Jordan are run by the city council of each municipality (Zash 1989, cited by Abu Shaikha and Younis 2006). There are 100 public libraries in Jordan. The first library was established in Irbid in 1957. The municipality of Greater Amman established Libraries Department to maintain its public libraries, and so did Irbid municipality (Qandeel, 2000). There are 38 public libraries and 11 IT centers supervised by the Municipality of Greater Amman (Alali 2007).

2.4 Kuwait

Al-Maktabah Al-Ahliyah or the people's library was the first public library in Kuwait; 18 citizens established it in 1923. It had 1500 books, most of which were lost or damaged (Abdel-Motey & Al-Ansari 2003). In 1936, the library received government supervision through the Department of Knowledge (later the Ministry of Education), and a branch library was opened in 1953. More public libraries were established as the means for the service was constantly increasing. In 1979, the supervision over public libraries was transferred from the Ministry of the Education to the National Council of Culture, Arts, and Literature. In 1988, public libraries came back under the supervision of the Ministry of Education. As of 2001, there were 25 public libraries (Alroomi, Alateeqi, Basha, Hafith, & Alali 2001).

2.5 Lebanon

The Ministry of Culture supervises public libraries in Lebanon, a country that still suffers from the aftermath of a long civil war.

The Ministry of Culture signed a number of agreements of cooperation with society and municipality libraries, making them "associate libraries" in the mission of promoting reading. As of February 2003, there were 22 associate libraries. And in 2005, ten more libraries joined (Ministry of Culture in Lebanon, 2007).

Baaklin National Library is actually a public rather than a national or depository library.

2.6 Oman

According to Al-Mufaraji (1992), the Ministry of National Heritage and Culture supervises public libraries in Oman. The oldest library is the Islamic Library of the Ministry, which was founded in 1980. A branch of the library was planned back then to be open in Salalah in southern Oman.

2.7 Palestine

Mosque libraries are common in the Islamic world and especially in Palestine. According to Alaqla (2002), Alaqsa Mosque Library is one of the most important public libraries in Palestine. Apart from mosque libraries which act as basically specialized public libraries, Bergan (2000) makes note of two types of public libraries in Palestine: municipal public libraries which are the official ones, and private public libraries that were founded by the citizens.

Ghanim (2002) points out that in 1948 Israel confiscated hundreds of Palestinian public libraries and thousands of private ones. Later 13 new public libraries were established; five in the West Bank, and eight in the East Bank. Bergan (2000) adds that Nablus Municipality Library was established in 1960 and that was the first public library. The catalogue of the library is partially computerized. There are other public libraries, such as Ramallah Public Library and El Bireh Library.

2.8 Qatar

According to Khalifa (1992), early public libraries in Qatar appeared in the form of "Majalis Al Elm" or knowledge circles in private libraries that were open to the public and even to the illiterate by offering reading circles. Khalifa adds that the first official public library was established in 1956. In 1962 it was merged with the Central Library of the Ministry of Education, and then it started to act as both the national and the public library. In 1977 new public libraries started to emerge. Ahmad (2005) points out that this national/public library named "Dar Alkutub" or the house of books is under the supervision of the National Council of Culture, Arts, and Heritage since 1998.

Apart from Dar Alkutub, there are five public libraries in Qatar:

Alkhor Public Library (established in 1977), Ashamaal Public Library (established in 1979), Alkhansaa Public Library (established in 1981) and it offers its services to females only, Arrayaan Public Library (established in 1982), and Alwakrah Public Library (established in 1985) (National Council of Culture, Arts, and Heritage n.d.).

Kahlifa (1992) points out that apart from these six public libraries, there are two public libraries run by the Ministry of Mass Communication, 15 libraries administered by the Qatari Armed Forces, and the private library of Abdullah Alansari, which was opened to the public by his family. Ahmad (2005) also adds Sheikh Ali Bin Abdullah Al Thani's Library, which is a private library that acts as a public one. Both of these libraries are run by the Ministry of Endowments and Islamic Affairs.

2.9 Saudi Arabia

As in the case of most countries in the Islamic world, the mosque is more than a place of worship; its role extends to act as a public activity center of education. According to Siddiqui (1995), most libraries evolved around the two Holy cities of Islam: Mecca and Medina.

Alharam Almakki (Meccan Haram Mosque) library (situated in Mecca, the spiritual capital of Muslims) is one of the oldest libraries in the Islamic world. Its roots date back to 160 H/776 A.D. In 1357 H/1938 A.D., King Abdulaziz formed a committee of scholars to study and organize its situation ("Library of the Holy Meccan Mosque" 2006). Alharam Almadani (The Medina Mosque) library, located in Medina, is the second holy city for Muslims after Mecca. It has also housed a public library for a long time. ("Library of the Holy Mosque of the Prophet", 2006). According to Siddiqui (1996), "Libraries of the two Holy Places (Makkah and Medina) are supervised by the Department of Holy Mosques" (p. 197).

Abbas (1993) points out that 1959 is the year when public libraries in Saudi Arabia were reborn. Abbas adds that this happened when the Ministry of Education established the General Directorate of Public Libraries (G.D.P.L.) with the responsibility to supervise public libraries. Technical operations such as acquisitions, cataloguing, indexing, and book selection are performed centrally by the G.D.P.L. There are 59 libraries, 47 of which are managed by the GDPL. The Ministry of Pilgrimage and Endowments manages seven public libraries, the Department of Holy Mosques manages three, while the Department of Religion, Ifta, Dawah, and Guidance manages one public library (Siddiqui, 1995).

Since 2004, the Ministry of Culture and Information took over the responsibility of public libraries. The total number of public libraries has now increased to 80 libraries ("Public Libraries", 2005).

2.10 Syria

Public libraries in Syria are called cultural centers and are supervised by the Ministry of Culture. There are 64 cultural centers that offer library services in addition to other activities such as workshops, exhibitions, and lectures. The collections are expected to have the diversity that meets everyone's taste. There are also mobile libraries that are called mobile cultural units (Al-Laham, 1992). Administratively, in each Syrian governorate, there is a Cultural Department (Mudeeriyat Althaqafah), which supervises cultural centers (Ministry of Culture in Syria n.d.). In the capital Damascus, there are eight cultural centers, three of which have a collection of 95300 volumes (Damascus Cultural Department, n.d.).

Al-Laham (1992) points out that very few centers have library specialists. The Cultural Department coordinates the standardization of cataloguing and classification, but the centers are supposed to take care of their catalogues and acquisitions.

A review of eight cultural department websites showed that none of them has an OPAC.

2.11 United Arab Emirates

The United Arab Emirates is a federal country, so it is normal that each state or emirate of the seven has its own way of dealing with public libraries. The Ministry of Culture, Youth, and Society Development, however, coordinates these efforts and offers a collective OPAC at: http://www.libraries.gov.ae.

There are six public libraries in Dubai. The main library was established in 1963. Five branch libraries were established later on as the need increased. In 2003, the Governor of Dubai issued a decree that organized public libraries . These are supervised by the Public Libraries Section, which falls under the Department of Administrative Affairs in the Municipality of Dubai (Abu Eed & Alareedy 2005).

Dubai public libraries' OPAC is available at: http://www.libraries.ae.

The Cultural Foundation Library (Daar Alkutub) is the main public library in Abu Dhabi. It was established in 1981 (Dubai Cultural Council n.d.). Daar Alkutub has an OPAC available at: http://horizon.cultural.org.ae

Sharjah Public Library was established in 1971 and it was supervised by the Ministry of Information and Culture. But in 1980, the Department of Culture and Information was established in Sharjah that assumed its role. Now the Sharjah Library has five branch libraries (Sharjah Library, n.d.). There are branch libraries in Kalbaa, and in Khor Fakken, both established in 1989 (Dubai Cultural Council n.d.).

Sharjah Library OPAC is available at: http://www.shjlib.gov.ae/

Fujairah Public Library was established in 1974, and it is under the supervision of Fujairah Cultural Center. While Ras Alkhaimah Public Library was established in 2004 under the supervision of Ras Alkhaimah Cultural Center (Dubai Cultural Council n.d.).

2.12 Yemen

According to Alqurashy (2003), Public libraries in Yemen are maintained by the Public Authority of Books, which was established in 1990 as a part of the Ministry of Culture. Between 1999 and 2003, 15 new libraries have been opened. . It is noteworthy that the Public Authority of Books provides books to some public libraries that were established by some citizens, and it also works on the "Books Corner" Project, which aims at making books available in schools.

3. RESOURCES, AND SERVICES

The statistics available about the collections and resources of public libraries were meager and outdated. Services available are mostly traditional such as circulation and basic reference service. Public libraries are commonly used by students who look for a quiet place during exams period. OPACs are not common and so are other electronic services.

3.1 Bahrain

Young and Ali (1992) pointed out that public libraries have had a big percentage of title redundancy, which is normal due to the need to provide basic collection to everyone.

3.2 Iraq

The collection of public libraries in Iraq is 2,110,000 items, and circulation is the main service provided due to the political unrest (Kazanchi 2000).

3.3 Jordan

The collections of public libraries in Jordan are around half a million books and 300 periodical titles. The libraries serve around 1000 users daily and loan 136,000 books yearly (Alali 2007).

3.4 Kuwait

By 1990, the total collection of all public libraries numbered 294,033 items and the total staff numbered 87. In addition, the central State Library, which was opened in 1986, had a collection of 140,000 volumes and a staff of 52 employees (Abdel-Motey & Al-Ansari,2003). Due to Iraqi invasion on Kuwait in 1990, a big percentage of these items were either looted or vandalized. Abdel-Motey and Al Humood (1992) point out that 261,752 items were lost with an estimated value of 4.5 million US dollars.

The holdings of public libraries are 442,262 volumes, 17% of which is on literature, 15% on geography and history, 17% on social studies, 12% on religion, 8% on pure sciences, 10% on applied sciences, and 7% are non-Arabic materials (The Libraries Administration, 2000, cited by Abdel-Motey & Al-Ansari 2003). Abdel-Motey and Al-Ansari also point out that this is way too far from IFLA/UNESCO standard for public libraries which requires 1.5-2.5 books per capita. To meet this standard, the public library collection has to add 3,957,738 books.

A section for technical services in the Libraries Department in the Ministry of Education takes care of cataloguing and classification of items. Public libraries receive books with catalogue cards ready to be used (Altammar & Badawi 1994).

Al-Qallaf and Al-Azmi's study in 2002 shows that only "eight (34.8%) libraries have at least one PC while 15 (65.2%) libraries are not using any form of information technology" (P. 294).

Libraries Administration has an OPAC that allows users to search the collections of eight of the 25 public libraries. It is available at: http://library.moe.edu. kw/.

3.5 Oman

As of 1992, the Islamic Library had 21,937 books and it also has a collection for children. Lack of staff was evident in the library (Al-Mufaraji, 1992).

3.6 Palestine

Alaqsa Mosque Library has 1000 manuscripts and over 10,000 books (Alaqla 2002) while Nablus Public Library has 70,000 volumes and 24 employees. Journal subscriptions are available but Israeli censorship and restrictions make the acquisition difficult. The library receives 500 visitors and 300 book loans a day. Other Public libraries include Ramallah Public Library, which has 40,000 volumes. El Bireh Library has 15,.000 volumes (Bergan 2000).

One of the private/public libraries is Ansari Library, which was founded in 1985 and is only 135 square meters in size. Its collection is relatively large compared to its size. According to Bergan (2000) it has:

"Over 40.000 books in Arabic, many of them unique, including about 65 % of all the books that were ever published in Palestine since 1862. It contains maybe the most extensive and growing collection of Palestinian newspapers and periodicals – dating back to 1910. It also contains a growing collection of some 25.000 books, periodicals and reference works in English and French" (Bergan, 2000).

3.7 Qatar

According to Ahmad (2005), the total number of users of the six public libraries and the two private/public libraries in 2004 was 25700, with Sheikh Ali Bin Abdullah Al Thani's Library being the most heavily used; it had 15875 patrons due to the religious nature of its collections which appeals to the public. Ahmad points out that the main collection in the eight libraries she studied is of traditional materials; there is a shortage of other materials such as audio-visual and electronic resources. Three of the eight libraries use software to enable their patrons to search the collection. In terms of buildings, only four public libraries have buildings that were initially constructed to be public libraries (Ahmad, 2005).

3.8 Saudi Arabia

Alharam Almakki (Meccan Mosque) library has more than 500,000 books, 3000 magazines, and more than 8000 manuscripts. Many public library owners donated their collections to Alharam Almakki Library. Its collection contains religious books, along with books on Arabic language, history, education, psychology, sociology, geography, economics, and even medicine ("Library of the Holy Meccan Mosque", 2006).

Alharam Almadani (The Medina Mosque) library has 60,000 book titles, 5000 manuscripts, and 31,829 audio items. The library has 75 employees ("Library of the Holy Mosque of the Prophet", 2006).

3.9 United Arab Emirates

The six public libraries in Dubai had a collection of 225,824 items in 2003 (Abu Eed & Alareedy 2005). Sharjah Public Library has 171,000 monograph titles and 794 periodical titles. Kalbaa branch library has 24,538 book titles, and 1500 periodical titles. Khor Fakkan branch library has 25,554 book titles and 1680 periodical titles (Dubai Cultural Council n.d.).

The Cultural Foundation Library (Daar Alkutub) in Abu Dhabi has 300,000 book titles, 1450 periodical titles, 4000 e-journals, 12,000 manuscripts, and 7000 audio-visual items (Dubai Cultural Council n.d.).

Fujairah Public Library has 14000 titles, while Ras Alkhaimah Public Library has 15000 titles (Dubai Cultural Council n.d.).

3.10 Yemen

On the average, the libraries in the capitals of the governorates have 10.00 monograph titles. Dar Alkutub (the House of Books), the public library in the Governorate of the Capital (Sanaa) was visited by 72,000 persons in 2003 clubs, universities, and societies (Alqurashy 2003).

4. PERSONNEL AND PHYSICAL FACILITIES

Availability and preparedness of professional staff is one of the primary concerns in most Asian Arab countries. A master's degree is not required for employing professional staff. Mostly they require a library degree, which is also not commonly found in these libraries in this part of the world; this appears to be a major challenge for staffing of public libraries.

In 1992, in Bahrain only one employee in public libraries had a master's degree in library science. And although this statistic is very old, h concern is found in almost all public libraries in the Arab world (Young & Ali, 1992). Only 17% of the employees in Iraqi public libraries are professional (Kazanchi, 2000). The situation in Kuwait is better, but does not meet the bottom-line though. There are 148 employees in public libraries in Kuwait. Only 25% of them have college degrees in librarianship. IFLA/UNESCO standard requires 33% (Abdel-Motey & Al-Ansari, 2003). In Qatar, the six public libraries and the two private/public libraries have a total of 115 employees (Ahmad, 2005).

The situation is not brighter when it comes to public library building, but documented information is not available on this issue. In Iraq only one third of the Iraqi public libraries have suitable buildings (Kazanchi 2000). In Kuwait, availability of suitable buildings has always been a concern in Kuwaiti public libraries. Zehery (1975) noted that the need is pressing for "functional, friendly, and accessible library buildings to replace the present poor facilities." (P. 169) In 1994, Altammar and Badawi pointed out that although that Libraries Administration in the Ministry of Education set standards for the buildings of school libraries in 1987, both school and public libraries do not meet these standards. The situation was not better in 2003, as reported in the findings of Abdel-Motey and Al-Ansari's study; 63% of public librarians complained that there is a shortage in buildings and areas, and 48% described the furniture as unsuitable.

5. NON-GOVERNMENTAL CONTRIBUTION

Non-governmental contribution is more visible in public libraries buildings that have been sponsored by benevolent personalities such as Abdul Hameed Shoman Public Library in Jordan, King Abdulaziz Public Library in Saudi Arabia, and Juma Almajed Center for Culture and Heritage Library in the UAE. There are libraries donated by the corporate sector such the Public Knowledge Library in Oman. Other examples include public libraries run by non-governmental institutions such as Assabil Association in Lebanon and other smaller libraries in Palestine and Oman.

5.1 Abdul Hameed Shoman Public Library in Jordan

A noted public library in Jordan is Abdul Hameed Shoman Public Library, established by Abdul Hameed Shoman Foundation in 1986 and it had a computerized reference system, the first of its kind in Jordan (Natour 1988:276). Alali (2007) points out that 96,666 users visited the library in 2006, and that it houses 118, 000 book and audio-visual titles and 10.000 journal issues. All the operations of the 2100 square meter library are fully digitized and it has several database subscriptions. It is the national distributor in Jordan for CDS/ISIS (currently WINISIS) library system which was developed by the UNESCO. Shoman Library offered the system to around 60 academic, school, and public libraries in Jordan. The library had 25400 subscribers in 2002. There are no fees to subscribe and the subscribers are entitled to receive a group of services including circulation, reference service, photocopying, and manual and electronic current awareness service. It has specialized services such as journal listings for researchers and library training for other librarians and library science students in Jordan. The library is active in several vital projects including a mobile library project since 1998, working on a unified union list of periodicals in Jordan since 1988, Arabising Dewey Decimal Classification System in cooperation with ALECO (Arab League Educational, Cultural and

Scientific Organization), and cooperating with Dubai Municipality and Juma Al-majed Center Library to publish a trilingual thesaurus, a CD version of which was launched in 2001 that had 50,000 terms. The library has also contributed to the establishment of several public libraries in Jordan and Palestine (Abu Eed 2000). Abdul Hameed Shoman Public Library has an OPAC available at: http://www.shoman.org

5.2 Lebanese Case

Assabil Association, Friends of Public Library, is a non-governmental organization that has been working on establishing public libraries in Lebanon. Assabil was founded in 1997 and it runs 25 public libraries and has distributed over 100,000 books to public libraries and schools, in addition to organizing training sessions to librarians. Between 2001and 2005, the two municipal public libraries in Beirut received 94,431 visitors, and 350 school visits (Assabil, 2007).

The Organisation Internationale de la Francophonie (OIF) established 14 Reading and Cultural Activity Centres. OIF is an intergovernmental organization that has more than 60 French speaking countries. During the period 2002-2004, these centers received 186,198 visits, had 10,086 annuals subscribers, and loaned 47,036 books (Weber, 2007).

5.3 Oman

There are public libraries in Oman that were established by foreign institutions. This includes the public library of the British Council, which had 80,000 volumes in 1991, and the library of the United States Information Services USIS that was established in 1986. The collections of both libraries are mostly in English (Karim 1991).

Back in 1990, the Petroleum Development Oman Company established the Technical Public Library that was renamed as the Public Knowledge Library because its collection expanded to cover other disciplines. 1996, Petroleum Development Oman Company gave the Library to the Diwan of Royal Court that now manages the library (Petroleum Development Oman n.d.).

The Public Knowledge Library has an OPAC at: http://www.publiclibrary.gov.om.

5.4 Palestine

There are some public libraries set up by non-governmental organizations such as Bethlehem Bible College Library which is open to the public, Pontifical Mission Library at Notre Dame, and the public library run by the Palestinian Red Crescent Society (Bergan 2000).

5.5 Saudi Arabia

One of the noted public libraries in Saudi Arabia is King Abdulaziz Public Library in Riyadh. The library is a non-profit organization and was established in 1985 (Aldobaian 1995). The library was opened to the public in 1987, and it added an independent building for female patrons in 1996, and opened a branch of the library in 1999 ("About the Library" n.d.). The library receives 250.,000 users annually, and houses one million items (Alali 2003). The library has an OPAC available at: http://ipac.kapl.org.sa/elib/.

5.7 United Arab Emirates

One of the noted public libraries in Dubai, United Arab Emirates is Juma Almajed Center for Culture and Heritage Library, named after Juma Almajed, a UAE businessman. It was established in 1988 and its main collection came from acquiring a number of private collections (Boumarafi 1996). The center has a collection of around 500.000 items ranging from privates collections which were acquired from 48 private collections and also a collection of references (Bamiflih 2003).

6. CHALLENGES

Public libraries in the Asian Arab are facing numerous challenges. Most serious problems are related to staff, physical infrastructure, and provision of services. In some countries, financial problems also pose a serious challenge while in other place organizational and management issues are aiding the development of public library systems and services. Affluent nations lack strategic planning. Specific problems reported in the case of distinct nations are reviewed in this section country-wise.

6.1 Jordan

Qandeel (2000) summarises the challenges the Jordanian public libraries face.

1. Little value is given to public libraries in the structure of municipalities. A crucial decision was taken that no municipality budget would be approved unless it has a library in the hope that it would promote the cause of public libraries at the lower grass root level.. The steps taken by Irbid and Greater Amman municipalities in establishing a department for pubic libraries was a very positive step to alleviate the status of public libraries;
2. Lack of awareness about the importance of public libraries; citizens are not fully aware of the potential role of the public library;
3. Lack of a plan to establish an infrastructure to expand public libraries;
4. Absence of adequate commitment on the part of the Ministry of Culture;

5. Weak children resources and services; and
6. Difficulties with regard to digitization due to lack of qualified staff.

6.2 Kuwait

After an exploratory study by Alansari, Abu Zayd, Alqudsi, Alabdullah, and Al-sharekh in 1999, 17 recommendations were made to develop the status of public libraries in Kuwait. The study pointed out that 50% of the surveyed members – in particular housewives and retired members of the community – did not use public libraries. A need was felt to make an improvement in the areas such as budgeting, collections, non-traditional media, buildings and furniture, computers and IT facilities, Internet service, children materials and services, availability of qualified staff, and circulation and reference service. These recommendations overlap with the findings of the study of Abdel-Motey and Al-Ansari study in 2003. Most obvious problems they had identified included lack of staff incentives, shortage in allocated budgets, lack of IT and modern communication, lack of user's information literacy, shortage in buildings and areas, lack of professional development, shortage in qualified personnel, lack of standards and guidelines, unsuitable furniture, problems/policies, procedures, shortage in collections and lack of cooperation (p. 33).

6.3 Palestine

The Palestinian public libraries are constrained due to the political unrest, financial limitations, availability of professional staff, and lack of standards (Bergan 2000).

6.4 Saudi Arabia

Sharayah (2007) noted that the Saudi public libraries faced several problems that included absence of needed legislation, the inadequacy of grants in annual budgets, shortage of qualified personnel, scarcity of suitably furnished buildings, absence of book selection policy, lack of coordination and cooperation between public libraries, and lack of media coverage and publicity, absence of libraries in larger community centers in cities as large as Riyadh and Jeddah.

6.5 Syria

Al-Laham (1992) analyzed the situation of the Syrian cultural centers and noted that these faced two main challenges. First, these are housed in buildings that were originally built as residential buildings. These buildings are so small for the functions of public libraries. Secondly, these centers are not located in suitable quarters. Another problem was related to the non-availability of professional staff.

7. DISCUSSION AND CONCLUSION

The rich history of knowledge and scholarship appreciation in the Arab world in general and in the Asian Arab world in particular has exhibited its effects on public libraries. Mosque libraries along with private libraries were often open to the public and these played the role of public library for an extended period of time. These served like gateways to knowledge, scholarship, and enlightenment.

Common characteristics that can be noted for the public library institution in this region is as follows

1. The parent institution or ministry responsible for organizing public library services in a country has its inherent merits or demerits. In some countries, the responsibility of public libraries has shifted from one place to another, which reflects the indecision about where this vital establishment fits. (See Table 1). Another observation is that public libraries are viewed differently in several nations. In some countries, public libraries have their own department as part of a ministry, while in others they are maintained by municipalities with little, or even no central coordination.

2. Benevolence and individual philanthropy have made a major contribution in the recent developments in public libraries in the region. Many of these individual donations provided the foundation for public libraries. The corporate sector rarely contributes to that. Only three libraries sponsored by the corporate sector could be tracked;: Shoman Public Library in Jordan, The Knowledge Library in Oman, and The National Bank Public Library.

3. The location and conditions of public library buildings are not inviting in most of the cases. Vast majority of public library buildings were not initially constructed for the specialized purposes of a public library. Equipping libraries with suitable furniture also needs to be addressed in many public libraries.

4. Professional staff is a prerequisite for public library services and most libraries in this region lack in this area.

5. Political circumstances always adversely affect public libraries in Palestine. Iraqi capture of Kuwait had a devastating effect on Kuwaiti public libraries.

6. Non-traditional materials are growing slowly and so is the IT infrastructure. Most public libraries do not have OPACs.

Table 1. Facts and Figures About Public Libraries in the Asian Arab World

Country	Population	Literacy Rate	Approximate Number of Public Libraries	Supervising Institution/ Minisrty	Notes
Bahrain	708,573	86.5%	9 (year not available)	Ministry of Education	

Iraq	27,499,638	74.1%	127 (as of 1998)	Ministry of Interior Affairs	
Jordan	6,053,193	89.9%	38 (as of 2007)	City Council of the Municipality	
Kuwait	2,505,559	93.3%	25 (as of 2001)	Ministry of Education	
Lebanon	3,925,502	87.4%	32 "associate libraries" (as of 2003)	Ministry of Culture	
Oman	3,204,897	81.4%	2 (as of 1992)	Ministry of National Heritage and Culture	
Palestine	Gaza Strip: 1,482,40 West Bank: 2,535,927	Gaza Strip: 92.4% West Bank: 92.4%	13 (year non available)	Municipalities	
Qatar	907,229	89%	5	Ministry of Education	
Saudi Arabia	27,601,038	78.8%	80 (as of 2005)	Ministry of Culture and Information	
Syria	19,314,747	79.6%	64 (as of 1992)	Ministry of Culture	Public libraries are called "cultural centres"
UAE	4,444,011	77.9%	Dubai: 6 (as of 2005) Abu Dhabi: 1 (data not ascertained) Sharjah: 1 with 5 branches Other Emierates: accurate data could not be warranted	Ministry of Culture, Youth, and Society Development with indepen- dency to each emirate's muni- cipality	
Yemen	22,230,531	50.2%	NA	Ministry of Culture	

Populations and latentcy rates are according to CIA Factbook available at: https://www.cia.gov/library/publications/the-world-factbook/index.html.

References

The Library of the Holy Meccan Mosque. (2006). [Online] Available: http://informatics.gov.sa/modules.php?name=Sections&op=viewarticle&artid=145. Retrieved October 11, 2007. The library of the Holy Mosque of the Prophet.

(2006). [Online] Available: http://informatics.gov.sa/modules.php?name= Sections&op=viewarticle&artid=135. Retrieved October 11, 2007. Public libraries: Between the Ministry of Education and the Ministry of Information and Culture. (2005). [Online] Available: http://informatics.gov.sa/modules. php?name=Sections&op=viewarticle&artid=108. Retrieved October 11, 2007

Abbas, H. B. (1993). The main pillars of the national system for public libraries in the Kingdom of Saudi Arabia. Riyadh: King Fahd National Library. (In Arabic)

Abdel-Motey, Y. Y., & Al-Ansari, H. (2003). Public libraries in Kuwait: a study of their resources, facilities and services. Public Library Quarterly, vol. 22, no.2, 23-37.

Abdel-Motey, Y. Y., & Al Humood, N. (1992). An overview of the impact of the Iraqi aggression on libraries, information and education for librarianship in Kuwait. Journal of Information Science, vol. 18, no. 6, 441-446.

Abu Eed I. (2000) The contribution of private sector to public libraries in the Arab world: Abdul Hameed Shoman Library as an example. [Online] Available: http://www.arabcin. net/arabic/5nadweh/pivot_6/shooman2.htm.   Retrieved November 14, 2007 (In Arabic).

Abu Eed, I., & Alareedy J. (2005). Public libraries in Dubai: The civilisational and cultural role in building and developing the community in Emirates. Alarabiyah 3000, vol. 5, no. 2. (In Arabic).

Ahmad, I. H. (2005). Planning for information services for the elderly in Qatar public libraries. Alarabiyah 3000, vol. 5, no. 4, 83-114. (In Arabic)

Al-Laham, G. (1992). Libraries and Information Infrastructure in Syria. Journal of Information Science, vol. 18, no. 6, 497-504.

Al-Mufaraji, M. N. (1992). Libraries and library education in Oman. Journal of Information Science, vol. 18, no. 6, 417-479.

Alali, N. (2007) Educationalists: The Arab verbal cultural caused the book to be unnecessary in the Arab family shopping basket. [Online] Available: http://www.alghad.jo/index. php?news=187129. Retrieved November 13, 2007 (In Arabic).

Alali, N. (2003 May). Quarter million visitors to King Abdulaziz Library and one million information source. [Online] Available: http://www.asharqalawsat. com/details.asp?section =28&issue=8923&article=168823. Retrieved November 20, 2007 (In Arabic).

Alansari, H. , Abu Zayd R., Alqdusi, T., Alabdullah, A., & Alsharekh, I. (1999). Developing the reality of public libraries in Kuwait: An exploratory study. Kuwait: Awqaf Public Foundation. (In Arabic).

Alaqla, S. B. (2002). Libraries in Palestine. [Online] Available: http://www. arabcin.net/arabiaall/2-2002/9.html. Retrieved November 22, 2007 (In Arabic).

Aldobaian, S. A. (1995). Studies on the public libraries in the Kingdom of Saudi Arabia. Riyadh: King Fahd National Library.

Alqurashy, O. (2003 May). The public authority of books is a part of the cultural system of Yemeni unity. [Online] Available: http://www.26sep.net/newsweekarticle.php?lng=arabic&sid=4489. Retrieved November 22, 2007 (In Arabic).

Alroomi, H. B., Alateeqi, K. S., Basha, N., Hafith, M., & Alali, A. (2001). Public libraries in Kuwait: Their establishment and development. Kuwait: Ministry of Education. (In Arabic)

Arnoult, J. (2004). Libraries in Iraq in 2003: A new chapter in the never-ending story of disasters. Quarterly Bulletin of the National Library of South Africa, vol. 58, no. 1, 31-38.

Assabil. (n.d.). Support for Assabil, friends of public libraries to establish a training and resource center in Lebanon. [Online] Available: http://www. assabil.com/documents/ pdfs/Assabil_Resource_Center_S.pdf Retrieved November 3, 2007

Bamiflih, F. S. (2003). Juma Almajed center. [Online] Available: http://infor matics.gov.sa/modules.php?name=Sections&op=viewarticle&artid=30a Retrieved November 2, 2007 (In Arabic).

Bergan, E. (2000). Libraries in the West Bank and Gaza: Obstacles and Possibilities. 66th IFLA Council and General Conference, 13-18 August, 2000, Jerusalem.

Boumarafi, B. M. (1996). Libraries and information services in the United Arab Emirates (UAE): An overview. International Information & Library Review, vol. 28, no. 4, 331-343.

Damascus Cultural Department. (n.d.) Cultural Centers. [Online] Available: http:// damascusculture. org/attach.html. Retrieved October 27, 2007 (In Arabic).

Dubai Cultural Council. (n.d.) Public libraries. [Online] Available: http://www. dubaiculturalcouncil. ae/ar/?T=1&ID=614. Retrieved November 2, 2007 (In Arabic).

Ghanim, H. (2002). The reality of Palestinian libraries: Alkhalidiyah library as an example. [Online] Available: http://www.arabcin.net/arabiaall/2-2002/21.html. Retrieved October 7, 2007 (In Arabic).

Ibraheem, H. M. (2006) The National Bank of Bahrain Public Library in Muharraq. [Online] Available: http://informatics.gov.sa/modules.php? name=Sections&op=view article&artid=153. Retrieved October 26, 2007. (In Arabic).

Johnson, I. M. (2005). The impact on libraries and archives in Iraq of war and looting in 2003. A preliminary assessment of the damage and subsequent reconstruction efforts. International Information and Library Review, vol. 37, no.3, 209-271.

Karim, B. M. (1991). The Emergence of Libraries in the Sultanate of Oman. International Library Review, vol. 23, no. 3, 229-236.

Kazanchi, F. Y. (2001). Libraries in Iraq: From the ancient times until nowadays. Baghdad: Ministry of Culture and Information, Cultural Affairs. (In Arabic).

Khalifa, S. A. (1992). Libraries and librarianship in Qatar. Journal of Information Science, vol. 18, no. 6, 481-489.

King Abdulaziz Library. (n.d.) About the Library. [Online] Available: http://www.kapl.org.sa/part.php?partid=17. Retrieved November 20, 2007. (In Arabic)

Ministry of Education in Bahrain. (n.d.) Public library. [Online] Available: http://www.education.gov. bh/english/library/index.asp. Retrieved October 27, 2007.

Ministry of Culture in Lebanon. (n.d.) Promoting Public Reading Policy. [Online] Available: http:// www.culture.gov.lb/SECTIONSAr/underLivresEtLitt/Under LecturePublique/Historique.asp. Retrieved November 3, 2007. (In Arabic).

Ministry of Culture in Syria. (n.d.) The cultural departments of ministry. [Online] Available:(http://www.moc.gov.sy/index.php?m=87. Retrieved October 27, 2007. (In Arabic).

National Council of Culture, Arts, and Heritage. (n.d.) Public libraries department. [Online] Available: http://www.nccah.org/arabic/divisions.asp?content=qatar_public_library. Retrieved November 4, 2007. (In Arabic).

Natour, N. (1988). Abdul-Hameed Shoman Public Library. In Advances in library administration and organization, vol. 7, 275-278. JAI Press.

Petroleum Development Oman. (n.d.) Public Knowledge Library. [Online] Available: http://www. pdo.co.om/pdoweb/tabid/79/Default.aspx. Retrieved November 4, 2007.

Qandeel, Y. (2000). Library institution in Jordan. In Libraries and information centers in Jordan: Reality and challenges. Beirut: Arab Foundation for Studies and Publishing. (In Arabic) Sharayah, A. (2007 August). Handicapped public libraries. [Online] Available: http://www.asharqalawsat.com/details.asp?section=43&issue=10479 &article=431394. Retrieved November 7, 2007. (In Arabic).

Sharjah Library. (n.d.) Sharjah Library. [Online] Available: http://www. shjlib.gov.ae. Retrieved November 2, 2007. (In Arabic).

Siddiqui, M. A. (1996). Library and information science education in Saudi Arabia. Education for Information, vol. 14, no. 3, 195-214.

Siddiqui, M. A. (1995). Management of libraries in Saudi Arabia practices and constraints. Library Management, vol.16, no.36, 24-32.

Weber, E. (2007). Improving the integration of public reading in cultural policies of Francophone developing countries. IFLA Journal, vol. 33, no. 1, 7-15.

Young, H. C. , & Ali, N. (1992). The Gulf war and its effect on information and library services in the Arabian Gulf with particular reference to the State of Bahrain. Journal of Information Science, vol. 18, no. 6, 453-462.

Zehery, M. H. (1975). Library service in Kuwait: a survey and analysis with recommendations for public library development. Texas: North Texas State University.

ACADEMIC LIBRARIES

Teresa M. Lesher and Yaser Abdel-Motey

1. INTRODUCTION

Although the first university is widely believed to have been an Arab one, (Al-Azhar University in Cairo founded in 970 AD), it is only within the past 40 years that many of the 305 universities in the Middle East were established, especially the private universities. While most countries have one to several public universities that offer usually free tuition to very large enrollments of students, several factors have justified the evolution of private universities in the Arab world, including the inability of state universities to accommodate the students desiring higher education, the resultant higher grades demanded for admission, the limited number of non-national students accepted into state universities, and other social, cultural and economic factors. Table 1 shows the number of universities in Middle East countries.

Table 1: Number of Universities in Middle East Countries*

Country	Number of Universities	Country	Number of Universities
Bahrain	10	Palestine	17
Iraq	42	Qatar	11
Jordan	26	Saudi Arabia	33
Kuwait	12	Syria	21
Lebanon	41	United Arab Emirates	47
Oman	30	Yemen	15

* International Association of Universities (2007); UAE Commission for Academic Accreditation (2007); Arabian Campus (2007); and the Ministries of Higher Education for Kuwait (2005), Jordan (2007), Saudi Arabia (2007), Iraq (2007), Palestine (2007), Lebanon (2007) and Oman (2007).

Each institution of higher education undoubtedly owns a library, or several if branch libraries are counted. The collections, services, automation, and staffing situations vary greatly among these libraries. Al-Khatib and Johnson (2001) feel that funding is the principal factor in determining the rate of development in academic libraries in the Middle East. Rich states are able to acquire the staff and resources to enable them to adopt new methods, while the poor states are unable to make the necessary investments.

Instability in the region has also impacted many university libraries, especially those in Lebanon, Palestine, Iraq and Kuwait. The war in Lebanon severely handicapped academic libraries; Al-Khatib and Johnson (2001:214) report that "[s]ome libraries were destroyed, burned or looted; the others were affected by migration of personnel, whilst frozen or reduced budgets, inflation, and the devaluation of the local currency contributed to a loss of purchasing power. Advances in library services were limited to a minimum in the majority of the surviving institutions...." As well, collections in Kuwait suffered from the looting and destruction of the Iraqi occupation; collections in some universities after ten years of rebuilding were less than half of their pre-invasion size (Fadhli and Johnson 2006:38). Academic and research libraries in occupied and war-torn areas require major financial provisions not only to restore their facilities, collections and services to their previous states but also to cope with fast-paced changes related to electronic information and remote access.

Many Middle Eastern countries provide higher education through Western Universities that open branches locally. For example, Qatar's Education City provides local access to American university degrees by contracting several universities to provide signature degree programs in a wide range of fields: Texas A&M University (TAMU) for several engineering programs, Weill-Cornell Medical College, Carnegie Mellon University for computer science and business, Georgetown University for international affairs, and Virginia Commonwealth University for art and design programs. Each institution functions autonomously and each academic library serves its own students and faculty. Gilreath (2006:55) describes an information service model that was adopted by TAMU and is used by most of the institutional partners in Education City: the library has a small but well selected print collection onsite that is complemented with ample electronic resources at each user's workstation and a highly responsive document delivery service. When the college accepted its first enrollment in 2003, the library provided access to about 500 databases and some 39,000 electronic full-text journals.

Most of the libraries in private academic institutions in the Middle East are relatively new and have similarly small in-house collections that provide access to targeted subject areas; online collections make up for the sparse collection. For example, the American University of Kuwait, four years into operation, has a total collection of 12,116 items serving approximately 1500 students and 100 staff, including faculty. However, their online collection features 14 databases providing access to 38,500 periodicals and more than 1500 e-books. (Varnet 2007).

The library of King Fahed University for Petroleum and Minerals (KFUPM) is reportedly the most modern in the region (Al-Baridi and Ahmed 2000:110) with its four stories housing a large collection of monographs, periodicals, research reports, educational films and resources on microfilm and other media. The collection supports undergraduate programs, as well as 18 Master's level and nine PhD level programs, in the fields of pure and applied sciences, computer science and engineering, industrial management and environmental design. King Saud University Library in Riyadh is the largest library in the GCC region with a collection of over one million volumes (Khurshid 2006) followed by the Islamic University of Imam Mohammed Ibn Saud with nearly one million (Khalid 2000:180). However, Khalid says that "[for] all their large stock and generous facilities, these libraries are not heavily used for a number of reasons," mainly a lack of user skills.

2. USER PROFILES

Unlike developed countries in the West whose information industry is highly developed, the Middle East does not have a "book culture." Although standards of literacy are relatively high, people do not generally rely on books to meet their information needs. Specialized Arabic magazines or scientific journals are few in number, although leisure magazines and newspapers are available extensively. User-centered research regarding user perceptions, information use and satisfaction with resources is not systematically undertaken in the Arab world.

Al-Khatib and Johnson (2000) note a situation in Lebanese academic libraries that is common across the Arab world: "A typical Lebanese student is unlikely to have used a library before arriving at the university and, with notions of independent learning still a novel concept in the country's universities, he/she may well graduate without ever entering the library, having relied solely on memorizing the lecturers' notes and whatever set books were required purchases."

Although there is a growing number of exceptions to rote learning from lectures and notes, the problem remains somewhat circular: lecturers give minimum encouragement for students to use the library, and the few demands made on them hinders the development of appropriate library facilities and the ability to respond effectively to information needs.

Speaking for academic libraries in Kuwait, Varnet (2007) says that "Our biggest challenge lies in the area of 'expectations.' With rote learning being the norm in Kuwaiti education, students do not know how to learn and search for relevant information on their own. They have no 'frame of reference' for becoming independent learners. Hence, when they come to the university and we expect them to do their course work independently, there is an initial disconnect – they are used to being told what to do, and university faculty don't do that. To become an independent learner, you must know how to use a library – frankly, students can't do this with any semblance of success. So, at AUK our biggest challenge is to assist students in becoming skilled library users. Virtually all our students are at the basic/beginning level, and that is where our training efforts go."

Ashoor (2005) feels that developing countries face a number of problems which stand in the way of developing their information literacy (IL) programs, including their traditional educational systems, the low literacy rate and the low level of publishing. Rudasill (1998) states that in developing countries "...students lack the qualities of independence, of self direction and even of simple curiosity in their attitudes to learning." Therefore, much preparation and planning need to be done to develop effective information literacy programs in Middle Eastern academic libraries.

3. LIBRARY RESOURCES

There is variation across the Middle East in library acquisitions, which depends primarily on sufficient funding. Some libraries are able to afford both quality and quantity of resources while others have virtually no budget for acquisitions. For example, Maguire (2001) reports that during his service at Birzeit University, considered among the top academic libraries in Palestine, he "assisted with selecting monographs for purchase, something that had not been done for ten years due to funding shortages." Library collections are also affected by local publishing trends as well as the availability of indexing services and electronic formats.

Research and publishing in the Arab world, especially those of scientific nature, is limited. Some countries have no national information policy and many Arabic publications do not have ISBNs (International Standard Book Numbers) or ISSNs (International Standard Serial Numbers). There is no annual listing of publications, and government publications are difficult to monitor for acquisition purposes. Not only is funding for research limited, but there is little incentive to undertake it since remunerations are often based solely on the last degree one earns, and promotions do not often require research. Most publishing is through university publishing houses or vanity press, resulting in low sales and distribution, especially outside of the country of origin. Further discouraging for Arab scholars is the non-standardization of terminology in Arabic in reference to contemporary developments, and the cross-dialect linguistic barriers. Articles published in Arabic will probably not be indexed and if they are, the indexes are poorly marketed and underutilized. Moreover, journals that have the highest international reputation and circulation tend to publish in English, a factor that deters many researchers from offering papers for publication in them (Fadhli and Johnson, 2006: 33).

Al-Fihrist indexing service for Arabic journals was the first, established in 1981; by 1987 it was indexing 216 periodicals from 21 countries. More recently, Arabia Inform initiated "AskZad" in 1998, which indexes over 200 newspapers and 2000 refereed journals primarily in Arabic, English and French, as well as e-books, theses, conference papers and other research, providing some full-text. The indexes require paid subscriptions for complete access. AskZad charges $2 per hour for viewing, 0.15 per page for printing general books, $0.25 per page for printing references in social sciences, and $0.50 per page for printing references in applied sciences. Despite reasonable prices, the database is underutilized.

Periodical indexing in the Arab world is irregular at best. Al-Khuraiji's study of 2282 Arabic periodical titles acquired by research libraries in Riyadh revealed that 7.8% of them (178 periodicals) have dedicated indexes and, of these, only ten are issued regularly. General indexes are incomplete, with only 48% coverage and no periodical being fully indexed. Four percent of the indexes were gathered in accumulated indexes, but most of them were issued only once. Less than 30% of the indexes use cross-referencing and 80% of the articles were indexed under a single subject heading, some of which are not standardized.

Researchers' limited benefit from Arabic periodicals is due to lack of complete indexes; variations in coverage, currency, and production accuracy; a lack of standardized indexing language; inaccurate indexing; and non-coordinated and non-institutionalized indexing efforts. Al-Khuraiji recommends that Arab and national authorities are assigned to prepare, issue and update the indexes, that libraries pool indexing efforts, that regulations and laws are issued to protect the intellectual and financial rights of publishers, and that indexers benefit from automated indexing applications as well as digitization of data for publishing in electronic formats.

A good portion of Middle Eastern academic libraries provide e-resources. Al-Baridi and Ahmed (2000) feel that the Arabian Gulf region, in particular, has the necessary infrastructure and expertise to set up digital libraries. They advise that when making the transition to electronic resources, librarians should weigh the experiences of other libraries and carefully consider selection criteria.

Kuwait became the first Arab country to access DIALOG, in 1978. By 1984 there were subscribers in seven Arab countries and by the late 1990s it was universally available (Zehery 1997). Abdulla (2005:48-49) reports that the United Arab Emirates University (UAEU) is much farther along in the transition to electronic-only access to journal literature than most libraries in the Arab world, with a collection of more than 10,000 e-journals and print journals being reduced to 452 titles. The Dean of the UAEU libraries said that the decision to migrate to electronic-only access to journals as "a strategic decision to meet our users' expectations of unrestricted, convenient and remote access, in addition to having them benefit from the powerful searching tools and features that the printed journal could not offer" (Diesnis 2003). Abdulla (2005:52) reported that document delivery requests at UAEU for articles fell from 966 in 2001 to 161 in 2003. However, Ibrahim (2004) reported that the use of electronic resources among university faculty members at UAEU was low; reasons cited include lack of time, lack of awareness of resources provided by the library and language barriers.

Many publishers offer a discount to subscribers of e-only access; further cost savings relate to binding and storing print journals. Worth mentioning is one of the library community's concerns about e-journal packages, summarized by Maxy-muk (2004): that libraries have no permanent access to the e-journal packages. Once a library subscribes, they are left with no choice but to continue renewing the contracts as it would be difficult to reduce the enormous amount of literature that users become accustomed to accessing. Especially in libraries where funding may not be stable, this is a grave concern.

4. ACADEMIC LIBRARY SERVICES

Library services in Middle Eastern academic institutions are developing in response to the changing collections and accessibility. The widespread automation of major library functions have naturally led to an increase in circulation transactions, reference transactions, interlibrary loans, and document delivery. Many libraries offer numerous classes in how to use resources and search engines, how to navigate the on-line catalogues, as well as providing web-based tutorials. For example, an e-classroom was inaugurated in Jafet Library at the American University in Beirut (AUB) in 2004 and is now used to teach hundreds of undergraduate and graduate students the tools they need to access the numerous electronic resources of the library. There are also special efforts to help instructors incorporate research methods in their courses that take advantage of these on-line resources (Maingate 2007).

In response to international trends in information literacy instruction, many librarians are shifting their focus from the general library orientation and course related instructions using traditional learning methods to a set of critical thinking skills involving the use of information. This may be the best approach since the requisite skills and attitudes from early training are largely lacking.

New patterns of services in Saudi academic libraries include online services, online database searching, some marketing efforts, some current awareness but not at the level of selective dissemination of information (SDI), and in some universities the reference services switched to electronic instead of print (Al-Hadad 2003:124). In 1995, KFUPM connected to the university's fiber optic backbone, allowing access to full-text periodical databases, encyclopedias and specialized reference sources (Al-Baridi and Ahmed 2000:113). In 1999, the university established full Internet connectivity. Khurshid (2006:441) reports that "the [KFUPM] library administration's current emphasis is more on developing digital collections, including electronic databases, e-journals, and multimedia. If an item is available with the vendor both in print and electronic formats, preference is given to the electronic format. The plan is also to replace hard copies of some existing materials with the electronic version, if available. This will mostly include retrospective holdings of key journals."

To assist users in accessing full-text journal databases on CD-ROM, the User Services Division (USD) at KFUPM requested that the online catalogue should also reflect the holdings of the titles in CD format so that users would be aware of their availability in the library (Khurshid, 2001:85). Lists posted at the user workstations or on the library's Web site were not consulted often or did not provide a sufficient description of the journals. To meet the USD's request, it was decided to undertake analytical cataloging, defined as "an entry for a part of an item for which a comprehensive entry is also made." (AACR2 1988: 615). Thus, the library provided catalogue records for the journals in their full-text abstracting and indexing services and other aggregator databases, despite the enormity of the project and no additional staffing.

Five years into the project, Khurshid (2001:88) reports that both users and library staff make better use of existing collection resources. Maintenance of the full-text journal information is difficult as it includes incorporating title changes and updating holdings information. However with the coordinated efforts of the cataloguing, collection development and user services divisions at KFUPM library, it has been successful.

5. AUTOMATION

Libraries across the Middle East have benefited from automated library systems since the early 1980s (Kurshid 2002:75) and have evolved their systems since then to modern standards. For example, the University of Yarmouk was the first to use an advanced automation system in Jordan, becoming a model for other libraries (Younis 1999:338). Automation has historically been problematic for libraries with collections in Arabic for several reasons. Arabic has special features, such as being written from right to left, the absence of capital letters and different letterforms depending on how it is connected to previous or subsequent letters in a word.

Most libraries in the Middle East have collections in both Arabic and English, and there are three options for managing electronic records in multiple scripts (Vassie 2000). One option is to create twin monolingual, monoscript catalogues, but users will have to toggle between them (or change locations) to search for materials. Circulation information would also be more labor intensive and less efficient. Secondly, monolingual with bi- or multi-script catalogues comprise records with notes in English script but with some data in vernacular scripts, like OCLC's WorldCAT or Research Libraries Information Network (RLIN). The only other option is to merge databases in a bilingual, bi-script catalogue such as that at the

UAEU (http://maktaba.uaeu.ac.ae), something that was accomplished with Arabic and Roman scripts in the early 1990s.

The library automation initiative started in Europe and North America in the early 1970s. Before Arabic automation systems were developed, Romanization of Arabic text was the only choice for libraries to catalogue Arabic resources on computer systems. However, because of the complexities of the Arabic language, Romanization is difficult at best and rarely produces records standardized enough to ensure successful searching. The advent of the Unicode universal character in 1991 with its capability to encode the characters of world languages paved the way for libraries with Arabic collections. Khurshid (2006:442-443) describes the Arabic language support that library automation system should include an Arabic character set based on Unicode and the regional coding system, ASMO449, developed by the Arab Organization for Standardization and Metrology, to translate Arabic information consisting of letters and numbers to equivalent binary numbers; entry and display of Arabic text from right to left but left-to-right collating sequence for numerals within the text; handling of diacritics; contextual analysis capability for Arabic words with several meanings; handling the various forms of each Arabic letter, among other features. One of the main concerns in Arabic automation systems is maintenance and technical support provision, and can be a deciding factor when considering equally attractive library automation options.

OCLC implemented the Basic Arabic and Extended Arabic character sets and, beginning June 1, 2000, members began inputting bibliographic records with Arabic characters using OCLC Arabic Cataloging software. Users can search for MARC records, edit them, create and add records that are not found in WorldCat, add the local library symbol to the WorldCat record, and download a copy of the MARC record to the local system (Kurshid 2002:75). Arabic characters now appear in several OCLC-MARC services and products.

Web-based OPACs are an advanced generation of traditional OPACs serving as a gateway to the resources not only held by particular library but also to the holdings of other linked libraries to full-text resources (Ibrahim 2005). The web-technology is underutilized; Ibrahim (2005) discovered that only four out of ten web-based OPACs in the Arabic script in GCC countries use MARC bibliographic format in spite of the fact that it is the backbone for the exchange of bibliographic data electronically. In addition, the Z39.50 protocol, which enables cataloguers to search in remote OPACs, is also underutilized. Networked OPACs and union catalogues are also very limited. The application of MARC format will facilitate communication between their OPACs.

Ibrahim (2005) describes a lack of uniformity in terms used for call number, subject and physical description labels in Arabic OPACs. For example, *raqm al-itisal* and *raqm al-talab* are used for call number label; *ras al-mawdu*, *mustalah mawdui* and *mawdu* are used for subject label; *al-tarqim* and *wasf madi* are used for physical description. He encourages librarians to employ the guidelines and interface features checklist in evaluating packages as part of the standards for the selection of automation systems. Furthermore, designers should pay more efforts to be in compliance with the guidelines. He offers a checklist of Arabic scripts web OPAC interface that covers 97 criteria in areas of search types and methods, search limits and strategy, access points, bibliographic display, output/services/facilities/ external links, user assistance, layout, labels, and text (Ibrahim, 2005:429-432).

Kurshid (2002) summarized problems typical to the cataloguing of Arabic materials: lack of standard authority lists; missing imprint information in some Arabic books and confusion between edition and imprint, for which there is a single word in Arabic (*tabaa*); publication dates based on different calendars (Gregorian or Hejri); difficulty in determining the entry element of classical names, which may have up to six different elements; and shortcomings in international classification systems and subject heading lists, which are oriented towards Western languages, literature, culture, customs and religion. In addition, Arabic cataloguers generally have a BLS degree, which does not give them the knowledge and skills needed for efficient cataloguing, as well as limited knowledge of the English language, which hinders their usage of basic cataloguing tools. These obstacles lead to lower productivity and quality of work among Arabic cataloguers.

6. STAFFING

Many of the problems in librarianship in the Middle East can be traced to issues related to library personnel and their qualifications. Generally, the bachelor degree in library and information science (LIS) is regarded as professional qualification; however, in spite of this relatively low standard, many libraries are forced to hire non-professionals, which include college graduates with or without some library training. Al-Khatib and Johnson (2001) reported that 13 staff are required at the American University of Beirut Saab Memorial Medical Library (AUB-SMML), but there are only 11 and among these, only one has a professional degree and two are volunteers. Similarly, among the Beirut Arab University (BAU) library staff of 30, only eight have a qualification in library science. Zehery's research (1997) revealed that only 8% of the 483 persons employed in six state universities libraries in the GCC had graduate or advanced degrees in LIS. The situation has since improved as more Gulf universities are offering post-graduate professional degrees. However, since academic libraries generally do not provide teaching status and salary to professional staff, librarianship will continue to be viewed as a low-status career.

　There has long been a shortage of indigenous LIS professionals in most Middle Eastern countries, a situation that has been remedied with the recruitment of library staff from Pakistan, India, Egypt, Europe and North America. However, many countries, particularly those of the GCC, are trying to replace expatriate staff with local citizens, a task unlikely to be accomplished until specialized educational programs, employment standards, and professional image improve.

Librarianship has not attracted many young professionals in Lebanon and elsewhere in the Middle East due to its low status and apparent irrelevance to academic needs, evidenced by the fact that professional academic librarians are usually denied faculty status. In addition, academic librarians are not always a part of academic planning, so librarians have to undertake proactive liaison activities with faculty to know when the universities add new programs so that they can build suitable collections. Gyeszly and Ismail (2003) did just that during a collection assessment at the American University of Sharjah (UAS) and reported a subsequent increase in faculty involvement in collection development.

Al-Hassan and Meadows (1994) report that once employed, library staff in Kuwait, with the exception of those in special libraries, appear to be poorly managed and motivated, and that there seems to be a general resistance to change in many libraries in Kuwait. Zehery (1997:36) reported that "inequity in salaries, increments, and fringe benefits between the indigenous and expatriate staff has been a source of dissatisfaction and apathy in the library work environment" in the Arab Gulf region. Abdel-Motey and Lesher (2007) identified seven variables that affect job satisfaction among academic librarians: salary and benefits; the work environment; the nature of the job; relations with colleagues; relations with superiors; professional development opportunities; and job stability. Professional librarians in the Public Authority for Applied Education (PAAET) in Kuwait were surveyed and reported general job satisfaction. However, most reported dissatisfaction with salary and benefits as well as with professional development opportunities.

Opportunity for continuing professional development (CPD) is crucial considering the lower professional standards in the Middle East and especially with the advent of multiple-script automation systems, e-resources, and information and communications technologies (ICT), which have dramatically changed librarians' tasks. For example, acquisitions librarians may now spend more time negotiating licenses for databases, CDs, or remote access to databases than they do for purchasing books.

Anwar and Al-Ansari (2002) studied continuing professional development (CPD) practices and employers' perceptions about academic library staff in publicly funded universities in the Gulf Cooperation Council (GCC). Their study revealed that the skills most preferred by employers relate to electronic resources, user education, policymaking and resource sharing. Preferred management skills for academic librarians relate to communication, leadership, motivation, problem-solving, staff development and the use of management information data skills. Preferred ICT skills relate to automation systems, electronic resources, networking and multimedia applications. However, there is no agreement on who is responsible for CPD among practitioners, professional associations, academic institutions, employers or government agencies. Some authors have emphasized the need for coordinated national strategies such as Australia's "Library Industry Competency Standards" (Cuthbert, 1997).

7. COOPERATIVE EFFORTS

In general, libraries today face budget cuts and difficulties in harnessing technological advances in the field. These and other reasons have encouraged, or rather necessitated, cooperative initiatives between libraries. One of the major forms of cooperation is the grouping of libraries into consortiums to help cut costs and develop services and resources. There are several benefits of consortiums, including discounts through group purchasing, improved user services, greater access to material, improved database services, and cooperative training programs for library employees within the consortium.

Cooperation often takes place on the local level, but lack of information provision policies and coordination limit their range of service. For example, the Educational Resources Department of PAAET in Kuwait initiated a project in 2006 to link the online catalogues of academic, school, public and research libraries in the country, most of which use the Horizon library system. However, only two libraries responded positively to the initiative: Gulf University of Science and Technology (GUST) and the American University of Kuwait (AUK). Users can now simultaneously search the catalogs of all three universities from any of their online catalogs. However, more coordination and cooperation is needed at an official level.

A very important form of cooperation is exemplified in the Committee of Deans and Directors of Academic Libraries of the GCC, which was established in 1983 to provide a forum for professionals to discuss common issues and policies. The committee meets at least once a year in one of the member countries, aiming to develop cooperation between academic libraries, the level of user services, technical services, and professional development. Committee members discuss their problems, offer proposed solutions, present ongoing projects and ideas for further cooperation. Publishers and service providers and invited to present their products and services to the committee. Recent achievements are the linking of catalogs through a single portal, enlarging the Saudi consortiums to include more libraries in member countries, and organizing training and workshops for the continuing professional development of academic librarians and staff in the GCC. Regarding the latter, Anwar and Al-Ansari (2002:238-239) recommend that the committee takes advantage of their annual meetings to 1) accept responsibility for promoting

CPD in the region, 2) designate selected LIS department and libraries to develop a range of CPD activities for all libraries, 3) promote training needs analyses among all libraries, 4) develop policies for CPD responsibilities, opportunities and incentives, and 5) develop regular CPD activities for LIS professionals as part of their academic library services.

Following the recommendations of the Saudi Deans of Academic Libraries, headed by the Saudi undersecretary of higher education, a Saudi consortium for academic universities was lunched in 2003. The consortium began with a project for Saudi universities to share subscriptions to specialized databases with the goals of activating cooperation, economizing spending, and drawing general guidelines for subscriptions to insure efficient and maximal access to databases for the benefit of users. In its first year, seven universities subscribed to 17 databases; the second year the membership and resources grew to ten universities subscribing in 27 databases, and the consortium continues to grow. Negotiations are underway to include not only Saudi but also other GCC academic libraries in the consortium, as well as plans for a unified portal through which users will be able to access all databases (Informatics 2005).

Cooperation varies in Middle Eastern libraries regarding document delivery and interlibrary loan (ILL). Abdulla (2005) reports that there has recently been strong cooperation among GCC university libraries, namely Sultan Qaboos University in Oman, Kuwait University, KFUPM in Saudi Arabia, American University of Sharjah and UAE University, the latter being a net document suppler rather than a receiver. However, Fadhli and Johnson (2006) report that the three major library services in Kuwait – Kuwait University, PAAET, and the National Scientific and Technical Information Center (NSTIC) – have not efficiently or effectively implemented electronic document delivery to enhance their interlibrary loan services. They point out that while there is no protocol or agreement in Kuwait for resources sharing or document exchange between libraries and other governmental establishments, there emerged in 2001/2002 a type of resource sharing between Kuwait University and NSTIC in the form of a union list of periodicals for both establishments in order to avoid duplication and facilitate ILL between them. This is a first and long-overdue step to a more comprehensive utilization of external sources.

Several authors have supported the idea of greater cooperation on progressive levels. Al-Baridi and Ahmed (2000:115) feel that libraries in the Arabian Gulf region should "actively cooperate and work seriously toward forming a regional digital library network for optimally using the resources, cost, space and time…. But what is important is to plan and design systems in a way that they can be integrated easily later into the national, regional and international digital library networking topologies." There should be national plans to connect all databases in each country in a national information network and, at a later stage, with other Arab and foreign universities.

One of the most recent developments in cooperative librarianship in the Middle East is the launching of the Arabic Union Catalogue (AUC) in 2006, sponsored and supervised by the King Abdulaziz Public Library in Saudi Arabia. The AUC is a non-profit project aiming to develop the infrastructure of Arabic libraries and to enable effective information exchange of resources, especially cataloging records. The goals of the AUC are to reduce efforts spent on original cataloging of Arabic resources, standardize bibliographic data through the application of international specifications and standards, increase bibliographical control of Arabic resources, and facilitate resource sharing on the Arab level. The basic services provided are:

- Bibliographic copy-cataloguing, allowing librarians to download records in MARC format from the AUC database to their local database;
- Uploading local holdings information;
- Original cataloguing on the AUC database through the web;
- Authority copy cataloguing, allowing librarians to download authority records in MARC format from the AUC database;
- References services such as online bibliographic search;
- Cataloging desktop, which provides members with permanent cataloguing assistance by highly qualified specialists and unlimited access to a specialized AUC knowledge base.

Other services include providing MARC records for retrospective conversion; reclassification support for libraries migrating from one classification system to another; MARC upgrades such as converting obsolete tags, indicators and subfield codes to their current equivalents, or deleting or adding fields; collections evaluation using different criteria; and technical support for interlibrary loaning.

The AUC, which is accessible to subscribers via the Internet against record-sharing and fee scales, currently has 400,000 downloadable bibliographic records in MARC format and 412,886 authority records in five categories, among other records. As of 2007, 17 academic libraries and 13 public, national and special libraries are members (Arabic Union Catalog, 2007).

8. CONCLUSION

Academic libraries in the Middle East, numbering over 300, vary considerably regarding collections, services, automation and staffing. Significant differences result largely from the availability of funds, the effects of instability, and affiliations with Western institutions of higher education. Some libraries have large collections in many formats while others have small onsite collections but ample access to electronic resources. Both types of libraries need well-planned information literacy programs to offset the traditional teaching methods and lack of requisite skills for independent research. Instructors, as well, need guidance in the use of electronic sources and how to incorporate research methods in their courses. Intra- and inter-library cooperation is necessary to guarantee the effectiveness of user education and services.

Professional development is a major concern in light of the fast-paced advances in information and communications technology. In addition, librarians' knowledge, skills, status and involvement in academic planning should increase to help overcome lack of motivation, resistance to change and job dissatisfaction.

Most libraries in the Middle East have collections in both Arabic and English, requiring automation systems that handle multiple scripts. The advent of Unicode in 1991 was a breakthrough for automation in the Arabic language, which is unique in many respects. Gradually libraries have converted card-catalogues and some have adopted web-based OPACs, but the MARC format and Z39.50 protocol remain underutilized. The launching of the Arabic Union Catalogue in 2006 will help to standardize bibliographic data and facilitate resource sharing. Indexing efforts are also in need of coordination and institutionalization to overcome problems in coverage, currency and accuracy.

Many academic libraries are taking advantage of consortiums to cut costs and boost collections and services. However, more coordination is needed to efficiently and effectively implement electronic document delivery and interlibrary loans. In addition, more promotional material, seminars, workshops and conferences, as well as media coverage at national, regional and local levels are important in order to develop awareness for the use of libraries and technology in libraries. Cooperative efforts with other professional bodies through formal and informal alliances seem to be the key to successful academic librarianship in the Middle East.

References

Abdel-Motey, Y. and Lesher, T. (2007). "Job satisfaction for professional librarians in the libraries and institutes of the Public Authority for Applied Education and Training in Kuwait" (in Arabic), *Al-Tarbiya Magazine*, no. 160, 88-99.

Ask Zad. [Online] Available: www.askzad.com. Retrieved November 11, 2007.

Abdulla, Ali Dualeh (2005). "The development of electronic journals in the United Arab Emirates University (UAEU)." *Collection Building*, vol. 24, no. 2.

Al-Ansari, Husain A. (1999). "Improving the organizational structure for an electronic environment: A case analysis of Kuwait University libraries." *Library Review*, vol. 48, no. 3.

Al-Baridi, Saleh and Ahmed, Syed Sajjad (2000). "Developing electronic resources at the KFUPM library." *Collection Building*, vol. 19, no. 3.

Al-Fadhli, Meshal Shehab and Johnson, Ian M. (2006). "Electronic document delivery in academic and research organizations in the Gulf States: A case study in Kuwait" *Information Development*, vol. 22, no. 1.

Al-Hadad, Faisal Abdulla (2003). Khadamat al-maktabat al-jamaiah al-Saudia: dirasat tatbeqiya lil-jowda ashamila. Riyadh: King Fahad National Library.

Al-Hassan, S. and Meadows, A.J. (1994). "Improving library personnel management: A case study of Kuwait." Library Management, vol. 15, no. 1, quoted in Al-Fadhli and Johnson (2006).

Al-Khatib, Sahar and Johnson, Ian M. (2001). "Libraries in major universities in Lebanon" *Libri*, vol. 51, no. 4.

Al-Khuraiji, Saleh (2003). Indexing of Arabic periodicals: A comparative analytical study. (In Arabic). [Online] Available: http://www.imamu.edu.sa/ccsi/dis/dissertations/alkhuragi. htm. Retrieved November 11, 2007.

Anwar, Mumtaz A. and Al-Ansari, Husain (2002). "Developing working LIS professionals in the Gulf Cooperation Council countries: A study of the perceptions of deans and directors of academic libraries." *The Electronic Library*, vol. 20, no. 3.

Arabian Campus. [Online] Available: www.arabiancampus.com/studyinqatar/uc.htm. Retrieved November 13, 2007.

Arabic Union Catalogue. (In Arabic). [Online] Available: http://ipublish.aruc.org/Detail.asp?InSectionID=39&InNewsItemID=122. Retrieved November 13, 2007.

Arabic Union Catalog. [Online] Available: http://www.aruc.org/uPortal/Initial ize?uP_tparam= props&props=AUCE&uP_reload_layout=true. Retrieved November 13, 2007.

Ashoor, Mohammed-Saleh (2005). "Information literacy: a case study of the KFUPM library." *The Electronic Library*, vol. 23, no. 4.

Bergan, Erling (2000). "Libraries in the West Bank and Gaza: Obstacles and possibilities" paper presented at the 66th IFLA Council and General Conference, Jerusalem, 13-18 August 2000. [Online] Available: http://www.ifla.org/IV/ifla66/papers/170-172e. htm. Retrieved November 11, 2007.

Cuthbert, Sheena (1997). "Library Industry Competency Standards: State of the Art – State Library of Victoria" *Australian Library Journal*, vol. 46, no. 3.

Diesnis, O. (2003). "Success stories from the field: Korea and United Arab Emirates" *(Elsevier) Library Connect Newsletter*, vol. 1, no. 4, quoted in Abdulla (2005).

Gilreath, Charles L. (2006). "Library development for Texas A&M at Quatar: Maximum access/minimum holdings." *Collection Building*, vol. 25, no. 2.

Gyeszly, Suzanne D. and Ismail, Matthew (2003). "American University of Sharjah library: A collection development project." *Collection Building*, vol. 22, no. 4.

Ibrahim, Ahmed Elhafiz (2005). "Displays of Arabic script on web-based OPACs in GCC institutions." *The Electronic Library*, vol. 23, no. 4.

Ibrahim, Ahmed Elhafiz (2004). "Use and user perception of electronic resources in the United Arab Emirates University (UAEU)." *Libri*, vol. 54, no. 1.

Informatics Magazine, (2005). (In Arabic). [Online] Available: http://www. informatics.gov.sa/modules. php?name=Sections&op=viewarticle&artid=90 Retrieved November 15, 2007.

Iraq Ministry of Higher Education and Scientific Research. [Online] Available: http://www.moheiraq. org/RelatedAgency.htm#تاعماجلا_ . Retrieved November 13, 2007.

Jordan Ministry of Higher Education and Scientific Research. [Online] Available: http://www.mohe. gov.jo/mohedesc/detailsar.asp?kind=2&p_id=57. Retrieved November 13, 2007.

Khalid, H.M. (2000). "The use of technology for housekeeping and bibliographic searching activities in the university libraries of Saudi Arabia: The need for acceleration." *Library Review*, vol. 49, no. 4.

Khurshid, Zahiruddin (2001). "Analytical cataloging of full-text journal databases at a Middle East university." *Cataloging & Classification Quarterly*, vol. 32, no. 2.

Kurshid, Zahiruddin (2002). "Arabic script materials: Cataloging issues and problems." *Cataloging and Classification Quarterly*, vol. 34, no. 4.

Khurshid, Zahiruddin (2006). "Migration from DOBIS/LIBIS to Horizon at KFUPM." *Library Hi Tech*, vol. 24, no. 3.

Lebanese ministry of Education& Higher Education. [Online] Available: http:// www.higher-edu. gov.lb/index_ar.asp. Retrieved November 13, 2007.

Maguire, John T. (2001). "A semester in Palestine: Volunteering in Birzeit University main library" *Australian Library Journal*, vol.50, issue 2. [Online] Available: http://alia.org. au/publishing/alj/50.2/full.text/semester.in.palestine. html. Retrieved October 13, 2007.

Maingate (2007). The American University of Beirut Quarterly Magazine. [Online] Available: http:// wwwlb.aub.edu.lb/~webmgate/spring2007/article7.htm. Retrieved November 13, 2007.

Maxymuk, J. (2004) "Internet: Electronic journals redux" *The Bottom Line: Managing Library Finances*, vol. 17, no. 2, quoted in Abdulla (2005).

Medawar, Katia (1999). "The implementation of the Arabic script in OLIB7 at the American University of Beirut Libraries." Program, vol. 33, no. 4.

OCLC (nd). "OCLC-MARC Records: 1993 November to Present" (section 5.3). [Online] Available: www.oclc.org/support/documentation/worldcat/records/subscription/5/5.pdf. Retrieved January 4, 2008.

Palestinian Ministry of Education & Higher Education. [Online] Available: http://www.moe.gov.ps/ links.html. Retrieved November 13, 2007.

Qari, Abdulghafoor A. (1999). "Training for information technology at King Abdulaziz University library." *Journal of Librarianship and Information Science*, vol. 31, no. 1.

Rehman, Sajjad Ur and Al-Obaidali, Luluwa Ahmad (2000). "Internet use and capabilities of library and information professionals at the Kuwait university libraries: Results of a survey." *Program*, vol. 34, no. 2.

Rudasill, L. (1998). "Global literacy initiatives: the United States and developing nations. [Online] Available: http://www.iatul.org/conferences/pastconferences/1998proceedings.asp. Retrieved November 17, 2007.

Saudi Ministry of Higher Education. [Online] Available: http://web.mohe.gov.sa/detail.asp?InService ID=247&intemplatekey=MainPage. Retrieved November 13, 2007.

Siddiqui, Moid A. (1998). "Academic libraries in Saudi Arabia: A survey report." *The Reference Librarian*, no. 60.

Siddiqui, Moid A. (2003). "Adoption of Internet for resource sharing by the Gulf academic libraries." *The Electronic Library*, vol. 21, no. 1.

Siddiqui, Moid A. (2000). "Brief communication: Document delivery in the Arabian Gulf." *Interlending & Document Supply*, vol. 28, no. 3.

Sultanate of Oman: Ministry of Higher Education. [Online] Available: http://www.mohe.gov.om. Retrieved November 13, 2007.

Syria Ministry of Higher Education. [Online] Available: www.mhe.gov.sy/ara/article/79-sub.htm. Retrieved November 13, 2007.

UAE Commission for Academic Accreditation. [Online] Available: www.caa.ae/CAweb/Desktop Modules/Institutions.aspx. Retrieved November 13, 2007.

Varnet, Harvey. Email communication with the author on November 10, 2007.

Vassie, Roderic (2000). "Improving access in bilingual, biscript catalogues through Arabised authority control." *Online Information Review*, vol. 24, no. 6.

Younis, Abdul Razeq (1999). "The effect of automated systems on Jordanian university libraries' organizational structure." *Library Review*, vol. 48, no. 7.

Zehery, M.H. (1997). University library development in the Arab Gulf region: A survey and analysis of six state university libraries." *International Information and Library Review*, vol. 29, no. 1.

SPECIAL LIBRARIES

Reham Al-Issa

1. INTRODUCTION

This chapter examines the state of special libraries and information centers in selected nations of the Asian Arab world including six countries of the Gulf Cooperation Council (GCC) namely Bahrain, Kuwait, Saudi Arabia, United Arab Emirates, Oman and Qatar will be reviewed. Special libraries in Syria, Lebanon and
Palestine have also been examined. The approach used is that the country's special
libraries have been examined for selected variables of overview and history, resources, human resources, automation and IT use, and other pertinent aspects of
marketing and quality management.

1.1 Definition and Scope

A special library is a library that is not classified as an academic, school or a public library. Some examples of special libraries include medical libraries, corporate
libraries, and museum libraries. The term information centers is also used interchangeably with special library. The special library deals with specific patrons,
and a specialized type of information. Special libraries have existed in the Arab
world for quite a while and have continued developing both gradually and progressively. They are usually part of corporate organizations, ministries and governmental agencies, and other public or private enterprises.

1.2 Overview

Generally speaking, special libraries in the region have not flourished as generously as other types of libraries and the funding in many cases has been limited.
Very few of them have been patterned along the standards and norms of special libraries in the West. Human resource polices have also greatly varied from one library to another. One common denominator found among these libraries is an emphasis on English language in their resource development and service policies and
practices.

Iraqi occupation of Kuwait stalled the development and growth of special libraries in Kuwait and other libraries in the neighboring countries. Salem (1992) examined the state of eight special libraries in Kuwait and their situation after the Iraqi
occupation and reported that the estimated cost of damage to these eight libraries
was two million Kuwaiti Dinars. The library that was hit the hardest was the National Scientific and Technological Information Center (NSTIC); also know to be
the most technologically advanced and rich in terms of its collection in the region.
There are a number of special libraries in various sectors of finance and investment, trade, industry, research and health and law libraries that have been developed. Notable examples of these include NSTIC of KISR, health and law libraries

of Kuwait University, Central bank of Kuwait library, and libraries in petroleum companies. Al-Babtain Library is the latest addition and it is dedicated to Arabic poetry and related arts. This library is the world's first library specializing in Arabic poetry. Its uniqueness stems from the interests of its founder and owner, poet Abdulaziz Saud Al-Babtain, who wanted the library to be a unique resource on the subject.

In Saudi Arabia, the majority of special libraries belong to governmental agencies. They are expected to provide crucial support to their parent organizations (Siddiqi 1995). Special libraries in the Kingdom of Saudi Arabia have extensive collections in respective areas of specialization. Additionally, they are well equipped electronically with the latest technology and databases. The libraries are well funded and are most often staffed by a professional librarian.

According to Young and Ali (1992), there are around 65 special libraries in the Kingdom of Bahrain, and 24 of these libraries are part of governmental agencies and ministries. Bahrain also has 12 special libraries that are Embassy libraries. Specialized information centers such as the Bait al Qur'an for Quranic research, Bahrain Center for Studies and Research (BCSR), and the Bahrain Historical Document Center (BHDC) are among the well-known special libraries in Bahrain. International information centers such as the United Nations Information Center (UNIC), and the British Council Library (BLDSC), and the American Embassy USIS and Commercial Library are also based in Bahrain. The management of these centers is usually done by expatriates due to a lack of nationals who have a professional degree in librarianship.

Qatar is a country encountering a boom in all aspects of education and economy. The infrastructural development has been immense during the recent years. It is estimated that Qatar is the home of about 150 special libraries. Khalifa (1992) examined these libraries and found their state rather discouraging. They are mostly lacking in substance and quality and are considered a place to house small collections. The overall organization and management of these information centers was also found to be poor. Most of the special libraries in Qatar are part of Ministries or government organizations. Some of the best special libraries in Qatar include the Gulf Organization for Industrial Consultations, Al Diwan Al Amiri, the Ministry of Foreign Affairs, just to name a few. The Gulf Organization for Industrial Consultations was founded in 1976 and is regarded as the best information center in Qatar because of its rich collection. Al-Mufaraji (1992) reported that there are four major special libraries in Oman. He also mentioned that 22 of such libraries existed in government departments and ministries. He found that these libraries generally lacked in organization and management. The deficiencies were attributed to the absence of professional librarians. Libraries located within corporate setup included the Central Bank of Oman Library, the Oman Mining Company

Library, the Oman Institute of Bankers, and the Oman Chamber of Commerce and Industry Library.

Little information was available in literature about special libraries in Syria, Amman, Palestine and Lebanon. The earliest special libraries in Syria were founded in during 1950's. A number of such libraries are located in government departments. Primary purpose of these libraries is reported to be supporting official work and academic and research activities. These are also reported to support cultural activities, typical of the nature of Syrian government and society. (Al-Laham 1992)

In Jordan as well, early special libraries were instituted back in 1950s. Subeihi (2001) reported the development of ten special libraries during this phase. It is reported that by the end of the 20th century, Jordan had a total of 104 special libraries out of a total of 1527 libraries. A main motivator for the progress in Amman is the Jordanian Library Association (JLA), which was established in 1963. The association has contributed toward cultivating professionalism "in these libraries. The association has been conducting training courses, issuing a quarterly newsletter (Risalat Al-Maktaba), hosting conferences and seminars, and cooperating with sister agencies in the region. Thus has contributed to the development of special libraries as well.

Bergan (2000) conducted a survey in 1996 and reported the existence of 295 libraries in Palestine, one third of which are supposed to be special in nature. Of these 295 over 100 are special libraries (Bergan 2000). It was maintained that majority of these libraries are rich in their collection and usually have a high number of users from the organization they serve. According to the researcher these institutions also have a symbolic expression of the will of the people in these countries. Some notable examples of these institutions include Women's Studies Center Library, Human Right Organization Library, and the Arab Studies Society in Orient House (Bergan 2000).

2. RESOURCES

The collections in the special libraries of this region vary in size and scope according to the role and status of the library itself and its parent organization. In Kuwait, (Al-Ansari, 2008) surveyed 14 special libraries and reported that each of them had a collection of less than 15,000 volumes. Many of the special libraries in Kuwait have small monographic collections, typical about this type of libraries. In terms of journal subscriptions, majority of these libraries subscribed to less than 100 periodical. The library with the richest collection in Kuwait and the GCC is the Health Center Library; it has the largest number of subscriptions to periodicals between 750-1599.

As a result of the Gulf war, many of the libraries were looted and burned; the total loss to special libraries was calculated to be about 2 million items at a cost of about 1.3 Kuwaiti Dinars. The center that was hit the hardest was National Scientific and Technological Center (NSTIC), another information center in Kuwait with an extensive collection. This center suffered great losses during the Gulf war, but the Kuwait Institute for Scientific Research has formulated a strategic plan to rebuild and develop their collection, and they have been keeping in line with their strategic plan. (Salem, 1992)

In Saudi Arabia, Saudi Aramco has a collection of over 55,000 volumes and 1,600 journal subscriptions. The average collection of 25 special libraries in Saudi Arabia is less than 10,000 volumes. King Abdulaziz City for Science and Technology has a strong collection in research management, solar energy, nuclear energy and related fields. In 1992 they had over 11,100 books, over 350,000 technical reports (Microfiche) and over 60,000 source documents. At that time the library subscribed to over 340 periodicals. They have also developed several databases to promote resource sharing in the Kingdom of Saudi Arabia (Al-Tasan 1992).

In Bahrain, according to Young and Ali (1992) the College of Health Science, Al-Farsi Library (AFL) has the largest collection in the group of special libraries. Other sizable collections are reported in the Arabian Gulf University Medicine and Medical Science Library. Al- Mufaraji (1992) stated that the Central Bank of Oman had a total of 5,000 books and 20 periodicals, the Oman Mining Company had 2,500 books and 18 periodicals and the Oman Chamber of Commerce and Industry Library had 3,110 books and 25 periodicals.

Special libraries in Qatar are reported to be dynamic and thriving. According to Khalifa (1992), two good examples of special libraries in Qatar are Hamad Central Hospital library that was established in 1981, and the Qatari General Petroleum Corporation Library which was also established during the early 80's.

Moving away from the GCC to Syria and it neighbors; Al-Laham (1992) reported that in Syria the collections of special libraries varied, depending upon the size of the library and its mission. Majority of special libraries in Syria are reportedly contributing to research and cultural activities and events. In Palestine the collections vary depending on the size of the library. Censorship in Palestine hinders the collection development of their libraries. The Israeli military has banned specific books over the years. In Beirut one of the high talked about libraries is the Imam Ouzal College of Islamic Studies Library, which was founded in 1979 and has over 40,000 volumes in its collection. (Al-Laham 1992)

From this review, it is apparent that health sciences libraries are always the richest in resources. They are technologically advanced and use electronic resources heavily. In the CGG region specifically in Saudi Arabia, Kuwait and Qatar, special libraries in the area of petroleum studies and research are also having substantial resources. Concurrently, rich mosque libraries abound and flourish in Syria, Lebanon, Amman, and Palestine. Valuable manuscript collections and rare books are found in these libraries. In their literary treasures, these libraries are like rich museums of history religion and culture.

3. HUMAN RESOURCES

No library can grow without having competent workforce, irrespective of its type, nature, resources, and location. This is the most crucial resource for all libraries and special libraries are no exception to this norm. When we find that a number of special libraries do not have a single professional on their roll, it becomes their most serious handicap. Special libraries require subject expertise on the top of professional qualifications. It is observed that special libraries in this region lack in these respects seriously.

With the continuing increase in special libraries in this region, demand for professional librarians is more pressing. One of the major obstacles that Saudi Arabia, Qatar, Bahrain, and Oman are faced with is the shortage of professional librarians. In a clear majority of the private enterprise libraries, professional staff is generally expatriates who are usually paid lesser salaries and do not have the same career prospect as their local counterparts. In the case of Bahrain, according to Young and Ali (1992) the number of Bahraini's who hold a Master's degree in Library Science from a library school was nine. Efforts have been made in producing librarians with a bachelor's degree who can assist in the operation and running of these information centers. In 1992 the only library in Bahrain with more than one professional librarian was the University of Bahrain and BCSR. Oman is confronted with many problems in librarianship and foremost of them is the lack of professional librarians, equipment and management support.

The number of special libraries in Kuwait was not determined, but according to Al Hassan and Meadow (1994) thirty such libraries existed prior to the Gulf war. Before the war there were about 33 information specialists working in them and NSTIC was considered the largest information center in Kuwait. NSTIC had the tradition of employing professionals with a Master's degree and they have the largest number of these professionals. The Health Center library is the library, equipped with professional librarians. Other special libraries in Kuwait have few staff members. The average number of staff is reported to be 1-3 persons. Almost every special library has one professional staff member on the team. It is clear that these libraries heavily depend on professional staff for day-to-day operations. There is a lesser need for non-professional and support staff. In Of all the special libraries in Kuwait, NSTIC offered the best packages in terms of compensation, training, development and appraisal of their staff.

In Jordan, the situation is not much different from other countries in the region. In a 2000 survey, it was reported that there were 14 doctorates in librarianship and about 35 Master's degree holders in Jordan. They are facing the same problems of lack of professional staff and resources. (Subeihi, 2001)

The situation in Palestine is also pretty much similar. Political and social uncertainties do not permit stability in situation. In Syria, it was noted that professional manpower was not available for services. Some of those who were managing these services had been allowed opportunities of overseas exposure and engagement with external agencies. The Syrian Libraries and Documents Society was founded in Damascus in 1972. The Ministry of Education has been trying to organize training courses in library science and systems. A number of Syrian professionals are working in richer Arabian nations that provide them better financial packages. That is an additional factor behind the non availability of professionals in this country (Al-Laham,1992).

4. AUTOMATION

One common problem impeding library automation in this region has been that a large part of the collection of each library is in Arabic, and the system does not have the capability to cater to the needs of Arabic script. However, a number of systems have not used multi-lingual features. Special libraries in the region have also followed suit in automating their libraries and using information technology.

Khurshid (2006) claims that one of the first institutions that was automated in the region is the King Fahad University of Petroleum & Minerals in Dahran. Back in the 1970's they acquired a system and made modifications so that it satisfies the needs of the resources of the library. Currently they use Horizon Information Portal (HIP) and they are focused on developing their collection digitally. Another pioneering information center in Saudi Arabia is King Abdulaziz City for Science (KACST), administered by the Directorate of Information Services. KACST's OPAC is also searchable through GULFNET and KACSTNET, providing crucial support for resource sharing in this country. Some other special libraries In Saudi Arabia, Saudi Aramco in Dahran and the Institute of Public Administration in Riyadh have been working with DOBIS/LIBIS system. The Ministry of Finance and National Economy in Riyadh is using the bilingual system of VTLS and it has been subscribing to OCLC for their cataloging. The MINISIS system is used at King Faisal Center for Islamic Research and Studies in Riyadh. Special libraries in Saudi Arabia have been using the latest IT applications and telecommunications systems such as Internet, fax and phone (Khurshid 2006).

Al-Ansari (2008) examined the state of automation in 32 special libraries in Kuwait. He found that 18 of the 25 respondent libraries were automated, 8 used

Horizon, and other libraries used other systems or those they had developed in-house. Seven of the 25 libraries reported that they had not automated. Al-Ansari also provided information about automated modules, hardware platforms, network configuration, number of workstations and other related aspects. He found that all the 18 libraries had automated their catalog, 7 had automated acquisitions, 7 had automated their circulation, and 7 had automated their serials.

In Bahrain, Qatar and Oman automation has been used in special libraries. Large operations are automated while this might not be the case with small libraries. In Jordan's libraries, computers were first introduced around late 80's. Major libraries have succeeded in the automation of their operations such as the Abdel Hameed Shoman Library. Subeihi (2001) reported that two major software packages used in Jordan are as follows:

- CDS/ISIS developed by UNESCO
- MINISIS a product of IDRC- Canada.

Both have been Arabized by the Arab League Documentation Center. Other libraries in Amman have developed their own in-house systems. Additionally, all libraries have access to the internet. In Palestine the automation initiative is slower than it is in Amman, but the need to automate has been established.

A system called LibSys has been developed locally in Ramallah and has a wide spread use among the libraries in Palestine. In the case of Lebanon, all the major academic libraries have been, automated, but we do not have enough information about automation initiatives in is special libraries (Subeihi 2001).

5. CONCLUSION

We have noted a great deal of diversity among special libraries in this region. Some libraries are well developed, advanced in their use of IT, resourceful, and vital within their organizations. At the same time, we find a large number of them weak, low on resources, and backward in their outlook and vitality within their organizations. Consistent with the roles and status of the parent organizations, this diversity seems to be natural and commonplace. These differences are evident in user community, budgeting, staffing, and other physical and intellectual resources.

In terms of development, it has been noted that special libraries, especially those in the GCC, started growing in number and in their resources around early 1980's. All available literature indicates that the Iraqi occupation not only impeded the growth of the libraries in Kuwait, but its impact reverberated throughout the GCC, encompassing all countries of the GCC. In particular special libraries in Bahrain and Saudi Arabia were most affected since they had established cooperation with their counterpart special libraries in Kuwait. Ties were also cut with Iraqi libraries as a result of the war. Since then Iraqi special libraries had little interaction or collaboration with sister libraries in the region, hampering their growth drastically.

It is obvious that the most developed special libraries are the health sector libraries. These are usually rich in their collections and they have the latest technology and best selection of databases. These are followed by libraries specializing in petroleum, and science and research. This also reflects the significance of these two fields to the socio-political-economic fabric of the Gulf community. The first field is healthcare, its development and the well being of the people. The second field, petroleum and science and technology provide major economic drive to the GCC countries. Both are equally important, and almost all countries need them for their well being and development.

When it comes to automation and information technology, it has been noted that while some of them are rich and advanced, others have not made any significant progress in this area. Organization strategies, staffing situation, leadership, and budget are the primary factors behind slow applications in this area. Large and resourceful libraries are automated and most promising among them are health, S&T and research libraries. Smaller special libraries are usually part of small organizations and organizational needs and finances do not allow major investments in IT applications. Many of them have thus developed in house systems with little application potential, primarily due to financial and human considerations. Some special libraries that had implemented automation early in the 1980's are at the forefront of IT use in the regions such as KACST and KFUPM library in Saudi Arabia and KISR in Kuwait. Additional important considerations have been the needs of Arabization of software and creation of bilingual systems.

The most serious problem in the regional special libraries is the availability of professional staff. Human resources are the most valuable asset for managing these libraries. An additional difficulty is that many of those who hold professional degrees in librarianship are opting for jobs outside the world of librarianship. In many countries they have to count on expatriate professionals to fill-in these positions. There is a need for these nations to be investing in the education of professionals and their continued development so that these libraries and information centers are run effectively and efficiently. Finding the right person to run a special library in the Arab world is somewhat of a challenge, and this needs to be strategically addressed.

With regard to resources, it is evident that majority of libraries, specifically health and S&T libraries, are well stocked and contain valuable resources in their respective fields. It is also clear that in some organizations, special libraries are given the task to house organizational archives, reports and other similar resources Also some of them are meant for satisfying the needs of selected few in the organization. Because of the nature of special libraries, they are often quiet places with little traffic, as they support their community and the public have limited access to them. Almost all of them are using Internet. Those libraries that lag behind in their use of electronic resources might be constrained in this aspect. Overall, it can be generalized that many of these libraries are playing a vital role for providing information support in their organizations. Those libraries in the public sector have definite sources of funding while this may not be the case with those located in the private sector.

The new trend of marketing has become popular amongst all kinds of libraries. The image a library has along with the services it provides need to be marketed positively. Librarians over the years have not really succeeded in marketing the libraries and the services they offer. Special libraries need to exert more effort in their marketing, because unlike public or academic libraries where patrons come to the library for pleasure, assignments, etc. special libraries have a specific focus and they serve a dedicated community. Thus, marketing their resources and services to their direct users is needed in order for the library to thrive. Quality management goes hand in hand with marketing and special libraries need to attend to that positively.

The future of special libraries in this region appears to hold some promise. Special libraries of the region will continue to evolve and grow to support their immediate institutions and ultimately their communities. Emphasis should be given to the education and training of the nationals of these countries in order to ensure that these libraries/information centers continue to operate and prosper. The efforts of the Special Libraries Association (Arabian Gulf Chapter) have really helped librarians in this region through their annual conference, training activities, publications and other activities. This has also provided a sense of collegiality and fraternity among the professionals of the region.

There is a need to conduct systematic research about special libraries in the region and various aspects of their management, resources and services. There appears to be a dearth of pertinent literature in this area. Most of the works cited in this chapter were published during the 1990's, and there is a strong need to have more current treatment of this vital sector of librarianship in this region.

References

Al-Ansari, Husain (2008). Special Libraries in Kuwait. Unpublished paper.

Aman, Mohammed M. (1992). Libraries and information systems in the ArabGulf States: after the war. Journal of Information Science, vol. 18, 447-451.

Bergan, Earling (2000). Libraries in the West Bank and Gaza: Obstacles and possibilities. Paper presented to 66th IFLA Council and General Conference. [Online] Available: http://www.ifla.org/IV/ifla66/papers/ 170-172e.htm. Retrieved November 26, 2007.

Al-Hassan, S., & Meadows, A.J. (1994). Improving Personnel Management. A Case Study of Kuwait. Library Management, vol. 15, 19-25.

Khalifa, Shaban A. (1992). Libraries and Librarianship in Qatar. Journal of Information Science, vol. 18, 481-489.

Khurshid, Zahiruddin (2006). Migration from DOBIS/LIBIS to Horizon at KFUPM. Library Hi Tech, vol. 24, 440-451.

Al-Laham, Ghassan (1992). Libraries and Infrastructure in Syria. Journal of Information Science. vol. 18, 497-504.

Lebanon (2008). Islamic Libraries and Information Centers.[Online] Available: http://www.geocities.com/Athens/Rhodes/9485/listofislamiclibraries.html? 200728. Retrieved on December 4, 2007.

Al-Mufaraji, Moosa N. (1992). Libraries and Library Education in Oman.Journal of Information Science. vol. 18, 471-479.

Salem, Shawky (1992). Tables and photos on the Iraqi aggression to the library and information infrastructure in Kuwait. Journal of Information Science, vol. 18, 425-440.

Scammell, Alison (1997). Handbook of special librarinaship and information work. London: ASLIB.

Al-Shara, Mohammed (2007). Marketing and total quality management in special libraries. (In Arabic) [Online] Available: http://www.informatics.gov. sa/mod ules.php?name=sections&op=printpage&artid=79. Retrieved on November 21, 2007.

Siddiqui, Moid Ahmad (1995). Management of libraries in Saudi Arabia: practices and constraints. Library Management, vol. 16, 24-32.

The Special Libraries Association (Arabian Gulf Chapter). [Online] Available: http://www.sla.org. Retrieved November 4, 2007.

Subeihi, Mohammad A (2001). Library Concepts in Jordan. BIBLIOTHEKS-DIENST, vol. 35, 833-840.

Al-Tasan, Mohammed Ali (1992).The role of the King Abdulaziz City for Science and Technology in Information Services in the Kingdom of Saudi Arabia. Journal of Information Science, vol. 18, 491-495.

Young, Harold C., & Ali, S. Nazim (1992). The Gulf War and its effect on information and library services in the Arabian Gulf with particular reference to the State of Bahrain. *Journal* of Information Science. vol. 18, 453-462.

SCHOOL LIBRARIES

Hamad Ibrahim Alomran

1. INTRODUCTION

Learning resource centers have emerged as a vital organ for the learning process in schools. School libraries or learning resource centers are now used interchangeably while other terms such as resource center, media center are also used with a similar connotation. The primary purpose of learning resource center is to support the learning process of school children in curricular, extra-curricular, and developmental needs. In this context, developing information literacy among school children becomes one of the essential functions of these centers.

2. STUDIES ABOUT SCHOOL RESOURCE CENTERS

AlSwedan (1996) examined the state of school libraries in the Arab Gulf countries. From his analysis, he brought forth the following points:

- School libraries in the Arab Gulf countries lack a solid foundation that would enable them to perform their functions appropriately.
- These are mostly monograph-oriented and do not have substantial collections of other media.
- These schools do not have specialist staff. Mostly these are managed by part-time staff or teachers who are given this additional job. More than half of them are not located in suitable physical quarters.
- Most of them are not furnished appropriately.
- Most of these schools do not use technology effectively. Book selection is not based on any scientific method. Hence these do not provide support to the academic process. Technical services are not performed using the bibliographic standards. These libraries provide weak services. Few libraries offer reference services and facilities for photocopying.

The study was conducted twelve years back and since then ministries of education in many of these countries have made efforts in improving their situation. Many of these libraries have now been converted into resource centers. Still, many of them lag behind. Al Omran (2007) focused on the school resource centers in Saudi Arabia and made the following observations:

- Most librarians are full time but they are not specialists in this kind of work, as their education and training were general in nature and had little to do with this type of work.

- Most centers are located in specifically built quarters. Yet many others are not housed in special purpose facilities, defying the standard of 150 cubic meters.
- Most centers are not equipped with technological equipment and facilities.
- Though these centers are well stocked, their collections appear to have deficiencies in the areas of science and language.
- Bibliographic work is not accomplished in most of these centers.
- Many of them lack adequate financial appropriations.

Al Manaey (2000) noted that in Bahrain, most of these centers did not have clarity of role and functions. These were thus removed from the learning process. She also noted that most of these centers offered traditional services such as borrowing, photocopying and searching references. There was little use of electronic resources. The teachers were not keen to bring students to these centers, as they did not have a clear idea about their role.

Al Musawy & Halwagy (1994) had earlier noted that the Bahraini resource centers did not have adequate facilities. Their collections were found to be weak and were housed in inadequate quarters.

Osman had examined the state of libraries in Qatar back in 1992. He had complained that the space provided to these libraries was inadequate. A very small ratio of Qatari schools (13%) had school libraries. No standard practices of bibliographic work had been adopted.

Al Amory, et al. (2004) tried to identify the problems that hindered the development of elementary school libraries. He observed that the staff members did not have proper training in their work.

3. SITUATION OF RESOURCE CENTERS

This writer developed contacts with the officers responsible for learning resource centers in the ministries of education in Jordan, United Arab Emirates, Bahrain, Saudi Arabia, Syria, Iraq, Oman, Palestine, Qatar, Kuwait, Lebanon and Yemen. The writer was also well familiar with the situation of these centers in Saudi Arabia and the neighboring nations who are members of the Gulf Cooperation Council. Also the writer made telephonic contacts with a number of principals of schools who had the insight to make comments on the situation of these learning resource centers. It is not easy to generalize from these observations and exchanges. The situation described in the following sections provides a general view of the overall condition prevailing in the centers of this region. Some primary observations are:

- The administrative authority responsible for the school libraries lies in the ministry of education. Normally this ministry has a department headed by deputies.
- Almost 30% of the schools in this region do not have adequate libraries.
- Most of them do not have professional librarians. Normally a part-time librarian may spend about twelve periods in a typical Saudi school.
- Library staff members are not professionally trained in technical and public services.

In the six nations of the GCC, the trend has been to establish Learning Resource Centers that receive well stocked collections and these have the needed equipment. But, those institutions that do not have these centers have the same old libraries, lacking in resources, services, and management.

3.1 Development

This region has a strong tradition of knowledge, scholarship and libraries. Great libraries were found in the centers of civilization located in Baghdad, Damascus, Jerusalem, and Hejaz. However, when we look at the modern state of school libraries, we can trace their development during the period when modern institutions of learning and education have been established since mid-80s.

We have noted that in some of the Asian Arab countries, a great deal of effort has been made in changing the role of the school libraries to learning resource centers, adding technology and media to their resources, and having adequate physical facilities in terms of space, furnishing, etc. Concurrently, we do not find similar developments in other Arab countries.

There is a need that these resource centers are integrated with the learning programs of these institutions. Then the teachers need to work hand-in-hand with the professional librarians so as to develop information literacy capabilities among students.

3.2 Technical Services

It has been found that almost all the libraries are using DDC and AACR2 for their technical operations. In Saudi Arabia, Kuwait and some other GCC member nations, technical processing is performed centrally in the designated offices of the ministries of education. This centralized processing is not found in other countries.

In Saudi Arabia, the Arabian Union Catalog project was initiated in 2006. King Abdulaziz Public Library in Riyadh has been managing this project. It is expected that other libraries in this region will benefit from that. School libraries can use this resource for copy cataloging and authority files.

3.3 Automation Packages

Some of the school libraries are automated. Different approaches have been used for automation. Ministries of education in certain countries have developed automated packages for their school libraries. These include:

- Alyaseer: It is a product of the Saudi Ministry of Education and used in Saudi schools.
- Aleph Baa Almaktabat (A B C libraries): It is a product of the Bahraini Ministry of Education and applied in Bahraini schools.
- Afaq Almarefah (scopes of knowledge): It is a product of the Omani Ministry of Education. It is applied in Oman.
- Winisis: This is an open source program supported by UNESCO.

Some private schools in the region are using Unicorn and Follett. Most of these automation packages have the modules of loans, acquisition, cataloguing, and serials control.

3.4 Acquisition

A number of countries such as Saudi Arabia and Kuwait have a centralized system of acquisition. The designated departments in the ministries of education acquire materials for all the school libraries under their control.

Certain collection development criteria have also been applied in some countries such as ten volumes per student in a school. Budgets are allocated using this formula and acquisitions are managed. A core of 1500-2000 books is considered to be the foundation collection. Once the books are received and catalogued, these are sent to school libraries. The system has both its merits and demerits.

Selection of books is done using principles of book selection and criteria developed for the purpose. These are expected to support instructional activity, promote reading habits among students, and cultivate positive values for personality development. Current materials are preferred in selection. In many of these states, some sort of censorship is also used, which is related to religious, political and cultural sensitivities.

A variety of sources are acquired that include fiction, other types of books, audiovisual materials, and electronic media containing instructional programs.

3.5 Services

Standard services in these libraries include loan, reference, and photocopying services. The learning resource centers support teachers in preparing lessons for classes. They help teachers in the use of instructional technology and resources. And the centers conduct activities for developing information literacy capabilities among students. Students are also encouraged to use the resources and services of the resource centers for participating in extra-curricular and cultural activities.

3.6 Buildings

Certain standards have been implemented for Saudi Arabian school libraries. The area specified for the school libraries is in the range of 40-80 cubic meters. This variation is related to the school area and number of schools and students. The area of a learning resource center is in the range of 80-150 cubic meters with provisions for administrative office, printed and non-printed resources, equipment, readers, and specialized services. Normally it has two halls for self-learning and collective learning. Figure 1 gives an overall layout scheme for a typical resource center. The hall meant for collective activities is suitable for group activities of information literacy and other cultural activities.

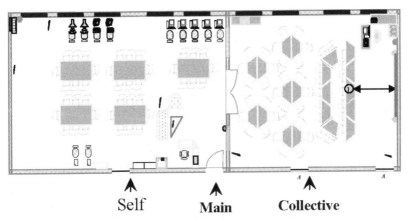

Self   Main   Collective

Figure 1. Layout of learning resource centers

3.7 Personnel

The person who is in-charge of a resource center should have a minimum of diploma in library and information science. In most cases the librarian has a bachelor degree in library and information science. The person should have educational, administrative and professional capabilities. The librarian is responsible for organizing resources, providing services, and maintaining liaison with teachers.

In some countries, no professional is available to organize the library or resource center. In this case, normally it is one of the teachers who is assigned the responsibility to provide library services. Such a person is expected to have 12 periods in a week meant for library services.

4. CONCLUSION

The situation of school libraries or learning resource centers in the Asian Arab nations varies from country to country. In Some GCC member nations, a great deal of effort has been made in transforming school libraries into learning resource centers. But, little development was noted in other countries.

In the six GCC nations, processing of materials is centralized. Materials are centrally selected, acquired, catalogued and delivered to these centers. This arrangement has both merits and demerits. While all school libraries receive resources, the process is bureaucratic and time consuming. Specialized needs of one school may not be as well satisfied in this process.

Physical facilities have been subjected to standards and criteria laid down by the ministries of education in some countries. But, no standards are uniformly applied in the region.

There is a strong need that information literacy skills are developed among school children. For this purpose, information literacy should be packaged and delivered to the school children. When these students become active and dynamic learners, the resource centers will be effectively used.

Teachers are the backbone in the learning process. They need to be integrated with the learning activities of the resource centers. Professionals responsible for managing these resource centers should have clear strategies for bringing teachers into the net of effective use of the resources and services of the resource centers. This is a major challenge for the resource center staff.

Learning resource centers can become effective only if these are managed by competent professional librarians. It is clear that the required qualification of the professional is diploma or a bachelor's degree in library and information science. There is no specialized track of education in library schools for school libraries. This is a major handicap in engaging specialist staff for these libraries. This problem can be somewhat addressed if training programs are designed and conducted for these librarians. This is an urgent need for the development of school resource centers in this region.

References

Alamory, and her colleagues (2004). The difficulties of activating the learning resource centers in the elementary education. Masqat: Sultan Qaboos University.

Almanay, Latifa Ali (2000). A Survey of the learning source centers in secondary schools in Bahrain: the final report. Bahrain: Ministry of Education.

Almusawi, Naser Hasan, Al halwagy, Fesal Ahmed (1994). An evaluative study to the reality of learning resource centers in the schools of Bahrain. Bahrain: University of Bahrain

Alomran, Hamad Ibrahim (2007). Learning resource centers in Saudi Arabia: a study to the Rrality with a plan for an ideal center. Riyadh: Riyadh Girls University.

Osman, Fawzia Mustafa (1992). The school libraries in Qatar. Doha: Qatar University.

LIS EDUCATION[*]

Sajjad ur-Rehman

1. INTRODUCTION

Library and information education has changed globally and the Asian Arab region has been no exception. This region had an unprecedented socio-political turmoil during the last many decades that affected the way library and information professionals have been produced and prepared in the region. Economic and geopolitical disparities have made LIS education traditions and practices diverse among different countries in this region. Six nations of this region are members of the Gulf Cooperation Council (GCC) and they are natural and bona fide members of this affinity as these share economic affluence, geographic proximity, and other similarities of faith and culture. It is quite natural to treat them as a bloc when we discuss their educational and professional profiles. The same approach has been used in this chapter and the six nations are treated together, followed by description of the situation of other nations.

2. DEVELOPMENT AND STATUS OF LIS EDUCATION PROGRAMS

Al-Khatib and Johnson (2001) assessed that LIS education in the region has generally been poor. Locally trained librarians have been few and even large Arab countries such as Iraq and Egypt have few locally educated senior librarians (Francis 1993). Though LIS education programs in the region are found in all the member nations, yet an apparent handicap is the serious paucity of reading materials in Arabic language. Weaknesses in the production and preparation of indigenous professional manpower have prompted affluent nations to employ a large number of expatriate professionals in order to manage their library and information centers (Siddiqui 1996). Aman (1992) made a case that Iraqi occupation of Kuwait and the Gulf War had a drastic effect on library situation in the region. He proposed several measures to remedy the situation. He also recommended that traditional and archaic methods of instruction be replaced in library schools. He urged that there was a need to make appropriate changes in the curricula of library schools.

---

[*] A number of initials have been used in this chapter. The key for these initials is as follows: KAU: King Abdulaziz University, Jeddah, Saudi Arabia, KU: Kuwait University, PAAET: Public Authority for Applied Education and Technology, Kuwait, UQ: Umm alqura University, Mecca, Saudi Arabia, QU: Qatar University, SQU: Sultan Qaboos University, Oman, GCC: Gulf Cooperation Council, LIS: library and information science, LU: Lebanese University

2.1 GCC Member Nations

Among the GCC nations, the program founded at King Abdulziz University, Saudi Arabia (KAU) in 1973 is the oldest in the region and Kuwait University's (KU) Master's program, established in 1996, is the latest. The undergraduate program at PAAET (Kuwait) was established in 1977. It seems that the period of 1984-88 was the most fertile for establishing new programs in this region as three Saudi programs at University of Al-Ummal Qura's (UQ) Men and Women wings (Mecca) and King Saud University (KSU) were established during this period. Also the undergraduate programs of Sultan Qaboos University SQU (Muscat, Oman) and Qatar University (QU) were founded in 1986 and 1988 respectively.

Rehman (2007a) gathered information about the placement of the LIS programs in the GCC higher education institutions. There appear to be two leading choices for the placement of these programs in different colleges. Three of these programs were located in the College of Social Sciences while two others in the College of Arts. SQU program was located in the College of Arts and Social Sciences while QU was placed in the College of Arts and Science. PAEET was the only program situated in the College of Education. It means that there are eight degree- awarding LIS programs in the six nations.

One distinctive feature of the LIS programs in the GCC nations is that seven of the eight are predominantly undergraduate. It is only KU that does not have an undergraduate major though it has been offering a minor in information studies. Among these programs, KAU is the only one that has three degree programs: bachelor's, master's, and Ph.D. The graduate programs of this university had 24 and 11 students in 2007 that were all pursuing research track in their degree programs, meaning there is no structured coursework required in these programs. It is worth noting that majors in the undergraduate programs in both the men and women wings of UQ and the minor of KU have a clear orientation toward information science or studies. These programs are not designed to cater for the traditional markets of LIS programs. Master's program at KU is a typical program patterned on the model of ALA-accredited programs with a coursework structure of 36 credit hours. All undergraduate programs in the region are designed on the semester system, requiring credit hours for major, minor, and other segments. The two Master degree programs at KU and KAU have 24 and 45 students respectively with an annual intake of 25-30 students at KU.

Rehman (2007a) found that the undergraduate programs in the GCC universities have large enrolments. UQU had an enrolment of about 1,800 students in both the wings of men and women. PAEET, Kuwait also had the enrolment of 700. The number of undergraduate students at QU was 400. Enrolment of undergraduates at KAU, KSU and SQU was in the range of 200-300.

Bahrain, a small GCC nation, also needs LIS professionals desperately. Young and Ali reported in 1992 that there were only nine Bahraini Master degree holders while the national needs were enormous. In response to these needs, University of Bahrain started a postgraduate diploma in learning and information resource centers and a large number of graduates had been produced in this program. Later the university abandoned this program. Also quite a few bachelor degree holders were hired from overseas and the number of professionals possessing bachelor and Master degree exceeded fifty around early 90s. Then University of Bahrain decided to send 2-3 bachelor degree holders to earn their Master's degree from the US or Europe.

Al-Mufaraji (1992) assessed Omani situation of library and information professionals and noted a serious dearth in the Sultanate. He had inventoried 189 libraries in the country and noted that an acute shortage of professionals hampered their development. Majority of the staff had no professional qualification and they heavily relied on expatriate workforce. Against this background, they had established the Department of Library and Documentation in the College of Arts at Sultan Qaboos University.

United Arab Emirates is a fast growing nation in this region. It has also developed an elaborate IT infrastructure and Dubai Media City and Computer City are attracting attention from all over the world. The growth in the higher education sector has been unprecedented in the region and a large number of institutions have been developed. All this has created a strong need of information professionals. Against this backdrop, non-availability of a formal degree program in this country makes it difficult for employers to manage library and information centers. Boumarafi (1996) had observed that these libraries were understaffed and consequently underutilized. She emphasized that the country needed professionals who were well familiar with the environmental conditions. She stressed that the need of a formal degree was imperative for the region. As of 2008, there has been no initiative in the country for establishing a formal degree program that could produce indigenous graduates, exposed to the ground realities.

2.2 LIS Education in Non-GCC Nations of the Asian Arab World

Among the non-GCC nations of the region, Jordan has made a bring stride in addressing the needs of education and training of LIS professionals. Degree awarding programs are well in place in Jordanian universities. The national library association has conducted hundreds of continuing education programs and thousands of LIS workforce have benefited from them. Lebanon also has a tradition of degree programs in two of its universities. Since 1980, Iraq has been involved in three successive wars that have severely damaged the higher education institutions of the country. Libraries have been on the end of low priority in the wake of national development and restoration. The country now lags behind in LIS education and training. Syrian situation of library and information landscape has received little attention in the literature. Yemen has had formal degree program at the undergraduate level, but the nation is more behind than its neighbouring nations in terms of IT resources, equipment and finances.

Qindeel et al. (2001) reviewed the situation of library and information organizations in Jordan. The nation had more than one hundred public libraries and 22 of them were located in the Greater Amman area. There are hundreds of additional libraries in the government sector, academic institutions and schools. A large number of special libraries also exist in the country. These authors noted that there was a big gap in the number of needed staff members for these libraries in general and school libraries in particular. There existed a need to develop and train personnel in the areas in which they had to function and offer services.

Alyan (2001) and Younis (1992) have presented an elaborate case for the education and training of Jordanian professionals. The first degree program, a postgraduate diploma, was founded at the University of Jordan in 1977. The degree was titled library science and documentation. This program went through a number of phases of course structure, orientation, and production of graduates. According to Alyan, in 1984, it developed its program in collaboration with Mustansiriyah University of Iraq, making major adjustments in the coursework. In 1992, the diploma in library and information science with 33 credit hours was replaced by a professional diploma of 24 hours, possibly with the duration of one academic year. It turned out to be the mainstream for producing professionals in the country and the number of graduates had reached hundreds. Major problems that this program encountered were: unclear objectives, inconsistency with the latest developments, oversight of the market needs, paucity of faculty members, and use of traditional and obsolete teaching methods. Despite all the odds, the postgraduate diploma has left a lasting mark on the scene of library and information studies in the country.

A highly significant development was the introduction of an undergraduate program and turning postgraduate into Master's degree program at Jordan University. Alyan (2001) premised that LIS education in Jordan had witnessed the following phases:

1. Introduction of the major of library science in 1979/80 in community colleges, essentially for school libraries that graduated more than six hundred students, primarily female.
2. Introduction of the major of library science and documentation in private community colleges.
3. Abandonment of the first two programs by the Ministry of Education in favour of a new major of library science and educational technology, later changing it to educational resources and information technology, majoring with 76 hours.

Alyan (2001) has been critical about these majors as being traditional, failing to fulfil the market needs, and having low quality. He observed that the faculty members were not qualified who could instil a spirit among the graduates.

Jordan is perhaps the first nation in the region that had a component of library science in its Teachers College of Amman back in 1965. However, lack of availability of teachers did not permit its continuation beyond the first year of its life. Jordanian Library Association is genuinely credited with making a worthy contribution for the training and continuing education of its working library staff. Since 1963, more than four thousand individuals have benefited from its more than two hundred activities. Mohssin et al. (2006) have described in detail the role of the Jordanian Library Association in the conduct of training activities since its founding in the year 1961. JLIA has organized (218) general and specialized training courses that covered a variety of subjects. JLIA began the training courses on using computers in libraries in 1987. The number of participants who have attended the training courses of JLIA has exceeded four thousand. This association has been the most active in the region and has left a big mark on the science of librarianship.

Lebanon has suffered tremendously from a long civil war that had an adverse effect on its social fabric and civil institutions. Libraries also suffered a great deal during this turmoil. When we look at the early history of LIS education in the country, we find that the first program of a 2-year duration was initiated at the Lebanese American University in 1970 for library technicians (Kent 1975). Naaman (1994) observed that in terms of methodology and content, the course was patterned on the American model, yet due to its duration, it was labelled as an Associate Degree (AA). The YWCA started a similar two year program in 1976 that was later abandoned during the civil war (Hafez 1986).

The first 4-year degree program of a bachelor degree was introduced at the Lebanese University in 1976. This course now leads to a French style "license" and the "Maitrise." The same university offers a 5th year qualification for in-depth studies and the degree is named as DEA. The focus of the program is on media and communication studies (Lebanese University, 2008). Quite recently, Balamand University, located outside Beirut, has started offering a bachelor's degree in library and information science (University of Balamand 2008). Common problems identified for the two degree programs of LU and the University of Balamand are related to traditional curricula, part-time faculty, and small number of students.

In Syria, the Syrian national government has been responsible for sponsoring and organizing library activities in all the sectors. Academic, public and special libraries have been developed with the sole support of the government. During 1950s and 60s, the government sent a large number of staff abroad for library training. Around mid-70s a library section was created within Damascus University that was made responsible for the education and training of library employees. In 1977, the Secretariat Institute of Damascus University started organizing a one-year training program for librarians. The Library Section, attached to the Faculty of Arts, started functioning as an academic entity in the year 1984, which was a formal degree program (Al-Laham 1992). Syrian Libraries and Documents Society, first established in 1972, had fluctuating periods for its membership and activities. Later, when Asad National Library was established in 1984, it also housed the secretariat of the society and provided funds. This society has been active in organizing training activities. Another development was the establishment of Scientific Society of Informatics in 1989 with the largest membership in the area. One of the regular activities of this society has been the conduct of training activities for its membership. Developments in Syria have been slow and bureaucratic, consistent with the national system of governance.

Kazanchi (2001) gave a detailed and critical account of libraries and librarianship in Iraq. He stated that though thousands of different types of libraries existed in the country, most of them could not prosper. Thousands of school libraries were without adequate housing premises. These libraries did not offer any service as no part-time or full-time staff members were deputed to manage them. At Mustansariyah University, the Department of Library Science was established in 1970 and had its first graduating class in 1972. The same department had organized training activities for elementary and middle school library staff. No matter how limited this program had been in its effect, it had made a significant change on the scene of librarianship in the country.

Bergan (2000) provided a detailed account of the development of libraries in Palestine. Israeli occupation and restrictions on movement have seriously hampered development of libraries in West Bank and Gaza. Tradition of libraries is old and mosque libraries have played a significant cultural role. There is a strong need for professional librarians in the region. Bergan noted that the librarians in Palestine got their education from all over the world: Leningrad, Cairo, Leeds, Amman, Kiev, Sofia, – and many others. The library cultures they brought back were very different and had an impact on the possibilities to standardize and cooperate. The libraries of Palestine are in need of an institution that could develop a Library and Information Science program adapted to their needs. A study conducted by the Palestinian Ministry of Higher Education had looked at the possibility of establishing a library education program at one of their universities. A British library expert evaluated the situation. If the political situation in this region improves, one of the Palestinian universities needs to take the much-needed initiative of developing a library education program.

3. FACULTY

The most critical factor in the effectiveness of LIS education programs is the faculty. Rehman (2007a) gathered data about the size of faculty members in the eight LIS programs in the GCC nations. It was found that PAEET had the largest faculty size of 21 faculty members for its 700 students, resulting in the student teacher ratio of 1:33. Other high faculty student ratios were noted for men and women wings of UQU that were found to be 1:57 and 1:73 respectively. This ratio for SQU and QU were noted to be 1:31 and 1: 44. For the combined strength of graduate and undergraduate students of KAU, the ratio was found to be 1:20. The ratio for KSU was found to be 1:11. For KU, ratios could be separated for graduate and undergraduate students, which were 1:11 and 1:20 respectively. These results indicate that five of the eight undergraduate programs had ratios exceeding 1:30 while two of the five even exceeded 1:50. It shows that there is a serious shortage of faculty members in these programs. Table 1 displays data about a number of factors of these eight LIS programs.

Ansari, Rehman and Yousef (2001) had evaluated the faculty performance in six GCC schools by collecting data from 49 faculty members through a survey. It was found that the mean age of these faculty members was 48.5. They all had a Ph.D. and most of them had earned it from Western countries during the 1980s and the 1990s. Majority of them had considerable professional and managerial experience. Their instructional assignments had primarily been in the traditional areas of library operations and services. It was found that most of them had weak research and publication records. It was found that with regard to journal articles, a majority of them had not produced anything in English while about one third of them reported no publication in Arabic or other languages. It is worth noting that with the mean of 13.3 years of teaching experience, there were only about one third of the respondents who had produced four articles or more in Arabic. For English language, less than ten percent reported as having produced anything. This indicates that a large number of these faculty members are making little scholarly contribution to the field. They are also quite inactive in professional service as few of them were engaged in continuing professional education activities and none of them reported to be active in any national or regional professional forum.

Naaman (1994) had identified the problems that inhibited the development of library education in Jordan. He pointed out that the paucity of faulty members had affected LIS education negatively.

4. CURRICULUM

The curriculum determines the academic focus, direction, content, and expected capabilities from the graduates of a program. Curriculum reflects the priorities of its designers about the market needs and the way the graduates would be absorbed in it. One common denominator among the LIS education programs in the region is the fact that almost all of them are undergraduate programs. There is only one notable exception to Kuwait University's MLIS program that has been structured in line with the ALA-accredited programs, and it is treated as the qualification that the entry-level professionals hold. In all other programs, the undergraduate program is the basic entry qualification. A postgraduate qualification is built on the top of that. Most undergraduate programs have a 4-year structure with the credit hour range of 120-140, more than half of which is meant for the major of LIS coursework. Master's degree in three Saudi Arabian schools is a research degree and the primary requirement is the satisfaction of thesis research. The coursework has the elements of core and electives. Studies reviewed in the preceding sections hold the coursework traditional. Significant components of the core coursework include foundation of LIS, cataloging, reference and information services, collection development, management, and IT fundamentals. One clear trend has been addition of multimedia and computing courses related to database, searching and retrieval, Internet applications, Web design and management, and networking.

Rehman (2003) premised that curriculum could be best designed if an inventory of the needed competencies is conducted. He surveyed 144 academics from the three regions of North America, East Asia and the Arabian Gulf countries and a select group of professionals from the GCC nations. The participants provided their input on an instrument containing competency segments in nine areas of information studies. Data were analyzed to validate core and elective components by using frequency counts and percentages. Thus ten competency segments were found in the primary core, focused on the human and social dynamics of the information process. It also contained the segments of information organization and information resource development. A supplementary core was also developed with 11 statements, each requiring focused deliberation in any school where curriculum design and revision are being contemplated. The breadth of elective offerings was also identified in primary and supplementary lists, having a certain degree of overlap with some segments listed in the two lists of core. The study provides a clear focus for any deliberations of curriculum design, based on a systematic effort of competency definition. From the findings of this study it was established that the academics from the three regions had little difference in their perceptions about the needed competencies.

5. FACILITIES AND RESOURCES

LIS programs can only function effectively if these are equipped with adequate physical facilities such as space, buildings, computer laboratories, and library and information resources. These facilities can be developed and managed if financial resources are made available. GCC nations have petroleum-based economies and most of them have used their affluence in the development of libraries. Their LIS programs are also expected to be equipped with the latest technology and information resources.

Rehman and Al-Ansari (2003) had collected data from six LIS programs in the GCC nations. They had found that most of these programs were quite weak in their hardware, software and networking capabilities. Availability of per capita computers was found to be alarmingly low. Likewise, monograph and periodical collections were also found to be deficient in majority of schools. One school with a large enrolment and substantial resources was found to be lacking computing and periodical resources altogether. Additionally, these schools did not have access to online systems and database search vendors.

In a follow-up study, Rehman (2007a) gathered information about computing facilities, electronic classrooms, audio-visual facilities, library resources, and teaching facilities in the eight LIS programs of the GCC region. It was found that all the eight programs had computing laboratories with varying extent of facilities. Among those that provided detailed information, UQU women were reported to have two laboratories with Internet connections. The men's wing of the same university had 80 personal computers networked with a server. It is worth mentioning that these two programs have the student strength of about 1,800. SQU reported 25 workstations in the laboratory for the student strength of about three hundred, meaning one workstation for about twelve students. Each of the KSU's four laboratories had 30 workstations and a server while the number of students was reported to be 200, meaning that there was one pc for every 3-4 students. KU reported to have elaborate facilities. Its graduate computing laboratory had 15 workstations; one for about three students. There was a dedicated undergraduate computer laboratory while the undergraduate students shared the college facilities. They however needed larger laboratories with additional pc units in order to accommodate larger classes. All the laboratories had Internet connections.

Five of the eight programs reported that they did not have electronic classrooms. The other three – KU, QU and UQU Men – had projection facilities and Internet connections in these classrooms. None of them reported that these classrooms were connected with the central media facilities of the university. Three programs did not report their audiovisual facilities. KSU reported of having 12 TVs, video equipment, and recorders, etc. Other schools reported projection facilities. At SQU, a central unit was equipped with learning technology and each college also had a small unit to facilitate local needs. This program reported two laboratories for children and bibliographic activities.

As far as library resources are concerned, 4 of the 8 programs did not report periodical subscriptions and 3 did not report monograph collection. Since all of these programs save KU's MLIS program use Arabic medium of instruction, information was gathered for both English and Arabic resources. Among those that provided information, KSU and QU had subscriptions for 11 and 13 titles; out of which 5 and 3 were Arabic. KAU subscribed to 9 Arabic and 27 English titles. KU had the largest number of subscriptions of 10 Arabic and 80 English titles. When it comes to monographs, the largest collection of seven and eight thousand volumes for Arabic and English titles was reported at KAU. The second largest collection was at KU, which had 2000 and 3000 Arabic and English language volumes. The respondent from QU commented that the collection was very poor. PAEET, with a student body of 700, reported the monograph collection of 1,500 and 700 for Arabic and English languages. This number was 1000 and 400 for KSU's LIS program. The information for periodical and monograph collections is incomplete, yet it indicates that most programs have inadequate resources while the number of students in these institutions is very high. If per capita number of periodical subscriptions and monograph collections is computed, it will not present an encouraging scenario. It is worth exploring what factors are responsible for this apparent weakness in these oil-rich nations.

Rehman (2007a) found that six of the eight programs used library automation package in the instruction of courses. Four of them accessed the automation package of Horizon while one used Unicorn. LIS program at SQU was in the process of converting from the locally developed system of Afaq to Unicorn. UQU Women also used the digital library system of Dspace. One important instructional resource is the use of bibliographic databases for search and retrieval and research. Among the databases that were accessible to these programs, all the eight reported of having access to LISA and ERIC. Six of them reported that they had access to Academic Search, ABI Inform, and Dissertation Abstracts Online. Five had access to Library Literature. Four reportedly accessed Emerald Full-text, Ulrich Plus, and General Science Index. Three of them were found to be accessing Encyclopaedia Britannica and Readers Guide. Two of them reported access to Web Dewey, Classification Web, and ISI Web of Knowledge. Only KU's program reported access to BIP, Psychinfo, and LISTA.

Published information is not available about the situation of physical resources and computing equipment in the LIS programs of non-GCC nations. Iraq is war-ravaged and it desperately needs to rebuild all sorts of infrastructure. Stark realities of civil war in Lebanon, a constant state of turmoil in Syria, and occupation of Palestinian territories have badly affected educational and informational infrastructure. Yemen also does not have the basic computing facilities in its LIS program. One possibility would be to establish strong cooperative links with the neighbouring affluent countries that might help in alleviating certain problems.

6. ACCREDITATION AND EVALUATION

Accreditation is a recognized measure for verifying the credibility, authenticity, and transferability of degrees. However, there are no standard criteria or practices available to accredit LIS degrees in developing regions or nations. Having realized this shortcoming, Khoo, Majid and Chaudhry (2003) proposed a model of accreditation for East Asian nations. They also proposed criteria for this purpose that included mission, goals and objectives, curriculum, faculty and staff, students, administration and financial support, instructional resources and facilities, regular review of the program, and documentation. Rehman (2007b) found that in the absence of any accreditation provisions in the GCC nations, the academic of the region strongly feel the need to institute regional accreditation practices. Rehman asked these academics whether they considered accreditation desirable. All the respondents responded affirmatively. They were asked to mark which agency they considered appropriate for accrediting these programs. Seven of them marked the option of a regional professional body such as SLA/AGC or a new body in the region. Three respondents considered the national professional association as the right forum while another three thought the regional consortium of universities should conduct evaluations. Only one of them marked the choice of an international agency.

In the absence of any formal accreditation practice in the region, Rehman (2007a) examined whether the LIS schools were engaged in formal evaluation practices. Two modes of evaluation were identified – self study and evaluation by external reviewers. UQU Women and KSU indicated that they had not conducted self study. Five programs gave the date of their last self study exercise. Accordingly, PAEET program had conducted the self study in 2000, KU in 2001-02, SQU in 2003-4, UQU Men in 2004, and KAU in 2005. KU conducted another self study in 2007 and it also had an external review in late 2007. It appears that most of the programs conducted a self study in a thorough and comprehensive manner.

Rehman (2007a) also collected information whether the 8 programs had received an external review. It was found that both the Men and Women wings of UQU had not conducted external evaluation. Five of them had used an external expert for review whereas KSU had been examined by an appointee of the Ministry of Education. Only the curriculum was examined in the external reviews of the LIS programs of KSU and QU, conducted in 2006 and 2007 respectively. In 2002 and 2003, KU program received an external review and another expert examined the program in November 2007.

7. CONCLSIONS

We have identified common features among LIS programs in the region. One common denominator is that the basic qualification for entry into professional cadres is an undergraduate degree in all the countries. This is the civil service policy in these countries and Master degree holders do not have any advantage in terms of remunerations, professional placement, or career advancement opportunities. Mostly Master's degree is considered to be a research degree. The only exception is that of Kuwait University's MLIS program that is coursework-based and designed with the assumption that Master's degree is an entry-level qualification.

Another resemblance among the LIS programs in the region is that almost 90% of them use Arabic as medium of instruction. This is consistent with the needs of the region. However, a serious problem is that there is a serious dearth of quality textbooks and professional literature in Arabic language. Most textbooks are translations or edited versions of outdated English language books. English language readings cannot be prescribed as students do not have adequate reading comprehension in the English language. Even if some courses are taught in a bilingual mode, treatment is mostly superficial.

Faculty members are required to have a Ph.D. degree in most of these countries. This policy is applied very rigidly. It means that those professionals who have a master's degree with strong academic and professional credentials cannot be engaged as adjunct faculty. It might deprive many schools from a strong resource. Faculty-student ratios in a number of schools are alarmingly high, meaning little interaction between the teacher and the taught. Faculty members are thus unable to serve as guides or mentors in a field that is professional in nature. Research, publication and service credentials of many faculty members are weak. This might be a point of serious concern for professional leadership.

Saudi Arabia has the largest number of LIS programs in this region. Two of its programs have lately decided to pursue a non-LIS track, specializing their graduates in information science and expecting them to be employable in the general information market. Some other schools are also seriously considering this possibility. Kuwait University's Master program has also been aggressively exploring the possibilities of information and knowledge management tracks. These initiatives are opening up new avenues for these programs and it may take quite a few years when a judgment can be made about the viability of these initiatives.

References

Alyan, R.M. Program for developing library professionals in Jordanian libraries. In Y. Qindeel et al. (Eds.) Jordanian library and information centers: status and constraints, (in Arabic). Amman: AbdulHameed Institute, 97-111.

Aman, M. (1992). Libraries and information systems in the Arab Gulf States: after the war. Journal of Information Science, vol. 18, 447-451.

Al-Ansari, H., Rehman, S. And Yousef, N. (2001). Faculty in the library schools of the Gulf Cooperation Council member nations: an evaluation. Libri, vol. 51, 173–181.

Bergan, E. (2000). Libraries in the West Bank and Gaza: Obstacles and possibilities. Paper presented to the 66th IFLA Annual Conference, held at Jerusalem, 18-23 August 2000. [Online] Available: File:///C:/Documents% 20and%20Settings/ Administrator/Desktop/library%20science%20middle%20east/palestine.htm. Retrieved February 22, 2008.

Boumarafi, B. M. (1996). Libraries and information services in the United Arab Emirates (UAE): an overview. International Information and Library Review, vol. 28, 331-343.

Francis, S. (1993). Libraries and information in the Middle East. London: British Library, 63-66.

Hafez, A. (1986). The training of professionals in library and information science: the needs of the Arab countries with special reference to Lebanon. Unpublished Ph.D. dissertation. London University.

Kazanchi, F.Y. (2001). Libraries in Iraq: from ancient times until nowadays. Baghdad: Ministry of Culture and Communication, 104-106.

Kent, F.L. (1975). Lebanon, libraries in. In A. Kent, H. Lancour, & J.E. Daily (eds.). Encyclopaedia of library and information science, v. 14, 120-130.

Al-Khatib, S. & Johnson, I.M. (2001). Libraries in major universities in Leanon. Libri, vol. 31, 209-224.

Al-Laham, G. (1992). Libraries and information infrastructure in Syria. Journal of Information Science, vol. 18, 497-504.

Lebanese University (2008). Faculty of Information and Documentation. Retrieved on 22 February 2008: http://www.ul.edu.lb/francais/faculte.htm

Majid, S., Chaudhry, A.S., Foo, S. & Logan, E. (2003). Accreditation of library and Information studies programs in Southeast Asia: A proposed model. Singapore Journal of Library & Information Management, vol. 32, 58-69.

Al-Mohssin, I, Al-Ahmad, N., Ali, A. & Troesch, M. (2006). Jordan library and information association (JLIA) and its role in the continuous training in the field of library and informatics. Journal of Social Sciences. [Online] Available: File:///C:/Documents%20and%20Settings/Administrator/Desktop/library% 20science %20middle%20east/JLIA%20training%20programs.htm. Retrieved February 22, 2008.

Al-Mufaraji, M. (1992). Libraries and library education in Oman. Journal of Information Science, vol., 471-479.

Naaman, A. (1994). Library and information science. Journal of Lebanese Library Association, vol. 1, 4-5.

Qindeel, Y. et al. (2001). The institution of library in Jordan. In Jordanian library and information centers: status and constraints, eds. Y. Qindeel et al.(in Arabic). Amman: AbdulHameed Institute, 17-24.

Rehman, S. (2003). Information studies curriculum based on competency definition. Journal of Education for Library and Information Science, VOL. 44 no3/4, 276-95.

Rehman, S. (2007a). Quality Assurance and LIS Education in the GCC Countries. Paper presented to the 73rd IFLA General Conference, held at Durban, South Africa, 19-23 August 2007. [Online] Available: http://www. ifla.org/IV/ifla73/papers/114-Rehman-en.pdf. Retrieved February 22, 2008.

Rehman, S. (2007b). Accreditation of the LIS programs in the Arabian Gulf region. Paper presented to the 2nd ALIEP held in Taipei, Taiwan on 23-24 Nov. 2007.

Rehman, S. & Al-Ansari, H. (2003). Digital marketplace and library and information education in the GCC nations: a critical review. Library Review, vol. 52, no. ¾, 170-179.

Siddiqui, M.A. (1997). The use of information technology in academic libraries in Saudi Arabia. Journal of Librarianship and Information Science, vol. 29, no. 4, 295-303.

University of Balamand (2008). Department of Library Science. [Online] Available: http://www.balamand.edu.lb/english/Majors.asp?id=1426&fid=49. Retrieved February 22, 2008.

Young, H.C. & Ali, N. (1992). The Gulf War and its effect on information and library services in the Arabian Gulf with particular reference to the state of Bahrain. Journal of Information Science, vol. 18, 453-462.

Younis, A.R. (1992). Professional library development, manpower education and training in Jordan. International Information and Library Review, vol. 24, no. 1, 15-43.

Table 1. Profile

Institution	Year established	College	Number of students	Number of faculty
KAU	1973	Arts	Bachelor: 242 Master: 24 Ph.D. 11	Prof.: 3 Assoc. Prof.:5 Asstt Prof. 4 Lecturer: 2 Ph.D. students: 5
QU	1988	Arts & Sciences	Bachelor: 400	Prof.: 1 Assoc. Prof. : 3 Asstt Prof. 5

488 Sajjad ur-Rehman

Institution	Year established	College	Number of students	Number of faculty
				TAs: 2
SQU	1986	Arts & Social Sciences	Bachelor: 275 Master: 22 Diploma: 8	Prof.: 1 Assoc. Prof.: 2 Asstt Prof.: 7 TAs: 4 Ph.D. students: 2
UQU Women	1987	Social Sciences	Bachelor and Media Center Certificate: 850	Assoc. Prof.: 4 Asstt Prof. 11 TAs: 7 Ph.D. students: 4
KU	1996	Social Sciences	Bachelor minor: 51 Master: 45 One required service course for 450 students and another required service course for 200 students every year.	Prof.: 2 Assoc. Prof.: 3 Asstt Prof. 5 TAs: 4 Ph.D. students: 5
PAAET	1977	Education	Bachelor: 700	Prof.: 1 Assoc. Prof.: 1 Asstt Prof. 14 Lecturer: 5 TAs: 14 Ph.D. students: 6
KSU	1986	Arts	Bachelor: 200	Prof.: 4 Assoc. Prof.: 5 Asstt Prof. 9 TAs: 5
UQU Men	1984	Social Sciences	Bachelor: 944	Assoc. Prof.: 2 Asstt Prof. 11 Ph.D. students: 4

Table 2. Resources and Facilities

Institution	Computer laboratories	Electronic classrooms	Audio-visual facileties	Periodical Subscriptions		Monograph collection		Automation package
				Arabic	English	Arabic	English	
KAU	X	None	None	9	27	7000	8000	Horizon
QU	X	X	None	3	10	Very poor	Very poor	Unicorn
SQU	X	None	X	No info.	No info.	No info.	No info.	Afaac (locally developed); library converting to Unicorn
UQU Women	X	None	None	No info.	No info.	No info.	No info.	Horizon; Dspace digital library system
KU	X	X	X	10	80	2000	3000	Horizon
PAAET	X pcs and printers	None	None	No info.	No info.	1500	700	None
KSU	X	None	X	5	6	1000	400	None
UQU Men	X	X	X	No info.	No info.	No info.	No info.	Horizon

PART 7
NORTH AMERICA

INTRODUCTION

Ismail Abdullahi
Regional Editor

In North America, library development went through many stages beginning in 1700 with the establishment of parish libraries in the U.S. and Canada. As settlements in both nations increased, private libraries were found in the colonial homes of prominent citizens, such as ministers, doctors and some businessmen. With the establishment of Harvard and Yale College, libraries began to organize collections of books. In the beginning these libraries lacked recognition and a professional librarian. Other libraries such as proprietary and subscription libraries were small and they were fee-based services. In 1700 the first circulating libraries in America were introduced. The industrial revolution brought special libraries to the scene.

Barbara Dewey writes about the changes academic libraries are going through in North America to meet the needs of twenty-first century students, scholars, and the many departments and schools they serve. She explores academic libraries' activities in terms of teaching and learning, research, and scholarly communication. She emphasizes other important issues facing academic libraries such as the digital initiatives, services and professional preparation to provide a twenty-first century library service.

Carol Brey-Casiano tells the history of public libraries from the ancient Greek period to the present and discusses various libraries serving the public that were established in North America from the time of the colonial settlers. She describes the work of Andrew Carnegie, who in the period 1886-1920 donated large sums of money that built more than 2,000 library buildings in 1,400 communities in the United States. Carnegie truly transformed the public library into a peoples place through out North America. Not all public libraries were for everyone; for example, public libraries in the South were not open to blacks until early in the twentieth century. Bre-Casiano cites the fact that the public libraries from 1992-2002 were visited by 2.1 billion users per year and served as cultural centers for all communities.

Rebecca Vergha writes about the development of special libraries in North America from the period 1909 to the present. She presents their purpose in providing services to the parent organization such as corporations, business, government and non-profit institutions. She describes the Special Libraries Association's contribution to the profession and emphasizes how special libraries evolved from being a reference service library to managing information services such as designing, developing, testing, marketing to packaging.

Blanche Wools writes about the different approaches to school library development in the United States and Canada. In the U.S., the responsibility for the school library rests with the states; in Canada, the responsibility is that of the federal government. The chapter further describes issues like early development of school libraries, education for school librarians, staffing for school libraries, and the influence and role of school library associations.

Irene Owens and Tom Leonhardt discuss the history and the processes by which Schools of Library and Information Science apply for, receive, and reaffirm, through established process, the standards of its accrediting body for North America, the American Library Association (ALA). Also, they provide the critical role its professional Association, the Association of Library and Information Science Education (ALISE) plays in the development of LIS Education in North America.

PUBLIC LIBRARIES

Carol Brey-Casiano

The Western World has enjoyed some of the finest public library systems in the world. Anyone can walk into a public library in most developed countries and use a computer, find a book, read a magazine, or enjoy a lecture. In fact, the ancient Greeks who first opened their libraries to the public would probably be amazed by the depth and breadth of today's public library programs and services.

THE FIRST PUBLIC LIBRARIES

The first library in ancient Greece reported to have been open to the public was a library founded at Heraclea, in Bithynia about 364 B.C. by the ruler Clearchus. Other libraries opened to the public were found on the Aegean islands, including Cos, Rhodes and Cnidos. Some things never change, as excavations on the islands of Cos and Rhodes show that fundraising drives were common even back then – with inscriptions on the wall of the library in Cos mentioning donations of "100 drachmas and 100 books" – indicating fairly wealthy donors for that time.[1]

A second "public" library was opened in Athens about the 4th century B.C. featuring the plays of Aeschylus, Sophocles and Euripedes. In order to ensure that only authentic versions of these great playwrights' works were performed, official copies were deposited in a public collection – one of the first examples of providing people with ready access to resources of public interest.

The most famous Greek library was actually located in Egypt, in the ancient coastal city of Alexandria. The Bibliotheca Alexandria was founded in 290 B.C. by descendants of Alexander the Great, and eventually acquired the largest collection of its time with 700,000 papyrus rolls – covering every subject and containing almost all of the literature of the ancient world. It is said that all ships and travelers passing through Egypt had to surrender any manuscripts they possessed so that they could be copied – with the originals placed in the library and the copies returned to the original owners. Sadly, this great library was slowly dismantled by Julius Caesar and others from the period of 47 B.C. to 642 A.D. A series of fires, which ravaged Alexandria, destroyed what was left of the library that had once been the world's vast storehouse of learning.

Today's concept of the public library can be traced all the way back to Julius Caesar, who planned one for the city of Rome to equal or surpass the one in Alexandria, and appointed the writer and book collector Terrentius Varro (116-27 B.C.) to make his dream a reality. Prior to this time only private libraries existed in Rome, their owners sharing the books with friends and elites. Unfortunately,

---

[1] Harris, Michael H. *History of Libraries in the Western World.* Scarecrow Press, 1984, p. 37

Julius Caesar was assassinated in 44 B.C., but his vision was carried out by his supporter G. Asinius Pollio in about 37 B.C. using wealth he had received from his conquest of Dalmatia to consolidate several important collections already in Rome – possibly including those of Varro and Sulla – to form a library in the Temple of Liberty. Following Caesar's original design, the library had two reading rooms – one for Latin books, and the other for Greek books – along with a variety of statues of poets and orators. Subsequently, all Roman libraries followed this model, a departure from the Greek model of libraries – such as the aforementioned famous one built in Alexandria, which did not have reading rooms.

Roman libraries were found everywhere, generally built by the Roman emperors, but these libraries were not just limited to important buildings and palaces. During Augustus' reign, public baths even included libraries, no doubt stocked with some of the more popular and classical literary works.[2] Augustus is also known for building two significant public libraries, the first in the Temple of Apollo, which was dedicated in 28 B.C. Located on the Palatine Hill, this library served as one of the major libraries in Rome and survived well into the 4th century. The second library was located in the Porticus Octaviae, which was built in honor of Augustus' sister Octavia, though the library was thought to have been founded by Octavia in memory of her son Marcellus who died in 23 B.C. The Octavian Library probably survived into the 2nd century.

Considered the greatest of the Roman libraries was the Ulpian Library founded by the Emperor Trajan in 114 A.D. and located in his Forum – although for a time the library was moved to the Baths of Diocletian, possibly while the Forum was being repaired. Additional public libraries continued to be founded by subsequent emperors, and there were reported to be 28 or 29 located in Rome before the 4th century. Some are surmised to have been located in public baths, others may have been Christian collections begun as private libraries and opened to congregations in the 4th century, while still others were large private collections charitably opened to the public.

MODERN PUBLIC LIBRARIES COME TO EUROPE

Sadly, after the 4th century little survived of the great public libraries from the Roman Empire, that had stretched at one time from Spain to Greece. But the Renaissance brought back libraries as well as culture, with the first modern "public" library thought to exist in Florence under the name of San Marco, founded by Cosimo de Medici in 1444. This library made its resources available to those who could read them (a limited number following the Middle Ages), but it was also

---

[2]   Battles, Matthew. *Library: An Unquiet History.* Norton, 2003, p. 48

"public" in the sense that it provided a vehicle for publicity for the powerful Medici family.

Many so-called "public" libraries were developed by governments in Europe, especially the totalitarian nations, to disseminate information selectively in order to benefit the State. Those countries favoring a more democratic political style emphasized the free flow of information. Overall, the development of public libraries in Europe presented a complex and diverse picture.

Libraries in the Western World by Michael H. Harris defines a "public library" as one that is "not only publicly owned but also open to any citizen who desires to use it...the municipal or regional circulating library."[3] The author goes on to say that, by this definition, the public library does not appear on the European scene until the late 19th century, and could even be considered a 20th-century development. A phenomenon known as the "public reference library" featuring largely scholarly collections did emerge, slowly, in Europe between the years of 1500 and 1900. These libraries often began as a gift of a private library, through the transfer of a monastery or cathedral library to public use, or as a professional collection. Their development was slow and uneven because they tended to prosper during times of peace but often were destroyed or dispersed during wartime. These libraries were often poorly housed and rarely had a librarian in charge –most had inexperienced or uninterested "library keepers."

PREDECESSORS OF THE PUBLIC LIBRARY: PAROCHIAL, SUBSCRIPTION AND CIRCULATING LIBRARIES

Great Britain tended to be the leader in the development of public libraries in Europe, and by the 18th century a few publicly owned libraries were opened there. However, the vast majority of libraries added during this period were known as parochial libraries, subscription/social libraries, and circulating libraries. These types of libraries would also make their way in large numbers to America.

Parochial libraries were largely established by Dr. Thomas Bray, who had taken part in the formation of the "Society for the Propagation of the Gospel in Foreign Parts" during the late 17th century. The primary purpose of this group was to provide ministers for the English colonies in America, but Dr.Bray also attempted to deliver books for the purpose of religious training and inspirational reading. Later, he founded similar church libraries in parishes throughout England, which may not have been heavily used but did provide some professional reading for local ministers and their parishioners.

---

[3]   Harris, Michael H. *History of Libraries in the Western World.* Scarecrow Press, 1984, p. 138

The commercial circulating libraries, which would be called rental collections today, provided popular reading material for a small fee. These "libraries" were established by booksellers, with the first one said to have existed in Edinburgh as early as 1725, and others in business in London and other prominent cities by 1750. Commercial circulating libraries could be found in most of the major British towns by 1800, and some remained profitable into the 20th century. Many of the books provided appealed to the romantic and erotic interests of the general public, causing the playwright Sheridan to call these libraries "evergreen trees of diabolical knowledge." Eventually, most of the commercial circulating libraries were replaced by paperbacks and libraries in the 20th century.[4]

Another type of library that developed in the British Isles was the subscription library, generally an extension of book clubs or reading societies that were formed by the more well-to-do readers of a community. Members paid fees by the month or the year, and the collections tended to feature material at a higher level and more serious nature than the commercial libraries. By 1900 subscription libraries were common, often housed in rented halls or rooms, though many had their own buildings by the mid-19th century.

There is no doubt that subscription libraries were the predecessors of today's public library, because they demonstrated the potential demand for large collections that were readily accessible to the people. However, it also became clear that voluntary support was not sufficient for public libraries to survive and flourish.

During this period, a public library movement swept through Great Britain that also set the stage for today's public library. In 1838, following two years of depression in England, London radical William Lovett proposed a bill in Parliament he called "The People's Charter." While the bill was rejected by Parliament, it fostered the "Chartist movement" which recognized the necessity of education for Britain's working poor. Chartist reading rooms sprang up across Brittan, cooperative lending libraries offering books to members of radical organizations. These reading rooms were extremely popular, and provided strong competition for the existing subscription libraries.

In 1847, Parliament passed an act appointing a Committee on Public Libraries "to consider the necessity of establishing libraries throughout Great Britain."[5] That Committee, headed by William Ewart and supported by library pioneer Edward Edwards, reported in 1849 on the poor condition of current library service and recommended the establishment of free public libraries across the country. This led to the passage of the Public Libraries Act in 1850, which allowed cities with populations over 10,000 to levy taxes for the support of public libraries. Subsequent laws extended this Act to Scotland, Ireland, and smaller towns in Britain.

---

[4]   Ibid, p. 141-142
[5]   Ibid, p. 143-144

By 1900 there were free public libraries in more than 300 cities across Great Britain, with many of the municipal libraries benefiting from the generosity of Andrew Carnegie who, in addition to providing many of the library buildings in the United States, also provided a number of the municipal libraries across the ocean in Britain. And, while many of these public libraries were not well-supported until after World War I, they met an important need for their communities.

Public library development in other parts of Europe from 1500 to the early 20th century did not always follow the patterns established by the British, and in fact could be called erratic – a situation that was exacerbated by the effects of two World Wars. Still, by 1914 most European governments agreed that some form of publicly supported library service was beneficial to their communities.

PUBLIC LIBRARY DEVELOPMENT IN THE UNITED STATES

Public libraries in the United States emerged in a similar fashion, slowly at first, with early public libraries made available by generous benefactors. One of the first known examples of this occurred in 1656, when Captain Robert Keayne, a merchant of Boston, willed his book collection to the town for a public library. He stipulated that the town build a suitable building to house the collection, which wound up in a room of the Town House but ended in a fire in 1747.

The Reverend Thomas Bray, mentioned earlier as the Anglican clergyman responsible for establishing parish libraries in England, also did his part to establish similar libraries in "the colonies" between 1695 and 1704 – when he succeeded in establishing some 70 libraries in America. Early library laws were even passed in Maryland and South Carolina to secure and maintain the Bray libraries, and at least one of the Bray collections – in Annapolis – was intended as a general public library with some 1,100 volumes. However, after Reverend Bray's death interest in the parish libraries declined and most of them disappeared – though Bray is to be commended for his vision of libraries almost two centuries before the idea of today's public library took hold in our society.

Several years later, in 1731, Benjamin Franklin and members of his Philadelphia literary society known as "Junto" founded the Library Company, which served as the first American subscription, or social, library. Franklin called this new library the "Mother of all N. American Subscription Libraries…" and stated that, "These Libraries have improved the general conversation of the Americans." However, access to these "social libraries" was limited to those who could pay to use them, as most were established by those who owned stock in the company –

though in time individuals who were not shareholders could "subscribe" to the library by paying fees.[6]

Social libraries were also considered to be a more serious source of knowledge for those pursuing self-improvement, and generally did not provide the more popular fiction and romances. This need was filled by the new circulating libraries – similar to those established in Great Britain – that appeared in printshops and bookstores just before the American Revolution, providing books for rent for a small fee.

The social and circulating libraries lasted well into the mid-1800's and are considered to be the significant predecessors of public libraries in America. The ultimate downfall of these libraries came from their reliance on voluntary support, in that many American communities lost their library service whenever they experienced difficult financial times. This instability eventually proved to be unacceptable to Americans who believed that libraries were essential to the success of the new Republic.

Books for children were also considered increasingly important, especially with the rise of the public school district. Horace Mann, then Secretary of the Massachusetts Board of Education, wrote in his Third Annual Report in 1839: "After the rising generation have acquired habits of intelligent reading, what shall they read? For, with no books to read, the power of reading will be useless…"[7] This question prompted educators to establish libraries associated with school districts, particularly in the seaboard states. New York's legislature was the first to pass an act in 1835 that made it permissible for school districts to levy taxes for school libraries, and Massachusetts, Michigan, Indiana and Ohio followed. However, in general the school-district libraries were not very successful – due in part to the lack of selections that were of interest to children, as well as the lack of adequate quarters in school buildings so that library books were often stored in the homes of teachers or school board members.

Still, the idea of public libraries – for children, for all – persisted. Sunday School libraries were established in practically every church by the mid 1800's, and academy libraries in private schools also thrived during this period. Public opinion had changed to concern about a perceived decline in the reading standards of the public at large, and clearly, something had to be done to bring reading material to all.

The American public library developed out of several social and political changes that occurred during what is commonly called the Jacksonian period (roughly 1824 to 1837), recognized as the period in our history when the so-called "aristocracy" was overthrown and true democracy came into power with Jackson's election as President. This was also the period of increased industrialization, re-

---

[6]   Ibid, p. 171-172
[7]   Ibid, p. 177

sulting in larger cities and their accompanying problems as well as the arrival of numerous immigrants to the United States – many of whom were often poorly educated.

During the late 1820's the general public began to identify publicly supported education as an important aspect of democracy, believing as Thomas Jefferson had written that "Whenever the people are well-informed, they can be trusted with their own government."[8] Educators and civic leaders began to seek successful ways to establish public libraries for the people, but the groundswell of support came after the Trustees of the Boston Public Library issued their famous *Report* written by Edward Everett and George Ticknor, which stated in part that "Reading ought to be furnished to all, as a matter of public policy and duty, on the same principle that we furnish free education...as...a most important part of the education of all."[9]

Boston Public Library was not the first public library established in the United States, but its founding gave real momentum to the public library movement. At the time Boston was considered by many to be the social and intellectual center of the country, and other major communities followed its example. It became clear that libraries should be supported by local taxation and open to all citizens in order to survive and flourish.

Other communities that deserve credit for establishing some of the first public libraries include Salisbury, Connecticut – home of the Bingham Library for Youth, which began with a collection of books donated by Caleb Bingham in 1803. This library later became a part of the modern Scoville Memorial Library. There were several other examples throughout New England of small collections that became publicly owned and supported, but the library considered to be the first true public library was the Peterborough (NH) Public Library, established in 1833 when the town decided to use part of its State Literary Fund for the purchase of books for a free public library.

Despite the opening of numerous public libraries in the early 1800's, it was not until state laws were passed giving local governments the power to levy taxes for the support of these libraries that the modern public library movement really took hold. New Hampshire was the first to pass such a law in 1849, followed by Massachusetts, Maine in 1854, and several other New England and Midwest states after the Civil War. Other developments during the last quarter of the 19th century strengthened public libraries even further, beginning with the organization of the American Library Association in Philadelphia in 1876. In addition, the classic 1876 *Report on Public Libraries in the United States of America* was published, serving as a standard handbook of library practice for many years.

---

8   Lewis, Jone Johnson, www.wisdomquotes.com.
9   Harris, Michael H. *History of Libraries in the Western World.* Scarecrow Press, 1984, p. 226

One of the most critical developments was the work of perhaps the greatest library benefactor ever, Andrew Carnegie. Between the years of 1881 and 1920 he provided some $50 million for the construction of 2,500 library facilities. Carnegie once said that, "I choose free libraries as the best agencies for improving the masses of the people, because they give nothing for nothing. They only help those who help themselves...They reach the aspiring, and open to these the chief treasures of the world – those stored up in books."[10]

During the late 19th and early 20th centuries, public libraries began to take hold in the United States with many new developments. Branch libraries were established in many major cities, the concept of open stacks was generally accepted, hours of service were increased, and the concept of reference service began to take hold. Access to the public library's resources were clearly important, but women and children had only recently been recognized as legitimate clientele, and some ethnic minorities were denied use of the public library altogether.

THE PUBLIC LIBRARY – NOT FOR EVERYONE

According to Eliza Atkins Gleason's study in 1941, *The Southern Negro and the Public Library*, public libraries in the South were not open to African-Americans until early in the 20th century.[11] Black colleges made their library resources available to the community, and they sometimes even trained librarians for public library service. But even those states with the most libraries rarely accommodated blacks. Out of 53 libraries in Georgia in 1936, only five served blacks; of the 44 public libraries in Florida, blacks could use only four. The same pattern existed in other southern states:

- Arkansas, 1 out of 19 public libraries served blacks;
- Alabama, 2 out of 18 public libraries;
- Kentucky, 14 out of 64;
- Louisiana, 3 out of 16; and
- Mississippi, 2 out of 22 (8.11% of the state's libraries, while 50.24% of the population was black.)

There were some exceptions: West Virginia had a state law requiring libraries receiving public monies to offer full access to blacks, while in Texas, the percentage of public libraries serving blacks exceeded the black percentage of the population.

The power of the public library can be demonstrated by a story Richard Wright (1908-1960) told in his autobiography *Black Boy*. He first became interested in books when, as a seventeen-year-old factory worker he came across a newspaper

---

[10] Ibid, p. 230
[11] Battles, Matthew. *Library: An Unquiet History*. Norton, 2003, p. 183

editorial condemning a book by H.L. Mencken. Understanding the oppression of blacks in the South, he suspected that the newspaper's condemnation of Mencken might mean that he really had something worthwhile to say! He wanted to read Mencken but his local library, was closed to blacks.

Remembering that he had been permitted entrance to the library in the past to pick up books requested by the white men he worked for, Wright decided to ask an acquaintance, Mr. Falk, if he could use his library card and forge his name on notes requesting books. Falk reluctantly agreed, but only if Wright accepted full responsibility if caught.

It may seem amazing to us today that such a seemingly simple act as visiting the public library and borrowing books could be seen as a criminal act. Upon his first visit to the library with Falk's library card, Wright says he waited at the desk with cap in hand for the whites in line to be served – looking "as unbookish" as possible. Upon reading the forged note asking for two books by Mencken, the librarian was incredulous, and asked if Wright was planning to use the books himself. Wright responded that he couldn't read, and the librarian went to fetch the books for him. He had won! Subsequently he continued to use the borrowed library card as a visa to the world, but it was a dangerous time for him as the white men around him became suspicious of the time he spent reading. He had to guard his every word and his facial expressions to hide all traces of his new learning.

In the North, access to public libraries by African-Americans was somewhat different, as freedmen formed literary societies and subscription libraries, much like those established by whites, to make books available in their communities.

The postwar 1950's continued to be a period of discrimination against public library users of color. Not only were African-Americans denied access to libraries, but other groups such as Mexicans and Mexican-Americans faced limited access – forced to use certain branches of the library and made to feel unwelcome at others. Ernesto Cortes, Jr., Founder of the San Antonio Communities Organized for Public Services (COPS) talks about growing up in San Antonio, Texas, during the 1950's, noting that "Mexicanos were not barred from using the public library...if they went to the downtown library. The problem was not discrimination, it was access."

AMERICAN PUBLIC LIBRARIES AT THE TURN OF THE 20TH CENTURY

In some rural areas, such as in the state Wisconsin, home libraries were an early predecessor to bookmobile service. The local librarian would gather up a set of books and deliver them to readers in a horse-drawn buggy.

In his book *The American Public Library*, Arthur Bostwick describes another kind of home library, in addition to the collections delivered to rural readers. This second home library was offered in urban settings, particularly to children of immigrants. A librarian or volunteer would go into neighborhoods and look for a child to whom she could lend books with confidence, hoping that the child would share the books with family or friends. In a week or so, the librarian would return to the immigrant-occupied tenements to collect the books, discuss them with the children, and offer more books to borrow. The goal of this program was to entice young readers into the children's room of the local branch, where they would help fulfill the goal of the public library in the early 20th century – to assimilate into American society, producing so-called "efficient" readers, people who used books to advance themselves and their society.

The change in the view of the American public library was evident from the change in the way libraries displayed their books. Libraries in the previous century displayed their books and encouraged browsing; the new libraries of the 20th century hid their books away, to be accessed only by staff using the latest technology: telephones, conveyor belts, and elevators. For example, the cover of the May 27, 1911 issue of *Scientific American* showed a cutaway view of the stacks of the newly opened New York Public Library, with the all-male staff sending volumes to the delivery room via a complex network of shafts and booklifts. Above, readers are blissfully unaware of the machinery employed to bring their books.[12]

In fact, the rapid growth of libraries in the early decades of the 20th century forced librarians to focus increasingly on internal matters of management, perhaps influenced by Melville Dewey's referral to librarianship as a "mechanical art." By the 1930's, however, the Nazi and Fascist movements had inspired librarians to be more deeply concerned with the purpose of the public library as a "guardian of the people's right to know."[13] This philosophy gained increasing acceptance during the 1940's and is reflected in all of the library profession's basic policy statements such as the American Library Association's "Library Bill of Rights."

THE PUBLIC LIBRARY IN WARTIME

International events during the 20th century also had an impact on public access to libraries and books. By World War I, public libraries in the United States had taken on a major role as cultural and community centers – particularly in large urban areas – providing reading material, free meeting space, free public lectures, reference service and other forms of assistance. During the War, public libraries served as a source of information, providing reading material for people who

---

[12] Ibid, p. 202-203
[13] Harris, Michael H. *History of Libraries in the Western World*. Scarecrow Press, 1984, p. 231

wanted to know more about the conflict in Europe. As a meeting place, the public library served as a refuge for all ages, particularly for children – who visited the library to enjoy story hours, books and spaces designed just for them.

As World War II began, a number of influential organizations – including the Library of Congress, the New York Public Library, and the American Library Association – joined together to safeguard their most treasured documents and books. And, when the United States entered the war, many libraries took the lead to inform the public by offering public programs, mounting exhibits, and creating information centers.

One of the most gripping stories to come out of World War II centered on a public library of sorts, the Theresienstadt Ghetto Central Library that served Jews in Nazi concentration camps from 1942-1945. This library, complete with bookmobile system, reading room, and branch libraries, provided a means for prisoners to escape momentarily the terrible humiliation and dehumanization they suffered at the hands of the Nazis. It might seem surprising to find a library in a Nazi concentration camp, but the population served here was somewhat different: it included wealthy and prominent Jews as well as many famous artists, writers, musicians and scholars – people whose sudden disappearance might be noticed by the international community.

The value of this library can hardly be imagined by those of us living in the Western World today. One library user who did not survive the War wrote an epic poem that stated in part:

"Be once more nice and send me something
Because here a body has time …
But please no thin and lightweight books.
No, rather something to chew on, heavy and hard…"[14]

THE MODERN PUBLIC LIBRARY

During the late 1950's and 1960's American public libraries began to reach out to diverse segments of their communities, a practice that continues today as the demographics of our cities and towns change rapidly. These early outreach efforts, coupled with the civil rights legislation of the 1960's, ensured that anyone could use the local public library by the 1970's. The Vietnam era also created a new sense of social responsibility among librarians, motivating them to help the poor and uneducated fit into a rapidly developing scientific society.

---

[14] Intrator, Miriam. "People were literally starving for any kind of reading": The Theresienstadt Ghetto Central Library, 1942-1945." *Library Trends*, vol. 55, no. 3, winter 2007, p. 514

The economic recessions of the 1970's and 1980's affected public libraries and the people they served in several ways. As governments began to struggle economically, libraries found themselves in the position of having to compete with other government services for funding. This caused the gap between the "have" and the "have not" populations – already broad due to a reduction in federally funded social programs and other economic factors – to widen even further.

This trend continued into the 1990's and the early 21st century, although ever-resourceful librarians and library stakeholders continue to advocate for increased library funding. The public library continues to thrive by making the most effective use of limited funding, utilizing the latest technologies, connecting with communities in new and innovative ways such as social networking, and staying relevant as a center for lifelong learning.

CONCLUSION: THE PUBLIC LIBRARY TODAY

Today's public library is one of our most popular institutions, with library use in the United States doubling from the decade of 1992-2002 to a high of 2.1 billion users per year. The library continues to serve as a cultural center for all, providing a sense of place – of community – for an increasingly isolated American society.

References

Battles, Matthew. (2003) *Library: An Unquiet History.* New York: W.W. Norton & Co.

Chernik, Barbara E. (1992) *Introduction to Library Services.* Englewood, CO: Libraries Unlimited, Inc.

Harris, Michael H. (1984) *History of Libraries in the Western World.* Metuchen, NJ: Scarecrow Press.

Intrator, Miriam. (2007) "People were literally starving for any kind of reading": The Theresienstadt Ghetto Central Library, 1942-1945." *Library Trends,* vol. 55, no. 3, 513-522

Kimball, Melanie A. (2007) "From Refuge to Risk: Public Libraries and Children in World War I." *Library Trends,* vol. 55, no. 3, 454-463.

Lewis, Jone Johnson. (2008). [Online] Available: http://www.wisdomquotes.com.

Peiss, Kathy. (2007) "Cultural Policy in a Time of War: The American Response to Endangered Books in World War II." *Library Trends*, vol. 55, no. 3, 370-386.

ACADEMIC LIBRARIES

Barbara I. Dewey

1. INTRODUCTION

Academic libraries in North America support institutions of higher education in the United States and Canada, both private and public in nature. They comprise an integral and important part of creating, preserving, and accessing the world's knowledge. This chapter will describe academic libraries as they transform to meet the needs of 21st century students, scholars, and the many communities they serve. Understanding academic libraries also requires a basic knowledge of the higher education environment in North America and how it has emerged. Important aspects of today's libraries will be explored in terms of teaching and learning, research, and scholarly communication. Other important aspects include digital initiatives, technical services, public services, professional preparation, and a summary of important issues facing academic libraries today as they strive to advance knowledge generally and in their specific institutions.

2. ACADEMIC LIBRARIES: TRANSFORMATION AND CHANGE

Academic libraries are in a state of major change and transformation moving from a just in case model anticipating student and faculty needs through largely print resources to a just in time digital content and delivery service model. "In the transitional or responsive academic library, the processes of information acquisition, synthesis, navigation, and archiving are increasingly focused on networked and interactive access to digital multimedia …at point of need, and on the innovative application of electronic technologies, according to Neal.[1] Academic libraries are both archive and dynamic learning and information-creation environments fueled by ever changing technology. All aspects of the academic library are affected by this transformation.

2.1 The Higher Education Environment

What is meant by higher education? In North America it generally means research universities, four-year colleges, two-year community colleges and technical schools. Transformation is also occurring in colleges and universities in an environment of inherent conservatism combined with cutting edge discover and creative achievement. This dichotomy is not unlike the tensions felt in academic librar-

---

[1] Neal, James G. "The Entrepreneurial Imperative: Advancing from Incremental to Radical Change in the Academic Library." portal: Libraries and the Academy, Vol. 1, No. 1 (2001), pp. 1-13.

ies in the early part of the 21st century. Libraries built on centuries of largely Western European intellectual development must now embrace different models of operation, collection building, ownership, and access.

North American institutions of higher education emerged built on European developments specifically from the earliest Western universities in Paris and Bologna beginning in the 12th century. The curriculum was based on seven liberal arts seen as the foundation of education – mathematics, astronomy, geometry, music, grammar, rhetoric, and logic. Professional areas such as law, medicine, and theology also emerged. Library catalogues were created, first in the Sorbonne, boosted by the advent of printing and growth in book production. Comprehensive research universities were modeled out of Germany but took on a strong individual freedom of inquiry model in North America.

The first university in North America is considered to be the University of Santiago in the Dominican Republic. Harvard University is the first university established in the United States followed by the College of William and Mary. The first public university was the University of Georgia opening in 1795. Libraries begun to appear, often started from collections of individual faculty members. In the 20th century the emphasis on research as well as teaching increased the number of journals and books published.[2] Professionalization of the disciplines including librarianship and the emergence of many learned societies (who also published journals) also increased the depth and size of library collections in academic institutions. Frequent funding crises and explosion of information technology fueled major changes that are accelerating today.

Academic libraries exist within their parent institutions' context. They confront major issues of funding, accountability, recruitment of the best and brightest, competition for research and private dollars, increased emphasis on diversity and internationalization, and a more user centered, diffuse approach fueled by innovative technologies supporting non-traditional learning, teaching, communication, and scholarship creation. Major philosophies of higher education including academic freedom, relative independence of faculty, loathing of corporate models and bureaucracy, the high value placed on cutting edge discovery coupled with higher education's conservative view of change, and ultimately the dedication to preparing young people for life's challenges inform the academic library's overall mission and strategic priorities.

Library deans and directors in academic libraries must identify and communicate effectively with key campus players including academic administrators (Provost, Chancellor, President, Deans, and department heads) and other administrators (Chief Information Officer, Chief Financial Officer, administrators for space, human resources, general counsel, etc.). Additionally key players in the library, it-

---

[2]   Budd, John. (1998). *The Academic Library: Its Context, Its Purpose, and Its Operation.* Englewood, Colorado: Libraries Unlimited.

self, include the library administrative team, department heads, librarians, other library professionals, staff, and student library assistants. Student and faculty constituencies are also critically important contacts.

Campus organizations must also be engaged by the library including the Faculty Senate, Deans Council, Library advisory committees, Student Senate, representative unions, student services, campus staff committees, and Library Friends groups. Librarians in successful North American academic libraries are at the table when important campus initiatives are pursued or should be. Examples are strategic planning, curriculum revision, efforts towards student and faculty recruitment, improving quality and ranking of programs, and the like.

3. TEACHING AND LEARNING

Academic librarians are increasing their focus on support of teaching and learning. Specifically, they see as crucial their role in lifelong student success for critical thinking and the ability to find and assess information as needed in the classroom and beyond. Major national initiatives to support these efforts include the American College and Research Libraries' (ACRL) information literacy initiatives, specifically the Information Literacy Competency Standards for Higher Education.[3] The Canadian Library Association sponsors the Information Literacy Interest Group with accompanying resources and activities.[4]

Given the major investment academic libraries make in providing extensive collections and access to many general and discipline-related databases, large collections of full text electronic journals, and legacy print collections, librarians are motivated to push for the use of these collections in student learning and research. This push is particular strong given the propensity for students to go directly to search engines, especially Google, exclusively for their research and information needs. Academic librarians and faculty throughout the institutions are challenged to work together to come up with strategies ensuring that students learn, at some level, comprehensive research skills, gaining an appreciation of scholarship in their chosen field regardless of where the student begins their research. The habits of students to ignore library websites and collections are well documented in the OCLC study, College Students' *Perceptions of Libraries and Information Resources*.[5] Academic librarians, in partnership with faculty, are developing a variety of strategies to imbed information literacy and critical thinking skills throughout

---

[3] ACRL Information Literacy Initiatives, http://www.ala.org/ala/acrl/acrlissues/acrlinfolit/information literacy.cfm
[4] Canadian Library Association. Information Literacy Group. http://cybrary.uwinnipeg.ca/ilig/
[5] OCLC. *College Students Perceptions of Libraries and Information Resources*. http://www.oclc.org/reports/perceptionscollege.htm

the curriculum. These include tutorials, Web components, peer advisor programs, course/subject guides, and comprehensive strategies for required courses and/or general education offerings.

Recent advances in teaching and learning include user-centered strategies focused on current generational characteristics of students and results of library assessment studies. These include development of technology-intensive shared spaces or learning commons which provide a variety of related services including library research support, information technology services, tutorial assistance, spaces for group/individual study, presentation spaces, social spaces, and the like. All of these functions are increasingly housed in attractive and widely accessible library spaces, which once featured legacy print collections no longer needed in our digital environment.

4. PUBLIC SERVICES

Public services in North American academic libraries traditionally have centered on reference librarians' work. Reference librarians still, in most academic libraries, work one-on-one with students and faculty pursuing information queries, assignments, and research. Additionally, they teach and develop subject-based tools and services. However, the Web has certainly changed the face of reference and public services in profound ways requiring that academic librarians develop new methods of publicizing their services and reaching their clientele including through virtual means. Information-seeking behavior increasingly depends on an individual's use of search engines independent of the library. However, the academic library and its public service librarians, regardless of what they are called, continue to play a critical role in developing the social, culture, and intellectual environment that is the North American research library. Students remain largely residential and do congregate in their institution's library to study, socialize, and attend events. Public service librarians including reference, access services, bibliographers, and digital media experts continue to provide the human touch for students who wish to be around others while studying. However, they are also providing this "touch" through innovative virtual services. These services compete with similar services such as Ask.Com[6] so they must be seen as effective and relevant to students. They must be "pushed" to students through a variety of means since students do not initially start with the library or its website.

Many North American academic libraries serve graduate students and all serve faculty. These constituents need different kinds of support from the library. They are involved in long-term and complex research agendas involving the need for

---

[6] Ask. www.ask.com

specific resources and the most up-to-date data and publications. They are asking for and getting specific types of spaces for quiet and contemplative study away from the lively information commons-type spaces. The term "research commons" is beginning to take hold to describe these kinds of spaces, some of which are virtual.

Large universities in North America still feature library systems that include branch or subject-based libraries. Given the increasing interdisciplinary nature of scholarship, the increased body of digital resources, and the competition for space campus-wide discussion of consolidation is becoming more common. On the other hand there is a movement to place librarians with subject expertise closer to their constituents or as part of research teams, centers, or other disciplinary initiatives.

5. SCHOLARLY COMMUNICATION, RESEARCH, AND COLLECTION MANAGEMENT

Faculty who make up North American colleges and universities are the primary creators of scholarship. The academic library role in the scholarship communication has evolved to one of advocacy for broad access and dissemination of scholarship. Institutes of higher education are in the strange position of paying faculty, in part, to create scholarship and then paying commercial and society publishers to obtain that scholarship. Over the past few years active national efforts, some spanning both the US and Canada higher education environments, have emerged to support the open access movement. In particular the Association for Research Libraries (ARL) launched the Create Change initiative to help administrators, faculty, and librarians understand and take appropriate action to remove barriers of access to scholarship.[7] The Canadian Association of Research Libraries (CARL) also has initiated specific actions to improve access to research in Canada.[8] Scholarly Publishing and Academic Resources Coalition (SPARC) is an alliance of universities, research libraries, and organizations dedicated to open access and has been successful in a number of arenas to advance new forms of digital scholarly publishing and communication.[9]

5.1 Institutional Repositories

Scholarly communication initiatives also include advocacy for setting up institutional and/or disciplinary repositories where an institution's scholarly output can be accessed by all. According to Lynch, "a university-based institutional reposi-

---

[7]   Association of Research Libraries. Create Change. http://www.createchange.org/
[8]   Canadian Association of Research Libraries. Scholarly Communication. http://www.carl-abrc.ca/ projects/scholarly_communication/scholarly_communication-e.html
[9]   Scholarly Publishing and Academic Resources Coalition. http://www.arl.org/sparc/

tory is a set of services that a university offers to the members of its community for the management and dissemination of digital materials created by the institution and its community members."[10] Institutional or digital repositories include, but are not limited to electronic theses and dissertations, faculty publications, university archival materials, conference proceedings, video of important university events, and digital material in any other form important to the output of the university. Examples include MIT's DSpace,[11] Ohio State's Knowledge Bank,[12] and Queen's University's QSpace.[13]

5.2 Copyright Education

Copyright education and application is another area of activity for North American academic libraries. ARL and CARL have worked on helpful tools for faculty to guide them in negotiating rights to their publications to ensure open access and the ability to deposit their work locally. Additionally, academic librarians are involved in ensuring appropriate application of fair use elements of copyright laws for educational purposes. Advocacy at the national level to monitor copyright legislation is a continuing and important activity. Resources related to copyright are found on both the ARL[14] and CARL[15] websites.

5.3 Digital Initiatives

If it is online it does not exist and thus, digital initiatives form the key foundation for advances in open access and scholarly communication. Scholars and librarians are hearing this sentiment from students but also from each other. The imperative to build digital collections and services is paramount for academic libraries in North American. Major initiatives are underway to, not only digitize unique collections and make them widely available, but to also digitize legacy print collections. Key players and programs in this arena include the Digital Library Federation,[16] Library of Congress American Memory Project,[17] Library Archives Canada,[18] Google Books Library Project,[19] Open Content Alliance,[20] and projects

---

[10] Clifford A. Lynch, "Institutional Repositories: Essential Infrastructure for Scholarship in the Digital Age," *ARL Bimonthly Report* 226 (February 2003), 1-7. Online at http://www.arl.org/newsltr/226/ir.html

[11] DSpace at MIT. http://dspace.mit.edu/

[12] The Knowledge Bank at Ohio State. https://kb.osu.edu/dspace/index.jsp

[13] QSpace at Queen's University. https://qspace.library.queensu.ca/

[14] ARL (2007). Know Your Copy Rights: Using Copyrighted Works in Academic Settings. http://www.knowyourcopyrights.org/index.shtml

[15] CARL. Copyright. http://www.carl-abrc.ca/projects/copyright/copyright-e.html

[16] Digital Library Federation (DLF). http://www.diglib.org/

[17] Library of Congress American Memory Project. http://memory.loc.gov/ammem/index.html

[18] Library Archives Canada. http://amicus.collectionscanada.ca/electroniccollection-bin/Main/AdvSearch?coll=11&l=0&v=1

[19] Google Books Library Project. http://books.google.com/googlebooks/library.html

[20] Open Content Alliance. http://www.opencontentalliance.org/

throughout North American academic libraries digitizing individual collections, especially manuscript and special collections. These efforts have the potential of changing the face of academic libraries in terms of collection, space, and service priorities.

Building the virtual academic library includes a heavy emphasis on services. If students and faculty are coming into the library from a virtual portal or gateway then academic libraries must provide services in the virtual sense. Initially these included email reference, ability to reserve or renew books, and the ability to manage citations. These services have broadened to include social networking and interactive capability such as instant messaging and chat services, tools available on the library website to help students and faculty manage scholarly resources in a variety of ways to support their teaching, learning, and research. Imbedding library resources, tools, and virtual assistance directly into course management systems such as Blackboard are common in today's academic library. Application of social networking technologies is underway through academic libraries' presence on sites such as Facebook and the creation of Blogs.

More global efforts to expand the virtual library and bring in to the forefront include OCLC WorldCat,[21] DLF's Acquifer Project,[22] and many other partnership projects to bring together formerly disparate research collections by subject. Canadian research libraries especially have made strategic progress on digitizing Canadian culture and heritage in a comprehensive way. Commercial publishers are adding to available digital content, not only in sciences and technology, but in large reformatting projects converting microfilm sets to full text digital content. Consortia of libraries throughout North America are engaged in collaborative digitization projects. Funding sources for these projects include foundations and federal grant programs.

Academic libraries in North America are beginning to work in partnership with other key players to develop cyber infrastructures for sciences, social sciences, and humanities scholarship and datasets. These efforts are still emerging but will provide access to and sustained support for important databases and other scholarly resources, which currently often exist in a largely ad hoc manner.

6. TECHNICAL SERVICES ARE HIGH TECH

Academic libraries continue to have significant operations focused on selecting, purchasing, cataloging, indexing, recording, and making available collections in all formats albeit increasingly digital. Large cooperative utilities emerged to enable sharing of expertise to process and gain access to scholarly resources. OCLC

---

[21] OCLC WorldCat. http://www.worldcat.org/
[22] DLF's Aquifer. http://www.diglib.org/aquifer/

stands out in the early 21st century as the primary utility for this work featuring, at this writing, 96 million records and evolving into the digital age with more cooperative services including Worldcat.org and Worldcat Local. Academic libraries still base their technical services operations on integrated library systems but we are on the cusp of major change where such products as Worldcat Local have the capability of supplanting many of the functions of an integrated library system. Additionally, the propensity for users to gain access to resources, not through library catalogs, but through browsers, notably Google, will change the landscape of technical services even more as we strive to better connect users with what Lougee terms as the "diffuse" library.[23] Currently, academic libraries are dependent on interlibrary loan increasingly providing desktop electronic delivery but also moving physical books from libraries to faculty and students through a variety of delivery services. Some academic libraries are pursuing a "digitize on demand" strategy when possible to delivery virtually everything in digital form but that direction is still evolving.

Scholarly journals are now largely digital, which calls into question the need to acquire and store print versions. Mass digitization of books will bring major changes to technical services operations as academic libraries strive to focus on core activities not done by other entities. The academic library's mission to preserve scholarly resources for future generations remains but in different forms. Currently two major efforts to preserve both commercial and locally digitized content exist – LOCKSS[24] and Portico.[25] These systems are providing academic librarians in North America with greater confidence in digital persistence over time and are changing the need to store redundant print copies.

7. PROFESSIONAL PREPARATION

The majority of academic librarians in North America obtain a master's degree from an American Library Association (ALA) accredited degree program to prepare for their career. Currently 57 institutions of higher education in North America offer the accredited master's program.[26] Many academic librarians also have a subject master's degree and a few have the Ph.D. in a specific field. However, an additional graduate degree, while desirable, is not typically required. Both the As-

---

[23] Lougee, Wendy Pradt (2002). *Diffuse Libraries: Emergent Roles for the Research Library in a Digital Age*. Washington DC: CLIR.
[24] LOCKSS (Lots of Copies Keeps Stuff Safe). http://www.lockss.org/lockss/Home
[25] Portico. http://www.portico.org/
[26] American Library Association. *Alphabetical List of ALA-Accredited Institutions*. http://www.ala.org/ala/accreditation/lisdirb/alphaaccred.cfm

sociation for Research Libraries[27] and the American Library Association[28] conduct annual salary surveys to benchmark salaries for different types of academic librarians as well as for administrators. Academic libraries are increasingly hiring professionals with other types of training, especially information technologists. Other non-librarian professionals in academic libraries include human resources specialist, fundraiser, accountant, and a wide range of supervisors. Additionally, university libraries are increasingly interested in individuals with graduate degrees in specialized areas, particularly foreign languages, to take on what was once considered responsibilities for traditionally trained librarians. A select number of specialized training programs for these specialists exist in individual libraries or in a consortia of libraries.

8. CONCLUSION

Academic libraries in North America are experiencing unprecedented change and transformation as scholarship becomes more digital and communication more networked. These changes affect physical and virtual spaces. They affect services and relationships. They affect education, training, and career development. They affect the library's organizational structure. Change in the 21st century is revitalizing the dynamics of the modern research library and the university in dramatic and long lasting ways. North American academic libraries will look very different by mid-century but will still persist as fundamental to faculty and student success. North Academic libraries will play an even larger role in the production and dissemination of scholarship but in a more interconnected way with international colleagues recognizing that knowledge encompasses the world.

---

[27] Association of Research Libraries. *ARL Annual Salary Survey*. http://www.arl.org/stats/annualsurveys/salary/index.shtml

[28] American Library Association. Office for Research and Statistics. *ALA Survey of Librarians Salaries 2006* (summary). http://www.ala.org/ala/ors/reports/2006_Salary_Survey_Final_Report.pdf

SPECIAL LIBRARIES

Rebecca B. Vargha

The purpose of this book chapter is to trace the development of special libraries in the United States and Canada. A primary central focus is the role, history and mission of the Special Libraries Association during the development of special libraries from the beginning of the association in 1909 to the current practices in North America. What is a special library? How is a special library different from other types of libraries? A traditional definition from the Oxford English Dictionary (Second Edition 1989) defines a library as "a place set apart to contain books for reading, study, or reference or a building, room, or set of rooms, containing a collection of books for the use of the public or of some particular portion of it, or of the members of some society or the like; a public institution or establishment, charged with the care of a collection of books, and the duty of rendering the books accessible to those who require to use them."[1]

To contrast the classic definition, author Michael H. Harris defines a "special library" as a unit, which is quite focused in content and has a very specific clientele to serve in terms of information needs. A decided difference between traditional libraries and special libraries is the capability to innovate new technologies and services more readily than standardized libraries. Corporate libraries have a reputation in the United States as being especially nimble and flexible in adopting new information technologies.[2] Generally, special libraries are either independent or related to general public or university libraries. The other three groups are government, professional and business. Since the founding of the Special Libraries Association in 1909, a number of famous leaders and writers within the special libraries field have authored definitions of special libraries.[3] John Cotton Dana who is credited with founding SLA stated:

"These special collections of books, reports and other printed material are so varied in their character and in the use made of them, that no definition will any longer satisfactorily include them all."[4]

Over time, the definition was expanded to include more factors such as the effectiveness, knowledge and skill of the special librarian. As early as 1923, Rebecca Rankin expressed her thoughts in the following manner, "the essential part of a special library, the part to be emphasized and that which gives it its greatest possibilities, is the personality behind the library, the special librarian."[5]

---

[1] Oxford English Dictionary, Second Edition, 1989.

[2] Harris, Michael H. "History of Libraries in the Western World," (Scarecrow Press) 1995, page 275.

[3] McKenna, Frank. "Special Libraries and the Special Libraries Association," Encyclopedia of Library and Information Science (Marcel Dekker) 1980, volume 28, page 391.

[4] Dana, John Cotton. "The President's Opening Remarks." Special Libraries 1 (1) (1909) page 5.

[5] Rankin, Rebecca B. "The Public Library and the Special Library," Special Libraries 14 (5) (1923) page 76.

More than twenty-five years later, Herman H. Henkle wrote that efficient service is a key ingredient in the definition of a special library:

"The primary characteristic of special librarianship is not so much the subject content of the collection or the type of organization in which the library is operating, nor the particular personnel it serves, but rather the kind of service it gives."[6]

In 1952, Rose Vormelker also thought service was a key component with her comments:

The distinguishing characteristic of special librarianship is service. It is service which stops at northing short of producing on request or without request information which is needed, at the time it is needed and in the form in which it is needed, and in a manner which inspires confidence and respect for the librarian on the part of the user.[7]

In summary a general definition includes: a specialized collection in any format, which is arranged for a specific customer base and special library service which also foresees and provides information to clientele in a rapid and proactive manner. Essentially, the purpose of a special library is to deliver the right information to the right people at the right time. The development of the special librarianship continues to evolve quickly during the 21st century.

In the United States, the forerunners of today's special libraries began early. As noted author, consultant and Past SLA President (1991-1992), Guy St. Clair states, "a community in the United States was judged as if good place to live if it had a house of worship, a school and a library."[8] The reference specifically refers to a public library, which is open to all citizens of the community. The general development of public libraries began in England and America during the nineteenth century and is beyond the scope of this article. The goal of the earliest special libraries is to provide immediate access to "practical and utilitarian information to meet the needs of the library's users."[9]

Pennsylvania Hospital Library in Philadelphia began in 1763 and is generally considered to be the first medical library established in the United States.[10] It has been suggested that the United States and Canada were the cradle of civilization for the development of special libraries. Early library developments began well

---

[6] Henkle, Herman H. "Education for Special Librarianship," B.R. Berelson, ed., Eucation for Librarianship, American Library Association, Chicago, 1949, pages 170-182.

[7] Voemelker, Rose L. "Special Library Potential of the Public Library," Library Trends, 1 (2) (1952) page 200.

[8] St. Clair, Guy. SLA at 100: From Putting Knowledge to Work To Building The Knowledge Culture. (SLA) 2009 (forthcoming).

[9] St. Clair, Guy. SLA at 100: From Putting Knowledge to Work To Building The Knowledge Culture. (SLA) 2009 (forthcoming).

[10] Harris, Michael H. "History of Libraries in the Western World," (Scarecrow Press) 1995, page 192.

before the American Revolution.[11] In Canada for example, in 1725 the first hospital library was founded in Quebec City and a legislative library was founded in 1773 in Prince Edward Island.[12] In 1724, the Carpenters' Company of the City and County of Philadelphia (Pennsylvania) was created and included a library with books on subjects such as architecture and handbooks of designs by members. The collection began with books printed in England and then with materials published in America.[13] Today the organization is the oldest trade guild in the United States and there are 3,600 books in the Carpenters' Hall library.

The first law libraries in the United States were founded in Philadelphia, Pennsylvania and Boston, Massachusetts respectively. The Law Association Library (Philadelphia) began in 1802 and the Social Law Library (Boston) began in 1804.[14] The National Library of Medicine originated in 1836 and the New York Times Editorial Reference Library was created in 1851.[15]

From a historical point of development, Elizabeth Ferguson states "specialized problems in librarianship were recognized almost simultaneously as evidenced by the formation of the National Association of State Libraries in 1889, the Medical Library Association in 1898, the American Association of Law Libraries in 1906. The American Library Association was founded in 1876. It progressed so rapidly that in 1910 the Encyclopedia Britannica called it the largest and most important library association in existence."[16] While all libraries possess a certain degree of specialty, the special library in the United States developed an unparalleled identity in the traditional library landscape at the time. All the necessary elements were in place for significant discussions and the subsequent development of a unique professional association for librarians working in the subject discipline of business occurred rapidly.

The Special Libraries Association was founded in 1909 in the United States by a forward-looking group of specialized business librarians to network and collaborate with their peers.[17] John Cotton Dana was visionary librarian and leader who founded the professional association. His management theory was that librarians should be ready for radical change in the work place and this philosophy has stood

---

[11] McKenna, Frank. "Special Libraries and the Special Libraries Association," Encyclopedia of Library and Information Science (Marcel Dekker) 1980, volume 28, page 388.

[12] McKenna, Frank. "Special Libraries and the Special Libraries Association," Encyclopedia of Library and Information Science (Marcel Dekker) 1980, volume 28, page 388.

[13] McKenna, Frank. "Special Libraries and the Special Libraries Association," Encyclopedia of Library and Information Science (Marcel Dekker) 1980, volume 28, page 389.

[14] Harris, Michael H. "History of Libraries in the Western World," (Scarecrow Press) 1995, page 193.

[15] Kruzas, Anthony. Business and Industrial Libraries in the United States, 1820-1940 (Special Libraries Association) 1965, page 8.

[16] Feguson, Elizabeth. "Association Highlights," Special Libraries Association-Its First Fifty Years 1909-1959. (Special Libraries Association) 1959, page 5.

[17] Bender, David. "Special Libraries Association," Encyclopedia of Library and Information Science (Marcel Dekker) 2003, page 2723.

the test of time from the founding of SLA through the first one hundred years of the association and field of special librarianship. During his tenure as Head Librarian at the Newark Public Library in New Jersey (US), John Cotton Dana established a business branch for this public library. He stated the library was for the "men of affairs, a business branch. This was in a rented store close to the business and transportation center of the city. The library's management believed that men and women who were engaged in manufacturing, commerce, transportation, finance, insurance and allied activities could profitably make greater use than they had heretofore of information to be found in print."[18] The goal of this specialized arrangement was to promote easy and convenient access to business information.

Sarah B. Ball was the librarian for the business collection at the Newark Public Library. She attended the New Jersey Library Association and Pennsylvania Library Club joint meeting in Atlantic City, which took place in 1909. During the meetings, she met Anna B. Sears from the Merchants' Association of New York Library. They discussed potential collaboration between their respective organizations and scheduled a planning session to take place in New York. This planning discussion was attended by John Cotton Dana and F.B. Deberard from the Merchants' Association plus Sarah B. Ball and Anna B. Sears.[19] As a direct result of that energizing conversation in 1909, letters proposing a meeting during the July meeting of ALA were dispatched to forty-five special libraries. The text of the May 20, 1909 letter is as follows:

"To the Librarian:
In a few public libraries a special effort has been made to discuss and meet the needs of businessmen. A few manufacturing, business and engineering firms, and a few civic and commercial bodies have established their own libraries to meet their own needs.

The librarians who are managing these special libraries and special departments could be of much help to one another if they could exchange experiences and talk over methods and results. This letter of inquiry is sent out as the first step toward mutual aid. If you will kindly answer the questions enclosed, make suggestions for further inquiries and add names of other libraries in this field to the brief list, enclosed, to which this first circular is sent, we will report results to you and ask your cooperation in the next step. We especially ask your opinion on the advisibility of attempting cooperative work."[20]

---

[18] Dana, John Cotton. "Evolution of the Special Library," Special Libraries 5 (1914) pages 70-76.

[19] Bender, David. "Special Libraries Association," Encyclopedia of Library and Information Science (Marcel Dekker) 2003, page 2723.

[20] McKenna, Frank. "Special Libraries and the Special Libraries Association," Encyclopedia of Library and Information Science (Marcel Dekker) 1980, volume 28, page 399.

The meeting was held on the veranda of the Mt. Washington Hotel in Bretton Woods, New Hampshire and twenty librarians were in attendance to discuss the concept of special librarianship. Elizabeth Ferguson outlined the meeting in the following terms: "The participants in this "Veranda Conference," as it has come to be known decided that the demands of their jobs had actually created a new kind of librarianship – that of library service geared to meet the needs of specialized situations. These librarians were breaking completely new ground."[21] Lively discussion occurred at the meeting and the vote was taken. The Special Libraries Association was created with the following purpose: "The object of the Association is to promote the interests of the commercial, industrial, technical, civic, municipal and legislative reference libraries, the special departments of the public libraries, universities, welfare associations and business organizations."[22]

The charter members of the Special Libraries Association included:[23]

Mary Eileen Ahern Editor, Public Libraries	Clement W. Andrews The John Crear Library	Sarah B. Ball Newark Free Public Library
(Mrs.)Helen Page Bates New York School of Philanthropy	Andrew Linn Bostwick Saint Louis Municipal Reference Library	George F. Bowerman Public Library of the District of Columbia
Richard Rogers Bowker Editor, The Library Journal	Beatrice E. Carr Fisk and Robinson School	Clara M. Clark Bible Teachers Training
John Cotton Dana Newark Free Public Library	F. B. DeBerard Merchants' Association of New York	Dr. Horace E. Flack Baltimore Legislative Reference Department
Anna Fossler Columbia University	Marilla W. Freeman Louisville Free Public Library	George S. Godard Connecticut State Library
Mabel R. Haines The Library Journal	Daniel N. Handy The Insurance Library Association of Boston	Dr. Frederic C. Hicks Columbia University

---

[21] Feguson, Elizabeth. "Association Highlights," Special Libraries Association-Its First Fifty Years 1909-1959. (Special Libraries Association) 1959, page 5.

[22] Constitution. Special Libraries Association-Its First Fifty Years 1909-1959. (Special Libraries Association) 1959, page 4.

[23] McKenna, Frank. "Special Libraries and the Special Libraries Association," Encyclopedia of Library and Information Science (Marcel Dekker) 1980, volume 28, page 436-437.

Dr. Frank Pierce Hill
Brooklyn, N.Y.

Jessie Fremont Hume
Queens Borough
Public Library

Dr. John A. Lapp
Indiana State Library

Mari Fay Lindholm
New York Public Service
Commission Library

John J. Macfarlane
Philadelphia
Commercial Museum

Grace W. Morse
Equitable Life
Assurance Company

Samuel H. Ranck
Grand Rapids Public
Library

Anna Sears
Merchants' Association
of New York

William Franklyn
Stevens
Carnegie Library

Henry M. Utley
Detroit Public Library

Miss L.E. Howard
United Engineering
Society

Maude E. Inch
Insurance Society
of New York

George W. Lee
Stone and Webster

Dr. Harry Miller Lyndenberg
New York Public Library

Milo Roy Malbie
New York Public Service
Commission Library

Edith Allen Phelps
Oklahoma City
Public Library

Frances L. (Mrs. Coe)
Rathbone
East Orange Free
Public Library

F. O. Stetson
Newton, Mass.

Ida M. Thiele
Association of Life
Insurance Presidents

Mary S. Wallis
(Mrs. Mary W.
MacTarnaghan)
Baltimore Legislative
Reference Bureau

Mrs. K. M. Howze
Commonwealth Edison
Company

Florence Johnson
Boston Town Room Library

Clarence B. Lester
New York State Library

Charles McCarthy
Wisconsin Free Library
Commission

Guy E. Marion
Arthur D. Little Associates

George E. Plumb
Chicago Association
of Commerce

Mary M. Rosemond
Iowa State Library

Edward F. Stevens
Pratt Institute Free Library

William Trelease
Missouri Botanical Garden

Miss M.F. Warner
U.S. Bureau of Plant Industry

Dr. Joseph L. Wheeler	Dr. Robert H. Whitten	T. J. Willis
Public Library of the	New York Public	Milwaukee Municipal
District of Columbia	Service Commission	Reference Library
F. Mabel Winchell	Beatrice Winser	
Manchester City	Newark Free Public	
Library	Library	

John Cotton Dana was elected as the new president of the fledgling association. The Special Libraries Association had its first annual conference on November 5, 1909 in New York City. The first one hundred years of the organization began in earnest.

In chronological order, the SLA Historical Highlights are as follows:

1909–1920
1909 Special Libraries Association (SLA) is officially established
1909 Membership count 57
1909 Dues $2 including subscription to *Special Libraries*
1910 Affiliation with American Library Association (ALA) begins
1910 Special Libraries begins publication. Subscription $2.
1910 Directory of Special Libraries published, listing 100 libraries and 24 fields
1914 Membership count 354
1915 "Putting Knowledge to Work®" Association slogan coined by John A. Lapp
1919 First Conference held completely independent of ALA
1919-1920 First Female President elected Maude A. Carabin Mann

1920–1930
1923 Five classes of membership were established: Individual, $3; Institutional, $5; Associate, $2; Life, $100; and Honorary
1924 Districts change names to Chapters
1927 Association incorporated in Rhode Island
1928 Membership count 1,129

1930–1940
1930 SLA list of members published
1931 SLA moves to Standard Statistics Building in New York City.
1931-1932 Special Libraries registered as a trade name with the U.S. Patent Office
1931 SLA staff count: Two
1932 First recruitment material. Putting Knowledge to Work-Special Librarianship as a Career
1939 SLA moves to the Stecher-Hafner Building , 31 East 10th Street New York, NY.

1940–1950

1940 SLA staff count: Three

1941–1942 Dues waived for all members drafted in the military or government service

1942 SLA extends services to all libraries engaged in national defense

1943 SLA opens headquarter library

1944 Membership count 3,491

1944 Dues set for new membership categories: Sustaining, $25; Student, $1

1946 SLA becomes a member of the International Federation of Library Associations (IFLA)

1947 Special Libraries subscription $7

1947 Salary Survey conducted and published in Special Libraries

1949 SLA staff count: Eight; Membership count 5,443; Dues Institutional, $20; Active, $7; Associate, $4

1949 Divisions were formed from groups

1949 SLA disaffiliated from the ALA

1950–1960

1954 Retired membership established, with dues of $5

1959 Translations Monthly publication replaced by Technical Translations

1959 First presentation of SLA Hall of Fame

1960–1970

1960 Publications department established

1961-1962 News and Notes quarterly publication replaces the Bulletin

1963 Subscription to Special Libraries and Technical Book Review, $10 each

1964 Membership count 5,697; Dues Active and Associate, $20

1967 Conventions renamed conferences to emphasize the professional program content

1967 SLA moves to 235 Park Avenue South, New York, NY

1968 Initiation of a study on mechanized records of membership and subscription

1970–1980

1970 Proceedings initiated to seek Internal Revenue Service (IRS) reclassification of SLA as an Internal Revenue Code (IRC) Section 501(c)(3) organization

1972 Reclassification as an IRC Section 510 (c)(3) approved by IRS

1973 SLA suspends membership in International Federation for Information and Documentation (FID) until South African National Representative to FID either withdraws or no longer represents a government with a policy of apartheid

1974 Special Libraries registered as a trademark

1976 Dues for Members and Associates, $40; Sustaining Members, $200

1978 Professional development department established

1978 Membership approves a resolution not to select conferences and meeting sites in states that have not ratified the Equal Rights Amendment

1979 David Bender is appointed executive director

1980–1990

1981 Dues: Member/Associate Member, $55; Sustaining Member, $250; Student, $12

1981 Special Libraries changes frequency from monthly to quarterly

1981 SpeciaList monthly newsletter begins publication.

1981 Electronic mail communication between the Board of Directors and Association Staff begin experimental basis

1981 First Who's Who in Special Libraries is published

1981 Building Fund is established

1982 Public Relations program is established

1982-1983 Middle Management Institute established

1983-1984 Association celebrates its 75th Anniversary

1984 Building at 1700 18th Street in Dupont Circle neighborhood of Washington DC is purchased as a new home for SLA

1984 Dues: Member/Associate Member, $75; Student Member/Retired Member, $15; Sustaining Member, $300

1985 SLA Headquarters moves from New York City to Washington, DC

1986 Fellows Award is established

1986 SLA initiates first annual State of the Art Institute

1987 Information Resources Center (IRC) implements online cataloging

1988 SLA introduces first computer-assisted study program at 79th annual conference

1988 SLA, ALA, District of Columbia Library Association (DCLA), hold Library Legislative Day

1989 Staff count: 26

1989 First Caucus established: Solo Librarian (which later became Solo Librarian Division)

1990–2000

1990 Information Services department established

1991 First annual International Special Librarians Day recognized

1993 SLA is connected to the Internet@ sla1@capcon.net

1995 Dues: Members, $105; Retired/Students, $25; Sustaining, $400

1995 SLA creates online discussion lists for members

1995 SLA launches its first videoconference training session

1996 SLA launches its own World Wide Web site (www.sla.org)

1996 SLA introduces the Legacy Club
1996 SLA publishes Competencies for Special Librarians of the 21st Century
1996 SpeciaList and Special Libraries are discontinued
1997 Information Outlook, the monthly four-color magazine is published
1997 New association management system acquired allowing members to update their records via the website
1997 SLA's Virtual Bookstore launched
1997 CONSULT Online launched on the website
1998 Information Outlook available online at www.informationoutlook.com
1998 SLA Chat room hosting service created
1998 New Vision Statement and Strategic Plan adopted
1998 Leadership Development Department created to develop, manage and coordinate the Association's leadership services
1999 Professional Development sponsors its first conference in Southern Europe, Management of the Library in the Electronic Era, in Barcelona, Spain
1999 SLA's first satellite broadcast videoconference, which included mock licensing activity and discussion groups before and after the broadcast.
1999 Asian Chapter formed
1999 Introduces online conference planner for Annual Conference in Minneapolis

2000–Present
Global 2000 conference held in Brighton, England. Members raised in excess of $80,000 to send 25 librarians from developing countries to the conference.
2000 SLA's Career Services Online revised to include online posting of job opportunities, resumes, Virtual Advisers, and greatly improved searching capabilities
2000 Launch of the Virtual Exhibit Hall integrated with the online conference planner
2000 Major redesign of SLA's website, Virtual SLA
2001 SLA Executive Director David R. Bender retires after 22 years of service
2001 SLA Board of Directors appoints Roberta I. Shaffer as new executive director
2001 Publication of the membership e-newsletter, SLA.COMmunicate
2001 Web version of Quicken made available to unit treasurers supporting their need to access their financial records anywhere and at anytime
2002 First publication made available electronically in PDF as well as hardback format
2002 Electronic newsletter, BOARD.COMmunicate, launched to improve communications between the Association's directors and members
2002 Bylaws revisions approved by members
2003 Vote on changing name
2003 SLA Board of Director appoints Janice R. Lachance as new executive director

2003 SLA members attending the annual business meeting in New York vote to retain Association's name
2003 SLA adopts new vision, mission, and core values statements
2003 SLA announces major web site redesign in response to member needs
2004 SLA accepts multiple currencies
2004 SLA offers multiple language translations on www.sla.org
2004 SLA adopts a new naming model and begins to use the acronym SLA publicly
2004 SLA moves to its new headquarters in historic Alexandria, VA
2009 SLA celebrates 100th year anniversary as a professional association
2009 Publication of Guy St. Clair's book, SLA at 100: From Putting Knowledge to Work to Building The Knowledge Culture. The Centennial History of SLA (Special Libraries Association) 1909–2009.

As the association grew and changed, the field of special librarianship developed rapidly at the beginning of the twentieth century. According to Marian C. Manley (Chair, SLA Committee on Training and Recruiting) the April 1910 issue of Special Libraries listed a directory of108 libraries showing marked development of legislative and municipal reference libraries, scientific and technical collections, some museum developments and a few business libraries.[24] As a contrast, the 1935 Special Libraries Directory listed 1,475 special libraries. By 1953 the number of special libraries was listed at 2,270.[25] The growth from the early days mirrors the value of information in business over the forty-year time span and the increased importance of the information professional in a business environment.

Edythe Moore wrote an article in 1987 which traced the progression of corporate libraries from their beginnings to the late 1980s. She cites three specific factors which influenced the early development of corporate libraries; "the expansion of research and scholarly publishing, the rapid acceleration in the growth of business and industry and the newly emerging library profession."[26] She cited the innovative activity of two noted librarians who were truly ahead of their time in terms of innovations in corporate settings. At the turn of the century (1900s) these librarians were George W. Lee at Stone and Webster and Guy E. Marion at Arthur D. Little Inc. They looked beyond traditional resources collected by libraries at that time to needs of their corporate clientele. In fact, George W. Lee called his special library "a business and information bureau" within the engineering firm in

---

[24] Manley, Marian C. "The Special Library Profession and What It Offers: A General Survey." *Special Libraries*, vol.29, No. 6, page 182.

[25] Kruzas, Anthony. *Business and Industrial Libraries in the United States, 1820-1940* (Special Libraries Association) 1965, page 13.

[26] Moore, Edythe. "Corporate science and technology libraries: one hundred years of progress," *Science & Technology Libraries*, vol.8 (Fall 1987) p. 51.

Boston, Massachusetts (United States) where he was employed.[27] Both Lee and Marion were early adaptors and recognized that an effective corporate library enhanced the competitive position of their respective companies. They also transformed their respective corporate libraries from mere professional collections to the "information center."[28] Lee identified the following list of materials as crucial for his special library:

1. Documents, mostly typewritten, the records of the business
2. Books, pamphlets, and periodicals.
3. Maps, atlases, etc.
4. Indexes, catalogs, lists, etc.
5. Other departments
6. Other libraries
7. Business undertakings, institutions and people in general.
8. Miscellany: some unappreciated publications, emergencies and matters of that sort.[29]

His remarks on the role of the special library or information center ring true in the 21st century. George W. Lee stated "Quick service is indeed called for and rightly expected. We need to realize that not only are we library workers, but that we are office workers, and that the department as a whole is merely incidental to the work of the engineers, financiers and general managers of public utilities.[30]

Guy E. Marion worked as the librarian for Arthur D. Little, Inc and that library began in 1886. The early focus of the company was consulting and research in the subject area of chemistry. The collection of the special library was comprised of a plethora of materials including as he stated, "made up of information culled from the laboratory's daily correspondence, out of the experiences of the various members of the laboratory staff, from experiments carried on in the laboratory, and from various technical reports and investigations made for clients."[31] The collection contained 1,000 bound volumes, 900 pamphlets, 20,000 clippings, 10,000 patents, and 800 blueprints indexed with a card catalog of 100,000 cards.[32] Marion

---

27 Kruzas, Anthony. Business and Industrial Libraries in the United States, 1820-1940 (Special Libraries Association) 1965, page 4.
28 Moore, Edythe. "Corporate science and technology libraries: one hundred years of progress," Science & Technology Libraries, vol.8 (Fall 1987) p. 53-54.
29 Kruzas, Anthony. Business and Industrial Libraries in the United States, 1820-1940 (Special Libraries Association) 1965, page 56.
30 Kruzas, Anthony. Business and Industrial Libraries in the United States, 1820-1940 (Special Libraries Association) 1965, page 57.
31 Marion, Guy E. "The Library As an Adjunct to Industrial Laboratories," Library Journal, 35 (September 1910, p.401.
32 Kruzas, Anthony. Business and Industrial Libraries in the United States, 1820-1940 (Special Libraries Association) 1965, page 58.

was also an early innovator since his library collection is generally considered to be the first special library in the United States to collect technical reports in a corporate library setting. The CEO of the company by today's standards, Dr. Arthur D. Little stressed the value of special libraries during his inaugural address at the American Chemical Society in 1912 when he stated, "These laboratories should each be developed around a special library."[33]

This early adaptation of library management concepts such as the consistent practice of high levels of customer satisfaction, rapid service, deliberate focus on the user, customization and systematic control of nontraditional information provided the very foundation of the librarianship which special librarians particularly in corporate settings put into practice with managing information assets so effectively today.

As commerce and industry grew after World War I, the number of special libraries also increased in number. With the new challenges at hand, librarians turned to each other for advice on building and maintaining their respective collections. As the essay by Edythe Moore outlines, "these librarians, without hesitation, turned to their colleagues who had the same or similar problems; to the Special Libraries Association which had been formed in 1909 and which was beginning to be organized into both geographically designated chapters and subject oriented divisions."[34] In other words, the powerful professional network that is cited as the number one benefit among SLA members continued to grow and flourish.

In particular after World War II, the sheer number of special libraries and information centers grew quite rapidly. The libraries in corporations expanded and additionally the special libraries in government, higher education and professional organizations also increased. Anthony Kruzacs conducted a census of special libraries for 1961-62 and identified 8,533 special libraries in the United States.[35]

With the growth of bibliographic databases in the 1970s, and in particular the formation of OCLC and the creation of their bibliographic utility now known as WorldCat, special librarians were poised strategically on the brink of what would later be called the "Information Age." The computer revolution has revolutionized the profession of special librarianship in ways which are almost beyond human imagination since the founding of SLA in 1909. In the words of futurist, Joseph Becker, "In this new information society, special librarians are destined to play an

---

[33] Kruzas, Anthony. *Business and Industrial Libraries in the United States, 1820-1940* (Special Libraries Association) 1965, page 59.

[34] Moore, Edythe. "Corporate science and technology libraries: one hundred years of progress," *Science & Technology Libraries*, vol.8 (Fall 1987) p.55.

[35] Kruzas, Anthony. *Business and Industrial Libraries in the United States, 1820-1940* (Special Libraries Association) 1965, page 115.

increasingly greater role in shaping and establishing new information connections among libraries, information centers and people."[36]

As technology advances, there are many exciting circumstances and shifts ahead for special librarians. One of those shifts took place in the 1990s for SLA and its members with the transition to a virtual association. By using electronic technology, the professional association was afforded an opportunity for special librarians to network and communicate with their peers on global basis. Two of the earliest available resources were the membership database and the online version of Information Outlook which is published monthly by SLA.

During the last decade, SLA created two pivotal documents which are particularly relevant to the profession of special librarianship. The first is the vision, mission and core values for the association.

SLA VISION, MISSION AND CORE VALUE STATEMENTS

These statements were revised and adopted in October 2003.

Vision: SLA is the global organization for innovative information professionals and their strategic partners.

Mission: SLA promotes and strengthens its members through learning, advocacy and networking initiatives.

The following five core value statements are based on values shared by SLA members:

1. Strengthening our roles as information leaders in our organizations and our communities, including shaping information policy.
2. Responding to our clients needs, adding qualitative and quantitative value to information services and products.
3. Embracing innovative solutions for the enhancement of services and intellectual advancement within the profession.
4. Delivering measurable results in the information economy and our organizations. The Association and its members are expected to operate with the highest level of ethics and honesty.
5. Providing opportunities to meet, communicate, collaborate, and partner with the information industry and the business community.[37]

The second document is the revised competencies for special librarians and information professionals. Members of SLA explored their interpretation and of the

---

[36] Becker, Joseph. "How to Integrate and Manage New Technology in the Library," Special Libraries vol. 74 (1) (Jan. 1983) pages 1-6.
[37] SLA Vision, Mission, and Core Value Statements http://www.sla.org/content/SLA/AssnProfile/ slanplan/index.cfm (Accessed April 9, 2008)

skills and competencies required in the current environment over several years. The following excerpt from the SLA web site highlights the professional and personal competencies needed by practicing special librarians.[38]

CORE COMPETENCIES

Information professionals contribute to the knowledge base of the profession by sharing best practices and experiences, and continue to learn about information products, services, and management practices throughout the life of his/her career.

Information professionals commit to professional excellence and ethics, and to the values and principles of the profession.

PROFESSIONAL COMPETENCIES

A. Managing Information Organizations

Information professionals manage information organizations ranging in size from one employee to several hundred employees. These organizations may be in any environment from corporate, education, public, government, to non-profit. Information professionals excel at managing these organizations whose offerings are intangible, whose markets are constantly changing and in which both high-tech and high-touch are vitally important in achieving organizational success.

A.1 Aligns the information organization with, and is supportive of, the strategic directions of the parent organization or of key client groups through partnerships with key stakeholders and suppliers.

A.2 Assesses and communicates the value of the information organization, including information services, products and policies to senior management, key stakeholders and client groups.

A.3 Establishes effective management, operational and financial management processes and exercises sound business and financial judgments in making decisions that balance operational and strategic considerations.

A.4 Contributes effectively to senior management strategies and decisions regarding information applications, tools and technologies, and policies for the organization.

A.5 Builds and leads an effective information services team and champions the professional and personal development of people working within the information organization.

---

[38] SLA Competencies for Information Professionals http://www.sla.org/content/learn/comp2003/index. cfm (accessed April 10, 2008)

A.6 Markets information services and products, both formally and informally, through web and physical communication collateral, presentations, publications and conversations.

A.7 Gathers the best available evidence to support decisions about the development of new service and products, the modification of current services or the elimination of services to continually improve the array of information services offered.

A.8 Advises the organization on copyright and intellectual property issues and compliance.

Managing Information Resources

Information professionals have expertise in total management of information resources, including identifying, selecting, evaluating, securing and providing access to pertinent information resources. These resources may be in any media or format. Information professionals recognize the importance of people as a key information resource.

B.1 Manages the full life cycle of information from its creation or acquisition through its destruction. This includes organizing, categorizing, cataloguing, classifying, disseminating; creating and managing taxonomies, intranet and extranet content, thesauri etc.

B. 2 Builds a dynamic collection of information resources based on a deep understanding of clients' information needs and their learning, work and/or business processes.

B.3 Demonstrates expert knowledge of the content and format of information resources, including the ability to critically evaluate, select and filter them.

B.4 Provides access to the best available externally published and internally created information resources and deploys content throughout the organization using a suite of information access tools.

B.5 Negotiates the purchase and licensing of needed information products and services.

B.6 Develops information policies for the organization regarding externally published and internally created information resources and advises on the implementation of these policies.

C. Managing Information Services

Information professionals manage the entire life cycle of information services, from the concept stage through the design, development, testing, marketing, packaging, delivery and divestment of these offerings. Information professionals may oversee this entire process or may concentrate on specific stages, but their expertise is unquestionable in providing offerings that enable clients to immediately integrate and apply information in their work or learning processes.

C.1 Develops and maintains a portfolio of cost-effective, client-valued information services that are aligned with the strategic directions of the organization and client groups.

C.2 Conducts market research of the information behaviors and problems of current and potential client groups to identify concepts for new or enhanced information solutions for these groups. Transforms these concepts into customized information products and services.

C.3 Researches, analyzes and synthesizes information into accurate answers or actionable information for clients, and ensures that clients have the tools or capabilities to immediately apply these.

C.4 Develops and applies appropriate metrics to continually measure the quality and value of information offerings, and to take appropriate action to ensure each offering's relevancy within the portfolio.

C.5 Employs evidence-based management to demonstrate the value of and continually improve information sources and services.

D. Applying Information Tools & Technologies

Information professionals harness the current and appropriate technology tools to deliver the best services, provide the most relevant and accessible resources, develop and deliver teaching tools to maximize clients' use of information, and capitalize on the library and information environment of the 21st century.

D.1 Assesses, selects and applies current and emerging information tools and creates information access and delivery solutions

D.2 Applies expertise in databases, indexing, metadata, and information analysis and synthesis to improve information retrieval and use in the organization

D.3 Protects the information privacy of clients and maintains awareness of, and responses to, new challenges to privacy

D.4 Maintains current awareness of emerging technologies that may not be currently relevant but may become relevant tools of future information resources, services or applications.

For a listing of the personal competencies and examples of applied scenarios consult the SLA web site: http://www.sla.org/content/learn/comp2003/index.cfm

From the beginning of the association in 1909 throughout the 21st century seismic shifts continue to occur in technology, from the invention of the automobile, television, radio to computer technology. Throughout the inventions of the last century, special libraries continue to innovate and embrace change quickly to fit their environments through professional development and competencies for special librarians and information professionals .

As a professional organization, SLA provides unique opportunities for members to actively participate in an association which is an integral part of staying ahead of constant change within the library and information science profession. There are a myriad of resources and activities which deliver valuable and tangible benefits from networking to continuing education through Click U, and career development. The very essence of daily work is changing with the constant impact of technology like rss feeds, podcasts, blogs and wikis.

Currently, over 11,000 SLA members work in a diverse range of environments such as business, government, law firms, banking industry, non-profit organizations, pharmaceutical companies and academic institutions. There are many additional information settings and learning environments such as news libraries, medical libraries, museum libraries, and engineering firms. The term "special libraries" is often used interchangeably with information centers. Other commonly used names include competitive intelligence units, intranet departments, knowledge resource centers, and content management organizations. In each unique setting librarians or information professionals use information strategically in their jobs to advance the mission of their respective parent organizations. Special librarians collect, analyze, evaluate, package and disseminate information to facilitate accurate decision making in corporate, academic, non-profit and government settings.

The author gratefully acknowledges the excellent support and advice of Guy St. Clair.

SCHOOL LIBRARIES

Blanche Woolls

School libraries in Canada and the United States have a very short history compared to other types of libraries in North America; however, their histories have many similarities and some differences. While school libraries in both countries developed within their educational systems, Canada launched a more nationalized approach for its provinces, and the U.S. systems grew state by state.

IN THE BEGINNING

Canadian education was modeled first after the French and then Great Britain, controlled by the church. Later the Ontario province passed legislation creating a school system with municipally elected boards, local taxation, and a central administration of education which was copied by the Constitution of 1867 giving control of education to the provinces. Designed by a Methodist minister, Egerton Ryerson, they copied the schools of the New England colonies. School libraries were often referred to as important in achieving the goals of education. (1) In the U.S., all government not covered by the Constitution is assigned to the individual states making education a part of state governance. The first schools in the United States were very small and in the hands of the headmaster. Students (usually male students) were asked to copy information from the board to their slates. They might learn how to read and write, but this came independently from what they were copying. Schooling was labor-intensive and available only to those who could pay.

As the country grew, those in charge wanted a citizenry able to read and write, live and vote in a democratic society. In some of the larger cities, societies were formed to provide free education to the masses so they would become responsible citizens. These nineteenth-century societies adopted a method in which many students were organized into groups based on ability. The older students learned from the master, and then taught the younger ones. They copied and were drilled on facts until they knew them. (2) Slowly, but steadily, state governments across the nation built public schools, teachers were hired to educate all children, and school attendance became compulsory.

Educational funding in the U.S. is left to state laws, and this varies by an individual state's ability and willingness to support education. Problems in equity arise. A current situation has to do with being able to find qualified teachers. In 1996, the National Commission on Teaching and America's future stated:

Although no state will allow a person to fix plumbing, guard swimming pools, style hair, write wills, design a building, or practice medicine without completing training and passing an examination, more than 40 states allow school districts to hire teachers on emergency licenses who have not met these basic requirements. States pay more attention to the qualifications of veterinarians treating the nation's cats and dogs than to those of teachers educating the nation's children and youth. (3)

EARLY DEVELOPMENT OF SCHOOL LIBRARIES

In both countries, schools were usually very small, and collections of library materials were kept on the corner of the teacher's desk and administered by the teacher or a headmaster if the school had more than one room. In Canada, a Common Schools Act of 1850 established school libraries. This was similar to public library legislation except that the libraries were in school buildings but administered by the public library board. Common school libraries in locations where no access to free reading materials was available were initially seen as a positive for the community members who were often barely literate. When the collections were not well used, they returned to the public library with their better-trained staff and "more public-oriented programs of service." (4)

Laws varied in each state in the U.S. According to the publication, *Public Libraries in the United States*, in 1876 in the U.S., there were 826 schools of secondary rank with libraries containing nearly 1 million volumes, or a little over 1,000 volumes per library. (5)

By 1900 in both countries, public libraries were offering services to schools. This could take the form of placing boxes of books or even complete collections in buildings. For some, a librarian was provided to staff the library. In some cases, these became branches of the public library or, as stated above, absorbed by the public library. Bookmobile service was also provided, and contracts between school library boards and the public library designated the services to be provided including a librarian to visit the schools and tell stories. Having the school share a facility with the public library remains one means of providing both public and school library service, particularly in smaller, rural areas where funding both becomes difficult.

Mary Kingsbury, the first professionally trained librarian in the U.S. was appointed to Erasmus Hall in 1900, and the second librarian, Mary E. Hall, was appointed to Girl's High School in Brooklyn in 1903. (6) Despite the appointment of these new librarians, the number of libraries grew slowly, and their collections were even slower to grow. Edward D. Greenman reported that in the 10,000 public high schools in the U.S. in 1913, "not more than 250 possess collections containing 3,000 volumes or over." (7) He noted that these libraries were well managed and often had a professional trained librarian who taught the students how to use the library and its reference books, and the classification of materials.

IN THE MIDDLE AND LATE 20TH CENTURY

By the 1940s, school libraries in secondary schools in Canada were common while elementary libraries, usually in smaller schools, were assigned to a teacher, and development was slower. In the 60s, the increase in population, changes in curriculum, and the change in the resources found in libraries led to the school librarian taking a broader teaching role. At that time, the name of the school library became the learning resource center, and the person in charge became the teacher librarian. (8)

Growth of secondary school libraries in the U.S. accelerated in the mid-1920s when regional accrediting agencies for schools specified a high school library with a trained librarian as a requirement for all schools seeking to be accredited. However, these did not cover elementary schools, and most had, if anything at all, classroom collections of reading materials. In cities with public libraries, these were sometimes supplemented with collections from the local public library.

The U.S.S.R.'s launching of Sputnik in the 50s turned the attention of U.S. educators and legislators to the fact that students were seriously behind in the study of science and foreign language as taught in schools. The National Defense Education Act provided matching funds for the purchase of resources and equipment for schools, and some of these found their way into the school library. Then in 1965, lobbying efforts of the American Library Association's Washington office and the concentrated efforts of key school librarians across the country resulted in passage of Title II of the Elementary and Secondary Education Act. Funds were specified to purchase library materials. These funds were then combined with local initiatives and volunteer efforts to build school libraries in elementary buildings and to expand libraries in secondary schools.

In the late 1980s and early 1990s, both in Canada and the U.S., educational decision-making began being decentralized. In Canada, the principal was given much more authority in choosing the educational programs within the school. (9)

Site-based management changes in the U.S. meant that a committee of teachers could choose whether or not to include a library media specialist as part of the essential program for students, or if one was in place, funding for library resources could be eliminated. In some U.S. states, certification requirements came under review, and it was no longer considered necessary for the library to be staffed with someone who held teacher certification. Much of what was lost, but not all, needs to be regained. It became the task of school library associations to encourage revitalization of school libraries.

EDUCATION FOR SCHOOL LIBRARIANS

For someone interested in becoming a school librarian, they must meet the requirements established by the province or state to hold a teaching certificate or credential with a specialty in school librarianship. To do this, they attend schools of education and schools of library and information science. Some accomplish this credential with their bachelor's degree while others must earn a master's degree. In many states in the U.S., a person must hold both a teaching certificate and a school library credential.

Courses typically offered include an introduction to the profession, technology in the library, reference, collection development, and management of libraries. More specialized courses for school librarians include literature and materials for children and young adults, curriculum integration, instructional design, building websites, online resources and searching, among others. Students in most programs are required to have a practicum experience working in a school library for a specific amount of time. When these are taken as a student in a college of education, students intend to work in a school. When they are taken in a master's of library and information science program, they are share classes with students who will become academic, public, and special librarians as well as those interested in school libraries.

Those who gain their certification as an undergraduate usually have a minor in library and information science, which may be as many as 24-30 hours or as few as 18 hours. These students usually have a teaching practicum and a library practicum before they graduate.

STAFFING FOR SCHOOL LIBRARIES

School libraries are managed by professional school librarians. If schools are very large, more than one librarian may be assigned to the library, and these librarians have additional staff to work with them.

Additional personnel working in the library may include someone with technical skills who will have earned a two-year certificate in a training program. This person helps manage the library or may be responsible for computer technology. In some situations, someone with clerical skills helps with the circulation of materials, ordering books and other resources, and other tasks.

In many situations, parent or community volunteers come into the library regularly to help with various tasks as assigned to them. These persons are very helpful with many activities in the library such as checking in and re-shelving books or helping with circulation.

Students often work in the library. It may be as a part of a school club program, or they may be given credit for their work. Students can be very useful in helping their fellow students locate resources on the OPAC and on the shelves. They can help their fellow students change bulletin boards,maintain a website, and make good use of the technologies available.

INFLUENCE OF NEW TECHNOLOGIES ON SCHOOL LIBRARIES

At first, the implementation of technology in schools meant that school library funds might be taken to purchase computers for classrooms. The rush to have computers available often resulted in poor choices of less expensive and limited hardware, and, even though less expensive, seldom were enough purchased for use by an entire classroom. One computer in a classroom had little application beyond learning stations or something for children to do if they finished their seatwork early. School librarians began to take the lead in helping their teachers and administrators select the best equipment and software to be used by students. Computer labs were set up, often in the library, so an entire class could use this technology simultaneously.

As computer technology was adopted by other types of libraries for a variety of management applications, such as circulation, serials control, and online public access catalogs, these applications were also implemented in school libraries. Vendors were quick to develop the software needed by schools for their smaller collections. The process of converting card catalogs into machine-readable records became the topic of many presentations at local, state or province and national library association meetings. The ability to bar code information made it much easier to protect the identity of a student who had checked out an item.

The expansion of information found in online resources continues to challenge school librarians today. The high cost of online databases and the need for more than one database often cuts into the book budget so that there is a constant struggle to maintain an up-to-date collection of print resources. The emergence of statewide purchase of online resources has been helpful in many states in the U.S.

THE SCHOOL LIBRARY FACILITY

Providing spaces in schools to house the information resources is always a challenge. It has become more of a challenge since new technologies have been added. Housing word-processing equipment and online resources in addition to print is different from the configurations found in media centers constructed before 1980.

Finding spaces and adequate electricity to contain a computer laboratory adjacent to the book shelving usually required some remodeling. When the servers to handle the schools online resources are the responsibility of the library media staff, being able to house them in a closed area that is both secure and air conditioned properly adds to the remodeling plans. Many school librarians are also responsible for wireless installations providing movable carts with a classroom of laptops. Although rearranging to accommodate new technologies is mandatory, all this is done in the context of the goals and objectives of the school's educational program.

Since differences exist in the goals and patterns of educational programs, facilities within a school are designed to reflect its curriculum and the particular instructional requirements of its students and teachers. The size and characteristics of school populations and the rapidly changing technologies for instruction demand alternatives and maximum flexibility in the design and relationship of functional spaces within the library media program facilities. (10)

Because of these differences in educational programs, facilities reflect the following:

- Size of the student body
- Attendance patterns of students
- Age and learning styles of students
- Teaching methods
- Number of staff in the media center
- Scheduling of students to the media center
- Size of the collection, materials, and equipment
- Technologies to be housed and managed from the media center

The size of the student body is a major consideration. Often state or provincial agencies mandate building specifications. If the guidelines for schools require the media center to seat 10 percent of the student body, this would require a larger facility for a school population of 2,000 students than 200. In addition, regional accrediting agencies often specify a ratio of building size to the size of the student body.

Although educators prefer to think that all teachers have moved beyond sole use of lecture and text, this is not yet true. It is unlikely that an entire staff is using this traditional teaching pattern; nevertheless, this pattern is a factor in the use of media center spaces. That is, spaces are used less for reference and more for recreational reading.

SCHOOL LIBRARY RESOURCE COLLECTIONS

The major change in resource collections for schools has come about with the argument that schools do not need libraries because of the ability to find all the information needed by students on the Internet. Some school districts in the U.S. have built new buildings without a room designated as the library media center. However, after the initial announcement, little has been heard about the success or failure of these ventures. The school librarian is needed to help students learn to use online resources, to separate relevant and accurate information from the flood of information available, and to recognize misinformation when it is found on websites or through a Google search. In addition, school librarians are essential in choosing which databases to purchase and keeping the subscriptions current. For teachers and students to understand how to access these commercial databases with their passwords and different search engines requires someone whose role it is to keep current. In some states in the U.S. the legislature is providing a statewide online collection with access to a variety of databases and other electronic resources. In this situation, the librarian is there to help teachers and students make the best use of these electronic resources.

Another resource available to students in schools today is access to 24/7 reference service. This may be through the school library's databases, or it may be through another agency such as the public library that provides reference service at all times of the day or night.

School librarians must continue to help teachers and students understand the rules of copyright. Because information is readily available, many ignore the right to make copies of material, distributing what is found on websites without gaining permission.

At all times school librarians have helped teachers explain to students how to use resource collections so that they are not copying entire passages and claiming them. It is very simple to download and cut and paste passages found through computer searches. Overcoming plagiarism and using papers being placed for sale on the web is a constant battle. One effective solution is to work collaboratively with teachers to make sure assignments require thoughtful responses.

SCHOOL LIBRARY PROGRAMMING

School librarians continue their role in encouraging students to read. The library is open during the school day for students to come and use materials. As computers were first available in the school library, students came to word process their papers and to conduct online research. Students continued to come to the library to conduct research and prepare research reports, but the school librarian was in a more cooperating role with the teacher, placing materials on reserve or sending them to the classroom for an extended period rather than actually collaborating with teachers to teach units of instruction. This change began as school librarians moved from teaching library skills in a sequence (often dictated by the school district and almost without relation to the curriculum being taught) to working with teachers to help students become information literate.

Perhaps the greatest change has come with the efforts of school librarians to collaborate with teachers to improve teaching and learning. Because school librarians know the curriculum taught throughout the school and they know the resources available in the library and online, they are able to plan with teachers to make units of instruction more effective. They share in teaching the units and thereby providing students with two teachers rather than a single teacher during the lesson. They are also able to make activities more exciting to students engaging their interest, and they are able to help create assignments that encourage students to use their critical thinking skills rather than being able to cut and paste simple answers to simple questions.

THE ROLE OF SCHOOL LIBRARY ASSOCIATIONS AND THEIR STANDARDS

The Canadian Association for School Librarians (CASL) is a recent association. It was formed when members of two associations, the Association for Teacher-Librarianship in Canada (ATLC) and the Canadian School Library Association (CSLA), determined that a strong, single national association would be preferable to having two. CASL's first annual general meeting was held on June 18, 2004 during the annual meeting of the Canadian Library Association conference. The mission of this merged association is:

> To provide a national forum for promoting school library programs, as an essential element in the educational process, through advocacy, continuing education, and leadership.

The association meets ever year during the Canadian Librarian Association national conference and tradeshow in late May or early June. Division and interest group meetings are held as well as an annual general meeting.

Prior to the forming of their new association, four sets of guidelines had been developed. The latest was the 2003 document, *Achieving Information Literacy: Standards for School Library Programs in Canada* (11) (#11 Edited by Marlene Asselin, Jennifer L. Branch, and Dianne Oberg. Ottawa, Ont.: 2003: Canadian School Library Association and Association of Teachers Librarianship in Canada) is the fourth and was created by Canadian school librarians working collaboratively. This document provides a vision and a framework for school library programs in Canada based upon anticipated outcomes. The standards list the numbers needed for staffing, collections, facilities, and information and communication technologies. These are cited at three levels, "below standard," "acceptable," and "exemplary."

The final section describes "A Collaborative Team for Achieving Information Literacy" and states, "Key to the success of teacher and teacher-librarian collaboration and the school-wide development of information literacy is the Principal." (12) This section, in stressing the need for a collaborative team, assigned responsibilities for the district superintendent, district coordinator, principal, teacher librarian, and the clerical and technical staff. Two appendixes, Appendix A, "Research in School Library Programs: Linking Teacher Librarians, School Librarians, and Student Achievement," written by Ken Haycock and the evaluation checklists found in Appendix B, offer important information.

This was not their first standards document, and their previous documents included: Canadian School Library Association. (1967); *Standards for Library Service for Canadian Schools*. Toronto: McGraw-Hill Ryerson; Association for Media and Technology in Education in Canada and Canadian School Library Association (1977); *Resource Services for Canadian Schools*. Toronto: McGraw-Hill Ryerson, Canadian School Library Association (1988-1992); and *Guidelines for Effective School Library Programs*. Ottawa, ON: Canadian School Library Association. They had also issued a policy statement developed by the Canadian School Library Association, a division of the Canadian Library Association, identifying these nine areas of competence:

- Administration of the program.
- Selection of learning resources.
- Acquisition and organization of learning resources.
- Reading, listening and viewing guidance.
- Design and production of learning resources.
- Information and reference services.
- Promotion of the effective use of learning resources and services.
- Cooperative program planning and teaching.
- Professionalism and leadership (13)

The mission of the American Association of School Librarians (AASL) is to advocate for excellence, facilitate change, and develop leaders in the school library media field. Their goals are to ensure that all members of the school library media field collaborate to

- Provide leadership in the total education program.
- Participate as active partners in the teaching/learning process.

- Connect learners with ideas and information, and
- Prepare students for life-long learning, informed decision-making, a love of reading, and the use of information technologies.

As one of 13 divisions of the American Library Association, AASL members meet during the ALA Midwinter and annual meetings in January and June. In addition, AASL hosts a Fall Forum during non-AASL National Conference years. They offer regional institutes and other library promotional events.

The development of standards and guidelines for school libraries began in 1919 for secondary schools and in 1925 for elementary schools, and they provided numbers of staff, collections, and size of facilities. The 1945 *School Libraries for Today and Tomorrow* included both elementary and high school libraries. (14) These were updated by *Standards for School Library Programs.* (15)

In the middle of the twentieth century in the U.S., the school library was renamed library media center, and the school librarian became a media specialist. This change of role was defined in 1988 with the American Association of School Librarians' publication, *Information Power: Guidelines for School Library Media Programs*. The mission statement written in 1988 was reconfirmed for the media center in 1998 in *Information Power: Building Partnerships for Learning*, and the mission statement read: "The mission of the library media program is to ensure that students and staff are effective users of ideas and information." (16) and (17) These are currently under revision.

While national associations may create guidelines for library services and library associations in states in the U.S. may develop their own guidelines, they are not legal documents. The only guidelines or standards that have governmental support are those developed by people responsible for education in their province or state. These often have very low requirements because they are a legal obligation, and government agencies must help support them. Finding these documents is possible through searches on the Internet.

The American Association of School Librarians is currently preparing new Standards. At their October 2007 conference, an outline was distributed. Committees have been established to turn this outline into a full document is underway. The finished product should be available in late 2008 or early 2009. Watch for it at: www.ala.org.

INTO A NEW CENTURY

At the close of the 20th century, school librarians in both Canada and the U.S. were challenged to provide programs to ensure their students left school able to survive in an information rich environment. The term "information literacy" was first used by Paul Zurkowski, president of the Information Industry Association, more than 30 years ago. He described persons who were information literate as "people trained in the application of information resources to their work.... They have learned techniques and skills for utilizing the wide range of information tools as well as primary sources in molding information-solutions to their problems." (18) In the new century, school librarians are being asked to help teachers teach technology literacy, health literacy, and many other literacies. The word, *literacy*, is easily added to a variety of information needs for students. This is a positive approach for school librarians while a change in legislation has been less helpful for the role.

A major change in the U.S. has been legislation turning the education of students into a national testing environment. Previously, curriculum was designed to meet the needs of individual students in their schools, and the determination of success or failure relied on something other than national testing. The effort to prepare students for the workplace and to make curriculum meaningful in their daily lives with its perspective on whether students have achieved the progress anticipated is being replaced by test scores, sometimes with teacher retention or merit salary increases based on these test scores.

The pressure to raise test scores means that any possible learning occurring outside the classroom is dismissed as irrelevant. This makes it very difficult for school library media specialists to collaborate with teachers in unit planning and the use of materials found in the media center. The new American Association of School Librarian's (AASL's) *Standards for the 21ˢᵗ Century Learner* are based on the premise that learners use skills, resources, and tools and how school libraries are essential to the development of these learning skills. Their outline was shared with school library media specialists in attendance at the AASL conference in October, 2007.

The lack of a national curriculum, mentioned earlier, led to the development of content standards by various national associations such as the National Council of Teachers of English (NCTE) and the National Council for the Social Studies (NCSS) among others. Standards have been proposed at the national level for fine arts, language arts, mathematics, physical education and health, science, social sciences, and technology, but they can only be useful when individual state departments of education adopt rather than ignore them.

THE READING PROGRAM

The emphasis on reading books provided in the school library at the beginning of the twentieth century has been maintained, but it now embraces a variety of formats including e-books, audio books, animated books, and interactive books.

These are useful in encouraging students who have not been avid readers in the past. Learning how to read and reading is essential in the lives of students. This is shown in the research literature.

A landmark publication in 1993 and updated in 2004, Stephen Krashen's *The Power of Reading*, perhaps explains the success of independent, free-choice reading. His first edition provides the justification needed for media specialists to embark on an expanded reading initiative:

> There is abundant evidence that literacy development can occur without formal instruction. Moreover, this evidence strongly suggests that reading is potent enough to do nearly the entire job alone. (19)

> The read and test studies reviewed earlier are among the most compelling cases of literacy development without instruction. Clearly, in these cases, acquisition of vocabulary and spelling occurred without skill building or correction. Similarly, students in in-school free reading programs "... who made gains equal to or greater than children in traditional programs have demonstrated acquisition of literacy without instruction as do reports of the success of 'whole language' programs." (20)

In the new edition of his book, Krashen summarizes:

> In-school free reading studies and "out of school" self-reported free voluntary reading studies show that more reading results in better reading comprehensive, writing style, vocabulary, spelling, and grammatical development. (21)

To apply these research findings in elementary schools, school library media specialists must allow as much free voluntary reading time as possible. A case can be made for using the entire time students are assigned to the media center to read and read and read. This research supports the value of having free voluntary reading in schools where students are assigned to the media center during the teacher's planning period. Rather than attempting to teach some isolated library skill, the librarian can teach reading by allowing students time to read. One group of students who will benefit very much by being able to read and read and read includes those students whose first language is not English.

While the financial endowments of school systems and the educational qualifications of teachers fall outside the responsibility of librarians, they are responsible for providing students with ready access to good books. Research confirms the need for a wide variety of materials to entice interest in reading for students.

The connection between the amount of reading done and reading proficiency has been well known and accepted for a number of years. Less well known but of equal importance has been the finding that more access to reading materials *leads* to more reading, and subsequently higher reading achievement, and can itself explain a great deal of variation in reading scores. (22)

Eley found that the size of the school library was the number one factor distinguishing the reading scores of nine-year-olds between the high- and low-scoring nations, with an impressive effect size of .82. Frequent silent reading time was the next most important variable, with an effect size of .78. (23)

McQuillan closes his book with

> There is now considerable evidence that the amount and quality of students' access to reading materials is substantively related to the amount of reading they engage in, which in turn is the most important determinant of reading achievement. Many students attend schools where the level of print access is abysmal, creating a true crisis in reading performance.... I do *not* wish to argue that simply providing books is all that is needed for schools to success... But just as we would not ask a doctor to heal without medicine, so we should not ask teachers and schools to teach without the materials to do so. (24)

REPORTING RESEARCH

School librarians through the library's professional periodicals have ready access to research findings in all areas of education, and they should share such findings with their administrators and teachers. One way to do this is to mark pages for them to read. Educators are often caught with the next educational fad that they must implement, and any information concerning best practice or lack of progress should be noted. Being informed and keeping the school community informed will help librarians structure programs throughout the school and within the library to meet new needs.

Of real importance to school librarians has been the research that shows having a professional librarian and an adequate collection improves student achievement. The first study was done by an independent research organization, School Match, for realtors who wanted to help families moving to a new location and to find the best school districts. This study has been updated by many states in the U.S., each new study confirming the results of the previous studies. A search for the name, Keith Curry Lance, will help one find these studies.

Whenever possible, school librarians should conduct their own action research projects to see how successful their efforts are. If they are not comfortable with such activities, they should ask other school librarians about their projects or even contact a local education institution or library and information science program. To learn what is successful provides an opportunity to share with teachers and administrators the activities in the library that are making a difference. If the research findings are less affirmative, making an effort to change the approach or try another methodology may improve the findings. Certainly school librarians need to continue doing those things that make a difference in the education of students, and they need to cease doing those things that make no difference at all.

A LEADERSHIP ROLE FOR SCHOOL LIBRARIANS

In the face of threats from educators who believe that all information their students might need can be found on the Internet and from reductions in funds available to school districts, school librarians are living in perilous times. Their leadership role can be very effectively instituted through collaboration with classroom teachers.

One of the challenges to collaborating with teachers has been the lack of time to plan. A remedy to this has been the establishment of professional learning communities, which are built on the premise that staff development should be focused on change processes to improve student learning. These professional learning communities have five attributes: supportive and shared leadership, shared values and vision, supportive conditions, shared personal practice, and collective creativity. The time allocated to the professional learning community gives the librarian the opportunity to become a part of the collaborative teaching team. Their knowledge of the resources available to teachers as they are planning is incomparable. Providing open access in the library allows teachers and students to find resources when they are needed.

School librarians also have a central role because they work with all the teachers, all the students, and all the curriculum, all the time. Because they have no vested interest in any grade level or any subject area, they provide an open mind to proposals being made. Because they are aware of the entire curriculum, they are able to make suggestions for integrating the different units across grade levels and subject areas. When planning is orchestrated by the school district and a definite time is set aside within the contract hours, then school librarians can make new relationships as decisions are made by groups who have come to consensus about their school culture and environment. They can work together to get their desired results.

Even when such time is not made available, taking the initiative to place the resources of the media center into a teacher's unit planning means that students will have two teachers working with students on that unit of instruction. To build this joint relationship, the library media specialist must make it clear to the teacher that the partnership will not substantially increase the workload of the teacher and will, substantially, increase the learning of the students. This will make it easier to demonstrate the necessities for a strong media program when allocation of funds occurs.

School librarians should also share the activities conducted in the media center with teachers, but most importantly with school administrators. Perceptions of what a school librarian does is often based upon past experience where the role was to distribute books to students who came to the library once a week with their teacher for book exchange and perhaps to hear a story. Other students came to learn how to do research and were given a topic to research. The role of the school librarian is much different in this new century, more like a teacher who works with other teachers to make learning easier for the student.

School librarians should also take leadership roles within their professional associations, preparing articles for professional periodicals. Sharing experiences through writing for publication or making a presentation at a professional meeting gives others the ability to learn best practices. Working with a larger group allows the best methods to be used to push legislation that is favorable to having strong information collections for students and teachers. School librarians should work to see that access to databases is done for the entire school district, if not for the region. This can only be done if funding is included in legislation at the province or state level. Also school librarians should join teacher groups and even school administration professional associations to make sure these bodies understand the role of the school librarian in this new century.

THE FUTURE

On Monday, October 15, 1999, the First International School Library Day was announced by the President of the International Association of School Librarianship (IASL) to be held the third Monday in October. Using the IASL website, members of the association were asked to carry out a theme and to promote school libraries around the globe. Other activities of school librarians in Canada and the U.S. are used to promote school libraries and to continue to let educators understand the role of the school librarian and their influence on students.

Student researchers and their teachers continue to rely less on printed reference materials and more on electronic sources, such as databases, online encyclopedias, atlases, dictionaries, and information found on the Internet, a change that has impact on a facility, its size, arrangement, and use by students. It further has an impact on the role of the school librarian in the education of students. School librarians who take that very important leadership role in getting teachers to collaborate makes teaching easier for the teachers and learning easier for their students. When lessons go beyond rote learning or absorbing facts to pass a test, students can become better able to lead productive lives and it is more likely that students will become lifelong learners.

The future of school libraries parallels that of other libraries and information agencies. School librarians must accept new technologies and design their programs to make the best use of resources and must help their patrons to make the best use of the wealth of information available to them. In this way school libraries and other types of libraries will remain viable agencies in their communities.

Notes

1. Dianne Oberg and John G. Wright. "Canada" in Jean E. Lowrie and M. Nagakura, Eds. *School Libraries: International Development*, 2nd ed. (Metuchen, N.J.: Scarecrow Press, 1991): 339-340.
2. Blanche Woolls. *School Library Media Manager*, 3rd ed. (Westport, Conn.: Libraries Unlimited, 2004): 1-2.
3. National Commission on Teaching & America's Future. *What Matters Most: Teaching for America's Future.* (New York: Teachers College, Columbia University, September, 1996): 14-15.
4. Oberg and Wright, *op. cit.*: 342.
5. U.S. Office of Education. Public Libraries in the United States: Their History, Condition, and Management: Special Report: Department of the Printing Office, 1876: Interior, Bureau of Education, Part I. (Washington, D.C.: Government Printing Office, 1976): 58.
6. Mary E. Hall. "The Development of the Modern High School." *Library Journal* 40 (September 1915): 627.
7. Edward D. Greenman. "The Development of Secondary School Libraries." *Library Journal* 38 (April 1913): 184.
8. Oberg and Wright, *op. cit.*: 343, 344.
9. Oberg, Dianne. "Principal Support: Research from Canada." In IFLA General Conference Programme and Proceedings, August 30-September 5, 1997.
10. American Association of School Librarian and Association for Educational Communications and Technology. *Information Power: Guidelines for School Library Media Programs.* (Chicago: American Library Associaiton, 1988): 85-101, 131-39.
11. Marlene Asselin, Jennifer L. Branch, and Dianne Oberg. *Achieving Information Literacy: Standards for School Library Programs in Canada.* (Ottawa, Ont.: The Canadian School Library Association and the Association for Teacher Librarianship ion Canada, 2003).
12. *Ibid.* pp. 52-59.
13. Oberg and Wright. *Op. cit.*: 347.
14. Committee on Post-War Planning of the American Library Association, *School Libraries for Today and Tomorrow: Functions and Standards* (Chicago: American Library Association, 1945).

15. American Association of School Librarians, *Standards for School Library Programs* (Chicago: American Library Association, 1960).

16. American Association of School Librarians and Association for Educational Communications and Technology. *Information Power: Guidelines for School Library Media Programs* (Chcago: American Library Association, 1988).

17. American Association of School Librarians and Association for Educational Communications and Technology. *Information Power: Building Partnerships for Learning.* (Chicago: American Library Association, 1988).

18. Paul G. Zurkowski. *The Information Service Environment Relationships and Priorities* (Washington, DC: National Commission on Libraries and Information Science, 1974), 6.

19. Stephen Krashen. *The Power of Reading* (Englewood, CO: Libraries Unlimited, 1993): 15.

20. Krashen, *ibid.*, 34.

21. Stephen Krashen. *The Power of Reading*, 2nd ed. (Englewood, CO: Libraries Unlimited, 2004): 17.

22. Jeff McQuillan. *The Literacy Crisis: False Claims, Real Solutions* (Portsmouth, N.H.: Heinemann, 1998): 72.

23. *Ibid.*, 78.

24. *Ibid.*, 86.

LIS EDUCATION IN NORTH AMERICA

Irene Owens and Tom Leonhardt

The history of education for librarianship in North American is rather well documented through numerous sources (bibliography, biography, research studies, dissertations, thesis, articles, archival materials, and the like) some areas to a better extent than others. There are other materials that do exist although there has not been appropriate collation or established canon. There are also extensive coverage of various histories of individual library schools, prominent individuals in the field, and histories of various types of librarianship (medical, school librarianship, archival training and education, etc). Also important to staffing in the field is the literature on education and traiing for paraprofessionals or support staff as well as student assistants. The field of Library and Information Sciences in North America is also well represented by professional organizations, through which the profession continues to critique itself, advance knowledge in the field, and make improvements through new initiatives. This chapter will dilineate a representative number of these sources in various eras of the history of Library and Information Sciences (LIS) in the first part of the chapter, and in the second half, show the processes by which Schools of Library and Information Sciences apply for, receive, and reaffirm, through established processes, the standards of its accrediting body for North America, the American Library Association (ALA).

In addition to the critical role of accreditation by the American Library Association (ALA), as well as its professional development role in annual and mid-winter conferences, there is an equally important organization that attends to LIS education specifically. The Association of Library and of Education (ALISE), grew out of a series of informal meetings of library school faculty at the American Library Association conferences which was known as the Round Table of Library School instructors. The association provides a forum for library educators to share ideas, to discuss issues, and to seek solutions to universal problems. Both ALISE and ALA have regularly published journals (*Library Journal, American Libraries*, and the *Journal of Library and Information Science Education*) that are critical to the continuing history of the profession. One of the more important of ALA's many roundtables related to this chapter, is the Library History Roundatable (LHRT) whose mission is to encourage research and publication on library history and promote awareness and discussion of historical issues in librarianship. The journal that best updates LIS education through addressing issues in library history is *Libraries and Culture* (name changed to *Libraries and the Cultural Record*). *Libraries and the Cultural Record* is an interdisciplinary journal that explores the significance of collections of recrrded knowledge in the contect of cultural and social history. The journal is edited by Dr. David B. Gracy, II, and is a publication of the University of Texas at Austin in Austin, Texas.

In more recent years, as the profession has grown, there are ALA affiliated associations that help to focus more closely on issues associated with various ethnic groups, these include but not limited to, the Black Caucus of the American Library Association (BCALA), the National Association to Promote Library and Information Services to Latinos and the Spanish-Speaking (REFORMA), the Asian Library Association (ALA), and the American Indian Library Association (AILA). These orgnaizations are explicit examples of how library education has grown since its first inception. In 2006, the above named special associations held a joint conference in Dallas, Texas, the first Joint Conference of Librarians of Color (JCLC).

LIBRARY EDUCATION HISTORY

The profession of library and Informaiton Science owes a significant debt of gratitude to several authors who helped to document its history. Edward G. Holley, Donald G. Davis, Wayne Weigand, Mark Tucker, Robert Sydney Martin, James Carmichael, Mary Miles Maack, Louis Round Wilson, Robert Downs, to name a few. Anyone interested in the historical development and continuing development, as the case may be, of library education in North America would be well advised to refer to these seminal authors.

A short sampling of resources documenting the history and development of library education in North America are as follows: Donald G. Davis, Jr. And John Mark Tucker's *American Library History: A Comprehensive Guide to the Literature* (1989); Gerald Bramley's *A History of Library Education* (1969), *Library Education: An International Survey,* (1968); and Charles Churchwell's, *The Shaping of American Library Education* (1975).

CLOSING, MERGING AND RENAMING OF LIS PROGRAMS

Identifying problems and finding solutions to historical isses, became the hallmark of the nearly one and one half decades (1985-2000) of the closing, merging (with other on-campus academic units) and renaming of schools of library and information sciences. These issues are addressed through dissertations, theses, books, articles, and symposia. Another convenient medium for discussions, of the Information and Digital Age has been in the use of blogs, and list serves. *The Closing of American Library Schools in North America: What Role Accreditation?* (1994) discusses the full gamut of associated topics including: accreditation standards, basic model and content, theoretical foundations, core curriculum, academic isolation, and responses to changing situations. Another important source is *The*

Closing of American Library Schools: Problems and Opportunities (1995), a book which places library schools in an historical context and discusses opportunities to reform library education. The renaming of library schools currently referred to as the I-School Movement is another change emerging from the era (http://www3. interscience.wiley.com/journal/116329617/abstract?CRETRY=18SRETRY=0). Mergers, renaming, and closings are having to a large extent positive effects on the profession as a whole, with some exception.

Schools like Clark Atlanta's School of Library and Information Studies, were created because of the Jim Crow laws of earlier years which prevented minorities from gaining access to higher education, until the remarkable Brown vs. Board of Education case in 1954 which outlawed seperate and unequal education in the United States. The closing of the Altlanta School of Library and Informatoin Studies (Atlanta, Georgia) was one such difference. It was the only accredited program in the state of Georgia and it was one of only two such programs in an Historically Black College or University (HBCU). The only current HBCU with a library and information science program is North Carolina Central University's School of Library and Informatoin Sciences in Durham, North Carolina (http:// nccuslis.org). The closing of Atlanta's program meant that without a lot of new initiatives in place to help provide professional education for minority librarians, North America would be at an even greater disadvantage in meeting the needs of a critcal shortage of minority librarians, the graying of the profession, and more importantly not having a sufficient number of libarians to address cultural and service needs of the diverse populations of the North America (Fullwood, 2006, and Mulligan, 2006). The ALA Spectrum scholarships (http://www.ala.org) are one such instance as well as grants made availble through the Laura Bush 21st Century Library program (http://www.imls.gov) to assist in improving the number of minorities in the field of librarianship.

SIGNIFICANT STUDIES ON LIBRARY AND INFORMATION SCIENCE EDUCATION

Library and Information Science (LIS) has been changing since the advent of the computer, and the pace of change in the LIS curriculum has increased with the increasing demands of technology and the concomitant sophistication of the technology available for the delivery of information and instruction, with the widespread availability of distance education programs throughout the United States. Chu examined about 3,000 courses in 45 ALA-accredited LIS master's programs and discovered several trends including more electives and fewer required core courses that, along with an increased interdisciplinary approach to LIS education, allow students to tailor programs to suit their individual needs. Information technology and courses addressing the Web and the Internet were identified by Chu as new clusters of courses that are new to LIS curricula over the past ten years or so. Chu's research seems to validate the conclusions of research done between 1998 and 2000 that was published as *Educating Library and Information Science Professionals for a New Century: The KALIPER Report* (http://www.si.umich.edu/~durrance/TextDocs/KaliperFinalR.pdf)

"KALIPER – the Kellog—ALISE Information Professions and Education Renewal project – is the most extensive examination of the library and information science (LIS) curriculum since the 1923 Williamson Report, the field's first examination of education for librarianship, which is credited with major changes in the education of librarians. In contrast to the Williamson Report's negative conclusions about the state of library education at the beginning of the 20th century, the KALIPER scholars find a vibrant, dynamic, changing field that is undertaking an array of initiatives." (http://www.si.umich.edu/~durrance/TextDocs/KaliperFinalR.pdf

The KALIPER scholars identified several trends, including the following, that show up as new courses in Chu's research:

- development of broader frameworks for examining information problems
- increased interdisciplinarity,
- stronger information technology infrastructure,
- more effective use of technology to support curricula,
- emergence of curricular innovations,
- more effective delivery of distance learning,
- greater flexibility in program delivery, and
- the emergence of a more user-centered curriculum.

Not mentioned by Chu or the *KALIPER Report* but related to the interdisciplinarity cited by both, is the opportunity of LIS students to finish with dual degrees. A cursory examination of the Web sites of Chu's 45 institutions shows that at least twenty programs offer opportunities for dual degrees. Several offer more than one dual degree choice with the two highest choices being eight (8) and twenty (20). Law, business, and history show up more than once.

DISTANCE EDUCATION

Distance delivery of LIS programs, while not new, has reached a point where at least 24 of Chu's 45 programs offer some kind of distance delivery, either synchronous, asynchronous, or hybrid. Even programs that do not offer distance delivery, as such, still participate in   Web-based information   science education through WISE (Web-based Information Science Education) a consortium of LIS programs in 15 universities, 13 of which are accredited by the American Library Association. The vision of this initiative is to provide a collaborative distance education model that will increase the quality, access, and diversity of online education opportunities in library and information science. (http://www.wiseconsortium.org)

Closely related to these 24 or so distance programs is the resurgent interest in LIS education as evidenced by growing enrollments. Prospective librarians can now earn an LIS master's degree without leaving home. Whether LIS programs are offered online, on campus, or as a hybrid, all LIS programs strive in their pursuit of excellence and continuous improvement, to attain and maintain accreditation through the ALA.

ACCREDITATION OF NORTH AMERICAN LIS PROGRAMS

ALA's accreditation of LIS programs in the United States, Canada, and Puerto Rico, is voluntary, non-governmental, and collegial. The overall purpose of accreditation in higher education and the ALA LIS programs is to "ensure that postsecondary educational institutions and their units, schools, or programs meet appropriate standards of quality and integrity and improve the quality of education these institutions offer. http://www.ala.org/ala/accreditation/accredstandards/AP3 SecondEdition1.pdf

Accreditation "assures the public that graduates have received a quality education, assures students and the profession that accredited programs meet the standards of the profession they seek to enter, [and] provides programs with an objective external vehicle for review ad a catalyst for improvement efforts." http://www.ala.org/ala/accreditation/accredstandards/AP3SecondEdition1.pdf

The Committee on Accreditation (COA), formerly the Board of Education for Librarianship (established in 1924), was created by the ALA Council in June 1956. Its charge is "To be responsible for the execution of the accreditation program of ALA and to develop and formulate standards of education for librarianship for the approval of the Council (*ALA Handbook of Organization*). http://www.ala.org/ala/accreditation/accredstandards/AP3SecondEdition1.pdf

"The Committee on Accreditation has developed an accreditation process that seeks to achieve the following objectives:

- To respond to the content and emphasis of the *2008 Standards for Accreditation* adopted by ALA Council.
- To incorporate suggestions of the LIS educational community and the LIS profession.
- To conform to good practices in the educational process in accord with provisions set forth by the Council for Higher Education Accreditation (CHEA

www.chea.org) and the Association of Specialized and Professional Educators (ASPA www.aspa-usa.org).

http://www.ala.org/ala/accreditation/accredstandards/AP3SecondEdition1.pdf

MEMBERSHIP

The COA is composed of twelve members and includes two public members, with the Chairperson to be appointed annually from among the Committee members. The President-Elect of ALA will appoint two regular members for one four-year term and one public member for a two-year term in uneven years. The President-Elect will appoint three regular members for one four-year term and one public member for a two-year term in even years. Members may not be re-appointed once they have served. http://www.ala.org/ala/accreditation/accredstandards/AP3 SecondEdition1.pdf

COA accredits master's programs in library and information studies that are offered under the degree-granting authority of regionally accredited institutions located in the United States and its territories, possessions, and protectorates. By agreement with the Canadian Library Association (CLA), the COA also accredits LIS master's programs in Canada. http://www.ala.org/ala/accreditation/accred standards/AP3SecondEdition1.pdf

COA is also responsible for overseeing the development of the standards for accrediting these master's programs in library and information studies, standards that are not prescriptive but rather are broadly based. The process for developing, revising, and applying the standards through policies and procedures is broad-based. In developing these standards for the profession, COA involves members of the profession – practitioners, employers, educators, and members of the public – and culminates in the approval of the standards. By the ALA Council.

The COA reviews the standards on a five-year schedule that led to the current revision, adopted in January 2008, of the 1992 standards. In fact, the latest standards are already under review as part of the COA charge and in response to the broad-based constituency that is the profession.

The Committee on Accreditation is composed of twelve members, ten of which are personal members of ALA. These ten, one of which is Canadian, represent practitioners and educators. The remaining two members are appointed from the public at large to represent public interest and may not be librarians or information professionals or have studies LIS. They cannot be currently or formerly professionally employed in a library, information center, or related industry (e.g., material or systems vendor), and they cannot be a current or former member of the

American Library Association or any other library association. http://www.ala.org/
ala/accreditation/accredstandards/AP3SecondEdition1.pdf

ALA personal members are appointed for four-year staggered terms without
possibility of reappointment. Public members are appointed to two-year terms
with the possibility of re-appointment. The COA chair (a COA member) is appointed for a year by the ALA President-Elect and may be re-appointed once.
http://www.ala.org/ala/accreditation/accredstandards/AP3SecondEdition1.pdf

To ensure that deliberations about accreditation are fair and ethical, COA conducts a conflict of interest polling at the beginning of each of its four sessions per
year. Members of COA may recuse themselves for any reason that might prevent
objectivity or cause a reasonable person to believe that the member is biased.
Typical situations requiring disclosure and review include:

- Current or recent employment by or consulting arrangements with LIS pro-
  grams;
- Close personal relationships with individuals at LIS programs;
- Current or recent student status at an LIS institution;
- Any other reason that might prevent objectivity or cause a reasonable person
  to believe that bias might exist.

Although the presence of seven of twelve COA members constitutes a quorum for
non-accreditation business, accreditation decisions require at least eight voting
members be present (a quorum) and further require at least eight affirmative votes
by voting members in order to make an accreditation decision. The Chair votes
only in order to break a tie. http://www.ala.org/ala/accreditation/accredstandards/
AP3SecondEdition1.pdf

The COA meets four times a year, in the ALA office in the spring and fall of
each year and during the Midwinter Meeting and Annual Conference of the
American Library Association.

Each of the 62 accredited programs at 57 institutions is reviewed for continuing
accreditations every seven years. In between visits, the COA is kept apprised of
program changes through annual statistical reports, biennial narrative reports, and
occasional special reports when situations warrant them.

A year or so prior to an accreditation visit by an External Review Panel (ERP)
(see Table below for complete review cycle), a program goes through a comprehensive review process that is documented in a Program Presentation (PP). The PP
addresses each of the six ALA Standards:

- Standard I: Mission, Goals, and Objectives
- Standard II: Curriculum
- Standard III: Faculty
- Standard IV: Students

- Standard V: Administration & Financial Support
- Standard VI: Physical Resources & Facilities

Eighteen months before a comprehensive review, COA appoints a six-member External Review Panel (ERP) that is reviewed by the program for acceptability, expertise, and conflicts of interest. Currently, four of the ERP members are site visitors and two are off-site members. Beginning in 2009, LIS programs up for review will have the option of having all six members visit the program.

The chair of the ERP works with the program and the ALA Office for Accreditation to develop the program presentation and review the process and logistics.

Once the ERP receives the PP, the chair assigns work to the panel members and aims to have as many questions answered as possible from a distance and a draft report is written before the site visitors travel to the program. There the panel interviews those within the program (faculty, students, staff, and administrators) and others such as deans, provosts, and library directors, as possible in addition to alumni and employers.

After the COA reviews the ERP final report and the PP, it meets with the program director/dean and the ERP chair to make statements and ask questions. It is not until then that it informs the program of its accreditation decision. There are six categories of accreditation:

- Precandidate for accreditation
- Candidate for accreditation
- Initial accreditation
- Continued accreditation
- Conditional accreditation
- Withdrawn accreditation

More information about the accreditation process and what the different categories mean can be found on the Office for Accreditation's web site at http://www.ala.org/ala/accreditation/accredstandards/AP3SecondEdition1.pdf

The Committee on Accreditation and the External Review Panels are composed of volunteers from the profession. Their work, essential as it is, could not be done without the help and support of the Office for Accreditation (http://www.ala.org/ala/accreditation/accreditation.cfm).

In broad terms, the Office provides planning, leadership, and clerical support. It coordinates and supports activities directly related to LIS accreditation, maintains relationships with other accrediting agencies (CHEA, ASPA), and is the main contact with programs in the process of review or interested in seeking accreditation.

The Office for Accreditation regularly provides information about all aspects of the accreditation process, policies, and procedures. In addition to providing educational programs, publications, and other activities to promote the awareness of and enhance knowledge about LIS programs, it answers questions from the graduate programs themselves, potential students and employers, ALA members, the press, and the general public.

It is the responsibility of the Office for Accreditation to maintain the schedule of evaluation reviews, past correspondence and records, and a listing of all accredited programs past and present.

The information in this summary about LIS accreditation in the United States and Canada comes directly from ALA documents, all of which can be found on the web site maintained by the Office for Accreditation. The Office welcomes enquiries from all interested parties including those from countries other than the United States and Canada and is already used to fielding those questions. The Office website is (http://www.ala.org/ala/accreditation/accreditation.cfm).

ALA Accreditation Cycle Timeline Synopsis

24 months before the review visit
0. Program seeking initial accreditation sends letter of intent to the Office for Accreditation (OA)
1. OA reminds accredited programs scheduled for reviews
2. Institution CEO (president/chancellor) requests review
3. Program sends letter confirming visit & focus, giving three sets of possible dates for visit

18 months before the visit
4. Committee on Accreditation (COA) appoints external review panel (ERP) chair
5. OA confirms ERP chair appointment and visit dates with program
6. OA sends letter of instruction to ERP chair
7. OA sends letter to program describing working relationship among the OA director, ERP chair and program dean

12 months before the visit
8. Program submits plan for program presentation to OA director and ERP chair
9. OA director, ERP chair and program review the plan through a conference call
10. OA proposes panel members to COA; COA appoints ERP members
11. OA proposes panel members to program and to ERP chair
12. Program reviews proposed ERP and notes any conflicts of interest
13. ERP members/chair submit signed conflict of interest forms to OA
14. OA repeats steps 12 – 14 until a complete panel is established
15. OA confirms final panel to program and ERP (summary sheet with roster and important dates)
16. ERP chair, members, and program review the AP3 manual and Standards for Accreditation

4 months before the visit
17. Program submits draft program presentation to OA director and ERP chair
18. OA director, ERP chair and program review the draft program presentation through a conference call
19. ERP chair begins planning the evaluation process, tentative assignments, and schedules for the review

6 weeks before the visit
20. Program submits final program presentation to ERP (1 copy to chair and each member), and OA (15 copies along with 1 declaration form)
21. ERP chair and program arrange visit agenda and travel details
22. ERP chair assigns responsibilities to panel members

4 weeks before the visit
23. ERP members complete pre-visit assignments
24. ERP chair provides schedule of activities

Visit
25. ERP meets with faculty, students and others during evaluation review

3 weeks after the visit
26. ERP chair submits draft ERP report to program, OA director, and ERP members
27. ERP members who incur expenses submit reimbursement forms to OA; OA processes reimbursements and invoices program

4 weeks after the visit
28. Program submits any corrections to OA director and ERP chair, or notifies them that there are no corrections

5 weeks after the visit
29. ERP chair submits final panel report to program and OA director

6 weeks after the visit
30. ERP members complete and submit peer evaluation forms to OA
31. Program submits response (optional) to OA director
32. ERP chair sends final ERP report and program response to panel

Month prior to the COA meeting
33. OA sends program presentation, ERP report and program's response to COA
34. OA notifies ERP chair and program dean/director of COA's meeting agenda

COA meeting
35. Head of program and ERP chair meet with COA at ALA Annual Conference (spring reviews) or ALA Midwinter Meeting (fall reviews)

Week following conference
36. OA sends COA decision document to program
37. OA notifies ALA/CLA Executive Directors of the COA decisions

2 weeks after COA meeting
38. OA sends COA decision document to ERP and institution's CEO
39. OA sends press release to PIO and American Libraries announcing accreditation decisions

A Select Chronology of North American LIS Accreditation	
1900	ALA Committee on Library Training established to formulate and enforce the first standards of quality for library education.
1924	ALA Board of Education for Librarianship (BEL) established to replace the Committee on Library Training and develop new set of standards of quality for library education.

1926	Twelve library and information studies programs are accredited.
1933	Standards revision approved by ALA Council.
1951	Standards revision approved by Council. The master's degree is established by policy as the professional degree.
1955	ALA Committee on Accreditation (COA) is established to replace BEL.
1972	Standards revision approved.
1992	Standards revision approved.
1993	New review process adopted.
1997	First virtual accreditation review visit is conducted at the University of Illinois, Urbana- Champaign.
2002	COA appoints external committee to review standards and provide a report with recommendations.
2003	Process documents reissued with more streamlined appeal process based on experience with two appeals.
2006	COA releases for comment a proposed update to the 1992 standards. ALA Office for Accreditation releases second edition of *Accreditation Process Policies and Procedures.*
2008	Standards revision approved.

Source: Karen L. O'Brien, Executive Director, ALA Office of Accreditation (http://www.ala.org/ala/accreditation/accredstandards/standards_2008.pdf

For a succinct history of LIS accreditation, please see "Accreditation of Library and Information Studies," by Karen L. O'Brien in *Encyclopedia of Library and Information Sciences*, 3rd edition, edited by Marcia J. Bates and Mary Niles Maack, Boca Raton, FL: CRC Press, 2009.

SUMMARY

LIS education in North America is a growing, self-examining, and corrective process while at the same time applying sensitivity to standards and accreditation with collegiality, respect and support for the profession, an entity critical to the continuing development of LIS in North America.

Bibliography and list of sources

Recommended reading for the discussion of the role individuals and professional associations had in the development of archival and library practice, technology and theory, focusing on the American Historical Association, the American Library Association, the Society of American Archivists and the Special Libraries Association

Jeannette Bastian and Elizabeth Yakel, "Are We There Yet? Professionalism and the Development of an Archival Core Curriculum in the United States," Journal of Education for Library and Information Science 46(2005):

Richard C. Berner, "Archival Education and Training in the United States, 1937 to Present," Journal of Education for Librarianship 22(1981): 3-19.

John Berry, (2002) "LIS Boom Spurs New Faculty Push," *Library Journal,* 127 no4 20.

William F. Birdsall, "Archivists, Librarians and Issues During the Pioneering Era of the American Archival Movement," Journal of Library History 14(1979): 457-79.

_____, "The Two Sides of the Desk; the Archivist and the Historian, 1909-1935," American Archivist 38(1975): 159-73.

Michael Carpenter, Corporate Authorship: Its Role in Library Cataloging (Westport, CT: Greenwood Press, 1981).

Edward Carroll, The Professionalization of Education for Librarianship with Special Reference to the Years 1940-1960 (Metuchen, NJ: Scarecrow Press, 1970).

Heting Chu (2006) ("Curricula of LIS Programs in the USA: A Content Analysis" in *Proceedings of the Asia-Pacific Conference on Library & Information Education & Practice 2006 (A-LIEP 2006), Singapore, 306 April 2006* (pp. 328-337), Singapore: School of Communication & Information, Nanyang Technological University.

John C. Colson, "On the Education of Archivists and Librarians, American Archivist 31(1968): 167-74.

Churchwell, Charles. The Shaping of American Library Education. Chicago: American Library Association, 1975.

J. Frank Cook, "The Blessings of Providence on the Association of Archivists," American Archivist 46(1983): 374-99.

Davis, Donald G and John Mark Tucker. *American Library History: A Comprehensive Guide to the Literature.* Santa Barbara, California: ABC-CLIO,Inc.

Fullwood, Steven G. (2006). „ Saving Ourselves: Archival treasures: the Closing of the Clark Atlanta Librry school renews interest in collections at historically black colleges and universities,"

Jacquelin Goggin, "That We Shall Truly Deserve the Title of Profession: The Training and Education of Archivists, 1930-1960," American Archivist 47(1984): 243-54.

Donald J. Lehnus, Milestones in Cataloging: Famous Catalogers and Their Writings, 1835-1969 (Littleton, CO: Libraries Unlimited, 1974).

Robert Sidney Martin, "The Development of Professional Education for Librarians and Archivists in the United States: A Comparative Essay," American Archivist 57(1994):544-58.

Francis L. Miksa, The Development of Classification at the Library of Congress (Urbana, IL: University of Illinois Press, 1984).

Frederic M. Miller, "The SAA as Sisyphus: Education since the 1960's," American Archivist 63(2000): 224-36.

Risa Mulligan, (2006). The Closing of the Clark Atlanta University School of Library and Information Studies. Master's Thesis. The University of North Carolina at Chapel Hill.

Jesse Shera, The Foundations of Education for Librarianship (New York, NY: Becker and Hayes, 1972).

Dennis Thomison, The History of the American Library Association, 1876-1972 (Chicago, IL: ALA, 1977).

Carl M. White, A Historical Introduction to Library Education: Problems and Progress to 1951 (Metuchen, NJ: Scarecrow Press, 1976).

_____, The Origins of the American Library School (Metuchen, NJ: Scarecrow Press, 1976).

Wayne Wiegand, "Politics of an Emerging Profession: ALA, 1876-1917," Contributions in Librarianship and Information Science 56(1986):

_____, The Politics of an Emerging Profession: The American Library Association, 1876-1917 (Westport, CT: Greenwood Press, 1986)

Robert V. Williams and M.J.K. Zachert, "Knowledge Put to Work: SLA at 75," Special Libraries 74(1983): 370-82.

Recommended reading for discussion of the educational and professional opportunities for women and minorities for leadership roles in archives and libraries during the 20th century

Kayla Barrett and Barbara Bishop, "Integration and the Alabama Library Association," Libraries & Culture 33(1998): 141-61.

Stephen Cresswell, "The Last Days of Jim Crow in Southern Libraries," Libraries & Culture 31(1996): 557-73.

el and Kathleen Heim, The Role of Women in Librarianship, 1876-1976 (Phoenix, AZ: Oryx Press, 1979).

Davis, Donald G. *Dictionary of American Biography.*

Ellen Elizabeth Dickey, "Serving the African American Population in Durham County, North Carolina: A History of the Bragtown Branch Library (Master's Thesis, NCCU, 1993).

Rosa Maria Fernandez de Zamora, "Mexican Library History: A Survey of the Literature of the Last Fifteen Years," Libraries & Culture 32(1997): 227-44.

Toby Patterson Graham, "Public Librarians and the Civil Rights Movement: Alabama, 1955-1965," Library Quarterly 71(2001): 1-27.

_____, A Right to Read: Segregation and Civil Rights in Alabama's Public Libraries, 1900-1965 (Tuscaloosa, AL: University of Alabama Press, 2002).

Steven R. Harris, "Civil Rights and the Louisiana Library Association: Stumbling Toward Integration," Libraries & Culture 38(2003): 322-50.

Suzanne Hildenbrand, ed., Reclaiming the American Library Past: Writing the Women In (Norwood, NJ: Ablex, 1996).

Edward G. Holley and Charles D. Churchwell, "Racial Integration at the University of Houston, A Personal Perspective, I & II," John M. Tucker, ed., Untold Stories. Civil Rights Libraries and Black Librarianship (Urbana, IL: University of Illinois, GSLIS, 1998): 126-140.

Reinette F. Jones, Library Service to African Americans in Kentucky from the Reconstruction Era to the 1960's (Jefferson, NC: McFarland, 2002).

E.J. Josey, "Edward Christopher Williams: A Librarian's Librarian," Journal of Library History 4(1969): 106-22.

_____, The Black Librarian in America (Metuchen, NJ: Scarecrow Press, 1970).

Dan Lee, "From Segregation to Integration: Library Services for Blacks in South Carolina, 1923-1962," Untold Stories pp. 93-109.

Cheryl K. Malone, "Accommodating Access: Colored Carnegie Libraries, 1905-1925," (Ph.D. Dissertation, University of Texas at Austin, 1995).

_____, "Quiet Pioneers: Black Women Public Librarians in the Segregated South," Vitae Scholasticae 19(2000): 59-76.

_____, "Toward a Multicultural American Public Library History," Libraries & Culture 35(2000): 77-87.

Kathleen de la Peja McCook, ed., Women of Color in Librarianship: An Oral History (Chicago, IL: ALA, 1998).

Elizabeth McHenry, "An Association of Kindred Spirits: Black Readers and Their Reading Rooms," in Thomas Augst and Kenneth Carpenter, eds., Institutions of Reading: The Social Life of Libraries in the United States (Amherst, MA: University of Massachusetts Press, 2007), 99-118.

Annie McPheeters, Library Service in Black and White: Some Personal Recollections (Metuchen, NJ: Scarecrow Press, 1988).

S.W. O'Donnell, "Equal Opportunities for Both: Julius Rosenwald, Jim Crow and the Charleston Free Library's Record of Service to Blacks, 1931-1960," (Master's Thesis, University of North Carolina, SILS, 2000).

Ostler, Larry J., Therrinn C. Dahlin, J.D. Willardson. (1994). *The Closing of American Library Schools: Problems and Opportunities.* Westport, Connecticut: Greenwood Publishing.

Joanne Passet, Cultural Crusaders: Women Librarians in the American West, 1900-1917 (Albuquerque, NM: University of New Mexico, 1994).

Annette L. Phinazee, ed., The Black Librarian in the Southeast: Reminiscences, Activities, Challenges (Durham, NC: SLS NCCU, 1980).

Pamela Spence Richards, "Library Services and the African-American Intelligensia Before 1960" Libraries & Culture 33(1998): 91-97.

Louise S. Robbins, "Changing the Geography of Reading in a Southern Border State: The Rosenwald Fund and the WPA in Oklahoma," Libraries & Culture 40(2005):

Saracevic, T. (1994) „Closing of Library Schools in North America: What role accreditaion? " *Libri,* 44 (3), 190-200.

O. Lee Shiflett and Robert S. Martin, "Hampton, Fisk and Atlanta: The Foundations, ALA and Library Education for Blacks, 1925-1941," Libraries & Culture 31(1996): 299-325.

Kathleen Weib el and Kathleen Heim, The Role of Women in Librarianship, 1876-1976 (Phoenix, AZ: Oryx Press, 1979).

Wingand, Wayne A. and Donald G. Davis. *Encyclopedia of Library History.* New York: Garland Publishing, Inc.

Ethelene Whitmire, "Breaking the Color Barrier: Regina Andrews and the New York Public Library," Libraries & the Cultural Record 42(2007): 408-21.

GLOBAL ROLES OF LIBRARY ASSOCIATIONS

Michael Dowling and Keith Michael Fiels

Library associations at the local, national, regional, and international levels are of great importance to libraries, the profession, and society. This chapter provides a brief overview of the general roles of library associations and a look at how associations are organized and challenges they face. It includes a review of the development of national, regional, and international associations, and examples that describe some of the ways national library associations engage in international activities. It concludes with a focus on the global activities of the International Federation of Library Associations and Institutions (IFLA).

The global community is a reality in the twenty-first century. Many of the issues that were national issues for libraries, such as copyright and technology standards, are now international issues. Decisions made in international venues can now have a dramatic impact on how libraries in a specific country are able to function, and determine what services they can provide. Therefore, library associations around the world need to work together, share experiences, and ideas on initiatives beyond their borders.

The information age has brought opportunity for libraries to exponentially expand the information and services provided to users through the Internet, digitization of collections, and new technologies. Libraries and librarians must be forward thinking in adapting and implementing new technologies and services. Without improving services to keep pace with the demands of users, libraries will find themselves on the fringe of the information age.

As Narayanan Rakunathan aptly describes:

"Library associations provide an opportunity for librarians to meet and share experiences and learn from each other. They offer a range of services to members and look after their interests. For outsiders, interested in dealing with the profession, they act as the ideal contact point. Although library associations do serve the needs of their members, ultimately, the long-term benefactors are the end uses of the services these members provide."[1]

Roles

Library associations provide the opportunity for members of the profession to work together toward common goals of improvement of the profession, libraries, and library services. Whether at the local, national, or international level, the roles of library associations are similar. Here are some of the major roles of library associations, which are very much interconnected.

---

[1] Rakunathan, Narayanan, "Library Associations," www.ifla.org/VII/s40/pub/rakunathan.pdf

Networking

Associations allow interaction to occur between members of the profession. All the other roles of library associations follow from individuals getting together to share experiences, knowledge, and ideas. Networking leads to the improvement of each individual and provides an opportunity to share visions and work together on collaborative activities for the greater good. Imagine how isolated a librarian on a small atoll of the Republic of Kiribati in the Pacific is. But through the Pacific Islands Association of Libraries and Archives (PIALA), he or she is able to connect with others in the region through conferences and trainings, and through PIALA to the rest of the library profession.

Leadership

Leadership is also what a library association brings to the profession and the world beyond libraries. Working together as a collective organization provides opportunities to improve the development of libraries and the profession. The Uganda Library Association (ULA) provided the leadership necessary to achieve passage of the National Library of Uganda Act of 2003, which established the National Library of Uganda and provided for the depositing and preserving of publications, and the creation of an information referral service.[2]

A Voice

Individually it is very hard to achieve recognition and to meet goals, and nearly impossible to make an impact on society. One voice is easily lost, but an organization representing hundreds or thousands, provides a unified voice representing all, a voice that can be heard, especially by those outside the library community on such issues as the importance of literacy, the need for information policy, and equal and equitable access to information. The voice of the Australian Library and Information Association (ALIA) helped get the state of New South Wales to establish library workers in a focus group on pay equity evaluation. This led to the recognition of professional status for librarians and pay increases.[3]

Education and Professional Development

Library associations are a key to continuing the development of the profession within this rapidly changing world. Librarians need to be educated to understand and adapt to new ideas, new technologies, and new services. Associations provide educational opportunities through conferences, workshops, publications, etc. The Association of Information Specialists in the Republic of Georgia provides much

---

[2]   Ikoja,-Odongo, J.R.., "Public library politics: the Uganda perspective"
      www.ifla.org/IV/ifla69/papers/171e-Ikoja-Odongo.pdf
[3]   Teece, Phil, "Raising Library Salaries in New South Wales, Australia,"
      www.ifla.org/IV/ifla71/papers/180e-Nicholson.pdf

needed computer training for librarians at its training center in Tbilisi. Associations can also be influential in the development of standards of education for the profession. The American Library Association is responsible for setting up the guidelines and accrediting library schools in the United States and Canada.

Standards and Best Practices

Library associations draft and adopt standards, guidelines, code of conducts, and best practices, etc., thereby codifying and improving the profession. Many associations, such as Korean Library Association, have created codes of ethics that serve as a foundation for the profession.[4] The Anglo-American Cataloging Rules were a combined effort of the Canadian Library Association, the Australian Library and Information Association, the Chartered Institute of Library and Information Professionals in the United Kingdom, and the American Library Association.

Advocacy

Library associations work to increase the visibility of libraries and librarians in society, to encourage the general public to advocate for libraries, and also to advocate directly to legislators and policy makers to pass laws and fund libraries. Like many others do to promote libraries, the Armenian Library Association organizes a National Library Week, which gains national publicity and puts the spotlight on libraries.[5] The Federacion Espanola de Sociedades de Archivistica, Biblioteconomia, Documentacion y Museistica (FESABID) created a "No Al Prestamo de Pago" campaign to fight the legislative efforts of authors and writers to receive royalties from the public lending of materials through libraries and institutions.[6]

Partnerships

Library associations build strategic relationships and partnerships with others interested in libraries, such as foundations, corporations, government entities, non-governmental organizations, and schools. These partnerships can be valuable to associations, which usually do not have enough resources on their own to achieve some of their goals and objectives. For example, IFLA's Advancement of Librarianship Programme (ALP) has been supported with cooperation by the Nordic Library Association by funds provided by the Swedish International Development Cooperation Agency (SIDA).

Organization and Challenges

Library Associations follow similar organizational structures, but vary funding support, staffing, and eligibility of members. Most library associations are set up

---

[4] www.ifla.org/faife/ethics/klacode.htm
[5] http://www.ala.am/eng/index.asp
[6] http://noalprestamodepago.org/

as independent non-governmental organizations, but in some countries, such as China or Cuba, there is a strong connection with the government. Even some independent library associations, such as the Danish Library Association, are eligible to receive direct financial support from the government for specific activities.

Each library association determines its membership based on its mission. Some associations limit their membership to just librarians. In others, institutions make up the membership. Some are strictly individual membership associations, while there are some that allow both personal and institutional membership. Some allow the membership of those outside the profession as well, such as the library vendor community, library supporters, and library staff.

Library associations around the world face similar challenges. Foremost is sustainability. Library associations, at any level, need resources, both human and financial, to survive and thrive. Human capital comes in two forms: members and staff. Library associations are not strong if they do not have members actively engaged in the association. Many associations are too small to pay for staff, and so they rely on the volunteer efforts of their members to run the association. For sustainability, library associations need to work hard to recruit new members in order to create and maintain initiatives.

Library associations need financial resources as well. Most library associations rely predominately on membership dues and conference revenue for their funds. In many cases, especially in the developing world, these revenue sources may be minimal. Other possible areas of revenue for library associations are publications, trainings, and grants.

Despite these challenges, there are very successful library associations around the world, even those with no staff and very little money.

National Associations

As might be expected, the development of national library associations has more or less mirrored the general historical development and transition of countries around the world. The creation of national library associations began in North America and in Europe near the end of the nineteenth century. In 1876 Melville Dewey, creator of the Dewey Decimal System, and others founded the American Library Association. The following year, in 1877, the Library Association (United Kingdom), now called the Chartered Institute of Library and Information Professionals (CILIP), was established.

Library associations began forming in countries across continental Europe, including the Vereinigung Österrechisher Bibliothekarinnend und Bibliotekare in Austria in 1896; the Association des Bibliotèques et Bibliothècaires Suisses in 1897; and Association des Bibliothécaires Français (ABS) in 1906.[7] With the

---

[7] *World Encyclopedia of Library and Information Sciences*, Third Edition, 1993, American Library Association, various country reports.

breakup of the Soviet Union, many new national library associations were reconstituted. The Lithuanian Library Association, originally founded in 1931, was reestablished in 1990, and the new Russian Library Association was organized in 1995.[8]

In addition to these national associations, library associations for specific disciplines were also being created in the United States and Europe. These include the American Association of Law Libraries in 1896, the Medical Library Association in 1898, the Special Libraries Association in 1909, and the Finnish Research Library Association in 1929.[9]

In Asia and the Pacific, the Japanese Library Association was the first national library association outside of the U.S. and Europe, founded in 1892. Other early national associations in the region included the New Zealand Library Association in 1910, and the Philippine Library Association in 1922. It took a little longer for the formation of national library associations to develop in Latin America with the first being the Asociación Mexicana de Bibliotecarios, A.C. (AMBAC) in 1924. Other national library associations in the region were not founded until the 1950s and later.[10]

The first national library association in Africa, the South African Library Association, was created in 1930 and became an all-white organization under apartheid in 1962. In 1964 the African Library Association of South Africa for black library workers was created. In 1997 a new national library association was formed through mergers of separate associations, called the Library and Information Association of South Africa (LIASA). The founding of what is now the Egyptian Library and Archives Association was in 1946. National library associations in other countries started with independence from colonial rule in the 1960s. The Zimbabwe Library Association was originally founded as the Library Association of Rhodesia and Nyasaland in 1959. The Nigerian Library Association was founded in 1962.[11]

The Indian Library Association was funded before independence, but the Pakistan Library Association was not created until 1967. National library associations that have been founded in Eurasia, such as the Uzbekistan Library Association, have formed after 2000. Library associations began to from in the Middle East region in the 1950s and 1960s with the Israeli Library Association 1952, the Lebanese Library Association in 1960, the Iranian Library Association in 1966, and the Iraqi Library Association in 1968.[12] Development of national library associations

---

[8] *IFLA Membership Directory*, 2002-2003
[9] *World Encyclopedia*, various country and association reports
[10] Ibid
[11] Ibid
[12] Ibid

in the Gulf region is just beginning with the Kuwait Library Association being established in 2005.

Regional Associations

In addition to national library associations, many regional library associations have formed so that librarians, libraries, and library associations can work together. Some work on a variety of issues, whereas others provide networking opportunities within their region. The European Bureau of Library, Information and Documentation Associations (EBLIDA) is an independent umbrella association of the national library, information, documentation and archive associations and institutions in Europe. EBLIDA concentrates on European information society issues, including copyright and licensing, culture and education, and EU enlargement. They promote unhindered access to information in the digital age and the role of archives and libraries in achieving this goal.[13]

In comparison, groups such as the Nordic Library Associations meet yearly to discuss matters of current interest, to inform each other of national developments, and to work together on various advocacy and professional activities.

In Africa, the Standing Conference of Eastern, Central and Southern African Library and Information Associations (SCECSAL) derives its origins from the East African Library Association (EALA), founded in 1957.[14] It organizes a biennial conference that provides networking and professional development. The West African Library Association (WALA) was established in 1954 and serves in much the same capacity as SCECSAL.[15]

The Congress of Southeast Asian Librarians (CONSAL) was founded in Singapore in 1970 in response to a growing sense of Southeast Asian identity, fostered particularly by the formation of the Association of Southeast Asian Nations (ASEAN). CONSAL represents 10 countries, holds a conference every three years, and promotes cooperation in the fields of librarianship, bibliography, documentation, and related activities.[16]

Regional associations are crucial to collaboration in the Caribbean and the Pacific Islands. The Association of Caribbean University Research Institutional Libraries (ACURIL) was established in 1969 and holds an annual conference.[17] The Pacific Islands Association of Libraries and Archives (PIALA) was created in 1991 to organize the librarians and archivists of the seven separate political juris-

---

[13] www.eblida.org/
[14] www.scecsal.org/
[15] www.nla-ng.org/aboutus.html
[16] www.consal.org
[17] www.acuril.uprrp.edu

dictions of Micronesia.[18] PIALA also holds an annual conference focusing on different training issues.

International Activities of National and Regional Associations

Whether national or regional, these library associations are the vital backbone of international librarianship. They make up the membership of IFLA, and include those who engage in international pursuits on their own. Most national and regional associations do have some international membership. The Special Libraries Association, though primarily a U.S.-based association, has members in 80 countries and chapters in regions around the world. Associations, such as the China Society for Library Science and ALA, have staff time dedicated to fostering international activities. Those who do not have staff undertake their activities through international committees. Many international activities of national library associations are supported through government or foundation grants.

National associations can help facilitate librarian exchanges or visits to and from their country. Some national associations have also partnered directly with other national associations to provide support and assistance. The Finnish Library Association works with the library associations of South Africa (LIASA) and Namibia, through scholarships and trainings. With a grant from the Carnegie Corporation, ALA has provided training for associations in the Caucasus region. Associations in France, the Netherlands, Denmark, and the United States pay the membership dues of other countries in IFLA.

National library associations also work to have representatives on their countries' various international delegations. For example, the Danish Library Association has an official voice in the Danish UNESCO National Commission. *It is critical for all national library associations to get a representative at as many tables as they can.*

National associations also provide international assistance in times of crisis. The Persatuan Pustakawan Malaysia (Library Association of Malaysia) has led the fundraising and support effort to help rebuild libraries in Aceh Province, Indonesia devastated by the tsunami in December, 2005.

Regional association conferences provide opportunities for IFLA-sponsored training and workshops to take place. Regional associations also serve as resources for exchange opportunities.

International Associations

The first transnational association was the Fédération Internationale de Documentation (FID), founded in 1895 for national organizations in the field of documenta-

---

[18] www.mangilao.uog.edu/rfk/piala/piala.html

tion. Its mission was to "provide encouragement for the study and of classification in general and to promote a uniform system of classification in particular." FID worked on the development of the Universal Decimal Classification (UDC), first published in 1905. FID's Universal Bibliographic Repertory, a database, grew to more than 11 million entries. It also established an international loan service, operated through the mail, in which 1500 requests were being received each year by 1912.[19]

For much of its existence, FID was really a regional organization with only seven members outside Europe as late as 1958. FID disbanded, ceasing operation in 2001 due to financial issues. Financial solvency is especially an issue for international associations whose objective reach is great, but whose budgets and staff support are often quite small.

With the proliferation and development of national associations in the early twentieth century, many believed that the time had come to create an international association of library associations. As a result, the International Federation of Library Associations and Institutions (IFLA) was established in 1927 in Edinburgh, Scotland. IFLA's development and activities are explored later in this chapter.

The International Council of Archives (ICA) was founded in 1948 by the United Nations Educational Scientific and Cultural Organizations (UNESCO) to establish a worldwide organization for the archive profession. It was "created to improve worldwide standards of archival administration and practice and to advance archival theory." ICA has a global network of more than 1,400 institutional members in 190 countries, with current priorities being advocacy and promotion, automation and electronic records, disaster prevention and preservation, and education and training.[20]

Mirroring library-specific associations in countries, a number of such international associations have been created. Here is just a sampling of some of these organizations.

- The International Association of Music Libraries Archives and Documentation Centers (IAML) has about 2,000 individual and institutional members in some 45 countries throughout the world. It was founded in 1951 to promote international cooperation and to support the interests of the profession.[21]
- The International Association of Law Libraries (IALL) was founded in 1959, and now has over 600 members in more than 50 countries on five continents. The members represent all types of legal collections, ranging from academic law libraries of all sizes to corporate libraries, and from national and parliamentary libraries to administrative agency and court libraries. IALL has an

[19] World Encyclopedia, FID article
[20] www.ica.org
[21] www.iaml.info

annual budget around $100,000. It hosts an Annual Course, as opposed to a conference, which focuses on a specific area of legal librarianship (e.g., its "Legal Information in Multiple Legal Systems" was held in sites around the world in 2008).[22]

- The International Association of School Libraries (IASL), inaugurated in 1971, provides an international forum for those people interested in promoting effective school library media programs as viable instruments in the educational process. IASL provides guidance and advice for the development of school library programs and the school library profession. IASL works in cooperation with other professional associations and agencies. In 2008, there were 730 members from 76 countries. IASL also has a very small budget of $50,000 annually.[23]

International Federation of Library Associations and Institutions (IFLA)

Founded in 1927, IFLA is the leading international body representing the interests of library and information services and their users. IFLA's aim is to:

"Promote high standards of provision and delivery of library and information services; Encourage widespread understanding of the value of good library & information services; Represent the interests of our members throughout the world."[24]

During its formative years, IFLA was a European- and North American–centric organization, as much of the rest of the world had not established library associations. By the 1930s, IFLA had recruited 41 members from 31 countries, including members in China, India, Japan, Mexico, and the Philippines.

IFLA's first 45 conferences were held in either Europe or North America. It was not until 1980, in Manila, that a conference was held elsewhere. The first IFLA Conference in Africa was Nairobi in 1984, and it did not meet in Latin America until 2005, in Buenos Aires.

Where to hold the IFLA conference can impact who can attend. When it was held in Jerusalem in 2000, the conference was not attended by any librarians from other Middle Eastern countries. When held in Havana in 1994, the conference was difficult for U.S. librarians to attend, and hard for Cuban librarians to attend in Boston in 2001.

In 2003, Kay Raseroka, Director of Library Services at the University of Botswana, became the first non-European/North American to be elected president-elect of IFLA. By 2008, IFLA's membership had risen to 1700 members from 150

[22] www.iall.org
[23] www.iasl-online.org
[24] www.ifla.org

countries. As with many international organizations, IFLA has a global reach, but that does not mean it has a lot of resources. In fact, IFLA's annual budget is only around 2 million euros and has a staff of only 11. Headquarters staff is assisted by only three colleagues, who oversee core activities, such as the library development program, and by the generosity of host institutions. IFLA has seven official languages: Arabic, Chinese, English, French, German, Russian, and Spanish.

IFLA's headquarters is located in The Hague at the Royal Library of the Netherlands (which provides free space). Three regional offices provide support in different parts of the world. They are at the National Library Board of Singapore, Biblioteca Pública do Estado do Rio de Janeiro, Brazil, and the University of South Africa. IFLA's website is hosted by Institut de l'Information Scientifique et Technique (INIST) in France.

IFLA'S GLOBAL ACTIVITIES

At the end of 2004, IFLA adopted its 3 Pillars: *Society, Members, and Profession.* These three pillars encompass the major roles of library associations mentioned previously: networking; leadership; a voice; education and professional development; standards and best practices; advocacy; and partnerships.

The Society Pillar

IFLA in the past was very much focused on internal activities within the library community. All IFLA's core activities were related to internally improving the profession. It has now, however, expanded its mission to reach out to those outside the profession.

Copyright and Other Legal Matters

Issues once considered the domain of nations, such as copyright and intellectual property, are now international issues. International organizations [e.g., the World Trade Organization (WTO) and World Intellectual Property Organization (WIPO)] construct treaties and agreements that will impact how libraries and library users around the world will be able to access information.

To ensure libraries' interests are represented, IFLA, in 1999, created a Copyright and Other Legal Maters Committee, with representatives from around the world. IFLA then applied for and achieved observer status with the ability to send accredited representatives to WIPO, WTO, and the International Organization for Standardization (ISO).

IFLA monitors the activities of these organizations and provides input through position papers and statements, such as "Library Related Principles for the International Development Agenda of the World Intellectual Property Organization" (2005) and "The IFLA Position on Copyright in the Digital Environment" (2000). IFLA has established good working relations with a variety of other bodies with similar interests, providing an opportunity for a regular exchange of information and views on issues of mutual concern. IFLA has Formal Associate Relations with UNESCO, observer status with the United Nations, and associate status with the International Council of Scientific Unions (ICSU). IFLA has offered consultative status to a number of non-governmental organizations operating in related fields, including the International Publishers Association (IPA), which, despite opposite views on some issues, has worked together with IFLA on joint statements in areas they agree upon.

Freedom of Access to Information and Freedom of Expression

In 1999, IFLA created the Freedom of Access to Information and Freedom of Expression Committee (FAIFE) to defend and promote the basic human rights defined in Article 19 of the United Nations "Universal Declaration of Human Rights."

IFLA, through FAIFE, furthers free access to information and freedom of expression in all aspects, directly or indirectly, related to libraries and librarianship. FAIFE monitors the state of intellectual freedom within the library community worldwide, supports IFLA policy development and co-operation with other international human rights organizations, and responds to violations of free access to information and freedom of expression.

FAIFE provides trainings on intellectual freedom, especially related to IFLA's "Internet Manifesto (2002)," which promotes unhindered access to the Internet by libraries and removal of barriers to the flow of information that lead to inequality. IFLA and FAIFE now produce "The World Report Series" that offers timely and detailed summaries of the state of intellectual freedom and libraries worldwide.

World Summit for the Information Society (WSIS)

Activities of CLM and FAIFE provided the base for IFLA's involvement in the United Nations World Summit for the Information Society (WSIS), a two-phased summit in Geneva, 2003, and in Tunis, 2005. IFLA, with support of the Swiss Library Association, was active in ensuring that the voice of libraries and society were represented at WSIS. Under the banner of "Libraries @ the heart of the information society," IFLA made the case for libraries in the information society in areas such as information literacy and lifelong learning, digital memory, the global information commons, equal access, and intellectual freedom.

Through IFLA's efforts, libraries were recognized as having a role in the Information Society in the WSIS Principles and Action Plan. IFLA is engaged in the follow-up meetings that are continuing after the summits, and has created "Libraries and the WSIS Action Lines: Guideline for international, regional and local advocacy for Libraries in relation with implementation of the WSIS by Action Line 2005–2015."

International Committee of the Blue Shield

Following the mass destruction of cultural property at the start of the Iraq War, IFLA became one of the co-founding organizations, along with other international cultural associations (e.g., the International Council of Archives and the International Council of Museums) on the International Committee of the Blue Shield (ICBS). ICBS is designed to serve as a cultural Red Cross, which protects cultural heritage by supporting the UN's International Committee for the Protection of Cultural Property in the Event of Armed Conflict, established under the Second Protocol of the 1954 Hague Convention.

THE PROFESSIONAL PILLAR

Under its Professional Pillar, IFLA focuses on its long-established core activities to improve practices in the profession and to help libraries and information services assist users in the rapidly changing global environment.

Development of Libraries and Library Associations

Through its Action for Development of Libraries Program Associations (ALP), IFLA works to further the library profession, library institutions and library and information services in the developing countries of Africa, Asia and Oceania, and Latin America and the Caribbean.

ALP, which is supported by funding from the Swedish International Development Agency (SIDA), funds conferences, seminars and workshops, pilot projects, and publications. By providing continuing education and training, ALP facilitates the establishment of new library associations, supports the functions of libraries (e.g., services to the general public, information literacy, lifelong learning, and combating functional illiteracy), and promotes the use of Information and Communication Technology (ICT) and the creation of electronic resources.

Within IFLA, there is the Section on Management of Library Associations (MLAS), which works to address the needs and promotes interests of all types and sizes of library associations. MLAS tries to foster and improve leadership skills, to share experiences, and to work in cooperation with ALP to develop useful seminars and workshops at regional meetings for association development. MLAS oversees the Global Library Association Development Program (GLAD), a mentor/mentee program designed to strengthen the skills and competencies of library association officers to help them operate their associations. MLAS also has created guidelines for library associations on developing policies and procedures, financial management, operation, government relations, and more.

Establishing Standards and Guidelines

IFLA and Conference of Directors of National Libraries (CDNL) through the "IFLA-CDNL Alliance for Bibliographic Standards" known as ICABS, assures the ongoing coordination, communication, and support of key activities in the areas of bibliographic and resource control for all types of resources, related formats and protocol standards. ICABS accomplishes its goals in collaboration with UNESCO and the International Standards Organization (ISO).

ICABS aims to maintain, promote, and harmonize existing standards and to advance understanding of issues related to long-term archiving of electronic resources, including the promotion of new and recommended conventions for such archiving. ICABS organizes seminars and workshops to enhance communication on these issues within the library and archive community.

In 2003 IFLA established the UNIMARC Core Activity (UCA) with the responsibility for maintaining, developing, and promoting the Universal MARC format (UNIMARC), which facilitates the international exchange of bibliographic data. UNIMARC is now a set of four formats: Bibliographic, Authorities, Classification, and Holdings.

IFLA was also contracted by UNESCO to create the "UNESCO Guidelines for Establishing Digitization Programs in Libraries and Archives." These guidelines serve decision makers as well as library and archives managers, particularly in developing countries, when planning digitization projects.

Preservation and Conservation

IFLA's Preservation and Conservation Core Activity (PAC) has as its major goal that significant library and archive materials, published and unpublished, in all formats, will be preserved in accessible form for as long as possible. PAC, with help from its regional centers, raises awareness to make information and heritage professionals, governments, and the public conscious of the fundamental position occupied by preservation in the management of an institution.

PAC achieves this transfer of knowledge through training staff and technicians, producing and disseminating information to raise awareness of preservation issues, assessing needs through surveys, and promoting national and international standards and guidelines as well as best practices in the field.

THE MEMBERSHIP PILLAR

The World Library and Information Congress

As with all library associations, the IFLA must work together to ensure it remains vibrant, attractive, and beneficial for members throughout the world, providing needed services to its members. IFLA provides the vehicle for the international library community to network. Every August between 3,000 and 5,000 delegates attend the IFLA World Library and Information Congress (WLIC). Each is held in different cities around the globe. The delegates meet to discuss professional issues, share experiences, review new products and services, and strategize.

CONCLUSION

Library associations are crucial to the development of libraries and the profession locally, nationally, and internationally. They represent libraries, the profession, and the needs of users to those outside the library community, advocating for and promoting positions on issues that impact everyone. It is important for those entering the profession to understand the value of library associations and the need to join and participate. Library associations need new members to provide energy and ideas, and future leadership to continue to succeed.

AUTHORS

Peter Johan Lor wrote the forword to this book. He was the Secretary General of IFLA 2005-2008. He is an extraordinary professor in the Department of Information Science, University of Pretoria, South Africa.

AFRICA SECTION AUTHORS

Reggie Raju is Librarian, University of KwaZulu Natal Library, University of KwaZulu Natal, South Africa

Jaya Raju is Associate Professor, Department of Library and Information Studies, Durban University of Technology, South Africa

Issac Kigongo-Bukenya is Professor, East African School of Library and Information Science, Makarere University, Uganda

Robert Ikoja Odongo is Professor and Deputy Director at the East African School of Library and Information Science, Makarere University, Uganda

Janneke Mostert is a Senior Lecturer, Department of Library and Information Science, University of Zululand, South Africa

Busire Omwoyo Onyancha is a Lecturer at the Department of Information Science, University of South Africa, South Africa.

Mabel Majanja is a Senior Lecturer and Head of the Department of Information Science, University of South Africa, South Africa

ASIA SECTION AUTHORS

Trishanjit Kaur is Reader& Head, Department of Library and Information Science Punjabi University, India

Christopher Khoo is Associate Professor
Division of Information Studies, Wee Kim Wee School of Communication and Information, Nanyang Technological University
Singapore

Shaheen Majid is Associate Professor
Division of Information Studies, Wee Kim Wee School of Communication and Information, Nanyang Technological University
Singapore

Chihfeng P. Lin is Associate Professor and Director
Department/Graduate Program of Information and Communications
Shih-Hsin University, Taipei, Taiwan

Mei-hwa Yang is Professor, Graduate School of Library, Information and Archival Studies, National Chengchi University, Taipei, Taiwan

Anthony W. Ferguson is Director of Libraries, The University of Hong Kong

AUSTRALIA AND NEW ZEALAND

Stuart Ferguson is Senior Lecturer, Information Studies, Faculty of Communication and International Studies, University of Canberra, Australia

Chris Jones is Manager – Library Services, Great Lakes Library Service, NSW, Australia

Anne Horn is University Librarian, Deakin University, Australia

Sue Henczel is Manager, Faculty Library Services, Deakin University, Australia

Julie Sibthorpe is Subject Librarian, University of Auckland, New Zealand

Gillian Ralph is Subject Librarian, University of Auckland, New Zealand

James E. Herring is Lecturer in Teacher Librarianship, Charles Sturt University, Australia

Gillian Hallam is Associate Professor, Queensland University of Technology, Australia

Philip Calvert is Senior Lecturer, Victoria University of Wellington, New Zealand

Stuart Ferguson is Senior Lecturer, University of Canberra, Australia

LATIN AMERICA SECTION AUTHORS

Mary Giraldo is Library Consultan, Regional Center for Book Promotion in Latin America, the Caribbean, Spain, and Portugal

Elsa Ramírez Leyva is Researcher University Center for Library Science Research, National Autonomous University of Mexico

Adolfo Rodríuez Gallardo is Director General Direction for Libraries, National Autonomous University of Mexico

Filiberto Felipe Martínez-Arellano is Researcher and Director, University Center for Library Science Research, Nacional Autonomous University of Mexico

MIDDLE EAST SECTION AUTHORS

Teresa Lesher, Department of Library and Information Science, PAAEET, Kuwait

Yaser Abdel-Motey, Department of Library and Information Science, PAAEET, Kuwait

Sajjad ur-Rehman is Professor and Director, MLIS, Kuwait University

Hayat Alyaqout is Teaching Associate, DLIS, Kuwait University

Sultan Al-Daihani, Department of Library and Information Science, Kuwait University

Ms. Reham Al-Issa, Research Fellow, Department of Library and Information Science, Kuwait University

NORTH AMERICA SECTION AUTHORS

Carol Brey-Casiano is the Director of El Paso Public Library and Past President of ALA, USA

Barbara Dewey is Dean of Libraries, University of Tennessee, Knoxville, USA

Blanche Wools is Professor and Director Emeritus, School of Library and Information Science, San Jose University, USA

Rebecca B. Vargha is Director of library at School of Information and Library Science, University of North Carolina at Chapel-Hil, USA

Irene Owens is Dean of School of Library and Information Sciences, North Carolina Central University, USA

Thomas Leonhardt is Director of Library, St. Edward's University, Austin, Texas, USA

REGIONAL EDITORS

Copenhagen
Denmark

Dr. Marian Koren
Head of Research Bureau
Netherlands Public Library Association
Netherlands

Latin America

Mr. Filiberto Felipe Martinez-Arellano
Director University Center for Library Science Research
National Autonomous University of Mexico
Mexico

Middle East

Dr. Sajjad ur Rehman
Professor and Director, MLIS Program
Department of Library and Information Science
Kuwait University
Kuwait

Dr. Leila Marouf
Assistant Professor
Department of Library and Information Science
Kuwait University
Kuwait

North America

Dr. Ismail Abdullahi,
Associate Professor
North Carolina Central University
School of Library and Information Sciences
USA

INDEX